CONTENTS

DAIRY & REFRIGERATED ITEMS

DELI & PACKAGED MEATS

DRIED FOODS & MIXES

FROZEN FOODS

MEAT & POULTRY

PRODUCE

SEAFOOD

SOUPS

FAST FOODS

INTRODUCTION

Your diet affects a lot more than just your waistline. Food choices and eating habits influence not only the shape of your body but your overall health as well. A low fat diet, for example, not only helps control blood cholesterol levels and body weight, it may enhance your defenses against certain types of cancer, too.

Indeed, there is a new focus on using food to optimize our physical potential as well as head off debilitating chronic disease. Witness the explosion of research on the antioxidant vitamins C and E and beta-carotene to prevent and treat heart disease, cancer, and cataracts. Scores of scientists are scrutinizing common foods such as broccoli, garlic, and tea for chemicals believed to prevent illness.

But, in general, many of our health problems stem from dietary excesses rather than deficiencies. As a nation, we consume too many calories and too much fat, saturated fat, cholesterol, and sodium. We don't get enough of the protective nutrients such as complex carbohydrates and fiber, and even with an abundant food supply fortified to the hilt with vitamins and minerals, we fall short on these nutrients.

Several studies suggest that we are losing the battle of the bulge. Despite the hundreds of delicious and nutritious nonfat and low fat foods on the market today, Americans are getting heavier. Yet our collective consciousness about the importance of diet has never been higher. So why the gulf between knowing that we should eat better and exercise more and actually doing what it takes to stay our healthiest?

According to the results of a survey of eating habits conducted by the American Dietetic Association, many Americans recognize the importance of good nutrition, but few actually take steps to improve their diets. The obstacles? Many say they don't want to give up their favorite foods. Others cite a lack of time as a reason for not keeping track of what they eat. Many others are just plain confused by the conflicting nature of nutrition information.

If these barriers to healthy eating sound familiar, you should know the following: First, remember the dietitians' mantra: There are no good or bad foods, just good and bad diets. No single food or food group will make or break a diet, no matter what anyone says, so you don't have to eliminate all the foods you love from your diet. Second, keeping track of the foods you eat isn't really a chore if you learn to read manufacturers' food labels and become familiar with the Dietary Guidelines for Americans and the Food Guide Pyramid. Finally, even if headlines about some nutrients appear to change with the wind, the basic tenets of a healthy diet do not.

DIETARY GUIDELINES FOR AMERICANS

The U.S. Department of Agriculture Dietary Guidelines for Americans are the most widely accepted nutrition guidelines for health. They represent the nutrition advice of a number of different authorities—the Surgeon General, National Research Council of the National Academy of Sciences, American Heart Association, American Cancer Society, and other organizations and experts in health and nutrition. The guidelines reinforce two major food messages—eat less fat and eat more carbohydrates and fiber. Bear in mind that the Dietary Guidelines were developed for Americans older than the age of two. The nutrition needs of infants and toddlers differ from those of adults. The official Dietary Guidelines follow:

Eat a variety of foods. If you don't eat different types of foods, you may miss out on important nutrients your body needs to function at its best. Variety also means picking different foods from within each food group.

Maintain a healthy weight. The Dietary Guidelines recommend exercise as the best way for you to lose weight. It burns calories and boosts overall health and fitness.

Choose a diet low in fat, saturated fat, and cholesterol. These three nutrients shoulder much of the blame for the amount of heart disease in the United States. Fat has also been fingered because of its links to obesity and some types of cancer. In addition, reducing fat intake is another step in losing excess body fat.

Choose a diet with plenty of vegetables, fruits, and grain products. Fruits and vegetables are packed with complex carbohydrates, fiber, and vitamins, especially the disease-fighting antioxidants beta-carotene (a form of vitamin A) and vitamin C. Furthermore, they tend to be low in fat and calories. The fiber from breads, cereals, pasta, rice, and other grain products lowers your risk of heart disease, constipation, diverticular disease, hemorrhoids, and numerous other ailments.

Use sugars in moderation only. It is virtually impossible to cut all sugars out of your diet. They serve as natural flavor enhancers, thickeners, and food preservatives. But they also add calories without contributing other nutrients; in other words, they add empty calories. By spending some of your daily calories on sugars, you have less to spend on foods with more nutrition value. For example, a 12-ounce can of regular soda pop has approximately 150 calories and no other nutrients, whereas the same 150 calories of orange juice provide well over the Recommended Dietary Allowance (RDA) for vitamin C and close to the RDA for folate. Sugars and starchy foods can also increase tooth decay.

Use salt and sodium in moderation only. Approximately one out of every three adults in the United States has high blood pressure. If you have high blood pressure and reduce sodium in your diet, chances are good your blood pressure will go down. Even if your blood pressure is not high, reducing your intake of sodium cannot hurt and may help prevent high blood pressure in the future.

If you drink alcoholic beverages, do so in moderation. Of course, you know that alcohol is a major factor in automobile and other types of accidents as well as a major contributor to liver disease. But alcohol also drains your body of water and B vitamins and is full of empty calories. Moderate drinking is no more than two drinks a day for men and one a day for women. One drink is 12 ounces of regular beer, 4 ounces of wine, or 1 ounce of 100-proof liquor (whisky, rum, vodka, and so on). Complete abstinence is best for women who are pregnant or trying to conceive because of the relationship between alcohol and birth defects.

THE FOOD GUIDE PYRAMID

The dietary guidelines for Americans are accompanied by the Food Guide Pyramid, which graphically illustrates the emphasis each food group should have in our diets. Using the Food Guide Pyramid, you will know what and how much to eat from each of the food groups. Your diet will not be too high in calories, fat, saturated fat, cholesterol, sugars, sodium, or alcohol. It will have plenty of complex carbohydrates and fiber. Overall, the Food Guide Pyramid is your picture of health.

At the base of the Pyramid, you'll find the foundation of healthy eating—the bread, cereal, rice, and pasta group. Foods in this group supply the complex carbohydrates you need for energy plus B vitamins, minerals, and fiber. You should eat 6 to 11 servings from this group. What is a serving? One slice of bread; 1 ounce of ready-to-eat cereal (usually between a ½ and 1 cup—check the label of your favorite brands); one small tortilla; ½ cup of cooked cereal, pasta, or rice; 3 cups of popped popcorn; or one half of a medium bagel, English muffin, or pita bread.

The Food Guide Pyramid

Fats, Oils & Sweets
Use sparingly

KEY
•Fat (naturally occurring and added)
▾Sugar (added)
These symbols show fats, oils, and added sugars in foods.

Milk, Yogurt & Cheese Group
2–3 Servings

Meat, Poultry, Fish, Dry Beans, Eggs & Nuts Group
2–3 Servings

Vegetable Group
3–5 Servings

Fruit Group
2–4 Servings

Bread, Cereal, Rice & Pasta Group
6–11 Servings

The next level of the Pyramid, right on top of the bread group, comprises the vegetable group and its close cousin, the fruit group. Vegetables are your best source of beta-carotene, vitamin C, and folic acid. They also supply iron, magnesium, and other key minerals. In general, the darker the color, the more vitamins and minerals a vegetable contains. For a high-fiber, low fat food, look no further than vegetables.

Be bean smart, too. Legumes, such as split peas, kidney beans, lentils, and chickpeas, are rich in vitamins and minerals and abundant in complex carbohydrates. They also supply both the soluble fiber that may help prevent heart disease and the insoluble fiber needed to keep your colon healthy. (Legumes are listed in both the vegetable and meat groups.)

According to the Pyramid, you should eat between three and five servings of vegetables daily. A serving is 1 cup of lettuce, raw spinach, or other raw leafy vegetables, ½ cup of cooked or chopped vegetables, or 6 ounces of tomato or vegetable juice.

Meeting the Pyramid's recommendation of two to four fruit servings should be relatively easy. What counts as a serving? A medium piece of fruit, such as an apple, banana, orange, or peach; ½ cup of cooked, chopped, or canned fruit; or 6 ounces of juice.

Fruit is packed with many of the same nutrients that you find in vegetables, especially fiber, vitamin C, and the mineral potassium. As with vegetables, you should eat a variety of fruits to ensure you get adequate amounts of the different types of nutrients and fiber they contain. For example, an apple with skin provides fiber but almost no vitamin C, while an orange has fiber plus vitamin C. When possible, eat whole fruit more often than you drink juice. While juice has the same vitamins as the fruit that it came from, it is missing fiber and some minerals that went out with the pulp. Juice also adds calories quickly without filling you up. A 6-ounce glass of orange juice is gone in a couple of gulps; a whole orange takes longer to eat, supplies you with fiber, and can help you feel full.

At the next level, the Pyramid becomes much narrower for a reason: You should eat less from the two food groups at this level than of the three groups closer to the base. That does not make these two food groups—the milk, yogurt, and cheese group and the meat, poultry, fish, dry beans, eggs, and nuts group—any less important. Your body still benefits from these nutrient-rich foods; it just doesn't need as many servings from these groups. Foods in these two food groups also tend to be higher in fat, saturated fat, and cholesterol and very low in fiber, with the exception of legumes.

One serving from the milk group is 1 cup of milk or yogurt, 1½ ounces of hard cheese such as cheddar or Swiss, or 2 ounces of processed cheese such as American. In addition to protein, B vitamins, and minerals, foods from this group supply you with the calcium you need for strong bones.

Some foods in the milk group are smarter nutrition choices than others. Skim and low fat milk and low fat and nonfat yogurt give you the most nutrition with the least amount of fat. Although frozen yogurt contains less fat than ice cream, it is heavily sweetened and lower in calcium. Lower-fat cheeses and ice creams have less fat, saturated fat, cholesterol, and calories than their full-fat counterparts, but they don't provide significant amounts of calcium and other important dairy nutrients.

The meat group is the most diverse group because it contains not only meats, poultry, and fish, but also dried peas and beans, eggs, nuts, and peanut butter. These foods are grouped together because they supply similar nutrients: All supply protein and B vitamins; many are good sources of iron, zinc, and other minerals. Dried beans and peas have the bonus of fiber.

The serving size for meat, poultry, or fish is 3 ounces cooked—a portion about the size and thickness of a deck of cards or the palm of your hand. The serving size for some other foods in the group includes ½ cup of cooked or canned legumes, one egg, or 2 tablespoons of peanut butter.

At the top of Pyramid, in the smallest space, you'll find fats, oils, and sweets. Use these high-calorie, low-nutrient foods sparingly to add flavor, texture, and some calories to your diet.

HOW MUCH SHOULD I EAT?

How do you know how many servings you should have of each food group? The answer depends on your age, sex, and activity level. At the very least, though, you should get the lowest number of servings from each group.

Sedentary women and older adults need the fewest calories, approximately 1,600 daily; this calorie level corresponds to the lowest serving numbers for each food group: Six servings from the bread group, three from the vegetable, two from the fruit, and so on. Most children older than two years of age, teenage girls, active women, and sedentary men need about 2,200 calories daily, or the middle of the range for each group on the Pyramid. Teenage boys, active men, or very active women should eat according to the high end of the range, about 2,800 calories—11 servings from the breads, 5 from the vegetables, and so on.

NUTRIENTS IN *THE COMPLETE FOOD COUNT GUIDE*

In addition to providing serving size and calories, *The Complete Food Count Guide* provides values for the following nutrients: total fat, saturated fat, cholesterol, sodium, total carbohydrates, and fiber. What follows is a discussion of each nutrient and its role in your diet.

FAT

Fat is a big part of the American diet. Clearly, dietary fat can make foods so appealing that they're hard to resist. But fully 37 percent of the total calories we consume come from fat, most of which is saturated fat. Compared with many countries around the world, our consumption of so much saturated fat and cholesterol is unusually high.

Although we need some fat in our diet for good health, too much of it can have exactly the opposite effect. One of the main reasons to adopt a low fat diet is to combat coronary heart disease (CHD)—the formation of fatty deposits and blood clots on the walls of the coronary arteries that supply blood to the heart. Over time, a buildup of these deposits leads to a narrowing of the arteries and, eventually, reduces the flow of blood to the heart—just as stepping on a garden hose cuts down the flow of water to a lawn sprinkler. A heart attack occurs when the blood flow through a coronary artery to a portion of the heart is completely blocked and part of the heart muscle dies. If enough of the heart muscle is damaged, the person may die. The seriousness of this disease is clear from the statistics: Heart attacks strike

1.25 million Americans each year, killing more than half a million. CHD is the leading cause of death in the United States.

Though it strikes many older people, CHD is not limited to the elderly. Indeed, nearly half of all heart attacks occur in people younger than age 65. What's more, the fatty deposits that may eventually block the arteries of adults can begin to form in childhood. CHD is not necessarily a part of growing older either. You can take steps now to protect your own heart and to reduce the possibility of one day becoming a heart attack statistic.

While some of the factors that increase your risk of CHD are beyond your control—such as being male or having a family history of heart disease—there are three major risk factors that you can control: cigarette smoking, high blood pressure, and a high level of cholesterol in the blood. If you smoke, you can stop. If you have high blood pressure, you can work with your doctor to get it under control. And if you have a high blood cholesterol level, you can make dietary changes to help reduce it. **Decreasing the amount of saturated fat in your diet is the most important way to reduce blood cholesterol levels**.

The benefits of a diet low in fat go well beyond reducing the risks of heart disease. The most common cancers found in this country, cancer of the breast, prostate, and colon, are also linked to high-fat diets. It would be misleading to oversimplify a complex issue and imply that a low fat diet will protect against these cancers. The fundamental point is that a low fat diet clearly helps combat CHD, and it may influence cancer protection as well.

What Is Fat?

Fat is nature's storehouse of energy-yielding fuel. Most fats are made up primarily of triglycerides. To use the energy stored in fat, the body breaks down triglycerides into fatty acids. Individual cells then burn the fatty acids for energy. Protein and carbohydrates such as sugars and starches also provide energy, but fat, with more than two times the energy available per gram, is a denser fuel.

All living organisms, including plants, have the ability to manufacture fatty acids and assemble them into molecules of fat to store energy. Different species tend to manufacture different types of fat. As a general rule, animals manufacture a fat composed mainly of **saturated** fatty acids, and plants manufacture a fat rich in **polyunsaturated** fatty acids. Some plants also manufacture **monounsaturated** fatty acids. The degree of saturation determines which form (solid or liquid) the fat takes at room temperature, how useful it is in cooking and baking, and how it affects blood cholesterol levels.

Saturated fats are typically solid at room temperature. Butter, lard, and the marbling and visible fat in meats are saturated fats. Much of the fat in milk (butterfat) is also saturated; the process of homogenization breaks the solid fat into fine particles and scatters it throughout the liquid portion of the milk. Saturated fats are implicated in raising the body's cholesterol level and in clogging the arteries.

Polyunsaturated fats are usually liquid at room temperature. These liquid oils are found mostly in the seeds of plants. The oils from safflowers, sunflowers, corn, soybeans, and cotton are polyunsaturated fats.

Monounsaturated fats are also liquid at room temperature. Examples of fats rich in monounsaturated fatty acids are olive oil and canola oil. Avocados and nuts are also rich in this fat.

Sometimes vegetable oils are chemically modified to change some of their polyunsaturated fatty acids to saturated ones. This process, called **hydrogenation,** is useful commercially because it improves the shelf life of the oils and allows the less expensive vegetable oils to acquire important baking properties found normally in the more costly animal fats. **Hydrogenated** or **partially hydrogenated** vegetable oils are more saturated than the original oils from which they're made. Margarine and vegetable shortening are examples of such vegetable oils. Hydrogenating a fat or oil creates *trans* fatty acids, which research has found to be potentially more harmful than saturated fats.

Although most animal fats are saturated and most vegetable fats unsaturated, there are some noteworthy exceptions. For example, a few vegetable fats are so rich in saturated fats they are solid at room temperature. Palm oil, coconut oil, and palm kernel oil contain between 50 and 80 percent saturated fat. Coconut oil and palm oil are widely used in the commercial production of nondairy creamers, snacks such as popcorn or chips, baked goods, and candy bars. Cocoa butter, the fat found in expensive chocolates, is also rich in saturated fatty acids.

The Importance of Fat

Humans also have the ability to manufacture fat. Your body uses energy from the foods you eat. When you provide your body with more energy than it can use right away, it packages that energy into fat and stores it. The amount of energy obtained from a particular food is represented by the number of calories it produces when burned in the body. Recent research suggests that if you consume excess energy from carbohydrates and you are physically active, the body may step up its rate of metabolism, burning calories. But when excess energy is consumed from fat, it is likely to be stored as fat. (Alcohol is an exception to this general rule, since sometimes energy consumed from alcohol can be stored as body fat.)

We all need some stored fat for vital functions, daily activities, and exercise. When an adult continually consumes more calories than the body needs, fat begins to accumulate, causing weight gain. Diabetes, high blood pressure, and heart disease are but a few of the negative health risks of being overweight.

CHOLESTEROL

Cholesterol is a white, odorless, fatlike substance that is a basic component of the human body. Cholesterol is essential to your body's chemistry. But you don't have to consume any: The body is able to manufacture all the cholesterol it needs. We also get it from many of the foods we eat. All animals produce cholesterol so foods from animal sources, such as egg yolks, meat, poultry, fish, and milk products, contain cholesterol. Plants do not produce cholesterol so grains, fruits, vegetables, and nuts do not contain cholesterol.

The body has several mechanisms that enable it to balance the cholesterol it produces against what it obtains from food. If you regularly consume foods from animal sources, your body slows down its production of cholesterol. If you eat mostly foods from plant sources, your body manufactures more cholesterol to get the amount it needs. However, these mechanisms aren't foolproof. In a very small minority of people (perhaps less than 1 percent of all those with high blood cholesterol), an inherited defect can cause blood cholesterol levels to rise: Receptor cells that pull cholesterol out of the bloodstream don't function properly, and the total amount of cholesterol in the blood rises. But for most people, high blood cholesterol is caused by diets that are high in total fat, saturated fat, and cholesterol.

How Dietary Fat Affects Blood Cholesterol

Cholesterol is transported through the bloodstream and distributed throughout the body by lipoproteins. Low-density lipoprotein, or LDL (often referred to as "bad" cholesterol), carries cholesterol to the cells. The cholesterol that is not used by the cells can build up on artery walls. Over time, this buildup, known as atherosclerosis, will decrease blood flow through the arteries and may lead to heart attacks or strokes or both. High-density lipoprotein, or HDL ("good" cholesterol), helps rid the body of cholesterol by carrying it to the liver where it is excreted. When more of the cholesterol in your blood is carried by HDLs, there is less danger of cholesterol accumulating in the body. If, on the other hand, most of the cholesterol in your blood is carried by LDLs, the risk of cholesterol accumulating increases. A blood test to determine blood cholesterol level reveals how efficiently your body manages its cholesterol.

The relationship between dietary fat and blood cholesterol levels is a close one; however, not all sources of fat have the same effect on blood cholesterol. Saturated fat is more of a culprit in disrupting the body's cholesterol balancing mechanism than unsaturated fat. For reasons that are not well understood, saturated fats suppress the production of the receptor cells that pull the cholesterol out of the low-density lipoproteins—and thus out of the bloodstream. When these receptors don't function properly, LDL cholesterol is stranded in the bloodstream, and the total amount of cholesterol in the blood rises. Thus, **saturated fats in the diet tend to increase blood cholesterol**. In fact, no other dietary factor increases blood cholesterol as much as a high intake of saturated fat, including consumption of dietary cholesterol. The degree to which dietary cholesterol affects blood cholesterol levels seems to depend on how much total fat and saturated fat are eaten along with it.

The richest source of dietary cholesterol is egg yolks: A single yolk contains about 213 milligrams (mg) of cholesterol. Additional sources of cholesterol that are also rich in total and saturated fat include beef, pork, veal, lamb, whole milk, butter, cheese, cream, ice cream, sausages, frankfurters, and most luncheon meats.

Commercially prepared baked goods, processed snack foods, and candy are frequently overlooked sources of large amounts of fat, saturated fat, and cholesterol. These "sweets" are often made with palm oil, coconut oil, or partially hydrogenated vegetable oils because these oils add flavor and are often cheaper than the more costly animal fats. Moreover, many of these products are prepared with eggs.

Is Your Blood Cholesterol Too High?

Periodic testing to measure the amount of cholesterol in the blood is important because such tests reveal how efficiently your body handles cholesterol. The most common test measures total cholesterol.

The National Cholesterol Education Program (NCEP) suggests that all adults aged 20 years or older have a cholesterol test. The NCEP also developed recommendations for classifying cholesterol levels and determining treatment. The level of cholesterol in your blood is expressed in milligrams per deciliter (mg/dL), the amount of cholesterol found in one deciliter of blood. According to these guidelines, a total blood cholesterol level below 200 mg/dL is considered *desirable* for all adults aged 20 and older. A test result between 200 and 239 mg/dL is regarded as *borderline high*, whereas 240 mg/dL or more is rated as *high*.

Research has shown that the risk of heart disease increases as the blood cholesterol level rises, especially as it climbs above 200 mg/dL. In the United States, adults who have a blood cholesterol level of 240 mg/dL or above appear to have more than twice the risk of developing CHD than those with readings below 200 mg/dL. Unfortunately, it has been estimated that more than 100 million Americans have a blood cholesterol level of 200 mg/dL or above. This means about two out of every five people living in the United States fall into this group.

Classification Based on Total Blood Cholesterol	
200 mg/dL	desirable
200–239 mg/dL	borderline high
240 mg/dL	high

If your test places you in the borderline-high or high range, you should undergo evaluation with another test, the lipoprotein analysis. A lipoprotein analysis determines how much of that cholesterol is in the form of HDLs and how much in LDLs. Perhaps more important than total cholesterol (LDL plus HDL) is this ratio of LDL to HDL. In other words, a high total cholesterol level may not be so bad if you have a high level of HDL. Likewise, a low total cholesterol may not be as good as it seems if the HDL is very low. Confused? Here's the straight scoop: A desirable level of LDL is below 130, and a desirable level of HDL is 35 and above.

Eating to Lower Your Blood Cholesterol Level

Whether you're among the thousands with a high blood cholesterol level or you just want to make sure your cholesterol level stays low, reducing saturated fat in your diet should be your top priority. As you will see, adopting a heart-healthy diet does not mean depriving yourself of all the foods you love. It simply means making wiser choices in food selection and preparation, eating certain foods only in moderation, and keeping an eye on the overall content of your diet.

You need to keep track of how much fat and cholesterol you consume each day. That may sound somewhat intimidating, but it doesn't have to be. By picking up this book, you've taken the important first step toward cleaning up your diet with a minimum amount of inconvenience. The Complete Food Count Guide lists the caloric, total fat, saturated fat, and cholesterol content of brand-name and common food items. It can help you make wise food choices when you plan meals and shop for groceries.

Controlling Fat

Because saturated fats are the main contributing factor in raising blood cholesterol, the primary health benefit of reducing dietary fat is reducing blood cholesterol levels. But another benefit of a low fat diet is greater control of body weight. A third benefit derives from the link between high-fat diets and cancers of the breast, prostate, and colon.

Fat should account for no more than 30 percent of the calories you eat in a day. You can figure out how much fat is the maximum you should eat in a day: Multiply the approximate number of calories you eat (see the Food Guide Pyramid, or use the 2,000 calorie standard that appears on food labels) by 0.3 to get the number of calories contributed by fat. For example, 2,000 times 0.3 equals 600 calories from fat. Then divide by 9, the calories in a gram of fat. The number you end up with, 67, is the maximum number of grams of fat you should eat in a day. You can reduce the percentage of fat you consume to 10 percent of calories without any adverse health effects. (The exception to this rule is for babies and children, who need a higher amount of fat in their diets to grow properly. Ask your child's pediatrician for details, and don't give skim or low fat milk to a child younger than two years of age.)

With the information provided in this book, you can limit your total fat intake. Note that it isn't necessary to eliminate all high-fat foods from your diet or even all foods that derive more than 30 percent of their calories from fat. When you do choose a food or a meal that contains more than the recommended amount of fat, balance it out with lower-fat choices the rest of the day. Keep in mind that you want your overall diet to provide less than 30 percent of your total calories from fat.

Controlling Cholesterol

To limit your dietary cholesterol intake to the recommended amount of less than 300 mg per day, you should cut back on foods that are high in cholesterol. *The Complete Food Count Guide* provides the cholesterol content for thousands of individual food items. When planning meals, simply add up the cholesterol values shown to find out if the foods you plan to eat fit into your daily cholesterol "budget" of less than 300 mg. The counter makes it easy to compare similar foods and pick the ones that are lower in cholesterol.

Here are some additional tips to help you choose and prepare foods that are low in fat and cholesterol:

- Eat less meat. Beef, pork, veal, lamb, poultry, and even some types of fish can be relatively high in fat and cholesterol. Also, we eat far larger portions than we need for nutrition and health. You should eat no more than six ounces of meat, poultry, or fish daily. That is the equivalent of two pieces, each the size of the palm of your hand.
- Have several meatless meals each week. Beans and peas are cholesterol free, naturally low in fat, and high in fiber. Experiment with tofu.
- When you do choose meat, select only lean cuts—beef round, loin, and sirloin; pork tenderloin; lamb leg and loin—and trim any fat. Take the skin off poultry. Choose lower-fat fish, such as cod, haddock, grouper, snapper, and halibut, and select fish canned in water instead of oil.
- Increase your consumption of high-fiber foods, such as whole grains, fruits, vegetables, and dried peas and beans. These foods fill your stomach without filling you up with fat and cholesterol. Also, high-fiber foods have a cholesterol-lowering effect.
- Limit eggs to four whole eggs per week. In recipes, use two egg whites for every whole egg called for. Accustom yourself to nonfat liquid egg substitutes.
- Choose skim or low fat milk and fat free or low fat yogurt and cheese most of the time. These days, a wide variety of tasty low fat and fat free dairy products is available.
- Limit your use of margarine and butter. Although margarine is not as high in saturated fat as butter, it is hydrogenated. Hydrogenated fat contains *trans* fatty acids, which may be as bad or worse for you than saturated fats. When you do use margarine, use varieties made from polyunsaturated oils—corn, safflower, soybean, or sunflower.
- Use oils lowest in saturated fat, including canola oil and safflower oil. (Remember, liquid vegetable oils are lower in saturated fat than solid fats.) Avoid palm oil and coconut oil, which are solid at room temperature and have the same effect on your health as saturated fats do.
- Substitute monounsaturated and polyunsaturated fat for much of the saturated fat in your diet. And keep your fat intake to no more than 30 percent of your total daily calories.

- Use low fat preparation and cooking techniques: In addition to trimming away all visible fat, broil, grill, bake, or roast foods instead of frying. When basting, use wine, lemon juice, or tomato juice rather than fatty drippings.
- When sautéing foods, use only a small amount of olive or canola oil. Use nonstick cooking spray or nonstick cookware.
- Commercially prepared baked goods—pies, cakes, and doughnuts—are often high in saturated fat and cholesterol. Look for low fat varieties, or prepare mixes at home with optional no-cholesterol recipes.

SODIUM

Even if you wanted to, you probably couldn't eliminate sodium completely from your diet. Sodium is in just about everything—from water to vegetables—and it is important to your health. But there are good reasons to watch your sodium intake.

Sodium controls fluid balance in the body. Too much sodium causes bloating, swelling, and excess water weight. In people who are sensitive to sodium's effects, it has been linked to elevated blood pressure (hypertension). Hypertension increases your risk of heart attack, stroke, kidney failure, and buildup of plaque in the arteries (atherosclerosis). Because no test can tell you if you're "salt sensitive," it makes sense to be careful about salt intake.

Follow these tips to reduce the salt in your diet:

- Keep the salt shaker off the table.
- Don't salt foods when cooking—even when a recipe calls for added salt.
- Choose fresh or plain frozen vegetables instead of canned or buy reduced-sodium canned products.
- Cook cereals, pasta, rice, and dried beans and peas without salt.
- Pick fresh meat, poultry, and fish over canned and processed varieties.
- Limit high-salt foods, such as frozen dinners, canned soup, pickles, olives, and certain condiments, such as catsup, mustard, and soy, barbecue, and Worcestershire sauces.
- Learn to spice up your foods with lemon, herbs, and spices instead of salt.

CARBOHYDRATES

Carbohydrates come in three varieties: simple, complex, and fibrous. All three types contain four calories per gram. Complex carbohydrates, or starches, are found in legumes, grains, vegetables, and fruits. Simple carbohydrates, or sugars, are found in table sugar, honey, natural fruit sugars, and molasses. Fiber is found in whole grains, legumes, vegetables, and fruits.

Carbohydrates are the body's principal source of energy. They fuel all bodily functions, including the digestion of other foods. While the body can also convert fat and some protein into energy, carbohydrates are the easiest fuel source for the body to process. According to the Food Guide Pyramid, more than half of our daily calories should come in the form of carbohydrates. Here's how to achieve this goal:

Consume the majority of your carbohydrate calories in the form of whole grains, beans, potatoes, fruits, and vegetables.

Limit your intake of foods made with white flour and white sugar, such as cake, cookies, and candy.

Eat high-fiber carbohydrates, such as bran cereal, apples, dry beans (kidneys, pintos, limas), peas, parsnips, and potatoes.

FIBER

By now you've heard all the claims about the benefits of fiber, a form of carbohydrate. This is one area where you can believe what you hear. Including a source of fiber at every meal can have the following benefits:

Fiber adds bulk to your diet, preventing constipation and hemorrhoids.

It may reduce the risk of colon and rectal cancers.

It lowers cholesterol.

Dietary fiber is found only in plant foods, not in animal products. Since it is not digested, the body absorbs no calories from fiber. Because of this, and because it gives the stomach a feeling of fullness, fiber is an excellent weight-control aid (when consumed in suggested amounts). There are two main types of fiber: insoluble and soluble. Insoluble fiber speeds up the movement of food through the intestines and promotes bowel regularity. It is found in foods such as asparagus, peas, kidney and pinto beans, and the wheat bran found in whole-wheat breads and cereals. Soluble fiber slows the movement of food through the intestines. It also appears to be effective at lowering blood cholesterol. Oat bran is a source of soluble fiber, as are rolled oats, broccoli, brussels sprouts, grapefruit, apples, and navy beans.

Although there is no Recommended Dietary Allowance (RDA) for fiber, most nutrition experts recommend an intake of 20 to 35 grams of fiber per day. Try the following tips for boosting your fiber intake:

- Choose whole-grain breads instead of refined white, bran cereal instead of plain cornflakes, brown rice instead of white, whole wheat instead of regular pasta.
- Leave the edible skins on fresh fruits and vegetables. These skins are an excellent source of fiber.
- Eat a piece of fresh fruit rather than drinking juice. An orange has more fiber than orange juice.

Resist the urge to boost your fiber intake to the recommended level overnight. Otherwise, you may be in for an uncomfortable gastric surprise, including gas, bloating, constipation, or diarrhea. Instead, increase your fiber intake gradually, going up to recommended levels over the course of a couple of weeks, even a month, and be sure to increase your fluid intake at the same time.

THE IMPORTANCE OF READING FOOD LABELS

If you're serious about eating healthfully, you'll have to master an important skill: reading the nutrition labels on food packages. Today's food package labels represent the efforts of government agencies, Congress, the food industry, and health and professional groups to create a label to help Americans make wise food choices. Nutrient and ingredient information on the label enables you to reduce your disease risk and improve your health profile through the foods you purchase and eat.

These new food labels have many advantages: First and foremost, they're designed to help consumers compare food products. For example, nutrition information is uniform. Labels must list the same nutrients—those most important to your health—such as total fat, cholesterol, sodium, and total carbohydrates. Serving sizes have been standardized: Because they're based on the average amount of the food usually eaten at one sitting, you can easily compare the nutritional value of similar products. The ingredient list is more complete so that you know what is really in a food. No more allergic reactions from eating caseinate and other milk derivatives that were not listed as being milk products. Another new feature is the Percent Daily Values: They let you see how the nutrients in a food fit into your daily nutrient needs.

Take a look at the food label pictured on page 22. You can easily spot the new labels with their **Nutrition Facts** boldly displayed. Serving size per container is listed first. Incidentally, when you assess calories and nutrients, be honest with yourself. If the serving size on the label of your favorite ice cream is ½ cup, but you usually fill your bowl to the brim, you need to figure your calories based on the amount you actually consume—not just the standard serving size. Notice also that the label provides the total calories and the number of calories from fat.

The **Percent Daily Values** appear next. The percentages show how these foods fit in a 2,000-calorie-a-day diet; for example, the % Daily Value for fat in the label pictured is 5%, so this food provides 5% of the recommended fat intake for the entire day. The government has set the Percent Daily Values based on current nutrition recommendations, such as the suggested limitation on calories from all sources of fat (**Total Fat** on the label) to no more than 30 percent of total calories. Label space permitting, a daily value footnote appears on the bottom portion of the label. This information is the same on every label, no matter what the food. It lists the recommended daily amounts for nutrients such as fat, cholesterol, sodium, and fiber.

In addition, the label provides the daily values for vitamins A and C, calcium, and iron based on the RDA. Now it is easier to find foods that have higher amounts of these nutrients that may lower your risk of heart disease, cancer, osteoporosis, and anemia.

You won't find nutrition information stamped or pasted onto the skin of an apple. Nor will you find a nutrition label dangling from a drumstick. The produce section of your market should have nutrition information handy for the 20 most popu-

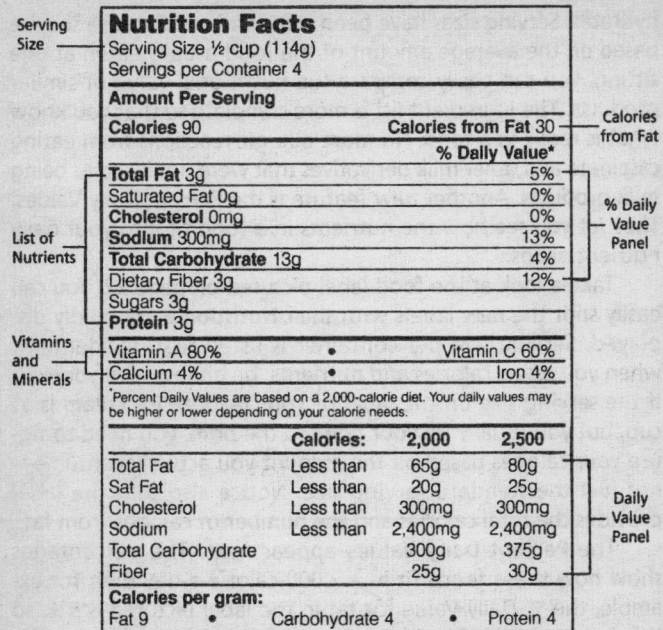

Serving Size

Nutrition Facts
Serving Size ½ cup (114g)
Servings per Container 4

Amount Per Serving

Calories 90	Calories from Fat 30

Calories from Fat

	% Daily Value*
Total Fat 3g	5%
Saturated Fat 0g	0%
Cholesterol 0mg	0%
Sodium 300mg	13%
Total Carbohydrate 13g	4%
Dietary Fiber 3g	12%
Sugars 3g	
Protein 3g	

% Daily Value Panel

List of Nutrients

Vitamin A 80%	•	Vitamin C 60%
Calcium 4%	•	Iron 4%

Vitamins and Minerals

*Percent Daily Values are based on a 2,000-calorie diet. Your daily values may be higher or lower depending on your calorie needs.

		Calories:	2,000	2,500
Total Fat	Less than		65g	80g
Sat Fat	Less than		20g	25g
Cholesterol	Less than		300mg	300mg
Sodium	Less than		2,400mg	2,400mg
Total Carbohydrate			300g	375g
Fiber			25g	30g

Daily Value Panel

Calories per gram:
Fat 9　•　Carbohydrate 4　•　Protein 4

lar fruits and 20 most popular vegetables. Some packages in the meat case carry nutrition information labels. Look for labeling materials such as posters or brochures near the meat case.

A Label Lexicon

In the case of the Nutrition Facts label, you can believe what you read. If it says good source of vitamin C, the food supplies between 10 and 19 percent of the vitamin C daily value in a standard serving. A sweet potato dish that says high in vitamin A has at least 20 percent of the daily value. Phrases such as good source of, high in, and extra lean have been standardized by law. Here are some other words you see frequently on labels along with their definitions per serving:

Sugarfree: less than ½ gram of sugar

Nonfat or Fat free: ½ gram of fat or less

Low fat: 3 grams of fat or less

Reduced fat: 25% less saturated fat than similar foods

Lean: less than 10 grams of fat, 4 grams of saturated fat, and 95 milligrams of cholesterol

Extra lean: less than 5 grams of fat, 2 grams of saturated fat, and 95 milligrams of cholesterol

Calorie free: less than 5 calories

Low calorie: 40 calories or less

Reduced calorie: At least 25% fewer calories than similar foods

Light or Lite: 1/3 fewer calories or 50% less fat

Low cholesterol: 20 milligrams or less cholesterol and 2 grams or less saturated fat

Cholesterol-free: Less than 2 milligrams cholesterol and 2 grams or less saturated fat

High fiber: 5 grams or more of fiber

Very low sodium: 35 milligrams or less of sodium

Low sodium: 140 milligrams or less of sodium

CONTROLLING YOUR WEIGHT

If you need to lose weight, dieting is not the answer, health experts agree. The best way to lose weight and maintain that weight loss is not by means of a "diet," but by adopting a healthier lifestyle. Unless you change your eating and health behaviors, shedding potentially unhealthy food and exercise habits and replacing them with habits that promote health, you will likely regain the weight you lost.

To start, even if you're the only one in your family trying to lose weight, you needn't eat foods that are different than what the rest of your family is eating. Weight control doesn't have to be an experience of sacrifice and denial. A low fat, well-balanced diet is something your whole family can enjoy. Learning to cook foods more healthfully, choosing leaner cuts of meat, lower fat snacks, carbohydrates over sweets—these are the components of a successful weight control plan.

The Dietary Guidelines recommend you lose weight slowly by following this advice:

- Eat less fat and fatty foods.
- Eat more fruits, vegetables, and breads and cereals—without fats and sugars added during cooking or at the table.
- Eat less sugars and sweets.

- Drink little or no alcohol
- Eat smaller portions and limit second helpings.

Think Moderation, Not Deprivation

All foods can have a place in a healthy diet. You just need to trade-off to make room for an occasional indulgence—less fat here for more fat there, and so on.

Pick a few high-fat foods you eat consistently, such as whole or 2 percent milk, ice cream, and blue cheese salad dressing. Then substitute lower fat versions such as skim or 1 percent milk, low fat frozen yogurt, and nonfat blue cheese dressing. These small changes will result in huge fat and calorie savings over a year's time. Another tip is to eat five servings of fruits and vegetables daily. That way, you'll crowd out more high-fat, refined foods, such as cookies, crackers, and chips, and you will pack more complex carbohydrates, fiber, and important vitamins and minerals into your day.

IMPROVING YOUR DIETARY HABITS

Busy lifestyles breed on-the-go feeding styles. In consuming more meals on the fly, we may consume more calories, fat, and sodium and fewer vitamins and minerals and less fiber than we need. With little time for food preparation, we may resort to commercially prepared and highly refined meals.

The key to a healthy diet is planning. Investing an hour or two thinking about meals and shopping for food can set you on your way to better nutrition in no time. Having healthy ingredients on hand enhances your chances for eating better. Even the most creative cook would be hard pressed to create something out of nothing. Keep these staples on the shelves to prevent you from consuming less-than-healthy fare.

- Whole-grain bread and low fat (less than 2 grams per serving) breads, rolls, bagels, and English muffins
- Safflower, sunflower, corn, olive, or canola oil
- Rice and pasta, preferably not in prepackaged flavored mixes (The seasoning packets are high in sodium and may require fat in the preparation.)
- Breakfast cereals with at least 2 grams of fiber per serving
- Graham crackers, gingersnaps, or animal crackers

- Low fat microwave popcorn or pretzels
- Frozen fruit juice bars or frozen yogurt
- Frozen vegetables without added sauces or salt
- Nonfat or low fat milk, yogurt, and cheese
- 100% fruit juice
- Lean deli meats (at least 90 percent fat free)
- Fresh fruit and vegetables
- Peanut butter
- Canned or dried beans (chickpeas, kidney beans, and so on)

Here are more easy ways to improve nutrition:

- Choose low fat snacks to stock your kitchen shelves, your briefcase, and your work area. Raisins, graham crackers, flavored rice cakes, pretzels, low fat popcorn, juice, and yogurt are great pick-me-ups.
- Buy frozen fruits and vegetables if you fear fresh will spoil before you can use them. Canned vegetables are the lowest in nutrient value and most have added salt.
- Prepare one or two dishes, such as roasted chicken or a bean soup, on the weekend. Reheat, adding a salad or steamed vegetables, bread or rolls, milk, and fruit for a nourishing, quick midweek meal with little preparation and cleanup time.
- Good intentions are hard to keep when you're hungry, tired, and aggravated after a long day at work. Pack low fat, nourishing snacks to munch on on the way home or eat them as soon as you get home to tide you over until dinner is ready.

DINING OUT

We love to eat out. Luckily, more restaurants—even fast food chains—are bending to consumer demand for healthier fare. You're more likely than ever to find egg substitutes, margarine, and lower-fat milk on the menu. Chefs and waitstaff are more accommodating, too. Many are willing to prepare and serve menu items with less fat and sodium. Even burger joints are joining in, adding salads, baked potatoes, and low fat shakes to their menus. When you eat out, follow this advice:

- Choose carefully at fast food restaurants. Stay away from cheeseburgers, sausages, most fried foods, and dishes prepared with eggs. Look for foods such as broiled chicken (without skin), plain baked potatoes, and salads with low fat, low cholesterol dressings.

- When portion sizes are large, ask for a doggy bag at the beginning of the meal. Remove half the food from your plate. That way, you won't be tempted to eat twice as much as you should. Eat the leftovers for lunch the next day. Or split a large entrée or oversized dessert with your dining companion to curb calorie and fat consumption.

- Know where fat hides. Avoid entrées described as creamed, buttery, au gratin, fried, or with gravy. Select grilled, steamed, poached, and braised dishes instead.

- Capitalize on fiber by ordering extra vegetables or a salad on the side (with reduced calorie dressing, of course). Forgo french fries in favor of a baked potato. Order a fruit cup for dessert and a fresh vegetable platter with dip as an appetizer.

- Limit alcoholic beverages. Alcohol has nearly twice the calories of carbohydrates or protein. And when you mix it with soda or sour mix, the calorie content soars. Stick with light beer or wine spritzers made with no more than four ounces of wine. Steer clear of cream based drinks; they have nearly four times the calories of wine or beer.

EXERCISE FOR HEALTH

Exercise has a major role in good health, particularly in fighting heart disease. And as rigid diet plans take a back seat to more flexible, and enjoyable, low fat eating styles, exercise has become even more central to a sensible and long lasting weight control regimen.

Exercise strengthens muscles, including your heart. Stronger muscles can do more work with less effort, and a healthy heart works smart: It beats less often to pump out the same amount of blood to the rest of the body. Physical activity can lower blood pressure and keep it low; it can also decrease total blood cholesterol levels and increase HDL, "good" cholesterol levels. Exercise can also help mitigate the effects of age by promoting calcium deposition in your bones: Studies confirm that regular exercisers have thicker and stronger bones. A daily walk, jog, or bike ride may also help you to relax and sleep more restfully. And exercise can be fun. You may actually look forward to it as a welcome distraction from a hectic day.

Researchers say that no matter how old you are, you can become stronger and more agile with regular workouts. Just 30 minutes of aerobic exercise daily may do the trick. Even moderate activity, such as gardening, strolling, and stair climbing, may help reduce the risk of disease.

HOW TO USE *THE COMPLETE FOOD COUNT GUIDE*

The Complete Food Count Guide provides values for thousands of common foods as well as more than 1,000 items from fast food menus. The data come from the United States Department of Agriculture, food manufacturers and processors, and directly from food labels.

Separate columns list the calorie (CAL), total fat, saturated fat (SAT FAT), cholesterol (CHOL), sodium, total carbohydrate (CARB), and fiber content of each food. Fats and carbohydrates appear in grams (g), cholesterol and sodium in milligrams (mg).

Foods are grouped according to the layout of most grocery stores. You'll find a produce section, a canned goods section, a frozen foods section, and so on. When looking for a food, think about where you might find it in a grocery store. The "aisles" are arranged alphabetically. We've taken an additional step to make looking for a food easier for you. Take nuts, for example. They're located in several areas of your grocery store: whole walnuts, pecans, and peanuts are often in the produce section; chopped, sliced, and ground nuts of all varieties are usually in the baking aisle; and macadamias, peanuts, and cashews are in the snack aisle. For your convenience, we've placed all these nuts together in one "aisle" called Chips, Nuts & Snacks.

After a brief description of each item, the brand name or manufacturer of the product appears. (Foods are arranged alphabetically by this description, which is consistent with the manufacturer's spelling and use of trademarks, or by brand name when there is no description. Fast foods are arranged by type of food.) If no brand name appears, the item is generic. After the description and brand name, the standard serving size appears, followed by the nutrient values for that serving size.

Keep in mind that when packaged in different-sized containers, nutrient values for the same product may differ—apple juice in an 11.5 ounce juice box will have different values than apple juice in a 64 oz bottle with a standard serving size of 8 ounces.

Unless indicated otherwise, nutrient values are for the product as packaged. When the food is prepared, the values represent the product prepared according to standard label directions. Values for meats, poultry, and seafood represent foods trimmed of fat and cooked without added salt or fat (oils, butter, margarine). Other foods, such as vegetables or dry beans, described as cooked or boiled are also prepared without added salt or fat.

The symbol "<" means "less than," so "<1" indicates the presence of less than one unit of whatever is measured (less than 1 mg, less than 1 gram). The abbreviation "na" (not available) indicates the manufacturer or label has not provided information for this value; "ns" (not significant) means the food is not a significant source of the nutrient(s) indicated. Fractional values have been rounded off in accordance with federal guidelines.

Finally, while every effort has been made to ensure that the values listed are as accurate as possible, they are subject to change as food manufacturers modify ingredients and methods of preparation. Be sure to check the actual product Nutrition Facts label.

BAKERY ITEMS & BREAD PRODUCTS

	CAL (g)	FAT (g)	SAT FAT (g)	CHOL (mg)	SODIUM (mg)	CARB (g)	FIBER (g)
BAGELS *See also Frozen Foods, Breads & Rolls.*							
Cinnamon raisin, Thomas', bagel	170	1.5	0	0	200	33	3
Egg, Thomas', 1 bagel	170	2	0	30	210	31	2
Multi-grain, Thomas', 1 bagel	150	1.5	0	0	290	32	2
Onion, Thomas', 1 bagel	160	2	0	0	200	33	2
Original, Roman Meal, bagel	230	1.5	0.5	0	400	47	4
Plain, Thomas', 1 bagel	170	2	0	0	220	32	2
BISCUITS							
Buttermilk, old fashioned, Arnold, 2 biscuits	130	5	1	0	250	18	<1
BREAD CRUMBS							
Italian style, Progresso, ¼ cup	110	1.5	0	0	430	20	1
Italian style, Wonder, ½ cup	180	2	0.5	0	320	34	na
Lemon herb, Progresso, ¼ cup	100	1	0	0	480	20	2
Panko, Dynasty, ½ cup	110	1	0	0	80	20	1
Plain, Contadina, ¼ cup	100	1.5	0	0	700	19	1
Plain, Progresso, ¼ cup	100	1.5	0	0	210	19	1
Tomato basil, Progresso, ¼ cup	120	1.5	0	0	750	22	2
BREADS							
Apple honey wheat, Brownberry, 1 slice	60	1	0	0	105	12	1
Apple walnut, Pepperidge Farm, 1 slice	80	2	1	0	120	14	1
Bran, country, light, Arnold Bakery Light, 2 slices	80	1	0	0	180	21	5

BREADS	CAL (g)	FAT (g)	SAT FAT (g)	CHOL (mg)	SODIUM (mg)	CARB (g)	FIB (g)
Bran, country, light, Brownberry Bakery Light, 2 slices	80	1.5	0	0	125	20	
Bran, honey, Wonder Light, 2 slices	80	0.5	0	0	190	18	
Bran, honey (1½ lb loaf), Pepperidge Farm, 1 slice	90	1	0	0	160	17	
Bran'nola, original, Arnold/Brownberry, 1 slice	90	2	0	0	125	18	
Brown, B&M Products, ½ slice	130	0.5	0	0	390	29	
Brown, raisin, B&M Products, ½ slice	130	0.5	0	0	360	29	
Buttermilk, country, Arnold, 1 slice	100	1.5	0	0	170	19	
Cinnamon, Pepperidge Farm, 1 slice	80	3	1	0	115	14	
Cinnamon & raisin, fat free, Natural Ovens, 2 slices	110	1	0	0	140	30	
Cinnamon raisin, Wonder, 1 slice	70	0.5	0	0	100	14	
Cranberry, Arnold, 1 slice	70	1	0	0	80	14	
Date-nut loaf, Thomas', 1 oz	80	2	0	<5	135	16	
Flax 'n honey, Natural Ovens, 2 slices	140	1	0	0	140	30	
Foccaccia, DiCarlo's, ⅛ loaf	130	1.5	0	0	260	25	
French, Bread Du Jour, 3" slice	130	1	0	0	300	26	
French, Wonder, 1 slice	80	1.5	0	0	160	15	
French, Wonder Light, 2 slices	80	1	0	0	210	18	
French, enriched, Arnold Francisco International, 1 oz	70	1	0	0	150	14	
French, enriched, Pepperidge Farm European Bake Shoppe, ⅑ loaf	130	2	1	0	280	25	
French, Parisian, DiCarlo's, 2 slices	70	1	0	0	150	14	
French, twin, Brownberry Francisco International, 1 slice	80	1	0	0	140	18	
French, twin, enriched, Pepperidge Farm European Bake Shoppe, ⅑ of 2 loaves	130	2	1	0	270	26	

BREADS	CAL (g)	FAT (g)	SAT FAT (g)	CHOL (mg)	SODIUM (mg)	CARB (g)	FIBER (g)
French roll, DiCarlo's, 1 slice	70	1	0	0	150	14	<1
French stick, Arnold Francisco International, 1 oz	70	1	0	0	150	14	1
Golden swirl, Vermont maple, Pepperidge Farm, 1 slice	90	3	1	0	100	15	<1
Grain, hearth, Brownberry, 1 slice	90	1.5	0	0	190	17	2
Granola, Wonder, 2 slices	100	1.5	0	0	210	19	2
Happiness, cinnamon, raisins & pecans, Natural Ovens, 2 slices	140	2	0	0	140	30	5
Hazelnut poppy seed, Roman Meal, 1 slice	110	4	0.5	0	180	16	1
Health nut, Brownberry, 1 slice	70	1.5	0	0	130	13	1
Hunger Filler, Natural Ovens, 2 slices	110	1	0	0	140	28	5
Indian (Navajo), 5 inch diameter	300	9	2	0	630	48	ns
Italian, Savoni's, 1 slice	60	0.5	0	0	125	13	<1
Italian, Wonder, 1 slice	80	1	0	0	190	15	<1
Italian, Wonder Light, 2 slices	80	1	0	0	230	18	5
Italian, brown & serve, enriched, Pepperidge Farm European Bake Shoppe, 1/9 loaf	130	2	1	0	260	24	1
Italian, family, Wonder, 1 slice	70	1	0	0	170	13	<1
Italian, light, Arnold Bakery Light, 2 slices	80	1	0	0	200	21	5
Italian, light, Brownberry Bakery Light, 2 slices	80	1	0	0	130	20	5
Italian, sliced, Arnold Francisco International, 2 slices	110	1	0	0	240	23	1
Italian, thick sliced, Brownberry Francisco International, 2 slices	110	1	0	0	250	23	1
Italian stick, Arnold Francisco International, 1 oz	70	1	0	0	135	14	1

BREADS	CAL (g)	FAT (g)	SAT FAT (g)	CHOL (mg)	SODIUM (mg)	CARB (g)	FIBER (g)
Italian stick, sliced, Arnold Francisco International, 2 slices	110	1	0	0	240	23	1
Millet, Natural Ovens, 2 slices	160	2	0	0	70	37	4
Nine grain, Wonder Light, 2 slices	80	1	0	0	230	18	6
Nutty grains, Brownberry Bran'nola, 1 slice	90	2.5	0	0	105	18	3
Oat, Roman Meal, 1 slice	70	1	0	0	150	13	1
Oat, country, Arnold Bran'nola, 1 slice	90	2.5	0.5	0	115	18	3
Oat, hearty crunchy, Pepperidge Farm, 1 slice	100	2	0	0	180	17	2
Oat bran, honey, Roman Meal, 1 slice	70	1	0	0	220	13	1
Oat bran, honey nut, Roman Meal, 1 slice	70	1.5	0	0	150	13	1
Oat bran, light, Roman Meal, 2 slices	80	1	0	0	200	19	5
Oatmeal, Brownberry, 1 slice	70	1	0	0	135	13	1
Oatmeal, Wonder Light, 2 slices	90	1	0	0	230	19	4
Oatmeal (1½ lb), Pepperidge Farm, 1 slice	80	1	0	0	200	15	1
Oatmeal, light, Arnold Bakery Light, 2 slices	80	1	0	0	200	20	4
Oatmeal, light, Brownberry Bakery Light, 1 slice	80	1	0	0	140	20	4
Oatmeal, light, Pepperidge Farm, 3 slices	140	1	0	0	310	27	5
Oatmeal, soft, Pepperidge Farm, 1 slice	60	1	0	0	0	12	0
Oatmeal, thin sliced, Pepperidge Farm, 1 slice	60	1	0	0	160	11	1
Orange raisin, Brownberry, 1 slice	70	1	0	0	70	14	0
Pita, Thomas' Sahara, 1 loaf	150	1	0	0	290	31	1
Pita, 100% whole wheat, Thomas' Sahara, 1 loaf	130	1	0	0	310	28	5

BREADS	CAL (g)	FAT (g)	SAT FAT (g)	CHOL (mg)	SODIUM (mg)	CARB (g)	FIBER (g)
Pita, 100% whole wheat, mini, Thomas' Sahara, 1 loaf	60	0.5	0	0	140	14	2
Pita, garlic & herb, Athens, 1 pita	210	2	0	0	480	40	1
Pita, large, Thomas' Sahara, 1 loaf	220	1	0	0	440	48	2
Pita, mini, Thomas' Sahara, 1 loaf	70	0	0	0	140	15	<1
Pita, oat, Athens, 1 pita	210	1.5	0	0	430	42	3
Pita, oat bran, Thomas' Sahara, 1 loaf	130	1	0	0	300	30	3
Pita, onion, Athens, 1 pita	220	1.5	0	0	430	42	2
Pita, onion, Thomas' Sahara, 1 loaf	140	0.5	0	0	270	31	2
Pita, pumpernickel, Athens, 1 pita	210	3	0.5	0	480	39	2
Pita, rye, Athens, 1 pita	220	2.5	0.5	0	480	42	3
Pita, sourdough, Athens, 1 pita	210	2.5	0.5	0	440	41	1
Pita, sourdough, Thomas' Sahara, 1 loaf	150	0.5	0	0	320	33	2
Pita, wheat, Athens, 1 pita	210	1.5	0	0	440	42	3
Pita, white, Athens, 1 pita	220	1.5	0	0	440	42	1
Potato, country, Arnold, 1 slice	100	2	0	0	150	18	1
Potato, hearty russet, Pepperidge Farm, 1 slice	90	2	1	<5	260	18	3
Protein, 1 slice	50	0	0	0	105	8	1
Pumpernickel, Arnold, 1 slice	80	1	0	0	150	16	1
Pumpernickel, Beefsteak, 1 slice	70	1	0	0	180	13	1
Pumpernickel, Levy's, 1 slice	80	0.5	0	0	150	16	1
Pumpernickel (1 lb loaf), August Bros., 1 slice	80	1	0	0	150	16	<1
Pumpernickel (24 oz loaf), August Bros., 1 slice	90	1	0	0	170	19	1
Pumpernickel, classic dark, Pepperidge Farm, 1 slice	80	1	1	0	230	15	1

BREADS	CAL (g)	FAT (g)	SAT FAT (g)	CHOL (mg)	SODIUM (mg)	CARB (g)	FIBER (g)
Pumpernickel, party slices, Pepperidge Farm, 8 slices	110	2	0	0	320	22	4
Pumpernickel rye, Brownberry, 1 slice	70	0.5	0	0	150	14	1
Pumpkin, 2 pieces	150	3	1	30	460	25	1
Raisin, Sun-Maid, 1 slice	70	1	0	0	85	14	0
Raisin, with cinnamon, Pepperidge Farm, 1 slice	80	2	0	0	105	14	1
Raisin & cinnamon, Arnold, 1 slice	70	1	0	0	90	14	0
Raisin cinnamon, Brownberry, 1 slice	70	1	0	0	110	14	<1
Raisin walnut, Brownberry, 1 slice	80	2.5	0	0	75	13	1
Rice bran, 1 slice	70	1.5	0	0	120	12	ns
Roman Meal, original, with oat bran, 1 slice	70	1	0	0	140	13	1
Roman Meal, round top, 1 slice	70	1	0	0	140	13	1
Rye, Arnold Deli, 1 slice	80	0.5	0	0	150	16	<1
Rye, Wonder, 1 slice	70	1	0	0	170	13	1
Rye, Wonder Light, 2 slices	70	1	0	0	220	17	5
Rye, caraway, Brownberry, 1 slice	70	1	0	0	160	15	1
Rye, country, soft, Arnold, 1 slice	70	1	0	0	140	13	<1
Rye, deli, hearty, Home Pride, 1/12 loaf	140	2	0	0	350	26	
Rye, dijon, thin sliced, Pepperidge Farm, 2 slices	100	2	1	0	340	18	
Rye, dill, Arnold, 2 slices	100	1	0	0	210	21	
Rye, dill, Brownberry, 1 slice	70	1	0	0	150	15	
Rye, German, Natural Ovens, 2 slices	130	1	0	0	140	33	
Rye, hearth, Brownberry, 1 slice	90	1.5	0	0	190	18	
Rye, hearty, Beefsteak, 1 slice	70	1	0	0	170	13	
Rye, Jewish dijon, Arnold, 1 slice	80	1	0	0	200	16	

BREADS	CAL (g)	FAT (g)	SAT FAT (g)	CHOL (mg)	SODIUM (mg)	CARB (g)	FIBER (g)
Rye, Jewish melba thin, Arnold, 2 slices	90	1	0	0	180	19	2
Rye, Jewish, seeded, Pepperidge Farm, 1 slice	80	1	1	0	210	15	1
Rye, Jewish, seedless, Arnold, 1 slice	70	1	0	0	150	16	1
Rye, Jewish, seedless, Pepperidge Farm, 1 slice	80	1	1	0	210	15	1
Rye, Jewish, 2 lb loaf, seedless, Arnold, 1 slice	70	0.5	0	0	140	15	<1
Rye, Jewish, with caraway seeds, Arnold/Levy's, 1 slice	70	1	0	0	150	16	1
Rye, light, Beefsteak, 2 slices	70	1	0	0	250	17	5
Rye, melba, thin sliced, Levy's, 2 slices	90	1	0	0	190	19	1
Rye, mild, Beefsteak, 2 slices	90	1	0	0	240	18	2
Rye, onion, August Bros., 1 slice	80	1	0	0	140	16	1
Rye, onion, Pepperidge Farm, 1 slice	80	1	1	0	210	15	1
Rye, onion, with seeds, August Bros., 1 slice	90	1	0	0	160	18	1
Rye, party slices, Pepperidge Farm, 8 slices	110	2	0	0	410	22	3
Rye, seedless, Brownberry, 1 slice	70	1	0	0	160	15	1
Rye, seedless, Levy's, 1 slice	70	0.5	0	0	150	16	1
Rye, seedless (1 lb loaf), August Bros., 1 slice	80	1	0	0	150	16	<1
Rye, seedless (24 oz loaf), August Bros., 1 slice	90	1	0	0	170	18	1
Rye, soft, Beefsteak, 1 slice	70	1	0	0	180	13	1
Rye, soft, light, Arnold Bakery Light, 2 slices	80	1	0	0	180	20	4
Rye, soft, seedless, Arnold Bakery, 1 slice	80	1	0	0	160	15	<1
Rye, soft, with seeds, Arnold Bakery, 1 slice	80	1	0	0	170	15	1
Rye, thin, seedless, August Bros., 2 slices	90	1	0	0	180	19	1

BREADS	CAL (g)	FAT (g)	SAT FAT (g)	CHOL (mg)	SODIUM (mg)	CARB (g)	FIBER (g)
Rye, thin sliced, seedless, Brownberry, 2 slices	100	1	0	0	250	20	1
Rye, with seeds (1 lb loaf), August Bros., 1 slice	80	1	0	0	140	16	<1
Rye, with seeds (24 oz loaf), August Bros., 1 slice	90	1	0	0	170	18	1
Rye n' pumpernickel, August Bros., 1 slice	90	1	0	0	170	18	1
Salt free, Natural Ovens, 1 slice	60	0.5	0	0	0	20	3
Sandwich, Roman Meal, 2 slices	110	1.5	0	0	230	21	2
Sandwich, soft, low fat, Natural Ovens, 2 slices	110	1	0	0	140	26	2
Sesame wheat, hearty, Pepperidge Farm, 1 slice	100	2	0	0	190	18	2
Seven grain, Home Pride, 1 slice	60	1	0	0	130	12	1
Seven grain, Roman Meal, 1 slice	70	1	0	0	180	16	1
Seven grain, hearty slice, Pepperidge Farm, 1 slice	100	2	0	0	180	18	2
Seven grain, light, Roman Meal, 2 slices	80	1	0	0	210	19	5
Seven grain, light style, Pepperidge Farm, 3 slices	140	1	0	0	320	28	5
Seven grain, multi grain, hearty, Home Pride, 1 slice	100	2	0	0	200	17	2
Seven grain herb, Natural Ovens, 2 slices	140	1	0	0	140	30	4
Seven grain white, Arnold Bran'nola, 1 slice	90	2	0	0	120	18	
Sourdough, Arnold/ Brownberry Francisco International, 1 slice	90	1	0	0	250	19	
Sourdough, August Bros., 1 slice	110	1	0	0	260	23	
Sourdough, Wonder, 1 slice	90	1.5	0	0	180	17	<
Sourdough, Wonder Light, 2 slices	80	1	0	0	250	18	

BREADS	CAL (g)	FAT (g)	SAT FAT (g)	CHOL (mg)	SODIUM (mg)	CARB (g)	FIBER (g)
Sourdough, brown n' serve, Arnold Francisco International, 1 oz	70	0.5	0	0	240	14	1
Sourdough, light, Arnold Bakery Light, 2 slices	80	0.5	0	0	180	20	4
Sourdough, light style, Pepperidge Farm, 3 slices	130	1	0	0	320	27	4
Sourdough, twin, Pepperidge Farm European Bake Shoppe, ⅑ of 1 loaf	130	2	1	0	270	26	1
Sourdough roll, Dicarlo's, 1 slice	100	1	0	0	230	20	1
Stay Slim, low sodium, low fat, Natural Ovens, 2 slices	100	1	0	0	140	20	4
Stick, sliced, August Bros., 2 slices	110	1	0	0	230	22	1
Stick, sliced, Brownberry Francisco International, 1 slice	100	0	0	0	180	21	1
Sun grain, Roman Meal, 1 slice	70	1.5	0	0	140	12	1
Supersub loaf, Arnold Francisco International, 1 oz	70	0.5	0	0	150	14	1
Texas toast, August Bros., 1 slice	150	3	0.5	0	260	28	1
Texas toast, Wonder, 1 slice	100	1	0	0	220	19	1
Toasting, cinnamon & raisin, Wolferman's, 1 slice	120	1	0	0	150	23	2
Toasting, heartland harvest, Wolferman's, 1 slice	80	0	0	0	230	22	2
Toasting, honey nut, Wolferman's, 1 slice	120	1.5	0.5	0	250	22	2
Toasting, oatmeal cinnamon, Wolferman's, 1 slice	120	2	1	0	160	23	2
Toasting, original, Wolferman's, 1 slice	80	0	0	0	170	15	1
Toasting, sourdough, Wolferman's, 1 slice	80	0	0	0	210	16	1
Twelve grain, Brownberry, 2 slices	110	2.5	0	0	180	20	2
Twelve grain, Roman Meal, 1 slice	70	1.5	0	0	150	12	1

BREADS	CAL (g)	FAT (g)	SAT FAT (g)	CHOL (mg)	SODIUM (mg)	CARB (g)	FIBER (g)
Vienna, Wonder, 1 slice	70	1	0	0	170	13	<1
Vienna, light, Pepperidge Farm, 3 slices	130	1	1	0	300	28	5
Vienna, regular & sourdough, 1 slice	70	1	0	0	150	13	<1
Vienna, thick sliced, enriched, Pepperidge Farm, 1 slice	70	1	0	0	150	12	<1
Wheat, Brownberry, 1 slice	80	1	0	0	200	17	2
Wheat, Home Pride, 1 slice	70	1	0	0	160	13	1
Wheat, Wonder Light, 2 slices	80	0.5	0	0	230	18	6
Wheat (1 lb loaf), Arnold Brick Oven, 2 slices	110	3	0.5	0	170	21	3
Wheat (2 lb loaf), Arnold Brick Oven, 1 slice	80	2	0	0	110	14	2
Wheat (8 oz loaf), Arnold Brick Oven, 2 slices	110	2.5	0.5	0	160	20	3
Wheat (1½ lb), Pepperidge Farm, 1 slice	90	2	0	0	190	16	1
Wheat (2 lb family), Pepperidge Farm, 1 slice	70	1	0	0	135	13	1
Wheat, Austrian, Bread Du Jour, 2 oz	130	1.5	0	0	280	26	2
Wheat, country, Arnold, 1 slice	90	1.5	0	0	170	18	1
Wheat, country, Brownberry, 1 slice	90	1.5	0	0	170	18	1
Wheat, cracked, 1 slice	70	1	0	0	135	12	1
Wheat, cracked, Wonder, 1 slice	70	1	0	0	150	14	1
Wheat, cracked, thin sliced, Pepperidge Farm, 1 slice	70	1	0	0	140	12	<1
Wheat, dark, Arnold/ Brownberry Bran'nola, 1 slice	90	2	0	0	130	16	3
Wheat, enriched, Arnold Sunny Valley, 2 slices	100	1.5	0	0	220	20	2
Wheat, golden, country style, Wonder, 2 slices	100	1.5	0	0	220	19	1
Wheat, golden, light, Arnold Bakery Light, 2 slices	80	0.5	0	0	180	20	5

BREADS	CAL (g)	FAT (g)	SAT FAT (g)	CHOL (mg)	SODIUM (mg)	CARB (g)	FIBER (g)
Wheat, golden, light, Brownberry Bakery Light, 2 slices	80	1	0	0	120	20	5
Wheat, golden honey, hearty, Home Pride, 1 slice	90	1.5	0	0	210	18	2
Wheat, hearty honey oats & cracked wheat, Home Pride, 1 slice	100	1.5	0	0	210	19	2
Wheat, hearth, Brownberry, 1 slice	90	1	0	0	190	18	2
Wheat, hearty, Arnold Bran'nola, 1 slice	90	3	0.5	0	130	16	3
Wheat, hearty, Beefsteak, 1 slice	70	1	0	0	160	13	1
Wheat, hearty, Brownberry Bran'nola, 1 slice	90	3	0.5	0	160	16	3
Wheat, hearty, light, Roman Meal, 2 slices	80	1	0	0	210	19	5
Wheat, honey, Home Pride, 1 slice	70	1	0	0	150	13	1
Wheat, light, Home Pride, 3 slices	110	1.5	0	0	300	25	6
Wheat, light, Pepperidge Farm, 3 slices	130	1	1	0	290	28	5
Wheat, light, Roman Meal, 2 slices	80	1	0	0	210	20	5
Wheat, natural, Roman Meal, 1 slice	90	1	0	0	140	12	2
Wheat, natural, 1½ lb, Pepperidge Farm, 1 slice	90	2	0	0	170	16	1
Wheat, nutty, natural, Natural Ovens, 2 slices	140	2	0	0	140	32	6
Wheat, sandwich, Old Home, 1 slice	70	1	0	0	140	13	<1
Wheat, soft, Beefsteak, 1 slice	70	1	0	0	150	13	<1
Wheat, soft, Brownberry, 1 slice	80	2	0	0	135	14	1
Wheat, very thin sliced, Pepperidge Farm, 3 slices	110	2	1	0	230	22	4
Wheat bran, 1 slice	60	1	0	0	120	11	2

BREADS	CAL (g)	FAT (g)	SAT FAT (g)	CHOL (mg)	SODIUM (mg)	CARB (g)	FIBER (g)
Wheat calcium, Wonder Light, 2 slices	80	0.5	0	0	240	18	6
Wheat germ, 1 slice	60	1	0	0	135	12	ns
Wheat berry, honey, Arnold, 1 slice	70	1	0	0	160	16	3
Wheatberry, hearty honey, Pepperidge Farm, 1 slice	100	2	0	0	200	18	2
Wheatberry, honey, Roman Meal, 1 slice	70	1	0	0	140	13	1
Wheatberry, light, Roman Meal, 2 slices	80	1	0	0	210	15	5
White, Brownberry, 2 slices	120	1.5	0	0	160	24	1
White, Home Pride, 1 slice	70	1	0	0	160	13	0
White, Wonder, 1 slice	70	1	0	0	150	13	<1
White, Wonder Kid, 1 slice	60	1	0	0	130	12	2
White, Wonder Light, 2 slices	80	1	0	0	230	18	5
White (2 lb loaf), Arnold Brick Oven, 1 slice	80	1.5	0	0	140	16	<1
White (8 oz loaf), Arnold Brick Oven, 2 slices	120	2.5	0	0	220	24	1
White, calcium, Wonder, 2 slices	100	1	0	0	240	20	1
White, calcium, Wonder Light, 2 slices	80	1	0	0	260	18	5
White, cottage, Hudson Bay, 1 slice	80	1	0	0	160	16	0
White, country, Arnold, 1 slice	100	1.5	0	0	190	19	<1
White, country, Brownberry, 1 slice	90	1.5	0	0	180	19	<1
White, country, soft, Arnold, 1 slice	80	1.5	0	0	150	16	<1
White, enriched, Arnold Sunny Valley, 2 slices	100	1.5	0	0	210	21	1
White, hearty, Pepperidge Farm, 1 slice	90	1	0	0	190	19	2
White, hearty buttermilk & biscuit, Home Pride, 1 slice	100	2	0	0	280	18	<1

BREADS	CAL (g)	FAT (g)	SAT FAT (g)	CHOL (mg)	SODIUM (mg)	CARB (g)	FIBER (g)
White, hearty country, Pepperidge Farm, 1 slice	90	1	0	0	190	19	2
White, light, Arnold Bakery Light, 2 slices	80	0.5	0	0	200	21	4
White, light, Home Pride, 3 slices	110	1.5	0	0	320	25	6
White, light, Roman Meal, 2 slices	80	1	0	0	210	20	5
White, low sodium, 1 slice	70	1	0	0	10	12	<1
White, premium, light, Brownberry Bakery Light, 2 slices	80	1	0	0	135	20	4
White, robust, Beefsteak, 1 slice	70	1	0	0	140	13	1
White, sandwich, Old Home, 1 slice	60	1	0	0	125	12	1
White, sandwich, enriched, Pepperidge Farm, 2 slices	130	2	1	0	260	23	<1
White, soft, Brownberry, 1 slice	80	1.5	0	0	120	14	1
White, thin sliced, enriched, Pepperidge Farm, 1 slice	80	2	0	0	135	13	0
White, thin sliced, family loaf, enriched, Pepperidge Farm, 1 slice	80	2	0	0	160	14	0
White, toasting, sliced, enriched, Pepperidge Farm, 1 slice	90	3	1	0	200	16	0
White, very thin sliced, enriched, Pepperidge Farm, 3 slices	110	2	0	0	270	23	2
White, with buttermilk, Wonder, 1 slice	80	1	0	0	180	14	<1
White grain, Home Pride, 1 slice	60	1	0	0	140	13	2
Whole bran, Brownberry, 1 slice	60	1	0	0	140	12	2
Whole grain, 100%, Natural Ovens, 2 slices	140	2	0	0	100	33	6
Whole grain, 100%, Roman Meal, 1 slice	90	1.5	0	0	150	12	2

BREADS	CAL (g)	FAT (g)	SAT FAT (g)	CHOL (mg)	SODIUM (mg)	CARB (g)	FIBER (g)
Whole grain, 100% whole wheat, Pepperidge Farm Natural Whole Grain, 1 slice	90	1	0	0	160	15	2
Whole grain, crunchy, Pepperidge Farm Natural Whole Grain, 1 slice	90	2	0	0	130	15	2
Whole grain, nine grain, Pepperidge Farm Natural Whole Grain, 1 slice	90	1	0	0	170	16	2
Whole grain sourdough, Roman Meal, 1 slice	70	1	0	0	220	13	1
Whole wheat, 1 slice	60	1	0	0	130	12	2
Whole wheat (1 lb 4 oz loaf), Arnold Stoneground 100%, 1 slice	60	1	0	0	115	12	2
Whole wheat (2 lb loaf), Arnold Stoneground 100%, 2 slices	100	1.5	0	0	170	19	3
Whole wheat, 100%, Roman Meal, 1 slice	60	1	0	0	140	13	2
Whole wheat, 100%, Wonder, 1 slice	70	1	0	0	180	12	2
Whole wheat, 100% stone-ground, Home Pride, 1 slice	90	1.5	0	0	250	18	3
Whole wheat, 100% stone-ground, Wonder, 1 slice	80	1.5	0	0	190	14	2
Whole wheat, 100%, light, Roman Meal, 2 slices	80	1	0	0	210	18	5
Whole wheat, 100%, soft, Pepperidge Farm, 1 slice	60	1	0	0	95	11	1
Whole wheat, light, Natural Ovens, 2 slices	80	1	0	0	140	30	5
Whole wheat, soft, Wonder, 2 slices	110	1.5	0	0	240	21	1
Whole wheat, soft hearth, Natural Ovens, 2 slices	100	2	0	0	140	30	4
Whole wheat, thin sliced, Pepperidge Farm, 1 slice	60	1	0	0	120	11	<1

AT A GLANCE: BREADS

Choose breads with less than 1 gram of saturated fat and no cholesterol.
Highest in Fiber: Wonder Light Honey Bran, Nine Grain, Wheat, and Wheat Calcium breads; Home Pride Wheat Light or White Light breads; and Natural Ovens Nutty Wheat and Whole Grain breads.

	CAL (g)	FAT (g)	SAT FAT (g)	CHOL (mg)	SODIUM (mg)	CARB (g)	FIBER (g)

BREADSTICKS

	CAL (g)	FAT (g)	SAT FAT (g)	CHOL (mg)	SODIUM (mg)	CARB (g)	FIBER (g)
Brown & serve, Pepperidge Farm, 1 breadstick	150	2	1	0	290	28	1
Cheddar cheese, thin, Pepperidge Farm, 7 breadsticks	70	3	1	5	120	10	<1
Classical, La Pace, 5 breadsticks	60	1	0	0	120	12	0
Garlic, Stella D'Oro, 1 breadstick	40	1	na	0	60	7	na
Garlic, fat free, Grissini, 3 breadsticks	60	0	0	0	120	12	na
Garlic, fat free, Stella D'Oro Deli, 5 breadsticks	60	0	0	0	120	12	na
Italian, Bread Du Jour, 1 breadstick	130	1	0	0	280	25	1
Onion, Stella D'Oro, 1 breadstick	40	1	na	0	35	6	na
Onion, thin, Pepperidge Farm, 7 breadsticks	70	2	0	0	115	11	<1
Original, fat free, Grissini, 3 breadsticks	60	0	0	0	130	12	1
Original, fat free, Stella D'Oro Deli, 5 breadsticks	60	0	0	0	130	12	na
Regular, Stella D'Oro, 1 breadstick	40	1	0	0	40	7	0
Regular, sodium free, Stella D'Oro, 1 breadstick	45	1	0	0	0	7	0
Sesame, La Pace, 5 breadsticks	60	1	0	0	120	12	0
Sesame, Stella D'Oro, 1 breadstick	50	2.5	0	0	45	7	<1
Sesame, low fat, Stella D'Oro, 3 breadsticks	70	1	na	0	90	14	na
Sesame, thin, Pepperidge Farm, 7 breadsticks	60	2	0	0	125	11	<1
Sourdough, Bread Du Jour, 1 breadstick	130	1	0	0	280	25	1
Wheat, Stella D'Oro, 1 breadstick	40	1	na	0	20	6	na

	CAL (g)	FAT (g)	SAT FAT (g)	CHOL (mg)	SODIUM (mg)	CARB (g)	FIBER (g)
BUNS & ROLLS							
Bavarian cracked wheat roll, Bread Du Jour, 1 roll	90	1	0	0	190	17	1
Brown & serve roll, Roman Meal, 2 rolls	140	2	0.5	0	290	26	2
Butter crescent roll, heat & serve, Pepperidge Farm, 1 roll	110	5	3	15	160	13	1
Buttermilk roll, brown 'n serve, Wonder, 1 roll	70	1	0	0	160	13	<1
Club roll, brown & serve, enriched, Pepperidge Farm European Bake Shoppe, 1 roll	120	2	0	0	240	22	2
Dinner roll, Arnold, 2 rolls	110	2.5	0.5	0	140	19	1
Dinner roll, Arnold Bran'nola, 1 roll	70	1	0	0	95	13	1
Dinner roll, August Bros., 1 roll	90	2	0	0	180	18	1
Dinner roll, Brownberry Francisco International, 1 roll	120	1	0	0	220	26	1
Dinner roll, Roman Meal, 2 rolls	150	2.5	0.5	0	290	27	2
Dinner roll, country style, Pepperidge Farm, 3 rolls	150	3	1	0	230	22	1
Dinner roll, gourmet, Natural Ovens, 1 roll	50	0.5	0	0	140	15	2
Dinner roll, plain or sesame, Arnold, 2 rolls	110	2.5	0	0	150	19	1
Dinner roll, potato, Arnold, 2 rolls	110	1.5	0	0	125	21	1
Dinner roll, rye, 1 roll	80	1	0	0	250	15	2
Dinner roll, tea, Wonder, 1 roll	80	1	0	0	210	19	5
Dinner roll, wheat, August Bros., 1 roll	100	2	0	0	160	19	1
Dinner roll, wheat, Home Pride, 1 roll	160	4	0.5	0	270	26	2
Dinner roll, white, August Bros., 1 roll	90	1	0	0	190	19	1

BUNS & ROLLS	CAL (g)	FAT (g)	SAT FAT (g)	CHOL (mg)	SODIUM (mg)	CARB (g)	FIBER (g)
Dinner roll, white, Wonder Light, 1 roll	60	1	0	0	150	9	4
Dinner roll, whole wheat, 1 roll	90	2	0	0	170	18	2
Finger roll, poppy seed, enriched, Pepperidge Farm, 3 rolls	150	5	2	5	230	20	1
Finger roll, sesame seeds, enriched, Pepperidge Farm, 3 rolls	150	5	2	5	230	20	1
Frankfurter bun, Pepperidge Farm, 1 bun	140	3	1	0	270	24	<1
Frankfurter bun, dijon, Pepperidge Farm, 1 bun	140	3	2	0	240	23	2
French roll, Brownberry Francisco International, 1 roll	170	1	0	0	260	35	1
French roll, 6", Arnold Francisco International, 1 roll	170	2.5	0	0	350	33	2
French roll, 7 grain, Pepperidge Farm European Bake Shoppe, 1 roll	80	2	0	0	270	19	2
French roll, brown & serve, enriched, Pepperidge Farm, ½ roll	180	2	1	0	400	34	2
French roll, brown & serve, enriched, Pepperidge Farm European Bake Shoppe, 1 roll	240	3	1	0	490	45	3
French roll, mini, Arnold Francisco International, 1 roll	110	1	0	0	200	22	<1
French roll, petite, Bread Du Jour, 1 roll	230	2	0	0	530	47	2
French roll, sourdough style, enriched, Pepperidge Farm European Bake Shoppe, 1 roll	100	1	0	0	240	18	1
French style roll, enriched, Pepperidge Farm European Bake Shoppe, 1 roll	100	1	0	0	230	19	1
German, hard roll, Natural Ovens, 1 roll	140	1	0	0	140	36	1
Golden twist roll, heat & serve, Pepperidge Farm, 1 roll	110	4	2	<5	160	13	1

BUNS & ROLLS	CAL (g)	FAT (g)	SAT FAT (g)	CHOL (mg)	SODIUM (mg)	CARB (g)	FIBER (g)
Hamburger, Arnold, 1 bun	130	2	0	0	240	25	1
Hamburger, Arnold Bran'nola, 1 bun	130	1.5	0	0	210	27	3
Hamburger, August Bros., 1 bun	140	2.5	0.5	0	210	26	1
Hamburger, Pepperidge Farm, 1 bun	130	3	1	0	230	22	1
Hamburger, Roman Meal, 1 bun	120	2	0.5	0	230	22	2
Hamburger or hot dog, Wonder Light, 1 bun	80	1.5	0	0	210	13	5
Hamburger or hot dog, enriched, Wonder, 1 bun	110	2	0	0	250	21	<1
Hamburger or hot dog, potato, Home Pride, 1 bun	130	1.5	0	0	270	27	2
Hamburger or hot dog, reduced calorie, 1 bun	80	1	0	0	190	18	3
Hamburger, wheat, August Bros., 1 bun	130	2	0	0	210	25	2
Hamburger, wheat, Wonder, 1 bun	170	2.5	0	0	370	31	1
Hard roll (includes Kaiser), 1 roll	150	2.5	0	0	270	26	1
Hearth, roll, assorted, Brownberry, 1 roll	120	1.5	0	0	220	22	1
Hearth roll, brown & serve, enriched, Pepperidge Farm European Bake Shoppe, 3 rolls	150	2	0	0	300	28	2
Hoagie, Pepperidge Farm Deli Classics, 1 roll	200	5	3	0	340	32	2
Hoagie, multigrain, Pepperidge Farm, 1 roll	200	5	3	0	340	32	2
Hot dog, Arnold Bran'nola, 1 bun	110	1.5	0	0	170	21	2
Hot dog, Roman Meal, 1 bun	110	2	0.5	0	220	20	2
Hot dog (8 pack/11 oz), Arnold, 1 bun	100	2	0	0	150	19	1
Hot dog (8 pack/12 oz), Arnold, 1 bun	110	2	0	0	210	21	1

BUNS & ROLLS	CAL (g)	FAT (g)	SAT FAT (g)	CHOL (mg)	SODIUM (mg)	CARB (g)	FIBER (g)
Hot dog, New England style, Arnold, 1 bun	110	2	0	0	210	21	1
Hot dog, potato, Arnold, roll	120	2	0	0	150	23	1
Hot dog, sliced, Brownberry, roll	110	2	0	0	210	22	1
Hot dog, wheat, Brownberry, roll	110	2	0	0	190	21	1
Italian roll, 8", Savoni, 1 roll	280	3.5	0.5	0	610	56	3
Italian roll, crusty, Bread Du Jour, 1 roll	80	0.5	0	0	190	16	<1
Kaiser roll, August Bros., roll	160	2	0	0	250	32	1
Kaiser roll, Brownberry Francisco International, 1 roll	170	1	0	0	260	35	1
Kaiser roll, Levy's, 1 roll	170	2	0	0	270	34	1
Kaiser roll, hearth, Brownberry, 1 roll	150	2.5	0	0	270	30	1
Kaiser sandwich, with sesame, Arnold, 1 bun	140	4	0.5	0	200	25	1
Onion roll, Arnold Deli, 1 roll	170	2	0	0	250	35	2
Onion roll, August Bros., roll	160	2	0	0	240	33	2
Onion roll, Levy's, 1 roll	160	3	0.5	5	210	31	3
Parker House roll, enriched, Pepperidge Farm, 3 rolls	150	5	2	5	230	20	1
Party roll, enriched, Pepperidge Farm, 5 rolls	170	5	2	10	240	26	2
Potato roll, Arnold, 1 roll	150	2	0	0	180	28	1
Potato roll, hearty, Pepperidge Farm Deli Classics, roll	80	3	1	0	110	12	1
Potato roll, sesame, Arnold, roll	150	3	0.5	0	180	28	1
Rye roll, Bread Du Jour, 1 roll	90	1.5	0	0	230	16	1
Sandwich, Roman Meal, 1 roll	190	3	0.5	0	390	35	3
Sandwich, 5", hearty, Pepperidge Farm, 1 bun	230	5	3	0	360	39	2
Sandwich, hearty, Natural Ovens, 1 bun	110	0.5	0	0	140	30	6

BUNS & ROLLS	CAL (g)	FAT (g)	SAT FAT (g)	CHOL (mg)	SODIUM (mg)	CARB (g)	FIBER (g)
Sandwich, multigrain, Pepperidge Farm, 1 bun	150	3	1	0	230	24	3
Sandwich, onion, Pepperidge Farm, 1 roll	150	3	2	0	270	26	1
Sandwich, potato, Brownberry, 1 roll	150	2.5	0	0	200	28	1
Sandwich, potato, Pepperidge Farm, 1 bun	160	4	1	0	260	28	<1
Sandwich, sesame, enriched, Pepperidge Farm, 1 bun	140	3	2	0	240	23	1
Sandwich, sesame, soft, Arnold, 1 roll	140	3.5	0.5	0	190	23	1
Sandwich, soft, Arnold, 1 roll	120	3	0.5	0	160	20	1
Sandwich, sourdough, Pepperidge Farm, 1 bun	170	4	2	0	290	28	1
Sandwich, wheat, Brownberry, 1 bun	130	2	0	0	230	24	2
Sandwich, wheat, Home Pride, 1 roll	160	4	0.5	0	270	26	2
Sandwich, white, Brownberry, 1 bun	140	2.5	0.5	0	210	25	1
Sandwich, white, seedless, Brownberry, 1 bun	140	2.5	0.5	0	220	26	1
Sandwich, white, with seeds, Brownberry, 1 bun	140	3	0.5	0	220	26	1
Sesame roll, August Bros., 1 roll	170	2.5	0	0	240	33	1
Sourdough roll, Arnold Francisco International, 1 roll	90	1	0	0	180	17	1
Sourdough roll, Bread Du Jour, 1 roll	140	1.5	0	0	230	29	2
Sourdough roll, brown n' serve, Francisco, 1 roll	80	1	0	0	180	17	1
Steak roll, Arnold, 1 roll	170	2.5	0	0	360	33	2
Steak roll, Arnold Francisco International, 1 roll	170	2	0	0	320	35	2
Steak roll, August Bros., 1 roll	170	2.5	0	0	360	33	2
Sub, August Bros., 1 roll	170	2.5	0	0	380	33	2
Sub, Levy's, 1 roll	140	1.5	0	0	250	30	1

BUNS & ROLLS	CAL (g)	FAT (g)	SAT FAT (g)	CHOL (mg)	SODIUM (mg)	CARB (g)	FIBER (g)
White & wheat roll, brown 'n serve, Wonder, 1 roll	70	0.5	0	0	135	14	<1
White roll, Home Pride, 2 rolls	130	4	0.5	0	230	22	1

AT A GLANCE: BUNS & ROLLS
Choose buns and rolls with less than 2 grams of saturated fat and no cholesterol.
Highest in Fiber: Natural Ovens Hearty Sandwich

CAKES *See also Coffee Cakes & Pastry; Snack Cakes.*

	CAL (g)	FAT (g)	SAT FAT (g)	CHOL (mg)	SODIUM (mg)	CARB (g)	FIBER (g)
All butter French crumb cake, Entenmann's, 1/8 cake	210	10	6	60	240	29	0
All butter loaf, Entenmann's, 1/6 loaf	220	10	6	80	290	31	0
Angel bar, Dolly Madison, 2 oz	170	1.5	0	0	190	35	1
Angel food ring, Dolly Madison, 2 oz	160	1.5	0	0	180	33	1
Angel food ring, Hostess, 1/6 cake	120	0	0	0	350	27	0
Apple spice crumb cake, fat free, cholesterol free, Entenmann's, 1/8 cake	130	0	0	0	140	30	2
Banana crunch cake, Entenmann's, 1/8 cake	220	9	2	40	280	32	<1
Banana crunch cake, fat free, cholesterol free, Entenmann's, 1/8 cake	140	0	0	0	150	33	2
Banana loaf, fat free, cholesterol free, Entenmann's, 1/8 loaf	150	0	0	0	190	34	1
Blueberry crunch cake, fat free, cholesterol free, Entenmann's, 1/8 cake	140	0	0	0	200	32	2
Carrot cake, Entenmann's, 1/8 cake	290	16	3.5	35	240	35	<1
Carrot cake, fat free, cholesterol free, Entenmann's, 1/8 cake	170	0	0	0	230	40	1
Chocolate cake, fudge iced, fat free, cholesterol free, Entenmann's, 1/6 cake	210	0	0	0	270	51	2

CAKES	CAL (g)	FAT (g)	SAT FAT (g)	CHOL (mg)	SODIUM (mg)	CARB (g)	FIBE (g)
Chocolate cake, mocha iced, fat free, cholesterol free, Entenmann's, ⅙ cake	200	0	0	0	270	46	
Chocolate crunch cake, fat free, cholesterol free, Entenmann's, ⅛ cake	130	0	0	0	170	32	
Chocolate fudge cake, Entenmann's, ⅙ cake	310	14	5	45	260	47	
Chocolate loaf, fat free, cholesterol free, Entenmann's, ⅛ loaf	130	0	0	0	250	30	
Coconut layer cake, Dolly Madison, 3 oz	300	9	2	5	290	53	
Devil's food bar, Dolly Madison, 2.8 oz	330	14	2	10	270	48	
Devil's food cake, marshmallow iced, Entenmann's, ⅙ cake	350	18	5	45	290	45	
Fruitcake, 1 piece	300	10	1.5	25	120	54	
Golden cake, fudge iced, fat free, cholesterol free, Entenmann's, ⅙ cake	220	0	0	0	200	52	
Golden cake, with fudge, Entenmann's, ⅙ cake	330	16	4	50	270	48	
Golden chocolate chip loaf, fat free, cholesterol free, Entenmann's, ⅛ loaf	130	0	0	0	220	31	
Golden French crumb cake, fat free, cholesterol free, Entenmann's, ⅛ cake	140	0	0	0	150	35	
Golden loaf, fat free, cholesterol free, Entenmann's, ⅛ loaf	120	0	0	0	160	28	<
Louisiana crunch cake, Entenmann's, ⅑ cake	310	13	3.5	50	290	45	<
Louisiana crunch cake, fat free, cholesterol free, Entenmann's, ⅙ cake	220	0	0	0	220	51	<
Marble loaf, Entenmann's, ⅛ loaf	200	10	6	65	230	25	<
Marble loaf, fat free, cholesterol free, Entenmann's, ⅛ loaf	130	0	0	0	190	29	

...AKES	CAL (g)	FAT (g)	SAT FAT (g)	CHOL (mg)	SODIUM (mg)	CARB (g)	FIBER (g)
...ound cake, Dolly Madison, ...oz	360	13	4	20	430	55	1
...ound cake, Hostess, 1/5 cake	350	16	4	55	360	48	1
...ound cake, ring, Dolly Madison, 2.5 oz	310	11	4	15	280	48	1
...aisin loaf, Entenmann's, ...e loaf	220	9	2	50	200	32	<1
...aisin loaf, fat free, ...olesterol free, ...ntenmann's, 1/8 loaf	140	0	0	0	150	33	1
...ortcake, Dolly Madison, ...cake	110	2	0.5	15	130	20	1
...our cream loaf, chip & nut, ...ntenmann's, 1/8 loaf	240	14	4	50	150	28	<1
...pice bar cake, Dolly ...adison, 2.8 oz	350	17	5	35	240	46	1
...ponge, 1 piece	190	2	0.5	65	160	40	0
...rawberry cream, ...pperidge Farm Special ...ecipe, 1/9 cake	230	9	3	30	115	38	1
...hite bar cake, Dolly ...adison, 2.7 oz	320	14	5	30	200	47	1

...T A GLANCE: CAKES

...you must have your cake and eat it too, choose from among the fat free cakes ...om Entenmann's or Hostess, but keep the calories under 200 grams per serving.

...HURROS

...nnamon, Tio Pepe's, ...churro	110	5	1.5	15	100	14	2

...OFFEE CAKES & PASTRY See also Snack Cakes.

...pple strudel, Entenmann's, ...strudel	310	14	3.5	0	230	44	2
...pricot Danish twist, fat free, ...olesterol free, ...ntenmann's, 1/8 Danish	150	0	0	0	110	34	<1
...ack forest pastry, fat free, ...olesterol free, ...ntenmann's, 1/9 Danish	130	0	0	0	115	32	2
...eese coffee cake, ...ntenmann's, 1/9 cake	190	8	3.5	30	160	24	0

COFFEE CAKES & PASTRY	CAL (g)	FAT (g)	SAT FAT (g)	CHOL (mg)	SODIUM (mg)	CARB (g)	FIBE (g)
Cheese filled crumb coffee cake, Entenmann's, 1/8 cake	210	10	4	40	190	25	<
Cinnamon apple coffee cake, fat free, cholesterol free, Entenmann's, 1/9 cake	130	0	0	0	110	29	
Cinnamon apple twist, fat free, cholesterol free, Entenmann's, 1/8 Danish	150	0	0	0	110	35	<
Cinnamon filbert ring, Entenmann's, 1/6 Danish	270	17	3	30	190	27	
Cinnamon swirl coffee cake, individual, Dolly Madison, 1 cake	170	6	2	15	170	29	
Crumb coffee cake, Entenmann's, 1/10 cake	250	12	3	15	210	33	
Crumb coffee cake, Sara Lee, 1/8 cake	220	9	1.5	15	210	32	<
Fruit slices, fat free, Stella D'Oro, 1 slice	50	0	0	0	60	12	n
Lemon twist, fat free, cholesterol free, Entenmann's, 1/8 Danish	130	0	0	0	140	31	
Pecan Danish ring, Entenmann's, 1/8 Danish	230	15	3	25	160	23	
Plain coffee cake, Dolly Madison, 2 cakes	270	11	3	15	240	41	
Raspberry cheese pastry, fat free, cholesterol free, Entenmann's, 1/9 Danish	140	0	0	0	110	32	
Raspberry Danish twist, Entenmann's, 1/8 Danish	220	11	3	20	170	28	<
Raspberry twist, fat free, cholesterol free, Entenmann's, 1/8 Danish	140	0	0	0	125	33	
Walnut Danish ring, Entenmann's, 1/8 Danish	230	14	3	25	160	23	

AT A GLANCE: COFFEE CAKES & PASTRY
Lowest in Fat: Entenmann's fat free selections

CROUTONS

	CAL (g)	FAT (g)	SAT FAT (g)	CHOL (mg)	SODIUM (mg)	CARB (g)	FIBE
Caesar, homestyle, Pepperidge Farm, 6 croutons	35	2	0	0	90	4	

CROUTONS	CAL (g)	FAT (g)	SAT FAT (g)	CHOL (mg)	SODIUM (mg)	CARB (g)	FIBER (g)
Caesar salad, Brownberry, 2 Tbsp	30	1.5	0	0	70	4	0
Cheddar & Romano cheese, Pepperidge Farm, 9 croutons	30	1	0	0	95	4	0
Cheddar cheese, Brownberry, 2 Tbsp	30	1.5	0	0	65	4	0
Cheese & garlic, Arnold, 2 Tbsp	30	1	0	0	50	5	0
Cheese & garlic, Brownberry, 2 Tbsp	30	1	0	0	60	5	0
Cheese & garlic, Pepperidge Farm, 9 croutons	35	2	0	0	80	4	0
Cracked pepper & Parmesan, Pepperidge Farm, 6 croutons	35	2	0	0	90	4	0
Fine herbs, Arnold, 2 Tbsp	30	1	0	0	60	5	0
French garlic, Country Hearth, ¼ cup	35	1	0	0	125	5	0
Italian, Arnold, 2 Tbsp	30	1	0	0	65	4	0
Olive oil & garlic, homestyle, Pepperidge Farm, 6 croutons	30	1	0	0	80	5	0
Onion & garlic, Arnold, 2 Tbsp	30	1	0	0	80	5	0
Onion & garlic, Brownberry, 2 Tbsp	30	1	0	0	80	4	0
Onion & garlic, Pepperidge Farm, 9 croutons	30	1	0	0	80	5	0
Plain, Country Hearth, ¼ cup	30	0	0	0	60	6	0
Ranch, Arnold, 2 Tbsp	30	1	0	0	75	5	0
Ranch, Brownberry, 2 Tbsp	30	1	0	0	80	4	0
Ranch, Pepperidge Farm, 9 croutons	35	2	1	<5	65	4	0
Reduced fat, Marie Callender's, 4 croutons	30	1	0	0	110	5	0
Seasoned, Brownberry, 2 Tbsp	30	1	0	0	70	4	0
Seasoned, Pepperidge Farm, 9 croutons	35	2	0	0	85	4	0
Seasoned, crispy, Arnold, 2 Tbsp	30	1	0	0	60	5	0
Sour cream & Parmesan, Marie Callender's, 4 croutons	30	1	0	0	100	4	0

CROUTONS	CAL (g)	FAT (g)	SAT FAT (g)	CHOL (mg)	SODIUM (mg)	CARB (g)	FIBER (g)
Sourdough cheese homestyle, Pepperidge Farm, 6 croutons	30	1	0	0	80	4	0
Toasted, Brownberry, 2 Tbsp	30	1	0	0	45	5	0
Zesty Italian homestyle, Pepperidge Farm, 9 croutons	35	2	1	<5	65	4	0

AT A GLANCE: CROUTONS
Lowest in Fat: Country Hearth Plain
Lowest in Sodium: Brownberry Toasted

CRUMPETS

	CAL (g)	FAT (g)	SAT FAT (g)	CHOL (mg)	SODIUM (mg)	CARB (g)	FIBER (g)
Blueberry, Wolferman's, 1 crumpet	100	0.5	0	0	250	21	1
Brown sugar cinnamon, Wolferman's, 1 crumpet	100	1.5	0	0	270	19	1
Lemon poppy seed, Wolferman's, 1 crumpet	90	0.5	0	0	280	19	2
Original, Wolferman's, 1 crumpet	90	0.5	0	0	260	19	1
Raspberry, Wolferman's, 1 crumpet	100	0	0	0	280	20	2
Whole grain, Wolferman's, 1 crumpet	100	1	0	0	310	19	2

CUPCAKES

	CAL (g)	FAT (g)	SAT FAT (g)	CHOL (mg)	SODIUM (mg)	CARB (g)	FIBER (g)
Butter cream, iced, creme filled, Tastykake, 2 cakes	250	8	2	10	280	42	2
Chocolate, Aunt Fanny's, 2 cakes	310	12	5	20	560	49	3
Chocolate, Dolly Madison, 1 cupcake	190	5	3	5	280	35	1
Chocolate, Hostess, 1 cake	170	5	2.5	<5	260	28	<1
Chocolate, Tastykake, 2 cakes	220	6	1.5	10	270	39	2
Chocolate, iced, creme filled, Tastykake, 2 cakes	250	8	2	10	270	41	2
Chocolate, light, Hostess, 1 cake	120	1.5	0	0	170	26	<1
Koffee Kake, creme filled, Tastykake, 2 cakes	240	9	2	35	150	35	0
Kreme Kup, Tastykake, 2 cakes	190	6	1.5	10	250	31	1

CUPCAKES	CAL (g)	FAT (g)	SAT FAT (g)	CHOL (mg)	SODIUM (mg)	CARB (g)	FIBER (g)
Orange, Aunt Fanny's, 2 cakes	310	12	4	15	370	50	1
Orange, Hostess, 1 cake	160	5	2	10	160	28	0
Spice, Dolly Madison, 1 cupcake	230	10	3	20	150	33	1
Tasty Too, chocolate, creme filled, Tastykake, 2 cakes	200	3	1	0	230	42	2
Tasty Too, vanilla, creme filled, Tastykake, 2 cakes	210	4	1.5	0	230	41	1

DONUTS

	CAL (g)	FAT (g)	SAT FAT (g)	CHOL (mg)	SODIUM (mg)	CARB (g)	FIBER (g)
Bismarck, yeast-leavened, creme filling, 1 bismarck	310	21	6	20	260	26	<1
Chocolate, cake-type, sugared or glazed, 1 donut	180	8	2.5	25	140	24	<1
Chocolate, mini, Hostess, 5 donuts	220	9	0	35	220	33	1
Chocolate iced, old fashion, Dolly Madison, 1 donut	300	14	7	20	310	32	1
Cinnamon, Hostess, 1 donut	110	5	2	5	140	15	<1
Cinnamon, Tastykake, 1 donut	210	12	2	15	240	24	1
Cinnamon crunch, Hostess, 4 donuts	160	2.5	0.5	20	170	34	0
Cinnamon stix, Dolly Madison, 1 donut	170	9	3.5	15	130	21	0
Cinnamon sugar, Dolly Madison, 2 donuts	230	12	5	10	270	29	1
Cruller, English, Dolly Madison, 1 cruller	260	14	6	30	190	32	1
Cruller, French, glazed, 1 cruller	170	8	2	<5	140	24	0
Crumb, Hostess, 1 donut	130	8	4	5	115	14	<1
Crumb topped, Entenmann's, 1 donut	260	13	3	15	230	34	<1
Crunch, Dolly Madison, 1 donut	140	6	3	10	120	15	0
Devil's food crumb, Entenmann's, 1 donut	250	12	3.5	15	240	33	1

DONUTS	CAL (g)	FAT (g)	SAT FAT (g)	CHOL (mg)	SODIUM (mg)	CARB (g)	FIBER (g)
Donut gems, chocolate (20 pack), Dolly Madison, 4 donuts	260	15	9	15	230	28	1
Donut gems, chocolate (6 pack), Dolly Madison, 6 donuts	400	23	14	20	340	42	1
Donut gems, cinnamon, Hostess Donettes, 6 donuts	340	14	5	15	410	48	2
Donut gems, cinnamon sugar, Dolly Madison, 6 donuts	360	17	7	25	400	46	1
Donut gems, crumb, Hostess Donettes, 6 donuts	320	11	4	10	390	53	1
Donut gems, crunch, Dolly Madison, 6 donuts	390	18	9	25	420	53	1
Donut gems, frosted, Hostess Donettes, 6 donuts	390	23	15	10	360	42	2
Donut gems, frosted strawberry, Hostess Donettes, 3 donuts	240	13	9	<5	210	29	1
Donut gems, powdered, Hostess Donettes, 6 donuts	350	16	6	10	380	47	1
Donut gems, powdered, strawberry filled, Hostess Donettes, 3 donuts	210	9	4	<5	210	31	<1
Donut gems, powdered sugar (20 or 38 pack), Dolly Madison, 4 donuts	240	11	5	15	270	31	1
Donut gems, powdered sugar (6 pack), Dolly Madison, 6 donuts	360	17	7	25	400	46	1
Donut sticks, Little Debbie, 1 pkg	210	13	3	5	210	25	1
Double chocolate crunch, Hostess, 4 donuts	160	3	0.5	20	170	32	1
Dunkin Stix (2 pack), Dolly Madison, 2 donuts	360	19	7	25	280	43	1
Dunkin Stix (3, 6, or 8 pack), Dolly Madison, 1 donut	170	9	4	15	130	21	1
Dunkin stix, Tastykake, 1 piece	190	11	4	5	150	21	1
Dunkin' Stix, cherry, Aunt Fanny's, 1.4 oz	180	11	3	5	150	21	1

DONUTS	CAL (g)	FAT (g)	SAT FAT (g)	CHOL (mg)	SODIUM (mg)	CARB (g)	FIBER (g)
Dunkin' Stix, chocolate, Aunt Fanny's, 1.4 oz	180	12	3	5	140	21	1
Dunkin' Stix, regular, Aunt Fanny's 1.4 oz	190	11	4	10	150	21	1
Frosted, regular, Dolly Madison, 1 donut	130	6	3	10	120	15	0
Frosted, rich, Entenmann's, 1 donut	280	19	6	10	220	27	1
Frosted, rich, Tastykake, 1 donut	270	16	5	5	180	30	2
Frosted, rich, mini, Tastykake, 6 donuts	400	23	11	20	370	44	3
Frosted jumbo, Hostess, 1 donut	260	16	10	10	240	28	1
Frosted mini, Entenmann's, 2 donuts	270	20	6	10	180	23	1
Frosted regular, Hostess, 1 donut	180	11	7	5	170	20	1
Glazed, Entenmann's, 6 pieces	240	11	2.5	15	210	33	0
Glazed, old fashion, Dolly Madison, 1 donut	300	14	7	20	310	32	1
Glazed, old fashioned, Hostess, 1 donut	250	12	5	15	230	33	<1
Glazed buttermilk, Entenmann's, 1 donut	270	13	3	10	270	36	0
Glazed chocolate, Entenmann's, 4 pieces	200	10	2.5	15	190	29	<1
Glazed honey wheat, old fashioned, Hostess, 1 donut	250	12	5	25	270	33	1
Glazed whirl, Hostess, 1 donut	180	7	3	<5	220	28	<1
Iced, jumbo, Dolly Madison, 1 donut	230	12	6	15	230	28	0
Jelly filled (bismarck), 1 donut	220	12	3	20	190	25	<1
Orange glazed, Tastykake, 1 donut	220	9	1.5	5	200	33	1
Plain, Dolly Madison, 2 donuts	170	10	6	10	200	18	0
Plain, Hostess, 1 donut	120	6	3	5	160	13	<1

DONUTS	CAL (g)	FAT (g)	SAT FAT (g)	CHOL (mg)	SODIUM (mg)	CARB (g)	FIBER (g)
Plain, Tastykake, 1 donut	180	11	2	15	210	19	1
Plain, cake-type, chocolate-coated or frosted, 1 donut	200	13	3.5	25	180	21	<1
Plain, cake-type, sugared or glazed, 1 donut	190	10	2.5	15	180	23	<1
Plain, jumbo, Dolly Madison, 1 donut	190	11	6	15	220	19	0
Plain, jumbo, Hostess, 1 donut	140	7	4	10	190	16	<1
Plain, old fashioned, Hostess, 1 donut	170	9	4	10	230	21	<1
Plain, yeast, glazed, Dolly Madison, 1 donut	180	8	4	10	125	24	0
Plain, yeast-leavened, glazed, enriched (includes honey buns), 1 donut	240	14	3.5	<5	210	27	1
Powdered, family pack, Hostess, 1 donut	110	6	2.5	5	135	15	0
Powdered, jumbo, Hostess, 1 donut	160	9	5	5	170	19	<1
Powdered, raspberry filled, Hostess, 1 donut	230	10	4	5	230	35	<1
Powdered sugar, Tastykake, 1 donut	210	11	2	15	210	24	1
Powdered sugar, mini, Tastykake, 6 donuts	290	12	2.5	25	350	40	1
Sugar, jumbo, Dolly Madison, 1 donut	230	12	6	15	240	27	0
Sugar, regular, Dolly Madison, 1 donut	110	6	3	10	120	15	1
Wheat, cake-type, sugared or glazed, 1 donut	160	9	1.5	10	160	19	1
Wheat, honey, Tastykake, 1 donut	230	10	2	5	180	33	1
Wheat, honey, mini, Tastykake, 6 donuts	280	13	2.5	20	300	39	1
White iced, old fashion, Dolly Madison, 1 donut	230	14	7	20	310	32	1

AT A GLANCE: DONUTS

As all these products are relatively high in fat, when you do choose a donut, choose one with less than 2.5 grams saturated fat.

	CAL (g)	FAT (g)	SAT FAT (g)	CHOL (mg)	SODIUM (mg)	CARB (g)	FIBER (g)
ENGLISH MUFFINS							
Bays, 1 muffin	140	1.5	0.5	0	530	27	1
Pepperidge Farm, 1 muffin	130	1	0	0	250	26	2
Roman Meal, 1 muffin	135	1	0	0	295	27	3
Thomas', 1 muffin	120	1	0	0	200	25	1
Wonder, 1 muffin	120	1	0	0	290	25	1
Apple strudel, Wolferman's, 1 muffin	250	5	1	0	370	44	4
Blueberry, Wolferman's, 1 muffin	240	1	0.5	0	520	50	3
Blueberry, mini, Wolferman's, 1 muffin	80	0	0	0	170	16	1
Cinnamon & raisin, Wolferman's, 1 muffin	240	2	1	0	310	48	6
Cinnamon & raisin, mini, Wolferman's, 1 muffin	80	0.5	0	0	100	16	2
Cinnamon raisin, Pepperidge Farm, 1 muffin	140	2	0	0	230	28	2
Cinnamon raisin, Tastykake, 1 muffin	110	1	0	0	170	20	3
Cranberry, Wolferman's, 1 muffin	240	1	0.5	0	340	49	3
Cranberry, mini, Wolferman's, 1 muffin	80	0	0	0	110	16	1
Golden raisin bran, Wolferman's, 1 muffin	250	1.5	na	0	540	51	na
Heartland harvest, Wolferman's, 1 muffin	230	1	0.5	0	460	46	5
Honey nut, Wolferman's, 1 muffin	240	2.5	0	0	510	45	7
Honey wheat, Thomas', 1 muffin	110	1	0	0	190	24	3
Low sodium, Wolferman's, 1 muffin	220	1	0.5	0	190	44	2
Mixed berry, Wolferman's, 1 muffin	230	1	0.5	0	290	49	4
Mixed berry, mini, Wolferman's, 1 muffin	80	0	0	0	100	16	1
Mixed grain, 1 muffin	140	1	0	0	250	28	4

ENGLISH MUFFINS	CAL	FAT (g)	SAT FAT (g)	CHOL (mg)	SODIUM (mg)	CARB (g)	FIBER (g)
Natural cheese, Wolferman's, 1 muffin	230	3.5	2.5	5	670	44	3
Oat bran, Thomas', 1 muffin	120	1	0.5	0	210	26	2
Oatmeal cinnamon, Wolferman's, 1 muffin	250	3.5	1	0	330	48	4
Onion, sandwich size, Thomas', 1 muffin	180	1.5	0	0	270	40	2
Original, Wolferman's, 1 muffin	220	1	0	0	410	45	3
Original, mini, Wolferman's, 1 muffin	70	0	0	0	135	15	<1
Raisin, Thomas', 1 muffin	140	1	0	0	170	31	1
Raisin rounds, Wonder, 1 muffin	150	2	0	0	240	30	2
Sandwich size (4 pack), Thomas', 1 muffin	190	2	0	0	280	38	2
Sandwich size (twin pack), Thomas', 1 muffin	190	1.5	0	0	300	41	2
Seven grain, Pepperidge Farm, 1 muffin	130	1	0	0	230	26	2
Sourdough, Pepperidge Farm, 1 muffin	130	1	0	0	250	26	2
Sourdough, Tastykake, 1 muffin	130	1	0	0	210	25	2
Sourdough, Thomas', 1 muffin	120	1	0	0	190	25	1
Sourdough, Wolferman's, 1 muffin	220	1	0.5	0	430	44	2
Sourdough, Wonder, 1 muffin	120	1	0	0	290	25	1
Sourdough, mini, Wolferman's, 1 muffin	70	0	0	0	140	15	<1
Sourdough, sandwich size, Thomas', 1 muffin	200	2	0	0	310	41	2
Traditional, Tastykake, 1 muffin	130	0.5	0	0	250	26	2
Wheat, sandwich size, Thomas', 1 muffin	180	1.5	0	0	300	39	4
Whole wheat, 1 muffin	100	1	0	0	320	20	5

AT A GLANCE: ENGLISH MUFFINS
A good low fat choice, choose English muffins with less than 2 grams of total fat and 1 gram of saturated fat.

	CAL (g)	FAT (g)	SAT FAT (g)	CHOL (mg)	SODIUM (mg)	CARB (g)	FIBER (g)
MUFFINS							
Almond poppy seed, Aunt Fanny's, 2 muffins	310	13	2	15	250	45	1
Apple bran, Aunt Fanny's, 2 muffins	290	11	2	15	220	45	2
Banana nut, Aunt Fanny's, 2 muffins	320	14	2	15	240	44	1
Banana nut, mini, Hostess, 5 muffins	260	16	2	40	160	28	<1
Banana walnut, Dolly Madison, 2 muffins	380	14	6	25	360	59	1
Blueberry, Aunt Fanny's, 2 muffins	290	11	2	15	230	45	1
Blueberry, Dolly Madison, 2 muffins	370	13	2.5	40	410	59	1
Blueberry, Entenmann's, 1 muffin	160	7	1.5	40	210	24	<1
Blueberry, fat free, cholesterol free, Entenmann's, 1 muffin	120	0	0	0	220	26	<1
Blueberry, mini, Hostess, 5 muffins	240	13	2	40	180	30	<1
Bran'nola, Arnold, 1 muffin	130	1.5	0	0	160	29	3
Chocolate chip, mini, Hostess, 5 muffins	260	15	5	35	170	29	1
Cinnamon apple, mini, Hostess, 5 muffins	260	16	2.5	45	180	28	<1
Extra crisp, Arnold, 1 muffin	120	1	0	0	190	25	1
Oat bran, Hostess, 1 muffin	160	8	1	0	150	22	<1
Oat bran banana nut, Hostess, 1 muffin	150	6	1	0	160	22	1
Raisin, Arnold, 1 muffin	150	1	0	0	160	32	1
Sourdough, Arnold, 1 muffin	120	1	0	0	200	25	1
PIES							
Apple, Entenmann's, 1/6 pie	300	14	3.5	0	300	42	2
Apple, fat free, cholesterol free, Entenmann's Beehive, 1/8 pie	270	0	0	0	330	65	2

PIES	CAL (g)	FAT (g)	SAT FAT (g)	CHOL (mg)	SODIUM (mg)	CARB (g)	FIBER (g)
Blueberry, ⅛ of 9" pie	360	17	4.5	0	270	49	2
Cherry, ⅛ of 9" pie	490	22	5	0	340	69	3
Cherry, fat free, cholesterol free, Entenmann's, ⅕ pie	270	0	0	0	310	64	1
Chocolate creme, ⅛ of 9" pie	400	23	7	75	350	44	na
Coconut creme, ⅛ of 9" pie	430	23	8	85	390	50	na
Coconut custard, ⅙ of 8" pie	270	14	6	35	350	31	2
Coconut custard, Entenmann's, ⅕ pie	340	19	8	135	310	35	1
Lemon, Entenmann's, ⅙ pie	340	17	4.5	45	420	45	<1
Lemon meringue, ⅛ of 9" pie	360	16	4	70	310	50	na
Peach, ⅛ of 9" pie	460	19	5	<5	470	67	2
Pecan, ⅛ of 9" pie	500	27	5	110	320	64	na
Pumpkin, ⅛ of 9" pie	320	14	5	65	350	41	na

AT A GLANCE: PIES
Lowest in Fat: Entenmann's fat free selections

SNACK CAKES

	CAL (g)	FAT (g)	SAT FAT (g)	CHOL (mg)	SODIUM (mg)	CARB (g)	FIBER (g)
Angel Cakes, raspberry, low fat, Little Debbie, 1 cake	120	1	0	0	120	28	1
Angel food bar, mini, Dolly Madison, 1 bar	170	2	0	0	200	35	1
Apple streusel coffee cake, Little Debbie, 1 cake	230	7	1	10	200	39	1
Banana Twins, Little Debbie, 1 cake	250	10	1.5	10	190	39	0
Baseball, yellow, Hostess, 1 cake	160	3	1	<5	160	32	0
Carrot cake, individual, Dolly Madison, 1 cake	360	8	3	0	530	69	1
Choco-Diles, Hostess, 1 cake	210	10	7	20	160	31	1
Choco Licious, Hostess, 1 cake	170	6	2.5	10	190	28	1
Chocolate, Tastykake, 1 cake	360	13	2.5	70	270	57	2
Chocolate chip, Little Debbie, 1 cake	290	15	3	0	200	41	1
Chocolate finger cakes, Aunt Fanny's, 2 cakes	290	10	4	20	430	47	2

SNACK CAKES	CAL	FAT (g)	SAT FAT (g)	CHOL (mg)	SODIUM (mg)	CARB (g)	FIBER (g)
Chocolate Twins, Little Debbie, 1 cake	250	9	1.5	20	290	43	1
Coconut, Little Debbie, 1 cake	270	13	2.5	5	180	38	0
Coconut, Tastykake, 1 cake	320	8	4	65	260	59	1
Coconut rounds, Little Debbie, 1 cake	140	7	2.5	0	85	22	1
Creamies, banana, Tastykake, 1 cake	170	7	1.5	10	125	27	0
Creamies, chocolate, Tastykake, 1 cake	180	7	2	15	120	26	0
Creamies, sprinkled, Tastykake, 1 cake	150	6	0.5	25	115	25	0
Creamies, vanilla, Tastykake, 1 cake	190	8	1.5	30	125	26	0
Creme, Dolly Madison, 3 cakes	340	12	6	40	360	53	1
Crumb cake, Hostess, 2 cakes	210	8	3	15	135	33	1
Crumb cake, apple (2 pack), Dolly Madison, 2 cakes	330	10	4	25	310	56	1
Crumb cake, apple (6 pack), Dolly Madison, 1 cake	170	5	2	15	150	28	0
Crumb cake, butter, Dolly Madison, 1 cake	170	6	2	15	170	29	0
Crumb cake, light, Hostess, 2 cakes	150	1	0	0	190	35	<1
Crumb cake, lowfat (2 pack), Dolly Madison, 2 cakes	280	3	0.5	0	300	59	1
Crumb cake, lowfat (6 pack), Dolly Madison, 1 cake	140	1.5	0	0	150	29	0
Dessert roll, lemon, Dolly Madison, 1 roll	260	2.5	0.5	20	280	56	1
Dessert roll, plain, Dolly Madison, 1 roll	230	2	0.5	20	260	49	1
Devil Cremes, Little Debbie, 1 cake	190	8	1.5	0	170	29	0
Devil Squares, Little Debbie, 1 cake	270	13	3	0	190	39	1
Ding Dongs, Hostess, 1 cake	160	9	6	5	110	21	<1
Fancy Cakes, Little Debbie, 1 cake	300	15	3	0	160	42	0

SNACK CAKES	CAL (g)	FAT (g)	SAT FAT (g)	CHOL (mg)	SODIUM (mg)	CARB (g)	FIBER (g)
Fruit loaf, Hostess, 1 cake	350	10	1	5	290	67	2
Fudge, frosted, Little Debbie, 1 cake	180	10	2	5	135	25	1
German chocolate, Dolly Madison, 1 cake	220	9	4	15	150	33	1
Golden Cremes, Little Debbie, 1 cake	170	7	2	0	180	25	0
Googles, Dolly Madison, 2 cakes	420	10	7	10	290	79	2
Ho Ho's, Hostess, 1 cake	130	6	4	10	75	17	<1
Hopper Cakes, Hostess, 1 cake	160	1	1	<5	160	32	0
Kandy Kakes, chocolate, Tastykake, 3 cakes	270	13	8	5	120	35	2
Kandy Kakes, coconut, Tastykake, 3 cakes	260	13	10	5	110	34	2
Kandy Kakes, frosty, Tastykake, 3 cakes	260	11	8	5	105	38	1
Kandy Kakes, peanut butter, Tastykake, 3 cakes	280	14	7	20	120	32	1
Koffee Kake, Tastykake, 1 cake	270	9	1.5	40	220	43	1
Koo Koo's, Dolly Madison, 2 cakes	400	17	12	5	190	60	1
Lil Angels, Hostess, 1 cake	90	2	1	<5	130	17	0
Marshmallow Supremes, Little Debbie, 1 cake	130	5	1	0	70	22	1
Pound cake, Aunt Fanny's, 1 cake	250	10	3	10	280	37	1
Pound cake, mini, Dolly Madison, 1 cake	370	13	5	30	450	57	1
Pound Kake, Tastykake, 1 cake	320	13	5	85	380	46	1
Raspberry finger cakes, Aunt Fanny's, 2 cakes	280	8	4	5	360	49	2
Sno Balls, Hostess, 1 cake	160	5	2.5	0	180	29	1
Spice, Little Debbie, 1 cake	300	15	3	10	240	43	1
Squares, Dolly Madison, 2 squares	400	19	11	15	270	53	1
Suzy Q's, Hostess, 1 cake	220	9	4	10	270	35	2

SNACK CAKES	CAL (g)	FAT (g)	SAT FAT (g)	CHOL (mg)	SODIUM (mg)	CARB (g)	FIBER (g)
Suzy Q's, banana, Hostess, 1 cake	220	10	1	25	280	32	<1
Swiss Cake Rolls, Little Debbie, 1 cake	260	12	2	15	180	39	1
Tiger Cakes, Little Debbie, 1 cake	310	15	3.5	0	190	44	1
Tiger Tails, Hostess, 1 cake	160	6	2.5	15	190	26	<1
Twinkie Lights, Hostess, 1 cake	120	1.5	0	0	200	24	0
Twinkies, Hostess, 1 cake	140	4	2	15	180	25	0
Twinkies, banana, Hostess, 2 cakes	300	13	1.5	35	370	42	<1
Twinkies, devil food, Hostess, 2 cakes	300	12	5	15	360	47	2
Twinkies, strawberry fruit 'n creme, Hostess, 1 cake	150	3	1	20	200	30	<1
Vanilla finger cakes, Aunt Fanny's, 2 cakes	290	10	4	10	430	47	2
Zebra Cakes, Little Debbie, 1 cake	330	16	3	0	180	45	0
Zingers, chocolate, Dolly Madison, 2 Zingers	260	8	3.5	5	230	46	1
Zingers, raspberry, Dolly Madison, 2 Zingers	300	11	5	10	180	46	1
Zingers, yellow, Dolly Madison, 3 Zingers	400	12	4	5	230	70	1

STUFFING MIX, DRY

	CAL (g)	FAT (g)	SAT FAT (g)	CHOL (mg)	SODIUM (mg)	CARB (g)	FIBER (g)
Apple & raisin, Pepperidge Farm, ½ cup	140	2	0	0	520	27	2
Chicken, classic, Pepperidge Farm, ½ cup	130	2	0	0	490	24	3
Chicken flavor, Stove Top, ⅙ box	110	1	0	0	440	20	<1
Chicken flavor, lower sodium, Stove Top, ⅙ box	110	1	0	0	270	21	<1
Chicken flavor, microwave, Stove Top, ⅙ box	130	3.5	0.5	0	450	20	<1
Corn bread, Arnold, 2 cups	250	4	1	0	800	49	2

STUFFING MIX, DRY	CAL (g)	FAT (g)	SAT FAT (g)	CHOL (mg)	SODIUM (mg)	CARB (g)	FIBER (g)
Corn bread, Brownberry, 2 cups	250	3.5	0.5	0	800	51	2
Corn bread, Pepperidge Farm, ¾ cup	170	2	0	0	480	33	2
Corn bread, Stove Top, ⅙ box	110	1	0	0	510	21	1
Corn bread, homestyle, microwave, Stove Top, ⅙ box	120	3.5	0.5	0	450	20	1
Country garden & herb, Pepperidge Farm, ½ cup	150	5	1	0	360	22	2
Country style, Pepperidge Farm, ¾ cup	140	2	0	0	380	27	2
Croutettes, Kellogg's, 1 cup	120	0	0	0	460	25	0
Cubes, Pepperidge Farm, ¾ cup	140	2	0	0	530	28	2
For beef, Stove Top, ⅙ box	110	1	0	0	520	22	1
For pork, Stove Top, ⅙ box	110	1	0	0	500	20	1
For turkey, Stove Top, ⅙ box	110	1	0	0	490	20	<1
Harvest vegetable & almond, Pepperidge Farm, ½ cup	140	3	1	0	300	23	2
Herb seasoned, Arnold, 2 cups	240	3	0.5	0	740	48	4
Herb seasoned, Brownberry, 1 cup	200	2.5	0.5	0	630	41	3
Herb seasoned, Pepperidge Farm, ¾ cup	170	2	0	0	600	33	3
Honey pecan corn bread, Pepperidge Farm, ½ cup	140	5	1	0	400	23	<1
Long grain & wild rice, Stove Top, ⅙ box	110	1	0	0	490	22	<1
Mushroom & onion, Stove Top, ⅙ box	110	1.5	0	0	410	20	<1
Sage & onion, Arnold, 2 cups	240	3	0.5	0	960	48	4
Sage & onion, Brownberry, 2 cups	240	3	0.5	0	980	49	3
Sage & onion, for turkey, Pepperidge Farm, ½ cup	150	2	0	0	520	28	2
San Francisco style, Stove Top, ⅙ box	110	1	0	0	510	20	1
Savory herbs, Stove Top, ⅙ box	110	1	0	0	510	20	<1

STUFFING MIX, DRY	CAL	FAT (g)	SAT FAT (g)	CHOL (mg)	SODIUM (mg)	CARB (g)	FIBER (g)
Seasoned, Arnold, 2 cups	250	3	0.5	0	820	49	2
Seasoned, Wonder, 1 cup	60	1	0	0	135	12	<1
Unseasoned cubes, Brownberry, 2 cups	240	3	0.5	0	500	51	3
Unspiced, Arnold, 2 cups	250	3	0.5	0	460	50	2
Wild rice & mushroom, Pepperidge Farm, ⅔ cup	170	6	2	0	410	22	2

AT A GLANCE: STUFFING
Lowest in Sodium: Wonder Seasoned Stuffing Mix

SWEET ROLLS *See also Frozen Foods, Breakfast Items.*

	CAL	FAT (g)	SAT FAT (g)	CHOL (mg)	SODIUM (mg)	CARB (g)	FIBER (g)
Almond twirls, Aunt Fanny's, 1 twirl	110	4	0.5	0	80	16	0
Apple bun, fat free, cholesterol free, Entenmann's, 1 bun	150	0	0	0	140	33	1
Apple cinnamon fruit delight, fat free, Stella D'Oro, 1 pastry	70	0	0	0	50	17	na
Apple Danish fruit roll, Hostess, 1 Danish	180	4	2	<5	170	33	1
Apple pocket, Tastykake, 1 pastry	380	23	6	5	170	40	2
Apple puffs, Entenmann's, 1 puff	260	12	3	0	220	36	1
Apple sweet roll (2 pack), Dolly Madison, 1 roll	230	6	2	10	270	38	1
Apple twist, Hostess, 1 twist	220	4	1.5	15	270	42	<1
Banana flip, Dolly Madison, 1 flip	410	15	3	30	240	61	1
Bear claw, Dolly Madison, 1 claw	310	11	5	25	360	48	1
Blueberry cheese bun, fat free, cholesterol free, Entenmann's, 1 bun	140	0	0	0	150	31	1
Caramel-pecan swirls, Hostess, 1 swirl	250	15	6	15	130	25	1
Cheese pocket, Tastykake, 1 pastry	410	27	8	10	210	38	2
Cherry bun, Dolly Madison, 1 bun	230	7	3	10	190	38	1

SWEET ROLLS	CAL	FAT (g)	SAT FAT (g)	CHOL (mg)	SODIUM (mg)	CARB (g)	FIBER (g)
Cherry pocket, Tastykake, 1 pastry	370	20	5	5	190	45	2
Cherry sweet roll (2 pack), Dolly Madison, 1 roll	210	6	3	10	170	34	1
Cinnaminis, original, Hostess, 5 rolls	300	17	4	20	230	37	2
Cinnamon bun, Dolly Madison, 1 bun	240	7	3	15	230	40	1
Cinnamon bun, Entenmann's, 1 bun	220	10	6	55	190	31	<1
Cinnamon raisin bun, fat free, cholesterol free, Entenmann's, 1 bun	160	0	0	0	125	36	1
Cinnamon roll, Dolly Madison, 1 roll	220	7	3	10	210	36	1
Cinnamon roll, Hostess, 1 roll	220	6	2.5	25	260	39	1
Cinnamon roll, honey wheat, Dolly Madison, 1 roll	240	8	2	10	200	40	1
Cinnamon twirls, Aunt Fanny's, 1 twirl	110	4	0.5	5	80	16	0
Coconut twirls, Aunt Fanny's, 1 twirl	110	4	1	0	80	17	1
Danish, apple, Hostess, 1 Danish	400	22	10	20	340	47	2
Danish, cinnamon, enriched, 1 Danish	350	17	3.5	30	330	47	0
Danish, coffee cake raspberry, Hostess, 1 Danish	110	2.5	1	<5	110	21	<1
Danish, cream cheese, Dolly Madison, 1 Danish	380	15	7	25	400	54	1
Danish, nut, 1 Danish	360	11	1	0	105	60	na
Devil's food flip, Dolly Madison, 1 flip	380	14	3	15	390	59	1
Honey bun, Little Debbie, 1 bun	210	13	3	0	180	22	1
Honey bun (3 oz), Dolly Madison, 1 bun	360	20	8	10	210	40	1
Honey bun (3.75 oz), Dolly Madison, 1 bun	450	25	11	15	260	50	1
Honey bun, applesauce filled, Aunt Fanny's, 1 bun	330	17	4	0	300	43	1

SWEET ROLLS	CAL	FAT (g)	SAT FAT (g)	CHOL (mg)	SODIUM (mg)	CARB (g)	FIBER (g)
Honey bun, banana or chocolate creme filled, Aunt Fanny's, 1 bun	350	18	4	0	290	32	2
Honey bun, glazed, Hostess, 1 bun	320	19	9	15	210	35	2
Honey bun, glazed, Tastykake, 1 bun	350	17	4	10	210	47	0
Honey bun, iced, Aunt Fanny's, 1 bun	350	18	4	0	290	32	2
Honey bun, iced, Hostess, 1 bun	390	20	9	15	220	49	2
Honey bun, iced, Tastykake, 1 bun	350	17	4	10	210	47	0
Honey bun, large, Aunt Fanny's, 1 bun	500	29	7	0	420	53	3
Honey bun, raspberry filled, Aunt Fanny's, 1 bun	350	17	5	0	290	45	2
Honey bun, regular, Aunt Fanny's, 1 bun	360	20	5	0	300	41	2
Honey bun, vanilla creme filled, Aunt Fanny's, 1 bun	350	18	4	0	290	32	2
Honey wheat cinnamon twirl, Dolly Madison, 1 twirl	450	14	4	15	380	75	1
Lemon sweet roll (2 pack), Dolly Madison, 1 roll	230	7	3.5	10	260	39	1
Peach apricot fruit delight, fat free, Stella D'Oro, 1 pastry	70	0	0	0	35	17	1
Pecan roller (2 pack), Dolly Madison, 2 rolls	210	7	1.5	0	95	33	1
Pecan roller (3 pack), Dolly Madison, 3 rolls	310	10	2	0	140	50	1
Pecan spinners, Hostess, 1 spinner	110	5	1	0	65	15	<1
Pecan Spinwheels, Little Debbie, 1 pkg	110	4	0.5	0	100	16	1
Pecan twirls, Aunt Fanny's, 1 twirl	100	4	0.5	0	100	16	0
Pecan twirls, Tastykake, 2 rolls	220	9	1	0	200	32	1
Pineapple cheese bun, fat free, cholesterol free, Entenmann's, 1 bun	140	0	0	0	150	30	<1

SWEET ROLLS	CAL (g)	FAT (g)	SAT FAT (g)	CHOL (mg)	SODIUM (mg)	CARB (g)	FIBER (g)
Raspberry cheese bun, fat free, cholesterol free, Entenmann's, 1 bun	160	0	0	0	135	36	1
Raspberry fruit delight, fat free, Stella D'Oro, 1 pastry	70	0	0	0	40	17	na
Raspberry sweet roll (2 pack), Dolly Madison, 1 roll	230	6	3.5	10	260	39	1
Strawberry shortcake rolls, Little Debbie, 1 pkg	240	8	1.5	15	160	41	0
Sweet potato flip, Dolly Madison, 1 flip	310	15	2	35	240	42	1
Whirly twirls, Tastykake, 2 rolls	260	14	7	10	210	36	1

AT A GLANCE: SWEET ROLLS
Lowest in Fat: Entenmann's and Stella D'Oro fat free selections

TACO SHELLS

	CAL (g)	FAT (g)	SAT FAT (g)	CHOL (mg)	SODIUM (mg)	CARB (g)	FIBER (g)
Gebhardt, 3 shells	160	9	2	0	10	20	4
Pancho Villa, 3 shells	190	11	2.5	0	0	19	3
Rosarita, 3 shells	160	9	2.5	0	10	19	4
Corn, hard, Ortega, 2 shells	140	7	1	0	200	20	2
Regular or white corn, Old El Paso, 3 shells	170	10	1.5	0	130	18	2
White corn, Chi-Chi's, 2 shells	130	6	1	0	0	17	2

TORTILLAS

	CAL (g)	FAT (g)	SAT FAT (g)	CHOL (mg)	SODIUM (mg)	CARB (g)	FIBER (g)
Corn, 2 tortillas	130	1.5	0	0	100	28	3
Flour, Old El Paso, 1 tortilla	150	3	0.5	0	340	27	0
Soft taco, Old El Paso, 2 tortillas	180	3.5	0.5	0	410	33	0
Wheat, low fat, Wonder, 1 tortilla	120	1.5	0.5	0	280	24	1
White, low fat, Wonder, 1 tortilla	110	1.5	0.5	0	280	22	1

TOSTADA SHELLS

	CAL (g)	FAT (g)	SAT FAT (g)	CHOL (mg)	SODIUM (mg)	CARB (g)	FIBER (g)
Old El Paso, 3 shells	160	10	2	0	220	19	2
Rosarita, 2 shells	130	5	1	40	20	17	0

BEVERAGES

	CAL (g)	FAT (g)	SAT FAT (g)	CHOL (mg)	SODIUM (mg)	CARB (g)	FIBER (g)
ALCOHOL							
Beer, light, 8 fl oz	70	0	0	0	10	3	0
Beer, regular, 8 fl oz	100	0	0	0	15	9	<1
Bloody Mary, 8 fl oz	200	0	0	0	560	40	0
Bourbon & soda, 8 fl oz	200	0	0	0	0	0	0
Coffee liqueur, 53 proof, 1.5 fl oz	180	0	0	0	0	24	0
Coffee liqueur, with cream, 34 proof, 1.5 fl oz	150	8	4.5	<5	45	11	0
Creme de menthe, 1.5 fl oz	180	0	0	0	0	21	0
Daiquiri, 8 fl oz	480	0	0	0	0	16	0
Gin, 90 or 86 proof, 1.5 fl oz	110	0	0	0	0	0	0
Gin, 100 or 94 proof, 1.5 fl oz	120	0	0	0	0	0	0
Gin & tonic, 8 fl oz	200	0	0	0	0	16	0
Malt liquor, 8 fl oz	100	0	0	0	15	9	1
Manhattan, 8 fl oz	480	0	0	0	0	10	0
Martini, 8 fl oz	480	0	0	0	0	0	0
Pina colada, 8 fl oz	480	4	0	0	0	72	0
Rum, 90 or 86 proof, 1.5 fl oz	110	0	0	0	0	0	0
Rum, 100 or 94 proof, 1.5 fl oz	120	0	0	0	0	0	0
Screwdriver, 8 fl oz	200	0	0	0	0	24	0
Tequila sunrise, 8 fl oz	280	0	0	0	0	24	0
Tom Collins, 8 fl oz	120	0	0	0	40	0	0
Vodka, 90 or 86 proof, 1.5 fl oz	110	0	0	0	0	0	0
Vodka, 100 or 94 proof, 1.5 fl oz	120	0	0	0	0	0	0
Whiskey, 90 or 86 proof, 1.5 fl oz	110	0	0	0	0	0	0
Whiskey, 100 or 94 proof, 1.5 fl oz	120	0	0	0	0	0	0
Whiskey sour, 8 fl oz	320	0	0	0	0	16	0
Wine, dessert, dry, 6 fl oz	240	0	0	0	0	6	0

ALCOHOL	CAL (g)	FAT (g)	SAT FAT (g)	CHOL (mg)	SODIUM (mg)	CARB (g)	FIBE (g)
Wine, dessert, sweet, 6 fl oz	270	0	0	0	0	24	0
Wine, red, 6 fl oz	120	0	0	0	0	10	0
Wine, rose, 6 fl oz	120	0	0	0	0	0	0
Wine, white, 6 fl oz	120	0	0	0	0	0	•

AT A GLANCE: ALCOHOL
Lowest in Calories: Beer, light

COCOA MIX

	CAL (g)	FAT (g)	SAT FAT (g)	CHOL (mg)	SODIUM (mg)	CARB (g)	FIBE (g)
25 calorie, fat free, Carnation, 1 envelope	25	0	0	0	135	4	•
70 calorie, Nestle, 1 envelope	70	0	0	0	140	15	<
Almond mocha, Swiss Miss Premiere, 1 pkg	140	3	1	0	210	28	
Chocolate English toffee, Swiss Miss Premiere, 1 pkg	140	2.5	1	0	220	29	<
Chocolate hazelnut, Ghirardelli, 1 pouch	90	1.5	1	0	35	21	•
Chocolate Irish creme, Nestle, 3 Tbsp	90	1.5	1.5	0	90	16	<
Chocolate mocha, Ghirardelli, 1 pouch	90	2	1	0	35	21	
Chocolate raspberry truffle, Swiss Miss Premiere, 1 pkg	140	3	1	0	220	28	
Chocolate Sensations, Swiss Miss, 1 pkg	150	4	1.5	0	170	27	
Cocoa & cream, Swiss Miss, 1 pkg	150	5	3	5	160	25	<
Diet, Swiss Miss, 1 pkg	25	0	0	0	210	4	<
Fat free, Swiss Miss, 1 pkg	50	0	0	<5	200	9	<
French chocolate creme, Nestle, 3 Tbsp	90	1	1	0	85	17	<
Lite, Swiss Miss, 1 pkg	70	0	0	0	200	17	
Marshmallow lovers, Swiss Miss, 1 pkg	140	3	1	<5	130	27	<
Milk chocolate, Carnation, 3 Tbsp	110	1	0	<5	95	24	<
Milk chocolate, Swiss Miss, 1 pkg	110	1.5	0	0	140	24	•

COCOA MIX	CAL	FAT (g)	SAT FAT (g)	CHOL (mg)	SODIUM (mg)	CARB (g)	FIBER (g)
Milk chocolate, sugar free, Swiss Miss, 1 pkg	50	0	0	0	180	10	<1
Mini-marshmallow, Swiss Miss, 1 pkg	110	1.5	0	0	150	24	<1
Mini-marshmallow, sugar free, Swiss Miss, 1 pkg	50	0.5	0	0	160	11	<1
No sugar added, Carnation, 3 Tbsp	50	0	0	<5	140	8	<1
Rich chocolate, Carnation, 3 Tbsp	110	1	0	<5	100	24	<1
Rich chocolate, Swiss Miss, 1 pkg	110	1.5	0	0	170	24	<1
Rich chocolate with or without marshmallows, Nestle, 1 envelope	110	1	0.5	0	60	24	<1
Rich sugar free, Swiss Miss, 1 pkg	50	0	0	0	170	10	<1
Rich with marshmallows, Carnation, 3 Tbsp	110	1	0	<5	95	24	<1
Sugar free, Swiss Miss, 1 pkg	70	0	0	0	240	13	<1
Suisse chocolate truffle, Swiss Miss Premiere, 1 pkg	140	2.5	1	0	230	28	1
Swiss chocolate truffle, Nestle, 3 Tbsp	90	1.5	1	0	65	17	<1
Weight Watchers, 0.675 oz	70	0	0	0	160	10	1
White chocolate, Swiss Miss, 1 pkg	110	1.5	0	0	130	21	0

COFFEE DRINKS

	CAL	FAT (g)	SAT FAT (g)	CHOL (mg)	SODIUM (mg)	CARB (g)	FIBER (g)
Cappuccino, cinnamon, instant, Maxwell House, 1 fl oz	90	1.5	0	0	70	16	0
Cappuccino, coffee flavor, iced, Maxwell House Cappio, 1 fl oz	130	2.5	1.5	5	120	24	0
Cappuccino, coffee flavor, instant, Maxwell House, 1 fl oz	90	1	0	0	65	18	0
Cappuccino, mocha, iced, Maxwell House Cappio, 1 fl oz	140	2.5	1.5	5	115	27	0

COFFEE DRINKS	CAL (g)	FAT (g)	SAT FAT (g)	CHOL (mg)	SODIUM (mg)	CARB (g)	FIBER (g)
Cappuccino, mocha, instant, Maxwell House, 8 fl oz	100	2.5	1	0	70	17	0
Cappuccino, mocha, instant, Nescafe, 1 pkg	110	2	0.5	0	30	21	<1
Cappuccino, mocha, instant, decaffeinated, Maxwell House, 8 fl oz	100	2.5	1	0	70	17	0
Cappuccino, sweetened, instant, Nescafe, 1 pkg	80	1.5	0.5	0	30	16	0
Cappuccino, unsweetened, instant, Nescafe, 1 pkg	90	2.5	0.5	0	45	13	0
Cappuccino, vanilla, iced, Maxwell House Cappio, 8 fl oz	140	2.5	1.5	5	110	27	0
Cappuccino, vanilla, instant, Maxwell House, 8 fl oz	90	1	0	0	65	19	0
Cappuccino, vanilla, instant, decaffeinated, Maxwell House, 8 fl oz	90	1	0	0	65	19	0
Coffee, brewed, made with distilled water, 8 fl oz	0	0	0	0	0	<1	0
Coffee, brewed, made with tap water, 1 cup	0	0	0	0	0	<1	0
Coffee, Cafe Amaretto, instant, General Foods International Coffee, 8 fl oz	60	3	0.5	0	105	8	0
Coffee, Cafe Francais, instant, General Foods International Coffee, 8 fl oz	60	3.5	1	0	25	7	0
Coffee, Cafe Vienna, instant, General Foods International Coffee, 8 fl oz	70	2.5	0.5	0	110	11	0
Coffee, Cafe Vienna, instant, sugar free, low calorie, General Foods International Coffee, 8 fl oz	30	1.5	0.5	0	75	3	0
Coffee, flavored, all flavors, instant, Taster's Choice, 1 tsp	5	0	0	0	0	1	0
Coffee, French Vanilla Cafe, instant, General Foods International Coffee, 8 fl oz	60	2.5	0.5	0	55	10	0

COFFEE DRINKS	CAL (g)	FAT (g)	SAT FAT (g)	CHOL (mg)	SODIUM (mg)	CARB (g)	FIBER (g)
Coffee, French Vanilla Cafe, instant, sugar free, low calorie, General Foods International Coffee, 8 fl oz	35	2	0.5	0	55	4	0
Coffee, Hazelnut Belgian Cafe, instant, General Foods International Coffee, 8 fl oz	70	2	0.5	0	65	12	0
Coffee, instant, regular or decaffeinated, Nescafe Mountain Blend, 1 tsp	5	0	0	0	0	1	0
Coffee, Italian Cappuccino, instant, General Foods International Coffee, 8 fl oz	50	1.5	0.5	0	50	10	0
Coffee, Kahlua Cafe, instant, General Foods International Coffee, 8 fl oz	60	2	0.5	0	55	10	0
Coffee, mocha cooler, Nescafe, 8 fl oz	170	4	3	15	150	25	0
Coffee, Orange Cappuccino, instant, General Foods International Coffee, 8 fl oz	70	2	0.5	0	100	11	0
Coffee, Orange Cappuccino, instant, sugar free, low calorie, General Foods International Coffee, 8 fl oz	30	1.5	0.5	0	75	3	0
Coffee, Suisse Mocha, instant, General Foods International Coffee, 8 fl oz	60	2.5	0.5	0	50	8	0
Coffee, Suisse Mocha, instant, sugar free, low calorie, General Foods International Coffee, 8 fl oz	30	2	0.5	0	30	4	0
Coffee, Suisse Mocha, instant, decaffeinated, General Foods International Coffee, 8 fl oz	60	3	0.5	0	40	8	0
Coffee, Suisse Mocha, instant, decaffeinated, sugar free, low calorie, General Foods International Coffee, 8 fl oz	30	1.5	0.5	0	35	4	0
Coffee, Viennese Chocolate Cafe, instant, General Foods International Coffee, 8 fl oz	60	2	1	0	30	10	0
Coffee, with chicory, instant, 1 tsp	5	0	0	0	0	1	0

COFFEE DRINKS	CAL (g)	FAT (g)	SAT FAT (g)	CHOL (mg)	SODIUM (mg)	CARB (g)	FIBER (g)
Coffee substitute, instant, Postum, 1 tsp (makes 8 fl oz)	10	0	0	0	110	3	0

AT A GLANCE: COFFEE DRINKS
Watch for higher fat values in some flavored coffees.
Lowest in Calories and Fat, Flavored Coffees: Taster's Choice

JUICE & JUICE DRINKS

Serving size for all frozen or unfrozen concentrate beverages is 8 fluid ounces reconstituted.

	CAL (g)	FAT (g)	SAT FAT (g)	CHOL (mg)	SODIUM (mg)	CARB (g)	FIBER (g)
Acrobat Apple juice drink, Squeezit 100, 1 bottle	110	0	0	0	20	27	0
Apple drink, Everfresh, 8 fl oz	110	0	0	0	0	28	ns
Apple drink, frozen concentrate, Bright & Early, 8 fl oz	120	0	0	ns	10	30	ns
Apple juice, Dole, 10 fl oz	160	0	0	0	25	39	0
Apple juice, Everfresh, 8 fl oz	120	0	0	0	10	29	ns
Apple juice, Indian Summer, 8 fl oz	110	0	ns	ns	30	27	0
Apple juice, Libby's Juicy Juice, 4.23 fl oz juice box	60	0	ns	ns	5	16	0
Apple juice, Minute Maid, 8.45 fl oz juice box	120	0	ns	ns	30	29	ns
Apple juice, Mott's, 8 fl oz	120	0	0	0	20	29	0
Apple juice, Musselman's, 8 fl oz	120	0	ns	ns	25	31	ns
Apple juice, Ocean Spray, 8 fl oz	110	0	ns	ns	35	28	0
Apple juice, R.W. Knudsen, 8 fl oz	110	0	0	ns	5	28	ns
Apple juice, Santa Cruz Natural, 8 fl oz	120	0	0	ns	25	30	ns
Apple juice, Tropicana Orchardstand Pure Premium, 8 fl oz	110	0	ns	ns	0	27	ns
Apple juice, Tropicana Season's Best, 8 fl oz	110	0	ns	ns	10	28	ns
Apple juice, Veryfine, 10 fl oz	130	0	0	0	35	32	2
Apple juice, Welch's, 11.5 fl oz	160	0	0	0	35	41	ns

JUICE & JUICE DRINKS	CAL (g)	FAT (g)	SAT FAT (g)	CHOL (mg)	SODIUM (mg)	CARB (g)	FIBER (g)
Apple juice, frozen concentrate, Minute Maid, 8 fl oz	110	0	ns	ns	5	28	ns
Apple juice, natural, Mott's, 8 fl oz	120	0	0	0	20	29	0
Apple juice, natural, regular or organic, R.W. Knudsen, 8 fl oz	120	0	0	ns	25	30	ns
Apple juice, organic, frozen concentrate, R.W. Knudsen, 8 fl oz	120	0	0	ns	25	30	ns
Apple juice cocktail, concentrate, Mott's Fruit Basket, 8 fl oz	120	0	0	0	5	29	0
Apple apricot juice, R.W. Knudsen, 8 fl oz	120	0	0	ns	35	30	ns
Apple banana juice, R.W. Knudsen, 8 fl oz	120	0	0	ns	25	30	ns
Apple Berry Burst juice drink, bottled or frozen concentrate, Dole, 8 fl oz	120	0	0	0	20	31	0
Apple boysenberry juice, Heinke's, 8 fl oz	120	0	0	ns	25	30	ns
Apple boysenberry juice, R.W. Knudsen, 8 fl oz	120	0	0	ns	25	30	ns
Apple cider, spiced, Swiss Miss, ¼ cup	80	0	0	0	60	20	<1
Apple cranberry juice, Mott's, 8 fl oz	120	0	0	0	20	30	0
Apple cranberry juice, R.W. Knudsen, 8 fl oz	120	0	0	ns	n	30	ns
Apple cranberry juice blend, Mott's, 10 fl oz	180	0	0	0	15	44	0
Apple cranberry juice drink, Dole, 10 fl oz	160	0	0	0	25	40	0
Apple cranberry juice drink, Welch's, 11.5 fl oz	210	0	0	0	30	52	ns
Apple cranberry kiwi juice drink, Tropicana Tropics, 8 fl oz	120	0	ns	ns	15	30	ns
Apple grape juice, Libby's Juicy Juice, 8 fl oz	130	0	ns	ns	10	30	0

JUICE & JUICE DRINKS	CAL	FAT (g)	SAT FAT (g)	CHOL (mg)	SODIUM (mg)	CARB (g)	FIBER (g)
Apple grape juice, Minute Maid, 8.45 fl oz juice box	130	0	ns	ns	30	32	ns
Apple grape juice, Mott's, 8 fl oz	120	0	0	0	20	30	0
Apple grape cherry juice drink, Welch's, 8.45 fl oz juice box	150	0	0	0	20	37	ns
Apple grape cherry juice drink, frozen concentrate, Welch's Orchard, 8 fl oz	140	ns	ns	ns	5	35	ns
Apple grape raspberry juice drink, Welch's, 8.45 fl oz juice box	150	0	0	0	20	37	ns
Apple grape raspberry juice drink, frozen concentrate, Welch's Orchard, 8 fl oz	140	ns	ns	ns	5	35	ns
Apple orange pineapple juice drink, Welch's, 11.5 fl oz	210	0	0	0	25	52	ns
Apple peach juice, R.W. Knudsen, 8 fl oz	120	0	0	ns	25	30	ns
Apple raspberry drink, Everfresh, 8 fl oz	120	0	0	0	0	30	ns
Apple raspberry juice, Heinke's, 8 fl oz	120	0	0	ns	25	30	ns
Apple raspberry juice, Mott's, 8.45 fl oz juice box	120	0	0	0	35	30	0
Apple raspberry juice, R.W. Knudsen, 8 fl oz	120	0	0	ns	25	30	ns
Apple raspberry juice blend, Mott's, 10 fl oz	140	0	0	0	10	33	0
Apple raspberry juice cocktail, concentrate, Mott's Fruit Basket, 8 fl oz	130	0	0	0	5	30	0
Apple raspberry blackberry juice drink, Tropicana Twister, 8 fl oz	120	0	ns	ns	20	31	ns
Apple strawberry juice, R.W. Knudsen, 8 fl oz	120	0	0	ns	25	30	ns
Apricot nectar, Kern's/Libby's, 8 fl oz	150	0	ns	ns	5	36	0
Apricot nectar, Santa Cruz Natural, 8 fl oz	120	0	0	ns	35	30	ns

JUICE & JUICE DRINKS	CAL (g)	FAT (g)	SAT FAT (g)	CHOL (mg)	SODIUM (mg)	CARB (g)	FIBER (g)
Apricot nectar juice blend, R.W. Knudsen, 8 fl oz	120	0	0	ns	35	30	ns
Apricot pineapple nectar, Kern's, 11.5 fl oz	220	0	ns	ns	5	53	2
Banana nectar, Kern's/Libby's, 11.5 fl oz	190	0	ns	ns	35	47	0
Banana pineapple nectar, Kern's, 11.5 fl oz	220	0	ns	ns	5	52	0
Beefamato, Mott's, 8 fl oz	80	0	0	0	780	20	1
Berry citrus juice drink, frozen concentrate, Five Alive, 8 fl oz	120	0	ns	ns	5	30	ns
Berry drink, Squeezit 100, 1 bottle	100	0	0	0	20	24	0
Berry juice, Libby's Juicy Juice, 8 fl oz	130	0	ns	ns	15	31	0
Berry nectar, Santa Cruz Natural, 8 fl oz	110	0	0	ns	25	27	ns
Berry patch juice drink, Heinke's, 8 fl oz	120	0	0	ns	25	30	ns
Berry punch, Minute Maid, 8 fl oz	130	0	ns	ns	25	31	ns
Berry punch, Minute Maid, 8.45 fl oz juice box	130	0	ns	ns	25	31	ns
Berry punch, Tropicana, 8 fl oz	120	0	ns	ns	25	29	ns
Berry punch, frozen concentrate, Minute Maid, 8 fl oz	130	0	ns	ns	5	31	ns
Black cherry juice, Everfresh, 8 fl oz	140	0	0	0	0	36	ns
Black cherry juice, Heinke's, 8 fl oz	180	0	0	ns	40	43	ns
Black cherry juice, R.W. Knudsen, 8 fl oz	180	0	0	ns	40	43	ns
Black cherry juice blend, concentrate, R.W. Knudsen, 8 fl oz	130	0	0	ns	15	32	ns
Black cherry white grape juice, Boku, 12 fl oz	180	0	0	0	50	44	0

JUICE & JUICE DRINKS	CAL	FAT (g)	SAT FAT (g)	CHOL (mg)	SODIUM (mg)	CARB (g)	FIBER (g)
Boppin Berry juice drink, Hi-C, 8 fl oz	130	0	ns	ns	30	32	ns
Boppin Berry juice drink, Hi-C, 8.45 fl oz juice box	140	0	ns	ns	30	33	ns
Boysenberry cider, Heinke's, 8 fl oz	120	0	0	ns	25	30	ns
Boysenberry juice, Farmer's Market, 8 fl oz	120	0	0	0	0	30	ns
Breakfast juice, frozen concentrate, R.W. Knudsen, 8 fl oz	110	0	0	ns	35	27	ns
Breakfast juice, natural, R.W. Knudsen, 8 fl oz	110	0	0	ns	35	27	ns
California punch, Heinke's, 8 fl oz	110	0	0	ns	20	28	ns
Calypso Breeze (strawberry kiwi) juice, Chiquita, 8 fl oz	120	0	0	0	60	30	0
Caped Grape drink, Squeezit 100, 1 bottle	100	0	0	0	20	24	0
Caribbean Colada (cranberry pineapple) juice drink, Ocean Spray, 8 fl oz	130	0	ns	ns	35	32	0
Caribbean Splash (pineapple guava mango) juice, Chiquita, 8 fl oz	130	0	0	0	70	30	<1
Carrot juice, canned, 8 fl oz	100	0	0	0	70	22	<1
Cherry cider, Heinke's, 8 fl oz	115	0	0	ns	5	28	ns
Cherry cider, frozen concentrate, R.W. Knudsen, 8 fl oz	130	0	0	ns	35	33	ns
Cherry cider juice blend, R.W. Knudsen, 8 fl oz	130	0	0	ns	35	33	ns
Cherry juice, Farmer's Market, 8 fl oz	120	0	0	ns	0	29	ns
Cherry juice, Libby's Juicy Juice, 4.23 fl oz juice box	70	0	ns	ns	5	17	0
Cherry juice, Libby's Juicy Juice, 8 fl oz	130	0	ns	ns	10	32	0
Cherry juice drink, Hi-C, 8 fl oz	130	0	ns	ns	30	33	ns

JUICE & JUICE DRINKS	CAL (g)	FAT (g)	SAT FAT (g)	CHOL (mg)	SODIUM (mg)	CARB (g)	FIBER (g)
Cherry juice drink, Hi-C, 8.45 fl oz juice box	140	0	ns	ns	30	35	ns
Cherry juice drink, frozen concentrate, Welchade, 8 fl oz	130	ns	ns	ns	15	31	ns
Cherry Cruz juice, Santa Cruz Natural, 8 fl oz	110	0	0	ns	20	26	ns
Cider & spice juice blend, R.W. Knudsen, 8 fl oz	120	0	0	ns	25	30	ns
Citrus juice drink, Five Alive, 8 fl oz	120	0	ns	ns	25	30	ns
Citrus juice drink, frozen concentrate, Five Alive, 8 fl oz	120	0	ns	ns	0	30	ns
Citrus cranberry juice drink, Ocean Spray Refreshers, 8 fl oz	120	0	ns	ns	35	30	0
Citrus peach juice drink, Ocean Spray Refreshers, 8 fl oz	120	0	ns	ns	35	30	0
Citrus punch, Minute Maid, 8 fl oz	130	0	ns	ns	25	31	ns
Citrus punch, Tropicana, 8 fl oz	140	0	ns	ns	20	36	ns
Citrus punch, frozen concentrate, Minute Maid, 8 fl oz	120	0	ns	ns	5	31	ns
Clamato, Mott's, 8 fl oz	100	0	0	0	720	24	2
Clamato Caesar, Mott's, 8 fl oz	100	0	0	0	780	24	0
Coconut nectar, R.W. Knudsen, 8 fl oz	140	5	4	ns	55	26	ns
Country raspberry juice, bottled or frozen concentrate, Dole, 8 fl oz	140	0	0	0	30	34	0
Cran-apple juice cocktail, Everfresh, 8 fl oz	120	0	0	0	0	31	ns
CranApple juice drink, Ocean Spray, 8 fl oz	160	0	ns	ns	35	41	1
CranApple juice drink, reduced calorie, Ocean Spray, 8 fl oz	50	0	ns	ns	35	13	0

JUICE & JUICE DRINKS	CAL (g)	FAT (g)	SAT FAT (g)	CHOL (mg)	SODIUM (mg)	CARB (g)	FIBER (g)
Cranberry juice, Farmer's Market, 8 fl oz	120	0	0	ns	0	31	ns
Cranberry juice, Heinke's, 8 fl oz	60	0	0	ns	25	14	ns
Cranberry juice, concentrate, R.W. Knudsen, 8 fl oz	70	0	0	ns	15	17	ns
Cranberry juice cocktail, Everfresh, 8 fl oz	140	0	0	ns	0	35	ns
Cranberry juice cocktail, Ocean Spray, 8 fl oz	140	0	ns	ns	35	34	0
Cranberry juice cocktail, frozen concentrate, Welch's, 8 fl oz	140	0	0	0	0	35	ns
Cranberry juice cocktail, light, frozen concentrate, Welch's, 8 fl oz	50	0	0	0	5	13	ns
Cranberry juice cocktail, low calorie, Ocean Spray Lightstyle, 8 fl oz	40	0	ns	ns	35	10	0
Cranberry juice cocktail, reduced calorie, Ocean Spray, 8 fl oz	50	0	ns	ns	35	13	0
Cranberry apple juice cocktail, frozen concentrate, Welch's, 8 fl oz	160	0	0	0	0	40	ns
Cranberry apricot juice, 8 fl oz	160	0	0	0	0	40	0
Cranberry cherry juice cocktail, frozen concentrate, Welch's, 8 fl oz	150	0	0	0	0	37	ns
Cranberry Cruz juice, Santa Cruz Natural, 8 fl oz	110	0	0	ns	25	27	ns
Cranberry lemon juice, Santa Cruz Natural, 8 fl oz	120	0	0	ns	35	29	ns
Cranberry lemonade, Heinke's, 8 fl oz	120	0	0	ns	35	29	ns
Cranberry lemonade, R.W. Knudsen, 8 fl oz	120	0	0	ns	35	29	ns
Cranberry medley juice, Tropicana Season's Best, 8 fl oz	120	0	ns	ns	20	29	ns

JUICE & JUICE DRINKS	CAL (g)	FAT (g)	SAT FAT (g)	CHOL (mg)	SODIUM (mg)	CARB (g)	FIBER (g)
Cranberry nectar, Heinke's, 8 fl oz	120	0	0	ns	5	30	ns
Cranberry nectar, bottled or frozen concentrate, R.W. Knudsen, 8 fl oz	150	0	0	ns	45	38	ns
Cranberry orange juice cocktail, frozen concentrate, Welch's, 8 fl oz	140	0	0	0	0	36	ns
Cranberry punch drink, Tropicana, 8 fl oz	140	0	ns	ns	10	34	ns
Cranberry raspberry juice blend, R.W. Knudsen, 8 fl oz	140	0	0	ns	35	36	ns
Cranberry raspberry juice cocktail, frozen concentrate, Welch's, 8 fl oz	150	0	0	0	0	37	ns
Cranberry raspberry juice cocktail, light, frozen concentrate, Welch's, 8 fl oz	50	0	0	0	5	13	ns
Cranberry raspberry strawberry juice drink, Tropicana Twister, 8 fl oz	120	0	ns	ns	5	31	ns
Cranberry raspberry strawberry juice drink, frozen concentrate, Tropicana Twister, 8 fl oz	120	0	ns	ns	5	29	ns
Cranberry raspberry strawberry juice drink, light, Tropicana Twister, 8 fl oz	45	0	ns	ns	10	11	ns
Cranberry Seabreeze (cranberry apple) juice, Chiquita, 8 fl oz	120	0	0	0	60	29	0
Cran-Blueberry juice drink, Ocean Spray, 8 fl oz	160	0	ns	ns	35	41	0
Cran-Cherry juice drink, Ocean Spray, 8 fl oz	160	0	ns	ns	35	39	0
Cran-Grape juice drink, Ocean Spray, 8 fl oz	170	0	ns	ns	35	41	0
Cran-Grape juice drink, low calorie, Ocean Spray Lightstyle, 8 fl oz	40	0	ns	ns	35	9	0
Cranicot (cranberry apricot) juice drink, Ocean Spray, 8 fl oz	160	0	ns	ns	35	40	0

JUICE & JUICE DRINKS	CAL	FAT (g)	SAT FAT (g)	CHOL (mg)	SODIUM (mg)	CARB (g)	FIBER (g)
Cran-Raspberry juice drink, Ocean Spray, 8 fl oz	140	0	ns	ns	35	36	0
Cran-Raspberry juice drink, low calorie, Ocean Spray Lightstyle, 8 fl oz	40	0	ns	ns	35	10	0
Cran-Raspberry juice drink, reduced calorie, Ocean Spray, 8 fl oz	50	0	0	ns	35	13	0
Cran-Strawberry juice drink, Ocean Spray, 8 fl oz	140	0	ns	ns	35	36	1
Crantastic fruit punch, Ocean Spray, 8 fl oz	150	0	ns	ns	35	37	0
Double fruit juice drink, Hi-C, 8 fl oz	130	0	ns	ns	30	31	ns
Double fruit juice drink, Hi-C, 8.45 fl oz juice box	130	0	ns	ns	35	32	ns
Ecto Cooler juice drink, Hi-C, 8 fl oz	130	0	ns	ns	25	32	ns
Ecto Cooler juice drink, Hi-C, 8.45 fl oz juice box	130	0	ns	ns	25	33	ns
Fruit fiesta juice drink, bottled or frozen concentrate, Dole, 8 fl oz	140	0	0	0	20	34	0
Fruit harvest punch juice drink, Welch's, 8.45 fl oz juice box	140	0	0	0	20	36	n
Fruit harvest punch juice drink, frozen concentrate, Welch's Orchard, 8 fl oz	140	0	0	0	5	34	n
Fruit punch, Everfresh, 8 fl oz	120	0	0	0	0	30	n
Fruit punch, Hi-C, 8 fl oz	130	0	ns	ns	30	32	n
Fruit punch, Hi-C, 8.45 fl oz juice box	140	0	ns	ns	30	33	n
Fruit punch, Minute Maid, 8 fl oz	120	0	ns	ns	25	31	n
Fruit punch, Minute Maid, 8.45 fl oz juice box	120	0	ns	ns	25	31	n
Fruit punch, Mott's, 8.45 fl oz juice box	120	0	0	0	20	29	n
Fruit punch, Ocean Spray, 8 fl oz	130	0	ns	ns	35	32	

JUICE & JUICE DRINKS	CAL (g)	FAT (g)	SAT FAT (g)	CHOL (mg)	SODIUM (mg)	CARB (g)	FIBER (g)
Fruit punch, Tropicana, 8 fl oz	130	0	ns	ns	25	32	ns
Fruit punch, Wagner, 8 fl oz	130	0	0	ns	0	30	ns
Fruit punch, Welch's, 11.5 fl oz	200	0	0	0	25	49	ns
Fruit punch, all natural, Capri Sun, 6.75 fl oz	100	0	0	0	20	26	0
Fruit punch, frozen concentrate, Minute Maid, 8 fl oz	120	0	0	ns	5	31	ns
Fruit punch, frozen concentrate (contains no fruit juice), Bright & Early, 8 fl oz	130	0	0	ns	5	31	ns
Fruit punch juice blend, Mott's, 10 fl oz	170	0	0	0	0	42	0
Fruity bubble gum juice drink, Hi-C, 8 fl oz	120	0	ns	ns	25	30	ns
Fruity bubble gum juice drink, Hi-C, 8.45 fl oz juice box	130	0	ns	ns	30	32	ns
Grape drink, Everfresh, 8 fl oz	130	0	0	0	0	37	ns
Grape drink, Mott's, 10 fl oz	170	0	0	0	50	42	0
Grape drink, Wagner, 8 fl oz	130	0	0	ns	0	33	ns
Grape drink, Welch's, 8 fl oz	150	0	0	0	20	36	ns
Grape drink, frozen concentrate, Bright & Early, 8 fl oz	140	0	0	ns	5	34	ns
Grape drink, frozen concentrate, Welchade, 8 fl oz	130	ns	ns	ns	10	31	ns
Grape juice, Everfresh, 8 fl oz	160	0	0	0	10	38	ns
Grape juice, Libby's Juicy Juice, 4.23 fl oz box	70	0	ns	ns	5	17	0
Grape juice, Libby's Juicy Juice, 8 fl oz	130	0	ns	ns	10	32	0
Grape juice, Minute Maid, 8 fl oz	130	0	ns	ns	5	33	ns
Grape juice, R.W. Knudsen, 8 fl oz	150	0	0	ns	30	37	ns
Grape juice, Tropicana Season's Best, 8 fl oz	160	0	ns	ns	25	39	ns

JUICE & JUICE DRINKS	CAL (g)	FAT (g)	SAT FAT (g)	CHOL (mg)	SODIUM (mg)	CARB (g)	FIBER (g)
Grape juice, Welch's, 8.45 fl oz juice box	150	0	0	0	20	38	ns
Grape juice, Concord, regular or organic, R.W. Knudsen/ Santa Cruz/Natural/Heinke's, 8 fl oz	160	0	0	ns	15	40	ns
Grape juice, frozen concentrate, Welch's, 8 fl oz	160	0	0	0	0	41	ns
Grape juice, frozen concentrate, sweetened, Welch's, 8 fl oz	130	0	0	0	0	33	ns
Grape juice, purple, Welch's, 8 fl oz	170	0	0	0	20	42	ns
Grape juice, red, Welch's, 8 fl oz	170	0	0	0	20	44	ns
Grape juice, red, sparkling, Welch's, 8 fl oz	170	0	0	0	45	44	ns
Grape juice, white, Welch's, 8 fl oz	160	0	0	0	20	39	ns
Grape juice, white, & cranberry, Welch's, 8 fl oz	160	0	0	0	15	39	ns
Grape juice, white, & peach, Welch's, 8 fl oz	150	0	0	0	15	37	ns
Grape juice, white, & raspberry, Welch's, 8 fl oz	140	0	0	0	15	36	ns
Grape juice, white, sparkling, Welch's, 8 fl oz	160	0	0	0	45	39	ns
Grape juice, white, sweetened, frozen concentrate, Welch's, 8 fl oz	140	0	0	0	40	35	ns
Grape juice blend, organic, frozen concentrate, R.W. Knudsen, 8 fl oz	150	0	0	ns	30	37	ns
Grape juice cocktail, concentrate, Mott's Fruit Basket, 8 fl oz	130	0	0	0	5	32	0
Grape juice cocktail, light, frozen concentrate, Welch's, 8 fl oz	50	0	0	0	5	13	ns
Grape juice cocktail, white, Welch's, 8.45 fl oz juice box	160	0	0	0	40	41	ns

JUICE & JUICE DRINKS	CAL	FAT (g)	SAT FAT (g)	CHOL (mg)	SODIUM (mg)	CARB (g)	FIBER (g)
Grape juice drink, Dole, 10 fl oz	150	0	0	0	25	38	0
Grape juice drink, Hi-C, 8 fl oz	130	0	ns	ns	30	32	ns
Grape juice drink, Hi-C, 8.45 fl oz juice box	130	0	ns	ns	30	33	ns
Grape juice drink, all natural, Capri Sun, 6.75 fl oz	110	0	0	0	20	28	0
Grape punch, Minute Maid, 8 fl oz	130	0	ns	ns	25	32	ns
Grape punch, frozen concentrate, Minute Maid, 8 fl oz	130	0	ns	ns	5	32	ns
Grape-apple drink, Welch's, 8 fl oz	150	0	0	0	20	36	ns
Grape-apple drink, frozen concentrate, Welch's Orchard, 8 fl oz	150	ns	ns	ns	5	36	ns
Grape-apple juice, Welch's, 8.45 fl oz juice box	150	0	0	0	20	38	ns
Grape apple juice blend, Mott's, 10 fl oz	170	0	0	0	10	41	0
Grape apple juice drink, Welch's, 11.5 fl oz	210	0	0	0	25	52	ns
Grapefruit juice, Dole, 10 fl oz	120	0	0	0	25	29	0
Grapefruit juice, Dole, 8 fl oz	130	0	0	0	30	31	0
Grapefruit juice, Everfresh, 8 fl oz	90	0	0	0	0	22	ns
Grapefruit juice, Minute Maid, 8 fl oz	100	0	ns	ns	25	23	ns
Grapefruit juice, Mott's, 10 fl oz	120	0	0	0	10	27	0
Grapefruit juice, Ocean Spray, 8 fl oz	100	0	ns	ns	35	24	<1
Grapefruit juice, R.W. Knudsen, 8 fl oz	100	0	0	ns	35	23	ns
Grapefruit juice, Tropicana Season's Best, 8 fl oz	90	0	ns	ns	5	22	ns
Grapefruit juice, Veryfine, 10 fl oz	110	0	0	0	20	25	3

JUICE & JUICE DRINKS	CAL	FAT (g)	SAT FAT (g)	CHOL (mg)	SODIUM (mg)	CARB (g)	FIBER (g)
Grapefruit juice, Welch's, 11.5 fl oz	150	0	0	0	30	37	ns
Grapefruit juice, frozen concentrate, Minute Maid, 8 fl oz	100	0	ns	ns	0	24	ns
Grapefruit juice, golden, Tropicana Pure Premium, 8 fl oz	90	0	ns	ns	0	23	ns
Grapefruit juice, organic, R.W. Knudsen, 8 fl oz	100	0	0	ns	35	23	ns
Grapefruit juice, pink, R.W. Knudsen, 8 fl oz	100	0	0	ns	35	23	ns
Grapefruit juice, ruby red, Tropicana Pure Premium, 8 fl oz	100	0	ns	ns	0	25	ns
Grapefruit juice, ruby red, & orange juice, Tropicana Pure Premium, 8 fl oz	120	0	ns	ns	0	28	ns
Grapefruit juice cocktail, pink, Ocean Spray, 8 fl oz	120	0	ns	ns	35	30	0
Grapefruit juice cocktail, pink, Veryfine, 10 fl oz	150	0	0	0	35	38	2
Grapefruit juice cocktail, pink, low calorie, Ocean Spray Lightstyle, 8 fl oz	40	0	ns	ns	35	9	0
Grapefruit juice cocktail, ruby red, Everfresh, 8 fl oz	130	0	0	0	0	32	ns
Grapefruit juice drink, Tropicana Twister, 8 fl oz	110	0	ns	ns	20	28	ns
Grapefruit juice drink, Pacific pink, bottled or frozen concentrate, Dole, 8 fl oz	140	0	0	0	20	34	0
Grapefruit juice drink, pink, frozen, Tropicana Twister, 8 fl oz	120	0	ns	ns	20	28	n
Grapefruit juice drink, pink, light, Tropicana Twister, 8 fl oz	40	0	ns	ns	20	10	n
Grapefruit juice drink, ruby red, Ocean Spray, 8 fl oz	130	0	ns	ns	35	33	•
Grapefruit juice drink, ruby red, & cranberry, Tropicana Twister, 8 fl oz	120	0	ns	ns	20	30	n
Grapefruit juice drink, ruby red, & tangerine, Ocean Spray, 8 fl oz	130	0	ns	ns	35	32	•

JUICE & JUICE DRINKS	CAL	FAT (g)	SAT FAT (g)	CHOL (mg)	SODIUM (mg)	CARB (g)	FIBER (g)
Guanabana nectar, Libby's, 11.5 fl oz	210	0	ns	ns	25	50	0
Guava juice, frozen concentrate, Welch's, 8 fl oz	140	0	0	0	5	34	ns
Guava nectar, Kern's, 8 fl oz	150	0	ns	ns	5	38	0
Guava nectar, Kern's/Libby's, 11.5 fl oz	220	0	ns	ns	10	54	0
Harvest blend juice drink, Welch's, 8 fl oz	140	0	0	0	20	35	ns
Harvest blend juice drink, Welch's, 8.45 fl oz juice box	150	0	0	0	20	37	ns
Harvest blend juice drink, frozen concentrate, Welch's Orchard, 8 fl oz	140	ns	ns	ns	5	35	ns
Hawaiian Punch, all flavors, 8 fl oz	120	0	0	0	30	30	0
Hawaiian Sunrise (pineapple orange banana) juice, Chiquita, 8 fl oz	120	0	0	0	60	30	<1
Hibiscus cranberry juice blend, R.W. Knudsen/ Heinke's, 8 fl oz	120	0	0	ns	35	30	ns
Hula Punch juice drink, Hi-C, 8 fl oz	120	0	ns	ns	30	29	ns
Hula Punch juice drink, Hi-C, 8.45 fl oz juice box	120	0	ns	ns	30	30	ns
Island Guava (Hawaiian guava fruit) juice drink, Mauna La'i, 8 fl oz	130	0	ns	ns	35	32	0
Jammin' Apple juice drink, Hi-C, 8 fl oz	130	0	ns	ns	30	31	ns
Jammin' Apple juice drink, Hi-C, 8.45 fl oz juice box	130	0	ns	ns	30	33	ns
Just Cranberry juice, R.W. Knudsen, 8 fl oz	60	0	0	ns	25	14	ns
Kiwi strawberry juice cocktail, Everfresh, 8 fl oz	120	0	0	0	0	30	ns
Kiwi strawberry juice drink, Ocean Spray, 8 fl oz	120	0	ns	ns	35	31	0
Lanai Breeze juice drink, bottled or frozen concentrate, Dole, 8 fl oz	120	0	0	0	20	30	0

JUICE & JUICE DRINKS	CAL (g)	FAT (g)	SAT FAT (g)	CHOL (mg)	SODIUM (mg)	CARB (g)	FIBER (g)
Lemon juice, fresh, 1 tsp	0	0	0	0	0	0	0
Lemon juice, ReaLemon, 1 tsp	0	0	0	ns	0	0	ns
Lemon juice, old fashioned, Heinke's, 8 fl oz	120	0	0	ns	35	29	ns
Lemon Ginger Cruz juice drink, Santa Cruz Natural, 8 fl oz	110	0	0	ns	35	27	ns
Lime juice, fresh, 1 tsp	0	0	0	0	0	0	0
Lime juice, ReaLime, 1 tsp	0	0	0	ns	0	0	ns
Lime cactus cooler juice blend, R.W. Knudsen, 8 fl oz	120	0	0	ns	35	29	ns
Macchu Pichu Punch, Heinke's, 8 fl oz	120	0	0	ns	25	30	ns
Mandarin Magic (mandarin orange) juice drink, Ocean Spray, 8 fl oz	120	0	ns	ns	35	31	0
Mandarin orange mango juice cocktail, Everfresh, 8 fl oz	120	0	0	0	0	29	ns
Mandarin tangerine juice, refrigerated or frozen concentrate, Dole, 8 fl oz	140	0	0	0	30	35	0
Mango Mango (mango & Hawaiian guava fruit) juice drink, Mauna La'i, 8 fl oz	130	0	ns	ns	35	33	0
Mango nectar, Kern's/Libby's, 8 fl oz	150	0	ns	ns	5	36	0
Mango orange nectar, Kern's, 8 fl oz	140	0	ns	ns	10	35	0
Mango peach juice blend, R.W. Knudsen, 8 fl oz	120	0	0	ns	50	30	ns
Maui Punch, all natural, Capri Sun, 6.75 fl oz	110	0	0	0	20	28	0
Mixed berry grape juice, Boku, 12 fl oz	180	0	0	0	100	44	0
Mixed fruit juice cooler, Dole, 8.45 fl oz juice box	130	0	0	0	20	33	0
Mountain cherry juice, all varieties, Dole, 8 fl oz	120	0	0	0	30	30	0
Mountain Cooler, all natural, Capri Sun, 6.75 fl oz	100	0	0	0	20	26	0

JUICE & JUICE DRINKS	CAL (g)	FAT (g)	SAT FAT (g)	CHOL (mg)	SODIUM (mg)	CARB (g)	FIBER (g)
Mountain raspberry juice, Heinke's, 8 fl oz	120	0	0	ns	25	30	ns
Orange drink, Bright & Early, 8 fl oz	120	0	0	ns	30	30	ns
Orange drink, Wagner, 8 fl oz	110	0	0	ns	0	27	ns
Orange drink, frozen concentrate, Bright & Early, 8 fl oz	120	0	0	ns	10	30	ns
Orange drink, frozen concentrate, Welchade, 8 fl oz	140	ns	ns	ns	40	34	ns
Orange float, R.W. Knudsen, 8 fl oz	140	0	0	ns	60	33	ns
Orange guava nectar, Kern's, 8 fl oz	150	0	ns	ns	10	36	0
Orange juice, Dean Foods, 8 fl oz	120	0	ns	ns	0	29	ns
Orange juice, Dole, 10 fl oz	140	0	0	0	25	33	0
Orange juice, Everfresh, 8 fl oz	100	0	0	0	0	24	ns
Orange juice, Florida's Natural, 8 fl oz	120	0	ns	ns	0	29	ns
Orange juice, Minute Maid, 8.45 fl oz juice box	120	0	ns	ns	25	28	ns
Orange juice, Mott's, 10 fl oz	130	0.5	0	0	20	29	0
Orange juice, Ocean Spray, 8 fl oz	120	0	ns	ns	35	31	0
Orange juice, R.W. Knudsen, 8 fl oz	100	0	0	ns	35	23	ns
Orange juice, Tropicana Pure Premium, 8 fl oz	110	0	ns	ns	0	27	ns
Orange juice, Tropicana Pure Premium Grovestand, 8 fl oz	110	0	0	ns	0	27	ns
Orange juice, Tropicana Season's Best Homestyle, 8 fl oz	110	0	ns	ns	5	27	ns
Orange juice, Veryfine, 10 fl oz	130	0	0	0	45	29	3
Orange juice, Welch's, 11.5 fl oz	170	0	0	0	30	43	ns

JUICE & JUICE DRINKS	CAL (g)	FAT (g)	SAT FAT (g)	CHOL (mg)	SODIUM (mg)	CARB (g)	FIBER (g)
Orange juice, all varieties, Minute Maid Premium Choice, 8 fl oz	110	0	ns	ns	0	27	ns
Orange juice, all varieties, Tropicana Season's Best, 8 fl oz	110	0	ns	ns	5	27	ns
Orange juice, all varieties except calcium rich, Minute Maid, 8 fl oz	110	0	ns	ns	25	27	ns
Orange juice, calcium rich, Minute Maid, 8 fl oz	120	0	ns	ns	25	27	ns
Orange juice, fresh, 8 fl oz	120	0	0	0	0	26	0
Orange juice, frozen concentrate, Tropicana, 8 fl oz	110	0	ns	ns	5	27	ns
Orange juice, frozen concentrate, all varieties except calcium rich, Minute Maid, 8 fl oz	110	0	ns	ns	0	27	n
Orange juice, frozen concentrate, calcium rich, Minute Maid, 8 fl oz	120	0	ns	ns	0	27	n
Orange juice, organic, frozen concentrate, R.W. Knudsen, 8 fl oz	100	0	0	ns	35	23	n
Orange juice blend, Welch's, 11.5 fl oz	170	0	0	0	30	42	n
Orange juice cooler, Dole, 8.45 fl oz juice box	130	0	0	0	20	33	•
Orange juice drink, Hi-C, 8 fl oz	130	0	ns	ns	25	32	r
Orange juice drink, Hi-C, 8.45 fl oz juice box	130	0	ns	ns	30	33	n
Orange juice drink, all natural, Capri Sun, 6.75 fl oz	100	0	0	0	20	26	
Orange & apricot juice, 8 fl oz	120	0	0	0	0	32	•
Orange banana strawberry drink, Everfresh, 8 fl oz	120	0	0	0	0	30	r
Orange cranberry juice drink, Ocean Spray Refreshers, 8 fl oz	130	0	ns	ns	35	33	

JUICE & JUICE DRINKS	CAL	FAT (g)	SAT FAT (g)	CHOL (mg)	SODIUM (mg)	CARB (g)	FIBER (g)
Orange cranberry juice drink, bottled or frozen concentrate, Tropicana Twister, 8 fl oz	120	0	ns	ns	15	29	ns
Orange cranberry juice drink, light, Tropicana Twister, 8 fl oz	30	0	ns	ns	20	7	ns
Orange kiwi passion juice drink, Tropicana Tropics, 8 fl oz	100	0	ns	ns	15	26	ns
Orange mango juice blend, R.W. Knudsen, 8 fl oz	120	0	0	ns	50	30	ns
Orange peach juice drink, Tropicana Twister, 8 fl oz	120	0	ns	ns	20	29	ns
Orange peach mango juice drink, Tropicana Tropics, 8 fl oz	110	0	ns	ns	15	28	ns
Orange pineapple juice drink, Tropicana, 8 fl oz	110	0	ns	ns	15	27	ns
Orange pineapple juice drink, Tropicana Tropics, 8 fl oz	110	0	ns	ns	15	27	ns
Orange pineapple apple drink, Welch's, 8 fl oz	140	0	0	0	20	35	ns
Orange pineapple apple juice drink, Welch's, 8.45 fl oz juice box	150	0	0	0	20	37	ns
Orange pineapple apple juice, frozen concentrate, Welch's, 8 fl oz	140	0	0	0	0	34	ns
Orange punch, Libby's Juicy Juice, 4.23 fl oz juice box	120	0	ns	ns	10	30	0
Orange punch, Minute Maid, 8.45 fl oz juice box	130	0	ns	ns	25	33	ns
Orange raspberry juice drink, bottled or frozen concentrate, Tropicana Twister, 8 fl oz	120	0	ns	ns	20	29	ns
Orange raspberry juice drink, light, Tropicana Twister, 8 fl oz	35	0	ns	ns	20	9	ns
Orange strawberry banana juice drink, Tropicana Tropics, 8 fl oz	110	0	ns	ns	5	27	ns

JUICE & JUICE DRINKS	CAL (g)	FAT (g)	SAT FAT (g)	CHOL (mg)	SODIUM (mg)	CARB (g)	FIBER (g)
Orange strawberry banana juice drink, bottled or frozen, Tropicana Twister, 8 fl oz	120	0	ns	ns	20	29	ns
Orange strawberry banana juice drink, light, Tropicana Twister, 8 fl oz	35	0	ns	ns	20	9	ns
Orange strawberry guava juice drink, Tropicana Twister, 8 fl oz	110	0	ns	ns	20	28	ns
Orchard peach juice, refrigerated or frozen concentrate, Dole, 8 fl oz	140	0	0	0	30	34	0
Orchard peach juice cocktail, concentrate, Mott's Fruit Basket, 8 fl oz	130	0	0	0	0	32	0
Pacific Cooler juice drink, all natural, Capri Sun, 6.75 fl oz	110	0	0	0	20	29	0
Papaya juice, creamed, R.W. Knudsen, 8 fl oz	40	0	0	ns	10	10	ns
Papaya juice cocktail, Everfresh, 8 fl oz	140	0	0	0	0	35	ns
Papaya juice drink, Farmer's Market, 8 fl oz	130	0	0	ns	0	32	ns
Papaya Cruz juice drink, Santa Cruz Natural, 8 fl oz	110	0	0	ns	35	28	ns
Papaya nectar, Kern's/Libby's, 11.5 fl oz	210	0	ns	ns	10	51	•
Papaya nectar, Libby's, 11.5 fl oz	210	0	ns	ns	10	51	•
Papaya nectar, R.W. Knudsen, 8 fl oz	130	0	0	ns	35	34	n
Papaya punch, Everfresh, 8 fl oz	120	0	0	0	0	29	n
Paradise Passion (Hawaiian guava and passion fruit flavor) juice drink, Mauna La'i, 8 fl oz	130	0	ns	ns	35	32	•
Paradise punch, Dole, 10 fl oz	150	0	0	0	25	38	•
Paradise punch, Heinke's, 8 fl oz	110	0	0	ns	20	28	n
Passion fruit juice, frozen concentrate, Welch's, 8 fl oz	140	0	0	0	60	34	n

JUICE & JUICE DRINKS	CAL (g)	FAT (g)	SAT FAT (g)	CHOL (mg)	SODIUM (mg)	CARB (g)	FIBER (g)
Passion fruit juice, purple, fresh, 8 fl oz	120	0	0	0	20	34	0
Passion fruit juice, yellow, fresh, 8 fl oz	140	0	0	0	20	36	0
Passionfruit mango juice, Heinke's, 8 fl oz	130	0	0	ns	25	33	ns
Passionfruit raspberry juice blend, R.W. Knudsen, 8 fl oz	130	0	0	ns	35	33	ns
Peach juice cocktail, Everfresh, 8 fl oz	110	0	0	0	0	28	ns
Peach juice drink, Farmer's Market, 8 fl oz	120	0	0	ns	0	30	ns
Peach nectar, Kern's/Libby's, 11.5 fl oz	210	0	ns	ns	5	52	0
Peach nectar, Libby's, 8 fl oz	150	0	ns	ns	0	36	0
Peach nectar, R.W. Knudsen, 8 fl oz	120	0	0	ns	25	30	ns
Pear juice, organic, R.W. Knudsen/Heinke's, 8 fl oz	120	0	0	ns	25	30	ns
Pear Cruz juice drink, Santa Cruz Natural, 8 fl oz	125	0	0	ns	30	30	ns
Pear nectar, Kern's/Libby's, 11.5 fl oz	220	0	ns	ns	5	54	3
Pear nectar, Libby's, 8 fl oz	150	0	ns	ns	0	38	2
Riot Punch, Squeezit 100, 1 bottle	100	0	0	0	20	24	0
Pineapple juice, Del Monte, 8 fl oz	110	0	0	0	10	26	0
Pineapple juice, Dole, 8 fl oz	130	0	0	0	20	29	0
Pineapple juice, Everfresh, 8 fl oz	130	0	0	0	0	32	ns
Pineapple juice, Minute Maid, 8.45 fl oz juice box	130	0	ns	ns	25	33	ns
Pineapple juice, frozen concentrate, Dole, 8 fl oz	130	0	0	0	20	30	0
Pineapple juice cooler, Dole, 8.45 fl oz juice box	130	0	0	0	20	33	0
Pineapple banana juice, frozen concentrate, Welch's, 8 fl oz	130	0	0	0	5	33	ns

JUICE & JUICE DRINKS	CAL	FAT (g)	SAT FAT (g)	CHOL (mg)	SODIUM (mg)	CARB (g)	FIBER (g)
Pineapple coconut juice blend, R.W. Knudsen, 8 fl oz	130	0	0	ns	50	32	ns
Pineapple coconut juice drink, Farmer's Market, 8 fl oz	120	0	0	ns	15	29	ns
Pineapple coconut nectar, Kern's, 11.5 fl oz	200	6	5	ns	40	36	2
Pineapple orange juice, Everfresh, 8 fl oz	130	0	0	0	0	31	ns
Pineapple orange juice, frozen concentrate, Minute Maid, 8 fl oz	120	0	ns	ns	0	31	ns
Pineapple orange juice drink, Mott's, 10 fl oz	170	0	0	0	15	42	0
Pineapple passion juice drink, Tropicana Tropics, 8 fl oz	120	0	ns	ns	25	30	ns
Pineapple pink grapefruit juice drink, Dole, 10 fl oz	160	0	0	0	25	40	0
Pineapple punch, Tropicana, 8 fl oz	120	0	ns	ns	15	31	ns
Pine-grapefruit juice, frozen concentrate, Dole, 8 fl oz	130	0	0	0	20	29	0
Pine-orange juice, Dole, 10 fl oz	150	0	0	0	25	36	0
Pine-orange juice, frozen concentrate, Dole, 8 fl oz	120	0	0	0	20	27	0
Pine-orange-banana juice, Dole, 8 fl oz	130	0	0	0	20	29	0
Pine-orange-banana juice, frozen concentrate, Dole, 8 fl oz	130	0	0	0	20	31	0
Pine-orange-berry juice, Dole, 8 fl oz	130	0	0	0	20	32	0
Pine-orange-berry juice, frozen concentrate, Dole, 8 fl oz	130	0	0	0	20	32	0
Pine-orange-guava juice, Dole, 8 fl oz	120	0	0	0	20	29	0
Pine-orange-guava juice, frozen concentrate, Dole, 8 fl oz	120	0	0	0	20	30	0

JUICE & JUICE DRINKS	CAL	FAT (g)	SAT FAT (g)	CHOL (mg)	SODIUM (mg)	CARB (g)	FIBER (g)
Pine-orange-strawberry juice, Dole, 8 fl oz	130	0	0	0	20	32	0
Pine-orange-strawberry juice, frozen concentrate, Dole, 8 fl oz	130	0	0	0	20	32	0
Pine-passion-banana juice, Dole, 8 fl oz	120	0	0	0	20	29	0
Pine-passion-banana juice, frozen concentrate, Dole, 8 fl oz	120	0	0	0	20	30	0
Polynesian Passion (raspberry passion fruit) juice, Chiquita, 8 fl oz	120	0	0	0	60	30	0
Pomegranate juice, R.W. Knudsen, 8 fl oz	150	0	0	ns	10	37	ns
Prune juice, Del Monte, 8 fl oz	170	0	0	0	20	43	1
Prune juice, Sunsweet, 8 fl oz	180	0	0	0	75	43	2
Prune juice, organic, R.W. Knudsen, 8 fl oz	170	0	0	ns	20	45	ns
Punch, Libby's Juicy Juice, 4.23 fl oz box	70	0	ns	ns	5	17	0
Punch, Libby's Juicy Juice, 8 fl oz	130	0	ns	ns	10	32	0
Rain forest punch juice blend, R.W. Knudsen, 8 fl oz	120	0	0	ns	20	29	ns
Raspberry juice, Farmer's Market, 8 fl oz	120	0	0	ns	0	30	ns
Raspberry Cruz juice drink, Santa Cruz Natural, 8 fl oz	100	0	0	ns	35	26	ns
Raspberry float, R.W. Knudsen, 8 fl oz	140	0	0	ns	60	33	ns
Raspberry Guava Cruz juice drink, Santa Cruz Natural, 8 fl oz	100	0	0	ns	25	24	ns
Raspberry lemon juice drink, Santa Cruz Natural, 8 fl oz	120	0	0	ns	35	29	ns
Raspberry lemon splash juice drink, bottled or frozen concentrate, Dole, 8 fl oz	120	0	0	0	20	31	0

JUICE & JUICE DRINKS	CAL (g)	FAT (g)	SAT FAT (g)	CHOL (mg)	SODIUM (mg)	CARB (g)	FIBER (g)
Raspberry nectar, frozen concentrate, R.W. Knudsen, 8 fl oz	120	0	0	ns	25	30	ns
Raspberry peach juice blend, R.W. Knudsen, 8 fl oz	120	0	0	ns	25	31	ns
Razzleberry juice blend, R.W. Knudsen, 8 fl oz	130	0	0	ns	35	33	ns
Red berry juice drink, all natural, Capri Sun, 6.75 fl oz	100	0	0	0	20	28	0
Safari Punch, all natural, Capri Sun, 6.75 fl oz	100	0	0	0	20	25	0
Seven fruit juice blend, Boku, 12 fl oz	180	0	0	0	10	44	0
Shasta Plus, all flavors, Shasta, 12 fl oz	170	0	0	0	45	42	0
Spritzer, apple, organic, R.W. Knudsen, 8 fl oz	160	0	0	ns	25	40	ns
Spritzer, black cherry, R.W. Knudsen, 8 fl oz	170	0	0	ns	20	42	ns
Spritzer, boysenberry, R.W. Knudsen, 8 fl oz	170	0	0	ns	20	42	ns
Spritzer, cherry cola, R.W. Knudsen, 8 fl oz	170	0	0	ns	20	42	ns
Spritzer, cranberry, R.W. Knudsen, 8 fl oz	190	0	0	ns	65	45	ns
Spritzer, ginger ale, R.W. Knudsen, 8 fl oz	160	0	0	ns	25	40	ns
Spritzer, grape, R.W. Knudsen, 8 fl oz	170	0	0	ns	30	41	ns
Spritzer, Jamaican lemonade, R.W. Knudsen, 8 fl oz	170	0	0	ns	25	41	ns
Spritzer, kiwi lime, R.W. Knudsen, 8 fl oz	160	0	0	ns	25	40	ns
Spritzer, lemon lime, R.W. Knudsen, 8 fl oz	170	0	0	ns	25	42	ns
Spritzer, mango, R.W. Knudsen, 8 fl oz	190	0	0	ns	30	45	ns
Spritzer, orange passionfruit, R.W. Knudsen, 8 fl oz	160	0	0	ns	25	40	ns
Spritzer, peach, R.W. Knudsen, 8 fl oz	160	0	0	ns	35	37	ns

JUICE & JUICE DRINKS	CAL (g)	FAT (g)	SAT FAT (g)	CHOL (mg)	SODIUM (mg)	CARB (g)	FIBER (g)
Spritzer, red raspberry, R.W. Knudsen, 8 fl oz	170	0	0	ns	25	42	ns
Spritzer, strawberry, R.W. Knudsen, 8 fl oz	170	0	0	ns	25	42	ns
Spritzer, tangerine, R.W. Knudsen, 8 fl oz	170	0	0	ns	35	39	ns
Squeezit, cherry, berry, red punch, grape, or green punch, 1 bottle	110	0	0	0	0	28	0
Squeezit, orange, 1 bottle	110	0	0	0	45	28	0
Squeezit, strawberry, 1 bottle	110	0	0	0	0	29	0
Squeezit, watermelon, tropical punch, or blue raspberry, 1 bottle	110	0	0	0	0	28	0
Stompin' Banana Berry juice drink, Hi-C, 8 fl oz	130	0	ns	ns	30	31	ns
Stompin' Banana Berry juice drink, Hi-C, 8.45 fl oz juice box	130	0	ns	ns	30	32	ns
Strawberry float, R.W. Knudsen, 8 fl oz	140	0	0	ns	60	33	ns
Strawberry juice drink, Farmer's Market, 8 fl oz	120	0	0	ns	0	30	ns
Strawberry banana juice blend, R.W. Knudsen, 8 fl oz	120	0	0	ns	25	30	ns
Strawberry banana nectar, Kern's, 8 fl oz	150	0	ns	ns	5	36	0
Strawberry banana nectar, Kern's/Libby's, 11.5 fl oz	220	0	ns	ns	10	52	0
Strawberry Cooler juice drink, all natural, Capri Sun, 6.75 fl oz	100	0	0	0	20	26	0
Strawberry guava juice blend, R.W. Knudsen, 8 fl oz	110	0	0	ns	25	27	ns
Strawberry guava juice blend, Santa Cruz Natural, 8 fl oz	100	0	0	ns	25	24	ns
Strawberry nectar, Kern's/Libby's, 11.5 fl oz	210	0	ns	ns	10	52	0
Strawberry nectar, Kern's/Libby's, 8 fl oz	150	0	ns	ns	5	36	0

JUICE & JUICE DRINKS	CAL	FAT (g)	SAT FAT (g)	CHOL (mg)	SODIUM (mg)	CARB (g)	FIBER (g)
Strawberry nectar, R.W. Knudsen, 8 fl oz	120	0	0	ns	25	30	ns
Summer cooler, Ocean Spray, 8 fl oz	120	0	ns	ns	35	31	0
Surfer Cooler, all natural, Capri Sun, 6.75 fl oz	100	0	0	0	20	27	0
Tangerine juice, fresh, 8 fl oz	100	0	0	0	0	26	0
Tangerine juice, frozen concentrate, Minute Maid, 8 fl oz	120	0	ns	ns	0	29	ns
Tomato juice, Campbell's, 10 fl oz	60	0	0	0	1070	12	2
Tomato juice, Campbell's, 11.5 fl oz	70	0	0	0	1230	13	2
Tomato juice, Campbell's, 5.5 fl oz	30	0	0	0	590	6	1
Tomato juice, Campbell's, 8 fl oz	50	0	0	0	860	9	1
Tomato juice, Del Monte, 8 fl oz	50	0	0	0	760	10	1
Tomato juice, Everfresh, 8 fl oz	45	0	0	0	490	11	ns
Tomato juice, Hunt's, 8 fl oz	25	0	0	0	400	5	1
Tomato juice, Welch's, 8 fl oz	50	0	0	0	730	10	2
Tomato juice, low sodium, Campbell's, 8 fl oz	50	0	0	0	140	10	1
Tomato juice, no salt added, Hunt's, 8 fl oz	35	0	0	0	15	8	2
Tomato juice, organic, R.W. Knudsen, 8 fl oz	60	0	0	ns	390	14	ns
Tomato & chile cocktail, Del Monte Snap-E-Tom, 8 fl oz	50	0	0	0	670	11	2
Tropical blend juice cocktail, concentrate, Mott's Fruit Basket, 8 fl oz	120	0	0	0	5	30	0
Tropical Breeze juice drink, bottled or frozen concentrate, Dole, 8 fl oz	120	0	0	0	20	30	0
Tropical citrus juice drink, Five Alive, 8 fl oz	120	0	ns	ns	25	29	ns

JUICE & JUICE DRINKS	CAL	FAT (g)	SAT FAT (g)	CHOL (mg)	SODIUM (mg)	CARB (g)	FIBER (g)
Tropical cocktail drink, Welch's, 11.5 fl oz	210	0	0	0	25	52	ns
Tropical fruit juice, Libby's Juicy Juice, 8 fl oz	130	0	ns	ns	10	31	0
Tropical fruit juice drink, Dole, 10 fl oz	130	0	0	0	25	33	0
Tropical fruit juice blend, bottled or frozen concentrate, Dole, 8 fl oz	140	0	0	0	30	34	0
Tropical nectar, Kern's Nectar, 11.5 fl oz	210	0	ns	ns	10	48	0
Tropical orange juice drink, Farmer's Market, 8 fl oz	120	0	0	0	0	29	ns
Tropical Paradise (orange strawberry banana) juice, Chiquita, 8 fl oz	120	0	0	0	60	29	0
Tropical punch, Farmer's Market, 8 fl oz	120	0	0	ns	0	29	ns
Tropical punch, Minute Maid, 8 fl oz	120	0	ns	ns	25	31	ns
Tropical punch, Minute Maid, 8.45 fl oz juice box	130	0	ns	ns	25	32	ns
Tropical punch, Santa Cruz Natural, 8 fl oz	110	0	0	ns	35	28	ns
Tropical punch, frozen concentrate, Minute Maid, 8 fl oz	120	0	ns	ns	5	31	ns
Tropical punch, frozen concentrate, R.W. Knudsen, 8 fl oz	120	0	0	ns	20	29	ns
Tropical punch juice blend, R.W. Knudsen, 8 fl oz	120	0	0	ns	20	29	ns
Vegetable juice, Mott's, 10 fl oz	60	0	0	0	800	13	2
Vegetable juice, V8, 11.5 fl oz	70	0	0	0	780	15	2
Vegetable juice, V8, 5.5 fl oz	35	0	0	0	430	7	1
Vegetable juice, V8, 8 fl oz	50	0	0	0	620	7	1
Vegetable juice, Welch's, 11.5 fl oz	70	0	0	0	1050	15	2
Vegetable juice, lightly tangy, V8, 11.5 fl oz	80	0	0	0	490	16	2
Vegetable juice, lightly tangy, V8, 5.5 fl oz	40	0	0	0	240	8	1

JUICE & JUICE DRINKS	CAL (g)	FAT (g)	SAT FAT (g)	CHOL (mg)	SODIUM (mg)	CARB (g)	FIBER (g)
Vegetable juice, lightly tangy, V8, 8 fl oz	60	0	0	0	340	11	1
Vegetable juice, low sodium, V8, 5.5 fl oz	40	0	0	0	95	7	1
Vegetable juice, low sodium, V8, 8 fl oz	60	0	0	0	140	11	2
Vegetable juice, picante, V8, 11.5 fl oz	70	0	0	0	990	14	2
Vegetable juice, picante, V8, 5.5 fl oz	35	0	0	0	470	7	1
Vegetable juice, picante, V8, 8 fl oz	50	0	0	0	680	10	1
Vegetable juice, spicy hot, V8, 11.5 fl oz	70	0	0	0	1120	15	2
Vegetable juice, spicy hot, V8, 5.5 fl oz	35	0	0	0	540	7	1
Vegetable juice, spicy hot, V8, 8 fl oz	50	0	0	0	780	10	1
Vegetable juice, Very Veggie, low sodium, R.W. Knudsen, 8 fl oz	50	1	ns	ns	30	10	ns
Vegetable juice, Very Veggie, original or spicy, R.W. Knudsen, 8 fl oz	50	1	ns	ns	610	10	ns
Vegetable juice, Vita Juice, fortified, R.W. Knudsen, 8 fl oz	110	0	0	ns	60	29	ns
Wild Berry juice drink, Hi-C, 8 fl oz	120	0	ns	ns	30	30	ns
Wild Berry juice drink, Hi-C, 8.45 fl oz juice box	130	0	ns	ns	30	32	ns
Wild cherry juice drink, all natural, Capri Sun, 6.75 fl oz	110	0	0	0	20	30	0
Yankee cranberry juice blend, R.W. Knudsen, 8 fl oz	120	0	0	ns	25	30	ns
Yo Yogi Berry juice drink, all natural, Capri Sun, 6.75 fl oz	100	0	0	0	20	27	0

AT A GLANCE: JUICE & JUICE DRINKS
Lowest in Calories, Vegetable Juice: Hunt's Tomato Juice (8 fl oz)
Lowest in Calories, Fruit Juice: Heinke's Cranberry Juice (8 fl oz); R.W. Knudsen Just Cranberry Juice (8 fl oz)
Lowest in Calories, Juice Drink: Tropicana Twister Orange Cranberry Juice Drink, Light (8 fl oz)

	CAL	FAT (g)	SAT FAT (g)	CHOL (mg)	SODIUM (mg)	CARB (g)	FIBER (g)
		(g)					

MIXERS

	CAL	FAT (g)	SAT FAT (g)	CHOL (mg)	SODIUM (mg)	CARB (g)	FIBER (g)
Banana daiquiri, frozen concentrate, Bacardi Mixer, 8 fl oz	150	0	0	ns	0	36	ns
Bitter lemon, Schweppes, 8 fl oz	110	0	0	0	45	28	0
Bloody Mary mix, extra spicy, Tabasco, 8 fl oz	60	0	0	0	1650	11	2
Bloody Mary mix, regular, Tabasco, 8 fl oz	60	0	0	0	1550	11	1
Collins, Canada Dry, 8 fl oz	100	0	0	0	15	21	0
Collins, Schweppes, 8 fl oz	100	0	0	0	55	24	0
Grenadine, Rose's, 2 Tbsp	90	0	0	0	10	22	0
Lemon sour, Schweppes, 8 fl oz	110	0	0	0	25	26	0
Lime, sweetened, Rose's, 1 tsp	10	0	0	0	0	2	0
Margarita, frozen concentrate, Bacardi Mixer, 8 fl oz	100	0	0	ns	0	25	ns
Pina colada, frozen concentrate, Bacardi Mixer, 8 fl oz	190	6	5	ns	25	33	ns
Quinine, Canfield's, 8 fl oz	80	0	ns	ns	10	21	ns
Quinine/tonic, Shasta, 12 fl oz	170	0	0	0	45	42	0
Rum Runner, frozen concentrate, Bacardi Mixer, 8 fl oz	140	0	0	ns	10	35	ns
Sour mix, Canada Dry, 8 fl oz	90	0	0	0	25	22	0
Strawberry daiquiri, frozen concentrate, Bacardi Mixer, 8 fl oz	140	0	0	ns	0	35	ns
Sweet & sour mix, ready-to-use, Rose's, 4 fl oz	100	0	0	0	50	23	0
Tonic water, Canada Dry, 8 fl oz	100	0	0	0	15	24	0
Tonic water, Canfield's, 8 fl oz	0	0	ns	ns	0	0	ns
Tonic water, Schweppes, 8 fl oz	90	0	0	0	45	22	0
Tonic water, citrus, Schweppes, 8 fl oz	90	0	0	0	25	20	0

MIXERS	CAL (g)	FAT (g)	SAT FAT (g)	CHOL (mg)	SODIUM (mg)	CARB (g)	FIBER (g)
Tonic water, cranberry, Schweppes, 8 fl oz	90	0	0	0	25	20	0
Tonic water, diet, Canada Dry, 8 fl oz	0	0	0	0	35	0	0
Tonic water, diet, Schweppes, 8 fl oz	0	0	0	0	85	0	0
Tonic water, lime, Canada Dry, 8 fl oz	100	0	0	0	20	24	0
Tonic water, lime, diet, Canada Dry, 8 fl oz	0	0	0	0	45	0	0
Tonic water, raspberry, Schweppes, 8 fl oz	90	0	0	0	25	20	0

NUTRITIONAL DRINKS

	CAL (g)	FAT (g)	SAT FAT (g)	CHOL (mg)	SODIUM (mg)	CARB (g)	FIBER (g)
Apple-cranberry-raspberry mix, Ultra Slim Fast, 1 can	220	1.5	0.5	10	190	53	5
Cafe mocha mix, Ultra Slim Fast, 3 Tbsp	110	1	0.5	<5	120	25	5
Chocolate almond, ready-to-drink, Nestle Sweet Success, 1 can	200	3	1	5	240	38	6
Chocolate almond, ready-to-drink, refrigerated, Nestle Sweet Success, 12 fl oz	220	1.5	1	<5	300	45	6
Chocolate almond mix, Nestle Sweet Success, 2 Tbsp	90	1.5	1	<5	210	19	6
Chocolate chip mix, Nestle Sweet Success, 2 Tbsp	90	2	1.5	<5	170	19	6
Chocolate chip mix, classic, Nestle Sweet Success, 2 Tbsp	90	1.5	1	<5	230	19	6
Chocolate fudge, ready-to-drink, Ultra Slim Fast, 1 can	220	3	1	10	180	42	5
Chocolate fudge shake mix, Weight Watchers, 0.75 oz	80	1	0	0	140	12	2
Chocolate malt mix, Ultra Slim Fast, 3 Tbsp	100	1	0.5	<5	120	20	2
Chocolate mix, Ultra Slim Fast, 3 Tbsp	100	1	0.5	<5	110	20	2
Chocolate mocha supreme, ready-to-drink, Nestle Sweet Success, 1 can	200	3	1	5	220	38	6

NUTRITIONAL DRINKS	CAL (g)	FAT (g)	SAT FAT (g)	CHOL (mg)	SODIUM (mg)	CARB (g)	FIBER (g)
Chocolate raspberry truffle, ready-to-drink, Nestle Sweet Success, 1 can	200	3	1	5	220	38	6
Chocolate raspberry truffle mix, Nestle Sweet Success, 2 Tbsp	90	1.5	1	<5	210	19	6
Chocolate royale, ready-to-drink, Ultra Slim Fast, 1 can	220	3	1	5	220	42	5
Chocolate royale mix, Ultra Slim Fast, 3 Tbsp	110	1	0.5	<5	100	25	5
Coffee, ready-to-drink, Ultra Slim Fast, 1 can	220	3	0.5	5	300	38	5
Dark chocolate fudge, ready-to-drink, Nestle Sweet Success, 1 can	200	3	1	5	220	38	6
Dark chocolate fudge, ready-to-drink, refrigerated, Nestle Sweet Success, 12 fl oz	220	1.5	1	<5	310	45	6
Dark chocolate fudge mix, Nestle Sweet Success, 2 Tbsp	90	1.5	1	<5	210	19	6
Dutch chocolate, Sego Lite, 1 can	150	3	na	na	400	21	0
French vanilla, Sego Lite, 1 can	150	4	na	na	380	18	0
French vanilla, ready-to-drink, Ultra Slim Fast, 1 can	220	3	0.5	5	250	38	5
French vanilla shake mix, Ultra Slim Fast, 3 Tbsp	110	0.5	0	<5	140	25	4
Fruit juice shake mix, Ultra Slim Fast, 5 Tbsp	110	0.5	0	10	120	18	5
GatorPro, vanilla, Gatorade, 11 fl oz	360	6	1	0	270	59	0
Golden apple, Ultra Slim Fast, 1 can	220	1.5	0.5	10	190	44	5
Milk chocolate, ready-to-drink, Nestle Sweet Success, 1 can	200	3	1	5	240	38	6
Milk chocolate, ready-to-drink, Ultra Slim Fast, 1 can	230	3	1	5	220	42	5
Milk chocolate, ready-to-drink, refrigerated, Nestle Sweet Success, 12 fl oz	220	1.5	1	<5	300	45	6

NUTRITIONAL DRINKS	CAL (g)	FAT (g)	SAT FAT (g)	CHOL (mg)	SODIUM (mg)	CARB (g)	FIBER (g)
Milk chocolate mix, Nestle Sweet Success, 2 Tbsp	90	1.5	1	<5	210	19	6
Orange-strawberry-banana, Ultra Slim Fast, 1 can	220	1.5	0.5	10	190	53	5
Strawberry, Sego Lite, 1 can	150	4	na	na	400	18	0
Strawberry shake mix, Ultra Slim Fast, 3 Tbsp	100	0.5	0	<5	130	20	2
Strawberry supreme, ready-to-drink, Ultra Slim Fast, 1 can	230	3	0.5	5	250	42	5
Strawberry supreme mix, Ultra Slim Fast, 3 Tbsp	110	0.5	0	<5	140	25	4
Vanilla, Sego Lite, 1 can	150	4	na	na	400	18	0
Vanilla creme, ready-to-drink, Nestle Sweet Success, 1 can	200	3	1	5	220	38	6
Vanilla delight mix, Nestle Sweet Success, 2 Tbsp	90	0.5	0	<5	180	20	6
Vanilla shake mix, Ultra Slim Fast, 3 Tbsp	100	0.5	0	<5	130	20	2
Very chocolate, Sego, 1 can	240	1.5	0	5	310	44	0
Very chocolate, Sego Lite, 1 can	150	3	na	na	400	21	0
Very chocolate malt, Sego, 1 can	240	1.5	0	5	310	44	0
Very strawberry, Sego, 1 can	240	5	1	5	280	37	0
Very vanilla, Sego, 1 can	240	5	1	5	280	37	0

AT A GLANCE: NUTRITIONAL DRINKS
Adding these drink mixes to 8 fl oz vitamin A & D skim milk contributes an additional 90 calories, 125 mg sodium, and 12 mg total carbohydrate.

SOFT DRINKS, CARBONATED

	CAL (g)	FAT (g)	SAT FAT (g)	CHOL (mg)	SODIUM (mg)	CARB (g)	FIBER (g)
50/50, Canfield's, 8 fl oz	110	ns	ns	ns	35	26	ns
50/50, diet, Canfield's, 8 fl oz	0	0	ns	ns	0	0	ns
7UP, 12 fl oz	160	0	0	0	75	39	0
Diet 7UP, 12 fl oz	0	0	0	0	35	0	0
Berry, Minute Maid, 8 fl oz	110	0	0	ns	10	30	ns
Birch beer, brown or clear, Canada Dry, 8 fl oz	110	0	0	0	40	27	0

SOFT DRINKS, CARBONATED	CAL	FAT (g)	SAT FAT (g)	CHOL (mg)	SODIUM (mg)	CARB (g)	FIBER (g)
Black cherry, Canfield's, 8 fl oz	130	ns	ns	ns	15	33	ns
Black cherry, Minute Maid, 8 fl oz	110	0	0	ns	10	29	ns
Black cherry, Shasta, 12 fl oz	170	0	0	0	45	41	0
Black cherry, diet, Shasta, 12 fl oz	0	0	0	0	45	0	0
Black cherry, sodium free, Diet Rite, 8 fl oz	0	ns	ns	ns	0	0	0
Black cherry Wishniak, Canada Dry, 8 fl oz	130	0	0	0	40	32	0
Blue, Nehi Lock Jaw, 8 fl oz	120	ns	ns	ns	35	29	ns
Blue raspberry, Nehi, 8 fl oz	120	ns	ns	ns	35	29	ns
Cactus cooler, Canada Dry, 8 fl oz	110	0	0	0	40	27	0
California strawberry, Canada Dry, 8 fl oz	110	0	0	0	45	27	0
Cherry, Crush, 8 fl oz	140	0	0	0	30	35	0
Cherry, Nehi, 8 fl oz	120	ns	ns	ns	35	29	ns
Cherry 7UP, 12 fl oz	160	0	0	0	35	39	0
Diet Cherry 7UP, 12 fl oz	0	0	0	0	35	0	0
Cherry chocolate fudge, diet, Canfield's, 8 fl oz	0	0	ns	ns	0	0	ns
Cherry Coke, 8 fl oz	100	0	0	ns	0	28	ns
Diet Cherry Coke, 8 fl oz	0	0	0	ns	0	0	ns
Cherry cola, Shasta, 12 fl oz	160	0	0	0	45	39	0
Cherry cola, diet, Shasta, 12 fl oz	0	0	0	0	45	0	0
Cherry RC, 8 fl oz	110	ns	ns	ns	35	29	ns
Cherry-lime, all natural, Spree, 12 fl oz	170	0	0	0	45	45	0
Cherry-ola cola, diet, Canfield's, 8 fl oz	0	0	ns	ns	0	0	ns
Cherry spice, Slice, 12 fl oz	150	0	ns	ns	35	39	ns
Chocolate fudge, diet, Canfield's, 8 fl oz	0	0	ns	ns	0	0	ns
Club soda, Canada Dry, 8 fl oz	0	0	0	0	60	0	0
Club soda, Canfield's, 8 fl oz	0	0	ns	ns	40	0	ns

SOFT DRINKS, CARBONATED	CAL (g)	FAT (g)	SAT FAT (g)	CHOL (mg)	SODIUM (mg)	CARB (g)	FIBER (g)
Club soda, Schweppes, 8 fl oz	0	0	0	0	70	0	0
Club soda, Shasta, 12 fl oz	0	0	0	0	90	0	0
Club soda, sodium free, Canada Dry, 8 fl oz	0	0	0	0	0	0	0
Club soda, sodium free, Schweppes, 8 fl oz	0	0	0	0	0	0	0
Coca-Cola Classic, regular and caffeine-free, 8 fl oz	100	0	0	ns	10	27	ns
Diet Coca-Cola, regular and caffeine-free, 8 fl oz	0	0	0	ns	0	0	ns
Coke II, 8 fl oz	110	0	0	ns	0	29	ns
Cola, Canfield's, 8 fl oz	110	ns	ns	ns	10	27	ns
Cola, Shasta, 12 fl oz	170	0	0	0	45	42	0
Cola, Slice, 12 fl oz	160	0	ns	ns	35	43	ns
Cola, all natural, Spree, 12 fl oz	170	0	0	0	45	42	0
Cola, caffeine free, Shasta, 12 fl oz	160	0	0	0	45	41	0
Cola, diet, Canfield's, 8 fl oz	0	0	ns	ns	0	0	ns
Cola, diet, Shasta, 12 fl oz	0	0	0	0	45	0	0
Cola, diet, caffeine free, Shasta, 12 fl oz	0	0	0	0	45	0	0
Cranberry, sodium free, Diet Rite, 8 fl oz	0	ns	ns	ns	0	0	ns
Cranberry-apple, sodium free, Diet Rite, 8 fl oz	0	ns	ns	ns	0	0	ns
Cream soda, A & W, 12 fl oz	170	0	0	0	55	44	0
Cream soda, Hires, 8 fl oz	130	0	0	0	30	32	0
Cream soda, I.B.C., 12 fl oz	180	0	0	0	30	42	0
Cream soda, blue, Nehi, 8 fl oz	120	ns	ns	ns	35	32	ns
Cream soda, diet, A & W 12 fl oz	0	0	0	0	70	0	0
Cream soda, diet, Hires, 8 fl oz	0	0	0	0	35	0	0
Cream soda, diet, I.B.C., 12 fl oz	5	0	0	0	35	0	0

SOFT DRINKS, CARBONATED	CAL (g)	FAT (g)	SAT FAT (g)	CHOL (mg)	SODIUM (mg)	CARB (g)	FIBER (g)
Cream soda, vanilla, Canada Dry, 8 fl oz	120	0	0	0	40	30	0
Creme soda, Mug, 12 fl oz	170	0	0	ns	65	48	ns
Creme soda, Shasta, 12 fl oz	170	0	0	0	45	42	0
Creme soda, diet, Mug, 12 fl oz	5	0	0	ns	80	0	ns
Creme soda, diet, Shasta, 12 fl oz	0	0	0	0	45	0	0
Diet Rite cola, sodium free, 8 fl oz	0	ns	ns	ns	0	0	ns
Diet Rite cola, sodium free, caffeine free, 8 fl oz	0	ns	ns	ns	0	0	ns
Doc Shasta, Shasta, 12 fl oz	160	0	0	0	45	39	0
Doc Shasta, diet, Shasta, 12 fl oz	0	0	0	0	45	0	0
Dr. Nehi, 8 fl oz	100	ns	ns	ns	35	26	ns
Dr. Pepper, 12 fl oz	160	0	0	0	55	40	0
Dr. Pepper, caffeine-free, 12 fl oz	160	0	0	0	55	40	0
Diet Dr. Pepper, 12 fl oz	0	0	0	0	55	0	0
Diet Dr. Pepper, caffeine-free, 12 fl oz	0	0	0	0	55	0	0
Dr. Slice, 12 fl oz	140	0	ns	ns	35	39	ns
Fresca, 8 fl oz	0	0	0	ns	0	0	ns
Fruit punch, Minute Maid, 8 fl oz	120	0	0	ns	10	32	ns
Fruit punch, Nehi, 8 fl oz	120	ns	ns	ns	35	34	ns
Fruit punch, Shasta, 12 fl oz	200	0	0	0	45	50	0
Fruit punch, Slice, 12 fl oz	190	0	ns	ns	55	48	ns
Fruit punch, sodium free, Diet Rite, 8 fl oz	0	ns	ns	ns	0	0	ns
Ginger ale, Canada Dry, 8 fl oz	90	0	0	0	15	25	0
Ginger ale, Canfield's, 8 fl oz	90	ns	ns	ns	10	22	ns
Ginger ale, Fanta, 8 fl oz	90	0	0	ns	0	23	ns
Ginger ale, Nehi, 8 fl oz	90	ns	ns	ns	35	24	ns
Ginger ale, Schweppes, 8 fl oz	90	0	0	0	50	22	0
Ginger ale, Shasta, 12 fl oz	130	0	0	0	45	32	0

SOFT DRINKS, CARBONATED	CAL	FAT (g)	SAT FAT (g)	CHOL (mg)	SODIUM (mg)	CARB (g)	FIBER (g)
Ginger ale, cherry, Canada Dry, 8 fl oz	100	0	0	0	25	27	0
Ginger ale, cherry, diet, Canada Dry, 8 fl oz	0	0	0	0	60	0	0
Ginger ale, cranberry, Canada Dry, 8 fl oz	90	0	0	0	15	25	0
Ginger ale, cranberry, diet, Canada Dry, 8 fl oz	0	0	0	0	50	<1	0
Ginger ale, diet, Canada Dry, 8 fl oz	0	0	0	0	60	0	0
Ginger ale, diet, Canfield's, 8 fl oz	0	0	ns	ns	0	0	ns
Ginger ale, diet, Schweppes, 8 fl oz	0	0	0	0	75	0	0
Ginger ale, diet, Shasta, 12 fl oz	0	0	0	0	45	0	0
Ginger ale, dry grape, Schweppes, 8 fl oz	100	0	0	0	50	26	0
Ginger ale, dry grape, diet, Schweppes, 8 fl oz	0	0	0	0	90	0	0
Ginger ale, golden, Canada Dry, 8 fl oz	100	0	0	0	10	24	0
Ginger ale, lemon, Canada Dry, 8 fl oz	90	0	0	0	15	25	0
Ginger ale, lemon, diet, Canada Dry, 8 fl oz	0	0	0	0	60	0	0
Ginger ale, raspberry, Schweppes, 8 fl oz	100	0	0	0	50	26	0
Ginger ale, raspberry, diet, Schweppes, 8 fl oz	0	0	0	0	75	0	0
Ginger beer, Schweppes, 8 fl oz	100	0	0	0	90	25	0
Grape, Canfield's, 8 fl oz	140	ns	ns	ns	15	34	ns
Grape, Crush, 8 fl oz	140	0	0	0	30	35	0
Grape, Fanta, 8 fl oz	120	0	0	ns	10	31	ns
Grape, Minute Maid, 8 fl oz	120	0	0	ns	10	32	ns
Grape, Nehi, 8 fl oz	120	ns	ns	ns	35	32	ns
Grape, Schweppes, 8 fl oz	130	0	0	0	55	33	0
Grape, Shasta, 12 fl oz	180	0	0	0	45	45	0

SOFT DRINKS, CARBONATED	CAL (g)	FAT (g)	SAT FAT (g)	CHOL (mg)	SODIUM (mg)	CARB (g)	FIBER (g)
Grape, Slice, 12 fl oz	190	0	ns	ns	70	50	ns
Grape, Concord, Canada Dry, 8 fl oz	120	0	0	0	45	29	0
Grape, diet, Shasta, 12 fl oz	0	0	0	0	45	0	0
Grape, white, sodium free, Diet Rite, 8 fl oz	0	ns	ns	ns	0	0	ns
Grapefruit, Minute Maid, 8 fl oz	110	0	0	ns	10	29	ns
Grapefruit, Schweppes, 8 fl oz	110	0	0	0	75	27	0
Grapefruit, all natural, Spree, 12 fl oz	170	0	0	0	45	41	0
Grapefruit, diet, Shasta, 12 fl oz	0	0	0	0	45	0	0
Grapefruit, pink, sodium free, Diet Rite, 8 fl oz	0	ns	ns	ns	0	0	ns
Green, Nehi Lock Jaw, 8 fl oz	120	ns	ns	ns	35	29	ns
Green apple, Nehi, 8 fl oz	120	ns	ns	ns	35	29	ns
Half & half soda, Canada Dry, 8 fl oz	110	0	0	0	25	27	0
Hi-Spot, Canada Dry, 8 fl oz	110	0	0	0	50	28	0
Island lime, Canada Dry, 8 fl oz	140	0	0	0	15	33	0
Jamaica cola, Canada Dry, 8 fl oz	110	0	0	0	10	27	0
Key lime, sodium free, Diet Rite, 8 fl oz	0	ns	ns	ns	0	0	ns
Kick, 8 fl oz	120	ns	ns	ns	35	32	ns
Diet Kick, sodium free, 8 fl oz	0	ns	ns	ns	0	0	ns
Kiwi strawberry, Shasta, 12 fl oz	170	0	0	0	45	43	0
Kiwi strawberry, diet, Shasta, 12 fl oz	0	0	0	0	45	0	0
Kiwi-strawberry, sodium free, Diet Rite, 8 fl oz	0	ns	ns	ns	0	0	ns
Lemon, Nehi, 8 fl oz	120	ns	ns	ns	35	29	ns
Lemon lime, Canfield's, 8 fl oz	100	ns	ns	ns	0	25	ns
Lemon-lime, Schweppes, 8 fl oz	100	0	0	0	75	25	0

SOFT DRINKS, CARBONATED	CAL (g)	FAT (g)	SAT FAT (g)	CHOL (mg)	SODIUM (mg)	CARB (g)	FIBER (g)
Lemon lime, Shasta, 12 fl oz	150	0	0	0	45	38	0
Lemon lime, Slice, 12 fl oz	150	0	ns	ns	55	40	ns
Lemon-lime, all natural, Spree, 12 fl oz	170	0	0	0	45	42	0
Lemon lime, diet, Shasta, 12 fl oz	0	0	0	0	45	0	0
Lemon lime, diet, Slice, 12 fl oz	0	0	ns	ns	35	1	ns
Lemon sour, Canada Dry, 8 fl oz	100	0	0	0	15	21	0
Lemon-tangerine, all natural, Spree, 12 fl oz	170	0	0	0	45	45	0
Lemonade, sodium free, Diet Rite, 8 fl oz	0	ns	ns	ns	0	0	ns
Mandarin-lime, all natural, Spree, 12 fl oz	170	0	0	0	45	42	0
Mandarin orange, Slice, 12 fl oz	190	0	ns	ns	55	51	ns
Mandarin orange, diet, Slice, 12 fl oz	0	0	ns	ns	50	0	ns
Mello Yello, 8 fl oz	120	0	0	ns	10	32	ns
Diet Mello Yello, 8 fl oz	0	0	0	ns	ns	0	ns
Mocha, Hires, 8 fl oz	100	0	0	0	45	24	0
Mocha, diet, Hires, 8 fl oz	5	0	0	0	45	0	0
Moon Mist, Shasta, 12 fl oz	180	0	0	0	45	46	0
Mountain Dew, 12 fl oz	170	0	ns	ns	70	46	ns
Diet Mountain Dew, 12 fl oz	0	0	ns	ns	35	0	ns
Caffeine-free Mountain Dew, 12 fl oz	170	0	ns	ns	70	46	ns
Diet Caffeine-free Mountain Dew, 12 fl oz	0	0	ns	ns	35	0	ns
Mr. PiBB, 8 fl oz	100	0	0	ns	10	26	ns
Diet Mr. PiBB, 8 fl oz	0	0	0	ns	0	0	ns
Orange, Canfield's, 8 fl oz	130	ns	ns	ns	15	33	ns
Orange, Crush, 8 fl oz	140	0	0	0	30	35	0
Orange, Fanta, 8 fl oz	120	0	0	0	10	32	0
Orange, Minute Maid, 8 fl oz	120	0	0	ns	0	32	ns

SOFT DRINKS, CARBONATED	CAL (g)	FAT (g)	SAT FAT (g)	CHOL (mg)	SODIUM (mg)	CARB (g)	FIBER (g)
Orange, Nehi, 8 fl oz	130	ns	ns	ns	35	35	ns
Orange, Shasta, 12 fl oz	180	0	0	0	45	46	0
Orange, diet, Canfield's, 8 fl oz	0	0	ns	ns	0	0	ns
Orange, diet, Crush, 8 fl oz	20	0	0	0	30	4	0
Orange, diet, Minute Maid, 8 fl oz	0	0	0	ns	0	0	ns
Orange, diet, Shasta, 12 fl oz	0	0	0	0	45	0	0
Passion plum, sodium free, Diet Rite, 8 fl oz	0	ns	ns	ns	0	0	ns
Peach, Canada Dry, 8 fl oz	120	0	0	0	40	30	0
Peach, Crush, 8 fl oz	140	0	0	0	40	34	0
Peach, Minute Maid, 8 fl oz	110	0	0	ns	10	29	ns
Peach, Nehi, 8 fl oz	130	ns	ns	ns	35	34	ns
Peach, Shasta, 12 fl oz	170	0	0	0	45	43	0
Peach, sodium free, Diet Rite, 8 fl oz	0	ns	ns	ns	0	0	ns
Peanut chocolate fudge, diet, Canfield's, 8 fl oz	0	0	ns	ns	0	0	ns
Pepsi, 12 fl oz	150	0	ns	ns	35	41	ns
Diet Pepsi, 12 fl oz	0	0	ns	ns	35	0	ns
Caffeine-free Pepsi, 12 fl oz	150	0	ns	ns	35	41	ns
Diet Caffeine-free Pepsi, 12 fl oz	0	0	ns	ns	35	0	ns
Pina pineapple, Canada Dry, 8 fl oz	110	0	0	0	40	26	0
Pineapple, Crush, 8 fl oz	140	0	0	0	30	35	0
Pineapple, Minute Maid, 8 fl oz	110	0	0	ns	10	30	ns
Pineapple, Nehi, 8 fl oz	130	ns	ns	ns	35	36	ns
Pineapple, Shasta, 12 fl oz	200	0	0	0	45	51	0
Pineapple, Slice, 12 fl oz	190	0	ns	ns	70	50	ns
Pineapple-orange, Shasta, 12 fl oz	180	0	0	0	45	46	0
Raspberry, Minute Maid, 8 fl oz	110	0	0	ns	10	30	ns

SOFT DRINKS, CARBONATED	CAL (g)	FAT (g)	SAT FAT (g)	CHOL (mg)	SODIUM (mg)	CARB (g)	FIBER (g)
Raspberry, sodium free, Diet Rite, 8 fl oz	0	ns	ns	ns	0	0	ns
Raspberry creme, Shasta, 12 fl oz	170	0	0	0	45	44	0
Raspberry creme, diet, Shasta, 12 fl oz	0	0	0	0	45	0	0
RC cola, 8 fl oz	110	ns	ns	ns	35	29	ns
Caffeine Free RC Cola, 8 fl oz	110	ns	ns	ns	35	29	ns
Red, Nehi Lock Jaw, 8 fl oz	120	ns	ns	ns	35	29	ns
Red, Slice, 12 fl oz	190	0	ns	ns	55	50	ns
Red pop, Canfield's, 8 fl oz	120	ns	ns	ns	15	30	ns
Red pop, Shasta, 12 fl oz	170	0	0	0	45	43	0
Red pop, diet, Canfield's, 8 fl oz	0	0	ns	ns	0	0	ns
Root beer, A & W, 12 fl oz	170	0	0	0	55	44	0
Root beer, Barrelhead, 8 fl oz	110	0	0	0	25	27	0
Root beer, Canfield's, 8 fl oz	120	ns	ns	ns	15	30	ns
Root beer, Dad's, 8 fl oz	110	0	ns	ns	40	28	ns
Root beer, Fanta, 8 fl oz	110	0	0	ns	0	29	ns
Root beer, Hires, 8 fl oz	130	0	0	0	45	31	0
Root beer, I.B.C., 12 fl oz	170	0	0	0	15	42	0
Root beer, Mug, 12 fl oz	160	0	0	ns	65	43	ns
Root beer, Nehi, 8 fl oz	120	ns	ns	ns	35	32	ns
Root beer, Ramblin', 8 fl oz	120	0	0	ns	0	33	ns
Root beer, Shasta, 12 fl oz	170	0	0	0	45	42	0
Root beer, all natural, Spree, 12 fl oz	170	0	0	0	45	42	0
Root beer, caffeine free, Dad's, 8 fl oz	110	0	ns	ns	25	28	ns
Root beer, diet, A & W, 12 fl oz	0	0	0	0	70	0	0
Root beer, diet, Canfield's, 8 fl oz	0	0	ns	ns	0	0	ns
Root beer, diet, Dad's, 8 fl oz	0	0	ns	ns	40	0	ns
Root beer, diet, Hires, 8 fl oz	0	0	0	0	70	0	0
Root beer, diet, I.B.C., 12 fl oz	0	0	0	0	80	0	0
Root beer, diet, Mug, 12 fl oz	0	0	0	ns	65	0	ns

SOFT DRINKS, CARBONATED	CAL (g)	FAT (g)	SAT FAT (g)	CHOL (mg)	SODIUM (mg)	CARB (g)	FIBER (g)
Root beer, diet, Shasta, 12 fl oz	0	0	0	0	45	0	0
Sprite, 8 fl oz	100	0	0	ns	30	26	ns
Diet Sprite, 8 fl oz	0	0	0	ns	0	0	ns
Strawberry, Canfield's, 8 fl oz	120	ns	ns	ns	15	30	ns
Strawberry, Crush, 8 fl oz	130	0	0	0	30	31	0
Strawberry, Minute Maid, 8 fl oz	120	0	0	0	10	33	ns
Strawberry, Nehi, 8 fl oz	120	ns	ns	ns	35	32	ns
Strawberry, Shasta, 12 fl oz	150	0	0	0	45	39	0
Strawberry, Slice, 12 fl oz	170	0	0	ns	55	46	ns
Strawberry-peach, Shasta, 12 fl oz	170	0	0	0	45	42	0
Sunripe orange, Canada Dry, 8 fl oz	140	0	0	0	45	35	0
Swiss creme, Canfield's, 8 fl oz	120	ns	ns	ns	15	30	ns
Swiss creme, diet, Canfield's, 8 fl oz	0	0	ns	ns	0	0	ns
Tab, 8 fl oz	0	0	0	ns	0	0	ns
Tahitian Treat, Canada Dry, 8 fl oz	150	0	0	0	45	36	0
Tangerine, sodium free, Diet Rite, 8 fl oz	0	ns	ns	ns	0	0	ns
Tropical blend, all natural, Spree, 12 fl oz	170	0	0	0	45	42	0
Tropical fruit punch, Crush, 11.5 fl oz	200	0	0	0	20	50	0
Tropical punch, Crush, 8 fl oz	210	0	0	0	65	51	0
Upper 10, 8 fl oz	100	ns	ns	ns	35	28	ns
Diet Upper 10, 8 fl oz	0	ns	ns	ns	0	0	ns
Sodium Free Diet Upper 10, 8 fl oz	0	ns	ns	ns	0	0	ns
Uptown, diet, Canfield's, 8 fl oz	0	0	ns	ns	0	0	ns
Wild cherry, Canada Dry, 8 fl oz	110	0	0	0	40	28	0
Wild Cherry Pepsi, Pepsi-Cola, 12 fl oz	160	0	ns	ns	35	43	ns

SOFT DRINKS, CARBONATED	CAL (g)	FAT (g)	SAT FAT (g)	CHOL (mg)	SODIUM (mg)	CARB (g)	FIBER (g)
Wild red soda, Nehi, 8 fl oz	120	ns	ns	ns	35	32	ns
Yellow, Nehi Lock Jaw, 8 fl oz	120	ns	ns	ns	35	29	ns

AT A GLANCE: SOFT DRINKS, CARBONATED

Many carbonated soft drinks from Canada Dry, Canfield's, Diet Rite, and Minute Maid contain no calories, sugar, or sodium.

SOFT DRINKS, NONCARBONATED

	CAL (g)	FAT (g)	SAT FAT (g)	CHOL (mg)	SODIUM (mg)	CARB (g)	FIBER (g)
Black cherry drink mix, unsweetened, Kool-Aid, 8 fl oz	100	0	0	0	20	25	0
Cherry, Kool-Aid Bursts, 6.75 fl oz	100	0	0	0	35	25	0
Cherry drink mix, sugar free, Kool-Aid, 8 fl oz	5	0	0	0	5	0	0
Cherry drink mix, sugar sweetened, Kool-Aid, 8 fl oz	60	0	0	0	0	16	0
Cherry drink mix, unsweetened, Kool-Aid, 8 fl oz	100	0	0	0	10	25	0
Chocolate flavored drink, Hershey's, 8 fl oz	130	1.5	0	0	150	27	0
Chocolate shake, Hershey's, 8 fl oz	230	4.5	2.5	20	290	41	1
Citrus blend drink mix, low calorie, Crystal Light, 8 fl oz	5	0	0	0	0	0	0
Cranberry Breeze drink mix, low calorie, Crystal Light, 8 fl oz	5	0	0	0	0	0	0
Fruit punch drink mix, low calorie, Crystal Light, 8 fl oz	5	0	0	0	0	0	0
Grape, Kool-Aid Bursts, 6.75 fl oz	100	0	0	0	30	25	0
Grape drink mix, sugar free, Kool-Aid, 8 fl oz	5	0	0	0	0	0	0
Grape drink mix, sugar sweetened, Kool-Aid, 8 fl oz	60	0	0	0	0	16	0
Grape drink mix, unsweetened, Kool-Aid, 8 fl oz	100	0	0	0	15	25	0
Great Bluedini, Kool-Aid Bursts, 6.75 fl oz	100	0	0	0	30	24	0

SOFT DRINKS, NONCARBONATED	CAL	FAT (g)	SAT FAT (g)	CHOL (mg)	SODIUM (mg)	CARB (g)	FIBER (g)
Great Bluedini drink mix, sugar free, Kool-Aid, 8 fl oz	5	0	0	0	0	0	0
Great Bluedini drink mix, sugar sweetened, Kool-Aid, 8 fl oz	60	0	0	0	0	16	0
Great Bluedini drink mix, unsweetened, Kool-Aid, 8 fl oz	100	0	0	0	10	25	0
Incrediberry (strawberry-raspberry), Kool-Aid Bursts, 6.75 fl oz	100	0	0	0	30	24	0
Incrediberry (strawberry-raspberry) drink mix, sugar free, Kool-Aid, 8 fl oz	5	0	0	0	0	0	0
Incrediberry (strawberry-raspberry) drink mix, sugar sweetened, Kool-Aid, 8 fl oz	60	0	0	0	0	16	0
Incrediberry (strawberry-raspberry) drink mix, unsweetened, Kool-Aid, 8 fl oz	100	0	0	0	10	25	0
Lemon-lime drink, Everfresh, 8 fl oz	130	0	0	0	0	34	ns
Lemon-lime drink mix, low calorie, Crystal Light, 8 fl oz	5	0	0	0	0	0	0
Lemon-lime drink mix, unsweetened, Kool-Aid, 8 fl oz	100	0	0	0	10	25	0
Lemonade, Everfresh, 8 fl oz	120	0	0	0	0	29	ns
Lemonade, Minute Maid, 8 fl oz	110	0	ns	ns	25	28	ns
Lemonade, Mott's, 10 fl oz	160	0	0	0	20	41	0
Lemonade, Nehi, 8 fl oz	130	ns	ns	ns	35	35	ns
Lemonade, Newman's Own Roadside Virgin, 8 fl oz	110	0	0	0	40	27	0
Lemonade, Ocean Spray, 8 fl oz	110	0	ns	ns	35	29	0
Lemonade, Santa Cruz Natural, 8 fl oz	120	0	0	ns	35	29	ns
Lemonade, Tropicana, 8 fl oz	110	0	ns	ns	20	28	ns
Lemonade, Welch's, 11.5 fl oz	190	0	0	0	95	47	ns

SOFT DRINKS, NONCARBONATED	CAL (g)	FAT (g)	SAT FAT (g)	CHOL (mg)	SODIUM (mg)	CARB (g)	FIBER (g)
Lemonade, blackberry, Everfresh, 8 fl oz	110	0	0	0	0	27	ns
Lemonade, cherry, R.W. Knudsen, 8 fl oz	120	0	0	ns	35	29	ns
Lemonade, cranberry, Minute Maid, 8 fl oz	120	0	ns	ns	25	31	ns
Lemonade, cranberry, frozen concentrate, Minute Maid, 8 fl oz	120	0	ns	ns	0	30	ns
Lemonade, diet, Tropicana, 8 fl oz	10	0	ns	ns	25	ns	ns
Lemonade, frozen concentrate, Bright & Early, 8 fl oz	120	0	0	ns	5	30	ns
Lemonade, frozen concentrate, Minute Maid, 8 fl oz	110	0	ns	ns	0	29	ns
Lemonade, natural, R.W. Knudsen, 8 fl oz	120	0	0	ns	35	29	ns
Lemonade, natural, frozen concentrate, R.W. Knudsen, 8 fl oz	120	0	0	ns	35	29	ns
Lemonade, organic, frozen concentrate, R.W. Knudsen, 8 fl oz	120	0	0	ns	35	29	ns
Lemonade, pink, Minute Maid, 8 fl oz	110	0	ns	ns	25	28	ns
Lemonade, pink, frozen concentrate, Minute Maid, 8 fl oz	120	0	ns	ns	0	30	ns
Lemonade, raspberry, Minute Maid, 8 fl oz	120	0	ns	ns	0	30	ns
Lemonade, raspberry, frozen concentrate, Minute Maid, 8 fl oz	120	0	ns	ns	0	30	ns
Lemonade, ruby red, Everfresh, 8 fl oz	110	0	0	0	0	27	ns
Lemonade, with cranberry juice, Ocean Spray, 8 fl oz	110	0	ns	ns	35	26	0
Lemonade, with raspberry juice, Ocean Spray, 8 fl oz	110	0	ns	ns	35	27	0

SOFT DRINKS, NONCARBONATED	CAL	FAT (g)	SAT FAT (g)	CHOL (mg)	SODIUM (mg)	CARB (g)	FIBER (g)
Lemonade mix, low calorie, Crystal Light, 8 fl oz	5	0	0	0	0	0	0
Lemonade mix, pink, sugar free, Country Time, 8 fl oz	5	0	0	0	0	0	0
Lemonade mix, pink, sugar sweetened, Country Time, 8 fl oz	70	0	0	0	15	17	0
Lemonade mix, pink, unsweetened, Kool-Aid, 8 fl oz	100	0	0	0	15	25	0
Lemonade mix, sugar free, Country Time, 8 fl oz	5	0	0	0	0	0	0
Lemonade mix, sugar free, Kool-Aid, 8 fl oz	5	0	0	0	0	0	0
Lemonade mix, sugar sweetened, Country Time, 8 fl oz	70	0	0	0	15	17	0
Lemonade mix, sugar sweetened, Kool-Aid, 8 fl oz	70	0	0	0	0	17	0
Lemonade mix, unsweetened, Kool-Aid, 8 fl oz	100	0	0	0	15	25	0
Limeade, frozen concentrate, Minute Maid, 8 fl oz	100	0	ns	ns	0	26	ns
Mango flavored drink mix, Tang, 8 fl oz	100	0	0	0	0	25	0
Orange drink mix, sugar sweetened, Kool-Aid, 8 fl oz	60	0	0	0	5	16	0
Orange drink mix, unsweetened, Kool-Aid, 8 fl oz	100	0	0	0	15	25	0
Orange flavored drink mix, Tang, 8 fl oz	100	0	0	0	0	24	0
Orange flavored drink mix, sugar free, Tang, 8 fl oz	5	0	0	0	0	1	0
Orange punch, Kool-Aid Bursts, 6.75 fl oz	100	0	0	0	30	24	0
Pina-pineapple drink mix, sugar sweetened, Kool-Aid, 8 fl oz	60	0	0	0	0	17	0
Pina-pineapple drink mix, unsweetened, Kool-Aid, 8 fl oz	100	0	0	0	10	25	0

SOFT DRINKS, NONCARBONATED	CAL (g)	FAT (g)	SAT FAT (g)	CHOL (mg)	SODIUM (mg)	CARB (g)	FIBER (g)
Pink grapefruit drink mix, low calorie, Crystal Light, 8 fl oz	5	0	0	0	0	0	0
Pink Swimmingo (watermelon-cherry), Kool-Aid Bursts, 6.75 fl oz	100	0	0	0	30	24	0
Pink Swimmingo (watermelon-cherry) drink mix, sugar free, Kool-Aid, 8 fl oz	5	0	0	0	0	0	0
Pink Swimmingo (watermelon-cherry) drink mix, sugar sweetened, Kool-Aid, 8 fl oz	60	0	0	0	0	16	0
Pink Swimmingo (watermelon-cherry) drink mix, unsweetened, Kool-Aid, 8 fl oz	100	0	0	0	15	25	0
Purplesaurus Rex drink mix, sugar free, Kool-Aid, 8 fl oz	5	0	0	0	5	0	0
Purplesaurus Rex drink mix, sugar sweetened, Kool-Aid, 8 fl oz	60	0	0	0	0	16	0
Purplesaurus Rex drink mix, unsweetened, Kool-Aid, 8 fl oz	100	0	0	0	30	25	0
Raspberry drink mix, sugar sweetened, Kool-Aid, 8 fl oz	60	0	0	0	0	17	0
Raspberry drink mix, unsweetened, Kool-Aid, 8 fl oz	100	0	0	0	35	25	0
Raspberry ice drink mix, low calorie, Crystal Light, 8 fl oz	5	0	0	0	0	0	0
Rock-A-Dile Red, Kool-Aid Bursts, 6.75 fl oz	100	0	0	0	30	24	0
Rock-A-Dile Red drink mix, sugar free, Kool-Aid, 8 fl oz	5	0	0	0	0	0	0
Rock-A-Dile Red drink mix, sugar sweetened, Kool-Aid, 8 fl oz	60	0	0	0	0	16	0
Rock-A-Dile Red drink mix, unsweetened, Kool-Aid, 8 fl oz	100	0	0	0	30	25	0

SOFT DRINKS, NONCARBONATED	CAL (g)	FAT (g)	SAT FAT (g)	CHOL (mg)	SODIUM (mg)	CARB (g)	FIBER (g)
Strawberry drink mix, sugar sweetened, Kool-Aid, 8 fl oz	60	0	0	0	0	16	0
Strawberry drink mix, unsweetened, Kool-Aid, 8 fl oz	100	0	0	0	35	25	0
Tropical lemonade, Squeezit, 1 bottle	100	0	0	0	15	25	0
Tropical punch, Kool-Aid Bursts, 6.75 fl oz	100	0	0	0	30	24	0
Tropical punch drink mix, sugar free, Kool-Aid, 8 fl oz	5	0	0	0	10	0	0
Tropical punch drink mix, sugar sweetened, Kool-Aid, 8 fl oz	60	0	0	0	0	16	0
Tropical punch drink mix, unsweetened, Kool-Aid, 8 fl oz	100	0	0	0	20	25	0

AT A GLANCE: SOFT DRINKS, NONCARBONATED

Lowest in Calories and Carbohydrates: Sugar Free Kool-Aid, Sugar Free Country Time, Crystal Light drink mixes, all flavors

SPORTS DRINKS

	CAL (g)	FAT (g)	SAT FAT (g)	CHOL (mg)	SODIUM (mg)	CARB (g)	FIBER (g)
Body Works, all flavors, Shasta, 12 fl oz	90	0	0	0	145	23	0
Fruit punch, All Sport, 8 fl oz	80	0	ns	ns	55	22	ns
Fruit punch, PowerAde, 8 fl oz	70	0	0	ns	30	19	ns
Gatorade, all flavors, 8 fl oz	50	0	0	0	110	14	0
GatorLode, all flavors, Gatorade, 11.6 fl oz	280	0	0	0	90	71	0
Grape, All Sport, 8 fl oz	80	0	0	ns	55	20	ns
Grape, PowerAde, 8 fl oz	70	0	0	ns	30	19	ns
Lemon, regular or organic, R.W. Knudsen, 8 fl oz	70	0	0	ns	25	18	ns
Lemon lime, All Sport, 8 fl oz	70	0	0	ns	55	20	ns
Lemon-lime, PowerAde, 8 fl oz	70	0	0	ns	30	19	ns

SPORTS DRINKS	CAL (g)	FAT (g)	SAT FAT (g)	CHOL (mg)	SODIUM (mg)	CARB (g)	FIBER (g)
Orange, All Sport, 8 fl oz	70	0	ns	ns	55	20	ns
Orange, PowerAde, 8 fl oz	70	0	0	ns	30	19	ns
Orange, R.W. Knudsen, 8 fl oz	70	0	0	ns	25	18	ns
Tropical, R.W. Knudsen, 8 fl oz	70	0	0	ns	25	18	ns

AT A GLANCE: SPORTS DRINKS
Highest in Carbohydrates: GatorLode (11.6 fl oz)
Highest in Sodium: Shasta Body Works (12 fl oz)

TEA DRINKS

	CAL (g)	FAT (g)	SAT FAT (g)	CHOL (mg)	SODIUM (mg)	CARB (g)	FIBER (g)
Tea, brewed, made with distilled water, 1 cup	0	0	0	0	0	<1	0
Tea, brewed, made with tap water, 1 cup	0	0	0	0	10	<1	0
Tea, herb, brewed, 1 cup	0	0	0	0	0	0	0
Tea drink, all flavors, instant, Nestea Ice Teasers, 8 fl oz	10	0	0	0	0	2	0
Tea drink, herbal, all flavors, R.W. Knudsen Herbal Tea Coolers, 8 fl oz	90	0	0	ns	40	23	ns
Tea drink, iced, Schweppes, 8 fl oz	90	0	0	0	60	22	0
Tea drink, lemon, Tropicana, 8 fl oz	100	0	ns	ns	25	25	ns
Tea drink, lemon, diet, Lipton, 8 fl oz	0	0	0	0	10	0	0
Tea drink, lemon, diet, Lipton Original, 8 fl oz	0	0	0	0	5	0	0
Tea drink, lemon, diet, Tropicana, 8 fl oz	15	0	ns	ns	25	4	ns
Tea drink, lemon, sweetened, Lipton, 8 fl oz	80	0	0	0	15	20	0
Tea drink, lemon, sweetened, Lipton Original, 8 fl oz	90	0	0	0	5	22	0
Tea drink, mountain berry, Lipton Original, 8 fl oz	90	0	0	0	5	24	0
Tea drink, peach, Lipton Original, 8 fl oz	110	0	0	0	5	26	0

TEA DRINKS	CAL (g)	FAT (g)	SAT FAT (g)	CHOL (mg)	SODIUM (mg)	CARB (g)	FIBER (g)
Tea drink, peach, Tropicana, 8 fl oz	140	0	ns	ns	20	35	ns
Tea drink, plain, Lipton Original, 8 fl oz	0	0	0	0	5	0	0
Tea drink, plain, sweetened, Lipton Original, 8 fl oz	60	0	0	0	5	15	0
Tea drink, raspberry, Lipton Original, 8 fl oz	110	0	0	0	5	26	0
Tea drink, raspberry, Tropicana, 8 fl oz	120	0	ns	ns	15	28	ns
Tea drink, raspberry or peach, Lipton, 8 fl oz	80	0	0	0	15	20	0
Tea drink, raspberry, light, Tropicana, 8 fl oz	15	0	ns	ns	25	4	ns
Tea drink, sparkling, all flavors, R.W. Knudsen Fruit TeaZers, 8 fl oz	110	0	0	ns	20	26	ns
Tea drink, sugar free, regular or decaffeinated, Nestea Iced Tea, 8 fl oz	5	0	0	0	0	1	0
Tea drink, tangerine, Tropicana, 8 fl oz	110	0	ns	ns	20	27	ns
Tea drink, tea & lemonade, Lipton Original, 8 fl oz	110	0	0	0	5	27	0
Tea drink, with lemon, Nestea Iced Tea, 8 fl oz	5	0	0	0	0	1	0
Tea drink, with lemon & sugar, Nestea Iced Tea, 8 fl oz	80	0	0	0	0	19	0
Tea mix, iced, & lemonade, Lipton, 1⅔ Tbsp	90	0	0	0	0	22	0
Tea mix, iced, calorie free, regular or decaffeinated, Lipton, 1 tsp	0	0	0	0	0	0	0
Tea mix, iced, citrus, lemon lime, tropical flavors, sweetened, Lipton, 1⅔ Tbsp	90	0	0	0	0	22	0
Tea mix, iced, lemon, Lipton, 1⅔ Tbsp	90	0	0	0	0	22	0
Tea mix, iced, lemon, decaffeinated, Lipton, 1⅔ Tbsp	90	0	0	0	0	22	0

TEA DRINKS	CAL (g)	FAT (g)	SAT FAT (g)	CHOL (mg)	SODIUM (mg)	CARB (g)	FIBER (g)
Tea mix, iced, lemon, sugar free, Lipton, 1 Tbsp	5	0	0	0	0	1	0
Tea mix, iced, no lemon, sugar free, Lipton, 1 Tbsp	0	0	0	0	0	1	0
Tea mix, iced, sugar free, fruit flavors, regular and decaffeinated, Lipton, 1 Tbsp	5	0	0	0	0	1	0
Tea mix, iced, sweetened, no lemon, Lipton, 1⅔ Tbsp	80	0	0	0	0	19	0
Tea mix, instant, pure, regular or decaffeinated, Lipton, 1 tsp	0	0	0	0	0	0	0
Tea mix, low calorie, Crystal Light, 8 fl oz	5	0	0	0	0	0	0
Tea mix, low calorie, decaffeinated, Crystal Light, 8 fl oz	5	0	0	0	0	0	0
Tea mix, lemon, instant, Lipton, 2 tsp	5	0	0	0	0	1	0
Tea mix, sugar sweetened, Country Time, 8 fl oz	70	0	0	0	0	17	0

WATER, MINERAL WATER & SELTZERS See also Mixers.

	CAL (g)	FAT (g)	SAT FAT (g)	CHOL (mg)	SODIUM (mg)	CARB (g)	FIBER (g)
Mineral water, all flavors, A Sante, 10 fl oz	0	0	0	0	30	0	0
Seltzer, all flavors, Canada Dry, 8 fl oz	0	0	0	0	10	0	0
Seltzer, all flavors, Canfield's, 8 fl oz	0	0	ns	ns	0	0	ns
Seltzer, all flavors, H2Oh!, 12 fl oz	0	0	ns	ns	35	0	ns
Seltzer, all flavors but raspberry, Schweppes, 8 fl oz	0	0	0	0	10	0	0
Seltzer, raspberry, Schweppes, 8 fl oz	0	0	0	0	0	0	0
Sparkling water, Canfield's, 8 fl oz	0	0	ns	ns	40	0	ns
Sparkling water, apple, Welch's, 12 fl oz	200	0	0	0	25	56	ns

WATER, MINERAL WATER & SELTZERS	CAL (g)	FAT (g)	SAT FAT (g)	CHOL (mg)	SODIUM (mg)	CARB (g)	FIBER (g)
Sparkling water, fruit punch, Welch's, 12 fl oz	210	0	0	0	30	53	ns
Sparkling water, grape, Welch's, 12 fl oz	200	0	0	0	40	51	ns
Sparkling water, orange, Welch's, 12 fl oz	200	0	0	0	25	51	ns
Sparkling water, peach, Welch's, 12 fl oz	220	0	0	0	10	52	ns
Sparkling water, pineapple, Welch's, 12 fl oz	210	0	0	0	50	53	ns
Sparkling water, strawberry, Welch's, 12 fl oz	200	0	0	0	25	51	ns
Water, bottled, noncarbonated, 8 fl oz	0	0	0	0	0	0	0
Water, municipal, 8 fl oz	0	0	0	0	10	0	0
Water, Vichy, Canada Dry, 8 fl oz	0	0	0	0	490	0	0

CANDY & CONFECTIONS

	CAL (g)	FAT (g)	SAT FAT (g)	CHOL (mg)	SODIUM (mg)	CARB (g)	FIBER (g)
CANDY							
3 Musketeers, M&M/Mars, 1 bar	260	8	4	5	110	46	1
3 Musketeers, fun size, M&M/Mars, 2 bars	140	4	2.5	5	60	25	0
100 Grand, Nestle, 1 bar	200	8	5	10	75	30	<1
Abra Cabubble, Brach's Pick-a-Mix, 1 piece	45	0	0	0	0	10	0
Aero Bar, Nestle, 1 bar	210	13	7	10	20	26	2
Alexander the Grape, Ferrara Pan, 10 pieces	60	0	0	0	0	14	ns
Almond Joy, Peter Paul, 1 bar	240	13	9	0	65	28	2
Almonds, assorted, Ferrara Pan, 3 pieces	60	1.5	0	0	0	12	ns
Anise bears, Ferrara Pan, 5 pieces	160	0	0	0	15	41	ns
Atomic Fireball, Ferrara Pan, 3 pieces	60	0	0	0	0	15	ns
Atomic Fireball, large, Ferrara Pan, 1 piece	40	0	0	0	0	9	ns
Baby Ruth, Nestle, 1 bar	280	12	7	ns	135	38	2
Baby Ruth, fun size, Nestle, 2 bars	200	9	5	ns	95	27	1
Bar None, Hershey's, 1 pkg	250	15	9	5	55	25	1
Boston Baked Beans, Ferrara Pan, 11 pieces	70	2.5	0	0	0	10	ns
Bottle Caps, Willy Wonka, 4 treat size pouches	60	0	0	ns	0	13	ns
Bridge mix, Brach's, 14 pieces	190	8	4	5	40	27	1
Buncha Crunch, Nestle, 1 bag	200	10	5	5	95	26	<1
Butter rum, LifeSavers, 2 candies	20	0	ns	ns	20	5	ns
Butterfinger, Nestle, 1 bar	280	11	6	ns	120	41	1
Butterfinger, fun size, Nestle, 2 bars	200	8	4	ns	85	30	1

CANDY	CAL (g)	FAT (g)	SAT FAT (g)	CHOL (mg)	SODIUM (mg)	CARB (g)	FIBER (g)
Butterfinger BB's, Nestle, 1 bag	230	10	7	0	90	34	1
Butterscotch, Callard & Bowser, 2 pieces	45	1	0.5	<5	40	9	0
Butterscotch disks, Brach's Pick-a-Mix, 3 pieces	70	0	0	0	95	17	0
California fruits, Starburst, 1 stick	240	4.5	1	2	35	48	0
California raisins, chocolate covered, Brach's, 34 pieces	170	7	5	5	20	27	2
Candy cane, roll, LifeSavers, 4 candies	40	0	ns	ns	0	10	ns
Candy corn, Brach's, 26 pieces	140	0	0	0	80	36	0
Caramel, Kraft, 5 pieces	170	3	1	<5	110	32	0
Care Bear, Ferrara Pan, 18 pieces	140	0	0	ns	10	31	ns
Carob, 1 oz	150	9	2.5	0	45	14	2
Cherry Clan, Ferrara Pan, 10 pieces	60	0	0	0	0	14	ns
Cherry Clan, large, Ferrara Pan, 1 piece	40	0	0	0	0	9	ns
Cherry cordials, Little Debbie, 1 pkg	170	8	1.5	0	105	23	1
Cherry slices, Ferrara Pan, 3 pieces	150	0	0	0	15	38	ns
Choc-o-Jels snacks, Little Debbie, 1 pkg	150	7	1.5	0	95	21	0
Chocolate almonds, Ferrara Pan, 11 pieces	210	16	6	2	30	17	ns
Chocolate cremes, assorted, Brach's Pick-a-Mix, 2 pieces	130	2.5	1.5	0	15	26	0
Chocolate peanuts, Ferrara Pan, 25 pieces	220	13	6	3	35	20	ns
Chocolate raisins, Ferrara Pan, 30 pieces	170	8	5	3	35	25	ns
Chunky Bar, Nestle, 1 bar	200	11	6	<5	20	22	2
Cinnamon bears, Brach's Pick-a-Mix, 4 pieces	150	0	0	0	15	38	0
Cinnamon disks, Brach's Pick-a-Mix, 3 pieces	70	0	0	0	10	17	0

CANDY	CAL (g)	FAT (g)	SAT FAT (g)	CHOL (mg)	SODIUM (mg)	CARB (g)	FIBER (g)
Cinnamon hearts, Ferrara Pan, 20 pieces	60	0	0	0	0	14	ns
Cinnamon imperials, Brach's, 52 pieces	60	0	0	0	0	15	0
Cinnamon imperials, red hots, Ferrara Pan, 20 pieces	70	0	0	0	0	17	ns
Cinnamon jelly hearts, Ferrara Pan, 7 pieces	130	0	0	0	14	33	ns
Circus Peanuts, Brach's, 6 pieces	160	0	0	0	10	39	0
Cookies 'n' Creme, Hershey's, 1 bar	230	13	7	5	85	24	0
Cookies 'n' Creme, fun size, Hershey's, 2 bars	180	10	6	5	65	19	0
Cookies 'n' Mint, Hershey's, 1 bar	230	12	6	10	80	27	1
Crunch, Nestle, 1 bar	230	12	7	5	60	28	1
Crunch, fun size, Nestle, 4 bars	200	10	6	5	55	25	1
Dinasour Eggs, Willy Wonka, 10 pieces	60	0	0	ns	0	15	ns
Dino-Slurps, Ferrara Pan, 1 piece	30	0	0	ns	0	6	ns
Double Dippers, Brach's, 15 pieces	220	14	6	5	50	19	2
Dove, dark chocolate, M&M/Mars, 1 bar	200	12	7	5	0	22	2
Dove, dark chocolate, miniatures, M&M/Mars, 7 pieces	220	14	8	5	0	26	2
Dove, milk chocolate, M&M/Mars, 1 bar	200	12	7	5	25	22	1
Dove, milk chocolate, miniatures, M&M/Mars, 7 pieces	230	13	8	10	30	25	1
Egg Breakers, Willy Wonka, 6 pieces	60	0	0	ns	0	15	ns
Fondant, 1 piece	60	0	0	0	5	15	ns
Fondant, sweet chocolate coated, 1 patty	40	1	0.5	0	0	9	0

CANDY	CAL (g)	FAT (g)	SAT FAT (g)	CHOL (mg)	SODIUM (mg)	CARB (g)	FIBER (g)
Freckled Eggs, Willy Wonka, 9 pieces	50	0	0	ns	0	13	ns
French Burnt Peanuts, Ferrara Pan, 15 pieces	70	2	0	0	0	11	ns
Fruit Bunch jellies, Brach's Pick-a-Mix, 2 pieces	110	0	0	0	0	28	0
Fruit cocktail, Ferrara Pan, 31 pieces	60	0	0	0	0	15	ns
Fruits on Fire, LifeSavers, 2 candies	20	0	ns	ns	0	5	ns
Fudge, brown sugar, with nuts, 1 piece	60	1.5	0	0	15	11	ns
Fudge, chocolate, 1 piece	60	1.5	1	<5	10	14	0
Fudge, chocolate, with nuts, 1 piece	80	3	1	<5	10	14	0
Fudge, chocolate marshmallow, 1 piece	80	3.5	2	<5	20	14	ns
Fudge, chocolate marshmallow, with nuts, 1 piece	100	4.5	2	<5	20	15	ns
Fudge, peanut butter, 1 piece	60	1	0	0	15	13	na
Fudge, vanilla, 1 piece	60	1	0.5	<5	10	13	0
Fudge, vanilla, with nuts, 1 piece	60	2	0.5	<5	10	11	0
Fudgies, Kraft, 5 pieces	180	5	2.5	0	90	32	0
Gobstoppers, Willy Wonka, 6 pieces	60	0	0	ns	0	15	ns
Goobers, Nestle, 1 bag	210	13	5	<5	20	19	3
Good & Plenty, snack size, 3 boxes	140	0	0	ns	80	34	ns
Gum drops, Ferrara Pan, 4 pieces	150	0	0	0	16	38	ns
Gummi Savers, all flavors, LifeSavers, 11 pieces	130	0	ns	ns	0	30	ns
Gummie bears, Ferrara Pan, 20 bears	150	0	0	0	10	31	ns
Gummie cherry hearts, Ferrara Pan, 9 pieces	150	0	0	0	10	33	ns
Gummie dinosaurs, Ferrara Pan, 3 pieces	120	0	0	0	10	28	ns

CANDY	CAL (g)	FAT (g)	SAT FAT (g)	CHOL (mg)	SODIUM (mg)	CARB (g)	FIBER (g)
Gummie Fercola, Ferrara Pan, 2 pieces	210	0	0	0	10	47	ns
Gummie fish, Ferrara Pan, 6 pieces	130	0	0	0	10	28	ns
Gummie Flintstones, Ferrara Pan, 15 pieces	150	0	0	0	10	31	ns
Gummie sharks, Ferrara Pan, 2 pieces	180	0	0	0	10	42	ns
Gummie tools, Ferrara Pan, 3 pieces	130	0	0	0	10	29	ns
Gummie trolls, Ferrara Pan, 9 pieces	140	0	0	0	10	31	ns
Gummie worms, Ferrara Pan, 4 pieces	130	0	0	0	10	28	ns
Gummy dolphins, Ferrara Pan, 10 dolphins	140	0	0	0	30	31	ns
Gummy mello rings, all varieties, Ferrara Pan, 6 rings	150	0	0	0	30	34	ns
Gummy worms, Wild 'n Fruity, Brach's, 5 pieces	120	0	0	0	5	29	0
Heart Breakers, Willy Wonka, 8 pieces	60	0	0	ns	0	15	ns
Hearts, assorted, Ferrara Pan, 20 pieces	60	0	0	0	0	14	ns
Heath, Leaf, 1 bar	210	13	7	20	180	25	0
Heath, fun size, Leaf, 4 bars	190	12	6	20	170	23	0
Heath Sensations, Leaf, 1 bag	210	12	7	15	140	25	0
Hershey's milk chocolate, 1 bar	230	13	9	10	40	25	1
Hershey's milk chocolate, snack size, 2 bars	190	11	7	5	30	20	<1
Hershey's milk chocolate, with almonds, 1 bar	230	14	7	5	35	20	1
Hershey's milk chocolate, with almonds, snack size, 2 bars	200	12	6	5	25	18	1
Hugs, Hershey's, 8 pieces	210	12	8	10	35	22	<1
Hugs, with almonds, Hershey's, 9 pieces	230	13	6	10	35	23	1

CANDY	CAL (g)	FAT (g)	SAT FAT (g)	CHOL (mg)	SODIUM (mg)	CARB (g)	FIBER (g)
J. P. Double Raptor Eggs, Ferrara Pan, 10 pieces	150	0	0	ns	15	37	ns
J. P. Gummie Dinosaur, all flavors, Ferrara Pan, 15 pieces	140	0	0	ns	10	31	ns
J. P. Juju Dinosaurs, Ferrara Pan, 15 pieces	140	0	0	ns	15	35	ns
Jaw Breakers, Ferrara Pan, 1 box	70	0	0	0	0	17	ns
Jaw Breakers, extra large, Ferrara Pan, 1 piece	40	0	0	0	0	9	ns
Jaw Breakers, mini, all varieties, Ferrara Pan, 1 Tbsp	60	0	0	0	0	15	ns
Jelly beans, Brach's, 14 pieces	140	0	0	0	0	36	0
Jelly beans, all varieties, Ferrara Pan, 16 pieces	150	0	0	0	10	38	ns
Jelly beans, jumbo, Ferrara Pan, 6 pieces	150	0	0	0	10	38	ns
Jelly bird eggs, all varieties, Ferrara Pan, 16 pieces	150	0	0	0	10	38	ns
Jelly chicks and rabbits, Ferrara Pan, 4 pieces	160	0	0	0	15	42	ns
Jelly hearts, Ferrara Pan, 7 pieces	130	0	0	0	15	33	ns
Jelly nougats, Brach's Pick-a-Mix, 5 pieces	160	2	0	0	35	34	0
Jelly rings, Ferrara Pan, 3 pieces	60	0	0	0	0	31	ns
Johnny Apple Treats, Ferrara Pan, 10 pieces	60	0	0	0	0	14	ns
Johnny Apple Treats, large, Ferrara Pan, 1 piece	40	0	0	0	0	9	ns
Jolly Jellies, Ferrara Pan, 6 pieces	150	0	0	0	15	38	ns
Jolly Rancher, assorted flavors, 3 pieces	60	0	0	ns	5	14	ns
Juju cinnamon hearts, Ferrara Pan, 8 pieces	140	0	0	0	15	35	ns
Jujubes, Heide, 58 pieces	160	0	0	ns	30	32	ns

CANDY	CAL (g)	FAT (g)	SAT FAT (g)	CHOL (mg)	SODIUM (mg)	CARB (g)	FIBER (g)
Jujus, assorted, Ferrara Pan, 14 pieces	140	0	0	0	15	35	ns
Jujyfruits, Heide, 15 pieces	160	0	0	ns	30	33	ns
Kisses, Hershey's, 8 pieces	210	12	8	10	35	23	1
Kisses, with almonds, Hershey's, 8 pieces	210	13	7	5	25	19	1
Kit Kat, Reese's, 1 bar	220	12	8	5	35	26	<1
Krackel, king size, Hershey's, 1 bar	390	21	13	10	110	45	1
Lemon & orange slices, Ferrara Pan, 3 pieces	150	0	0	0	15	38	ns
Lemon drops, Brach's, 4 pieces	70	0	0	0	5	16	0
Lemonheads, Ferrara Pan, 10 pieces	60	0	0	0	0	14	ns
Lemonheads, large, Ferrara Pan, 1 piece	40	0	0	0	0	9	ns
Licorice lozenges, Ferrara Pan, 31 pieces	150	0	0	0	10	38	ns
LifeSavers, assorted (five) flavors, 2 candies	20	0	ns	ns	0	5	ns
LifeSavers Holes, all flavors, 20 holes	20	0	ns	ns	0	5	ns
Lollipops, assorted flavors, LifeSavers, 1 pop	40	0	0	ns	0	11	ns
M&M's, almond, 1.5 oz	220	12	4	5	20	24	2
M&M's, almond, single bag, 1 bag	200	11	3.5	5	20	21	2
M&M's, mint, 1.5 oz	200	9	5	5	30	30	1
M&M's, mint, single bag, 1 bag	230	10	6	10	35	34	1
M&M's, peanut, 1.5 oz	220	11	4	5	20	25	2
M&M's, peanut, fun size, 1 bag	110	5	2	5	10	13	1
M&M's, peanut, single bag, 1 bag	250	13	5	5	25	30	2
M&M's, peanut butter, 1.5 oz	220	12	8	5	90	24	2
M&M's, peanut butter, fun size, 1 bag	110	6	4	0	45	12	1

CANDY	CAL	FAT (g)	SAT FAT (g)	CHOL (mg)	SODIUM (mg)	CARB (g)	FIBER (g)
M&M's, peanut butter, single bag, 1 bag	240	13	8	5	100	27	2
M&M's, plain, 1.5 oz	200	9	5	5	30	30	1
M&M's, plain, fun size, 1 bag	100	4	2.5	5	15	15	0
M&M's, plain, single bag, 1 bag	230	10	6	10	35	34	1
Malts (malted milk balls), Brach's, 15 pieces	190	9	5	10	55	27	1
Mars, 1 bar	240	13	4	5	70	31	1
Mars, fun size, 2 bars	190	10	3	5	55	23	1
Merry Mix, Willy Wonka, 11 pieces	60	0	0	ns	0	14	ns
Milk chocolate, Nestle, 1 bar	220	13	7	10	30	23	2
Milk Duds, Leaf, 1 box	230	8	6	0	115	38	0
Milk Maid caramels, Brach's Pick-a-Mix, 4 pieces	160	4	1	5	50	28	1
Milky Way, M&M/Mars, 1 bar	280	11	5	5	90	43	1
Milky Way, fun size, M&M/Mars, 2 bars	180	7	3.5	5	60	28	0
Milky Way, dark, M&M/Mars, 1 bar	220	8	4.5	5	85	36	1
Milky Way, dark, fun size, M&M/Mars, 1 bar	90	3	1.5	0	35	14	0
Mint cremes, dark chocolate covered, Brach's Pick-a-Mix, 2 pieces	130	2.5	2	0	10	26	1
Mints, butter, Kraft, 7 pieces	60	0	0	0	25	14	0
Mints, cinnamon, sugar free, Breath Savers, 1 mint	10	0	ns	ns	0	2	ns
Mints, Cryst-O-Mint, LifeSavers, 2 candies	20	0	ns	ns	0	5	ns
Mints, dessert, Brach's, 37 pieces	160	0	0	0	30	40	0
Mints, iced, sugar free, Breath Savers, 1 mint	10	0	ns	ns	0	2	ns
Mints, party, Kraft, 7 pieces	60	0	0	0	35	14	0
Mints, Pep-O-Mint, LifeSavers, 3 mints	20	0	ns	ns	0	5	ns

CANDY	CAL (g)	FAT (g)	SAT FAT (g)	CHOL (mg)	SODIUM (mg)	CARB (g)	FIBER (g)
Mints, peppermint, sugar free, Breath Savers, 1 mint	10	0	ns	ns	0	2	ns
Mints, Spear-O-Mint, LifeSavers, 3 mints	20	0	ns	ns	0	5	ns
Mints, spearmint, sugar free, Breath Savers, 1 mint	10	0	ns	ns	0	2	ns
Mints, vanilla, sugar free, Breath Savers, 1 mint	10	0	ns	ns	0	2	ns
Mints, wintergreen, Beech-Nut, 3 mints	20	0	0	0	0	5	ns
Mints, wintergreen, sugar free, Breath Savers, 1 mint	10	0	ns	ns	0	2	ns
Mints, Wint-O-Green, LifeSavers, 3 mints	20	0	ns	ns	0	5	ns
Mr. Goodbar, Hershey's, 1 bar	280	18	7	5	20	23	2
Mr. Melon, Ferrara Pan, 16 pieces	150	0	0	0	10	38	ns
Mounds, Peter Paul, 1 bar	250	13	11	0	80	31	3
Neapolitan coconut, Brach's Pick-a-Mix, 3 pieces	160	5	4	0	75	28	1
Nerds, Willy Wonka, 1 Tbsp	60	0	0	ns	0	14	ns
Nips, butter rum, Pearson, 2 pieces	60	1.5	1.5	ns	35	12	ns
Nips, caramel, Pearson, 2 pieces	60	1.5	1.5	ns	40	12	ns
Nips, chocolate mint, Pearson, 2 pieces	60	1.5	1.5	ns	40	11	ns
Nips, chocolate parfait, Pearson, 2 pieces	60	2	2	ns	35	11	ns
Nips, coffee, Pearson, 2 pieces	60	1.5	1	ns	45	12	ns
Nips, licorice, Pearson, 2 pieces	60	1.5	1.5	ns	40	12	ns
Nips, peanut butter parfait, Pearson, 2 pieces	60	2	2	ns	40	11	ns
Nutrageous, Hershey's, 1 bar	240	14	4.5	<5	85	22	1
Oh Henry!, Nestle, 1 bar	230	9	4	<5	125	32	2
Orange slices, Ferrara Pan, 3 pieces	150	0	0	ns	15	38	ns
Orangettes jellies, Brach's Pick-a-Mix, 2 pieces	110	0	0	0	0	28	0

CANDY	CAL (g)	FAT (g)	SAT FAT (g)	CHOL (mg)	SODIUM (mg)	CARB (g)	FIBER (g)
PB Krunch, Tastykake, 1 bar	140	8	1.5	0	50	18	<1
Peanut brittle, Kraft, 5 pieces	170	5	1	0	310	29	1
Peanut clusters, Little Debbie, 1 pkg	190	11	2	0	125	23	1
Pee Wee, Ferrara Pan, 30 pieces	150	0	0	0	10	37	ns
Perkys jellies, Brach's Pick-a-Mix, 2 pieces	110	0	0	0	0	28	0
Rainbow Bears jelly candy, Brach's Pick-a-Mix, 4 pieces	150	0	0	0	15	38	0
Raisinets, Nestle, 1 bag	200	8	0	<5	15	31	2
Reese's peanut butter cups, 2 pieces	190	11	4	<5	190	18	18
Riesen chocolate caramels, 5 pieces	180	7	3	<5	30	29	3
Rolo, Hershey's, 1 pkg	260	12	8	10	95	35	<1
Root beer barrels, Brach's Pick-a-Mix, 2 pieces	45	0	0	0	5	12	0
Royals, Brach's Pick-a-Mix, 5 pieces	150	4	1	0	70	27	0
Runts, chewy, Willy Wonka, 14 pieces	60	0.5	0	ns	0	13	ns
Runts, fruit, Willy Wonka, 15 pieces	60	0	0	ns	0	14	ns
Shock Tarts, 8 pieces	60	0.5	0	0	0	13	ns
Skittles, bulk, M&M/Mars, 1.5 oz	170	2	0	0	5	38	0
Skittles, single bag, M&M/Mars, 1 bag	250	2.5	0.5	0	10	55	0
Skittles, tropical, M&M/Mars, 1.5 oz	170	1.5	0	0	5	38	0
Skittles, tropical, single bag, M&M/Mars, 1 bag	250	2.5	0.5	0	10	56	0
Skittles, wild berry, bulk, M&M/Mars, 1.5 oz	170	1.5	0	0	5	38	0
Skittles, wild berry, single bag, M&M/Mars, 1 bag	250	2.5	0.5	0	10	56	0
Skor, Hershey's, 1 bar	220	13	9	20	110	23	<1

CANDY	CAL (g)	FAT (g)	SAT FAT (g)	CHOL (mg)	SODIUM (mg)	CARB (g)	FIBER (g)
Slime Slurps, Ferrara Pan, 1 piece	30	0	0	ns	0	6	ns
Slush Puppy, Ferrara Pan, 26 pieces	150	0	0	0	5	36	ns
Snickers, M&M/Mars, 1 bar	280	14	5	10	150	36	1
Snickers, fun size, M&M/Mars, 2 bars	190	9	4	5	100	24	1
Snickers Munch, M&M/Mars, 1 bar	230	15	3.5	10	150	17	2
Sno Caps, Nestle, 1 box	300	13	8	ns	0	48	3
Sour balls, Brach's Pick-a-Mix, 3 pieces	70	0	0	0	10	17	0
Sours, assorted, Ferrara Pan, 1 piece	40	0	0	0	0	9	ns
Sparkles, Brach's Pick-a-Mix, 3 pieces	70	0	0	0	30	17	0
Spearmint leaves, Ferrara Pan, 4 pieces	140	0	0	ns	15	34	ns
Spice drops, Ferrara Pan, 13 pieces	150	0	0	0	15	35	ns
Sprinkles, milk chocolate nonpareils, Brach's, 17 pieces	200	9	6	10	25	28	1
Star Brites peppermint starlight mints, Brach's, 3 pieces	60	0	0	0	10	15	0
Star Brites spearmint starlight mints, Brach's Pick-a-Mix, 3 pieces	60	0	0	0	10	15	0
Star Crunch, Little Debbie, 1 pkg	140	6	1	0	85	21	0
Starburst, original or tropical fruits, M&M/Mars, 1 stick pkg	240	5	1	0	35	48	0
Sunshine fruits, LifeSavers, 2 candies	20	0	ns	ns	0	5	ns
Super Sour bears, Ferrara Pan, 30 pieces	150	0	0	0	5	37	ns
Super Sour blue raspberry soda, Ferrara Pan, 10 pieces	150	0	0	0	5	37	ns
Super Sour chicks and rabbits, Ferrara Pan, 4 pieces	170	0	0	0	10	40	ns

CANDY	CAL (g)	FAT (g)	SAT FAT (g)	CHOL (mg)	SODIUM (mg)	CARB (g)	FIBER (g)
Super Sour mini-rings, Ferrara Pan, 13 pieces	140	0	0	0	5	35	ns
Super Sour trolls, Ferrara Pan, 16 pieces	140	0	0	0	5	35	ns
Super Sour tropical slices, Ferrara Pan, 28 pieces	150	0	0	0	5	36	ns
SweetTarts, 8 pieces	60	0	0	0	0	14	0
Symphony, milk chocolate, Hershey's, 1 bar	230	14	9	10	40	24	<1
Symphony, milk chocolate, almonds & toffee chips, Hershey's, 1 bar	240	15	8	10	60	22	1
Taffy, 1 piece	60	0.5	0	0	15	14	ns
Tangy fruit, LifeSavers, 2 candies	20	0	ns	ns	0	5	ns
Tart'n Tinys, Willy Wonka, 1 Tbsp	60	0	0	0	0	14	ns
Toffee, butter, Special Treasures, Brach's Pick-a-Mix, 3 pieces	80	2	1	10	95	15	0
Toffee, caramel, Storck Golden Best, 6 pieces	190	6	1.5	0	45	34	3
Toffee, chocolate, Callard & Bowser, 2 pieces	80	3.5	2	0	35	12	<1
Toffee, coffee, Callard & Bowser, 2 pieces	80	3.5	2	<5	45	12	0
Toffee, English, Callard & Bowser, 2 pieces	80	4	2.5	<5	45	12	0
Toffee, licorice, Callard & Bowser, 2 pieces	80	3.5	2	<5	45	12	0
Toffee, mint, Callard & Bowser, 2 pieces	80	3.5	2	<5	45	12	0
Tropical fruits, LifeSavers, 2 candies	20	0	ns	ns	0	5	ns
Turtles, Nestle, 2 pieces	160	9	3	<5	30	20	1
Twisters, cherry, Brach's, 5 pieces	160	1	0	0	10	35	1
Twisters, cherry, Brach's Pick-a-Mix, 1 pkg	100	1	0	0	5	22	0
Twisters, licorice, Brach's, 5 pieces	150	1.5	0	0	65	32	1

CANDY	CAL (g)	FAT (g)	SAT FAT (g)	CHOL (mg)	SODIUM (mg)	CARB (g)	FIBER (g)
Twix, M&M/Mars, 2 cookies	280	14	5	5	115	37	0
Twix, fun size, M&M/Mars, 1 cookie	80	4	1.5	0	30	10	0
Twix, peanut butter, family size, M&M/Mars, 1 cookie	130	8	3	0	70	13	1
Wacky Wafers, Willy Wonka, 4 treat size pouches	60	0	0	ns	0	13	ns
Whatchamacallit, Hershey's, 1 bar	250	13	10	5	125	29	1
Wild cherry, LifeSavers, 2 candies	20	0	ns	ns	0	5	ns
Wild sour berries, LifeSavers, 2 candies	20	0	ns	ns	0	5	ns

CONFECTIONS

CANDY	CAL (g)	FAT (g)	SAT FAT (g)	CHOL (mg)	SODIUM (mg)	CARB (g)	FIBER (g)
Confectioner's coating, butterscotch, 1 oz	150	8	7	0	30	19	0
Confectioner's coating, peanut butter, 1 oz	140	8	4	0	70	13	0
Confectioner's coating, white, 1 bar	450	26	15	20	75	52	0
Marshmallow creme, Kraft, 2 Tbsp	40	0	0	0	10	10	0
Marshmallow Fluff, 2 Tbsp	60	0	0	ns	20	5	ns
Marshmallows, Funmallows, 4 pieces	110	0	0	0	20	26	0
Marshmallows, Kraft Jet-Puffed, 5 pieces	110	0	0	0	40	27	0
Marshmallows, miniature, Funmallows, ½ cup	100	0	0	0	20	25	0
Marshmallows, miniature, Kraft, ½ cup	100	0	0	0	30	25	0
Marshmallows, teddy bear, cocoa-flavored, Kraft, ½ cup	100	0	0	0	25	23	0
Yokan (adzuki beans), ¼" slice	35	0	0	0	15	9	0

CANNED & BOTTLED FOODS

	CAL (g)	FAT (g)	SAT FAT (g)	CHOL (mg)	SODIUM (mg)	CARB (g)	FIBER (g)
APPLESAUCE							
Chunky, Mott's, ½ cup	90	0	0	0	0	23	2
Chunky, Musselman's, ½ cup	100	0	0	0	10	25	2
Cinnamon, Mott's, ½ cup	110	0	0	0	0	28	1
Cinnamon, Mott's, 4 oz container	90	0	0	0	0	23	1
Cinnamon, Musselman's, ½ cup	100	0	ns	ns	10	25	2
Dutch apple spiced, Mott's, 4 oz container	70	0	0	0	0	18	1
Golden delicious, Musselman's, ½ cup	90	0	0	0	10	22	2
Granny Smith, Musselman's, ½ cup	90	0	0	0	10	22	2
Natural, Mott's, ½ cup	50	0	0	0	0	14	1
Natural, Musselman's, ½ cup	50	0	0	0	20	13	2
Regular, Mott's, ½ cup	100	0	0	0	0	26	1
Regular, Musselman's, ½ cup	90	0	0	0	10	22	2
Strawberry, Mott's, 4 oz container	80	0	0	0	0	19	1
Sweetened, Mott's, 4 oz container	90	0	0	0	0	22	1
Sweetened, Musselman's, ½ cup	90	0	0	0	10	22	2
Unsweetened, Musselman's, ½ cup	50	0	0	0	20	13	2
FRUIT							
Apples, stewed, ½ cup	70	0	0	0	25	19	2
Apples, sweetened, sliced, drained, ½ cup slices	70	0.5	0	0	0	17	2
Apricots, extra-light syrup, with skin, ½ cup	60	0	0	0	0	16	3
Apricots, heavy syrup, with skin, ½ cup	110	0	0	0	5	28	2

FRUIT	CAL (g)	FAT (g)	SAT FAT (g)	CHOL (mg)	SODIUM (mg)	CARB (g)	FIBER (g)
Apricots, heavy syrup, without skin, ½ cup	110	0	0	0	15	28	2
Apricots, in juice, with skin, ½ cup	60	0	0	0	0	15	2
Apricots, light syrup, with skin, ½ cup	80	0	0	0	5	21	2
Apricots, halves, heavy syrup, Del Monte, ½ cup	100	0	0	0	10	26	1
Apricots, halves, lite, Del Monte, ½ cup	60	0	0	0	10	16	1
Apricots, stewed, ½ cup	160	0	0	0	5	40	4
Blackberries, Allen-Wolco, ⅔ cup	60	0.5	0	0	20	13	9
Blackberries, heavy syrup, ½ cup	120	0	0	0	0	30	4
Blueberries, heavy syrup, ½ cup	110	0	0	0	0	28	2
Boysenberries, heavy syrup, ½ cup	110	0	0	0	0	29	3
Cherries, dark, pitted, heavy syrup, Del Monte, ½ cup	100	0	0	0	10	24	<1
Cherries, sour, red, heavy syrup, ½ cup	120	0	0	0	10	30	1
Cherries, sour, red, in water, ½ cup	45	0	0	0	10	11	<1
Cherries, sour, red, light syrup, ½ cup	90	0	0	0	10	24	2
Cherries, sweet, pitted, heavy syrup, ½ cup	110	0	0	0	0	27	<1
Cherries, sweet, pitted, in juice, ½ cup	70	0	0	0	0	17	<1
Cherries, sweet, pitted, in water, ½ cup	60	0	0	0	0	15	<1
Cherries, sweet, pitted, light syrup, ½ cup	80	0	0	0	0	22	<1
Cranberry sauce, sweetened, ½ cup	210	0	0	0	40	54	1
Cranberry-orange relish, ½ cup	250	0	0	0	45	64	4
Figs, heavy syrup, ½ cup	110	0	0	0	0	30	3

FRUIT	CAL (g)	FAT (g)	SAT FAT (g)	CHOL (mg)	SODIUM (mg)	CARB (g)	FIBER (g)
Figs, light syrup, ½ cup	90	0	0	0	0	23	2
Fruit cocktail, heavy syrup, Del Monte, ½ cup	100	0	0	0	10	24	1
Fruit cocktail, in juice, Del Monte Fruit Naturals, ½ cup	60	0	0	0	10	15	1
Fruit cocktail, in juice, Dole, ½ cup	60	ns	ns	ns	5	19	ns
Fruit cocktail, in light syrup, Dole, ½ cup	70	ns	ns	ns	5	19	ns
Fruit cocktail, lite, extra lite syrup, Del Monte, ½ cup	60	0	0	0	10	15	1
Fruit salad, tropical, light syrup, Del Monte, ½ cup	80	0	0	0	10	21	1
Fruit salad, tropical, light syrup, Dole, ½ cup	80	0	0	0	10	20	1
Gooseberries, light syrup, ½ cup	90	0	0	0	0	24	3
Grapefruit sections, in juice, ½ cup	45	0	0	0	10	11	0
Grapefruit sections, light syrup, ½ cup	80	0	0	0	0	20	<1
Grapes, Thompson seedless, heavy syrup, ½ cup	90	0	0	0	5	25	<1
Grapes, Thompson seedless, in water, ½ cup	50	0	0	0	10	13	1
Lychee, heavy syrup, Dynasty, 8 pieces	70	0	0	0	30	16	<1
Mandarin oranges, in juice, ½ cup	45	0	0	0	5	12	<1
Mandarin oranges, lite syrup, Del Monte, ½ cup	80	0	0	0	10	19	<1
Mandarin oranges, segments, light syrup, Dole, ½ cup	80	0	0	0	10	19	1
Mandarin oranges, slices, heavy syrup, Dole, ½ cup	90	0	0	0	10	23	1
Mandarin oranges, slices, in clarified juice, Dole, ½ cup	60	0	0	0	10	15	1
Mandarin oranges, tidbits, heavy syrup, Dole, ½ cup	90	0	0	0	10	24	1

FRUIT	CAL (g)	FAT (g)	SAT FAT (g)	CHOL (mg)	SODIUM (mg)	CARB (g)	FIBER (g)
Mixed fruit, heavy syrup, Del Monte, ½ cup	100	0	0	0	10	24	1
Mixed fruit in juice, Del Monte Fruit Naturals, ½ cup	60	0	0	0	10	15	1
Mixed fruit, lite, extra light syrup, Del Monte, ½ cup	60	0	0	0	10	15	1
Peaches, all varieties, extra light syrup, Del Monte, ½ cup	60	0	0	0	10	15	1
Peaches, all varieties, heavy syrup, Del Monte, ½ cup	100	0	0	0	10	24	1
Peaches, sliced, in juice, Del Monte Fruit Naturals, ½ cup	60	0	0	0	15	15	1
Peaches, spiced, heavy syrup, Del Monte, ½ cup	100	0	0	0	10	24	<1
Pears, in juice, Del Monte Fruit Naturals, ½ cup	60	0	0	0	10	15	1
Pears, all varieties, heavy syrup, Del Monte, ½ cup	100	0	0	0	10	24	1
Pineapple, all varieties except sliced, heavy syrup, Del Monte, ½ cup	90	0	0	0	10	24	1
Pineapple, all varieties except sliced, in juice, Del Monte, ½ cup	70	0	0	0	10	17	1
Pineapple, chunks, heavy syrup, Dole, ½ cup	90	0	0	0	10	24	1
Pineapple, crushed, extra heavy syrup, Dole, ½ cup	110	0	0	0	10	29	1
Pineapple, crushed, in juice, Dole, ½ cup	70	0	0	0	10	17	1
Pineapple, cubes, extra heavy syrup, Dole, ½ cup	200	0	0	0	10	50	1
Pineapple, cubes, light syrup, Dole, ½ cup	80	0	0	0	10	20	1
Pineapple, sliced, heavy syrup, Del Monte, 2 slices	90	0	0	0	10	23	1
Pineapple, sliced, heavy syrup, Dole, 2 slices	90	0	0	0	10	23	1
Pineapple, sliced, in clarified juice, Dole, 2½ slices	60	0	0	0	10	16	1

FRUIT	CAL (g)	FAT (g)	SAT FAT (g)	CHOL (mg)	SODIUM (mg)	CARB (g)	FIBER (g)
Pineapple, sliced, in juice, Del Monte, 2 slices	60	0	0	0	10	16	1
Pineapple, sliced, light syrup, Dole, 3½ slices	60	0	0	0	10	16	1
Pineapple, tidbits, in clarified juice, Dole, ½ cup	60	0	0	0	10	15	1
Plums, purple, heavy syrup, ½ cup	110	0	0	0	25	30	1
Plums, purple, in juice, ½ cup	70	0	0	0	0	19	1
Plums, purple, in water, ½ cup	50	0	0	0	0	14	1
Plums, purple, light syrup, ½ cup	80	0	0	0	25	21	1
Prunes, heavy syrup, Sunsweet, ⅔ cup	150	0	0	0	15	37	3
Prunes, stewed, ½ cup	160	0	0	0	0	42	7
Raspberries, red, heavy syrup, ½ cup	120	1	0	0	0	30	4
Strawberries, heavy syrup, ½ cup	120	0	0	0	5	30	2

MEALS & SIDE DISHES

	CAL (g)	FAT (g)	SAT FAT (g)	CHOL (mg)	SODIUM (mg)	CARB (g)	FIBER (g)
Beans & wieners, microwave-ready, Kid's Kitchen, 1 cup	310	13	5	45	760	37	8
Beef chow mein, bi-pack, La Choy, 1 cup	110	2	1	15	760	15	3
Beef pepper, bi-pack, La Choy, 1 cup	100	3	1.5	25	1070	11	3
Beef stew, Hunt's, 1 cup	160	4.5	2	20	1140	20	5
Chicken, spicy, bi-pack, La Choy, 1 cup	100	2.5	1	20	860	11	<1
Chicken, sweet & sour, bi-pack, La Choy, 1 cup	160	2.5	1	25	660	29	1
Chicken, teriyaki, bi-pack, La Choy, 1 cup	110	3.5	1.5	30	1250	15	2
Chicken & dumplings, Swanson Main Dish, 1 cup	260	13	5	65	1120	22	0
Chicken & dumplings, microwave-ready, Dinty Moore, 1 cup	190	6	1.5	25	670	20	1

MEALS & SIDE DISHES	CAL (g)	FAT (g)	SAT FAT (g)	CHOL (mg)	SODIUM (mg)	CARB (g)	FIBER (g)
Chicken a la king, Swanson Main Dish, 1 cup	320	21	7	60	1080	17	0
Chicken and noodles, Dinty Moore American Classics, 1 bowl	260	8	4	80	1150	26	2
Chicken chow mein, La Choy, 1 cup	80	3.5	1	10	1350	6	3
Chicken chow mein, bi-pack, La Choy, 1 cup	110	4.5	1.5	10	1080	12	4
Chicken stew, Swanson Main Dish, 1 cup	180	8	3	35	1110	17	2
Chili, Gebhardt, ½ cup	130	1	0	0	630	31	7
Chili, Hunt's, ½ cup	90	1	0	0	600	17	6
Chili, chunky, with beans, Hormel, 1 cup	330	16	6	60	1040	30	8
Chili, meatless, Worthington, 1 cup	290	15	2.5	0	1130	21	9
Chili, no beans, Hormel, 1 cup	410	30	13	75	950	16	3
Chili, no beans, micro cup, Hormel, 1 cup	290	17	8	65	830	15	3
Chili, San Antonio, Chi-Chi's, 1 cup	240	19	1	60	900	23	6
Chili, thick, Nalley, 1 cup	290	9	4	30	1100	32	11
Chili, turkey, no beans, Hormel, 1 cup	190	3	1	70	1210	17	3
Chili, turkey, with beans, Hormel, 1 cup	220	3	1	55	1280	28	7
Chili, vegetarian, all varieties, fat free, Health Valley, ½ cup	80	0	0	0	160	15	7
Chili, Walla Walla onion, Nalley, 1 cup	290	9	4	25	1060	32	8
Chili bean, spicy, Ultra Slim Fast, 1 can	240	3	1	<5	930	42	7
Chili fixings, Hunt's, ½ cup	80	1.5	0	0	860	19	6
Chili mac, micro cup, Hormel, 1 cup	200	9	4	25	980	17	2
Chili with beans, Gebhardt, 1 cup	320	15	6	30	670	32	15
Chili with beans, Hormel, 1 cup	340	17	7	60	1200	30	9

MEALS & SIDE DISHES	CAL	FAT (g)	SAT FAT (g)	CHOL (mg)	SODIUM (mg)	CARB (g)	FIBER (g)
Chili with beans, Just Rite, 1 cup	380	27	13	35	1230	31	13
Chili with beans, hot, Nalley, 1 cup	300	9	4	30	1110	32	12
Chili with beans, micro cup, Hormel, 1 cup	250	11	5	50	980	23	6
Chili with beans, regular, Nalley, 1 cup	290	9	4	25	1220	31	13
Corned beef hash, microwave cup, Dinty Moore, 1 cup	350	22	9	60	850	19	2
Enchiladas, Gebhardt, 2 enchiladas	260	19	9	25	690	20	3
Hash, corned beef, Mary Kitchen, 1 cup	390	24	10	70	930	22	2
Hash, roast beef, Mary Kitchen, 1 cup	390	24	10	70	790	22	2
Lasagna, micro cup, Hormel, 1 cup	230	7	2	35	650	34	2
Lasagna & beef, in tomato sauce, micro cup, Hormel, 1 cup	360	19	7	35	1380	34	3
Macaroni, beefy, microwave-ready, Kid's Kitchen, 1 cup	190	6	2.5	30	790	23	2
Macaroni, cheezy mac & beef, microwave-ready, Kid's Kitchen, 1 cup	250	7	2.5	30	1180	34	0
Macaroni & beef with vegetables, micro cup, Hormel, 1 cup	285	8	3	25	920	37	6
Macaroni & cheese, Franco-American, 1 cup	200	7	3	10	1060	29	4
Macaroni & cheese, micro cup, Hormel, 1 cup	260	11	6	35	690	30	1
Macaroni & cheese, microwave-ready, Kid's Kitchen, 1 cup	260	11	6	35	690	30	1
Noodle rings & chicken, microwave-ready, Kid's Kitchen, 1 cup	150	5	1.5	20	860	16	1
Noodles & beef, Hunt's, 1 cup	150	4	2	20	1240	22	5
Noodles & chicken, Hunt's Homestyle, 1 cup	180	6	2	40	1280	21	2

MEALS & SIDE DISHES	CAL (g)	FAT (g)	SAT FAT (g)	CHOL (mg)	SODIUM (mg)	CARB (g)	FIBER (g)
Noodles & chicken, micro cup, Hormel, 1 cup	180	8	2	30	1010	19	1
Noodles & chicken, with mushrooms, Hunt's, 1 cup	200	4.5	2	25	910	32	4
Noodles & chicken cacciatore, Hunt's, 1 cup	180	6	2	40	1280	21	2
Noodles with beef, bi-pack, La Choy, 1 cup	150	1.5	0.5	15	1100	24	3
Noodles with chicken, bi-pack, La Choy, 1 cup	160	4	1	15	1160	23	4
Noodles with chicken, sweet & sour, La Choy, 1 cup	260	3	1.5	10	700	49	9
Noodles with vegetables, La Choy, 1 cup	130	1.5	0.5	0	1310	27	3
Noodles with vegetables & beef, La Choy, 1 cup	160	3.5	1.5	5	1330	27	3
Noodles with vegetables & chicken, La Choy, 1 cup	160	3.5	1.5	20	860	24	1
Pepper steak, bi-pack, La Choy, 1/5 pkg	35	0	0	0	940	7	1
PizzOs, Garfield, Franco-American, 1 cup	190	2	1	5	990	36	2
Pork chow mein, bi-pack, La Choy, 1 cup	80	2.5	1	10	1180	9	2
Ravioli, beef, Franco-American, 1 cup	300	10	4	25	1160	42	3
Ravioli, beef, Hunt's, 1 cup	220	8	3	15	1120	32	4
Ravioli, beef, Progresso, 1 cup	260	5	2	5	940	45	4
Ravioli, beef, in meat sauce, Franco-American, 1 cup	280	9	4	20	1160	38	3
Ravioli, beef, mini, Franco-American, 1 cup	270	9	4	20	1210	35	2
Ravioli, cheese, Progresso, 1 cup	220	2	1	<5	930	43	4
Ravioli, in tomato sauce, micro cup, Hormel, 1 cup	260	10	4.5	20	990	34	3
Ravioli, mini, microwave-ready, Kid's Kitchen, 1 cup	240	7	3	20	920	35	3
RavioliO's, beef, Franco-American, 1 can	250	7	4	15	1000	36	3

MEALS & SIDE DISHES	CAL	FAT (g)	SAT FAT (g)	CHOL (mg)	SODIUM (mg)	CARB (g)	FIBER (g)
Rice, Spanish, Bush's Best, 1 cup	170	4	1	0	1200	29	4
Rigatoni with Italian garden style sauce, Hunt's, 1 cup	170	5	1.5	0	830	28	4
Scalloped potatoes, flavored with ham, micro cup, Hormel, 1 cup	260	16	5	35	920	20	2
Shrimp chow mein, bi-pack, La Choy, 1 cup	50	1	0	10	950	10	2
Spaghetti, Bush's Best, 1 cup	180	3	1	0	1450	30	2
Spaghetti & meat sauce, micro cup, Hormel, 1 cup	220	5	2	30	670	33	4
Spaghetti in tomato & cheese sauce, Franco-American, 1 cup	210	2	1	5	1020	41	3
Spaghetti ring & meatballs, microwave-ready, Kid's Kitchen, 1 cup	250	7	3	20	1200	35	3
Spaghetti rings, Bush's Best, 1 cup	170	2.5	1	0	1500	30	2
Spaghetti rings & franks, microwave-ready, Kid's Kitchen, 1 cup	230	6	3	15	880	36	3
Spaghetti with meatballs in tomato sauce, Franco-American, 1 cup	270	10	5	30	1060	35	4
SpaghettiO's, in tomato & cheese sauce, Franco-American, 1 cup	190	2	1	5	990	36	2
SpaghettiO's, with sliced franks, Franco-American, 1 cup	250	11	5	25	1210	32	4
Stew, beef, Dinty Moore, 1 cup	230	14	7	40	950	16	2
Stew, beef, big chunk, Nalley, 1 cup	210	9	4	35	740	19	3
Stew, beef, micro cup, Hormel, 1 cup	180	9	4	30	880	15	2
Stew, beef, microwave cup, Dinty Moore, 1 cup	190	10	4	30	870	15	2
Stew, burger, microwave cup, Dinty Moore, 1 cup	240	13	5	40	930	19	3

MEALS & SIDE DISHES	CAL (g)	FAT (g)	SAT FAT (g)	CHOL (mg)	SODIUM (mg)	CARB (g)	FIBER (g)
Stew, chicken, Dinty Moore, 1 cup	220	11	3	40	980	16	2
Stew, country, Worthington, 1 cup	210	9	1.5	0	830	20	5
Stew, meatball, Dinty Moore, 1 cup	260	16	7	35	1110	16	3
Stew, meatball, microwave cup, Dinty Moore, 1 cup	240	15	7	30	990	14	2
Sweet & sour, bi-pack, La Choy, ¼ pkg	90	0	0	0	840	22	2
Tamales, Derby, 3 tamales	250	17	8	25	1030	21	4
Tamales, Gebhardt, 2 tamales	270	21	10	30	770	19	3
Tamales, beef, Hormel, 3 tamales	280	21	8	35	1010	20	3
Tamales, chicken, Hormel, 3 tamales	210	10	4	60	1040	23	2
Tamales, jumbo, Gebhardt, 2 tamales	330	25	12	35	930	24	3
Tortellini, cheese, with tomato sauce, Franco-American, 1 cup	240	4	2	25	1140	44	2
Tortellini, meat, with meat sauce, Franco-American, 1 cup	260	9	4	30	1140	36	2
Vegetables and sauce, Cantonese classic, House of Tsang, ½ cup	70	1	0	0	930	13	1
Vegetables and sauce, Hong Kong sweet & sour, House of Tsang, ½ cup	160	0	0	0	580	40	0
Vegetables and sauce, Szechwan hot & spicy, House of Tsang, ½ cup	70	1	0	0	1090	14	1
Vegetables and sauce, Tokyo teriyaki, House of Tsang, ½ cup	100	0	0	0	1240	22	0

AT A GLANCE: MEALS & SIDE DISHES

Look for products with less than 5 grams of fat. If the product requires you to add meat, choose lean cuts to keep the fat value low. Canned foods are often high in sodium; look for products with less than 1,000 mg per serving.
Lowest in Sodium: Health Valley Vegetarian Chili, Fat Free.

	CAL	FAT (g)	SAT FAT (g)	CHOL (mg)	SODIUM (mg)	CARB (g)	FIBER (g)
MEAT & POULTRY							
Chicken, chunk, in water, Swanson Premium, ¼ cup	90	3	1	40	240	1	0
Chicken, chunk white, in water, Swanson Premium, ¼ cup	80	1	1	15	240	1	0
Chicken, chunky, Underwood, ¼ cup	120	8	2.5	40	470	2	0
Ham spread, deviled, Hormel, 4 Tbsp	150	12	4	40	430	1	0
Ham spread, deviled, Underwood, ¼ cup	160	14	4.5	45	440	0	0
Ham spread, honey, Underwood, ¼ cup	180	16	6	45	330	3	0
Liverwurst, Underwood, ¼ cup	160	14	5	65	380	3	1
Pate, liver, Underwood, ¼ cup	160	14	5	65	380	3	1
Potted meat spread, Hormel, 4 Tbsp	100	7	3	50	580	1	0
Roast beef spread, Underwood, ¼ cup	130	11	4.5	45	390	0	0
Spam, Hormel, 2 oz	170	16	6	40	750	0	0
Spam, less salt, Hormel, 2 oz	170	16	6	40	560	0	0
Spam, lite, Hormel, 2 oz	110	8	3	45	560	0	0
Turkey, chunk, in water, Swanson Premium, ¼ cup	100	4	1	50	230	2	0
Turkey, chunk white, in water, Swanson Premium, ¼ cup	90	2	1	35	220	4	1

AT A GLANCE: MEAT & POULTRY
Lowest in Fat: Swanson Premium Chicken, Chunk White, in Water
Lowest in Sodium: Swanson Premium Turkey, Chunk White, in Water

MEAT & POULTRY ALTERNATIVES							
Beef, meatless, sliced, with gravy, Worthington Savory Slices, 3 slices	150	9	3.5	0	540	6	3
Burger, meatless, Loma Linda Redi-Burger, ⅝" slice	170	10	1.5	0	460	5	4

MEAT & POULTRY ALTERNATIVES	CAL (g)	FAT (g)	SAT FAT (g)	CHOL (mg)	SODIUM (mg)	CARB (g)	FIBER (g)
Burger, meatless, Loma Linda Vege-Burger, ¼ cup	70	1.5	0.5	0	115	2	2
Burger, meatless, Worthington Vegetarian Burger, ¼ cup	60	2	0	0	270	2	1
Chicken, meatless, Worthington Diced Chik, ¼ cup	80	4.5	1	0	360	1	<1
Chicken, meatless, diced, Worthington, ¼ cup	60	3.5	0.5	0	240	1	1
Chicken, meatless, fried, with gravy, Loma Linda Fried Chik'n, 2 pieces	390	31	4.5	5	810	6	<1
Chicken, meatless, sliced, Worthington Sliced Chik, 3 slices	90	6	1	0	390	1	1
Chicken, meatless, Southern fried with gravy, Worthington FriChik, 2 pieces	120	8	1	0	430	1	1
Cutlet, meatless, Worthington, 1 slice	70	1	0	0	340	3	2
Cutlet, meatless, Worthington Multigrain Cutlets, 1 slice	80	1.5	0.5	0	300	4	3
Cuts, meatless, Loma Linda Tender Bits, 6 pieces	110	4.5	0.5	0	440	7	3
Dinner cuts, patties, meatless, Loma Linda, 1 slice	80	1.5	0.5	0	350	3	3
Hot dog, meatless, Loma Linda Big Franks, 1 link	110	7	1	0	240	2	2
Hot dog, meatless, Loma Linda Linketts, 1 link	70	4.5	0.5	0	160	1	1
Hot dog, meatless, Worthington Veja-Links, 1 link	50	3	0.5	0	190	1	0
Meatballs, meatless, Loma Linda Tender Rounds, 8 pieces	120	5	1	0	330	5	3
Patties, meatless, Worthington Choplets, 2 slices	90	1.5	1	0	500	3	2
Sandwich spread, bean & peanut, Loma Linda, ¼ cup	80	4.5	1	0	260	7	3

MEAT & POULTRY ALTERNATIVES	CAL (g)	FAT (g)	SAT FAT (g)	CHOL (mg)	SODIUM (mg)	CARB (g)	FIBER (g)
Sausage, breakfast, meatless, Worthington Saucettes, 1 link	90	6	1	0	200	1	1
Sausage, meatless, Loma Linda Little Links, 2 links	90	6	1	0	230	2	2
Sausage, Polish, meatless, mild, Worthington Super-Links, 1 link	110	8	1	0	350	2	1
Steak, meatless, Worthington Vegetable Steaks, 1 pattie	80	1.5	0.5	0	300	3	3
Steak, Swiss, meatless, Loma Linda, 1 piece	120	6	1	0	430	8	4
Steak, Swiss, with gravy, meatless, Worthington Prime Stakes, 1 piece	140	9	1.5	0	440	4	4
Turkey, meatless, with gravy, Worthington Turkee Slices, 2 slices	190	14	2.5	0	580	3	2

AT A GLANCE: MEAT & POULTRY ALTERNATIVES
Lowest in Fat: Worthington Cutlets
Lowest in Sodium: Loma Linda Vege-Burger

OLIVES

	CAL (g)	FAT (g)	SAT FAT (g)	CHOL (mg)	SODIUM (mg)	CARB (g)	FIBER (g)
Chopped or sliced, Vlasic, 1 tsp	25	3	0	0	115	1	0
Colossal, Vlasic, 2 olives	20	2	0	0	110	1	0
Extra large, Vlasic, 3 olives	25	3	0	0	115	1	0
Jumbo, Vlasic, 3 olives	25	2	0	0	135	1	0
Large, pitted, Vlasic, 4 olives	15	3	0	0	55	1	0
Oil cured, Progresso, 6 olives	80	6	0.5	0	330	3	1
Olive salad, Progresso, 2 Tbsp	25	2.5	0	0	360	1	1
Small, medium, or large, Vlasic, 4–6 olives	25	3	0	0	115	1	0
Small, pitted, Vlasic, 6 olives	25	3	0	0	115	1	0
Spanish, petite, whole, Vlasic, 10 olives	20	2	0	0	320	1	0
Spanish, pitted, Vlasic, 5 olives	20	2	0	0	280	1	0
Spanish, queen, whole, Vlasic, 5 olives	20	2	0	0	320	1	0

OLIVES	CAL (g)	FAT (g)	SAT FAT (g)	CHOL (mg)	SODIUM (mg)	CARB (g)	FIBER (g)
Spanish, salad, sliced, Vlasic, 1 tsp	20	2	0	0	320	1	0
Spanish, stuffed, Vlasic, 6 olives	20	2	0	0	350	1	0
Spanish, stuffed queen, Vlasic, 2 olives	20	2	0	0	340	1	0
Super colossal, Vlasic, 1 olive	15	1	0	0	75	1	0

AT A GLANCE: OLIVES
Lowest in Fat: Vlasic Super Colossal
Lowest in Sodium: Vlasic Large, Pitted

PICKLES

	CAL (g)	FAT (g)	SAT FAT (g)	CHOL (mg)	SODIUM (mg)	CARB (g)	FIBER (g)
Bread 'n butter chips, Claussen, 4 slices	20	0	0	0	170	4	0
Bread 'n butter sandwich slices, Claussen, 2 slices	20	0	0	0	190	5	0
Bread 'n butter slices, Heinz, 1 oz	25	0	0	0	135	6	0
Bread and butter, Vlasic Sandwich Stackers, 2 slices	30	0	0	0	170	7	0
Bread and butter chips, original, Vlasic, 5 chips	25	0	0	0	170	6	0
Bread and butter chips, zesty, Vlasic, 10 chips	45	0	0	0	220	11	0
Bread and butter chunks, old fashioned, Vlasic, 3 chunks	25	0	0	0	135	6	0
Bread and butter midgets, Milwaukee's, 1 oz	40	0	0	0	230	10	0
Bread and butter stix, original, Vlasic, 1 spear	20	0	0	0	130	5	0
Dill, Heinz, 1 oz	0	0	0	0	360	1	0
Dill, Milwaukee's, 1 oz	5	0	0	0	260	1	0
Dill, genuine, Heinz, 1 oz	0	0	0	0	420	0	0
Dill, halves, Del Monte, ¼ pickle	5	0	0	0	370	<1	<1
Dill, hamburger chips, Del Monte, 5 chips	5	0	0	0	310	1	0
Dill, hamburger chips, Vlasic, 10 chips	5	0	0	0	390	1	0

PICKLES	CAL (g)	FAT (g)	SAT FAT (g)	CHOL (mg)	SODIUM (mg)	CARB (g)	FIBER (g)
Dill, hamburger slices/chips, Claussen, 10 slices	5	0	0	0	420	1	0
Dill, kosher, Claussen, ½ pickle	5	0	0	0	330	1	0
Dill, kosher, baby, Vlasic, 1 pickle	5	0	0	0	220	1	0
Dill, kosher, barrel cured, regular or hot, Hebrew National, 1 pouch	25	0	0	0	1570	4	0
Dill, kosher, crunchy, Vlasic, ½ pickle	5	0	0	0	220	1	0
Dill, kosher, halves, deli, refrigerated, Vlasic, ½ pickle	5	0	0	0	310	1	0
Dill, kosher, mini, Claussen, 1 pickle	5	0	0	0	300	1	0
Dill, kosher, sandwich, Vlasic Sandwich Stackers, 1 oz	5	0	0	0	210	1	0
Dill, kosher, sandwich slices, Claussen, 2 slices	5	0	0	0	390	1	0
Dill, kosher, slices, Claussen, 4 slices	5	0	0	0	320	1	0
Dill, kosher, snack chunks, Vlasic, 2 chunks (1 oz)	5	0	0	0	220	1	0
Dill, kosher, spears, Claussen, 1 spear	5	0	0	0	310	1	0
Dill, kosher, spears, Vlasic, 1 spear	5	0	0	0	220	1	0
Dill, kosher, tiny, Del Monte, 1½ pickles	5	0	0	0	240	1	<1
Dill, kosher, whole, refrigerated, Vlasic Deli, ⅓ pickle (1 oz)	5	0	0	0	310	1	0
Dill, no garlic, crunchy, Vlasic, ½ pickle	5	0	0	0	220	1	0
Dill, no garlic, spears, Vlasic, 1 spear	5	0	0	0	220	1	0
Dill, Polish, crunchy, Vlasic, ½ pickle	5	0	0	0	280	1	0
Dill, Polish, spears, Vlasic, 1 spear (1 oz)	5	0	0	0	280	1	0

PICKLES	CAL (g)	FAT (g)	SAT FAT (g)	CHOL (mg)	SODIUM (mg)	CARB (g)	FIBER (g)
Dill, whole, Del Monte, 1½ pickles	5	0	0	0	370	<1	<1
Dill, zesty, spears, Vlasic, 1 spear	5	0	0	0	280	1	0
Garlic, hearty, halves, refrigerated, Vlasic Deli, ½ pickle (1 oz)	5	0	0	0	310	1	0
Half sour, Hebrew National/Rosoff's/Schorr's, ⅓ pickle	0	0	0	0	210	1	0
Half sour, New York deli style, Claussen, ½ pickle	5	0	0	0	260	1	0
Half sour, spears, Rosoff's/Schorr's, ½ spear	0	0	0	0	200	1	0
Kosher, chips, Hebrew National, 3 slices	0	0	0	0	300	1	0
Kosher, halves, Hebrew National/Rosoff's/Schorr's, ⅓ pickle	0	0	0	0	290	1	0
Kosher, spears, Hebrew National/Schorr's, ½ spear	0	0	0	0	260	1	0
Kosher, whole or halves, Hebrew National/Rosoff's/Schorr's, ⅓ pickle	0	0	0	0	260	1	0
Sour garlic, Hebrew National/Schorr's, ⅓ pickle	0	0	0	0	250	1	0
Sweet, Heinz, 1 oz	30	0	0	0	180	8	0
Sweet, Vlasic, 1 pickle (1 oz)	40	0	0	0	170	10	0
Sweet, chips, Del Monte, 5 chips	40	0	0	0	210	10	<1
Sweet, gherkins, Del Monte, 2 pickles	40	0	0	0	210	10	<1
Sweet, gherkins, Heinz, 1 oz	30	0	0	0	170	7	0
Sweet, gherkins, Vlasic, 3 pickles (1 oz)	40	0	0	0	170	10	0
Sweet, midgets, Del Monte, 3 pickles	40	0	0	0	210	10	<1
Sweet, midgets, Vlasic, 3 pickles	40	0	0	0	170	10	0

PICKLES	CAL (g)	FAT (g)	SAT FAT (g)	CHOL (mg)	SODIUM (mg)	CARB (g)	FIBER (g)
Sweet, whole, Del Monte, 1 pickle	40	0	0	0	210	10	<1

AT A GLANCE: PICKLES
Lowest in Sodium: Vlasic Bread and Butter Stix

SEAFOOD

	CAL (g)	FAT (g)	SAT FAT (g)	CHOL (mg)	SODIUM (mg)	CARB (g)	FIBER (g)
Anchovy, fillets, flat, in olive oil, King Oscar, 6 fillets	25	1.5	0	15	700	0	0
Anchovy, paste, Reese, 1 Tbsp	30	2.5	0.5	55	940	0	0
Caviar, black lumpfish, Romanoff, 1 Tbsp	15	1	0	50	380	0	0
Caviar, black whitefish, Romanoff, 1 Tbsp	25	1.5	0	45	300	1	0
Caviar, red lumpfish, Romanoff, 1 Tbsp	15	1	0	50	380	0	0
Clams, baby, Polar, 2 oz	60	1.5	1	25	200	2	0
Clams, baby, boiled, Dynasty, 2 oz	30	0	0	20	270	3	0
Clams, minced, Polar, ¼ cup	30	0	0	10	290	1	0
Clams, minced, Progresso, ¼ cup	25	0	0	10	250	2	0
Clams, minced, Snow's, ¼ cup	25	0	0	10	320	2	0
Clams, ocean, chopped & minced, Gorton's, ¼ cup	20	0	0	10	360	1	0
Cod, Atlantic, with liquid, 3 oz	90	1	0	45	190	0	0
Crab, blue, 3 oz	80	1	0	75	280	0	0
Mackerel, Jack, 3 oz	130	5	1.5	65	320	0	0
Mussels, whole, smoked, Polar, 1.65 oz	90	5	1.5	50	250	3	0
Oysters, Southern Shellfish, ¼ cup	60	3	2.5	20	480	0	2
Oysters, petite, smoked, Reese, 2 oz	110	6	3.5	50	220	6	0
Oysters, whole, Polar, 2 oz	70	3	1	25	170	3	2
Oysters, whole, smoked, Polar, 1 oz	50	3	1	20	105	3	2
Salmon, chum, Sound Beauty, ¼ cup	90	4	1	40	270	0	0

SEAFOOD	CAL (g)	FAT (g)	SAT FAT (g)	CHOL (mg)	SODIUM (mg)	CARB (g)	FIBER (g)
Salmon, keta, Pink Beauty, ¼ cup	90	4	1	40	270	0	0
Salmon, medium red, Icy Point, ¼ cup	90	5	1	40	270	0	0
Salmon, pink, Bay Beauty/Icy Point/Pillar Rock/Pink Beauty/ Searchlight/Surf King, ¼ cup	90	4	1	40	270	0	0
Salmon, pink, Bumble Bee, ¼ cup	90	5	1	40	270	0	0
Salmon, pink, in water, Chicken of the Sea, ¼ cup	90	5	1	40	270	0	0
Salmon, pink, skinless, boneless, Bumble Bee, ¼ cup	60	2	0	40	220	0	0
Salmon, pink, skinless, boneless, Pillar Rock, ⅓ cup	60	2	0	40	190	0	0
Salmon, red, Bumble Bee, ¼ cup	110	7	1.5	40	270	0	0
Salmon, red, in water, Chicken of the Sea, ¼ cup	110	7	1.5	40	270	0	0
Salmon, red, sockeye, Pillar Rock/Icy Point, ¼ cup	110	7	1.5	40	270	0	0
Sardines, in mustard sauce, Underwood, 1 can	180	12	3	105	820	2	1
Sardines, in olive oil, King Oscar, 1 can	290	24	6	140	350	<1	<1
Sardines, in soy oil, Underwood, 1 can	220	16	3.5	100	310	1	0
Sardines, in soya oil, King Oscar, 1 can	200	16	7	130	70	0	0
Sardines, in tomato sauce, Del Monte, ½ fish w/sauce	80	4	1.5	35	170	1	<1
Sardines, in tomato sauce, King Oscar, 1 can	220	18	7	120	480	2	0
Sardines, in tomato sauce, Underwood, 1 can	180	11	3	115	960	4	1
Sardines, in water, King Oscar, 1 can	290	24	6	120	70	<1	<1
Sardines, lightly smoked, in oil, Polar, 4.5 oz	260	20	0.5	70	360	<1	0

SEAFOOD	CAL (g)	FAT (g)	SAT FAT (g)	CHOL (mg)	SODIUM (mg)	CARB (g)	FIBER (g)
Sardines, skinless & boneless, Nice, ½ pkg	120	7	1.5	20	350	0	0
Shrimp, broken, Chicken of the Sea, 2 oz	45	0.5	0	145	400	<1	0
Shrimp, medium, deveined, Chicken of the Sea, 2 oz	45	0	0	115	650	0	0
Shrimp, medium, deveined, Polar, 2 oz	44	0	0	115	650	0	0
Shrimp, tiny, Chicken of the Sea, 2 oz	45	0.5	0	145	400	<1	0
Shrimp, whole, tiny, Polar, ¼ cup	60	0.5	0	105	365	1	0
Tuna, albacore, solid white in oil, Chicken of the Sea, ¼ cup	90	3	0	25	250	0	0
Tuna, albacore, solid white in water, Chicken of the Sea, ¼ cup	70	1	0	25	250	0	0
Tuna, chunk light in oil, Bumble Bee, 2 oz	110	6	1	30	250	0	0
Tuna, chunk light in oil, Chicken of the Sea, ¼ cup	110	6	0	30	250	0	0
Tuna, chunk light in oil, Starkist, 2 oz	110	6	1	30	250	0	0
Tuna, chunk light in water, Bumble Bee, 2 oz	60	0.5	0	30	250	0	0
Tuna, chunk light in water, Chicken of the Sea, ¼ cup	60	0.5	0	30	150	0	0
Tuna, chunk light in water, Starkist, 2 oz	60	0.5	0	30	250	0	0
Tuna, chunk light in water, 50% less sodium, Chicken of the Sea, ¼ cup	60	0.5	0	30	125	0	0
Tuna, chunk light in water, low sodium, low fat, Starkist, 2 oz	60	0.5	0	25	100	0	0
Tuna, chunk light in water, very low sodium, Chicken of the Sea, 2 oz	60	0.5	0	25	35	0	0
Tuna, chunk white in oil, Bumble Bee, 2 oz	100	5	1	25	250	0	0
Tuna, chunk white in water, Bumble Bee, 2 oz	60	1	0	25	250	0	0

SEAFOOD	CAL (g)	FAT (g)	SAT FAT (g)	CHOL (mg)	SODIUM (mg)	CARB (g)	FIBER (g)
Tuna, chunk white in water, Starkist, 2 oz	60	1	0	25	250	0	0
Tuna, chunk white in water, diet, Bumble Bee, 2 oz	70	1	0	25	35	0	0
Tuna, solid, in olive oil, Progresso, ¼ cup	160	12	2	30	250	0	0
Tuna, solid light in water, hickory smoke, Starkist, 2 oz	60	1	0	30	250	0	0
Tuna, solid white in oil, Bumble Bee, 2 oz	90	3	0.5	25	250	0	0
Tuna, solid white in oil, Pillar Rock, ⅓ cup (2 oz)	80	1.5	0	20	230	0	0
Tuna, solid white in water, Bumble Bee, 2 oz	70	1	0	25	250	0	0
Tuna, solid white in water, Pillar Rock, ⅓ cup (2 oz)	80	1	0	25	230	0	0
Tuna, solid white in water, Starkist, 2 oz	70	1	0	25	250	0	0
Tuna, tonno, light in oil, Genova/Chicken of the Sea, 2 oz	130	8	1	30	250	0	0

AT A GLANCE: SEAFOOD
For a low fat dish, choose seafood packed in water rather than oil.
Lowest in Sodium: Chicken of the Sea Tuna, Chunk Light in Water, Very Low Sodium; Bumble Bee Tuna, Chunk White in Water, Diet

SEAFOOD ALTERNATIVES

	CAL (g)	FAT (g)	SAT FAT (g)	CHOL (mg)	SODIUM (mg)	CARB (g)	FIBER (g)
Scallops alternative, Worthington Vegetable Skallops, ½ cup	90	1.5	0.5	0	410	10	3
Tuna alternative, Worthington Tuno, ½ cup	80	6	1	0	290	2	1

VEGETABLES

	CAL (g)	FAT (g)	SAT FAT (g)	CHOL (mg)	SODIUM (mg)	CARB (g)	FIBER (g)
Artichoke hearts, Progresso, 2 pieces	35	0	0	0	240	6	1
Artichoke hearts, marinated, Progresso, ⅓ cup	160	14	2	0	290	6	1
Asparagus, all varieties, Del Monte, ½ cup	20	0	0	0	420	3	1

VEGETABLES	CAL (g)	FAT (g)	SAT FAT (g)	CHOL (mg)	SODIUM (mg)	CARB (g)	FIBER (g)
Asparagus spears, Green Giant, 4.5 oz	20	0	0	0	450	3	1
Asparagus spears, cut, Bush's Best, 4 oz	25	0	0	0	380	2	1
Asparagus spears, cut, Green Giant, ½ cup	20	0	0	0	420	3	1
Asparagus spears, cut, 50% less sodium, Green Giant, ½ cup	20	0	0	0	210	3	1
Asparagus spears, extra large, LeSueur Green Giant, 4.5 oz	20	0	0	0	440	3	1
Asparagus spears, extra long, Green Giant, 4.5 oz	20	0	0	0	400	3	1
Bamboo shoots, La Choy, 2 Tbsp	0	0	0	0	0	<1	0
Bamboo shoots, sliced, Dynasty, 3 oz	45	0	0	0	5	8	3
Bean sprouts, La Choy, 1 cup	10	0	0	0	20	1	1
Beans, adzuki, Eden, ½ cup	110	0	0	0	10	19	5
Beans, adzuki, sweetened, ½ cup	350	0	0	0	320	81	4
Beans, baked, Allen, ½ cup	150	1	0.5	0	350	29	8
Beans, baked, Bush's Best, 4 oz	150	1	0	<5	550	29	7
Beans, baked, Grandma Brown's, ½ cup	160	1.5	0	0	340	28	8
Beans, baked, Green Giant/Joan of Arc, ½ cup	160	1.5	1	<5	580	31	7
Beans, baked, Heartland Iron Kettle, ½ cup	150	1	0	<5	400	29	5
Beans, baked, 99% fat free, B&M, ½ cup	160	1	0	0	220	31	7
Beans, baked, barbecue, B&M, ½ cup	170	2	0.5	<5	360	32	6
Beans, baked, barbecue, old fashioned, Campbell's, ½ cup	170	3	1	5	460	29	6
Beans, baked, barbecue, tangy, Campbell's, ½ cup	170	3	1	5	460	29	6
Beans, baked, brick oven, B&M, ½ cup	180	2	0.5	5	390	32	7

VEGETABLES	CAL (g)	FAT (g)	SAT FAT (g)	CHOL (mg)	SODIUM (mg)	CARB (g)	FIBER (g)
Beans, baked, brown sugar & bacon, Campbell's, ½ cup	170	3	1	5	490	29	7
Beans, baked, extra hearty, B&M, ½ cup	190	2	0.5	<5	450	36	8
Beans, baked, honey, vegetarian, fat free, Health Valley, ½ cup	110	0	0	0	135	24	7
Beans, baked, honey, vegetarian, no salt, fat free, Health Valley, ½ cup	110	0	0	0	25	24	7
Beans, baked, New England style, Campbell's, ½ cup	180	3	1	5	460	32	6
Beans, baked, original, Friend's, ½ cup	170	1	0	<5	390	32	7
Beans, baked, red kidney, B&M, ½ cup	170	2	0.5	<5	440	32	6
Beans, baked, red kidney, Friend's, ½ cup	160	1	0	<5	510	32	6
Beans, baked, vegetarian, ½ cup	120	0.5	0	0	500	26	6
Beans, baked, with honey, B&M, ½ cup	170	1.5	0	0	450	30	8
Beans, baked, with onions, Bush's Best, 4 oz	150	1.5	0.5	0	500	26	6
Beans, baked, with onions, Green Giant/Joan of Arc's, ½ cup	150	1.5	0.5	0	620	28	5
Beans, baked, yellow eye, B&M, ½ cup	170	2	0.5	<5	460	28	7
Beans, barbeque, Green Giant/Joan of Arc, ½ cup	140	0.5	0	0	460	28	5
Beans, black, Eden, ½ cup	100	0	0	0	15	18	6
Beans, black, Green Giant/Joan of Arc, ½ cup	100	0	0	0	520	18	5
Beans, black, La Preferida, ½ cup	110	1	0	0	100	19	7
Beans, black, Old El Paso, ½ cup	100	1	0	0	400	17	7
Beans, black, Progresso, ½ cup	100	1	0	0	400	17	7

VEGETABLES	CAL (g)	FAT (g)	SAT FAT (g)	CHOL (mg)	SODIUM (mg)	CARB (g)	FIBER (g)
Beans, black, refried, Las Palmas, ½ cup	120	2	0	0	340	18	6
Beans, black, refried, Old El Paso, ½ cup	120	2	0	0	340	18	6
Beans, black, refried, low fat, Rosarita, ½ cup	110	0.5	0	0	570	23	7
Beans, black, seasoned, Allen/Trappey, ½ cup	120	1.5	0.5	0	410	20	7
Beans, black turtle, Hain, ½ cup	100	1	0	0	140	17	7
Beans, blackeye peas, Bush's Best, 4 oz	100	0.5	0	0	410	19	4
Beans, blackeye peas, Green Giant/Joan of Arc, ½ cup	90	0	0	0	250	16	3
Beans, blackeye peas, fresh shell, Allen/East Texas Fair/Homefolks/Dorman, ½ cup	120	1	0.5	0	350	21	6
Beans, blackeye peas, from fresh, Bush's Best, 4 oz	110	1	0	0	500	18	5
Beans, blackeye peas, with bacon, Allen/Sunshine, ½ cup	105	1.5	0.5	0	390	20	5
Beans, blackeye peas, with bacon, Bush's Best, 4 oz	110	1	0.5	<5	630	18	5
Beans, blackeye peas, with bacon, Trappey, ½ cup	120	2	0.5	0	350	19	5
Beans, blackeye peas, with bacon & jalapeno, Bush's Best, 4 oz	120	2.5	1	<5	660	16	5
Beans, blackeye peas, with bacon & jalapeno, Trappey, ½ cup	110	1.5	0.5	0	470	19	5
Beans, blackeye peas, with jalapeno, Homefolks, ½ cup	120	1	0.5	0	580	20	5
Beans, blackeye peas, with snaps, Allen/East Texas Fair/Homefolks, ½ cup	120	1	0.5	0	420	20	5
Beans, blackeye peas, with snaps, Bush's Best, 4 oz	110	0.5	0	0	550	17	5
Beans, brown sugar & bacon, old fashioned, Campbell's, ½ cup	170	3	1	5	490	29	7

VEGETABLES	CAL (g)	FAT (g)	SAT FAT (g)	CHOL (mg)	SODIUM (mg)	CARB (g)	FIBER (g)
Beans, butter, Green Giant/Joan of Arc, ½ cup	90	0	0	0	450	16	4
Beans, butter, baby, Allen, ½ cup	120	0.5	0.5	0	460	22	6
Beans, butter, baby, Bush's Best, 4 oz	120	0.5	0	0	510	19	5
Beans, butter, baby green, with bacon, Trappey, ½ cup	120	1	0.5	0	330	22	6
Beans, butter, green, Bush's Best, 4 oz	110	1	0	0	340	19	6
Beans, butter, green, Sunshine, ½ cup	120	0.5	0	0	370	23	8
Beans, butter, large, Allen, ½ cup	120	0.5	0	0	290	20	7
Beans, butter, large, Bush's Best, 4 oz	100	0.5	0	0	450	18	5
Beans, butter, light white, with sausage, Trappey, ½ cup	110	1	0	0	300	21	6
Beans, butter, Reber, Aunt Nellie's Farm Kitchen, ½ cup	140	1.5	0.5	<5	480	25	6
Beans, butter, speckled, Bush's Best, 4 oz	110	0.5	0	0	420	19	5
Beans, cannelini, Progresso, ½ cup	100	0.5	0	0	270	18	5
Beans, chick peas, Hain, ½ cup	120	2.5	0	0	140	20	7
Beans, chick peas, La Preferida, ½ cup	100	0	0	0	470	21	5
Beans, chick peas, Progresso, ½ cup	120	2.5	0	0	280	20	7
Beans, chili, hot, Bush's Best, 4 oz	120	1	0.5	0	480	20	6
Beans, chili, in zesty sauce, Campbell's, ½ cup	130	3	1	5	490	21	6
Beans, chili, Mexican, Allen/Brown Beauty, ½ cup	120	1	0	0	300	22	8
Beans, chili, spicy, Green Giant/Joan of Arc, ½ cup	110	1	0	0	490	20	5
Beans, cowboy peas, Bush's Best, 4 oz	120	1	0	0	500	19	5

VEGETABLES	CAL (g)	FAT (g)	SAT FAT (g)	CHOL (mg)	SODIUM (mg)	CARB (g)	FIBER (g)
Beans, cranberry (Roman), ½ cup	110	0	0	0	430	20	12
Beans, crowder peas, Allen/East Texas Fair/Homefolks, ½ cup	110	1	0.5	0	460	19	8
Beans, crowder peas, Bush's Best, 4 oz	110	1	0	0	500	18	5
Beans, fava, Progresso, ½ cup	110	0.5	0	0	250	20	5
Beans, gandules, La Preferida, ½ cup	80	0	0	0	480	17	5
Beans, garbanzo, Allen/East Texas Fair, ½ cup	120	2.5	0.5	0	330	19	8
Beans, garbanzo, Bush's Best, 4 oz	130	2	0.5	0	500	22	9
Beans, garbanzo, Eden, ½ cup	120	1.5	0	0	10	19	5
Beans, garbanzo, Green Giant/Joan of Arc, ½ cup	110	1.5	0	0	380	18	5
Beans, garbanzo, Old El Paso, ½ cup	120	2.5	0	0	280	20	7
Beans, great Northern, Allen, ½ cup	100	0.5	0	0	310	19	7
Beans, great Northern, Bush's Best, 4 oz	110	0.5	0	0	400	18	7
Beans, great Northern, Green Giant/Joan of Arc, ½ cup	100	0.5	0	0	290	18	6
Beans, great Northern, Hain, ½ cup	120	0.5	0	0	140	21	8
Beans, great Northern, with pork, Bush's Best, 4 oz	110	1.5	0.5	<5	460	17	6
Beans, great Northern, with sausage, Trappey, ½ cup	100	1	0.5	0	460	18	7
Beans, green, Bush's Best, 4 oz	25	0	0	0	430	5	2
Beans, green & shelly, Bush's Best, 4 oz	45	0	0	0	400	7	3
Beans, green, all cuts, Del Monte, ½ cup	20	0	0	0	360	4	2
Beans, green, and potatoes, Allen/Sunshine, ½ cup	35	0	0	0	220	7	2

VEGETABLES	CAL (g)	FAT (g)	SAT FAT (g)	CHOL (mg)	SODIUM (mg)	CARB (g)	FIBER (g)
Beans, green, cut, Allen/ Sunshine/GaBelle/Alma/Crest Top/Stone Mountain, ½ cup	30	0.5	0	0	320	6	3
Beans, green, cut, Green Giant, ½ cup	20	0	0	0	400	4	1
Beans, green, cut, 50% less sodium, Green Giant, ½ cup	20	0	0	0	200	4	1
Beans, green, cut, no salt added, Allen, ½ cup	15	0	0	0	10	3	2
Beans, green, French style, Allen, ½ cup	25	0	0	0	300	4	2
Beans, green, French style, Green Giant, ½ cup	20	0	0	0	390	4	1
Beans, green, Italian, Allen/Sunshine, ½ cup	35	0.5	0	0	320	7	3
Beans, green, kitchen sliced, Green Giant, ½ cup	20	0	0	0	400	4	1
Beans, green, kitchen sliced, 50% less sodium, Green Giant, ½ cup	20	0	0	0	200	4	1
Beans, green, no salt added, all cuts, Del Monte, ½ cup	20	0	0	0	10	4	2
Beans, green, seasoned, French style, Del Monte, ½ cup	20	0	0	0	360	4	2
Beans, green, with ham flavor, Bush's Best, 4 oz	35	0	0	0	500	6	2
Beans, green, with ham flavor & potatoes, Bush's Best, 4 oz	40	0	0	0	560	7	3
Beans, homestyle, Campbell's, ½ cup	150	2	1	5	490	27	7
Beans, honey bacon flavored, Green Giant/Joan of Arc, ½ cup	160	0.5	0	0	490	34	6
Beans, Italian, Del Monte, ½ cup	30	0	0	0	360	6	3
Beans, Italian, Green Giant/Joan of Arc, ½ cup	130	1	0	0	480	24	5
Beans, kidney, Eden, ½ cup	100	0	0	0	15	18	10
Beans, kidney, Hunt's, ½ cup	90	0.5	0	0	480	20	5

VEGETABLES	CAL (g)	FAT (g)	SAT FAT (g)	CHOL (mg)	SODIUM (mg)	CARB (g)	FIBER (g)
Beans, kidney, dark red, Allen/East Texas Fair/Trappey, ½ cup	130	0.5	0	0	310	22	8
Beans, kidney, dark red, Bush's Best, 4 oz	130	1	0.5	0	260	21	7
Beans, kidney, dark red, Green Giant/Joan of Arc, ½ cup	110	0	0	0	340	20	6
Beans, kidney, dark red, Hain, ½ cup	110	0	0	0	140	18	8
Beans, kidney, light red, Allen/Trappey, ½ cup	120	0.5	0	0	340	22	8
Beans, kidney, light red, Bush's Best, 4 oz	110	0.5	0	0	260	20	7
Beans, kidney, light red, Green Giant/Joan of Arc, ½ cup	110	0	0	0	340	20	6
Beans, kidney, light red, New Orleans style, with bacon, Trappey, ½ cup	110	1	0.5	0	410	20	6
Beans, kidney, light red, with jalapeno, Trappey, ½ cup	110	1	0	0	420	19	6
Beans, kidney, red, La Preferida, ½ cup	120	1	0	0	210	21	7
Beans, kidney, red, Progresso, ½ cup	110	0.5	0	0	280	20	8
Beans, kidney, red, with chili gravy, Trappey, ½ cup	110	1	0	0	510	20	7
Beans, lima, baby white, with bacon, Trappey, ½ cup	130	1.5	0.5	0	350	21	6
Beans, lima, green, Allen/East Texas Fair, ½ cup	120	0.5	0	0	370	23	8
Beans, lima, green, Del Monte, ½ cup	80	0	0	0	360	15	4
Beans, lima, green & white, Allen, ½ cup	110	1	0.5	0	280	20	9
Beans, lima, green & white, Bush's Best, 4 oz	110	0.5	0	0	360	20	5
Beans, lima, medium green, Bush's Best, 4 oz	110	1	0	0	310	17	5
Beans, lima, small green, Bush's Best, 4 oz	100	1	0	0	320	16	5

VEGETABLES	CAL (g)	FAT (g)	SAT FAT (g)	CHOL (mg)	SODIUM (mg)	CARB (g)	FIBER (g)
Beans, Mexe, Old El Paso, ½ cup	110	0.5	0	0	630	19	7
Beans, Mexican, Green Giant/Joan of Arc, ½ cup	120	1.5	0	0	530	21	5
Beans, Mexican, with jalapeno, Brown Beauty, ½ cup	120	1	0	0	370	21	7
Beans, Mexican, with jalapeno, Trappey, ½ cup	130	1.5	0.5	0	460	22	8
Beans, mixed, Bush's Best, 4 oz	110	0	0	0	500	19	6
Beans, navy, Allen, ½ cup	110	1	0	0	380	19	6
Beans, navy, Bush's Best, 4 oz	110	0.5	0	0	450	19	6
Beans, navy, Eden, ½ cup	110	0.5	0	0	15	20	7
Beans, navy, with bacon, Trappey, ½ cup	110	1.5	0.5	0	420	17	7
Beans, navy, with bacon & jalapeno, Trappey, ½ cup	120	1.5	0.5	0	420	17	7
Beans, pink, La Preferida, ½ cup	90	0	0	0	490	21	5
Beans, pinto, Allen/East Texas Fair/Brown Beauty, ½ cup	110	0.5	0	0	290	20	7
Beans, pinto, Bush's Best, 4 oz	110	0.5	0	0	430	18	6
Beans, pinto, Eden, ½ cup	100	0	0	0	15	18	6
Beans, pinto, Gebhardt, ½ cup	90	1.5	0	0	510	18	7
Beans, pinto, Green Giant/Joan of Arc, ½ cup	110	0.5	0	0	280	20	5
Beans, pinto, Hain, ½ cup	110	1	0	0	140	18	8
Beans, pinto, La Preferida, ½ cup	90	0	0	0	480	19	5
Beans, pinto, Old El Paso, ½ cup	110	0.5	0	0	420	19	7
Beans, pinto, Progresso, ½ cup	110	1	0	0	250	18	7
Beans, pinto, cowboy, Bush's Best, 4 oz	120	1	0.5	0	360	20	6
Beans, pinto, jalapinto, with bacon, Trappey, ½ cup	120	1	0.5	0	540	22	8

VEGETABLES	CAL (g)	FAT (g)	SAT FAT (g)	CHOL (mg)	SODIUM (mg)	CARB (g)	FIBER (g)
Beans, pinto, with bacon, Bush's Best, 4 oz	110	1	0.5	0	540	18	6
Beans, pinto, with bacon, Trappey, ½ cup	120	1	0.5	0	270	20	7
Beans, pinto, with bacon & jalapeno, Bush's Best, 4 oz	110	1.5	0.5	<5	550	17	6
Beans, pinto, with pork, Bush's Best, 4 oz	120	2.5	1	<5	530	17	6
Beans, pork & beans, Bush's Best, 4 oz	120	1.5	0.5	<5	550	22	6
Beans, pork & beans, Bush's Best Fanci Pak, 4 oz	160	1.5	0.5	<5	350	28	7
Beans, pork & beans, Crest Top, ½ cup	130	1	0.5	0	330	21	6
Beans, pork & beans, Hunt's, ½ cup	130	1.5	0	0	520	28	4
Beans, pork & beans, Wagon Master, ½ cup	110	1	0.5	0	710	21	7
Beans, pork & beans, Wagon Master/Trappey, ½ cup	110	1	0.5	0	710	21	7
Beans, pork & beans (2 lb 10 oz), Wagon Master, ½ cup	130	1	0	0	420	23	9
Beans, pork & beans, deluxe, Bush's Best, 4 oz	160	1.5	0.5	5	480	28	8
Beans, pork & beans, in tomato sauce, Campbell's, ½ cup	130	2	1	5	420	24	6
Beans, pork & beans, with jalapeno, Trappey, ½ cup	130	2	0.5	0	610	24	6
Beans, pork & beans, with tomato sauce, Green Giant/Joan of Arc, ½ cup	120	1	0	0	490	23	4
Beans, ranchero, Chi-Chi's, ½ cup	100	0.5	0	0	540	18	3
Beans, red, Allen, ½ cup	160	0.5	0	0	310	19	9
Beans, red, Bush's Best, 4 oz	110	0.5	0	0	460	19	6
Beans, red, Green Giant/Joan of Arc, ½ cup	100	0.5	0	0	350	19	6
Beans, red, small, Hunt's, ½ cup	90	0.5	0	0	710	19	6
Beans, refried, Allen, ½ cup	150	2.5	1	0	360	24	11

VEGETABLES	CAL (g)	FAT (g)	SAT FAT (g)	CHOL (mg)	SODIUM (mg)	CARB (g)	FIBER (g)
Beans, refried, Chi-Chi's, ½ cup	130	6	1	0	570	16	4
Beans, refried, Las Palmas, ½ cup	110	2	1	<5	500	17	5
Beans, refried, Old El Paso, ½ cup	110	2	1	<5	500	17	5
Beans, refried, & bacon, Rosarita, ½ cup	120	3	1	0	490	19	8
Beans, refried, & cheese, Old El Paso, ½ cup	130	3.5	1.5	5	500	18	6
Beans, refried, & green chiles, Old El Paso, ½ cup	110	0.5	0	<5	720	19	6
Beans, refried, & sausage, Old El Paso, ½ cup	200	13	5	10	360	14	8
Beans, refried, fat free, Old El Paso, ½ cup	110	0	0	0	480	20	6
Beans, refried, green chile, Rosarita, ½ cup	110	3	2	0	500	20	7
Beans, refried, jalapeno, Gebhardt, ½ cup	110	3	1.5	0	380	19	6
Beans, refried, nacho cheese, Rosarita, ½ cup	140	3.5	2	0	700	24	7
Beans, refried, no fat, Gebhardt, ½ cup	90	0	0	0	480	20	6
Beans, refried, no fat, Las Palmas, ½ cup	110	0	0	0	470	19	6
Beans, refried, no fat, Rosarita, ½ cup	120	0	0	0	570	28	6
Beans, refried, onion, Rosarita, ½ cup	110	3	1.5	0	510	21	6
Beans, refried, spicy, Old El Paso, ½ cup	140	3	1.5	<5	560	22	6
Beans, refried, spicy, Rosarita, ½ cup	120	3	1	0	570	22	6
Beans, refried, traditional, Gebhardt, ½ cup	110	3	1.5	0	500	20	6
Beans, refried, traditional, Rosarita, ½ cup	130	3	1.5	0	590	22	8
Beans, refried, vegetarian, Gebhardt, ½ cup	120	2.5	0	0	550	21	7

VEGETABLES	CAL (g)	FAT (g)	SAT FAT (g)	CHOL (mg)	SODIUM (mg)	CARB (g)	FIBER (g)
Beans, refried, vegetarian, Old El Paso, ½ cup	100	1	0	0	490	16	6
Beans, refried, vegetarian, Rosarita, ½ cup	120	2	0	0	560	23	6
Beans, refried, with green chiles & lime, no fat, Rosarita, ½ cup	100	0	0	0	570	22	8
Beans, refried, with zesty salsa, no fat, canned, Rosarita, ½ cup	100	0	0	0	550	22	8
Beans, saucepan, with bacon, Grandma Brown's, ½ cup	150	2.5	1	0	300	26	7
Beans, shell outs, Allen, ½ cup	30	0	0	0	460	6	2
Beans, three bean salad, Green Giant, ½ cup	70	0	0	0	470	16	3
Beans, vegetarian, Bush's Best, 4 oz	140	1	0	0	550	24	6
Beans, vegetarian, in tomato sauce, Campbell's, ½ cup	130	2	1	0	460	24	6
Beans, vegetarian, in tomato sauce, Heinz, ½ cup	130	0.5	0	0	490	24	7
Beans, wax, Bush's Best, 4 oz	25	0	0	0	400	4	2
Beans, wax, golden, Del Monte, ½ cup	20	0	0	0	360	4	2
Beans, white, small, La Preferida, ½ cup	110	1	0	0	260	20	7
Beans and fixin's, Big John's, ½ cup	130	3.5	1.5	<5	590	23	6
Beets, Bush's Best, 4 oz	40	0	0	0	370	9	2
Beets, Del Monte, ½ cup	35	0	0	0	290	8	2
Beets, baby whole, LeSueur Green Giant, ½ cup	35	0	0	0	260	8	2
Beets, Harvard, Aunt Nellie's Farm Kitchen, ⅓ cup	60	0	0	0	270	15	2
Beets, Harvard, Green Giant, ⅓ cup	60	0	0	0	270	15	2
Beets, pickled, Del Monte, ½ cup	80	0	0	0	380	19	2

VEGETABLES	CAL (g)	FAT (g)	SAT FAT (g)	CHOL (mg)	SODIUM (mg)	CARB (g)	FIBER (g)
Beets, pickled, and onions, Aunt Nellie's Farm Kitchen, 4 beets slices and 1 onion	20	0	0	0	110	5	0
Beets, pickled, sliced, Aunt Nellie's Farm Kitchen, 4 slices	20	0	0	0	100	5	0
Beets, pickled, whole, Aunt Nellie's Farm Kitchen, 2 beets	25	0	0	0	130	6	0
Beets, sliced, Green Giant, ½ cup	35	0	0	0	260	8	2
Beets, sliced, no salt added, Green Giant, ½ cup	35	0	0	0	60	8	2
Beets, whole, Green Giant, ½ cup	35	0	0	0	260	8	2
Beets, whole or sliced, Aunt Nellie's Farm Kitchen, ½ cup	40	0	0	0	300	8	2
Butterbur (fuki), 3 stalks	0	0	0	0	0	0	0
Cabbage, red, Aunt Nellie's Farm Kitchen, 2 Tbsp	20	0	0	0	150	5	1
Cactus, La Preferida, ½ cup	25	0	0	0	940	5	2
Capers, drained, Progresso, 1 tsp	0	0	0	0	105	0	0
Carrots, baby whole, LeSueur Green Giant, ½ cup	35	0	0	0	410	8	3
Carrots, sliced, Allen/Crest Top, ½ cup	35	0.5	0	0	230	8	3
Carrots, sliced, Bush's Best, 4 oz	30	0	0	0	240	5	2
Carrots, sliced, Del Monte, ½ cup	35	0	0	0	300	8	3
Carrots, sliced, Green Giant, ½ cup	25	0	0	0	380	6	2
Chiles, green, chopped, Old El Paso, 2 Tbsp	5	0	0	0	110	1	1
Chiles, green, diced, Pancho Villa, 2 Tbsp	5	0	0	0	110	1	1
Chiles, green, whole, Old El Paso, 1 chile	10	0	0	0	230	2	1
Chilies, green, diced, Rosarita, 2 Tbsp	5	0	0	0	85	1	<1
Chilies, green, whole, Rosarita, 2 Tbsp	0	0	0	0	75	1	<1

VEGETABLES	CAL (g)	FAT (g)	SAT FAT (g)	CHOL (mg)	SODIUM (mg)	CARB (g)	FIBER (g)
Collard greens, Allen/Sunshine, ½ cup	30	0.5	0	0	20	5	3
Collard greens, Bush's Best, 4 oz	30	0.5	0	0	410	4	2
Corn, Green Giant Niblets, ⅓ cup	70	0	0	0	230	15	2
Corn, 50% less sodium, Green Giant Niblets, ⅓ cup	60	0	0	0	115	14	1
Corn, baby sweet, Dynasty, 3 oz	45	0	0	0	340	8	6
Corn, cream style, Bush's Best, 4 oz	110	1	0	0	420	20	2
Corn, cream style, Del Monte, ½ cup	90	0.5	0	0	360	20	2
Corn, cream style, Green Giant, ½ cup	100	0.5	0	0	430	22	1
Corn, cream style, no salt added, Del Monte, ½ cup	90	0.5	0	0	10	20	2
Corn, cream style, supersweet, Del Monte, ½ cup	60	0.5	0	0	360	14	2
Corn, extra sweet, Green Giant Niblets, ⅓ cup	50	0.5	0	0	200	10	2
Corn, no added salt or sugar, Green Giant Niblets, ⅓ cup	60	0	0	0	0	13	2
Corn, white, cream style, Del Monte, ½ cup	100	0	0	0	360	21	2
Corn, white, whole kernel, sweet corn, Del Monte, ½ cup	80	0	0	0	360	17	2
Corn, white shoepeg, Green Giant, ⅓ cup	80	0.5	0	0	220	16	1
Corn, whole kernel, Bush's Best, 4 oz	80	0.5	0	0	340	15	2
Corn, whole kernel, Del Monte, ½ cup	90	1	0	0	360	18	3
Corn, whole kernel supersweet, no salt added, Del Monte, ½ cup	60	1	0	0	10	11	3
Corn, whole kernel supersweet, no sugar, Del Monte, ½ cup	60	1	0	0	360	11	3

VEGETABLES	CAL (g)	FAT (g)	SAT FAT (g)	CHOL (mg)	SODIUM (mg)	CARB (g)	FIBER (g)
Corn, whole kernel sweet, Green Giant, ½ cup	80	0.5	0	0	360	18	2
Corn, whole kernel sweet, 50% less sodium, Green Giant, ½ cup	80	0.5	0	0	180	17	2
Corn, with peppers, Green Giant Mexicorn, ⅓ cup	60	0	0	0	430	14	2
Cucumber garden salad, Rosoff's/Schorr's, 3 slices	10	0	0	0	220	3	0
Eggplant, appetizer, Progresso, 2 Tbsp	30	2	0	0	130	2	2
Greens, mixed, Allen/Sunshine, ½ cup	30	0.5	0	0	10	8	4
Greens, mixed, Bush's Best, 4 oz	25	0.5	0	0	300	3	2
Hominy, golden, Allen/Uncle William, ½ cup	120	0.5	0	0	340	27	4
Hominy, golden, Bush's Best, 4 oz	60	0.5	0	0	550	13	3
Hominy, golden with peppers, Bush's Best, 4 oz	70	1	0	0	570	14	3
Hominy, Mexican, Allen/Uncle William, ½ cup	120	1	0	0	340	25	3
Hominy, white, Allen/Uncle William, ½ cup	100	0.5	0	0	340	22	4
Hominy, white, Bush's Best, 4 oz	70	1	0	0	530	14	4
Hominy, white with peppers, Bush's Best, 4 oz	80	1	0	0	500	16	4
Hominy, yellow, ½ cup	60	1	0	0	170	11	na
Kale, Allen/Sunshine, ½ cup	25	0.5	0	0	20	3	2
Kale, Bush's Best, 4 oz	30	0.5	0	0	330	4	2
Mixed vegetables, Bush's Best, 4 oz	40	0	0	0	250	7	3
Mixed vegetables, Del Monte, ½ cup	40	0	0	0	360	8	2
Mixed vegetables, Green Giant, ½ cup	60	0	0	0	460	12	2
Mixed vegetables, Green Giant Garden Medley, ½ cup	40	0	0	0	360	9	2

VEGETABLES	CAL	FAT (g)	SAT FAT (g)	CHOL (mg)	SODIUM (mg)	CARB (g)	FIBER (g)
Mixed vegetables, Chinese, La Choy, ⅔ cup	10	0	0	0	35	1	<1
Mixed vegetables, for chop suey, La Choy, ½ cup	15	0	0	0	320	3	1
Mixed vegetables, stir fry, Dynasty, 3 oz	30	1	0	0	20	5	3
Mushrooms, Seneca, ½ cup	25	0	0	0	15	5	3
Mushrooms, all styles, in jars, Seneca, ½ cup	30	0	0	0	490	4	3
Mushrooms, broiled in butter, sliced, whole or pieces/stems, Green Giant BinB, 1 can	30	0	0	0	460	4	2
Mushrooms, in brine, Seneca, ½ cup	25	0	0	0	500	5	3
Mushrooms, marinated, Seneca, 1 oz	90	9	1.5	0	190	2	<1
Mushrooms, pickled, Seneca, 1 oz	5	0	0	0	220	1	<1
Mushrooms, salad, Seneca, 1 Tbsp	5	0	0	0	80	<1	0
Mushrooms, salad, hot, Seneca, 1 Tbsp	5	0	0	0	60	<1	0
Mushrooms, Shiitake, Dynasty, 3 oz	30	0	0	0	0	5	4
Mushrooms, sliced, broiled in butter with garlic, Green Giant BinB, 1 can	35	0.5	0	0	410	4	1
Mushrooms, straw, whole, peeled, Dynasty, ½ cup	60	0	0	0	75	12	10
Mushrooms, teriyaki, sliced, Seneca, ½ cup	80	0	0	0	900	15	2
Mushrooms, whole, sliced or pieces/stems, Green Giant, ½ cup	30	0	0	0	440	4	2
Mustard greens, Allen/Sunshine, ½ cup	30	0.5	0	0	10	5	3
Mustard greens, Bush's Best, 4 oz	25	0.5	0	0	400	3	2
Okra and tomatoes, Allen/Trappey, ½ cup	25	0	0	0	380	5	3

VEGETABLES	CAL	FAT (g)	SAT FAT (g)	CHOL (mg)	SODIUM (mg)	CARB (g)	FIBER (g)
Okra and tomatoes, cut, Bush's Best, 4 oz	25	0.5	0	0	640	3	3
Okra, Creole gumbo, Trappey, ½ cup	35	0	0	0	290	6	3
Okra, cut, Allen/Trappey, ½ cup	25	0	0	0	400	6	3
Okra, cut, Bush's Best, 4 oz	25	0.5	0	0	760	3	3
Okra, tomatoes and corn, Allen/Trappey, ½ cup	30	0	0	0	280	6	4
Onions, Aunt Nellie's Farm Kitchen, ½ cup	40	0	0	0	410	8	1
Onions, French fried, Durkee, 2 Tbsp	45	3.5	1	0	45	3	0
Onions, sweet, in jar, Pride of Holland, 10 onions	45	0	0	0	440	11	0
Onions, whole, Green Giant, ½ cup	35	0	0	0	410	8	1
Peas, cream, East Texas Fair, ½ cup	100	1	0.5	0	460	17	5
Peas, early, LeSueur Green Giant, ½ cup	60	0	0	0	380	12	3
Peas, early June, Bush's Best, 4 oz	80	1	0	0	340	12	4
Peas, early June, Crest Top, ½ cup	100	0.5	0	0	300	20	6
Peas, early, 50% less sodium, LeSueur Green Giant, ½ cup	60	0	0	0	190	11	4
Peas, early, with mushrooms & pearl onions, LeSueur Green Giant, ½ cup	60	0	0	0	380	11	2
Peas, field, Sunshine, ½ cup	120	1	0.5	0	350	21	6
Peas, field, with bacon, Trappey, ½ cup	90	1	0.5	0	380	15	5
Peas, field, with snaps, Allen/East Texas Fair/Homefolks, ½ cup	120	1	0	0	300	21	6
Peas, field, with snaps, La Preferida, ½ cup	110	0.5	0	0	550	17	5
Peas, field, with snaps & bacon, Trappey, ½ cup	110	1	0.5	0	380	19	4
Peas, lady, Sunshine, ½ cup	100	1	0.5	0	460	17	5

VEGETABLES	CAL (g)	FAT (g)	SAT FAT (g)	CHOL (mg)	SODIUM (mg)	CARB (g)	FIBER (g)
Peas, lady, with snaps, East Texas Fair, ½ cup	100	1	0.5	0	420	17	4
Peas, pepper, East Texas Fair, ½ cup	120	1	0.5	0	580	22	6
Peas, purple hull, Allen/East Texas Fair/Homefolks, ½ cup	120	1	0.5	0	350	21	6
Peas, sweet, Bush's Best, 4 oz	90	1	0	0	380	14	5
Peas, sweet, Del Monte, ½ cup	60	0	0	0	360	11	4
Peas, sweet, Green Giant, ½ cup	60	0	0	0	390	11	4
Peas, sweet, LeSueur Green Giant, ½ cup	60	0	0	0	380	12	3
Peas, sweet, 50% less sodium, Green Giant, ½ cup	60	0	0	0	190	11	3
Peas, sweet, 50% less sodium, LeSueur Green Giant, ½ cup	60	0	0	0	190	11	4
Peas, sweet, no salt added, Del Monte, ½ cup	60	0	0	0	10	11	4
Peas, sweet, very young, small, Del Monte, ½ cup	60	0	0	0	360	10	4
Peas, sweet, with tiny pearl onions, Green Giant, ½ cup	60	0	0	0	520	11	4
Peas, white acre, East Texas Fair, ½ cup	100	1	0.5	0	460	17	5
Peas & carrots, Bush's Best, 4 oz	60	1	0	0	360	9	3
Peas & carrots, Del Monte, ½ cup	60	0	0	0	360	11	2
Peas & carrots, Green Giant, ½ cup	50	0	0	0	410	11	3
Peas 'n pork, East Texas Fair, ½ cup	110	1.5	0.5	0	540	19	5
Pepper salad, Progresso, Tbsp	25	2	0	0	80	1	1
Peppers, banana, hot or mild, Vlasic, 1 oz	5	0	0	0	480	1	0
Peppers, cherry, Progresso, Tbsp	30	2	0	0	30	2	1
Peppers, cherry, hot, Hebrew National, ⅓ pepper	10	0	0	0	270	2	0

VEGETABLES	CAL	FAT (g)	SAT FAT (g)	CHOL (mg)	SODIUM (mg)	CARB (g)	FIBER (g)
Peppers, cherry, hot, Progresso, 1 pepper	15	0	0	0	250	3	0
Peppers, cherry, mild, Vlasic, 2 peppers (1 oz)	10	0	0	0	480	2	0
Peppers, filet, Hebrew National/Schorr's, ¼ pepper	10	0	0	0	310	2	0
Peppers, fried, Progresso, 2 Tbsp	60	5	0.5	0	60	3	1
Peppers, hot chili, Del Monte, 4 peppers	10	0	0	0	610	3	<1
Peppers, jalapeno, chilpotle peppers, in spicy sauce, Del Monte, 2 Tbsp	20	0.5	0	0	430	4	1
Peppers, jalapeno, diced, Rosarita, 2 Tbsp	5	0	0	0	120	<1	<1
Peppers, jalapeno, green, whole, Chi-Chi's, 1 oz	10	0	0	0	110	2	0
Peppers, jalapeno, hot, Vlasic, ¼ cup	10	0	0	0	490	2	0
Peppers, jalapeno, nacho sliced, Rosarita, 2 Tbsp	0	0	0	0	450	1	<1
Peppers, jalapeno, peeled, Old El Paso, 3 peppers	10	0	0	0	200	1	1
Peppers, jalapeno, pickled, Old El Paso, 2 peppers	5	0	0	0	380	1	0
Peppers, jalapeno, pickled, sliced, Del Monte, 2 Tbsp	5	0	0	0	530	1	<1
Peppers, jalapeno, pickled, sliced, nachos, Del Monte, 2 Tbsp	5	0	0	0	340	1	<1
Peppers, jalapeno, pickled, slices, Old El Paso, 2 Tbsp	15	0	0	0	400	3	1
Peppers, jalapeno, pickled, whole, Del Monte, 2 or 3 peppers	5	0	0	0	560	1	<1
Peppers, jalapeno, red, whole, Chi-Chi's, 1 oz	15	0	0	0	110	3	0
Peppers, jalapeno, red or green, wheels, Chi-Chi's, 1 oz	10	0	0	0	110	1	0
Peppers, jalapeno, sliced, La Preferida, 2 Tbsp	20	0	0	0	490	4	0

VEGETABLES	CAL (g)	FAT (g)	SAT FAT (g)	CHOL (mg)	SODIUM (mg)	CARB (g)	FIBER (g)
Peppers, jalapeno, whole, Del Monte, 1 pepper	3	0	0	0	230	<1	<1
Peppers, jalapeno, whole, La Preferida, 4 peppers	20	0	0	0	430	4	0
Peppers, jalapeno, whole, Rosarita, 2 Tbsp	10	0	0	0	430	1	<1
Peppers, Mexican, tiny, hot, Vlasic, 9 peppers (1 oz)	10	0	0	0	480	2	0
Peppers, pepperoncini, salad, Vlasic, 2 peppers (1 oz)	5	0	0	0	440	1	0
Peppers, rings, mild, Vlasic, 12 rings (1 oz)	5	0	0	0	480	1	0
Peppers, roasted, Progresso, 2 Tbsp	10	0	0	0	60	1	0
Peppers, serrano, whole, La Preferida, 5 peppers	15	0	0	0	530	3	1
Peppers, sweet, Rosoff's, ¼ pepper	10	0	0	0	310	2	0
Peppers, sweet, rings, Vlasic, 1 oz	25	0	0	0	170	6	0
Peppers, Tuscan, Progresso, 3 peppers	10	0	0	0	330	1	1
Pimiento, 1 slice	0	0	0	0	0	0	0
Poke greens, Allen, ½ cup	35	1	0	0	5	5	3
Potato sticks, Butterfield, ⅔ cup	150	9	3	0	90	16	2
Potatoes, new, sliced, Del Monte, ⅔ cup	60	0	0	0	360	13	2
Potatoes, new, whole, Del Monte, 2 medium	60	0	0	0	360	13	2
Potatoes, white, Bush's Best, 4 oz	50	0	0	0	400	10	1
Potatoes, white, diced, Butterfield, ⅔ cup	100	0	0	0	350	22	3
Potatoes, white, sliced, Butterfield, ½ cup	100	0	0	0	390	22	4
Potatoes, white, whole, Butterfield/Sunshine, 5.6 oz	90	0	0	0	330	20	2
Rutabagas, diced, Sunshine, ½ cup	30	0	0	0	220	7	3

VEGETABLES	CAL (g)	FAT (g)	SAT FAT (g)	CHOL (mg)	SODIUM (mg)	CARB (g)	FIBER (g)
Sauerkraut, Bush's Best, 4 oz	30	0.5	0	0	780	5	2
Sauerkraut, Claussen, ¼ cup	5	0	0	0	210	1	1
Sauerkraut, Del Monte, ½ cup	15	0	0	0	700	4	2
Sauerkraut, Rosoff's, ½ cup	50	1	0	0	550	11	0
Sauerkraut, Bavarian kraut, Bush's Best, 4 oz	60	0.5	0	0	470	14	3
Sauerkraut, new kraut, Hebrew National/Schorr's, ½ cup	50	1	0	0	550	11	0
Spinach, Bush's Best, 4 oz	30	0.5	0	0	390	4	2
Spinach, Del Monte, ½ cup	30	0	0	0	360	4	2
Spinach, Popeye, ½ cup	45	1	0	0	310	7	4
Spinach, chopped, Popeye/Sunshine, ½ cup	40	1	0	0	310	6	4
Spinach, leaf, Popeye, ½ cup	45	1	0	0	310	7	4
Spinach, low sodium, Popeye, ½ cup	35	1	0	0	35	4	3
Spinach, no salt added, Del Monte, ½ cup	30	0	0	0	85	4	2
Squash, summer, crookneck & straightneck, ½ cup	15	0	0	0	5	3	na
Squash, summer, zucchini, Italian style, ½ cup	35	0	0	0	430	8	2
Squash, yellow, Allen/Sunshine, ½ cup	25	0	0	0	160	5	2
Squash, yellow sliced, Bush's Best, 4 oz	20	0	0	0	350	3	1
Succotash, with cream style corn, ½ cup	100	1	0	0	330	23	6
Succotash, with whole kernel corn, with liquid, ½ cup	80	0.5	0	0	280	18	7
Sweet potatoes, candied, Royal Prince, ½ cup	210	0.5	0	0	30	50	2
Sweet potatoes, halves, Royal Prince, 5.7 oz	190	0.5	0	0	40	46	4
Sweet potatoes, mashed, Princella/Sugary Sam, ⅔ cup	120	0.5	0	0	30	28	3

VEGETABLES	CAL (g)	FAT (g)	SAT FAT (g)	CHOL (mg)	SODIUM (mg)	CARB (g)	FIBER (g)
Sweet potatoes, orange-pineapple, Royal Prince, ½ cup	210	0.5	0	0	30	43	3
Tomatillos, La Preferida, ½ cup	40	0	0	0	910	9	2
Tomato puree, Hunt's, ¼ cup	25	0	0	0	100	5	2
Tomato puree, Progresso, ¼ cup	25	0	0	0	15	5	1
Tomato puree, thick style, Progresso, ¼ cup	30	0	0	0	15	5	1
Tomatoes, Bush's Best, 4 oz	35	0	0	0	160	5	1
Tomatoes, Contadina Recipe Ready, ½ cup	30	0	0	0	210	5	1
Tomatoes, Del Monte, ¼ cup	20	0	0	0	340	4	<1
Tomatoes, Angela Mia crushed, Hunt's, ½ cup	30	0	0	0	380	6	2
Tomatoes, choice cut, Hunt's Choice Cut, ½ cup	25	0	0	0	330	5	1
Tomatoes, crushed, Contadina, ¼ cup	20	0	0	0	150	4	1
Tomatoes, crushed, Hunt's, ½ cup	30	0	0	0	290	7	2
Tomatoes, crushed, Progresso, ¼ cup	20	0	0	0	95	4	1
Tomatoes, diced, Eden, ½ cup	30	0	0	0	5	6	2
Tomatoes, diced, and green chilies, Hunt's Choice Cut, Tbsp	0	0	0	0	25	0	0
Tomatoes, diced, and roasted garlic, Hunt's Choice Cut, ½ cup	25	0	0	0	510	5	<1
Tomatoes, diced, peeled, Del Monte, ½ cup	25	0	0	0	25	6	2
Tomatoes, half sour, Rosoff's, 1 tomato	5	0	0	0	290	1	0
Tomatoes, halves, Claussen, 1 oz	5	0	0	0	320	1	<1
Tomatoes, Italian recipe, Green Giant, ½ cup	30	0	0	0	360	7	2

VEGETABLES	CAL	FAT (g)	SAT FAT (g)	CHOL (mg)	SODIUM (mg)	CARB (g)	FIBER (g)
Tomatoes, Italian style, Contadina, ½ cup	25	0	0	0	220	4	1
Tomatoes, Mexican recipe, Green Giant, ½ cup	35	0	0	0	400	7	2
Tomatoes, no salt added, Del Monte, ¼ cup	20	0	0	0	20	4	<1
Tomatoes, pear shaped, Hunt's, ½ cup	20	0	0	0	360	4	<1
Tomatoes, peeled, regular or with basil, Progresso, ½ cup	25	0	0	0	220	4	1
Tomatoes, pickled, Hebrew National/Schorr's, ⅓ tomato	0	0	0	0	280	1	0
Tomatoes, stewed, Contadina, ½ cup	40	0	0	0	250	9	1
Tomatoes, stewed, Green Giant, ½ cup	35	0	0	0	360	7	2
Tomatoes, stewed, Hunt's, ½ cup	35	0	0	0	360	7	2
Tomatoes, stewed, cajun style, Del Monte, ½ cup	35	0	0	0	460	9	2
Tomatoes, stewed, chunky chili, Del Monte, ½ cup	30	0	0	0	670	8	2
Tomatoes, stewed, chunky pasta, Del Monte, ½ cup	45	0	0	0	560	11	2
Tomatoes, stewed, chunky salsa, Del Monte, ½ cup	35	0	0	0	560	8	2
Tomatoes, stewed, Italian style, Contadina, ½ cup	40	0	0	0	260	8	1
Tomatoes, stewed, Italian style, Del Monte, ½ cup	30	0	0	0	420	8	2
Tomatoes, stewed, Mexican style, Contadina, ½ cup	40	0	0	0	220	9	1
Tomatoes, stewed, Mexican style, Del Monte, ½ cup	35	0	0	0	400	9	2
Tomatoes, stewed, no salt added, Hunt's, ½ cup	35	0	0	0	30	7	2
Tomatoes, stewed, original style, Del Monte, ½ cup	35	0	0	0	360	9	2
Tomatoes, stewed, original style, no salt added, Del Monte, ½ cup	35	0	0	0	50	9	2

VEGETABLES	CAL (g)	FAT (g)	SAT FAT (g)	CHOL (mg)	SODIUM (mg)	CARB (g)	FIBER (g)
Tomatoes, wedges, Del Monte, ½ cup	35	0	0	0	380	9	2
Tomatoes, whole, Contadina, ½ cup	25	0	0	0	220	4	1
Tomatoes, whole, Hunt's, 2 tomatoes	25	0	0	0	400	4	<1
Tomatoes, whole, no salt added, Hunt's, 2 tomatoes	25	0.5	0	0	0	5	1
Tomatoes, whole, peeled, Del Monte, ½ cup	25	0	0	0	160	6	2
Tomatoes, with green chilies, ½ cup	20	0	0	0	480	4	2
Turnip greens, Allen/Sunshine, ½ cup	25	0.5	0	0	15	3	2
Turnip greens, Bush's Best, 4 oz	25	0.5	0	0	300	3	2
Turnip greens, chopped, with diced turnips, Allen/Sunshine, ½ cup	30	0.5	0	0	20	5	3
Turnip greens with diced turnips, Bush's Best, 4 oz	30	0.5	0	0	380	5	2
Water chestnuts, sliced, La Choy, 2 Tbsp	10	0	0	0	0	3	1
Water chestnuts, whole, La Choy, 2 chestnuts	10	0	0	0	0	2	<1
Water chestnuts, whole or sliced, Dynasty, ½ cup	20	0	0	0	5	5	1
Yams, Bush's Best, 4 oz	110	0	0	0	25	26	2
Yams, cut, Allen/Princella/ Sugary Sam, ⅔ cup	160	0.5	0	0	35	40	3
Yams, whole, Royal Prince/Trappey, 6 oz	200	0.5	0	0	40	48	4
Zucchini, Italian style, Progresso, ½ cup	40	2	0	0	400	7	2
Zucchini, with Italian style tomato sauce, Del Monte, ½ cup	30	0	0	0	490	7	1

AT A GLANCE: VEGETABLES

Choose products labeled "No Salt Added," "Low Salt," or "50% Less Sodium" from names such as Allen, Del Monte, Eden, and Green Giant.

CEREAL & BREAKFAST ITEMS

	CAL (g)	FAT (g)	SAT FAT (g)	CHOL (mg)	SODIUM (mg)	CARB (g)	FIBER (g)
BREAKFAST DRINKS See also Beverages, Nutritional Drinks.							
Cafe mocha, Carnation Instant Breakfast, 1 envelope	220	0.5	0	<5	100	28	<1
Cafe mocha, ready-to-drink, Carnation Instant Breakfast, 10 fl oz	220	2.5	0.5	5	210	35	0
Chocolate, Pillsbury Instant Breakfast, 1 envelope	140	1	0.5	<5	190	28	0
Chocolate malt, Carnation Instant Breakfast, 1 envelope	130	1.5	0.5	<5	130	26	1
Chocolate malt, no sugar added, Carnation Instant Breakfast, 1 envelope	70	1.5	1	<5	120	11	0
French vanilla, Carnation Instant Breakfast, 1 envelope	130	0	0	<5	110	27	0
French vanilla, no sugar added, Carnation Instant Breakfast, 1 envelope	70	0	0	<5	90	12	0
French vanilla, ready-to-drink, Carnation Instant Breakfast, 10 fl oz	200	3	0.5	<5	180	31	0
Milk chocolate, Carnation Instant Breakfast, 1 envelope	220	1	0.5	<5	100	28	1
Milk chocolate, no sugar added, Carnation Instant Breakfast, 1 envelope	70	1	0.5	<5	90	12	1
Milk chocolate, ready-to-drink, Carnation Instant Breakfast, 10 fl oz	220	2.5	1	5	230	37	1
Strawberry creme, Carnation Instant Breakfast, 1 envelope	220	0	0	<5	160	28	0
Strawberry creme, no sugar added, Carnation Instant Breakfast, 1 envelope	70	0	0	<5	90	12	0
Strawberry creme, ready-to-drink, Carnation Instant Breakfast, 10 fl oz	220	3	0.5	5	210	35	0

AT A GLANCE: BREAKFAST DRINKS
Mixing drink mix with 8 fl oz vitamin A & D skim milk contributes an additional 90 calories, 125 mg sodium, and 12 mg total carbohydrates.

	CAL (g)	FAT (g)	SAT FAT (g)	CHOL (mg)	SODIUM (mg)	CARB (g)	FIBER (g)

CEREAL, HOT

Serving sizes are for dry product. See also Dried Foods & Mixes, Grains.

	CAL (g)	FAT (g)	SAT FAT (g)	CHOL (mg)	SODIUM (mg)	CARB (g)	FIBER (g)
4 Grain Plus Flax, Arrowhead Mills, ¼ cup	150	2	0	0	0	28	6
7 Grain, Arrowhead Mills, ⅓ cup	140	1.5	0	0	0	25	5
Banana nut barley, Fantastic, 1 pkg	180	2.5	0	0	230	35	4
Barley Plus, Erehwon, ¼ cup	170	1	0	0	0	37	4
Bear Mush, Arrowhead Mills, ¼ cup	160	1	0	0	0	33	2
Bits o Barley, Arrowhead Mills, ⅓ cup	140	1	0	0	0	35	6
Brown rice cream, Erehwon, ¼ cup	170	1	0	0	30	36	1
Bulgur wheat, Arrowhead Mills, ¼ cup	150	0.5	0	0	0	33	4
Cracked wheat, Arrowhead Mills, ¼ cup	140	0.5	0	0	0	29	6
Cream of Rice, Nabisco, ¼ cup	170	0	0	0	0	38	0
Cream of rye, Roman Meal, ⅓ cup	110	1	0	0	0	20	5
Cream of Wheat, instant, Nabisco, 1 packet	100	0	0	0	260	21	1
Cream of Wheat, quick, Nabisco, 3 Tbsp	120	0	0	0	85	25	1
Farina, Farina Mills, 3 Tbsp	100	0	0	0	0	22	<1
Fruit'n Wheat, Erehwon, ¼ cup	170	1.5	0	0	105	39	5
Grits, bulgur wheat with soy, Hodgson Mill, ¼ cup	120	1	0	0	0	24	1
Grits, corn, cheese flavor, instant, 1 packet	110	1	0	0	480	21	0
Grits, corn, with imitation bacon bits, instant, 1 packet	100	0.5	0	0	530	21	0
Grits, corn, with imitation ham bits, instant, 1 packet	100	0	0	0	660	21	0

CEREAL, HOT	CAL (g)	FAT (g)	SAT FAT (g)	CHOL (mg)	SODIUM (mg)	CARB (g)	FIBER (g)
Grits, hominy, quick, Albers, ¼ cup	140	0.5	0	0	0	31	1
Grits, soy, Arrowhead Mills, ¼ cup	140	6	1	0	0	12	6
Grits, white corn, Arrowhead Mills, ¼ cup	140	0	0	0	0	30	<1
Grits, yellow corn, Arrowhead Mills, ¼ cup	130	0	0	0	0	29	1
Malt-O-Meal, chocolate, ⅓ cup	220	0.5	0	0	0	50	2
Malt-O-Meal, maple brown sugar, ⅓ cup	220	0	0	0	10	51	1
Malt-O-Meal, quick, 3 Tbsp	120	0	0	0	0	28	1
Maypo, maple, instant, ½ cup	190	2	0	0	0	36	3
Milled wheat, 100%, Ralston, ½ cup	150	1	ns	ns	0	31	5
Multigrain, Mother's, ½ cup	130	1.5	0	0	10	29	5
Oat bran, Hodgson Mill, ¼ cup	120	3	1	0	0	23	8
Oat bran, Mother's, ½ cup	150	3	1	0	0	24	6
Oat bran, Quaker, ½ cup	150	3	1	0	0	24	6
Oat bran with toasted wheat germ, Erewhon, ⅓ cup	170	2.5	0.5	0	0	31	5
Oatmeal, instant, Mother's, ½ cup	150	3	0.5	0	0	27	4
Oatmeal, apple 'n cinnamon, instant, Quaker, 1 packet	130	1.5	0.5	0	105	26	3
Oatmeal, apple cinnamon, instant, Erehwon, 1 packet	130	2	0.5	0	100	24	3
Oatmeal, apple raisin, instant, Erehwon, 1 packet	140	2	0.5	0	100	26	3
Oatmeal, apple, raisin & walnut, instant, Quaker, 1 packet	140	2.5	0.5	0	160	27	3
Oatmeal, blueberries & cream, instant, Quaker, 1 packet	130	2.5	0.5	0	140	27	2
Oatmeal, cinnamon graham cookie, instant, Quaker, 1 packet	150	2.5	0.5	0	170	30	3

CEREAL, HOT	CAL (g)	FAT (g)	SAT FAT (g)	CHOL (mg)	SODIUM (mg)	CARB (g)	FIBER (g)
Oatmeal, cinnamon raisin almond, instant, Arrowhead Mills, 1 pkg	130	3	0	0	0	24	4
Oatmeal, cinnamon spice, instant, Quaker, 1 packet	170	2	0	0	290	36	3
Oatmeal, cinnamon toast, instant, Quaker, 1 packet	130	2	0	0	160	27	2
Oatmeal, cranberry orange, Fantastic, 1 pkg	210	3	0.5	0	220	42	3
Oatmeal, honey nut, instant, Quaker, 1 packet	130	3	0.5	0	210	25	2
Oatmeal, maple apple spice, instant, Arrowhead Mills, 1 pkg	130	2	0	0	40	25	3
Oatmeal, maple brown sugar, instant, Quaker, 1 packet	160	2	0.5	0	240	33	3
Oatmeal, maple spice, instant, Erehwon, 1 packet	130	2	0.5	0	100	25	3
Oatmeal, old fashioned, Quaker, ½ cup	150	3	0.5	0	0	27	4
Oatmeal, peaches & cream, instant, Quaker, 1 packet	130	2	0.5	0	150	27	2
Oatmeal, quick, Quaker, ½ cup	150	3	0.5	0	0	27	4
Oatmeal, radical raspberry, instant, Quaker Kids Choice, 1 packet	150	3	0.5	0	170	29	3
Oatmeal, raisin, date & walnut, instant, Quaker, 1 packet	130	2.5	0.5	0	240	27	3
Oatmeal, raisins, dates & walnuts, instant, Erehwon, 1 packet	130	2.5	0.5	0	40	24	3
Oatmeal, raisin-spice, instant, Quaker, 1 packet	160	2	0.5	0	250	32	3
Oatmeal, regular, instant, Arrowhead Mills, 1 pkg	110	2	0	0	0	19	3
Oatmeal, regular, instant, Quaker, 1 packet	130	2.5	0.5	0	95	22	3
Oatmeal, strawberries 'n stuff, instant, Quaker Kids Choice, 1 packet	150	2	0.5	0	170	30	3

CEREAL, HOT	CAL	FAT (g)	SAT FAT (g)	CHOL (mg)	SODIUM (mg)	CARB (g)	FIBER (g)
Oatmeal, strawberries and cream, instant, Quaker, 1 packet	130	2	0.5	0	160	27	2
Oatmeal, with added oat bran, instant, Erehwon, 1 packet	130	2.5	0.5	0	0	25	4
Oats, steel cut, Arrowhead Mills, ¼ cup	170	3	0.5	0	0	29	5
Oats, wheat, coconut, almonds, honey, Roman Meal, ⅓ cup	160	6	3	0	10	22	3
Oats, wheat, dates, raisins, almonds, Roman Meal, ⅓ cup	130	1.5	0	0	0	24	3
Oats, wheat, rye, bran, flax, Roman Meal, ⅓ cup	110	1.5	0	0	0	19	5
Rice & Shine, Arrowhead Mills, ¼ cup	150	1	0	0	0	32	2
Wheat Hearts, General Mills, ¼ cup	130	1	0	0	0	26	2
Wheat-free 7 grain, Arrowhead Mills, ¼ cup	120	1.5	0	0	0	25	2
Whole wheat natural, Mother's, ½ cup	130	1	0	0	0	30	4

AT A GLANCE: HOT CEREAL
Lowest in Calories: Nabisco Cream of Wheat, Instant; Farina Mills Farina
Lowest in Carbohydrates (Sugar): Arrowhead Mills Soy Grits
Highest in Fiber: Hodgson Mill Oat Bran

CEREAL, READY-TO-EAT

	CAL	FAT	SAT FAT	CHOL	SODIUM	CARB	FIBER
100% Bran, Nabisco, ⅓ cup	80	0.5	0	0	270	23	8
100% Natural, crispy wholegrain with raisins, low fat, Quaker, ½ cup	190	3	1	0	95	40	3
100% Natural, oats & honey, Quaker, ½ cup	220	8	3.5	0	25	32	3
100% Natural, oats, honey & raisins, Quaker, ½ cup	220	8	3.5	0	20	35	4
100% natural oat, cinnamon & raisin, Nature Valley, ¾ cup	240	8	1	0	90	38	3
100% natural oat, fruit & nut, Nature Valley, ⅔ cup	250	11	2	0	75	34	3

CEREAL, READY-TO-EAT	CAL (g)	FAT (g)	SAT FAT (g)	CHOL (mg)	SODIUM (mg)	CARB (g)	FIBER (g)
100% natural oat, toasted oats & honey, Nature Valley, ¾ cup	250	10	1.5	0	90	36	3
All-Bran, Kellogg's, ½ cup	80	1	0	0	280	22	10
All-Bran Extra Fiber, Kellogg's, ½ cup	50	1	0	0	150	22	15
Almond raisin, Breadshop's Nectarsweet Premium, ½ cup	240	9	1	0	0	35	5
Alpha-Bits, Post, 1 cup	130	1	0	0	210	27	1
Alpha-Bits, marshmallow, Post, 1 cup	120	1	0	0	160	25	1
Amaranth flakes, Arrowhead Mills, 1 cup	130	2	0	0	0	25	3
Apple cinnamon, Roman Meal, ⅓ cup	110	2	0	0	5	18	6
Apple Cinnamon Rice Krispies, Kellogg's, ¾ cup	110	0	0	0	220	27	1
Apple Cinnamon Squares, Kellogg's, ¾ cup	180	1	0	0	15	44	5
Apple corns, Arrowhead Mills, 1 cup	150	1.5	0	0	110	35	4
Apple Jacks, Kellogg's, 1 cup	110	0	0	0	135	27	1
Apple Raisin Crisp, Kellogg's, 1 cup	180	0	0	0	340	46	4
Apple Stroodles, Erehwon, ¾ cup	110	0.5	0	0	15	25	1
Aztec, Erehwon, 1 cup	110	0	0	0	70	25	1
Banana nut, Sunbelt, ½ cup	250	9	4	0	60	37	4
Banana Nut Crunch, Post, 1 cup	250	6	1	0	200	43	4
Banana-O's, Erehwon, ¾ cup	110	0	0	0	15	26	2
Basic 4, General Mills, 1¼ cups	210	3	0	0	320	42	3
Blueberry 'n cream, Breadshop's Nectarsweet Gourmet, ½ cup	220	8	1	0	0	32	4
Blueberry 'n cream, with organic grains, Breadshop's Organic Honey Gourmet, ½ cup	220	8	1	0	0	34	4

CEREAL, READY-TO-EAT	CAL (g)	FAT (g)	SAT FAT (g)	CHOL (mg)	SODIUM (mg)	CARB (g)	FIBER (g)
Blueberry Morning, Post, 1¼ cups	230	3.5	0.5	0	250	45	2
Blueberry Squares, Kellogg's, ¾ cup	180	1	0	0	15	44	5
Body Buddies natural fruit, General Mills, 1 cup	120	1	0	0	290	26	0
Boo Berry, General Mills, 1 cup	120	0.5	0	0	230	27	0
Bran, unprocessed, Quaker, ⅓ cup	30	0	0	0	0	11	8
Bran Buds, Kellogg's, ⅓ cup	70	1	0	0	210	24	11
Bran flakes, Arrowhead Mills, 1 cup	100	1	0	0	80	22	4
Bran flakes, Malt-O-Meal, ¾ cup	100	0.5	0	0	210	24	5
Bran flakes, Post, ⅔ cup	90	0.5	0	0	210	22	6
Bran'nola original, Post, ½ cup	200	3	0.5	0	240	43	5
Bran'nola raisin, Post, ½ cup	200	3	0.5	0	220	44	5
Brown rice, fat free, Health Valley, 1 cup	110	0	0	0	0	30	1
Cap'n Crunch, Quaker, ¾ cup	110	1.5	0	0	210	23	1
Cap'n Crunch's Crunch Berries, Quaker, ¾ cup	100	1.5	0	0	190	22	1
Cap'n Crunch's Deep Sea Crunch, Quaker, 1 cup	130	2	0.5	0	150	26	1
Cap'n Crunch's Peanut Butter Crunch, Quaker, ¾ cup	110	2.5	0.5	0	210	21	1
Cheerios, General Mills, 1 cup	110	2	0	0	280	23	3
Cheerios, apple cinnamon, General Mills, ¾ cup	120	2.5	0	0	190	24	1
Cheerios, honey nut, General Mills, 1 cup	120	1.5	0	0	270	24	1
Cheerios, multi-grain, General Mills, 1 cup	110	1	0	0	240	24	3
Chex Multi Bran, Ralston, 1¼ cups	220	1	0	0	300	48	7
Cinnamon Grins, Breadshop's, ¾ cup	110	0.5	0	0	0	25	2

CEREAL, READY-TO-EAT	CAL (g)	FAT (g)	SAT FAT (g)	CHOL (mg)	SODIUM (mg)	CARB (g)	FIBER (g)
Cinnamon mini buns, Kellogg's, ¾ cup	120	0.5	0	0	210	27	1
Cinnamon Toast Crunch, General Mills, ¾ cup	130	3.5	0.5	0	210	24	1
Clusters, General Mills, 1 cup	220	4	0.5	0	270	43	4
Cocoa Comets, Malt-O-Meal, ¾ cup	120	1	0	0	190	27	na
Cocoa Krispies, Kellogg's, ¾ cup	120	0.5	0	0	190	27	0
Cocoa Pebbles, Post, ¾ cup	120	1	1	0	160	25	<1
Cocoa Puffs, General Mills, 1 cup	120	1	0	0	190	27	0
Common Sense oat bran, Kellogg's, ¾ cup	110	1	0	0	270	23	4
Complete bran flakes, Kellogg's, ¾ cup	100	0.5	0	0	230	25	5
Cookie Crisp multi-grain, chocolate chip, Ralston, 1 cup	120	1.5	0	0	110	25	0
Corn Chex, Ralston, 1¼ cups	110	0	0	0	270	26	1
Corn flakes, Arrowhead Mills, 1 cup	130	0	0	0	65	30	2
Corn flakes, Erehwon, ¾ cup	100	1	0	0	50	22	1
Corn flakes, Kellogg's, 1 cup	110	0	0	0	330	26	1
Corn flakes, Malt-O-Meal, 1 cup	110	0	0	0	310	26	1
Corn flakes, Country, General Mills, 1 cup	120	0.5	0	0	290	26	0
Corn flakes, Krispie, Breadshop's, ¾ cup	110	0.5	0	0	130	26	1
Corn Pops, Kellogg's, 1 cup	110	0	0	0	95	27	1
Count Chocula, General Mills, 1 cup	120	1	0	0	190	27	0
Cracklin' Oat Bran, Kellogg's, ¼ cup	230	8	3	0	180	40	6
Crispix, Kellogg's, 1 cup	110	0	0	0	230	26	1
Crispy brown rice, Erehwon, 1 cup	110	0	0	0	180	25	1
Crispy brown rice, no salt added, Erehwon, 1 cup	110	0	0	0	10	25	1

CEREAL, READY-TO-EAT	CAL (g)	FAT (g)	SAT FAT (g)	CHOL (mg)	SODIUM (mg)	CARB (g)	FIBER (g)
Crispy puffs, Arrowhead Mills, 1 cup	80	1	0	0	0	16	1
Crispy rice, Malt-O-Meal, 1 cup	110	0	0	0	250	26	0
Crispy Wheats 'n Raisins, General Mills, 1 cup	190	1	0	0	270	44	4
Crunchy bran, Quaker, ¾ cup	90	1	0	0	250	23	5
Crunchy oat bran, Breadshop's Nectarsweet Gourmet, ½ cup	210	8.5	1	0	0	31	5
C.W. Post hearty granola, Post, ⅔ cup	280	9	1	0	150	45	4
Double Chex, Ralston, 1¼ cups	120	0	0	0	230	27	0
Double Dip Crunch, Kellogg's, ¾ cup	110	0	0	0	160	27	0
Fiber One, General Mills, ½ cup	60	1	0	0	140	24	13
Frankenberry, General Mills, 1 cup	120	0.5	0	0	220	27	0
Frosted Bran, Kellogg's, ¾ cup	100	0	0	0	200	26	3
Frosted Flakes, Kellogg's, ¾ cup	120	0	0	0	200	28	0
Frosted Krispies, Kellogg's, ¾ cup	110	0	0	0	230	27	0
Frosted Mini-Wheats, original or bite size, Kellogg's, 1 cup	190	1	0	0	0	45	6
Frosted Wheat Bites, Nabisco, 1 cup	190	1	0	0	170	44	5
Fruit & Fibre, dates, raisins & walnuts, Post, 1 cup	210	3	0.5	0	260	46	6
Fruit & Fibre, peaches, raisins & almonds, Post, 1 cup	210	3	0.5	0	270	46	6
Fruit & Frosted O's, Malt-O-Meal, 1 cup	110	1	0	0	150	26	0
Fruit Juice Gone Nuts!, Breadshop's Nectarsweet Premium, ½ cup	240	10	1	0	0	34	5
Fruit Loops, Kellogg's, 1 cup	120	1	0.5	0	150	26	1

CEREAL, READY-TO-EAT	CAL	FAT (g)	SAT FAT (g)	CHOL (mg)	SODIUM (mg)	CARB (g)	FIBER (g)
Fruit Wheats, blueberry, Nabisco, ¾ cup	170	0.5	0	0	170	41	4
Fruit Wheats, raspberry, Nabisco, ¾ cup	160	0.5	0	0	160	40	4
Fruit Wheats, strawberry, Nabisco, ¾ cup	170	0.5	0	0	160	41	4
Fruitful Bran, Kellogg's, 1¼ cups	170	1	0	0	330	44	6
Fruity Marshmallow Krispies, Kellogg's, ¾ cup	110	0	0	0	180	27	0
Fruity Pebbles, Post, ¾ cup	110	1	0.5	0	150	24	0
Galaxy Grahams, Erehwon, ¾ cup	100	0.5	0	0	60	23	2
Golden Crisp, Post, ¾ cup	110	0	0	0	40	25	0
Golden Grahams, General Mills, ¾ cup	120	1	0	0	280	25	1
Graham Chex and crispy mini grahams, multi-grain, sweetened, Ralston, 1 cup	210	1.5	0	0	340	45	1
Granola, almond flavor, fat free, Health Valley Granola O's, ⅔ cup	120	0	0	0	10	26	3
Granola, apple cinnamon, fat free, Health Valley Granola O's, ⅔ cup	120	0	0	0	10	26	3
Granola, Cinnapple Spice, Breadshop's, ½ cup	230	9	1	0	0	34	4
Granola, cocoa, Breadshop's, ½ cup	200	9	1.5	0	0	29	4
Granola, date & almond, fat free, Health Valley, ⅔ cup	180	0	0	0	25	45	6
Granola, date nut, Erehwon, ⅓ cup	220	9	1	0	85	29	4
Granola, fruit, low fat, Nature Valley, ⅔ cup	210	2.5	0	0	200	44	3
Granola, fruit & nut, Sunbelt, ½ cup	230	7	2.5	0	100	38	4
Granola, honey almond, Erehwon, ⅓ cup	210	9	1	0	60	29	4

CEREAL, READY-TO-EAT	CAL (g)	FAT (g)	SAT FAT (g)	CHOL (mg)	SODIUM (mg)	CARB (g)	FIBER (g)
Granola, honey apple blueberry, Breadshop's, ½ cup	210	8	1	0	0	31	4
Granola, honey crunch, fat free, Health Valley Granola O's, ⅔ cup	120	0	0	0	10	26	3
Granola, Honey Gone Nuts, Breadshop's, ½ cup	240	10	1	0	0	33	4
Granola, low fat, Heartland, ½ cup	210	3	1	0	50	40	3
Granola, low fat, Kellogg's, ½ cup	210	3	0.5	0	120	43	3
Granola, low fat, Sunbelt, ½ cup	200	3	1	0	80	42	4
Granola, maple, Erehwon, ⅓ cup	220	9	1	0	90	31	4
Granola, maple nut, Breadshop's, ½ cup	230	10	1.5	0	0	32	4
Granola, Oregon Blue Crunch, Breadshop's, ½ cup	230	9	1.5	0	0	33	4
Granola, original, Heartland, ½ cup	290	11	1.5	0	160	41	4
Granola, raisin, Heartland, ½ cup	290	10	1.5	0	140	42	4
Granola, raisin & date, Sun Country, ½ cup	260	8	1	0	15	43	4
Granola, raisin cinnamon, fat free, Health Valley, ⅔ cup	180	0	0	0	25	45	6
Granola, spiced apple, Erehwon, ⅓ cup	210	8	1	0	65	29	4
Granola, sunflower crunch, Erehwon, ⅓ cup	220	9	1	0	90	30	4
Granola, super, Breadshop's, ½ cup	230	9	1.5	0	0	31	4
Granola, supernatural, Breadshop's, ½ cup	200	10	1.5	0	0	34	7
Granola, tropical fruit, fat free, Health Valley, ⅔ cup	180	0	0	0	25	45	6
Granola, with almonds, Sun Country, ½ cup	270	9	1.5	0	20	38	3

CEREAL, READY-TO-EAT	CAL	FAT (g)	SAT FAT (g)	CHOL (mg)	SODIUM (mg)	CARB (g)	FIBER (g)
Granola, with bran, Erehwon, 1/3 cup	220	8	1	0	25	31	5
Granola, with raisins, low fat, Kellogg's, 1/2 cup	210	3	1	0	135	43	3
Grape-Nuts, Post, 1/2 cup	200	1	0	0	350	47	5
Grape-Nuts flakes, Post, 3/4 cup	100	1	0	0	140	24	3
Great Grains, crunchy pecan, Post, 2/3 cup	220	6	1	0	150	38	4
Great Grains, raisin, date, pecan, Post, 3/4 cup	210	5	0.5	0	150	39	4
Health nuggets, Breadshop's Organic Honey Gourmet, 1/2 cup	170	1	0	0	0	38	4
Healthy Choice, multi-grain flakes, Kellogg's, 1 cup	100	0	0	0	210	25	3
Healthy Choice, multi-grain squares, Kellogg's, 1 1/4 cups	190	1	0	0	0	45	6
Healthy Choice, multi-grains, raisins, oats & almonds, Kellogg's, 1 cup	200	2	0	0	240	45	4
Hearty wheat, Breadshop's, 2/3 cup	230	9	1	0	0	34	4
Hidden Treasures, General Mills, 3/4 cup	130	2	0	0	135	26	0
Honey Almond Delight, sliced almonds & clusters, Ralston, 1 cup	210	3	0	0	410	41	4
Honey Bunches Of Oats, honey roasted, Post, 3/4 cup	120	1.5	0.5	0	190	25	1
Honey Bunches Of Oats, with almonds, Post, 3/4 cup	130	3	0.5	0	180	24	1
Honey clusters and flakes, all flavors, fat free, Health Valley, 3/4 cup	130	0	0	0	20	31	4
Honey crisp corn, Erehwon, 1 cup	210	2.5	0	0	100	45	2
Honey Puffed Kashi, Kashi Company, 1 cup	120	1	0	0	6	25	2
Honeycomb, Post, 1 1/3 cups	110	0	0	0	190	26	<1

CEREAL, READY-TO-EAT	CAL	FAT (g)	SAT FAT (g)	CHOL (mg)	SODIUM (mg)	CARB (g)	FIBER (g)
Just Right, fruit & nut, Kellogg's, 1 cup	210	1.5	0	0	260	46	3
Just Right, with crunchy nuggets, Kellogg's, 1 cup	200	1.5	0	0	340	46	3
Kaboom, General Mills, 1¼ cups	120	1.5	0	0	280	24	1
Kamut 'n Honey, Breadshop's, 1 cup	120	3	0.5	0	0	22	0
Kamut flakes, Arrowhead Mills, 1 cup	120	1	0	0	65	25	3
Kamut flakes, Erehwon, ⅔ cup	110	0	0	0	75	25	4
Kashi Medley, Kashi Company, ½ cup	100	1	0	0	50	20	2
Kashi Pilaf, Kashi Company, ½ cup	170	3	0	0	15	30	6
King Vitaman, Quaker, 1½ cups	120	1	0	0	260	26	1
Kix, General Mills, 1⅓ cups	120	1	0	0	270	26	1
Kix, Berry Berry, General Mills, ¾ cup	120	1	0	0	170	26	0
Krinklie Grains, Breadshop's, ¾ cup	110	1	0	0	135	23	2
Life, Quaker, ¾ cup	120	1.5	0	0	170	25	2
Life, cinnamon, Quaker, 1 cup	190	2	0	0	220	39	4
Low fat cinnamon raisin, Breadshop's, ⅔ cup	200	1	0	0	0	45	5
Low fat raisin, Breadshop's, ⅔ cup	200	1	0	0	0	45	5
Low fat with organic grains, Breadshop's Organic Honey Gourmet, ½ cup	200	2	0.5	0	0	40	5
Lucky Charms, General Mills, 1 cup	120	1	0	0	210	25	1
Maple corns, Arrowhead Mills, 1 cup	190	3	0.5	0	140	43	6
Marshmallow Stars, Quaker Kids Favorites, ¾ cup	120	1.5	0.5	0	180	25	1
Marshmallow Treasures, Malt-O-Meal, 1 cup	120	1	0	0	210	25	1

CEREAL, READY-TO-EAT	CAL (g)	FAT (g)	SAT FAT (g)	CHOL (mg)	SODIUM (mg)	CARB (g)	FIBER (g)
Muesli, blueberry pecan, Ralston, 1 cup	200	2.5	1.5	0	170	41	4
Muesli, cranberry walnut, Ralston, ¾ cup	200	3	0	0	180	40	4
Muesli, five whole grains, Sunbelt, ½ cup	210	2	0.5	0	70	44	3
Muesli, oat bran, Breadshop's, ½ cup	200	3.5	0.5	0	0	37	4
Muesli, peach pecan, Ralston, ¾ cup	200	3	0	0	170	39	4
Muesli, raisin graham, Breadshop's, ½ cup	190	3	0.5	0	15	39	4
Muesli, raspberry almond, Ralston, ¾ cup	220	3	0	0	170	44	4
Muesli, rye date, Breadshop's, ½ cup	200	3.5	0.5	0	0	37	3
Muesli, Sierra crunch, Breadshop's, ¾ cup	190	3	0.5	0	60	38	3
Muesli, strawberry pecan, Ralston, 1 cup	210	2.5	0	0	170	42	3
Mueslix, crispy blend, Kellogg's, ⅔ cup	200	3	0	0	190	42	4
Mueslix, golden crunch, Kellogg's, ¾ cup	210	5	1	0	280	40	6
Multigrain flakes, Arrowhead Mills, 1 cup	140	1.5	0	0	130	29	3
Multi-grain flakes, Healthy Choice, 1 cup	110	0	0	0	210	26	3
Multi-grain Grins, Breadshop's, 1 cup	110	1	0	0	0	22	3
Multi-grain squares, Healthy Choice, 1¼ cups	190	1	0	0	0	45	6
Multi-grains, raisins & almonds, Healthy Choice, 1¼ cups	200	2	0	0	240	44	4
Nature Os, Arrowhead Mills, 1 cup	130	2	0.5	0	5	24	3
New England Supernatural, Breadshop's, ½ cup	220	9	1	0	0	31	3
Nut & Honey Crunch, Kellogg's, 1¼ cups	220	4	1	0	370	45	1

CEREAL, READY-TO-EAT	CAL (g)	FAT (g)	SAT FAT (g)	CHOL (mg)	SODIUM (mg)	CARB (g)	FIBER (g)
Nut & Honey Crunchy O's, Kellogg's, 1¼ cups	120	2.5	0	0	200	23	2
Nutri-Grain, almond raisin, Kellogg's, 1¼ cups	200	3	0	0	330	44	4
Nutri-Grain, golden wheat, Kellogg's, ¾ cup	100	0.5	0	0	240	24	4
Nutri-Grain, golden wheat & raisin, Kellogg's, 1¼ cups	180	1	0	0	310	45	6
Nutty Corn, Pacific Grain, ¾ cup	220	1	0	0	135	50	6
Nutty Rice, Pacific Grain, ¾ cup	210	1.5	0	0	110	46	2
Nutty Wheat and barley, Pacific Grain, ¾ cup	220	0.5	0	0	135	47	3
Oat bran, Quaker, 1¼ cups	210	3	0.5	0	210	41	7
Oat bran flakes, Arrowhead Mills, 1 cup	110	2	1	0	60	22	4
Oatmeal crisp, almond, General Mills, 1 cup	230	6	1	0	320	40	3
Oatmeal crisp, apple cinnamon, General Mills, 1 cup	210	2.5	0	0	350	44	3
Oatmeal crisp, raisin, General Mills, 1 cup	210	3	0	0	260	42	2
Oatmeal squares, Quaker, 1 cup	220	3	0.5	0	260	44	4
Oatmeal squares, cinnamon, Quaker, 1 cup	230	2.5	0.5	0	260	48	5
Oh!s, honey graham, Quaker, ¾ cup	110	2	0.5	0	180	23	1
Orange almond, Breadshop's Nectarsweet Premium, ½ cup	240	9	1	0	0	35	5
Peaches 'n cream, Breadshop's Nectarsweet Gourmet, ½ cup	220	8	1	0	0	32	4
Peaches 'n cream, with organic grains, Breadshop's Organic Honey Gourmet, ½ cup	220	8	1	0	0	34	4
Pop-Tarts Crunch, frosted brown sugar cinnamon, Kellogg's, ¾ cup	120	1	0	0	160	26	1

CEREAL, READY-TO-EAT	CAL (g)	FAT (g)	SAT FAT (g)	CHOL (mg)	SODIUM (mg)	CARB (g)	FIBER (g)
Pop-Tarts Crunch, frosted strawberry, Kellogg's, ¾ cup	120	1	0	0	125	27	0
Pop-Tarts Crunch, strawberry, Kellogg's, ¾ cup	120	1	0	0	125	27	0
Popeye Cocoa Blasts, Quaker, 1 cup	130	1.5	0.5	0	125	29	1
Popeye Fruit Curls, Quaker, 1 cup	120	1	0	0	170	27	1
Popeye Jeepers, Quaker, 1⅓ cups	110	1	0	0	140	24	1
Popeye Jeepers crispy corn puffs, Quaker, 1⅓ cups	110	0.5	0	0	150	24	1
Popeye Oat'mmms, Quaker, 1 cup	120	2	0.5	0	300	25	2
Popeye Oat'mmms toasted oat, Quaker, 1 cup	110	1.5	0	0	160	22	2
Poppets, Erehwon, 1 cup	120	1	0	0	10	25	<1
Post Toasties, Post, 1 cup	100	0	0	0	270	24	1
Product 19, Kellogg's, 1 cup	110	0	0	0	280	25	1
Puffed corn, Arrowhead Mills, 1 cup	80	0	0	0	0	16	1
Puffed corn, fat free, Health Valley, 1 cup	80	0	0	0	0	20	2
Puffed kamut, Arrowhead Mills, 1 cup	50	0	0	0	0	11	2
Puffed Kashi, Kashi Company, 1 cup	70	<1	0	0	0	19	2
Puffed millet, Arrowhead Mills, 1 cup	90	0.5	0	0	0	19	1
Puffed rice, Arrowhead Mills, 1 cup	90	0	0	0	0	19	1
Puffed rice, Malt-O-Meal, 1 cup	60	0	0	0	0	13	0
Puffed rice, Quaker, 1 cup	50	0	0	0	0	12	0
Puffed wheat, Arrowhead Mills, 1 cup	90	0.5	0	0	0	20	2
Puffed wheat, Malt-O-Meal, 1 cup	50	0	0	0	0	11	1
Puffed wheat, Quaker, 1¼ cups	50	0	0	0	0	11	1

CEREAL, READY-TO-EAT	CAL (g)	FAT (g)	SAT FAT (g)	CHOL (mg)	SODIUM (mg)	CARB (g)	FIBER (g)
Puffs 'n Honey, Breadshop's, ¾ cup	120	3	0	0	0	21	0
Quisp/Popeye Sweet Crunch, Quaker, 1 cup	110	1.5	0.5	0	190	23	1
Raisin bran, Erehwon, 1 cup	170	1	0	0	100	40	6
Raisin bran, Kellogg's, 1 cup	170	1	0	0	310	43	7
Raisin bran, Malt-O-Meal, 1 cup	180	1	0	0	260	43	7
Raisin bran, Post, 1 cup	190	1	0	0	300	46	8
Raisin bran, Skinner's, 1 cup	170	1	0	0	85	41	7
Raisin grahams, Erehwon, 1 cup	190	1	0	0	105	43	6
Raisin nut bran, General Mills, 1 cup	210	4.5	0.5	0	260	42	5
Raisin squares, Kellogg's, ¾ cup	180	1	0	0	0	44	5
Raspberry 'n cream, Breadshop's Nectarsweet Gourmet, ½ cup	220	8	1	0	0	32	4
Raspberry 'n cream, with organic grains, Breadshop's Organic Honey Gourmet, ½ cup	220	8	1	0	0	34	4
Reese's Peanut Butter Puffs, General Mills, ¾ cup	130	3	0.5	0	180	23	0
Rice Chex, Ralston, 1 cup	120	0	0	0	230	27	0
Rice Krispies, Kellogg's, 1¼ cups	110	0	0	0	320	26	1
Rice Krispies Treats, Kellogg's, ¾ cup	120	1.5	0	0	170	25	0
Ripple Crisp, honey bran, General Mills, 1¼ cups	190	1	0	0	410	48	5
Ripple Crisp, honey corn, General Mills, ¾ cup	110	0.5	0	0	290	26	0
Shapes 'n Honey, Breadshop's, 1 cup	110	0.5	0	0	0	24	2
Shredded wheat, Nabisco, 2 biscuits	160	0.5	0	0	0	38	1
Shredded wheat, Quaker, 3 biscuits	220	1.5	0.5	0	0	50	

CEREAL, READY-TO-EAT	CAL	FAT (g)	SAT FAT (g)	CHOL (mg)	SODIUM (mg)	CARB (g)	FIBER (g)
Shredded wheat, Spoon Size, Nabisco, 1 cup	170	0.5	0	0	0	41	5
Shredded Wheat 'N Bran, Nabisco, 1¼ cups	200	1	0	0	0	47	8
Smacks, Kellogg's, ¾ cup	110	0.5	0	0	75	26	1
S'mores Grahams, General Mills, ¾ cup	120	1.5	0	0	230	26	0
Special K, Kellogg's, 1 cup	110	0	0	0	250	21	1
Spelt flakes, Arrowhead Mills, 1 cup	100	1	0	0	60	22	3
Sprinkle Spangles, General Mills, 1 cup	120	1	0	0	130	27	0
Strawberry 'n cream, Breadshop's Nectarsweet Gourmet, ½ cup	220	8	1	0	0	32	4
Strawberry 'n cream, with organic grains, Breadshop's Organic Honey Gourmet, ½ cup	220	8	1	0	0	34	4
Strawberry Squares, Kellogg's, ¾ cup	180	1	0	0	10	44	5
Sugar frosted flakes, Malt-O-Meal, ¾ cup	110	0	0	0	200	27	0
Sugar frosted flakes, Quaker Kids Favorites, ¾ cup	110	0	0	0	250	26	1
Sun Crunchers, General Mills, 1 cup	210	3	0	0	390	44	3
Sun Flakes, Ralston, ¾ cup	110	1	0	0	210	23	1
Sweet Puffs, Quaker, 1 cup	130	0.5	0	0	80	30	1
Team flakes, Nabisco, 1¼ cups	220	0	0	0	360	49	1
Temptations, French vanilla almond, Kellogg's, ¾ cup	120	2	1	0	210	24	1
Temptations, honey roasted pecan, Kellogg's, 1 cup	120	2.5	0	0	240	24	1
Toasted Oatmeal, honey nut, Quaker, 1 cup	200	4.5	1	0	180	37	3
Toasted Oatmeal, original, Quaker, ¾ cup	120	1	0	0	210	25	2
Toasted oats, Malt-O-Meal, 1 cup	110	2	0	0	280	22	3

CEREAL, READY-TO-EAT	CAL (g)	FAT (g)	SAT FAT (g)	CHOL (mg)	SODIUM (mg)	CARB (g)	FIBER (g)
Toasted oats, apple & cinnamon, Malt-O-Meal, ¾ cup	120	1.5	0	0	190	24	2
Toasted oats, honey & nut, Malt-O-Meal, 1 cup	110	1	0	0	270	24	2
Total, corn flakes, General Mills, 1⅓ cups	110	0.5	0	0	210	25	0
Total, raisin bran, General Mills, 1 cup	180	1	0	0	240	43	5
Total, whole grain, General Mills, ¾ cup	110	1	0	0	200	24	3
Triples, General Mills, 1 cup	120	1	0	0	190	25	0
Trix, General Mills, 1 cup	120	1.5	0	0	140	26	0
Uncle Sam, U.S. Mills, 1 cup	190	5	0.5	0	135	38	10
Wheat Chex, 100% whole wheat grain, Ralston, ¾ cup	190	1	0	0	390	41	5
Wheat flakes, Erehwon, 1 cup	180	1	0	0	135	42	6
Wheat germ, Kretschmer, 2 Tbsp	50	1	0	0	0	6	2
Wheat germ, honey crunch, Kretschmer, 1⅔ Tbsp	50	1	0	0	0	8	1
Wheat puffs, frosted, Malt-O-Meal, ¾ cup	120	0	0	0	40	26	1
Wheat, rye, bran, flax, Roman Meal, ⅓ cup	90	0.5	0	0	0	15	5
Wheaties, General Mills, 1 cup	110	1	0	0	220	24	3
Wheaties, Dunk-A-Balls, General Mills, ¾ cup	110	1	0	0	160	26	2
Wheaties, Honey Gold, General Mills, ¾ cup	110	0.5	0	0	200	26	1

AT A GLANCE: READY-TO-EAT CEREAL
Highest in Fiber: Kellogg's All-Bran Extra Fiber

SNACK BARS *See also Chips, Nuts & Snacks, Snacks.,*

	CAL (g)	FAT (g)	SAT FAT (g)	CHOL (mg)	SODIUM (mg)	CARB (g)	FIBER (g)
Apple breakfast bar, fat free, Health Valley, 1 bar	110	0	0	0	25	26	3
Apple breakfast bar, fat free, Ultra Slim Fast, 1 bar	160	0	0	0	180	38	2

SNACK BARS	CAL (g)	FAT (g)	SAT FAT (g)	CHOL (mg)	SODIUM (mg)	CARB (g)	FIBER (g)
Apple-cinnamon cereal bar, SnackWell's, 1 bar	120	0	0	0	105	29	1
Apricot breakfast bar, fat free, Health Valley, 1 bar	110	0	0	0	25	26	3
Blueberry breakfast bar, fat free, Ultra Slim Fast, 1 bar	170	0	0	0	170	39	3
Blueberry cereal bar, SnackWell's, 1 bar	120	0	0	0	105	28	1
Cherry breakfast bar, fat free, Health Valley, 1 bar	110	0	0	0	25	26	3
Chocolate breakfast bar, fat free, Health Valley, 1 bar	110	0	0	0	30	26	4
Chocolate chip breakfast bar, Carnation, 1 bar	150	6	2.5	0	80	22	<1
Dutch chocolate breakfast bar, Ultra Slim Fast, 1 bar	140	5	2	<5	45	20	2
Fiber 7 Flakes with strawberry cereal bar, fat free, Health Valley, 1 bar	110	0	0	0	25	0	3
Fig breakfast bar, fat free, Ultra Slim Fast, 1 bar	160	0	0	0	270	37	3
Granola bar, all flavors, fat free, Health Valley, 1 bar	140	0	0	0	5	35	3
Granola bar, almond, chewy, Sunbelt, 1 pkg	130	7	2	0	65	17	2
Granola bar, almond & brown sugar, crunchy, low fat, Kellogg's, 1 bar	80	1.5	0	0	60	16	1
Granola bar, apple brown sugar, chewy, low fat, Nature Valley, 1 bar	110	2	0	0	70	21	1
Granola bar, apple spice, crunchy, low fat, Kellogg's, 1 bar	80	1.5	0	0	60	16	1
Granola bar, chocolate chip, Nature Valley, 2 bars	220	9	2	0	110	33	2
Granola bar, chocolate chip, chewy, Sunbelt, 1 pkg	160	7	3	0	65	23	2
Granola bar, chocolate chip, chewy, low fat, Nature Valley, 1 bar	110	2	0.5	0	85	21	1

SNACK BARS	CAL (g)	FAT (g)	SAT FAT (g)	CHOL (mg)	SODIUM (mg)	CARB (g)	FIBER (g)
Granola bar, chocolate chip, fudge dipped, Sunbelt, 1 pkg	200	10	4	0	70	27	2
Granola bar, chocolate chunk breakfast bar, Carnation, 1 bar	140	5	2	0	55	22	1
Granola bar, cinnamon, Nature Valley, 2 bars	210	8	1	0	140	33	2
Granola bar, cinnamon graham, Nature Valley, 2 bars	170	6	1	0	140	26	2
Granola bar, cinnamon raisin, crunchy, low fat, Kellogg's, 1 bar	80	1.5	0	0	60	16	1
Granola bar, fudge iced, with peanuts, chewy, Sunbelt, 1 pkg	200	9	2.5	0	90	28	2
Granola bar, honey & oats breakfast bar, Carnation, 1 bar	130	4	1.5	0	55	23	1
Granola bar, honey nut, chewy, low fat, Nature Valley, 1 bar	110	2	0	0	70	21	1
Granola bar, macaroon, fudge dipped, Sunbelt, 1 pkg	200	12	7	0	60	21	2
Granola bar, oat bran, Nature Valley, 2 bars	210	8	1	0	170	32	3
Granola bar, oatmeal raisin, chewy, low fat, Nature Valley, 1 bar	110	2	0	0	65	21	1
Granola bar, oats 'n honey, Nature Valley, 2 bars	210	8	1	0	150	32	2
Granola bar, oats and honey, chewy, Sunbelt, 1 pkg	120	5	2	0	60	19	1
Granola bar, orchard blend, chewy, low fat, Nature Valley, 1 bar	110	2	0	0	65	21	1
Granola bar, peanut butter, Nature Valley, 2 bars	220	10	1.5	0	150	30	2
Granola bar, raisins, chewy, Sunbelt, 1 pkg	150	6	2	0	65	24	2
Granola bar, triple berry, chewy, low fat, Nature Valley, 1 bar	110	2	0	0	60	22	1

SNACK BARS	CAL (g)	FAT (g)	SAT FAT (g)	CHOL (mg)	SODIUM (mg)	CARB (g)	FIBER (g)
Nutri-Grain cereal bars, all flavors, Kellogg's, 1 bar	140	3	0.5	0	60	27	1
Oat bran flakes with blueberry cereal bar, fat free, Health Valley, 1 bar	110	0	0	0	26	0	3
Peanut butter breakfast bar, Ultra Slim Fast, 1 bar	150	5	3	<5	45	19	2
Peanut butter chocolate chip breakfast bar, Carnation, 1 bar	150	5	2	0	90	21	<1
Raisin bran flakes with raisin apple cereal bar, fat free, Health Valley, 1 bar	110	0	0	0	26	0	3
Rice Krispies cereal bar, chocolate chip, Kellogg's, 1 bar	120	4	1.5	0	60	20	1
Rice Krispies Treats cereal bar, Kellogg's, 1 bar	90	2	0	0	75	18	0
Strawberry breakfast bar, fat free, Ultra Slim Fast, 1 bar	170	0	0	0	190	39	2
Strawberry cereal bar, SnackWell's, 1 bar	120	0	0	0	100	29	1
Strawberry apple breakfast bar, fat free, Health Valley, 1 bar	110	0	0	0	25	26	3
Whole grain, blueberry, lowfat, Kudos, 1 bar	90	1.5	0	0	90	15	1
Whole grain, chocolate chip, Kudos, 1 bar	120	5	2.5	5	75	18	1
Whole grain, chocolate chunk, Kudos, 1 bar	90	3	1	0	60	13	1
Whole grain, milk & cookies, Kudos, 1 bar	130	5	2.5	5	70	18	1
Whole grain, nutty fudge, Kudos, 1 bar	130	5	2.5	5	65	18	1
Whole grain, peanut butter, Kudos, 1 bar	130	5	2.5	5	85	18	1
Whole grain, strawberry, lowfat, Kudos, 1 bar	80	1.5	0	0	90	15	1

AT A GLANCE: SNACK BARS

Lowest in Fat: Health Valley Breakfast Bars; SnackWells Cereal Bars; Ultra Slim Fast Breakfast Bars (fruit flavors)

Highest in Fiber: Health Valley Chocolate Breakfast Bar, Fat Free

	CAL (g)	FAT (g)	SAT FAT (g)	CHOL (mg)	SODIUM (mg)	CARB (g)	FIBER (g)

TOASTER PASTRIES *See also Chips, Nuts & Snacks, Snacks.*

	CAL (g)	FAT (g)	SAT FAT (g)	CHOL (mg)	SODIUM (mg)	CARB (g)	FIBER (g)
Apple cinnamon, Kellogg's Pop-Tarts, 1 pastry	210	5	1	0	170	38	1
Blueberry, Kellogg's Pop-Tarts, 1 pastry	210	7	1	0	210	36	1
Blueberry, frosted, Kellogg's Pop-Tarts, 1 pastry	200	5	1	0	210	37	1
Blueberry, frosted, Nabisco Toastettes, 1 tart	190	5	1.5	0	190	35	1
Blueberry, low fat, Kellogg's Pop-Tarts, 1 pastry	190	3	0.5	0	220	40	1
Brown sugar cinnamon, Kellogg's Pop-Tarts, 1 pastry	220	9	1	0	210	32	1
Brown sugar cinnamon, frosted, Kellogg's Pop-Tarts, 1 pastry	210	7	1	0	180	34	1
Brown sugar cinnamon, frosted, Nabisco Toastettes, 1 tart	190	5	1.5	0	180	35	1
Cherry, Kellogg's Pop-Tarts, 1 pastry	200	5	1	0	220	37	1
Cherry, frosted, Kellogg's Pop-Tarts, 1 pastry	200	5	1	0	220	37	1
Cherry, frosted, Nabisco Toastettes, 1 tart	190	5	1.5	0	190	35	1
Cherry, low fat, Kellogg's Pop-Tarts, 1 pastry	190	3	0.5	0	220	40	1
Chocolate fudge, frosted, Kellogg's Pop-Tarts, 1 pastry	200	5	1	0	220	37	1
Chocolate fudge, frosted, Kellogg's Pop-Tarts Minis, 1 pouch	170	4	1	0	200	30	1
Fudge, frosted, Nabisco Toastettes, 1 tart	190	5	1.5	0	280	34	1
Grape, frosted, Kellogg's Pop-Tarts, 1 pastry	200	5	1	0	200	38	1
Grape, frosted, Kellogg's Pop-Tarts Minis, 1 pouch	170	4	1	0	180	32	0
Milk chocolate graham, Kellogg's Pop-Tarts, 1 pastry	210	6	1	0	220	36	1

TOASTER PASTRIES	CAL (g)	FAT (g)	SAT FAT (g)	CHOL (mg)	SODIUM (mg)	CARB (g)	FIBER (g)
Raspberry, frosted, Kellogg's Pop-Tarts, 1 pastry	210	6	1	0	210	37	1
S'mores, frosted, Kellogg's Pop-Tarts, 1 pastry	200	5	0.5	0	200	37	1
Strawberry, Kellogg's Pop-Tarts, 1 pastry	200	5	1.5	0	180	37	1
Strawberry, Nabisco Toastettes, 1 tart	190	5	1.5	0	200	35	1
Strawberry, frosted, Kellogg's Pop-Tarts, 1 pastry	200	5	1.5	0	170	38	1
Strawberry, frosted, Kellogg's Pop-Tarts Minis, 1 pouch	170	4	1	0	180	32	0
Strawberry, frosted, Nabisco Toastettes, 1 tart	190	5	1.5	0	190	35	1
Vanilla creme, frosted, Kellogg's Pop-Tarts, 1 pastry	200	5	1	0	230	37	1

AT A GLANCE: TOASTER PASTRIES
Lowest in Fat: Kellogg's Low Fat Pop-Tarts

CHIPS, NUTS & SNACKS

	CAL (g)	FAT (g)	SAT FAT (g)	CHOL (mg)	SODIUM (mg)	CARB (g)	FIBER (g)
CHIPS							
Apple chips, Weight Watchers Smart Snackers, 0.75 oz	70	0	0	0	125	18	3
Bagel chips, onion multigrain, Pepperidge Farm, 1 oz	120	4	0	0	200	19	1
Bagel chips, three cheese, Pepperidge Farm, 1 oz	140	7	1	5	240	16	<1
Bagel chips, toasted onion & garlic, Pepperidge Farm, 1 oz	110	5	1	0	280	18	2
Corn chips, Old Dutch, ¾ cup	170	10	1.5	0	180	16	2
Corn chips, Planters, 34 chips	170	10	1.5	0	180	17	2
Corn chips, barbecue, Fritos, 1 oz	150	9	1.5	0	310	16	1
Corn chips, barbecue, Old Dutch, ¾ cup	165	10	1.5	0	200	16	2
Corn chips, king size, Planters, 17 chips	160	10	1.5	0	180	16	2
Corn chips, original, Fritos, 1 oz	160	10	1.5	0	160	15	1
Corn chips, snack size bag, Fritos, 1 bag	120	8	1	0	125	11	1
Multi-grain, cheddar cheese, Old Dutch Golden Multi-Crisps, 18 chips	130	4.5	1	0	180	20	1
Pizza chips, cheese, Keebler Pizzarias, 14 chips	150	7	1.5	<5	210	19	1
Pizza chips, pizza supreme, Keebler Pizzarias, 14 chips	150	7	1.5	0	200	19	1
Pizza chips, zesty pepperoni, Keebler Pizzarias, 14 chips	150	7	1.5	<5	210	20	<1
Pop Chips, butter, Pop-Secret, 31 chips (1 oz)	120	3	0.5	0	380	21	1
Pop Chips, cheddar cheese, Pop-Secret, 31 chips (1 oz)	120	3	0.5	0	430	21	1
Pop Chips, original, Pop-Secret, 31 chips (1 oz)	120	3	0.5	0	380	21	1

CHIPS	CAL (g)	FAT (g)	SAT FAT (g)	CHOL (mg)	SODIUM (mg)	CARB (g)	FIBER (g)
Pop Chips, sour cream & onion, Pop-Secret, 31 chips (1 oz)	120	3.5	0.5	0	430	21	1
Potato chips, Cape Cod, 19 chips (1 oz)	150	8	2	0	110	17	1
Potato chips, Keebler O'Boisies, 16 chips	150	9	2	0	180	15	1
Potato chips, Keebler Ripplin's, 13 chips	160	11	2	0	210	15	1
Potato chips, Old Dutch, 12–15 chips	150	9	1	0	160	16	1
Potato chips, baked, Lay's, 1 oz	110	1.5	0	0	230	23	2
Potato chips, baked potato flavor, Keebler Tato Skins, 18 chips	150	8	1.5	0	150	17	0
Potato chips, barbecue, Jays, 1 oz	160	10	1.5	0	300	15	1
Potato chips, barbecue, Keebler Ripplin's, 12 chips	150	9	2	0	240	16	1
Potato chips, barbecue, Old Dutch, 12–15 chips	150	9	1	0	300	15	1
Potato chips, barbecue, baked, Lay's, 1 oz	110	1.5	0	0	260	23	2
Potato chips, cheddar, Keebler O'Boisies, 16 chips	150	10	2	0	135	15	1
Potato chips, cheddar & sour cream, Old Dutch, 12-15 chips	160	9	1.5	0	190	16	1
Potato chips, cheddar & sour cream, Ruffles, 1 oz	160	10	2.5	0	230	15	1
Potato chips, cheddar & sour cream, ripples, crispy cooked, Eagle, 16 chips (1 oz)	160	11	1	0	200	14	2
Potato chips, cheese 'n bacon, Keebler Tato Skins, 18 chips	150	9	1.5	0	170	17	1
Potato chips, Crazy Calypso, Jays, 1 oz	160	10	3	0	130	15	1
Potato chips, dill, Old Dutch, 12–15 chips	140	8	1	<5	330	16	1
Potato chips, fat free, Louise's, 30 chips	110	0	0	0	180	23	2

CHIPS	CAL (g)	FAT (g)	SAT FAT (g)	CHOL (mg)	SODIUM (mg)	CARB (g)	FIBER (g)
Potato chips, Hawaiian kettle, extra crunchy, Eagle, 19 chips (1 oz)	150	8	2	0	150	17	1
Potato chips, hickory BBQ, Frito Lay's, 1 oz	150	10	2	0	220	15	1
Potato chips, HotStuff, Jays, 1 oz	160	10	1.5	0	270	15	<1
Potato chips, Idaho russet, dark and crunchy, Eagle, 22 chips (1 oz)	140	7	1.5	0	150	17	1
Potato chips, jalapeno, Kruncher's, 1 oz	140	8	1.5	0	210	16	1
Potato chips, jalapeno & cheddar, kettle style, Old Dutch, 15–20 chips	130	6	1.5	0	190	17	1
Potato chips, jalapeno jack, Kettle Chips, 1 oz	150	9	1	0	110	15	na
Potato chips, kettle style, Old Dutch, 15–20 chips	130	6	1	0	140	18	2
Potato chips, lightly salted, Kettle Chips, 1 oz	150	9	1	0	80	15	na
Potato chips, Louisiana spicy hot, crispy cooked, Eagle, 18 chips (1 oz)	150	8	2	0	160	17	1
Potato chips, mesquite barbecue, Kruncher's, 1 oz	140	8	1.5	0	200	16	1
Potato chips, mesquite barbecue, kettle style, Old Dutch, 15–20 chips	130	6	1	0	230	19	2
Potato chips, mesquite barbecue, thins or ripples, Eagle, 19 chips (1 oz)	160	10	2	0	170	15	1
Potato chips, mesquite grille BBQ, Ruffles, 1 oz	150	9	3	0	120	15	1
Potato chips, New York cheddar, Kettle Chips, 1 oz	150	9	1	0	100	15	na
Potato chips, no salt, Kettle Chips, 1 oz	150	9	1	0	10	15	na
Potato chips, no salt added, Jays, 1 oz	150	10	1.5	0	0	14	1
Potato chips, onion & garlic, Old Dutch, 12–15 chips	140	8	1	<5	420	16	1

CHIPS	CAL	FAT (g)	SAT FAT (g)	CHOL (mg)	SODIUM (mg)	CARB (g)	FIBER (g)
Potato chips, organically grown, with sea salt, Kettle Chips, 1 oz	150	9	1	0	80	15	na
Potato chips, original, Ruffles, 1 oz	160	10	3	0	180	14	1
Potato chips, original or crispy ridged, Jays, 1 oz	150	10	1.5	0	190	14	1
Potato chips, ranch, Keebler Ripplin's, 12 chips	150	9	2	0	240	16	1
Potato chips, reduced fat, Ruffles, 1 oz	140	5	1	0	130	18	1
Potato chips, ripple style, Old Dutch, 12–15 chips	150	9	1	0	150	16	1
Potato chips, ripples, Eagle, 17 chips (1 oz)	150	10	2.5	0	170	14	<1
Potato chips, salsa with mesquite, Kettle Chips, 1 oz	150	9	1	0	120	15	na
Potato chips, salt & vinegar, Lay's, 1 oz	150	10	2.5	0	340	15	1
Potato chips, salt & vinegar, kettle style, Old Dutch, 15–20 chips	130	6	1	0	360	18	1
Potato chips, sea salt & vinegar, Cape Cod, 18 chips (1 oz)	150	8	2	0	130	17	1
Potato chips, sea salt & vinegar, Kettle Chips, 1 oz	150	9	1	0	120	15	na
Potato chips, sea salt & vinegar, ripples, crispy cooked, Eagle, 16 chips (1 oz)	150	8	2	0	135	17	1
Potato chips, sour cream & onion, Frito Lay's, 1 oz	150	9	2.5	0	180	15	1
Potato chips, sour cream & onion, Keebler O'Boisies, 15 chips	150	9	2	0	190	15	1
Potato chips, sour cream & onion, Old Dutch, 12–15 chips	150	9	1	<5	220	17	1
Potato chips, sour cream & onion, thins or ripples, Eagle, 9 chips (1 oz)	160	10	2	<5	180	14	1
Potato chips, sour cream 'n onion, Jays, 1 oz	150	10	2	0	200	14	1

CHIPS	CAL (g)	FAT (g)	SAT FAT (g)	CHOL (mg)	SODIUM (mg)	CARB (g)	FIBER (g)
Potato chips, sour cream 'n onion, Keebler Tato Skins, 18 chips	150	10	1.5	0	160	16	1
Potato chips, spicy fiesta, thins, Eagle, 19 chips (1 oz)	160	9	2.5	0	220	15	1
Potato chips, thins, Eagle, 20 chips (1 oz)	150	10	2.5	0	180	14	<1
Potato chips, thins, crispy cooked, Eagle, 19 chips (1 oz)	150	8	2	0	110	15	1
Potato chips, yogurt & green onion, Kettle Chips, 1 oz	150	9	1	0	120	15	na
Potato skins, cheese & bacon, snack size bag, Keebler Tato Wilds, 1 bag	190	12	2	0	220	21	1
Potato skins, criss cross, snack size bag, Keebler Tato Wilds, 1 bag	150	9	2	0	170	16	<1
Potato skins, sour cream n' onion, snack size bag, Keebler Tato Wilds, 1 bag	190	12	2	0	190	20	1
Taro chips, 1 oz	140	7	2	0	100	19	2
Tortilla chips, Doritos Cooler Ranch!, 12 chips (1 oz)	140	7	1	0	170	18	1
Tortilla chips, Doritos Nacho Cheesier!, 11 chips (1 oz)	140	7	1	0	200	17	1
Tortilla chips, Doritos Thins, 9 chips (1 oz)	140	7	1	0	135	18	1
Tortilla chips, Doritos Zesty Salsal, 11 chips (1 oz)	140	7	1.5	0	180	17	1
Tortilla chips, Old Dutch Tostados, 11 chips	150	7	1	0	200	19	1
Tortilla chips, Old El Paso, 9 chips	140	8	1	0	60	16	1
Tortilla chips, baked, Tostitos, 1 oz	110	1	0	0	140	24	2
Tortilla chips, blue corn, lightly salted, Kettle Tias, 1 oz	140	6	0.5	0	80	18	2
Tortilla chips, cheesy quesadilla, Keebler Chacho's, 14 chips	150	8	1.5	<5	270	18	<1

CHIPS	CAL (g)	FAT (g)	SAT FAT (g)	CHOL (mg)	SODIUM (mg)	CARB (g)	FIBER (g)
Tortilla chips, cinnamon Crispana, Keebler Chacho's, 13 chips	150	7	1	0	75	20	<1
Tortilla chips, cool ranch, baked, Tostitos, 1 oz	120	3	0.5	0	170	21	1
Tortilla chips, deli style, Jays, 1 oz	150	8	1.5	0	60	18	1
Tortilla chips, El Grande restaurant style rounds, Eagle, 9 chips (1 oz)	140	6	1	0	70	19	1
Tortilla chips, five-grain, lightly salted, Kettle Tias, 1 oz	140	6	0.5	0	80	18	2
Tortilla chips, nacho or ranch, thins, Eagle, 12 chips (1 oz)	150	7	1	0	170	18	1
Tortilla chips, nacho cheese, Jays, 1 oz	150	8	1.5	0	200	18	1
Tortilla chips, nacho cheese, Old Dutch, 17 chips	155	8	1.5	0	250	19	1
Tortilla chips, restaurant style, Old Dutch, 7 chips	140	6	1.5	0	125	18	1
Tortilla chips, restaurant style, original, Keebler Chacho's, 15 chips	150	8	1	0	210	18	<1
Tortilla chips, restaurant style rounds, Eagle, 11 chips (1 oz)	140	6	0.5	0	80	19	1
Tortilla chips, restaurant style strips, salt free, baked in canola oil, Eagle, 14 chips (1 oz)	140	6	0.5	0	0	19	1
Tortilla chips, restaurant style yellow, Eagle, 13 chips (1 oz)	140	7	1	0	80	18	1
Tortilla chips, rounds and strips, baked in canola oil, restaurant style, Eagle, 1 oz	140	6	0.5	0	80	19	1
Tortilla chips, unsalted, baked, Tostitos, 1 oz	110	1	0	0	10	24	2
Tortilla chips, white corn, Old El Paso, 11 chips	150	8	1.5	0	85	17	2
Tortilla chips, white corn, lightly salted, Kettle Tias, 1 oz	140	6	0.5	0	80	18	2
Tortilla chips, white corn, bite size, Tostitos, 1 oz	140	8	1	0	110	17	1

CHIPS	CAL (g)	FAT (g)	SAT FAT (g)	CHOL (mg)	SODIUM (mg)	CARB (g)	FIBER (g)
Tortilla chips, white corn, rounds or restaurant style, Jays, 1 oz	150	8	1.5	0	80	18	1
Tortilla chips, yellow corn, lime & chili, Kettle Tias, 1 oz	140	6	0.5	0	210	18	2
Tortilla chips, yellow corn, tomato & basil, Kettle Tias, 1 oz	140	6	0.5	0	150	18	2
Tortilla crisps, chili cheese, Pepperidge Farm, 36 pieces	130	7	1	<5	340	18	2
Tortilla crisps, nacho, Nabisco Mr. Phipps, 28 crisps	130	4	0	0	150	20	3
Tortilla crisps, original, Nabisco Mr. Phipps, 28 crisps	130	4	0.5	0	130	21	3
Tortilla crisps, original, Pepperidge Farm, 36 pieces	130	6	1	<5	290	18	2
Tortilla crisps, salsa, Pepperidge Farm, 36 pieces	130	7	1	<5	350	18	3
Zings, Nabisco, 1 bag	240	11	2	0	420	34	2

AT A GLANCE: CHIPS
Lowest in Fat: Louise's Fat Free Potato Chips; Tostitos Baked Tortilla Chips; Weight Watcher's Apple Chips

NUTS & SEEDS

	CAL (g)	FAT (g)	SAT FAT (g)	CHOL (mg)	SODIUM (mg)	CARB (g)	FIBER (g)
Acorns, dried, 1 oz	140	9	1.5	0	0	15	na
Acorns, raw, 1 oz	100	7	1	0	0	12	na
Almonds, Planters, 1 oz	170	15	1	0	0	5	3
Almonds, dried, Dole, 1 oz	170	14	na	ns	4	5	na
Almonds, dried, Timber Crest Farms, ¼ cup	180	15	0	0	0	6	4
Almonds, dried, blanched, 1 oz	170	15	1.5	0	0	5	2
Almonds, dried, unblanched, 1 oz	170	15	1.5	0	0	6	3
Almonds, dry roasted, unblanched, salted, 1 oz	170	15	1.5	0	220	7	4
Almonds, dry roasted, unblanched, unsalted, 1 oz	170	15	1.5	0	0	7	4
Almonds, honey roasted, Planters, 1 oz	160	14	1	0	190	7	2

NUTS & SEEDS	CAL (g)	FAT (g)	SAT FAT (g)	CHOL (mg)	SODIUM (mg)	CARB (g)	FIBER (g)
Almonds, oil roasted, blanched, salted, 1 oz	170	16	1.5	0	220	5	3
Almonds, oil roasted, blanched, unsalted, 1 oz	170	16	1.5	0	0	5	3
Almonds, oil roasted, unblanched, salted, 1 oz	180	16	1.5	0	220	5	3
Almonds, oil roasted, unblanched, unsalted, 1 oz	180	16	1.5	0	0	5	3
Beechnuts, dried, 1 oz	160	14	1.5	0	10	10	na
Black walnuts, Planters, 1 pkg	340	31	2	0	0	8	3
Black walnuts, dried, 1 oz	170	16	1	0	0	3	1
Brazilnuts, dried, unblanched, oz	190	19	4.5	0	0	4	2
Breadfruit seeds, raw, 1 oz	50	1.5	0	0	10	8	na
Breadfruit seeds, roasted, oz	60	1	0	0	10	11	na
Breadnut tree seeds, dried, oz	100	0	0	0	15	23	4
Breadnut tree seeds, raw, oz	60	0	0	0	10	13	na
Butternuts, dried, 1 oz	170	16	0	0	0	3	1
Cashews, dry roasted, salted, oz	160	13	2.5	0	180	9	<1
Cashews, dry roasted, unsalted, 1 oz	160	13	2.5	0	0	9	<1
Cashews, fancy, oil roasted, Planters, 1 oz	170	14	3	0	120	8	1
Cashews, halves, oil roasted, Planters, 1 oz	170	14	2.5	0	120	8	2
Cashews, halves, oil roasted, lightly salted, Planters, 1 oz	160	13	2.5	0	55	9	2
Cashews, honey roast, Eagle, 3 nuts (1 oz)	180	14	3	0	130	9	1
Cashews, honey roasted, Planters, 1 oz	150	12	2	0	120	11	1
Cashews, lightly salted, Eagle, nuts (1 oz)	190	14	3	0	65	8	1
Cashews, oil roasted, Planters, 1 oz	160	14	3	0	120	8	1

NUTS & SEEDS	CAL	FAT (g)	SAT FAT (g)	CHOL (mg)	SODIUM (mg)	CARB (g)	FIBER (g)
Cashews, oil roasted, salted, Kettle Snacks, 1 oz	160	14	2.5	0	180	8	1
Cashews, oil roasted, unsalted, Kettle Snacks, 1 oz	160	14	2.5	0	0	8	1
Cashews, with almonds and macadamias, oil roasted, Planters, 1 oz	170	16	2.5	0	90	6	2
Cashews, with almonds and pecans, oil roasted, Planters, 1 oz	170	15	2	0	95	7	2
Cashews and peanuts, honey roasted, Planters, 1 oz	150	12	2	0	125	10	2
Chestnuts, Chinese, boiled or steamed, 1 oz	45	0	0	0	0	10	na
Chestnuts, Chinese, dried, 1 oz	100	0.5	0	0	0	23	na
Chestnuts, Chinese, roasted, 1 oz	70	0	0	0	0	15	na
Chestnuts, European, boiled or steamed, 1 oz	40	0	0	0	10	8	na
Chestnuts, European, dried, 1 oz	100	1	0	0	10	22	na
Chestnuts, European, roasted, 1 oz	70	0.5	0	0	0	15	4
Chestnuts, Japanese, boiled or steamed, 1 oz	15	0	0	0	0	4	n
Chestnuts, Japanese, dried, 1 oz	100	0	0	0	10	23	na
Chestnuts, Japanese, roasted, 1 oz	60	0	0	0	5	13	n
Chia seeds, dried, 1 oz	130	7	3	0	10	14	n
Cottonseed kernels, roasted, 1 oz	140	10	3	0	10	6	
Fruit 'n nut mix, Planters, 1 oz	140	9	2	0	105	13	
Ginkgo nuts, canned, 1 oz	35	0	0	0	90	6	
Ginkgo nuts, dried, 1 oz	100	0.5	0	0	0	21	n
Ginkgo nuts, raw, 1 oz	50	0	0	0	0	11	n
Hazelnuts, dried, blanched, 1 oz	190	19	1.5	0	0	5	n

NUTS & SEEDS	CAL	FAT (g)	SAT FAT (g)	CHOL (mg)	SODIUM (mg)	CARB (g)	FIBER (g)
Hazelnuts, dried, unblanched, 1 oz	180	18	1.5	0	0	4	2
Hazelnuts, dry roasted, unblanched, salted, 1 oz	190	19	1.5	0	220	5	na
Hazelnuts, dry roasted, unblanched, unsalted, 1 oz	190	19	1.5	0	0	5	na
Hazelnuts, oil roasted, unblanched, salted, 1 oz	190	18	1.5	0	220	5	2
Hazelnuts, oil roasted, unblanched, unsalted, 1 oz	190	18	1.5	0	0	5	2
Hickory nuts, dried, 1 oz	190	18	2	0	0	5	2
Macadamia nuts, dried, 1 oz	200	21	3	0	0	4	3
Macadamia nuts, oil roasted, salted, 1 oz	200	22	3.5	0	75	4	3
Macadamia nuts, oil roasted, unsalted, 1 oz	200	22	3.5	0	0	4	na
Mixed nuts, Eagle, ¼ cup	200	17	3	0	140	6	2
Mixed nuts, deluxe, oil roasted, Planters, 1 oz	170	16	2	0	110	6	2
Mixed nuts, dry roasted, Planters, 1 oz	170	14	2	0	250	7	2
Mixed nuts, honey roasted, Planters, 1 oz	140	13	2	0	80	9	2
Mixed nuts, lightly salted, Eagle, ¼ cup	200	17	3	0	65	6	2
Mixed nuts, no Brazils, oil roasted, Planters, 1 oz	170	15	2	0	110	6	2
Mixed nuts, no Brazils, oil roasted, lightly salted, Planters, 1 oz	170	15	2	0	55	6	2
Mixed nuts, oil roasted, Planters, 1 oz	170	15	2.5	0	115	5	2
Mixed nuts, oil roasted, lightly salted, Planters, 1 oz	170	15	2	0	55	6	2
Mixed nuts, oil roasted, unsalted, Planters, 1 oz	170	15	2	0	0	6	3
Mixed nuts, without peanuts, Eagle, ¼ cup	200	17	3	0	110	6	2
Nut topping, Planters, 2 Tbsp	100	9	1	0	0	3	1

NUTS & SEEDS	CAL	FAT (g)	SAT FAT (g)	CHOL (mg)	SODIUM (mg)	CARB (g)	FIBER (g)
Peanuts, Planters Sweet 'N Crunchy, 1 oz	140	7	1	0	20	16	2
Peanuts, ballpark, Eagle, 28 nuts (1 oz)	180	15	3	0	110	5	1
Peanuts, cocktail, oil roasted, Planters, 1 oz	170	14	2	0	115	6	3
Peanuts, cocktail, oil roasted, lightly salted, Planters, 1 oz	170	15	2	0	55	5	2
Peanuts, cocktail, oil roasted, unsalted, Planters, 1 oz	160	14	2	0	0	6	2
Peanuts, dry roasted, Planters, 1 oz	160	13	2	0	250	6	3
Peanuts, dry roasted, lightly salted, Planters, 1 oz	160	14	2	0	110	5	3
Peanuts, dry roasted, unsalted, Planters, 1 oz	160	14	2	0	0	6	3
Peanuts, honey roast, Eagle, 35 nuts (1 oz)	170	13	3	0	130	7	2
Peanuts, honey roasted, Planters, 1 oz	160	13	1.5	0	90	8	2
Peanuts, honey roasted, Weight Watchers Smart Snackers, 0.70 oz	100	5	1	0	100	7	2
Peanuts, hot spicy, oil roasted, Planters Heat, 1 oz	160	14	2	0	190	5	9
Peanuts, lightly salted, Eagle, 29 nuts (1 oz)	180	15	3	0	65	5	2
Peanuts, mild spicy, oil roasted, Planters Heat, 1 oz	160	14	2	0	130	5	2
Peanuts, oil roasted, Planters, 1 oz	170	14	2	0	115	6	3
Peanuts, oil roasted, salted, Planters, 1 oz	170	15	2	0	110	5	2
Peanuts, roasted, Eagle, 28 nuts (1 oz)	180	15	2	0	135	5	2
Peanuts, Spanish, oil roasted, Planters, 1 oz	170	14	2.5	0	105	5	2
Peanuts, Spanish, oil roasted, no salt, Kettle Snacks, 1 oz	160	14	2	0	0	5	2
Peanuts, Spanish, oil roasted, salted, Kettle Snacks, 1 oz	160	14	2	0	125	5	2

NUTS & SEEDS	CAL (g)	FAT (g)	SAT FAT (g)	CHOL (mg)	SODIUM (mg)	CARB (g)	FIBER (g)
Peanuts, Spanish, raw, Kettle Snacks, 1 oz	160	14	2	0	5	4	3
Peanuts, Spanish, raw, Planters, 1 oz	150	13	3	0	5	6	3
Peanuts, Valencia, oil-roasted, salted, 1 oz	170	15	2.5	0	220	5	na
Peanuts, Valencia, oil-roasted, unsalted, 1 oz	160	14	2.5	0	0	5	na
Peanuts, Valencia, raw, 1 oz	160	14	2	0	0	6	na
Peanuts, Virginia, oil roasted, no salt, Kettle Snacks, 1 oz	160	14	2	0	0	6	3
Peanuts, Virginia, oil roasted, salted, Kettle Snacks, 1 oz	160	14	2	0	125	6	3
Peanuts & cashews, honey roast, Eagle, ¼ cup	180	14	3	0	130	8	2
Pecans, dried, 1 oz	190	19	1.5	0	0	5	2
Pecans, dry roasted, salted, 1 oz	190	18	1.5	0	220	6	2
Pecans, halves and pieces, Planters, 1 oz	190	20	1.5	0	0	4	2
Pecans, honey roasted, Planters, 1 oz	180	16	1.5	0	75	9	2
Pecans, oil roasted, salted, 1 oz	190	20	1.5	0	210	5	2
Pecans, oil roasted, unsalted, 1 oz	190	20	1.5	0	0	5	na
Pignoli, Progresso, 1 oz jar	170	13	1	0	0	2	0
Pilinuts-canarytree, dried, 1 oz	200	23	9	0	0	1	na
Pine nuts (pignolia), dried, 1 oz	150	14	2.5	0	0	4	1
Pinon, dried, 1 oz	160	17	3	0	20	5	3
Pistachios, Dole, 1 oz in shell	90	7	na	ns	250	3	na
Pistachios, Dole, 1 oz shelled	160	14	na	ns	na	7	na
Pistachios, no shell, dry roasted, Planters, 1 oz	160	14	2	0	220	7	3
Pistachios, red, dry roasted, salted, Planters, 1 oz	160	14	2	0	250	7	3
Pistachios, uncolored, dry roasted, Planters, 1 oz	160	14	2	0	180	7	3

NUTS & SEEDS	CAL (g)	FAT (g)	SAT FAT (g)	CHOL (mg)	SODIUM (mg)	CARB (g)	FIBER (g)
Pumpkin and squash seeds, whole, roasted, salted, 1 oz	130	6	1	0	160	15	na
Pumpkin and squash seeds, whole, roasted, unsalted, 1 oz	130	6	1	0	5	15	na
Pumpkin and squash kernels, dried, 1 oz	150	13	2.5	0	5	5	4
Pumpkin and squash kernels, roasted, salted, 1 oz	150	12	2.5	0	160	4	2
Pumpkin and squash kernels, roasted, unsalted, 1 oz	150	12	2.5	0	5	4	na
Sesame nut mix, oil roasted, Planters, 1 oz	150	12	2	0	240	9	2
Soybean kernels, roasted and toasted, salted, 1 oz	130	7	1	0	45	9	na
Soybean kernels, roasted and toasted, unsalted, 1 oz	130	7	1	0	0	9	1
Soybean seeds, dry roasted, ½ cup	390	19	3	0	0	28	7
Soybean seeds, raw, 1 cup	770	37	5	0	0	56	17
Soybean seeds, roasted, ½ cup	410	22	3.5	0	140	29	na
Sunflower kernels, BBQ, oil roasted, Planters, 3 Tbsp	150	13	1.5	0	100	6	3
Sunflower kernels, dried, 1 oz	160	14	1.5	0	0	5	3
Sunflower kernels, honey roasted, Planters, 1 pkg	280	22	2.5	0	105	15	6
Sunflower kernels, oil roasted, lightly salted, Planters, ¼ cup	200	17	2	0	180	6	4
Sunflower kernels, salted, Planters, 1 oz	170	14	1.5	0	140	5	4
Sunflower nuts, dry roasted, Planters, ¼ cup	190	17	1.5	0	230	6	
Sunflower seeds, dry roasted, Planters, ¾ cup with shell	160	15	1.5	0	90	5	
Sunflower seeds, dry roasted, no salt, Kettle Snacks, 1 oz	170	14	1.5	0	0	7	
Sunflower seeds, dry roasted, salted, Kettle Snacks, 1 oz	170	14	1.5	0	65	7	

NUTS & SEEDS	CAL (g)	FAT (g)	SAT FAT (g)	CHOL (mg)	SODIUM (mg)	CARB (g)	FIBER (g)
Sunflower seeds, hulled, Arrowhead Mills, ¼ cup	180	15	1.5	0	10	6	2
Walnuts, halves, Planters, ⅓ cup	220	22	2.5	0	0	5	1
Walnuts, pieces, Planters, ¼ cup	190	20	2	0	0	4	1
Watermelon seed kernels, dried, 1 oz	160	13	3	0	30	4	na

AT A GLANCE: NUTS & SEEDS
Lowest in Fat, Nuts: Chestnuts; Ginkgo Nuts
Lowest in Fat, Seeds: Breadnut Tree Seeds

SNACKS

	CAL (g)	FAT (g)	SAT FAT (g)	CHOL (mg)	SODIUM (mg)	CARB (g)	FIBER (g)
Bugles, nacho, 1⅓ cup	160	9	7	0	300	18	<1
Bugles, original, 1⅓ cup	160	9	8	0	310	18	<1
Bugles, ranch, 1⅓ cup	160	9	8	0	310	18	<1
Bugles, sour cream & onion, 1⅓ cup	160	9	8	0	260	18	0
Crisp Baked Bugles, 1½ cup	130	2.5	0.5	0	380	24	<1
Crisp Baked Bugles, BBQ, 1½ cup	130	2.5	0.5	0	390	24	<1
Crisp Baked Bugles, cheddar cheese, 1½ cup	130	3	0.5	0	430	22	0
Cheese and pretzels, MooTown Snackers, 1 pkg	90	3	2	10	320	12	0
Cheese and sticks, all varieties, MooTown Snackers, 1 pkg	100	4	2.5	10	260	13	0
Cheese balls, Eagle Cheegles, 1 cup	160	10	2	0	260	15	0
Cheese balls, reduced fat, Eagle Cheegles, 1 cup	150	6	1.5	0	200	18	0
Cheese crunch, Eagle Cheegles, 1 cup	160	10	2	0	240	15	0
Cheese curls, Ultra Slim Fast, 1 oz	120	3	0.5	0	190	22	2
Cheese puff snack, Pacific Grain No Fries, 1 oz	120	2	0	0	190	23	1
Cheese puffs, all varieties, fat free, Health Valley, 1½ cups	110	0	0	0	260	23	2

SNACKS	CAL (g)	FAT (g)	SAT FAT (g)	CHOL (mg)	SODIUM (mg)	CARB (g)	FIBER (g)
Cheese snack, Old Dutch Crunchy Curls, 1⅓ cups	130	6	1	0	230	19	0
Cheez Balls, Planters, 1 oz	150	10	2	<5	300	15	1
Cheez Curls, Planters, 1 oz	150	10	2	<5	310	15	1
Cheez'n breadsticks, Handi-Snacks, 1 pkg	130	7	4	15	340	11	0
Combos, cheddar cheese cracker, 1 oz	140	8	2	5	300	16	0
Combos, cheddar cheese pretzel, 1 oz	130	5	1	0	310	18	0
Combos, chili cheese with corn shell, 1 oz	140	6	1	0	420	17	1
Combos, mustard pretzel, 1 oz	130	4	0.5	0	270	19	1
Combos, nacho cheese pretzel, 1 oz	130	5	0.5	0	320	19	1
Combos, nacho cheese with tortilla shell, 1 oz	140	6	1	0	380	17	1
Combos, peanut butter cracker, 1 oz	140	8	1.5	0	260	15	1
Combos, pepperoni & cheese pizza, 1 oz	140	7	1	5	280	17	0
Combos, pizzeria pretzel, 1 oz	130	4	0.5	0	290	19	1
Combos, tortilla ranch flavor, 1 oz	140	7	1.5	5	350	17	1
Cornnuts, barbecue, 1 oz	120	4	1	0	280	20	2
Cornnuts, nacho, 1 oz	120	4	1	0	180	20	2
Cornnuts, plain, 1 oz	120	4	1	0	160	21	2
Curls, barbecue flavored, Weight Watchers Smart Snackers, ½ oz	60	1.5	0	0	110	11	1
Curls, cheese, Weight Watchers Smart Snackers, ½ oz	70	2.5	1	0	65	10	0
Curls, pizza flavored, Weight Watchers Smart Snackers, ½ oz	60	2	0	0	125	11	1
Curls, ranch flavored, Weight Watchers Smart Snackers, ½ oz	60	2	0	0	170	10	1

SNACKS	CAL (g)	FAT (g)	SAT FAT (g)	CHOL (mg)	SODIUM (mg)	CARB (g)	FIBER (g)
Fruit roll, all varieties, Fruit Roll-Ups, 2 rolls	110	1	0.5	0	105	24	0
Fruit roll, all varieties, Fruit by the Foot, 1 roll	80	1.5	0.5	0	40	17	<1
Fruit roll, apple, Sunkist, 1 roll	70	0	0	0	20	17	1
Fruit roll, apricot, Sunkist, 1 roll	70	0	0	0	15	17	2
Fruit roll, cherry, Sunkist, 1 roll	70	0	0	0	16	17	2
Fruit roll, fruit punch, Sunkist, 1 roll	70	0	0	0	25	17	2
Fruit roll, grape, Sunkist, 1 roll	80	0	0	0	0	17	2
Fruit roll, raspberry, Sunkist, 1 roll	70	0	0	0	20	17	1
Fruit roll, strawberry, Sunkist, 1 roll	70	0	0	0	20	17	2
Fruit snack, Bugs Bunny & Friends, 1 pouch	90	1	0	0	25	21	0
Fruit snack, Sunbelt Fruit Jammers, 1 pkg	100	1	0.5	0	20	23	0
Fruit snack, all flavors, String Thing, 1 pouch	80	1	0	0	40	17	0
Fruit snack, all flavors, Weight Watchers Smart Snackers, ½ oz	50	0	0	0	125	13	2
Fruit snack, cherry, Gushers, 1 pouch	90	1.5	0.5	0	40	20	0
Fruit snack, Flintstone, Ferrara Pan, 1 pouch	100	0	0	ns	15	22	ns
Fruit snack, Fruitomic Punch, Gushers, 1 pouch	90	1.5	0.5	0	45	20	0
Fruit snack, grape, Gushers, 1 pouch	90	1.5	0.5	0	40	20	0
Fruit snack, Samurai, Ferrara Pan, 1 pouch	100	0	0	ns	25	22	ns
Fruit snack, sour berry, Gushers, 1 pouch	90	1.5	0.5	0	50	20	0
Fruit snack, strawberry, Gushers, 1 pouch	90	1.5	0.5	0	40	20	0

SNACKS	CAL (g)	FAT (g)	SAT FAT (g)	CHOL (mg)	SODIUM (mg)	CARB (g)	FIBER (g)
Fruit snack, Yogi, Ferrara Pan, 1 pouch	100	0	0	ns	15	22	ns
Granola snack, apple cinnamon, low fat, Betty Crocker Granola Bites, 1 pouch	120	2	0	0	110	24	1
Granola snack, chocolate chip, low fat, Betty Crocker Granola Bites, 1 pouch	120	2	0.5	0	110	24	1
Granola snack, oats & honey, low fat, Betty Crocker Granola Bites, 1 pouch	120	2	0	0	110	24	1
Ice cream cone, chocolate, Nabisco Oreo, 1 cone	50	1	0	0	110	10	<1
Ice cream cone, cinnamon, Nabisco Teddy Grahams, 1 cone	80	3	0.5	0	140	13	1
Ice cream cone, cup, Comet, 1 cone cup	20	0	0	0	20	4	0
Ice cream cone, sugar, Comet, 1 cone	50	0	0	0	40	11	<1
Ice cream cone, waffle, Comet, 1 cone	70	0.5	0	0	30	14	1
Meat snack, beef, dried, Hormel Pillow Pack, 10 slices	45	1	0.5	20	810	1	0
Meat snack, beef, dried, sliced, Hormel, 10 slices	50	1.5	0.5	25	1240	1	0
Meat snack, beef jerky, Tombstone, 1 stick	35	0	0	15	310	<1	
Meat snack, beef pepperoni sausage stick, Eagle, 1.25 oz	150	11	5	25	740	3	
Meat snack, beef stick, Eagle, 1 stick	110	9	5	20	490	1	
Meat snack, beef stick, Tombstone, 1 stick	110	10	4.5	20	270	0	
Meat snack, beef stick, smoked, Slim Jim Giant Jerk, 1 package	70	4	2	10	360	2	
Meat snack, beefsteak, kippered, Eagle, 1 strip	50	0.5	0.5	20	560	1	
Meat snack, beefsteak, kippered, hot, Eagle, 1 strip	50	0.5	0.5	20	560	2	

SNACKS	CAL (g)	FAT (g)	SAT FAT (g)	CHOL (mg)	SODIUM (mg)	CARB (g)	FIBER (g)
Meat snack, Snappy sticks, Tombstone, 1 stick	110	10	4.5	20	260	<1	0
Meat snack, turkey steak, kippered, Eagle, 1 strip	60	1.5	0.5	20	580	2	0
PB Crisps, graham, Mr. Peanut, 1 oz	140	7	1.5	0	90	17	1
Peanut bar, original, Planters, 45 g	230	14	1.5	0	70	22	2
Peanut butter'n graham sticks, Handi-Snacks, 1 unit	170	10	2.5	0	130	14	1
Popcorn, Arrowhead Mills, 1/4 cup	180	2.5	0	0	0	36	6
Popcorn, Newman's Own Oldstyle Picture Show Popcorn, 5 cups popped	110	1	0	0	0	27	0
Popcorn, air-popped, 1 oz	110	1.5	0	0	0	22	4
Popcorn, all natural, Cape Cod, 3 1/2 cups	160	9	2	0	200	18	3
Popcorn, butter, Pop-Secret, 1 cup popped	35	2.5	0.5	0	50	4	<1
Popcorn, butter, Pop-Secret By Request, 1 cup popped	20	0	0	0	45	4	<1
Popcorn, butter, light, Pop-Secret, 1 cup popped	25	1	0	0	35	4	<1
Popcorn, butter, microwave, Act II, 3 Tbsp	170	11	2.5	0	400	19	4
Popcorn, butter, microwave, Act II Flavor Lovers, 3 Tbsp	170	9	2	0	420	21	3
Popcorn, butter, microwave, America's Best, 5 cups popped	90	2.5	0.5	0	210	23	8
Popcorn, butter, microwave, Jolly Time, 4 cups popped	140	9	1.5	0	320	18	6
Popcorn, butter, microwave, 95% fat free, Act II, 3 Tbsp	130	1.5	0	0	560	26	4
Popcorn, butter, microwave, light, Act II, 3 Tbsp	130	5	1	0	400	24	6
Popcorn, butter, microwave, light, Jolly Time, 5 cups popped	120	5	1	0	290	24	7

SNACKS	CAL (g)	FAT (g)	SAT FAT (g)	CHOL (mg)	SODIUM (mg)	CARB (g)	FIBER (g)
Popcorn, butter, old fashioned, Cape Cod, 3 cups	170	10	3	<5	220	16	2
Popcorn, butter flavor, Ultra Slim Fast, 4⅓ cups	130	3.5	0.5	0	170	20	4
Popcorn, butter flavor, microwave, Orville Redenbacher's, 2 Tbsp	170	13	3	0	390	15	4
Popcorn, butter flavor, microwave, light, Newman's Own Oldstyle Picture Show Popcorn, 3.5 cups popped	110	3	1	0	90	20	0
Popcorn, butter flavor, microwave, light, Orville Redenbacher's, 2 Tbsp	120	6	1	0	350	19	5
Popcorn, butter flavor, microwave, no salt added, Orville Redenbacher's, 2 Tbsp	180	12	2.5	0	0	19	4
Popcorn, butter flavored, Weight Watchers Smart Snackers, 0.66 oz	90	2.5	0	0	100	14	3
Popcorn, butter lovers, microwave, Act II, 3 Tbsp	170	11	2.5	0	340	19	4
Popcorn, butter toffee, Cracker Jack, ⅔ cup	130	4.5	2	5	160	21	<1
Popcorn, butter toffee, Weight Watchers Smart Snackers, 0.90 oz	110	2.5	1	0	90	21	1
Popcorn, butter toffee, fat free, Cracker Jack, 1 cup	110	0	0	0	95	26	<1
Popcorn, butter toffee, premium, with pecans & almonds, Cracker Jack, ½ cup	130	6	2	5	135	19	<1
Popcorn, Buttery Burst, Pop-Secret, 1 cup popped	35	2.5	0.5	0	50	4	<1
Popcorn, Buttery Burst, light, Pop-Secret, 1 cup popped	25	1	0	0	45	4	<1
Popcorn, candied popcorn, and peanuts, Cracker Jack, ⅔ cup	120	2.5	0.5	0	90	23	1
Popcorn, caramel, Jays, ⅔ cup	125	2	0	0	85	25	1
Popcorn, caramel, Ultra Slim Fast, ½ cup	120	1.5	0	<5	80	25	2

SNACKS	CAL (g)	FAT (g)	SAT FAT (g)	CHOL (mg)	SODIUM (mg)	CARB (g)	FIBER (g)
Popcorn, caramel, Weight Watchers Smart Snackers, 0.90 oz	100	1	0	0	45	22	1
Popcorn, caramel, microwave, Act II Flavor Lovers, 3 Tbsp	170	7	1.5	0	20	30	5
Popcorn, caramel, microwave, Orville Redenbacher's, 2 Tbsp	180	10	2.5	0	50	23	2
Popcorn, caramel coated popcorn, fat free, Cracker Jack, 1 cup	110	0	0	0	85	26	<1
Popcorn, caramel corn puffs, all varieties, fat free, Health Valley, 1 cup	110	0	0	0	60	24	2
Popcorn, caramel corn, fat free, Louise's, 1 cup	100	0	0	0	80	24	1
Popcorn, caramel corn with peanuts, Old Dutch, ⅔ cup	130	3	1	0	75	23	1
Popcorn, cheddar cheese, Pop-Secret, 1 cup popped	30	2	0.5	0	45	3	<1
Popcorn, cheddar cheese, microwave, Orville Redenbacher's, 2 Tbsp	140	9	1	0	280	16	4
Popcorn, cheese, Jays Oke-Doke, 1 oz	160	11	2.5	10	270	13	2
Popcorn, cheese, microwave, Act II Flavor Lovers, 3 Tbsp	180	10	2	0	370	21	3
Popcorn, cinnamon toffee, microwave, Act II Flavor Lovers, 3 Tbsp	170	7	1.5	0	20	30	5
Popcorn, corn pops, Jays, 1 oz	170	13	3	0	230	13	1
Popcorn, herb and garlic, microwave, Redenbudder's, Tbsp	180	13	3	0	500	16	4
Popcorn, hot air, Orville Redenbacher's, 2 Tbsp	90	1	0	0	0	24	6
Popcorn, microwave, Jolly Time, 4 cups popped	150	10	2	0	410	15	6
Popcorn, microwave, Orville Redenbacher's Smart Pop, Tbsp	100	3	0.5	0	450	20	5

SNACKS	CAL (g)	FAT (g)	SAT FAT (g)	CHOL (mg)	SODIUM (mg)	CARB (g)	FIBER (g)
Popcorn, microwave, Weight Watchers Smart Snackers, 1 oz	90	1	0	0	0	22	8
Popcorn, microwave, light, Jolly Time, 5 cups popped	120	5	1	0	320	20	7
Popcorn, movie theatre, microwave, Redenbudder's, 2 Tbsp	180	13	3	0	500	16	4
Popcorn, movie theatre, microwave, light, Redenbudder's, 2 Tbsp	110	5	1	0	320	19	5
Popcorn, nacho cheese, Pop-Secret, 1 cup popped	30	2	0.5	0	50	3	<1
Popcorn, natural, Pop-Secret, 1 cup popped	35	2.5	0.5	0	65	4	<1
Popcorn, natural, Pop-Secret By Request, 1 cup popped	20	0	0	0	45	4	<1
Popcorn, natural, light, Pop-Secret, 1 cup popped	25	1	0	0	45	4	<1
Popcorn, natural, microwave, Act II, 3 Tbsp	180	12	2.5	0	260	19	4
Popcorn, natural, microwave, light, Act II, 3 Tbsp	130	5	1	0	180	24	6
Popcorn, natural, microwave, no salt flavor, Newman's Own Oldstyle Picture Show Popcorn, 3.5 cups popped	160	10	2	0	0	16	0
Popcorn, natural butter flavor, microwave, Newman's Own Oldstyle Picture Show Popcorn, 3.5 cups popped	170	11	2	0	180	16	0
Popcorn, natural flavor, microwave, Orville Redenbacher's, 2 Tbsp	160	11	2.5	0	510	18	4
Popcorn, natural flavor, microwave, light, Newman's Own Oldstyle Picture Show Popcorn, 3.5 cups popped	110	3	1	0	90	20	
Popcorn, natural flavor, microwave, light, Orville Redenbacher's, 2 Tbsp	110	5	1	0	360	18	

SNACKS	CAL	FAT (g)	SAT FAT (g)	CHOL (mg)	SODIUM (mg)	CARB (g)	FIBER (g)
Popcorn, natural flavor, microwave, no salt added, Orville Redenbacher's, 2 Tbsp	170	12	2.5	0	0	19	5
Popcorn, original or white, Orville Redenbacher's, 2 Tbsp	90	1.5	0	0	0	22	5
Popcorn, Sante Fe butter, microwave, Act II, 3 Tbsp							
Popcorn, white, air-popped, Jolly Time, 5 cups popped	100	0.5	0	0	0	24	6
Popcorn, white, gourmet, Old Dutch, 2¾ cups	160	9	1	0	200	17	2
Popcorn, white cheddar, Cape Cod, 2⅓ cups	170	12	2.5	8	270	13	2
Popcorn, white cheddar, premium, Old Dutch, 2⅓ cups	160	10	1.5	<5	380	15	2
Popcorn, white cheddar, Weight Watchers Smart Snackers, 0.66 oz	90	4	1	0	125	12	2
Popcorn, yellow, air-popped, Jolly Time, 5 cups popped	100	1	0	0	0	24	5
Popcorn, yellow, buttered, low-fat, Louise's, 3½ cups	130	2.5	0.5	0	180	20	3
Popcorn, yellow, cheddar cheese, Old Dutch, 2½ cups	160	9	1.5	5	400	16	2
Popcorn, zesty, microwave, Redenbudder's, 2 Tbsp	180	13	3	0	430	16	4
Popcorn cakes, apple cinnamon, mini, Orville Redenbacher's, 11 cakes	100	0	0	0	40	26	5
Popcorn cakes, butter, Orville Redenbacher's, 3 cakes	110	2	0	0	190	26	7
Popcorn cakes, butter, mini, Orville Redenbacher's, 13 cakes	100	2	0	0	170	23	6
Popcorn cakes, caramel, Orville Redenbacher's, 2 cakes	80	0	0	0	30	23	4
Popcorn cakes, caramel, mini, Orville Redenbacher's, 11 cakes	100	0	0	0	35	26	5

SNACKS	CAL (g)	FAT (g)	SAT FAT (g)	CHOL (mg)	SODIUM (mg)	CARB (g)	FIBER (g)
Popcorn cakes, honey nut, mini, Orville Redenbacher's, 11 cakes	100	0	0	0	30	26	5
Popcorn cakes, white cheddar, Orville Redenbacher's, 3 cakes	110	2	0	0	110	26	7
Popcorn cakes, white cheddar, mini, Orville Redenbacher's, 13 cakes	100	1.5	0	0	100	23	6
Popcorn rice cakes, butter, fat free, Hain, 1 cake	40	0	0	0	60	9	0
Popcorn rice cakes, butter, mini, fat free, Hain, 7 cakes	60	0	0	0	65	13	0
Popcorn rice cakes, caramel, mini, fat free, Hain, 5 cakes	60	0	0	0	25	14	0
Popcorn rice cakes, white cheddar, Hain, 1 cake	40	1	0	<5	150	7	0
Popcorn rice cakes, white cheddar, mini, Hain, 6 cakes	70	3	0	<5	75	10	0
Pork rinds, hot and spicy, Old Dutch Bac'n Puffs, ½ oz	80	5	2	15	340	0	0
Pork skins, barbecue flavored, Jays, ½ oz	80	5	2	15	280	0	0
Pork skins, hot sauce flavored, Jays, ½ oz	80	5	2	15	260	0	0
Pork skins, original, Jays, ½ oz	80	5	2	15	230	0	0
Potato snack, Pacific Grain No Fries, 1 oz	120	2	0	0	200	23	1
Potato snack, all varieties, fat free, Health Valley, 1½ cup	110	0	0	0	260	23	2
Potato snack, barbecue, Pacific Grain No Fries, 1 oz	120	2	0	0	140	23	1
Potato sticks, ketchup flavored, Durkee, 1 oz	160	11	na	0	630	14	na
Potato sticks, regular, Durkee, 1 oz	160	9	na	0	210	16	na
Pretzel chips, Mister Salty, 16 chips	110	2.5	0	0	620	21	<1
Pretzel chips, fat free, Mister Salty, 16 chips	100	0	0	0	620	22	1

SNACKS	CAL (g)	FAT (g)	SAT FAT (g)	CHOL (mg)	SODIUM (mg)	CARB (g)	FIBER (g)
Pretzel chips, lower sodium, Nabisco Mr. Phipps, 16 chips	120	2.5	0	0	410	21	<1
Pretzel chips, original, Nabisco Mr. Phipps, 16 chips	120	2.5	0	0	630	21	<1
Pretzel chips, original, fat free, Nabisco Mr. Phipps, 16 chips	100	0	0	0	630	22	<1
Pretzel nuggets, oat bran, Weight Watchers Smart Snackers, 1.50 oz	170	2.5	0	0	250	33	3
Pretzel nuggets, soft, Superpretzel Soft Pretzel Bites, 4 bites	110	0	0	0	95	23	<1
Pretzel sticks, fat free, Mister Salty, 1 oz	110	0	0	0	370	23	1
Pretzel sticks, soft, cheddar cheese filled, Superpretzel Softstix, 2 softstix	110	2	1	0	290	19	1
Pretzel sticks, soft, nacho cheese filled, Superpretzel Softstix, 2 softstix	110	2	1	0	370	18	1
Pretzel sticks, soft, pizza cheese filled, Superpretzel Softstix, 2 softstix	110	2	1	0	310	19	2
Pretzels, Bavarian sourdough, Sunshine 2 pretzels	110	0	0	0	490	23	1
Pretzels, Bavarian, sourdough, no fat, Eagle, 1 oz	110	0	0	0	430	24	<1
Pretzels, Bavarian, traditional, Keebler, 3 pretzels	120	2	0.5	0	600	23	1
Pretzels, Butter Braids, Keebler, 22 pretzels	100	1	0	0	680	21	1
Pretzels, Butter Knots, Keebler, 7 pretzels	100	1	0	0	600	21	1
Pretzels, Butter Knots, minis, Keebler, 18 pretzels	100	1	0	0	770	22	1
Pretzels, Cheez'n pretzels, Handi-Snacks, 1 pkg	110	6	4	15	420	11	<1
Pretzels, Dutch, Mister Salty, 2 pretzels	120	1	0	0	580	25	1

SNACKS	CAL (g)	FAT (g)	SAT FAT (g)	CHOL (mg)	SODIUM (mg)	CARB (g)	FIBER (g)
Pretzels, fat free, Mister Salty, 1 oz	110	0	0	0	380	23	1
Pretzels, honey mustard and onion, Old Dutch, ½ cup	140	5	0.5	0	240	21	1
Pretzels, Knots, traditional, Keebler, 7 pretzels	110	1	0	0	530	20	1
Pretzels, mini, Mister Salty, 1 oz	110	1	0	0	440	22	1
Pretzels, mini bites, low fat, Eagle, ¾ cup (1 oz)	110	1	0	0	470	22	<1
Pretzels, multigrain, no fat, Cape Cod, 30 pretzels	110	0	0	0	310	25	3
Pretzels, rods, Old Dutch, 3 pieces	130	1.5	0	0	440	26	<1
Pretzels, salt & pepper rounds, Newman's Own Second Generation, 10 pretzels	110	1	0	0	400	24	1
Pretzels, salted rounds, Newman's Own Second Generation, 10 pretzels	110	1	0	0	400	24	<1
Pretzels, soft, Superpretzel, 1 pretzel	170	0	0	0	140	37	2
Pretzels, sticks, Old Dutch, 32 pieces	110	1.5	0	0	280	22	<1
Pretzels, sticks, fat free, Rold Gold, 1 oz	110	0	0	0	530	23	1
Pretzels, sticks, low fat, Eagle, 46 sticks (1 oz)	110	1	0	0	470	24	<1
Pretzels, thin twists, Rold Gold, 1 oz	110	1	0	0	510	22	1
Pretzels, thin twists, low fat, Eagle, 10 pretzels (1 oz)	110	1	0	0	470	22	<1
Pretzels, thin twists, no fat, Eagle, 10 pretzels (1 oz)	100	0	0	0	470	22	<1
Pretzels, thins, fat free, Old Dutch, 13 pieces	110	0	0	0	280	24	<1
Pretzels, thins, fat free, Rold Gold, 1 oz	110	0	0	0	340	23	1
Pretzels, tinys, fat free, Rold Gold, 1 oz	100	0	0	0	420	23	1

SNACKS	CAL (g)	FAT (g)	SAT FAT (g)	CHOL (mg)	SODIUM (mg)	CARB (g)	FIBER (g)
Pretzels, twists, Old Dutch, 7 pieces	110	1.5	0	0	260	22	<1
Pretzels, twists, Planters, 1 oz	100	0.5	0	0	420	23	1
Pretzels, twists, Ultra Slim Fast, 1 oz	110	1.5	0	0	420	22	3
Raisins, strawberry yogurt, Del Monte, 0.9 oz	110	3	2.5	0	25	20	<1
Raisins, vanilla yogurt, Del Monte, 0.9 oz	110	3	2.5	0	25	20	<1
Rice cakes, apple cinnamon, Hain, 1 cake	50	0	0	0	10	11	0
Rice cakes, banana split, mini, fat free, Hain Mini Munchies, 5 cakes	60	0	0	0	15	13	0
Rice cakes, brown rice, buckwheat, 1 cake	35	0	0	0	10	7	0
Rice cakes, brown rice, corn, 1 cake	35	0	0	0	25	7	0
Rice cakes, brown rice, multigrain, 1 cake	35	0	0	0	25	7	0
Rice cakes, brown rice, plain, 1 cake	35	0	0	0	30	7	0
Rice cakes, brown rice, rye, 1 cake	35	0	0	0	10	7	0
Rice cakes, brown rice, sesame seed, unsalted, 1 cake	35	0	0	0	0	7	na
Rice cakes, cheese, mini, Hain, 6 cakes	70	2.5	0.5	<5	135	11	0
Rice cakes, chocolate mint crunch, mini, fat free, Hain Mini Munchies, 5 cakes	60	0	0	0	15	12	0
Rice cakes, honey nut, Hain, 1 cake	50	0.5	0	0	40	11	0
Rice cakes, mild cheddar, mini, Hain, 6 cakes	70	2	0	<5	115	10	0
Rice cakes, peach cobbler, mini, fat free, Hain Mini Munchies, 5 cakes	60	0	0	0	15	12	0
Rice cakes, peanut butter crunch, mini, low fat, Hain Mini Munchies, 5 cakes	50	1	0	0	60	11	0

SNACKS	CAL (g)	FAT (g)	SAT FAT (g)	CHOL (mg)	SODIUM (mg)	CARB (g)	FIBER (g)
Rice cakes, ranch, mini, Hain, 6 cakes	80	3.5	0	0	190	9	0
Rice cakes, strawberry cheesecake, mini, fat free, Hain Mini Munchies, 5 cakes	60	0	0	0	15	12	0
Sesame sticks, 1 oz	150	10	2	0	420	13	<1
Shamu shapes, baked, Eagle, 1 cup	160	10	2	0	260	15	0
Shoestring potatoes, Jays, 1 oz	150	9	1.5	0	190	16	1
Snack bar, apple, Sunbelt Fruit Boosters, 1 pkg	130	2	0	0	60	27	0
Snack bar, apple, fat free, Health Valley, 1 bar	140	0	0	0	0	35	3
Snack bar, apple, fat free, Health Valley Apple Bakes, 1 bar	70	0	0	0	30	18	2
Snack bar, apple raisin, Weight Watchers Smart Snackers, ¾ oz	70	2	0.5	0	60	14	2
Snack bar, apricot, fat free, Health Valley, 1 bar	140	0	0	0	5	35	4
Snack bar, blueberry, Sunbelt Fruit Boosters, 1 pkg	130	2	0	0	60	27	1
Snack bar, blueberry apple, fat free, Health Valley Fat-Free Bakes, 1 bar	110	0	0	0	25	26	3
Snack bar, chewy caramel crunch, Ultra Slim Fast, 1 bar	120	3.5	2	<5	45	22	2
Snack bar, chocolate, Pillsbury Figurines, 2 bars	220	11	2.5	<5	110	24	1
Snack bar, chocolate brownie, Nestle Sweet Success, 1 bar	120	4	2	<5	35	23	3
Snack bar, chocolate caramel, Pillsbury Figurines, 2 bars	220	11	2.5	<5	130	24	1
Snack bar, chocolate chip, Nestle Sweet Success, 1 bar	120	4	2	<5	40	23	3
Snack bar, chocolate chip crunch, Ultra Slim Fast, 1 bar	120	4	2	0	25	16	3
Snack bar, chocolate flavor sandwich bars, all varieties, fat free, Health Valley, 1 bar	150	0	0	0	35	0	3

SNACKS	CAL (g)	FAT (g)	SAT FAT (g)	CHOL (mg)	SODIUM (mg)	CARB (g)	FIBER (g)
Snack bar, chocolate peanut butter, Nestle Sweet Success, 1 bar	120	4	2	<5	35	23	3
Snack bar, chocolate peanut butter, Pillsbury Figurines, 2 bars	220	11	3	<5	110	23	2
Snack bar, chocolate raspberry, Nestle Sweet Success, 1 bar	120	4	2	<5	35	23	3
Snack bar, cocoa almond crunch, Ultra Slim Fast, 1 bar	120	4	2	0	35	20	3
Snack bar, date, fat free, Health Valley, 1 bar	140	0	0	0	5	34	3
Snack bar, date, fat free, Health Valley Date Bakes, 1 bar	70	0	0	0	30	18	2
Snack bar, GatorBar, Gatorade, 1 bar	110	1	0	0	10	25	1
Snack bar, marshmallow, all flavors, fat free, Health Valley, 1 bar	90	0	0	0	0	22	1
Snack bar, oatmeal raisin, Nestle Sweet Success, 1 bar	120	4	2	<5	30	23	3
Snack bar, peanut butter, Sunbelt Naturals, 1 pkg	230	13	2	0	80	24	3
Snack bar, peanut butter crunch, Ultra Slim Fast, 1 bar	120	4	2	0	45	20	2
Snack bar, peanut caramel crunch, Ultra Slim Fast, 1 bar	120	4	2	<5	35	22	2
Snack bar, raisin, fat free, Health Valley, 1 bar	140	0	0	0	5	35	3
Snack bar, raisin, fat free, Health Valley Raisin Bakes, 1 bar	70	0	0	0	30	18	2
Snack bar, raspberry, fat free, Health Valley Fat-Free Bakes, 1 bar	110	0	0	0	25	26	3
Snack bar, rice bars, all varieties, fat free, Health Valley, 1 bar	110	0	0	0	5	26	1
Snack bar, s'mores, Pillsbury Figurines, 2 bars	220	11	2.5	<5	115	25	0

SNACKS	CAL (g)	FAT (g)	SAT FAT (g)	CHOL (mg)	SODIUM (mg)	CARB (g)	FIBER (g)
Snack bar, strawberry, Sunbelt Fruit Boosters, 1 pkg	130	2	0	0	60	27	0
Snack bar, strawberry, fat free, Health Valley Fat-Free Bakes, 1 bar	110	0	0	0	25	26	3
Snack bar, vanilla, Pillsbury Figurines, 2 bars	220	11	2.5	<5	115	25	0
Snack bar, vanilla almond crunch, Ultra Slim Fast, 1 bar	120	4	2	0	25	20	3
Snack curls, Old Dutch Puffcorn, 2 ½ cups	180	14	2	0	240	14	<1
Snack curls, caramel flavor, Old Dutch Puffcorn, ¾ cup	110	2	0.5	0	95	23	0
Snack curls, gourmet ranch, Pacific Grain Ranch-O's, 1 oz	110	0	0	0	240	23	1
Snack mix, Eagle, ½ cup	150	7	1	0	270	17	<1
Snack mix, Old Dutch Party Mix, ⅔ cup	150	7	1	0	248	19	1
Snack mix, Planters Heat, 1 oz	140	8	1	0	230	13	2
Snack mix, camping mix, Kettle Snacks, 1 oz	140	10	2	0	0	11	2
Snack mix, cheddar cheese, Cheerios, ¾ cup	130	5	1	0	360	20	1
Snack mix, Cheez-It party mix, Sunshine, ½ cup	140	5	1	0	270	19	1
Snack mix, Chex Mix, bold & zesty, ½ cup	160	7	1.5	0	390	17	5
Snack mix, Chex Mix, golden cheddar cheese, ⅔ cup	140	4.5	1	0	250	24	2
Snack mix, Chex Mix, traditional, ⅔ cup	130	3.5	1	0	280	22	1
Snack mix, chocolate lover's mix, Kettle Snacks, 1 oz	130	7	2	0	0	16	2
Snack mix, deluxe nut mix, Kettle Snacks, 1 oz	170	16	2	0	65	6	2
Snack mix, Doo Dads, original flavor, 1 oz	130	5	0	0	360	18	2
Snack mix, ecstasy mix, Kettle Snacks, 1 oz	140	9	2	0	35	15	2
Snack mix, extra nutty, Pepperidge Farm, ½ cup	180	9	2	25	330	20	2

SNACKS	CAL (g)	FAT (g)	SAT FAT (g)	CHOL (mg)	SODIUM (mg)	CARB (g)	FIBER (g)
Snack mix, Goldfish, Pepperidge Farm, ½ cup	150	7	1	10	230	18	2
Snack mix, Goldfish, zesty cheddar, Pepperidge Farm, ½ cup	180	10	2	<5	390	19	1
Snack mix, healthy mix, Kettle Snacks, 1 oz	130	7	2	0	5	14	2
Snack mix, honey mustard & onion, Pepperidge Farm, ½ cup	180	10	2	<5	390	19	1
Snack mix, honey roast harvest mix, Kettle Snacks, 1 oz	130	6	1.5	0	50	16	2
Snack mix, Kenai river mix, Kettle Snacks, 1 oz	160	13	1.5	0	40	7	3
Snack mix, lightly seasoned, Pepperidge Farm, ½ cup	170	8	1	<5	400	22	1
Snack mix, Mooseberry mix, Kettle Snacks, 1 oz	110	5	1.5	0	5	17	2
Snack mix, nutri-nut mix, Kettle Snacks, 1 oz	170	15	2.5	0	0	6	2
Snack mix, raw hiker's mix, Kettle Snacks, 1 oz	120	6	0.5	0	0	15	2
Snack mix, savory, seasoned, or spicy varieties, Pepperidge Farm, ½ cup	170	8	1	<5	400	22	1
Snack mix, Scandinavian mix, Kettle Snacks, 1 oz	120	6	2	0	20	16	2
Snack mix, smoky cheddar, Pepperidge Farm, ½ cup	180	10	2	<5	390	19	1
Snack mix, sour cream & onion, Cheerios, ¾ cup	130	5	1	0	370	20	1
Snack mix, sporting mix, Kettle Snacks, 1 oz	150	11	2	0	0	10	2
Snack mix, with peanuts, Cheerios, ¾ cup	140	5	1	0	320	20	1
Snack sticks, pretzel, Pepperidge Farm, 9 sticks	130	3	0	0	440	23	<1
Snack sticks, pumpernickel, or sesame Pepperidge Farm, 9 sticks	150	6	1	0	340	20	1
Snack sticks, sesame & cheese, Nabisco Twigs, 15 sticks	150	7	1.5	0	300	17	<1

SNACKS	CAL (g)	FAT (g)	SAT FAT (g)	CHOL (mg)	SODIUM (mg)	CARB (g)	FIBER (g)
Snack sticks, three cheese, Pepperidge Farm, 9 sticks	140	5	2	<5	410	20	<1
Snack tarts, all flavors, fat free, Health Valley, 1 tart	150	0	0	0	30	35	3
Tater crisps snacks, bar-b-que, Nabisco Mr. Phipps, 21 crisps	130	4	0.5	0	270	21	1
Tater crisps snacks, original, Nabisco Mr. Phipps, 23 crisps	120	4.5	0.5	0	220	20	1
Tater crisps snacks, sour cream 'n onion, Nabisco Mr. Phipps, 22 crisps	130	4	0.5	0	210	21	1
Tortilla snacks, cheddar jalapeno, Pacific Grain No Fries, 30 pieces	120	2	0	0	170	25	1
Tortilla snacks, ranch, Pacific Grain No Fries, 30 pieces	120	2	0	0	180	24	1
Tortilla snacks, salsa and sour cream, Pacific Grain No Fries, 30 pieces	110	0	0	0	150	25	1
Trail mix, California style, Dole, 2 oz	220	4	0.5	0	0	38	4
Trail mix, Hawaiian style, Dole, 2 oz	250	6	1.5	0	35	44	4
Trail mix, sierra, Del Monte, 0.9 oz	110	6	2	0	45	15	2
Trail mix, with chocolate chips, salted nuts & seeds, 1 oz	140	9	2	0	35	13	na
Trail mix, with chocolate chips, unsalted nuts & seeds, 1 oz	140	9	2	0	10	13	na

AT A GLANCE: SNACKS
Fat Free Snacks: Fruit snacks (rolls, leather, pieces); fat free popcorn; fat free pretzels; rice cakes

CONDIMENTS, DIPS, SAUCES & SPREADS

	CAL (g)	FAT (g)	SAT FAT (g)	CHOL (mg)	SODIUM (mg)	CARB (g)	FIBER (g)
BARBECUE SAUCE							
Bill's recipe, Texas Best, 2 Tbsp	20	0	0	0	430	5	0
Bold, K.C. Masterpiece, 2 Tbsp	60	0	0	0	240	12	na
Bold, hickory, Hunt's, 2 Tbsp	50	0	0	0	280	11	<1
Bold, original, Hunt's, 2 Tbsp	45	0	0	0	320	11	<1
Cajun, Texas Best, 2 Tbsp	45	3	1.5	0	260	5	0
Char-grill, Kraft, 2 Tbsp	60	1	0	0	440	12	0
Extra rich original, Kraft, 2 Tbsp	50	0	0	0	360	12	0
Garlic, Christopher Ranch, 2 Tbsp	40	0	0	ns	290	10	ns
Garlic, Kraft, 2 Tbsp	40	0	0	0	420	9	0
Hawaiian, Texas Best, 2 Tbsp	60	0	0	0	310	14	0
Hickory, Healthy Choice, 2 Tbsp	25	0	0	0	230	6	0
Hickory, Hunt's, 2 Tbsp	40	0	0	0	410	9	1
Hickory, K.C. Masterpiece, 2 Tbsp	60	0	0	0	220	13	na
Hickory & brown sugar, Hunt's, 2 Tbsp	70	0	0	0	380	18	<1
Hickory flavor, Open Pit, 2 Tbsp	50	0	0	0	380	11	0
Hickory smoke, Heinz, 2 Tbsp	35	0	0	0	580	9	0
Hickory smoke, Kraft, 2 Tbsp	40	0	0	0	440	10	0
Hickory smoke, Kraft Thick 'N Spicy, 2 Tbsp	50	0	0	0	440	12	0
Hickory smoke onion bits, Kraft, 2 Tbsp	50	0	0	0	340	11	<1
Honey, Kraft, 2 Tbsp	50	0	0	0	320	13	0
Honey, Kraft Thick 'N Spicy, 2 Tbsp	60	0	0	0	350	13	0
Honey dijon, K.C. Masterpiece, 2 Tbsp	50	1	na	0	570	10	na

BARBECUE SAUCE	CAL (g)	FAT (g)	SAT FAT (g)	CHOL (mg)	SODIUM (mg)	CARB (g)	FIBER (g)
Honey hickory, Hunt's, 2 Tbsp	40	0	0	0	410	9	1
Honey mustard, Hunt's, 2 Tbsp	50	0	0	0	450	12	<1
Honey mustard, Texas Best, 2 Tbsp	50	1	0	0	340	9	1
Hong Kong, House of Tsang, 1 tsp	10	0	0	0	150	2	0
Hot, Kraft, 2 Tbsp	40	0	0	0	540	9	0
Hot, Open Pit, 2 Tbsp	50	0	0	0	380	11	0
Hot & spicy, Healthy Choice, 2 Tbsp	25	0	0	0	230	6	0
Hot and spicy, Hunt's, 2 Tbsp	50	0	0	0	450	12	<1
Hot hickory smoke, Kraft, 2 Tbsp	40	0	0	0	360	9	0
Italian seasonings, Kraft, 2 Tbsp	45	0.5	0	0	280	10	0
Kansas City style, Kraft, 2 Tbsp	45	0	0	0	280	11	<1
Kansas City style, Kraft Thick 'N Spicy, 2 Tbsp	60	0	0	0	280	13	<1
Light, Hunt's, 2 Tbsp	25	0	0	0	170	6	<1
Mesquite, Hunt's, 2 Tbsp	40	0	0	0	360	9	<1
Mesquite, K.C. Masterpiece, 2 Tbsp	60	0	0	0	210	13	na
Mesquite, Open Pit, 2 Tbsp	50	1	0	0	440	11	0
Mesquite, Texas Best, 2 Tbsp	45	0	0	0	420	11	0
Mesquite smoke, Kraft, 2 Tbsp	40	0	0	0	410	9	0
Mesquite smoke, Kraft Thick 'N Spicy, 2 Tbsp	50	0	0	0	440	12	0
Mild, Hunt's, 2 Tbsp	40	0	0	0	380	10	<1
Mild dijon, Hunt's, 2 Tbsp	40	0	0	0	400	9	0
Old fashioned, Heinz, 2 Tbsp	40	0	0	0	370	10	0
Onion bits, Kraft, 2 Tbsp	50	0	0	0	340	11	0
Onion flavor, Open Pit, 2 Tbsp	50	0	0	0	480	11	0
Original, Healthy Choice, 2 Tbsp	25	0	0	0	230	6	0
Original, Hunt's, 2 Tbsp	40	0	0	0	400	9	<1

BARBECUE SAUCE	CAL (g)	FAT (g)	SAT FAT (g)	CHOL (mg)	SODIUM (mg)	CARB (g)	FIBER (g)
Original, K.C. Masterpiece, 2 Tbsp	60	0	0	0	210	13	na
Original, Kraft, 2 Tbsp	40	0	0	0	460	10	0
Original, Kraft Thick 'N Spicy, 2 Tbsp	50	0	0	0	440	12	0
Original, Open Pit, 2 Tbsp	50	0	0	0	490	11	0
Original, Texas Best, 2 Tbsp	40	2.5	1.5	0	430	4	0
Original, no salt, K.C. Masterpiece, 2 Tbsp	60	0	0	0	40	13	na
Original recipe, Heinz, 2 Tbsp	35	0	0	0	510	9	0
Salsa, Kraft, 2 Tbsp	40	0	0	0	420	9	0
Spicy, K.C. Masterpiece, 2 Tbsp	60	0	0	0	200	13	na
Sweet & sour, Open Pit, 2 Tbsp	45	0	0	0	420	10	0
Sweet flavor, Open Pit, 2 Tbsp	50	0	0	0	300	12	0
Tangy honey & spice, Open Pit, 2 Tbsp	45	0	0	0	340	11	0
Teriyaki, Hunt's, 2 Tbsp	45	0	0	0	350	11	<1
Teriyaki, Kraft, 2 Tbsp	60	1	0	0	430	12	0
Teriyaki, honey, K.C. Masterpiece, 2 Tbsp	60	1	na	0	720	13	na
Thick & tangy hickory, Open Pit, 2 Tbsp	50	0	0	0	390	12	0
Thick & tangy onion, Open Pit, 2 Tbsp	50	0	0	0	380	12	0

AT A GLANCE: BARBECUE SAUCE
Lowest in Calories: House of Tsang Hong Kong
Lowest in Sodium: K. C. Masterpiece Original, No Salt

BROWN SAUCE

Brown bean sauce, spicy, House of Tsang, 1 tsp	15	0	0	0	125	3	0
Brown gravy sauce, La Choy, ¼ cup	280	0	0	0	320	66	0
Brown sauce, spicy, House of Tsang, 1 Tbsp	15	0	0	0	125	3	0

	CAL	FAT (g)	SAT FAT (g)	CHOL (mg)	SODIUM (mg)	CARB (g)	FIBER (g)

CHILI SAUCE

	CAL	FAT (g)	SAT FAT (g)	CHOL (mg)	SODIUM (mg)	CARB (g)	FIBER (g)
Del Monte, 1 Tbsp	20	0	0	0	480	5	0
Heinz, 1 Tbsp	15	0	0	0	230	4	0
Hot dog, Gebhardt, ¼ cup	60	3.5	1.5	<5	260	6	2
Red, Las Palmas, ¼ cup	15	0.5	0	0	310	2	1

COCKTAIL SAUCE

	CAL	FAT (g)	SAT FAT (g)	CHOL (mg)	SODIUM (mg)	CARB (g)	FIBER (g)
Sauceworks, ¼ cup	60	0.5	0	0	800	13	<1
Seafood, Del Monte, ¼ cup	100	0	0	0	910	24	0
Seafood, Heinz, ¼ cup	60	0	0	0	680	14	1
Seafood, Silver Spring, ¼ cup	55	0	0	0	690	12	1

DIPS

	CAL	FAT (g)	SAT FAT (g)	CHOL (mg)	SODIUM (mg)	CARB (g)	FIBER (g)
Avocado, Kraft, 2 Tbsp	60	4	3	0	240	4	0
Avocado, pulp, Calavo, 1 oz	50	6	na	0	105	2	na
Bacon & horseradish, Kraft, 2 Tbsp	60	5	3	0	220	3	0
Bacon & horseradish, premium, Kraft, 2 Tbsp	50	5	3	15	200	2	0
Bacon & onion, premium, Kraft, 2 Tbsp	60	5	3	15	160	2	0
Bacon & onion sour cream, Breakstone's, 2 Tbsp	60	5	3	20	170	2	0
Bacon & onion sour cream, premium, Knudsen, 2 Tbsp	60	5	3	20	170	2	0
Bacon ranch, Marie's, 2 Tbsp	150	16	2	15	200	3	0
Bean, fiesta, Marie's, 2 Tbsp	140	14	2	10	160	1	<1
Bean, mild, Eagle, 2 Tbsp	40	1.5	0	0	160	5	2
Black bean, Eagle, 2 Tbsp	35	1	0	0	220	5	1
Black bean, Old El Paso, 2 Tbsp	20	0	0	0	150	4	1
Black bean, Tostitos, 2 Tbsp	25	0	0	0	190	5	1
Black bean, fat free, Taco Bell, 2 Tbsp	25	0	0	0	200	5	1
Black bean mix, Knorr, ¹⁄₁₆ pkg	10	0	0	ns	170	2	ns

DIPS	CAL (g)	FAT (g)	SAT FAT (g)	CHOL (mg)	SODIUM (mg)	CARB (g)	FIBER (g)
Blue cheese, premium, Kraft, 2 Tbsp	45	4	2.5	10	200	2	0
Buttermilk spice ranch style, Marie's, 2 Tbsp	180	18	3	15	230	4	0
Buttermilk veggie, Marzetti, 2 Tbsp	170	18	2.5	<5	240	1	0
Cheese and salsa, Eagle, 2 Tbsp	40	3	1	<5	300	3	0
Cheese and salsa, Old El Paso, 2 Tbsp	40	3	1	<5	300	3	0
Chili caliente mix, Knorr, 1/20 pkg	5	0	0	ns	80	1	ns
Clam, Kraft, 2 Tbsp	60	4	3	0	250	3	0
Clam, Chesapeake, sour cream, Breakstone's, 2 Tbsp	50	4	2.5	30	190	2	0
Clam, premium, Kraft, 2 Tbsp	45	4	2.5	10	210	2	0
Cracked pepper ranch mix, Knorr, 1/20 pkg	5	0	0	ns	100	1	ns
Cucumber, creamy, premium, Kraft, 2 Tbsp	50	4	3	15	140	2	0
Fiesta mix, Hidden Valley Ranch, mix to make 2 Tbsp	5	0	0	0	250	1	0
French onion, Kraft, 2 Tbsp	60	4	3	0	230	4	0
French onion, premium, Kraft, 2 Tbsp	50	4	2.5	10	160	2	0
French onion mix, Hidden Valley Ranch, mix to make Tbsp	5	0	0	0	140	1	0
French onion sour cream, Breakstone's, 2 Tbsp	50	4	3	20	160	2	0
French onion sour cream, Sealtest, 2 Tbsp	50	4	3	20	160	2	0
French onion sour cream, fat free, Borden, 2 Tbsp	25	0	0	0	170	4	0
French onion sour cream, premium, Knudsen, 2 Tbsp	50	4	3	20	160	2	0
Fruit dip, caramel, Marie's, Tbsp	150	5	4	5	75	24	1
Fruit dip, caramel, fat free, Smucker's, 2 Tbsp	130	0	0	0	85	30	0

DIPS	CAL (g)	FAT (g)	SAT FAT (g)	CHOL (mg)	SODIUM (mg)	CARB (g)	FIBE (g)
Fruit dip, caramel, low fat, Marie's, 2 Tbsp	140	2	2	5	90	29	0
Fruit dip, chocolate, fat free, Smucker's, 2 Tbsp	130	0	0	0	75	31	<1
Garden dill mix, Knorr, 1/20 pkg	0	0	0	ns	110	0	ns
Garden vegetable mix, Hidden Valley Ranch, mix to make 2 Tbsp	5	0	0	0	140	1	0
Green onion, Kraft, 2 Tbsp	60	4	3	0	190	4	0
Guacamole, California supreme, Calavo, 1 oz	60	6	na	0	130	2	na
Guacamole, hot'n spicy, Calavo, 1 oz	60	6	na	0	130	2	na
Guacamole, original, Calavo, 1 oz	60	6	na	0	105	2	na
Guacamole, western style, Calavo, 1 oz	60	6	na	0	130	2	na
Hidden Valley Ranch, original mix, mix to make 2 Tbsp	5	0	0	0	210	1	•
Hidden Valley Ranch, original mix, reduced calorie, mix to make 2 Tbsp	5	0	0	0	230	1	•
Hummus mix, Casbah, 1/4 cup prepared	120	5	0	0	180	14	
Hummus mix, Fantastic Foods, 2 Tbsp	60	2	0	0	220	8	
Jalapeno, Kraft, 2 Tbsp	60	4	3	0	260	3	•
Jalapeno, Old El Paso, 2 Tbsp	30	1	0	<5	125	4	
Jalapeno cheddar sour cream, Breakstone's, 2 Tbsp	60	4	3	15	170	2	•
Jalapeno cheese, premium, Kraft, 2 Tbsp	60	5	3	15	250	1	•
Mexican bean mix, Knorr, 1/16 pkg	10	0	0	ns	100	2	r
Nacho cheese, premium, Kraft, 2 Tbsp	60	5	3	15	270	2	
Nacho cheese mix, Knorr, 1/16 pkg	10	0	0	ns	140	1	r
Nacho cheese sour cream, premium, Knudsen, 2 Tbsp	60	4	3	15	200	3	

DIPS	CAL	FAT (g)	SAT FAT (g)	CHOL (mg)	SODIUM (mg)	CARB (g)	FIBER (g)
Onion, creamy, premium, Kraft, 2 Tbsp	45	4	2.5	10	160	2	0
Onion, toasted, sour cream, Breakstone's, 2 Tbsp	50	4	3	20	180	2	0
Onion chive mix, Knorr, 1/20 pkg	5	0	0	ns	110	1	ns
Parmesan garlic, Marie's, 2 Tbsp	140	14	2	10	140	2	<1
Ranch, Kraft, 2 Tbsp	60	4	3	0	210	3	0
Ranch, homestyle, Marie's, 2 Tbsp	150	15	2	15	140	3	0
Sour cream mix, Durkee, 1/4 pkg	25	0.5	0	0	200	4	0
Sun-dried tomato, Marie's, Tbsp	140	14	2	15	135	2	<1
Vegetable mix, Mrs. Grass Homestyle, 1/4 packet	35	0	0	0	900	7	1

AT A GLANCE: DIPS
Add dip mix to nonfat or low fat sour cream to keep fat values low.
Lowest in Sodium, Dip Mix: Knorr Chili Caliente

ENCHILADA SAUCE

	CAL	FAT (g)	SAT FAT (g)	CHOL (mg)	SODIUM (mg)	CARB (g)	FIBER (g)
Gebhardt, 1/4 cup	35	2	1	0	220	4	<1
Las Palmas, 1/4 cup	15	0.5	0	0	310	2	1
Green chile, Las Palmas, 1/4 cup	25	1.5	0	0	260	3	0
Green chile, Old El Paso, 1/4 cup	30	1.5	ns	0	330	3	0
Hot, Las Palmas, 1/4 cup	20	0.5	0	0	330	3	1
Hot, Old El Paso, 1/4 cup	30	1.5	ns	0	190	4	0
Mild, Old El Paso, 1/4 cup	25	1	ns	0	160	4	0
Mild, Rosarita, 1/4 cup	25	1	0	0	410	3	0

GRAVY & GRAVY MIX

	CAL	FAT (g)	SAT FAT (g)	CHOL (mg)	SODIUM (mg)	CARB (g)	FIBER (g)
Au jus gravy, Franco-American, 1/4 cup	10	1	0	<5	310	2	0
Au jus gravy mix, Durkee/French's, 1/8 pkg	5	0	0	0	220	1	0

GRAVY & GRAVY MIX	CAL	FAT (g)	SAT FAT (g)	CHOL (mg)	SODIUM (mg)	CARB (g)	FIBER (g)
Beef gravy, Franco-American, ¼ cup	30	2	1	<5	300	4	0
Beef gravy, hearty, with beef pieces, Pepperidge Farm, ¼ cup	25	1	0	<5	360	4	0
Brown gravy, with onions, Franco-American, ¼ cup	25	1	0	<5	340	4	0
Brown gravy mix, Durkee/French's, ¼ pkg	10	0.5	0	0	250	3	0
Brown gravy mix, Knorr Gravy Classics, ⅙ pkg	20	0.5	ns	0	400	3	ns
Brown gravy mix, Pillsbury, 2 tsp	10	0	0	0	270	3	0
Brown gravy mix, Weight Watchers, ¼ pkg	5	0	0	0	270	0	0
Brown gravy mix, herb, Durkee/French's, ¼ pkg	15	0.5	0	0	350	3	0
Brown gravy mix, Lyonnaise and onion, Knorr Gravy Classics, ⅕ pkg	20	0.5	ns	0	320	4	ns
Brown gravy mix, mushroom, Durkee, ¼ pkg	15	0	0	0	300	3	0
Brown gravy mix, onion, Durkee, ¼ pkg	15	0	0	0	290	4	0
Brown gravy mix, vegetarian, Loma Linda Gravy Quik, 1 Tbsp	20	0	0	0	370	4	0
Brown gravy mix, with mushroom or onion, Weight Watchers, ¼ pkg	10	0	0	0	300	2	0
Chicken gravy, Franco-American, ¼ cup	45	4	1	5	270	3	0
Chicken gravy, giblet, Franco-American, ¼ cup	30	2	0	10	310	3	0
Chicken gravy, rotisserie flavored, Pepperidge Farm, ¼ cup	25	1	0	5	280	3	0
Chicken gravy, with chicken pieces, Pepperidge Farm, ¼ cup	25	1	0	<5	270	3	0
Chicken gravy mix, Durkee, ¼ pkg	20	0.5	0	0	350	4	0

GRAVY & GRAVY MIX	CAL (g)	FAT (g)	SAT FAT (g)	CHOL (mg)	SODIUM (mg)	CARB (g)	FIBER (g)
Chicken gravy mix, French's, ¼ pkg	25	0.5	0	0	250	4	0
Chicken gravy mix, Weight Watchers, ¼ pkg	10	0	0	0	400	1	0
Chicken gravy mix, roasted, Knorr Gravy Classics, ⅕ pkg	30	1	ns	5	330	3	ns
Chicken flavor gravy mix, vegetarian, Loma Linda Gravy Quik, 1 Tbsp	20	0	0	0	410	3	0
Chicken style gravy mix, Pillsbury, 2 tsp	10	0	0	0	250	3	0
Country gravy mix, Durkee/French's, ⅛ pkg	35	2	1	0	370	5	0
Country style gravy mix, vegetarian, Loma Linda Gravy Quik, 1 Tbsp	25	0.5	0	0	260	4	0
Cream of chicken gravy, Pepperidge Farm, ¼ cup	30	1	1	5	280	3	0
Gravy additive, Gravymaster, ¼ tsp	10	0	0	0	65	2	0
Gravy maker, Kitchen Bouquet, 1 tsp	15	0	0	ns	10	3	ns
Homestyle gravy mix, Durkee, ¼ pkg	15	0.5	0	0	240	3	0
Homestyle gravy mix, French's, ¼ pkg	10	0.5	0	0	230	3	0
Homestyle gravy mix, Pillsbury, 2 tsp	10	0	0	0	270	3	0
Hunter mushroom gravy mix, Knorr Gravy Classics, ⅕ pkg	25	1	ns	0	270	4	ns
Mushroom gravy, Franco-American, ¼ cup	20	1	0	5	300	3	0
Mushroom gravy, creamy, Franco-American, ¼ cup	20	1	0	<5	310	4	0
Mushroom and wine gravy with mushrooms, Pepperidge Farm, ¼ cup	60	1	0	5	300	4	0
Mushroom gravy mix, Durkee, ¼ pkg	15	0	0	0	230	3	0
Mushroom gravy mix, French's, ¼ pkg	10	0.5	0	0	250	3	0

GRAVY & GRAVY MIX	CAL (g)	FAT (g)	SAT FAT (g)	CHOL (mg)	SODIUM (mg)	CARB (g)	FIBER (g)
Mushroom gravy mix, Loma Linda Gravy Quik, 1 Tbsp	15	0	0	0	300	3	<1
Onion & garlic gravy, roasted, Pepperidge Farm, ¼ cup	25	1	1	<5	350	4	0
Onion gravy mix, Durkee, ¼ pkg	10	0	0	0	310	3	0
Onion gravy mix, French's, ¼ pkg	15	1	0	0	260	4	0
Onion gravy mix, Loma Linda Gravy Quik, 1 Tbsp	20	0	0	0	230	3	<1
Pork gravy, golden, Franco-American, ¼ cup	45	4	2	<5	340	3	1
Pork gravy mix, Durkee, ¼ pkg	10	0	0	0	240	3	0
Pork gravy mix, French's, ¼ pkg	10	0.5	0	0	250	3	0
Sausage gravy mix, Durkee/French's, ⅛ pkg	35	2	1	0	570	5	0
Stroganoff gravy with sliced mushrooms, Pepperidge Farm, ¼ cup	30	1	1	<5	240	4	0
Swiss steak gravy mix, Durkee, ⅐ pkg	15	0	0	0	370	4	0
Turkey gravy, Franco-American, ¼ cup	25	1	0	<5	290	3	0
Turkey gravy, seasoned, with turkey pieces, Pepperidge Farm, ¼ cup	30	1	0	<5	330	4	0
Turkey gravy mix, Durkee/French's, ¼ pkg	20	0	0	0	270	4	0
Turkey gravy mix, roasted, Knorr Gravy Classics, ⅕ pkg	25	0.5	ns	5	290	4	ns

AT A GLANCE: GRAVY & GRAVY MIX
Lowest in Sodium, Gravy Mix: Durkee/French's Au Jus Gravy

HOISIN SAUCE

House of Tsang, 1 tsp	15	0	0	0	105	3	0

HONEY

Glorybee, 1 Tbsp	60	0	0	0	0	17	0
Sioux Bee, 1 Tbsp	60	0	0	0	0	17	0

	CAL	FAT (g)	SAT FAT (g)	CHOL (mg)	SODIUM (mg)	CARB (g)	FIBER (g)
HORSERADISH							
Beaverton Foods, 1 tsp	0	0	0	0	40	<1	0
Kraft, 1 tsp	0	0	0	0	50	0	0
Miller, 1 tsp	0	0	0	ns	0	0	ns
Sauceworks, 1 tsp	20	1.5	0	<5	35	<1	0
Silver Spring, 1 tsp	0	0	ns	ns	10	0	ns
Cream, Beaverton Foods, 1 tsp	10	1	0	0	20	<1	0
Cream style, Kraft, 1 tsp	0	0	0	0	50	0	0
Cream style, Silver Spring, 1 tsp	0	0	ns	ns	10	0	ns
Fresh ground, Silver Spring, 1 tsp	0	0	ns	ns	10	0	ns
Red, Hebrew National, ½ cup	25	0	0	0	800	4	0
Red, Rosoff's/Schorr's, 1 Tbsp	10	0	0	0	160	2	0
Sauce, Heinz, 1 tsp	25	2.5	0	0	35	1	0
Sauce, Silver Spring, 1 tsp	15	1	ns	ns	40	1	ns
White, Hebrew National/Rosoff's/Schorr's, 1 Tbsp	10	0	0	0	160	1	0
With beets, Silver Spring, 1 tsp	0	0	ns	ns	40	0	ns
HOT SAUCE							
Gebhardt, 1 tsp	0	0	0	0	90	0	0
Texas Best, 1 Tbsp	0	0	0	0	125	0	0
Jalapeno, Tabasco, 1 tsp	0	0	0	ns	70	0	ns
Pepper, Tabasco, 1 tsp	0	0	0	ns	30	0	ns
JAMS, JELLIES & FRUIT SPREADS							
Apple butter, Dutch Girl/Mary Ellen, 1 Tbsp	35	0	0	0	0	9	0
Apple butter, spiced, cider, Smucker's Simply Fruit, 1 Tbsp	45	0	0	0	10	11	0
Fruit spread, all flavors, Smucker's Homestyle, 1 Tbsp	45	0	0	0	0	11	0
Fruit spread, all flavors, Smucker's Simply Fruit, 1 Tbsp	50	0	0	0	0	13	0

JAMS, JELLIES & FRUIT SPREADS	CAL (g)	FAT (g)	SAT FAT (g)	CHOL (mg)	SODIUM (mg)	CARB (g)	FIBER (g)
Fruit spread, all flavors but blueberry, Polaner All Fruit, 1 Tbsp	40	0	0	ns	0	10	ns
Fruit spread, all flavors but grape, Welch's Totally Fruit, 1 Tbsp	35	0	0	0	5	9	ns
Fruit spread, blueberry, Polaner All Fruit, 1 Tbsp	40	0	0	ns	5	10	ns
Fruit spread, grape, Welch's Totally Fruit, 1 Tbsp	40	0	0	0	5	10	ns
Fruit spread, grape, reduced calorie, Kraft, 1 Tbsp	20	0	0	0	20	5	0
Fruit spread, reduced calorie, Smucker's Slenderella, 1 Tbsp	20	0	0	0	10	5	0
Fruit spread, strawberry, Welch's, 1 Tbsp	50	0	0	0	10	13	ns
Fruit spread, strawberry, reduced calorie, Kraft, 1 Tbsp	20	0	0	0	20	5	0
Jam, all flavors, Smucker's, 1 Tbsp	50	0	0	0	0	13	0
Jam, all flavors, Sorrell Ridge, 1 Tbsp	35	0	0	0	0	9	0
Jam, grape, Kraft, 1 Tbsp	60	0	0	0	10	14	0
Jam, grape, Welch's, 1 Tbsp	50	0	0	0	10	13	ns
Jam, red plum, Kraft, 1 Tbsp	60	0	0	0	10	13	0
Jam, strawberry, Kraft, 1 Tbsp	50	0	0	0	10	13	0
Jelly, all flavors, Smucker's, 1 Tbsp	50	0	0	0	0	13	0
Jelly, apple, Kraft, 1 Tbsp	60	0	0	0	10	14	0
Jelly, apple-strawberry, Kraft, 1 Tbsp	50	0	0	0	10	13	0
Jelly, blackberry, Kraft, 1 Tbsp	50	0	0	0	10	13	0
Jelly, grape, Kraft, 1 Tbsp	50	0	0	0	10	14	0
Jelly, grape, Welch's, 1 Tbsp	50	0	0	0	10	13	ns
Jelly, guava, Kraft, 1 Tbsp	50	0	0	0	10	13	0
Jelly, red currant, Kraft, 1 Tbsp	50	0	0	0	10	13	0
Jelly, strawberry, Kraft, 1 Tbsp	60	0	0	0	10	14	0

JAMS, JELLIES & FRUIT SPREADS	CAL	FAT (g)	SAT FAT (g)	CHOL (mg)	SODIUM (mg)	CARB (g)	FIBER (g)
Marmalade, all flavors, Smucker's, 1 Tbsp	50	0	0	0	0	13	0
Marmalade, orange, Kraft, 1 Tbsp	50	0	0	0	10	14	0
Peach butter, Smucker's, 1 Tbsp	45	0	0	0	10	11	0
Preserves, all flavors, Smucker's, 1 Tbsp	50	0	0	0	0	13	0
Preserves, all flavors, Smucker's Light Fruit Preserves, 1 Tbsp	20	0	0	0	5	5	0
Preserves, all flavors, Smucker's Low Sugar Preserves, 1 Tbsp	25	0	0	0	0	6	0
Preserves, apricot, Kraft, 1 Tbsp	50	0	0	0	10	13	0
Preserves, blackberry, Kraft, 1 Tbsp	50	0	0	0	10	13	<1
Preserves, peach, Kraft, 1 Tbsp	50	0	0	0	10	14	0
Preserves, pineapple, Kraft, 1 Tbsp	50	0	0	0	10	14	0
Preserves, red raspberry, Kraft, 1 Tbsp	50	0	0	0	10	13	0
Preserves, strawberry, Kraft, 1 Tbsp	50	0	0	0	10	13	0
Pumpkin butter, Smucker's Autumn Harvest, 1 Tbsp	45	0	0	0	25	11	0

AT A GLANCE: JAMS, JELLIES, & FRUIT SPREADS
Lowest in Calories: Kraft Fruit Spreads; Smucker's Light Fruit Preserves; Smucker's Slenderella Fruit Spread

KETCHUP

	CAL	FAT (g)	SAT FAT (g)	CHOL (mg)	SODIUM (mg)	CARB (g)	FIBER (g)
Del Monte, 1 Tbsp	15	0	0	0	190	4	0
Healthy Choice, 1 Tbsp	10	0	0	0	100	2	0
Smucker's, 1 Tbsp	25	0	0	0	110	7	0
Hot, Heinz, 1 Tbsp	15	0	0	0	190	4	0
Lite, Heinz, 1 Tbsp	10	0	0	0	95	3	0
No salt added, Hunt's, 1 Tbsp	15	0	0	0	5	3	0

AT A GLANCE: KETCHUP
Lowest in Sodium: Hunt's No Salt Added

	CAL (g)	FAT (g)	SAT FAT (g)	CHOL (mg)	SODIUM (mg)	CARB (g)	FIBER (g)
MARINADES See also Cooking & Baking Products, Seasoning Mix							
Beef, Lawry's, ¾ tsp	0	0	0	0	590	1	0
Cajun, Mr. Marinade, 1 Tbsp	10	0	0	0	190	2	0
Italian, Mr. Marinade, 1 Tbsp	10	0	0	0	120	2	0
Mandarin, House of Tsang, 1 packet	25	0	0	0	680	6	0
Mustard honey, Mr. Marinade, 1 Tbsp	20	0	0	0	320	4	0
Teriyaki, Kikkoman, 1 Tbsp	15	0	0	0	610	2	0
Teriyaki, Mr. Marinade, 1 Tbsp	20	0	0	0	620	3	0
Teriyaki, lite, Kikkoman, 1 Tbsp	15	0	0	0	320	3	0
Teriyaki, baste & glaze, Kikkoman, 2 Tbsp	50	0	0	0	810	11	0
Teriyaki, baste & glaze, with honey and pineapple, Kikkoman, 2 Tbsp	80	0	0	0	770	18	0
Wine, red, Mr. Marinade, 1 Tbsp	15	0.5	0	0	490	<1	0
Wine, white, Mr. Marinade, 1 Tbsp	15	0.5	0	0	490	2	0

AT A GLANCE: MARINADES
Lowest in Calories and Sodium: Mr. Marinade Cajun

MAYONNAISE & MAYONNAISE-TYPE DRESSING

See also Salad Dressings.

	CAL (g)	FAT (g)	SAT FAT (g)	CHOL (mg)	SODIUM (mg)	CARB (g)	FIBER (g)
Mayonnaise, Hellmann's/Best Foods, 1 Tbsp	100	11	1.5	5	80	0	ns
Mayonnaise, Kraft, 1 Tbsp	100	11	2	10	75	0	0
Mayonnaise, Mrs. Filbert's, 1 Tbsp	100	12	2	10	80	0	ns
Mayonnaise, canola light, reduced fat, Smart Beat, 1 Tbsp	35	3	0	0	110	2	na
Mayonnaise, honey mustard, Beaverton Foods, 1 Tbsp	80	8	1	5	45	2	0
Mayonnaise, light, Weight Watchers, 1 Tbsp	25	2	0	5	130	1	0

MAYONNAISE & MAYONNAISE-TYPE DRESSING	CAL (g)	FAT (g)	SAT FAT (g)	CHOL (mg)	SODIUM (mg)	CARB (g)	FIBER (g)
Mayonnaise, light, low sodium, Weight Watchers, 1 Tbsp	25	2	0	5	40	1	0
Mayonnaise, reduced calorie, Mrs. Filbert's, 1 Tbsp	30	3	0	0	130	1	ns
Mayonnaise, sandwich & salad sauce, Durkee, 1 Tbsp	60	6	0.5	15	330	2	0
Mayonnaise, super light, reduced fat, Smart Beat, 1 Tbsp	35	3	0	0	110	2	na
Mayonnaise dressing, fat free, Kraft Free, 1 Tbsp	10	0	0	0	105	2	0
Mayonnaise dressing, fat free, Smart Beat, 1 Tbsp	10	0	0	0	135	3	na
Mayonnaise dressing, fat free, Weight Watchers, 1 Tbsp	10	0	0	0	105	3	0
Mayonnaise dressing, light, Kraft Light, 1 Tbsp	50	5	1	0	110	1	0
Mayonnaise dressing, light, reduced calorie, Hellmann's/Best Foods, 1 Tbsp	50	5	1	5	115	1	ns
Mayonnaise dressing, reduced fat, cholesterol free, Hellmann's/Best Foods, 1 Tbsp	40	3	0.5	0	120	3	ns
Mayonnaise dressing, whipped, fat free, Weight Watchers, 1 Tbsp	15	0	0	0	95	3	0
Miracle Whip Free dressing, nonfat, Kraft, 1 Tbsp	15	0	0	0	120	3	0
Miracle Whip Light dressing, Kraft, 1 Tbsp	40	3	0	0	120	3	0
Miracle Whip salad dressing, Kraft, 1 Tbsp	70	7	1	5	85	2	0
Nayonaise, cholesterol free, Nasoya, 1 Tbsp	35	3	0	0	100	1	0

AT A GLANCE: MAYONNAISE & MAYONNAISE-TYPE DRESSINGS

Lowest in Fat and Cholesterol: Kraft Mayonnaise Dressing, Fat Free; Kraft Miracle Whip, Nonfat; Smart Beat Mayonnaise Dressing, Fat Free; Weight Watchers Mayonnaise Dressing

	CAL (g)	FAT (g)	SAT FAT (g)	CHOL (mg)	SODIUM (mg)	CARB (g)	FIBER (g)
MUSTARD							
French's Creamy Spread, 1 tsp	10	0.5	0	0	65	<1	0
Kraft, 1 tsp	0	0	0	0	60	0	0
Bavarian, hearty, Plochman's, 1 tsp	0	0	0	0	60	0	0
Beer'n brat, Silver Spring, 1 tsp	0	0	ns	ns	55	0	ns
Bold & spicy, French's, 1 tsp	5	0.5	0	0	80	<1	0
Brown, spicy, Jack Daniel's, 1 tsp	5	0	0	0	85	1	0
Brown, spicy, Plochman's, 1 tsp	0	0	0	0	60	0	0
Country dijon, Grey Poupon, 1 tsp	5	0	0	0	120	<1	0
Deli, Hebrew National, 1 tsp	0	0	0	ns	65	0	0
Deli, with horseradish, Hebrew National, 1 tsp	0	0	0	0	65	0	0
Dijon, French's, 1 tsp	10	0.5	0	0	130	<1	0
Dijon, Grey Poupon, 1 tsp	5	0	0	0	120	<1	0
Dijon, Jack Daniel's, 1 tsp	5	0	0	0	120	1	0
Dijon, Plochman's, 1 tsp	5	0	0	0	80	0	0
Dijon, Silver Spring, 1 tsp	0	0	ns	ns	100	0	ns
Dijon, honey, Jack Daniel's, 1 tsp	10	0	0	0	80	2	0
Dijon, strong, Beaverton Foods, 1 tsp	10	0	0	0	115	<1	0
Dijonnaise mustard blend, Hellmann's/Best Foods, 1 tsp	10	1	0	0	60	1	ns
Dill, Silver Spring, 1 tsp	0	0	ns	ns	60	0	ns
Honey, Beaverton Foods, 1 tsp	10	0.5	0	0	45	2	0
Honey, Grey Poupon, 1 tsp	10	0	0	0	5	2	0
Honey, spicy, Plochman's, 1 tsp	10	0	0	0	20	2	0
Horseradish, French's, 1 tsp	5	0.5	0	0	95	<1	0
Horseradish, Grey Poupon, 1 tsp	5	0	0	0	55	<1	0

MUSTARD	CAL (g)	FAT (g)	SAT FAT (g)	CHOL (mg)	SODIUM (mg)	CARB (g)	FIBER (g)
Horseradish, Jack Daniel's, 1 tsp	5	0	0	0	80	1	0
Horseradish, Kraft, 1 tsp	0	0	0	0	55	0	0
Horseradish, beer 'n brat style, Silver Spring, 1 tsp	0	0	ns	ns	55	0	ns
Horseradish, zesty, Plochman's, 1 tsp	5	0	0	0	60	0	0
Jalapeno, Silver Spring, 1 tsp	0	0	ns	ns	85	0	ns
Old No. 7, Jack Daniel's, 1 tsp	5	0	0	0	110	1	0
Peppercorn, Grey Poupon, 1 tsp	5	0	0	0	50	<1	0
Peppercorn, Jack Daniel's, 1 tsp	5	0	0	0	110	1	0
Polish, Silver Spring, 1 tsp	5	0	ns	ns	70	0	ns
Stone ground, Plochman's, 1 tsp	5	0	0	0	60	0	0
Sweet hot, Beaverton Foods, 1 tsp	10	0.5	0	0	35	2	0
Sweet 'n hot, Silver Spring, 1 tsp	10	0	ns	ns	45	1	ns
Sweet onion, French's, 1 tsp	10	0.5	0	0	70	1	0
Yellow, French's, 1 tsp	0	0.5	0	0	60	<1	0
Yellow, extra fancy mild salad, Plochman's, 1 tsp	0	0	0	0	55	0	0

AT A GLANCE: MUSTARD
Lowest in Sodium: Grey Poupon Honey Mustard

PASTA SAUCE See also Pesto Sauce.

	CAL (g)	FAT (g)	SAT FAT (g)	CHOL (mg)	SODIUM (mg)	CARB (g)	FIBER (g)
Alfredo, Contadina, ½ cup	400	38	21	80	510	8	0
Alfredo, Di Giorno, ¼ cup	230	22	10	45	550	2	0
Alfredo, Five Brothers, ½ cup	110	10	6	40	430	3	0
Alfredo, Progresso, ½ cup	310	27	15	75	670	5	0
Alfredo, reduced fat, Di Giorno Light Varieties, ¼ cup	170	10	6	30	600	16	0
Alfredo sauce mix, Betty Crocker Recipe Sauces, ½ cup	220	20	6	20	750	8	0
Alfredo sauce mix, Knorr, ⅙ pkg	35	1.5	ns	ns	360	4	ns

PASTA SAUCE	CAL (g)	FAT (g)	SAT FAT (g)	CHOL (mg)	SODIUM (mg)	CARB (g)	FIBER (g)
Alfredo with mushrooms, Five Brothers, ½ cup	80	6	4	20	460	3	0
Bandito spicy simmer sauce, Newman's Own, ½ cup	70	3	0	0	600	10	0
Beef and pork, Classico d'Abruzzi, ½ cup	90	5	1	10	610	7	2
Bombolina sauce, Newman's Own, ½ cup	100	5	0	0	690	12	0
Carbonara sauce mix, Knorr, ⅙ pkg	30	2	0.5	5	380	3	ns
Clam, creamy, Progresso, ½ cup	100	6	1.5	10	560	8	0
Clam, red, Progresso, ½ cup	80	3	0.5	5	620	8	1
Clam, white, Progresso, ½ cup	120	9	1.5	15	310	1	0
Clam, white, authentic, Progresso, ½ cup	90	7	1.5	10	470	2	0
Classic Italian, with garlic & onion, Hunt's, ½ cup	60	2	0	0	600	10	2
Classic Italian, with Parmesan, Hunt's, ½ cup	50	2	0	0	630	8	2
Classic Italian, with tomato & basil, Hunt's, ½ cup	50	2	0	0	610	8	4
Diced onion & garlic, Prego, ½ cup	120	5	1	0	500	18	3
Extra garlic & onion, Campbell's, ½ cup	60	1	0	0	370	12	2
Florentine spinach & cheese, Classico di Firenze, ½ cup	80	4.5	1	<5	450	7	3
Four cheese, Classico di Parma, ½ cup	70	4	1	<5	480	7	1
Four cheese, Di Giorno, ¼ cup	200	19	11	45	410	2	0
Four cheese sauce mix, Knorr, ⅙ pkg	30	2	0.5	ns	360	2	ns
Garden combination, Prego Extra Chunky, ½ cup	90	1	0.5	0	480	16	3
Garden combination, chunky, Ragu Chunky Gardenstyle, ½ cup	110	3.5	0.5	0	540	18	3

PASTA SAUCE	CAL (g)	FAT (g)	SAT FAT (g)	CHOL (mg)	SODIUM (mg)	CARB (g)	FIBER (g)
Garden harvest, Ragu Light, ½ cup	50	0	0	0	390	11	3
Garden style, Del Monte, ½ cup	60	1	0	0	510	11	<1
Garden vegetable primavera, Five Brothers, ½ cup	70	2	0	0	490	11	3
Garden zucchini & Parmesan, Classico di Milano, ½ cup	60	2.5	1	0	470	6	2
Garlic & herb, Del Monte, ½ cup	60	1.5	0	0	490	11	<1
Garlic & herbs, Healthy Choice, ½ cup	50	0.5	0	0	390	10	2
Garlic & herbs, Hunt's Old Country, ½ cup	60	3	0	0	520	9	3
Garlic & onion, Del Monte, ½ cup	70	1	0	0	470	15	<1
Garlic & onions, extra chunky, Healthy Choice, ½ cup	50	0.5	0	0	390	11	2
Garlic herb sauce mix, Knorr, ⅙ pkg	35	2	0.5	ns	450	4	ns
Green & red pepper, chunky, Ragu Chunky Gardenstyle, ½ cup	110	3.5	0.5	0	570	19	2
Green peppers & mushrooms, Del Monte, ½ cup	70	1	0	0	320	13	<1
Ground beef flavored, Campbell's, ½ cup	100	2	0	0	600	19	2
Homestyle, Campbell's, ½ cup	90	1	0	0	510	18	2
Homestyle, traditional, Hunt's, ½ cup	60	2.5	0	0	600	7	2
Homestyle, with meat, Hunt's, ½ cup	60	2.5	1.5	0	600	7	2
Homestyle, with mushrooms, Hunt's, ½ cup	60	2.5	0	0	590	7	2
Italian herb sauce, Del Monte, ½ cup	60	1	0	0	520	12	<1
Italian sausage, Hunt's, ½ cup	80	3	0.5	<5	600	12	2
Italian style, cheese & garlic, Hunt's, ½ cup	60	2.5	0.5	0	690	9	2

PASTA SAUCE	CAL (g)	FAT (g)	SAT FAT (g)	CHOL (mg)	SODIUM (mg)	CARB (g)	FIBER (g)
Italian style, vegetable, chunky, Hunt's, ½ cup	60	1	0	0	530	13	2
Italian style vegetables, Hunt's Old Country, ½ cup	60	2.5	0	0	620	9	3
Italian tomato, hearty, Ragu Hearty, ½ cup	110	3	0.5	0	580	18	3
Light, no sugar added, Ragu Light, ½ cup	60	1.5	0	0	390	9	3
Marinara, Barilla, ½ cup	80	4	1	0	450	10	3
Marinara, Di Giorno, ½ cup	100	4.5	1	<5	530	12	3
Marinara, Prego, ½ cup	110	6	2	0	670	12	3
Marinara, Prince, ½ cup	50	1	na	<1	500	8	na
Marinara, Progresso, ½ cup	90	4.5	0.5	<5	480	8	2
Marinara, Ragu Old World Style, ½ cup	80	4.5	1	0	820	9	3
Marinara, authentic, Progresso, ½ cup	100	5	1.5	<5	440	9	5
Marinara, chunky, Hunt's, ½ cup	60	1.5	0	0	530	12	2
Marinara with burgundy wine, Five Brothers, ½ cup	80	4	0.5	0	480	9	2
Marinara with mushrooms, Newman's Own Sockarooni, ½ cup	60	2	0	0	700	9	0
Meat, Del Monte, ½ cup	70	1.5	0	<5	390	13	<1
Meat, Hunt's, ½ cup	60	2.5	0.5	<5	600	11	2
Meat, Hunt's Old Country, ½ cup	60	2.5	0.5	0	470	7	3
Meat flavored, Healthy Choice, ½ cup	50	1	0	0	390	8	2
Meat flavored, Prego, ½ cup	160	6	2	5	700	23	3
Meat flavored, Prince, ½ cup	80	4	na	<1	510	8	na
Meat flavored, Progresso, ½ cup	100	4.5	1	5	610	12	3
Meat flavored, Ragu Old World Style, ½ cup	80	3.5	1	<5	820	9	3
Meat flavored, chunky, Prince, ½ cup	80	3	na	<1	540	11	na
Meatless, Prince, ½ cup	70	3	na	<1	520	8	na

PASTA SAUCE	CAL (g)	FAT (g)	SAT FAT (g)	CHOL (mg)	SODIUM (mg)	CARB (g)	FIBER (g)
Meatless, chunky, Prince, ½ cup	70	2	na	<1	560	11	na
Mushroom, Campbell's, ½ cup	100	1	0	0	530	22	2
Mushroom, Del Monte, ½ cup	80	1.5	0	0	520	15	<1
Mushroom, Healthy Choice, ½ cup	50	0.5	0	0	390	10	2
Mushroom, Hunt's, ½ cup	60	2.5	0	0	600	11	2
Mushroom, Hunt's Old Country, ½ cup	50	3	0	0	540	7	3
Mushroom, Prego, ½ cup	150	5	2	0	500	20	3
Mushroom, Prince, ½ cup	70	3	na	<1	520	8	na
Mushroom, Progresso, ½ cup	100	4.5	1	<5	580	12	4
Mushroom, Ragu Old World Style, ½ cup	80	3	0.5	0	820	10	3
Mushroom, Weight Watchers, ½ cup	60	0	0	0	420	11	4
Mushroom, chunky, Prince, ½ cup	70	2	na	<1	560	11	na
Mushroom, chunky, Ragu Light, ½ cup	50	0	0	0	390	11	2
Mushroom, extra chunky, Healthy Choice, ½ cup	50	0.5	0	0	390	10	2
Mushroom, super, Ragu Chunky Gardenstyle, ½ cup	120	3.5	0.5	0	540	19	3
Mushroom & diced onion, Prego Extra Chunky, ½ cup	120	6	2	0	570	16	3
Mushroom & diced tomato, Prego Extra Chunky, ½ cup	110	4	1	0	510	19	3
Mushroom & garlic, Barilla, ½ cup	80	4	1	0	500	9	3
Mushroom & garlic, Campbell's, ½ cup	90	1	0	0	540	19	2
Mushroom & green pepper, Prego Extra Chunky, ½ cup	100	4	1	0	430	16	3
Mushroom & green pepper, chunky, Ragu Chunky Gardenstyle, ½ cup	110	3.5	0.5	0	570	18	3

PASTA SAUCE	CAL (g)	FAT (g)	SAT FAT (g)	CHOL (mg)	SODIUM (mg)	CARB (g)	FIBER (g)
Mushroom & onion, chunky, Ragu Chunky Gardenstyle, ½ cup	120	3.5	0.5	0	560	19	3
Mushroom & ripe olives, Classico di Sicilia, ½ cup	50	1	0.5	0	490	8	2
Mushroom & sweet peppers, super chunky, Healthy Choice, ½ cup	50	0.5	0	0	390	11	2
Mushroom supreme, Prego Extra Chunky, ½ cup	130	5	1	5	490	21	3
Mushroom with extra spice, Prego Extra Chunky, ½ cup	120	4	0	0	510	19	3
Olive, green & black, Barilla, ½ cup	100	6	1.5	0	710	9	3
Olive oil & garlic sauce with grated cheeses, Di Giorno, ¼ cup	370	36	8	20	540	3	0
Onion & garlic, Classico di Sorrento, ½ cup	80	4	0.5	0	410	9	2
Parma rosa sauce mix, Knorr, ⅕ pkg	30	1	ns	ns	280	4	v
Parmesan, Ragu Hearty, ½ cup	120	3.5	1	<5	570	18	3
Plum tomato & mushroom, Di Giorno, ½ cup	70	0	0	0	310	15	2
Red hot chili pepper, organic, fat free, Enrico's, 3.5 oz	60	0	0	0	460	9	3
Rock lobster, Progresso, ½ cup	100	7	1	5	430	6	2
Sausage & pepper, Prego Extra Chunky, ½ cup	180	9	3	10	570	22	3
Sauteed beef flavored, Ragu Hearty, ½ cup	120	4	1	<5	530	18	3
Sauteed mushroom, Five Brothers, ½ cup	70	3	0.5	0	440	10	3
Sauteed onion & garlic, Ragu Hearty, ½ cup	120	4	0.5	0	510	18	4
Sauteed onion & mushroom, Ragu Hearty, ½ cup	110	3.5	0.5	0	540	17	3
Spicy pepper, Barilla, ½ cup	80	4	1	0	570	9	3

PASTA SAUCE	CAL (g)	FAT (g)	SAT FAT (g)	CHOL (mg)	SODIUM (mg)	CARB (g)	FIBER (g)
Spicy red pepper, Classico di Roma Arrabbiata, ½ cup	60	2.5	0.5	0	270	6	2
Spicy red pepper, Ragu Hearty, ½ cup	100	2	0	0	530	18	3
Summer tomato basil, Five Brothers, ½ cup	60	1.5	0	0	470	10	3
Sun-dried tomato, Classico di Capri, ½ cup	80	4.5	1	0	430	8	2
Sweet pepper & garlic, Barilla, ½ cup	70	3.5	0.5	0	580	8	3
Sweet peppers & onions, Classico di Salerno, ½ cup	70	4	0.5	0	380	8	3
Three cheese, Prego, ½ cup	100	2	1	0	480	20	3
Tomato, garlic & onion, chunky, Hunt's, ½ cup	60	1	0	0	530	13	2
Tomato, garlic & onion, chunky, Ragu Chunky Gardenstyle, ½ cup	120	3.5	0.5	0	550	19	3
Tomato, onion & garlic, Prego Extra Chunky, ½ cup	120	6	2	0	550	17	3
Tomato & basil, Barilla, ½ cup	70	2.5	0.5	0	570	10	3
Tomato & basil, Classico di Napoli, ½ cup	60	1.5	0	0	430	9	2
Tomato & basil, Prego, ½ cup	110	3	1	0	420	19	3
Tomato & herb, Ragu Light, ½ cup	50	0	0	0	390	11	2
Tomato & pesto, Classico di Genoa, ½ cup	110	6	1.5	<5	450	10	2
Tomato basil sauce, Del Monte, ½ cup	60	1	0	0	480	11	<1
Tomato with basil, chunky, Di Giorno Light Varieties, ½ cup	70	0	0	0	290	16	2
Traditional, Campbell's, ½ cup	120	2	0	<5	550	25	2
Traditional, Del Monte, ½ cup	80	1	0	0	470	15	<1
Traditional, Healthy Choice, ½ cup	50	0.5	0	0	390	10	2
Traditional, Hunt's, ½ cup	60	2.5	0	0	620	11	4

PASTA SAUCE	CAL	FAT (g)	SAT FAT (g)	CHOL (mg)	SODIUM (mg)	CARB (g)	FIBER (g)
Traditional, Hunt's Old Country, ½ cup	50	3	0	0	540	7	3
Traditional, Prego, ½ cup	150	6	2	0	640	22	2
Traditional, Ragu Old World Style, ½ cup	80	3	0.5	0	820	10	3
Traditional meat, Di Giorno, ½ cup	120	6	2	15	610	12	3
Vegetable, Italian style, extra chunky, Healthy Choice, ½ cup	50	0.5	0	0	390	11	2
Vegetable primavera, super, Ragu Chunky Gardenstyle, ½ cup	110	3.5	0.5	0	480	17	4
Vegetable primavera, super chunky, Healthy Choice, ½ cup	50	0.5	0	0	390	11	2
Vegetable supreme, Prego Extra Chunky, ½ cup	90	3	1	5	490	15	3
Zesty basil, Prego Extra Chunky, ½ cup	110	2	1	0	510	22	3
Zesty garlic & cheese, Prego Extra Chunky, ½ cup	130	4	1	0	610	22	3
Zesty oregano with mushrooms, Prego Extra Chunky, ½ cup	140	3	1	0	580	25	3

AT A GLANCE: PASTA SAUCE

Choose from the dozens of sauces with less than 4 grams of fat and 1 gram or less of saturated fat.

Lowest in Sodium: Classico di Roma Arrabbiata Spicy Red Pepper

PEANUT BUTTER & NUT SPREADS

	CAL	FAT (g)	SAT FAT (g)	CHOL (mg)	SODIUM (mg)	CARB (g)	FIBER (g)
Almond butter, Roaster Fresh, 1 oz	180	16	1.5	0	0	6	na
Almond butter, smooth, unsalted, Woodstock, 2 Tbsp	180	16	1.5	0	0	7	4
Cashew butter, Roaster Fresh, 1 oz	170	14	3	0	0	9	na
Cashew butter, unsalted, Woodstock, 2 Tbsp	180	15	2.5	0	0	9	1
Hazelnut butter, Roaster Fresh, 1 oz	190	19	2	0	0	5	na

PEANUT BUTTER & NUT SPREADS	CAL	FAT (g)	SAT FAT (g)	CHOL (mg)	SODIUM (mg)	CARB (g)	FIBER (g)
Peanut butter, Roasted Honey Nut Skippy Super Chunk, 2 oz	190	17	3	0	120	2	na
Peanut butter, Roaster Fresh, 1 oz	170	14	2.5	0	0	5	na
Peanut butter, chunky or creamy, Jif, 2 Tbsp	190	16	13	0	150	7	2
Peanut butter, chunky or creamy, Peter Pan, 2 Tbsp	190	16	3	0	150	7	2
Peanut butter, chunky or creamy, Smucker's, 2 Tbsp	190	15	3	0	160	6	2
Peanut butter, chunky or creamy, no salt added, Smucker's, 2 Tbsp	200	16	2	0	0	7	2
Peanut butter, creamy, Peter Pan, 2 Tbsp	190	16	3.5	0	150	7	2
Peanut butter, creamy, Real, 2 Tbsp	190	16	3	0	95	5	3
Peanut butter, creamy, Roasted Honey Nut Skippy, 2 oz	190	17	3	0	120	2	na
Peanut butter, creamy, Skippy, 2 Tbsp	190	17	3.5	0	150	5	2
Peanut butter, creamy, old fashioned, Adams, 2 Tbsp	200	16	3	0	115	4	1
Peanut butter, creamy, very low sodium, Peter Pan, 2 Tbsp	200	18	2.5	0	10	6	2
Peanut butter, creamy, whipped, Peter Pan, 2 Tbsp	150	13	2.5	0	120	5	2
Peanut butter, crunchy, Peter Pan, 2 Tbsp	190	16	3.5	0	120	6	2
Peanut butter, crunchy, Real, 2 Tbsp	190	16	3	0	95	5	4
Peanut butter, crunchy, old fashioned, Adams, 2 Tbsp	200	16	3	0	90	5	1
Peanut butter, crunchy, very low sodium, Peter Pan, 2 Tbsp	200	17	2.5	0	10	6	2
Peanut butter, crunchy, whipped, Peter Pan, 2 Tbsp	150	13	2.5	0	95	5	2
Peanut butter, natural, Smucker's, 2 Tbsp	200	16	2	0	120	7	2

PEANUT BUTTER & NUT SPREADS	CAL	FAT (g)	SAT FAT (g)	CHOL (mg)	SODIUM (mg)	CARB (g)	FIBER (g)
Peanut butter, with nuts, Skippy Super Chunk, 2 Tbsp	190	17	3.5	0	140	5	2
Peanut butter spread, creamy, reduced fat, Peter Pan Smart Choice, 2 Tbsp	180	11	2.5	0	190	15	2
Peanut butter spread, creamy, reduced fat, Skippy, 2 Tbsp	190	12	2.5	0	200	13	1
Peanut butter spread, crunchy, reduced fat, Peter Pan Smart Choice, 2 Tbsp	200	12	1.5	0	150	15	2
Peanut butter spread, crunchy, reduced fat, Skippy Super Chunk, 2 Tbsp	190	12	2.5	0	170	12	1
Sesame butter, Roaster Fresh, 1 oz	170	15	2.5	0	0	6	na
Sunflower butter, Roaster Fresh, 1 oz	160	14	1.5	0	0	5	na
Sunflower seed butter, salted, 1 oz	160	14	1.5	0	150	8	na

AT A GLANCE: PEANUT BUTTER
Lowest in Fat: Peter Pan Smart Choice Peanut Butter Spread, Creamy, Reduced Fat

PESTO SAUCE

	CAL	FAT (g)	SAT FAT (g)	CHOL (mg)	SODIUM (mg)	CARB (g)	FIBER (g)
Pesto, Christopher Ranch, ¼ cup	230	23	4	0	330	4	3
Pesto Classic, Christopher Ranch, ¼ cup	190	15	3	0	360	12	2
Pesto sauce, Di Giorno, ¼ cup	320	31	7	15	500	3	0
Pesto sauce mix, Knorr, ⅓ pkg	15	0.5	ns	ns	510	2	ns
Pesto sauce mix, creamy, Knorr, ⅕ pkg	30	1	ns	ns	440	3	ns

PIZZA SAUCE

	CAL	FAT (g)	SAT FAT (g)	CHOL (mg)	SODIUM (mg)	CARB (g)	FIBER (g)
Boboli, ¼ cup	40	0	0	0	410	9	1
Progresso, ½ cup	35	1	0	0	140	5	1
Chunky, Contadina, ¼ cup	30	0	0	0	280	6	1
Garlic & basil, Ragu Pizza Quick, ¼ cup	40	1.5	0	0	340	6	1

PIZZA SAUCE	CAL (g)	FAT (g)	SAT FAT (g)	CHOL (mg)	SODIUM (mg)	CARB (g)	FIBER (g)
Italian cheese, Contadina, ¼ cup	30	1	0	0	350	4	1
Italian cheese, Contadina Pizza Squeeze, ¼ cup	40	1.5	0	0	420	6	1
Mushroom, chunky, Contadina, ¼ cup	30	0	0	0	290	5	1
Mushroom, chunky, Ragu Pizza Quick, ¼ cup	40	1.5	0	0	340	6	1
Original, Contadina, ¼ cup	25	0.5	0	0	300	4	1
Original, Contadina Pizza Squeeze, ¼ cup	35	1.5	0	0	350	6	1
Pepperoni chunks, Prego, ½ cup	70	3	1	10	330	7	1
Pepperoni flavored, Contadina, ¼ cup	30	1	0	0	360	4	1
Pepperoni flavored, Ragu Pizza Quick, ¼ cup	60	2	1	<5	420	5	1
Three cheese, chunky, Contadina, ¼ cup	35	0.5	0	0	190	5	1
Tomato, chunky, Ragu Pizza Quick, ¼ cup	50	1.5	0	0	300	7	1
Traditional, Prego, ½ cup	40	2	0	0	230	6	2
Traditional, Ragu Pizza Quick, ¼ cup	40	1.5	0	0	340	5	1
Traditional, 100% natural, Ragu Pizza Quick, ¼ cup	40	1.5	0	0	340	5	1

AT A GLANCE: PIZZA SAUCE
Lowest in Fat: Boboli; Contadina Chunky; Contadina Chunky Mushroom
Lowest in Sodium: Progresso

PLUM SAUCE

La Choy, 1 Tbsp	25	0	0	0	0	6	0

RELISH

Corn, canned, Green Giant, 1 Tbsp	20	0	0	0	40	5	0
Dill, Vlasic, 1 Tbsp	5	0	0	0	240	1	0
Green, sweet, Hebrew National, 1 Tbsp	20	0	0	0	50	4	0
Hamburger, Heinz, 1 Tbsp	10	0	0	0	180	3	0

RELISH	CAL (g)	FAT (g)	SAT FAT (g)	CHOL (mg)	SODIUM (mg)	CARB (g)	FIBER (g)
Hamburger pickle, Del Monte, 1 Tbsp	20	0	0	0	220	6	<1
Hot dog, Heinz, 1 Tbsp	15	0	0	0	105	4	0
Hot dog, Silver Spring, 1 tsp	5	0	ns	ns	45	1	ns
Hot dog pickle, Del Monte, 1 Tbsp	15	0	0	0	140	4	<1
India, Heinz, 1 Tbsp	20	0	0	0	100	5	0
India, sweet, flavored with curry, Vlasic, 1 Tbsp	15	0	0	0	140	4	0
Jalapeno, Old El Paso, 1 Tbsp	5	0	0	0	110	1	0
Sweet, Heinz, 1 Tbsp	15	0	0	0	110	4	0
Sweet, Vlasic, 1 Tbsp	15	0	0	0	140	4	0
Sweet pickle, Claussen, 1 Tbsp	15	0	0	0	85	3	0
Sweet pickle, Del Monte, 1 Tbsp	20	0	0	0	125	5	0

SALAD DRESSING

	CAL (g)	FAT (g)	SAT FAT (g)	CHOL (mg)	SODIUM (mg)	CARB (g)	FIBER (g)
Bacon, Hidden Valley Ranch, 2 Tbsp	150	15	1.5	10	230	1	ns
Bacon mix, Hidden Valley Ranch, mix to make 2 Tbsp	10	0	0	0	130	1	0
Bacon & tomato, Henri's, 2 Tbsp	140	12	1.5	0	290	8	0
Bacon & tomato, Kraft, 2 Tbsp	140	14	2.5	<5	260	2	0
Bacon & tomato, reduced calorie, Kraft Deliciously Right, 2 Tbsp	60	5	1	<5	300	3	0
Bacon spinach salad, Marzetti, 2 Tbsp	80	2	0.5	0	260	16	0
Blue cheese, Hidden Valley Ranch, 2 Tbsp	160	17	2.5	10	260	1	ns
Blue cheese, Marzetti, 2 Tbsp	160	17	3	20	230	0	0
Blue cheese, chunky, Marie's, 2 Tbsp	180	19	4	15	170	3	0
Blue cheese, chunky, Marzetti, 2 Tbsp	150	16	3	25	300	1	0
Blue cheese, chunky, Seven Seas, 2 Tbsp	90	7	4	10	470	5	0

SALAD DRESSING	CAL	FAT (g)	SAT FAT (g)	CHOL (mg)	SODIUM (mg)	CARB (g)	FIBER (g)
Blue cheese, chunky, Wish-Bone, 2 Tbsp	170	17	3	10	280	2	0
Blue cheese, chunky, Wish-Bone Lite, 2 Tbsp	80	7	1.5	0	380	2	0
Blue cheese, chunky, fat free, Wish-Bone, 2 Tbsp	35	0	0	0	310	7	0
Blue cheese, chunky, light, Marzetti, 2 Tbsp	80	7	1.5	15	330	4	0
Blue cheese, chunky, reduced calorie, Marie's, 2 Tbsp	100	7	1	5	240	7	<1
Blue cheese, creamy, low fat, Marie's Luscious Low Fat Dressing, 2 Tbsp	45	2	0	0	270	7	<1
Blue cheese, fat free, Hidden Valley Ranch, 2 Tbsp	20	0	0	0	270	4	ns
Blue cheese, light, Henri's, 2 Tbsp	60	2	0.5	0	430	9	0
Blue cheese flavor, fat free, Kraft Free, 2 Tbsp	50	0	0	0	340	12	1
Blue cheese mix, Hidden Valley Ranch, mix to make 2 Tbsp	100	0	0	0	110	1	0
Blue cheese mix, Weight Watchers, 1/5 pkg	10	0	0	0	170	1	0
Buttermilk and herb, Marzetti, 2 Tbsp	180	20	3	3	260	1	0
Buttermilk bacon ranch, Marzetti, 2 Tbsp	180	19	3	10	270	1	0
Buttermilk blue cheese, Marzetti, 2 Tbsp	170	18	3	10	220	1	0
Buttermilk Parmesan pepper, Marzetti, 2 Tbsp	170	18	2.5	10	310	1	0
Buttermilk Parmesan ranch, Marzetti, 2 Tbsp	160	17	2.5	10	240	1	0
Buttermilk ranch, Kraft, 2 Tbsp	150	16	3	<5	230	2	0
Buttermilk ranch, Marzetti, 2 Tbsp	180	20	3	<5	250	1	0
Buttermilk ranch, light, Marzetti, 2 Tbsp	90	9	1.5	10	280	3	0

SALAD DRESSING	CAL (g)	FAT (g)	SAT FAT (g)	CHOL (mg)	SODIUM (mg)	CARB (g)	FIBER (g)
Buttermilk ranch mix, original, Hidden Valley Ranch, mix to make 2 Tbsp	0	0	0	0	140	0	0
Caesar, Kraft, 2 Tbsp	130	13	2.5	<5	370	2	0
Caesar, Marzetti, 2 Tbsp	150	16	2.5	0	390	1	0
Caesar, Newman's Own, 2 Tbsp	150	16	1.5	0	450	1	0
Caesar, Seven Seas Viva, 2 Tbsp	120	12	0	0	500	2	0
Caesar, 3 cheese, Weight Watchers Salad Celebrations, 2 Tbsp	40	2	0	10	190	5	0
Caesar, creamy, Seven Seas, 2 Tbsp	140	15	2.5	10	300	1	0
Caesar, fat free, Weight Watchers Salad Celebrations, 2 Tbsp	10	0	0	0	390	1	0
Caesar, house, Marzetti, 2 Tbsp	150	16	2.5	5	340	1	0
Caesar, olde world, Marzetti, 2 Tbsp	150	16	2.5	5	340	1	0
Caesar, reduced calorie, Kraft Deliciously Right, 2 Tbsp	60	5	1	<5	560	2	0
Caesar, Romano cheese, Marzetti, 2 Tbsp	150	16	2.5	15	370	1	0
Caesar mix, gourmet, prepared, Good Seasons, 2 Tbsp	150	16	2.5	0	300	3	0
Caesar ranch, Henri's, 2 Tbsp	170	18	3	10	290	2	0
Caesar ranch, Kraft, 2 Tbsp	140	15	2.5	10	300	1	0
Caesar ranch, Marzetti, 2 Tbsp	190	20	3	5	300	2	0
Caesar with olive oil, Wish-Bone, 2 Tbsp	100	9.5	1.5	0	400	2	0
Caesar with olive oil, Wish-Bone Lite, 2 Tbsp	60	5	1	<5	380	2	0
Catalina French, Kraft, 2 Tbsp	140	11	2	0	390	8	0
Catalina French, fat free, Kraft Free, 2 Tbsp	45	0	0	0	360	11	<1

SALAD DRESSING	CAL (g)	FAT (g)	SAT FAT (g)	CHOL (mg)	SODIUM (mg)	CARB (g)	FIBER (g)
Catalina French, reduced calorie, Kraft Deliciously Right, 2 Tbsp	80	4	0.5	0	400	9	0
Catalina with honey, Kraft, 2 Tbsp	140	12	2	0	310	8	0
Celery seed, Marzetti, 2 Tbsp	160	13	2	0	180	10	0
Champagne, vintage, Marzetti, 2 Tbsp	150	16	2	0	460	2	0
Cheese Fantastico!, Bernstein's Light Fantastic, 2 Tbsp	30	1	0	0	360	5	0
Cheese garlic mix, prepared, Good Seasons, 2 Tbsp	140	16	2.5	0	330	1	0
Coleslaw, Hidden Valley Ranch, 2 Tbsp	150	15	1.5	10	170	5	ns
Coleslaw, Kraft, 2 Tbsp	150	12	2	25	420	8	0
Coleslaw, Marie's, 2 Tbsp	150	13	2	10	210	6	0
Coleslaw, fat free, Hidden Valley Ranch, 2 Tbsp	35	0	0	0	200	9	1
Cucumber, creamy, light, Henri's, 2 Tbsp	60	2	0	5	430	11	0
Cucumber ranch, Kraft, 2 Tbsp	150	15	2.5	0	220	2	0
Cucumber ranch, reduced calorie, Kraft Deliciously Right, 2 Tbsp	60	5	1	0	450	2	0
Dijon honey mustard, Marzetti, 2 Tbsp	140	13	2	20	180	6	0
Dijon ranch, Marzetti, 2 Tbsp	170	18	3	25	190	2	0
Dijon vinaigrette, Wish-Bone, 2 Tbsp	60	5	1	0	400	3	0
Dill, creamy, cholesterol- & dairy-free, Nasoy Vegi-Dressing, 2 Tbsp	60	5	0	0	135	3	ns
Dutch sweet 'n sour, refrigerated, Marzetti, 2 Tbsp	160	13	2	0	200	10	0
Fiesta, Hidden Valley Ranch, 2 Tbsp	140	14	2	10	280	2	ns
French, Kraft, 2 Tbsp	120	12	2	0	260	4	0
French, California, Marzetti, 2 Tbsp	160	13	2	0	240	11	0

SALAD DRESSING	CAL (g)	FAT (g)	SAT FAT (g)	CHOL (mg)	SODIUM (mg)	CARB (g)	FIBER (g)
French, country, Marzetti, 2 Tbsp	150	13	2	10	220	7	0
French, deluxe, Wish-Bone, 2 Tbsp	120	11	1.5	0	170	5	0
French, fat free, Henri's, 2 Tbsp	45	0	0	0	240	11	0
French, hearty, Henri's, 2 Tbsp	140	11	1.5	0	190	9	0
French, hearty, light, Henri's, 2 Tbsp	60	2	0	0	200	10	0
French, original, Henri's, 2 Tbsp	120	11	1.5	0	210	6	0
French, original, light, Henri's, 2 Tbsp	70	2	0	0	280	13	0
French, reduced calorie, Kraft Deliciously Right, 2 Tbsp	50	3	0.5	0	260	6	0
French, sweet 'n spicy, Wish-Bone, 2 Tbsp	130	12	2	0	330	6	0
French, sweet and spicy, fat free, Wish-Bone, 2 Tbsp	30	0	0	0	220	7	0
French, tangy, Marie's, 2 Tbsp	130	11	2	0	260	8	0
French mix, Weight Watchers, ⅙ pkg	0	0	0	0	220	<1	0
French style, Wish-Bone Lite, 2 Tbsp	50	2	0.5	<5	250	9	0
French style, fat free, Kraft Free, 2 Tbsp	50	0	0	0	300	12	<1
French style, fat free, Weight Watchers Salad Celebrations, 2 Tbsp	40	0	0	0	200	9	0
French style, fat free, Western, 2 Tbsp	45	0	0	0	250	11	<1
Garden herb, cholesterol- & dairy-free, Nasoy Vegi-Dressing, 2 Tbsp	60	5	0	0	135	3	ns
Garlic, creamy, Kraft, 2 Tbsp	110	11	2	0	350	2	0
Garlic, Italian, creamy, Marzetti, 2 Tbsp	160	17	2.5	15	140	1	0
Garlic, roasted, creamy, Wish-Bone, 2 Tbsp	140	13	2	0	240	3	0
Garlic, roasted, creamy, fat free, Wish-Bone, 2 Tbsp	40	0	0	0	280	9	0

SALAD DRESSING	CAL (g)	FAT (g)	SAT FAT (g)	CHOL (mg)	SODIUM (mg)	CARB (g)	FIBER (g)
Garlic & herbs mix, prepared, Good Seasons, 2 Tbsp	140	15	2	0	340	1	0
Green goddess, Seven Seas, 2 Tbsp	120	13	2	0	260	1	0
Herb mix, zesty, fat free, prepared, Good Seasons, 2 Tbsp	10	0	0	0	260	2	0
Herb vinaigrette, classic, fat free, Marie's Zesty Fat Free, 2 Tbsp	30	0	0	0	250	7	0
Herbs and spices, Seven Seas, 2 Tbsp	120	12	2	0	320	1	0
Honey dijon, Hidden Valley Ranch, 2 Tbsp	140	15	2	5	250	3	ns
Honey dijon, Kraft, 2 Tbsp	150	15	2	0	200	4	0
Honey dijon, Marzetti, 2 Tbsp	140	13	2	15	170	6	0
Honey dijon, Wish-Bone, 2 Tbsp	130	10	1.5	0	390	9	0
Honey dijon, fat free, Hidden Valley Ranch, 2 Tbsp	35	0	0	0	270	7	ns
Honey dijon, fat free, Kraft Free, 2 Tbsp	50	0	0	0	330	11	1
Honey dijon, fat free, Marzetti, 2 Tbsp	60	0	0	0	190	14	1
Honey dijon, fat free, Weight Watchers Salad Celebrations, 2 Tbsp	45	0	0	0	150	11	0
Honey dijon, fat free, Wish-Bone, 2 Tbsp	45	0	0	0	270	10	0
Honey dijon mix, Hidden Valley Ranch, mix to make 2 Tbsp	15	0	0	0	120	3	0
Honey dijon ranch, Marzetti, 2 Tbsp	150	15	2.5	25	200	2	0
Honey dijon vinaigrette, fat free, Marie's, 2 Tbsp	50	0	0	0	125	11	0
Honey French, fat free, Marzetti, 2 Tbsp	45	0	0	0	330	11	0
Honey French, light, Marzetti, 2 Tbsp	80	4	0.5	0	250	12	0

SALAD DRESSING	CAL (g)	FAT (g)	SAT FAT (g)	CHOL (mg)	SODIUM (mg)	CARB (g)	FIBER (g)
Honey French blue cheese, Marzetti, 2 Tbsp	160	13	2	0	260	11	0
Honey mustard, Henri's, 2 Tbsp	100	6	1	0	230	10	0
Honey mustard, Marie's, 2 Tbsp	160	15	2	5	160	8	<1
Honey mustard, fat free, Henri's, 2 Tbsp	50	0	0	0	180	12	0
Honey mustard mix, fat free, prepared, Good Seasons, 2 Tbsp	20	0	0	0	280	5	0
Honey mustard mix, prepared, Good Seasons, 2 Tbsp	150	15	2	0	240	3	0
Honey ranch, Marzetti, 2 Tbsp	160	14	2	0	230	11	0
Italian, Ott's, 2 Tbsp	90	10	1.5	ns	210	1	ns
Italian, Seven Seas Viva, 2 Tbsp	110	11	1.5	0	580	2	0
Italian, Wish-Bone, 2 Tbsp	100	9	1.5	0	590	3	0
Italian, Wish-Bone Lite, 2 Tbsp	15	0.5	0	0	380	2	0
Italian, cheese & garlic, Bernstein, 2 Tbsp	110	11	1	0	340	2	0
Italian, cheese & garlic, fat free, Bernstein, 2 Tbsp	10	0	0	0	380	2	0
Italian, classic house, Wish-Bone, 2 Tbsp	140	14	2	<5	360	2	0
Italian, creamy, Kraft, 2 Tbsp	110	11	4	0	230	3	0
Italian, creamy, Marzetti, 2 Tbsp	150	16	2.5	15	170	1	0
Italian, creamy, Seven Seas, 2 Tbsp	110	12	2	0	510	2	0
Italian, creamy, Wish-Bone, 2 Tbsp	100	10	2	0	310	3	0
Italian, creamy, Wish-Bone Lite, 2 Tbsp	60	3.5	1	<5	240	7	0
Italian, creamy, cholesterol- & dairy-free, Nasoy Vegi-Dressing, 2 Tbsp	60	5	0	0	170	3	ns

SALAD DRESSING	CAL (g)	FAT (g)	SAT FAT (g)	CHOL (mg)	SODIUM (mg)	CARB (g)	FIBER (g)
Italian, creamy, fat free, Weight Watchers Salad Celebrations, 2 Tbsp	30	0	0	0	360	7	0
Italian, creamy, fat free, Wish-Bone, 2 Tbsp	35	0	0	0	170	8	1
Italian, creamy, light, Henri's, 2 Tbsp	50	2	0	0	420	8	0
Italian, creamy, reduced calorie, Kraft Deliciously Right, 2 Tbsp	50	5	1	0	250	3	0
Italian, creamy, reduced calorie, Seven Seas, 2 Tbsp	60	5	1	0	490	2	0
Italian, creamy garlic, Henri's, 2 Tbsp	110	9	1.5	0	290	6	0
Italian, fat free, Henri's, 2 Tbsp	15	0	0	0	320	2	0
Italian, fat free, Kraft Free, 2 Tbsp	10	0	0	0	290	2	0
Italian, fat free, Marzetti, 2 Tbsp	15	0	0	0	450	3	0
Italian, fat free, Seven Seas, 2 Tbsp	10	0	0	0	480	2	0
Italian, fat free, Weight Watchers Salad Celebrations, 2 Tbsp	10	0	0	0	360	2	0
Italian, fat free, Wish-Bone, 2 Tbsp	15	0	0	0	280	2	0
Italian, house, Kraft, 2 Tbsp	120	12	2	<5	240	3	0
Italian, oil-free, fat free, Kraft, 2 Tbsp	5	0	0	0	450	2	0
Italian, olde Venice, Marzetti, 2 Tbsp	130	13	2	0	490	2	0
Italian, presto, Kraft, 2 Tbsp	140	15	2.5	0	290	2	0
Italian, reduced calorie, Kraft Deliciously Right, 2 Tbsp	70	7	1	0	240	3	0
Italian, reduced calorie light, Newman's Own, 2 Tbsp	20	0.5	0	0	380	3	0
Italian, restaurant recipe, Bernstein, 2 Tbsp	130	13	1.5	5	350	1	0
Italian, robusto, Wish-Bone, 2 Tbsp	100	10	1.5	0	610	4	0

SALAD DRESSING	CAL (g)	FAT (g)	SAT FAT (g)	CHOL (mg)	SODIUM (mg)	CARB (g)	FIBER (g)
Italian, Romano, Marzetti, 2 Tbsp	160	17	3	0	390	1	0
Italian, traditional, Henri's, 2 Tbsp	110	11	1.5	0	560	3	0
Italian, two cheese, Seven Seas, 2 Tbsp	70	7	1	0	240	3	0
Italian, wine country, Bernstein, 2 Tbsp	110	11	1	0	250	2	0
Italian, with olive oil, Marzetti, 2 Tbsp	120	13	2	0	480	1	0
Italian, with olive oil, reduced calorie, Seven Seas, 2 Tbsp	50	5	1	0	450	2	0
Italian, zesty, Kraft, 2 Tbsp	110	11	1.5	0	530	2	0
Italian mix, Weight Watchers, ⅙ pkg	0	0	0	0	300	0.5	0
Italian mix, creamy, Weight Watchers, ⅙ pkg	5	0	0	0	390	1	0
Italian mix, creamy, fat free, prepared, Good Seasons, 2 Tbsp	20	0	0	0	280	3	0
Italian mix, fat free, prepared, Good Seasons, 2 Tbsp	10	0	0	0	290	3	0
Italian mix, mild, prepared, Good Seasons, 2 Tbsp	150	15	2.5	0	370	2	0
Italian mix, prepared, Good Seasons, 2 Tbsp	140	15	2	0	320	1	0
Italian mix, reduced calorie, prepared, Good Seasons, 2 Tbsp	50	5	1	0	280	2	0
Italian mix, zesty, prepared, Good Seasons, 2 Tbsp	140	15	2	0	220	1	0
Italian mix, zesty, reduced calorie, prepared, Good Seasons, 2 Tbsp	50	5	1	0	260	2	0
Italian garlic, creamy, Marie's, 2 Tbsp	180	19	3	15	220	3	0
Italian garlic, creamy, reduced calorie, Marie's, 2 Tbsp	90	7	1	5	240	6	1
Italian herb, Henri's, 2 Tbsp	110	11	1.5	0	410	2	0

SALAD DRESSING	CAL	FAT (g)	SAT FAT (g)	CHOL (mg)	SODIUM (mg)	CARB (g)	FIBER (g)
Italian herb, creamy, low fat, Marie's Luscious Low Fat Dressing, 2 Tbsp	40	2	0	0	290	6	0
Italian Parmesan, fat free, Hidden Valley Ranch, 2 Tbsp	20	0	0	0	240	4	ns
Italian vinaigrette, fat free, Marie's Zesty Fat Free, 2 Tbsp	35	0	0	0	280	8	0
Mexican spice mix, with vinegar, water & oil, Good Seasons, 2 Tbsp	140	15	2.5	0	310	2	0
Nacho cheese, Hidden Valley Ranch, 2 Tbsp	130	14	2	10	180	2	ns
Olive oil, Italian, Wish-Bone, 2 Tbsp	70	6	1	0	400	4	0
Olive oil & vinegar, Newman's Own, 2 Tbsp	150	16	2.5	0	150	1	0
Olive oil vinaigrette, Wish-Bone, 2 Tbsp	60	5	0.5	0	250	4	0
Oriental sesame mix, with vinegar, water, & oil, Good Seasons, 2 Tbsp	150	16	2.5	0	360	3	0
Ott's Famous Salad dressing, 2 Tbsp	80	6	1	ns	210	9	ns
Ott's Famous salad dressing, fat free, 2 Tbsp	35	0	0	ns	310	9	ns
Ott's Famous salad dressing, reduced calorie, 2 Tbsp	60	3	0	ns	210	8	ns
Parmesan, creamy, Hidden Valley Ranch, 2 Tbsp	140	15	3	10	260	1	ns
Parmesan, creamy, fat free, Hidden Valley Ranch, 2 Tbsp	30	0	0	0	250	5	ns
Parmesan, creamy, low fat, Marie's Luscious Low Fat Dressing, 2 Tbsp	45	2	0	0	270	7	0
Parmesan pepper, Marzetti, 2 Tbsp	160	17	3	10	260	1	0
Parmesan ranch, Henri's, 2 Tbsp	160	16	2.5	10	290	4	na
Parmesan ranch, Marie's, 2 Tbsp	180	19	3	15	160	3	0
Parmesan ranch, light, Henri's, 2 Tbsp	60	2	0.5	5	310	10	na

SALAD DRESSING	CAL (g)	FAT (g)	SAT FAT (g)	CHOL (mg)	SODIUM (mg)	CARB (g)	FIBER (g)
Peppercorn, cracked, Marzetti, 2 Tbsp	140	14	3	30	280	1	0
Peppercorn ranch, Kraft, 2 Tbsp	170	18	3	10	340	1	0
Peppercorn ranch, Marzetti, 2 Tbsp	180	19	3	10	220	1	0
Peppercorn ranch, fat free, Kraft Free, 2 Tbsp	50	0	0	0	360	11	1
Peppercorn ranch, fat free, Marzetti, 2 Tbsp	30	0	0	0	420	7	1
Pizza, Hidden Valley Ranch, 2 Tbsp	140	14	2	10	240	2	ns
Poppyseed, Marie's, 2 Tbsp	150	12	2	10	200	8	0
Poppyseed, Marzetti, 2 Tbsp	160	13	2	20	310	10	0
Poppy seed, reduced calorie, Ott's, 2 Tbsp	90	7	1	ns	210	9	ns
Poppyseed, refrigerated, Marzetti, 2 Tbsp	140	11	1.5	10	220	10	0
Ranch, Henri's, 2 Tbsp	170	17	2.5	10	270	4	0
Ranch, Kraft, 2 Tbsp	170	18	3	5	270	2	0
Ranch, Marzetti, 2 Tbsp	180	20	3	<5	260	1	0
Ranch, Newman's Own, 2 Tbsp	180	19	3	5	170	2	0
Ranch, Ott's, 2 Tbsp	140	15	2	ns	120	1	ns
Ranch, Seven Seas, 2 Tbsp	150	16	2.5	5	250	2	0
Ranch, Wish-Bone, 2 Tbsp	160	17	2.5	10	210	1	0
Ranch, Wish-Bone Lite, 2 Tbsp	100	8	1.5	5	240	5	0
Ranch, creamy, Marie's, 2 Tbsp	190	20	3	15	170	3	0
Ranch, creamy, reduced calorie, Marie's, 2 Tbsp	100	7	1	5	240	7	<1
Ranch, creamy herb, fat free, Bernstein, 2 Tbsp	30	0	0	0	300	7	0
Ranch, fat free, Henri's, 2 Tbsp	40	0	0	0	340	9	0
Ranch, fat free, Kraft Free, 2 Tbsp	50	0	0	0	310	11	<1
Ranch, fat free, Seven Seas, 2 Tbsp	50	0	0	0	330	12	1

SALAD DRESSING	CAL (g)	FAT (g)	SAT FAT (g)	CHOL (mg)	SODIUM (mg)	CARB (g)	FIBER (g)
Ranch, fat free, Weight Watchers Salad Celebrations, 2 Tbsp	35	0	0	0	270	7	0
Ranch, fat free, Wish-Bone, 2 Tbsp	40	0	0	0	270	9	0
Ranch, garden, Marzetti, 2 Tbsp	180	19	3	<5	250	1	0
Ranch, light, Henri's, 2 Tbsp	60	2	0	5	290	11	0
Ranch, nacho cheese, Hidden Valley Ranch, 2 Tbsp	130	14	1.5	10	180	1	ns
Ranch, original, Hidden Valley Ranch, 2 Tbsp	140	14	1.5	10	260	1	ns
Ranch, original, fat free, Hidden Valley Ranch, 2 Tbsp	45	0	0	0	320	9	ns
Ranch, Parmesan garlic, reduced calorie, Bernstein's Light Fantastic, 2 Tbsp	45	1	0.5	5	280	7	0
Ranch, reduced calorie, Kraft Deliciously Right, 2 Tbsp	110	11	2	10	310	2	0
Ranch, reduced calorie, Seven Seas, 2 Tbsp	100	9	1.5	0	320	5	0
Ranch, sour cream & onion, Kraft, 2 Tbsp	170	18	3	10	240	1	0
Ranch, super creamy, Hidden Valley Ranch, 2 Tbsp	140	14	1	5	250	2	ns
Ranch mix, original, Hidden Valley Ranch, mix to make 2 Tbsp	5	0	0	0	130	1	0
Ranch mix, original, lowfat, Hidden Valley Ranch, mix to make 2 Tbsp	10	0	0	0	210	2	0
Ranch mix, original, reduced calorie, Hidden Valley Ranch, mix to make 2 Tbsp	5	0	0	0	190	1	0
Ranch mix, prepared, Good Seasons, 2 Tbsp	120	12	2	10	220	2	0
Ranch mix, reduced calorie, prepared, Good Seasons, 2 Tbsp	60	4.5	1	5	240	3	0
Ranch style, Marzetti, 2 Tbsp	160	13	2	0	240	11	0

SALAD DRESSING	CAL (g)	FAT (g)	SAT FAT (g)	CHOL (mg)	SODIUM (mg)	CARB (g)	FIBER (g)
Ranch Italian mix, Hidden Valley Ranch, mix to make 2 Tbsp	15	0	0	0	250	3	0
Raspberry, fat free, Marzetti, 2 Tbsp	70	0	0	0	150	18	0
Raspberry vinaigrette, fat free, Marie's, 2 Tbsp	35	0	0	0	35	8	0
Red wine vinaigrette, fat free, Marie's Zesty Fat Free, 2 Tbsp	40	0	0	0	300	10	0
Red wine vinegar, fat free, Kraft Free, 2 Tbsp	15	0	0	0	400	3	0
Red wine vinegar, fat free, Seven Seas, 2 Tbsp	15	0	0	0	400	3	0
Red wine vinegar & oil, Marzetti, 2 Tbsp	130	14	2	0	460	2	0
Red wine vinegar & oil, Seven Seas, 2 Tbsp	110	11	2	0	510	2	0
Red wine vinegar & oil, reduced calorie, Seven Seas, 2 Tbsp	60	5	1	0	310	2	0
Roka blue cheese, Kraft, 2 Tbsp	90	7	4	10	470	5	0
Roquefort cheese, 2 Tbsp	150	16	3	5	330	2	0
Russian, Henri's, 2 Tbsp	120	10	1.5	0	190	9	0
Russian, Kraft, 2 Tbsp	130	10	1.5	0	280	10	0
Russian, Seven Seas Viva, 2 Tbsp	150	16	2.5	0	230	3	0
Russian, Weight Watchers Salad Celebrations, 2 Tbsp	45	1.5	0	10	190	8	0
Russian, Wish-Bone, 2 Tbsp	110	6	1	0	350	15	0
Russian mix, Weight Watchers, ⅙ pkg	0	0	0	0	200	1	0
Salsa ranch, Kraft, 2 Tbsp	130	13	2	10	320	1	0
Salsa zesty garden, Kraft, 2 Tbsp	70	6	1	0	280	3	<1
Santa Fe, Wish-Bone, 2 Tbsp	150	15	2.5	5	220	3	0
Sesame garlic, cholesterol- & dairy-free, Nasoy Vegi-Dressing, 2 Tbsp	60	5	0	0	125	3	ns

SALAD DRESSING	CAL (g)	FAT (g)	SAT FAT (g)	CHOL (mg)	SODIUM (mg)	CARB (g)	FIBER (g)
Sierra, Wish-Bone, 2 Tbsp	150	16	2.5	0	260	2	0
Slaw, light, Marzetti, 2 Tbsp	100	7	1	30	380	10	0
Slaw, original, Marzetti, 2 Tbsp	170	16	2.5	30	360	6	0
Sour cream & dill, Marie's, 2 Tbsp	190	20	3	15	160	3	0
Sweet & saucy, Marzetti, 2 Tbsp	140	12	1.5	0	290	9	0
Sweet & sour, Marzetti, 2 Tbsp	160	13	2	0	210	10	0
Sweet & sour, Old Dutch, 2 Tbsp	50	0	0	0	480	13	0
Tas-Tee, Henri's, 2 Tbsp	110	9	1.5	0	200	8	0
Tas-Tee, light, Henri's, 2 Tbsp	60	2	0	0	220	11	0
Teriyaki stir-fry, Marzetti, 2 Tbsp	80	1.5	0	0	820	14	0
Thousand island, Henri's, 2 Tbsp	100	9	1.5	5	230	5	0
Thousand island, Kraft, 2 Tbsp	110	10	1.5	10	310	5	0
Thousand island, Marie's, 2 Tbsp	240	23	4	20	320	7	0
Thousand island, Marzetti, 2 Tbsp	140	14	2	20	220	4	0
Thousand island, Weight Watchers Salad Celebrations, 2 Tbsp	45	1.5	0	10	190	8	0
Thousand island, Wish-Bone, 2 Tbsp	130	12	2	10	340	7	0
Thousand island, Wish-Bone lite, 2 Tbsp	80	5	1	10	250	7	0
Thousand island, cholesterol-dairy free, Nasoy Vegi-ressing, 2 Tbsp	60	4	0	0	140	6	ns
Thousand island, fat free, Henri's, 2 Tbsp	40	0	0	0	260	9	0
Thousand island, fat free, Kraft Free, 2 Tbsp	45	0	0	0	300	11	1
Thousand island, fat free, Marzetti, 2 Tbsp	35	0	0	0	370	9	0

SALAD DRESSING	CAL (g)	FAT (g)	SAT FAT (g)	CHOL (mg)	SODIUM (mg)	CARB (g)	FIBER (g)
Thousand island, fat free, Wish-Bone, 2 Tbsp	35	0	0	0	290	8	0
Thousand island, light, Henri's, 2 Tbsp	50	2	0	15	310	8	0
Thousand island, reduced calorie, Kraft Deliciously Right, 2 Tbsp	70	4	1	5	320	8	0
Thousand island, refrigerated, Marzetti, 2 Tbsp	150	15	2	25	230	5	0
Thousand island, Rio Grande, fat free, Bernstein, 2 Tbsp	40	0	0	0	270	10	0
Thousand island, with bacon, Kraft, 2 Tbsp	120	12	2	0	190	5	0
Thousand island mix, Weight Watchers, 1/6 pkg	0	0	0	0	260	1	0
Vinegar & oil, 2 Tbsp	140	16	3	0	0	<1	0
Viva Italian, reduced calorie, Seven Seas, 2 Tbsp	45	4	1	0	390	2	0
White wine vinaigrette, fat free, Marie's Zesty Fat Free, 2 Tbsp	40	0	0	0	310	10	0
Wilde raspberry, Marzetti, 2 Tbsp	150	12	1.5	0	65	12	0
Zesty ranch, low fat, Marie's Luscious Low Fat Dressing, 2 Tbsp	45	2	0	0	330	7	0

AT A GLANCE: SALAD DRESSING

Choose from among the dozens of fat free dressings (many with less than 10 calories per serving) from Bernstein, Good Seasons, Henri's, Hidden Valley Ranch, Kraft Free, Marzetti's, Seven Seas, Wish-Bone, Weight Watchers Salad Celebrations, and Western.

Lowest in Sodium: Vinegar & Oil

SALAD TOPPINGS

	CAL (g)	FAT (g)	SAT FAT (g)	CHOL (mg)	SODIUM (mg)	CARB (g)	FIBER (g)
Bacon bits, Betty Crocker Bac'Os, 1 Tbsp	30	1	0	0	130	2	0
Bacon bits, Durkee, 1 Tbsp	0	0	0	0	180	2	<1
Bacon bits, Hormel, 1 tsp	30	1.5	1	5	250	0	0
Bacon bits, real, Oscar Mayer, 1 Tbsp	25	1.5	0.5	5	220	0	0

SALAD TOPPINGS	CAL	FAT (g)	SAT FAT (g)	CHOL (mg)	SODIUM (mg)	CARB (g)	FIBER (g)
Bacon cheddar, Pepperidge Farm Salad Toppers, 1 Tbsp	35	2	0	0	85	4	0
Bacon chips, Durkee, 1 Tbsp	0	0	0	0	190	2	<1
Bacon pieces, Hormel, 1 tsp	25	1.5	0.5	10	170	0	0
Caesar salad bar mix, Pepperidge Farm Salad Toppers, 1 Tbsp	35	2	0	0	85	4	0
Cinnamon raisin, Pepperidge Farm Salad Toppers, 1 Tbsp	35	2	0	0	15	4	0
Garlic Italian, Pepperidge Farm Salad Toppers, 1 Tbsp	35	2	0	0	70	4	0

SALSA & PICANTE SAUCE

	CAL	FAT (g)	SAT FAT (g)	CHOL (mg)	SODIUM (mg)	CARB (g)	FIBER (g)
Garlic, roasted, Marie's, 2 Tbsp	10	0	0	0	230	2	0
Picante, Old El Paso, 2 Tbsp	10	0	0	0	230	2	0
Picante, Pace, 2 Tbsp	10	0	0	0	210	2	<1
Picante, hot, Chi-Chi's, 2 Tbsp	10	0	0	0	270	2	0
Picante, jalapeno, zesty, hot, Rosarita, 2 Tbsp	10	0	0	0	250	2	<1
Picante, jalapeno, zesty, medium, Rosarita, 2 Tbsp	10	0	0	0	250	2	<1
Picante, jalapeno, zesty, mild, Rosarita, 2 Tbsp	10	0	0	0	240	2	0
Picante, medium, Chi-Chi's, 2 Tbsp	10	0	0	0	200	2	0
Picante, thick & chunky, hot, Old El Paso, 2 Tbsp	10	0	0	0	160	2	0
Picante, thick & chunky, medium, Old El Paso, 2 Tbsp	10	0	0	0	140	2	0
Picante, thick & chunky, mild, Old El Paso, 2 Tbsp	10	0	0	0	130	2	0
Picante sauce, mild, Chi-Chi's, 2 Tbsp	10	0	0	0	210	2	0
Pico de gallo, Old El Paso, 2 Tbsp	5	0	0	0	260	2	<1
Salsa, Eagle, 2 Tbsp	10	0	0	0	250	2	<1
Salsa, Tostitos, 2 Tbsp	15	0	0	0	240	3	1

SALSA & PICANTE SAUCE	CAL	FAT (g)	SAT FAT (g)	CHOL (mg)	SODIUM (mg)	CARB (g)	FIBER (g)
Salsa, chunky, Old El Paso, 2 Tbsp	15	0	0	0	230	3	1
Salsa, chunky, hot, Enrico's, 2 Tbsp	15	0	0	0	90	3	0
Salsa, extra chunky, Rosarita, 2 Tbsp	10	0	0	0	230	1	0
Salsa, garlic, Christopher Ranch, 2 Tbsp	15	1	ns	ns	120	2	ns
Salsa, green chili, Territorial House, 2 Tbsp	10	0	0	0	180	2	1
Salsa, green chili, medium, Old El Paso, 2 Tbsp	10	0	0	0	110	2	<1
Salsa, homestyle, Old El Paso, 2 Tbsp	5	0	0	0	110	1	0
Salsa, hot, Chi-Chi's, 2 Tbsp	10	0	0	0	160	1	0
Salsa, hot, Newman's Own Bandito, 2 Tbsp	10	0	0	0	150	2	0
Salsa, hot, organic, Enrico's, 2 Tbsp	10	0	0	0	90	2	0
Salsa, medium, Chi-Chi's, 2 Tbsp	10	0	0	0	140	1	0
Salsa, medium, Newman's Own Bandito, 2 Tbsp	10	0	0	0	105	2	0
Salsa, mild, Chi-Chi's, 2 Tbsp	10	0	0	0	150	1	0
Salsa, mild, Newman's Own Bandito, 2 Tbsp	10	0	0	0	105	2	0
Salsa, roasted, Rosarita, 2 Tbsp	10	0	0	0	230	2	<1
Salsa, thick & chunky, Old El Paso, 2 Tbsp	10	0	0	0	140	2	0
Salsa, thick & chunky, Pace, 2 Tbsp	10	0	0	0	210	2	0
Salsa, thick 'n chunky, mild, Taco Bell, 2 Tbsp	15	0	0	0	340	3	1
Salsa, tomatillo, green, Rosarita, 2 Tbsp	10	0	0	0	190	2	<1
Salsa, traditional, medium, Rosarita, 2 Tbsp	10	0	0	0	230	2	<1
Salsa, traditional, mild, Rosarita, 2 Tbsp	10	0	0	0	250	1	<1

SALSA & PICANTE SAUCE	CAL	FAT (g)	SAT FAT (g)	CHOL (mg)	SODIUM (mg)	CARB (g)	FIBER (g)
Salsa, wild, Taco Bell, 2 Tbsp	15	0	0	0	240	3	1
Salsa Mexicana, Del Monte, 2 Tbsp	5	0	0	0	200	2	1
Salsa Mexicana, hot, Las Palmas, 2 Tbsp	10	0	0	0	75	2	0
Salsa Mexicana, medium, Las Palmas, 2 Tbsp	10	0	0	0	85	2	0
Salsa Mexicana, mild, Las Palmas, 2 Tbsp	10	0	0	0	90	1	0
Salsa Taquera, Del Monte, 2 Tbsp	5	0	0	0	220	2	1
Salsa verde, Chi-Chi's, 2 Tbsp	15	0	0	0	180	3	0
Salsa verde, Del Monte, 2 Tbsp	10	0	0	0	280	2	<1
Salsa verde, Old El Paso, 2 Tbsp	10	0	0	0	95	2	0
Tomato, Marie's, 2 Tbsp	10	0	0	0	250	2	0

AT A GLANCE: SALSA & PICANTE SAUCE
Lowest in Sodium: Las Palmas Salsa Mexicana, Hot

SAUCES

	CAL	FAT (g)	SAT FAT (g)	CHOL (mg)	SODIUM (mg)	CARB (g)	FIBER (g)
A la king sauce mix, Durkee, ½ pkg	60	4	1	0	800	8	0
Au jus sauce mix, Knorr Gravy Classics, ⅕ pkg	15	0	0	0	310	3	ns
Barbecue cooking sauce, Hunt's Chicken Sensations, 1 Tbsp	35	3	0	0	310	3	0
Bearnaise sauce mix, Knorr, ⅕ pkg	20	0.5	ns	0	210	3	ns
Beef cooking sauce, homestyle, Uncle Ben's, ½ cup	70	1	0	0	770	13	1
Broccoli cooking sauce, creamy, Betty Crocker Recipe Sauces, ½ cup	210	20	7	25	700	7	0
Broccoli cooking sauce, creamy, Campbell's Simmer Chef, ½ cup	100	6	2	10	630	9	1
Burrito sauce, Hunt's Manwich, ¼ cup	25	0	0	0	560	6	4

SAUCES	CAL (g)	FAT (g)	SAT FAT (g)	CHOL (mg)	SODIUM (mg)	CARB (g)	FIBE (g)
Cacciatore cooking sauce, Uncle Ben's, ½ cup	70	2	0	0	560	11	2
Cacciatore cooking sauce, old country, Campbell's Simmer Chef, ½ cup	90	4	1	0	400	13	2
Cheese sauce, Franco-American, ¼ cup	40	2	1	5	390	4	0
Cheese sauce mix, Durkee, ¼ pkg	25	1.5	1	2	260	4	0
Cheese sauce mix, French's, ¼ pkg	25	0.5	0	0	250	4	0
Chicken cooking sauce, country, Uncle Ben's, ½ cup	130	9	5	30	510	12	1
Chicken cooking sauce, country French, Ragu Chicken Tonight, ½ cup	130	11	2	15	860	6	1
Chicken cooking sauce, zesty southwestern, Uncle Ben's, ½ cup	80	3	0	0	710	13	1
Chicken cacciatore cooking sauce, Ragu Chicken Tonight, ½ cup	80	1.5	0	0	530	14	2
Chicken Parmesan cooking sauce, creamy, Ragu Chicken Tonight, ½ cup	90	6	1	10	750	7	2
Chicken with mushrooms cooking sauce, creamy, Ragu Chicken Tonight, ½ cup	110	9	1.5	10	750	5	1
Chicken with wine cooking sauce, herbed, Ragu Chicken Tonight, ½ cup	80	6	1.5	5	670	6	1
Curry sauce mix, Knorr, ⅕ pkg	30	1.5	ns	0	220	4	ns
Demi-glace sauce mix, Knorr, ⅕ pkg	30	1	0	0	380	4	ns
Hollandaise sauce mix, Durkee, ⅒ pkg	10	0	0	5	70	2	0
Hollandaise sauce mix, French's, ⅒ pkg	10	0	0	5	75	2	0
Honey mustard cooking sauce, golden, Campbell's Simmer Chef, ½ cup	150	2	0	0	400	30	1

SAUCES	CAL (g)	FAT (g)	SAT FAT (g)	CHOL (mg)	SODIUM (mg)	CARB (g)	FIBER (g)
Italian garlic cooking sauce, Hunt's Chicken Sensations, 1 Tbsp	30	3	0	0	330	1	1
Lemon butter sauce mix, Weight Watchers, ¼ pkg	5	0	0	0	410	1	0
Lemon herb cooking sauce, Hunt's Chicken Sensations, 1 Tbsp	30	3	0	0	380	2	0
Mushroom sauce, House of Tsang, 1 Tbsp	10	0.5	0	0	210	2	0
Mushroom sauce mix, Knorr, ⅕ pkg	20	1	ns	0	200	2	ns
Mushroom & herb cooking sauce, creamy, Campbell's Simmer Chef, ½ cup	90	5	2	5	670	9	1
Mustard herb sauce mix, Knorr, ¼ pkg	40	1.5	ns	0	380	5	ns
Nacho cheese sauce mix, Durkee, ⅕ pkg	25	2	0	0	180	2	0
Newburg sauce mix, Knorr, ⅕ pkg	20	0.5	0	0	160	3	0
Onion & mushroom cooking sauce, Campbell's Simmer Chef, ½ cup	50	1	0	0	670	9	1
Oriental sweet & sour cooking sauce, Campbell's Simmer Chef, ½ cup	110	1	0	0	340	25	1
Peppercorn sauce mix, Knorr, ⅕ pkg	25	1	ns	0	350	3	ns
Sloppy Joe sauce, Betty Crocker Hamburger Helper, ¼ cup	50	0	0	0	310	12	0
Sloppy Joe sauce, Hormel Not-So-Sloppy Joe, ¼ cup	70	0	0	0	720	15	1
Sloppy Joe sauce, barbecue, Hunt's Manwich, ¼ cup	60	0	0	0	890	14	1
Sloppy Joe sauce, bold, Hunt's Manwich, ¼ cup	60	1	0	0	800	13	<1
Sloppy Joe sauce, hickory flavor, Del Monte, ¼ cup	70	0	0	0	700	18	0
Sloppy Joe sauce, Italian style, Del Monte, ¼ cup	70	0	0	0	700	16	0

SAUCES	CAL (g)	FAT (g)	SAT FAT (g)	CHOL (mg)	SODIUM (mg)	CARB (g)	FIBER (g)
Sloppy Joe sauce, meat, Green Giant, ½ cup	200	11	4	20	470	11	2
Sloppy Joe sauce, Mexican, Hunt's Manwich, ¼ cup	30	0	0	0	550	5	<1
Sloppy Joe sauce, original, Hunt's Manwich, ¼ cup	35	0	0	0	370	6	<1
Sloppy Joe sauce, original recipe, Del Monte, ¼ cup	70	0	0	0	680	16	0
Sloppy Joe sauce, plain, Green Giant, ½ cup	50	0	0	0	420	11	2
Sloppy Joe sauce, thick & chunky, Hunt's Manwich, ¼ cup	45	0	0	0	740	9	<1
Sloppy Joe sauce mix, barbecue, Betty Crocker Hamburger Helper, ¼ cup	80	0	0	0	470	19	0
Sloppy Joe sauce mix, pepperoni pizza, Betty Crocker Hamburger Helper, ¼ cup	45	0.5	0	0	440	8	0
Sloppy Joe sauce mix, taco, Betty Crocker Hamburger Helper, ¼ cup	45	0	0	0	510	10	0
Southwestern cooking sauce, Hunt's Chicken Sensations, 1 Tbsp	30	2.5	0	0	280	1	0
Stroganoff cooking sauce, Campbell's Simmer Chef, ½ cup	100	6	2	5	740	8	1
Sweet & sour cooking sauce, Betty Crocker Recipe Sauces, ½ cup	160	0	0	0	350	40	0
Sweet & sour cooking sauce, Ragu Chicken Tonight, ½ cup	120	0	0	0	320	30	1
Taco sauce, Hunt's Manwich, ¼ cup	30	0	0	0	590	7	1
Tomato Mexicali cooking sauce, zesty, Campbell's Simmer Chef, ½ cup	80	2	1	0	390	15	2
White sauce mix, Durkee, ¼ pkg	20	0.5	0	0	330	5	0
White sauce mix, Knorr, ⅑ pkg	25	1	0.5	0	200	4	ns

AT A GLANCE: SAUCES
Lowest in Sodium: Durkee Hollandaise Sauce Mix

	CAL	FAT (g)	SAT FAT (g)	CHOL (mg)	SODIUM (mg)	CARB (g)	FIBER (g)

SOY SAUCE

	CAL	FAT (g)	SAT FAT (g)	CHOL (mg)	SODIUM (mg)	CARB (g)	FIBER (g)
Kikkoman, 1 Tbsp	10	0	0	0	920	0	0
La Choy, 1 Tbsp	10	0	0	0	1230	1	0
Light, House of Tsang, 1 Tbsp	5	0	0	0	900	0	0
Lite, Kikkoman, 1 Tbsp	10	0	0	0	605	1	0
Lite, La Choy, 1 Tbsp	15	0	0	0	540	2	0
Mandarin, for stir fry, La Choy, ½ cup	70	0	0	0	850	16	1

STEAK SAUCE

	CAL	FAT (g)	SAT FAT (g)	CHOL (mg)	SODIUM (mg)	CARB (g)	FIBER (g)
A.1., 1 Tbsp	15	0	0	0	250	3	0
A.1. Bold, 1 Tbsp	20	0	0	0	190	5	0
Hunt's, 1 Tbsp	10	0	0	0	260	2	0
Texas Best, 1 Tbsp	15	0	0	0	220	4	0
57 Sauce, Heinz, 1 Tbsp	15	0	0	0	220	4	0
Caribbean style, Tabasco, 1 Tbsp	15	0	0	ns	130	4	ns
New Orleans style, Tabasco, 1 Tbsp	10	0	0	ns	90	2	ns
Pepper, Betty Crocker Recipe Sauces, ½ cup	50	1.5	0.5	0	600	8	0
Traditional, Heinz, 1 Tbsp	10	0	0	0	190	2	0

STIR FRY SAUCE

	CAL	FAT (g)	SAT FAT (g)	CHOL (mg)	SODIUM (mg)	CARB (g)	FIBER (g)
Kikkoman, 1 Tbsp	15	0	0	0	530	3	0
Saigon Sizzle, House of Tsang, 1 Tbsp	40	1	0	0	350	8	0
Soy, Mandarin, La Choy, ½ cup	70	0	0	0	850	16	1
Sweet & sour, House of Tsang, 1 Tbsp	35	0	0	0	50	8	0
Sweet & sour, spicy, La Choy, ½ cup	140	0	0	0	750	36	3
Szechwan, spicy, La Choy, ½ cup	80	0	0	0	620	18	0
Szechwan Spicy, House of Tsang, 1 Tbsp	20	0.5	0	0	490	4	0
Teriyaki, La Choy, ½ cup	90	0	0	0	1150	22	2

	CAL	FAT (g)	SAT FAT (g)	CHOL (mg)	SODIUM (mg)	CARB (g)	FIBER (g)
SWEET & SOUR SAUCE							
House of Tsang, 1 Tbsp	30	0	0	0	45	7	0
Kikkoman, 2 Tbsp	35	0	0	0	190	9	0
Kraft, 2 Tbsp	80	0.5	0	0	180	19	0
La Choy, 2 Tbsp	60	0	0	0	105	14	0
Sauceworks, 2 Tbsp	60	0	0	0	125	14	0
Texas Best, 2 Tbsp	60	0.5	0	0	140	17	0
Concentrate, House of Tsang, 1 tsp	10	0	0	0	15	3	0
SYRUPS & TOPPINGS							
Aunt Jemima syrup, lite, ¼ cup	100	0	0	0	160	27	0
Banana split fudge topping, Hershey's Chocolate Shoppe, 2 Tbsp	130	4.5	1.5	<5	50	22	<1
Butter maple syrup, Pillsbury Hungry Jack, ¼ cup	210	0	0	0	90	52	0
Butter rich syrup, Aunt Jemima, ¼ cup	210	0	0	0	170	52	0
Butterlite syrup, Aunt Jemima, ¼ cup	100	0	0	0	150	26	0
Butterscotch topping, Mrs. Richardson's, 2 Tbsp	130	1	0.5	0	200	30	0
Butterscotch & caramel topping, fat free, Smucker's, 2 Tbsp	130	0	0	0	110	31	1
Butterscotch caramel fudge topping, Mrs. Richardson's, 2 Tbsp	130	1.5	1.5	<5	60	30	0
Butterscotch caramel syrup, Smucker's Special Recipe, 2 Tbsp	110	0	0	0	70	27	1
Butterscotch caramel topping, Smucker's Special Recipe, 2 Tbsp	130	1	0.5	5	70	30	<1
Butterscotch flavored topping, Kraft, 2 Tbsp	130	1.5	1	<5	150	28	0
Caramel topping, Kraft, 2 Tbsp	120	0	0	0	90	28	0

SYRUPS & TOPPINGS	CAL	FAT (g)	SAT FAT (g)	CHOL (mg)	SODIUM (mg)	CARB (g)	FIBER (g)
Caramel topping, fat free, Mrs. Richardson's, 2 Tbsp	130	0	0	0	55	32	0
Chocolate flavored topping, Kraft, 2 Tbsp	110	0	0	0	30	26	1
Chocolate fudge topping, Smucker's, 2 Tbsp	130	1.5	0.5	0	60	28	1
Chocolate sundae flavor topping, Smucker's, 2 Tbsp	110	0	0	0	70	27	1
Chocolate syrup, Hershey's, 2 Tbsp	100	0	0	0	25	24	0
Chocolate syrup, lite, Hershey's, 2 Tbsp	50	0	0	0	35	12	0
Chocolate malt syrup, Hershey's, 2 Tbsp	100	0	0	0	55	25	0
Country best recipe syrup, Mrs. Butterworth's, ¼ cup	230	0	0	ns	95	56	ns
Fruit syrup, all flavors, Smucker's Natural, ¼ cup	210	0	0	0	0	52	0
Fruit syrup, all flavors, light, Smucker's, ¼ cup	130	0	0	0	0	33	0
Fudge topping, dark chocolate, Mrs. Richardson's, 2 Tbsp	140	6	5	0	75	20	1
Golden griddle syrup, Karo, 4 Tbsp	240	0	0	0	55	57	ns
Hot caramel topping, Smucker's, 2 Tbsp	120	3	0.5	0	60	29	0
Hot fudge topping, Kraft, 2 Tbsp	140	4	2	0	100	24	<1
Hot fudge topping, Smucker's, 2 Tbsp	140	4	1	0	60	24	1
Hot fudge topping, Smucker's Special Recipe, 2 Tbsp	140	4	1	0	70	22	<1
Hot fudge topping, fat free, Mrs. Richardson's, 2 Tbsp	110	0	0	0	60	25	<1
Hot fudge topping, light, fat free, Smucker's, 2 Tbsp	90	0	0	0	90	23	2
Hungry Jack syrup, lite, all flavors, Pillsbury, ¼ cup	100	0	0	0	90	24	0

SYRUPS & TOPPINGS	CAL	FAT (g)	SAT FAT (g)	CHOL (mg)	SODIUM (mg)	CARB (g)	FIBER (g)
Hungry Jack syrup, regular, Pillsbury, ¼ cup	210	0	0	0	90	52	0
Log Cabin Country Kitchen syrup, ¼ cup	200	0	0	0	110	53	0
Log Cabin Country Kitchen syrup, butter flavored, ¼ cup	200	0	0	0	200	53	0
Log Cabin Country Kitchen Lite syrup, reduced calorie, ¼ cup	100	0	0	0	160	26	0
Log Cabin syrup, ¼ cup	200	0	0	0	60	52	0
Log Cabin Lite syrup, reduced calorie, ¼ cup	100	0	0	0	180	26	0
Magic Shell topping, all flavors, Smucker's, 2 Tbsp	220	16	6	0	25	16	0
Marshmallow topping, Smucker's, 2 Tbsp	120	0	0	0	0	29	0
Mrs. Butterworth's syrup, ¼ cup	230	0	0	ns	95	56	ns
Mrs. Butterworth's syrup, lite, ¼ cup	100	0	0	ns	100	25	ns
Mrs. Richardson's syrup, ¼ cup	210	0	0	0	115	52	ns
Mrs. Richardson's syrup, lite, ¼ cup	100	0	0	0	160	26	ns
Pancake syrup, Karo, 4 Tbsp	240	0	0	0	85	62	ns
Pancake and waffle syrup, Aunt Jemima, ¼ cup	210	0	0	0	120	53	0
Peanut butter caramel topping, Smucker's, 2 Tbsp	150	4.5	0.5	0	125	24	<1
Pecans in syrup, Smucker's, 2 Tbsp	190	11	1	0	0	22	0
Pineapple topping, Kraft, 2 Tbsp	110	0	0	0	15	28	0
Pineapple topping, Smucker's, 2 Tbsp	110	0	0	0	0	28	0
Strawberry topping, Kraft, 2 Tbsp	110	0	0	0	15	29	0
Strawberry topping, Smucker's, 2 Tbsp	100	0	0	0	0	26	0

SYRUPS & TOPPINGS	CAL	FAT (g)	SAT FAT (g)	CHOL (mg)	SODIUM (mg)	CARB (g)	FIBER (g)
Strawberry topping, fat free, Mrs. Richardson's, 2 Tbsp	70	0	0	0	15	18	<1
Walnuts in syrup, Smucker's, 2 Tbsp	190	10	1	0	0	23	0

AT A GLANCE: SYRUPS & TOPPINGS
Lowest in Sodium: Hershey's Lite Chocolate Syrup

TACO SAUCE

Old El Paso, 1 Tbsp	5	0	0	0	85	1	0
Pancho Villa, 2 Tbsp	15	0	0	0	170	3	0
Extra chunky, Old El Paso, 1 Tbsp	5	0	0	0	80	1	0
Hot, Old El Paso, 1 Tbsp	5	0	0	0	90	1	0
Medium, Old El Paso, 1 Tbsp	5	0	0	0	70	1	0
Mild, Old El Paso, 1 Tbsp	5	0	0	0	85	1	0
Thick & chunky, Chi-Chi's, 2 Tbsp	10	0	0	0	75	1	0
Thick & smooth, Ortega, 1 Tbsp	10	0	0	0	120	2	0

TAHINI

Joyva, 2 Tbsp	200	18	2.5	0	75	3	1
From raw & stone ground sesame seed kernels, 1 oz	160	14	2	0	20	7	3
From roasted & toasted sesame seed kernels, 1 oz	170	15	2	0	35	6	3
Organic, Once Again Nut Butter, 2 Tbsp	180	15	2	0	10	8	5
Tahini sauce mix, prepared, Casbah, ¼ cup	160	13	0	0	160	10	<1

TARTAR SAUCE

Heinz, 2 Tbsp	140	14	2	5	250	4	0
Hellmann's/Best Foods, 2 Tbsp	140	16	2.5	10	260	1	ns
Sauceworks, 2 Tbsp	100	10	4	10	180	4	0
Silver Spring, 2 Tbsp	80	6	1	5	210	7	1
Natural lemon & herb flavor, Sauceworks, 2 Tbsp	150	16	2.5	15	170	<1	0

TARTAR SAUCE	CAL	FAT (g)	SAT FAT (g)	CHOL (mg)	SODIUM (mg)	CARB (g)	FIBER (g)
Nonfat, Kraft, 2 Tbsp	25	0	0	0	210	5	<1
Reduced fat, Hellmann's/Best Foods, 2 Tbsp	60	4.5	0.5	0	340	6	ns

TERIYAKI SAUCE

	CAL	FAT (g)	SAT FAT (g)	CHOL (mg)	SODIUM (mg)	CARB (g)	FIBER (g)
La Choy, 1 Tbsp	20	0	0	0	920	3	0
Hot, Chun King, 1 Tbsp	20	0	0	0	990	3	0
Lite, La Choy, 1 Tbsp	20	0	0	0	440	4	0

TOMATO PASTE & SAUCE

	CAL	FAT (g)	SAT FAT (g)	CHOL (mg)	SODIUM (mg)	CARB (g)	FIBER (g)
Tomato & green chile sauce, Old El Paso, ¼ cup	10	0	0	0	310	2	0
Tomato paste, Contadina, 2 Tbsp	30	0	0	0	20	6	1
Tomato paste, Del Monte, 2 Tbsp	30	0	0	0	25	7	2
Tomato paste, Hunt's, 2 Tbsp	30	0	0	0	90	6	2
Tomato paste, Progresso, 2 Tbsp	30	0	0	0	20	6	1
Tomato paste, Italian, Contadina, 2 Tbsp	40	1	0	0	330	7	1
Tomato paste, Italian, Hunt's, 2 Tbsp	30	0	0	0	260	6	2
Tomato paste, no salt added, Hunt's, 2 Tbsp	30	0	0	0	10	6	2
Tomato paste, with garlic, Hunt's, 2 Tbsp	30	0	0	0	280	6	2
Tomato puree, Contadina, ¼ cup	20	0	0	0	15	4	<1
Tomato sauce, Contadina, ¼ cup	20	0	0	0	280	4	<1
Tomato sauce, Hunt's, ¼ cup	15	0	0	0	370	3	<1
Tomato sauce, Progresso, ¼ cup	20	0	0	0	260	4	1
Tomato sauce, chunky chili, Hunt's Ready Sauce, ¼ cup	25	0	0	0	320	4	1
Tomato sauce, chunky Italian, Hunt's Ready Sauce, ¼ cup	25	0	0	0	250	5	1

TOMATO PASTE & SAUCE	CAL (g)	FAT (g)	SAT FAT (g)	CHOL (mg)	SODIUM (mg)	CARB (g)	FIBER (g)
Tomato sauce, chunky Mexican, Hunt's Ready Sauce, ¼ cup	20	0	0	0	390	4	1
Tomato sauce, chunky special, Hunt's Ready Sauce, ¼ cup	20	0.5	0	0	140	4	<1
Tomato sauce, chunky tomato, Hunt's Ready Sauce, ¼ cup	15	0	0	0	400	3	1
Tomato sauce, country herb, Hunt's Ready Sauce, ¼ cup	35	1.5	0	0	260	5	<1
Tomato sauce, garlic, Hunt's Ready Sauce, ¼ cup	30	1	0	0	270	5	2
Tomato sauce, garlic & herb, Hunt's Ready Sauce, ¼ cup	25	0	0	0	200	5	<1
Tomato sauce, Italian, Hunt's, ¼ cup	35	1.5	0	0	210	5	1
Tomato sauce, Italian style, Contadina, ¼ cup	15	0	0	0	320	4	1
Tomato sauce, Meatloaf Fixins, Hunt's Ready Sauce, ¼ cup	25	0	0	0	600	4	<1
Tomato sauce, no salt added, Hunt's, ¼ cup	15	0	0	0	15	3	<1
Tomato sauce, original, Contadina Pasta Ready, ½ cup	40	2	0	0	620	5	1
Tomato sauce, original Italian, Hunt's Ready Sauce, ¼ cup	30	1.5	0	0	180	4	1
Tomato sauce, primavera, Contadina Pasta Ready, ½ cup	50	1.5	0	0	600	8	1
Tomato sauce, puree, Hunt's, ¼ cup	25	0	0	0	100	4	<1
Tomato sauce, salsa, Hunt's Ready Sauce, ¼ cup	20	0	0	0	360	3	<1
Tomato sauce, thick & zesty, Contadina, ¼ cup	20	0	0	0	340	3	1
Tomato sauce, three cheese, Contadina Pasta Ready, ½ cup	70	4	0	0	650	8	<1

TOMATO PASTE & SAUCE	CAL (g)	FAT (g)	SAT FAT (g)	CHOL (mg)	SODIUM (mg)	CARB (g)	FIBER (g)
Tomato sauce, with herb, Hunt's, ¼ cup	35	1	0	0	270	5	<1
Tomato sauce, with mushrooms, Contadina Pasta Ready, ½ cup	50	1.5	0	0	640	9	1
Tomato sauce, with olives, Contadina Pasta Ready, ½ cup	60	3	0.5	0	640	8	1
Tomato sauce, with red peppers, Contadina Pasta Ready, ½ cup	60	3	0.5	0	690	8	1
Tomatoes & jalapenos sauce, Old El Paso, ¼ cup	15	0	0	0	290	3	1

AT A GLANCE: TOMATO PASTE & SAUCE
Lowest in Sodium, Tomato Paste: Hunt's, No Salt Added
Lowest in Sodium, Tomato Sauce: Hunt's, No Salt Added

WORCESTERSHIRE SAUCE

French's, 1 Tbsp	8	0	0	0	180	2	0
Heinz, 1 tsp	0	0	0	0	60	0	0
Lea & Perrins Original, 1 tsp	5	0	ns	0	55	1	ns
Hickory, French's, 1 Tbsp	8	0	0	0	180	2	0

COOKIES & CRACKERS

	CAL (g)	FAT (g)	SAT FAT (g)	CHOL (mg)	SODIUM (mg)	CARB (g)	FIBER (g)
COOKIES							
Almond crescents, Archway, 2 cookies	100	3.5	0.5	<5	75	17	<1
Almond crescents, Sunshine, 4 cookies	150	6	1.5	0	105	22	<1
Anginetti, Stella D'Oro, 4 pieces	140	4	1	40	10	23	<1
Animal, Little Debbie, 1 pkg	190	5	2	0	110	33	0
Animal crackers, Nabisco Barnum's Animals, 12 crackers	140	4	0.5	0	160	23	1
Animal crackers, Sunshine, 14 crackers	140	4	1	0	125	24	<1
Animal-shaped shortbread, iced, Keebler, 6 cookies	140	4.5	2	0	130	24	<1
Anisette toast, Stella D'Oro, 3 pieces	130	1	0	35	150	27	<1
Apple, Sunshine Golden Fruit, 1 cookie	80	1.5	0	0	55	15	<1
Apple bar, fat free, Archway, 1 cookie	60	0	0	0	30	15	0
Apple bran, low fat, Archway, 1 cookie	130	1.5	0	0	140	27	2
Apple cinnamon, Sunshine Golden Fruit, 1 cookie	60	0	0	0	50	13	<1
Apple cinnamon bar, Tastykake, 1 bar	180	7	1.5	0	160	29	1
Apple Delights, Little Debbie, 1 pkg	130	4.5	1.5	5	125	23	1
Apple fruit bars, fat free, Famous Amos, 2 cookies	100	0	0	0	60	21	1
Apple n' raisin, Archway, 1 cookie	130	4.5	1	<5	105	20	1
Apple Newtons, fat free, Nabisco, 2 cookies	100	0	0	0	60	24	1
Apple spice, fat free, Health Valley, 3 cookies	100	0	0	0	50	24	3
Apricot delight, fat free, Health Valley, 3 cookies	100	0	0	0	50	24	3

COOKIES	CAL (g)	FAT (g)	SAT FAT (g)	CHOL (mg)	SODIUM (mg)	CARB (g)	FIBER (g)
Apricot filled, Archway, 1 cookie	110	4	1	5	90	18	<1
Apricot raspberry, Pepperidge Farm, 3 cookies	140	6	2	5	110	22	<1
Arrowroot biscuits, Nabisco National, 1 cookie	20	0.5	0	0	15	3	<1
Back-to-School, Little Debbie, 1 pkg	200	7	2	0	290	30	1
Banana bran, low fat, Archway, 1 cookie	120	1.5	0	0	115	27	2
Banana spice, fat free, Health Valley, 3 cookies	100	0	0	0	50	24	3
Beacon Hill, chocolate walnut, Pepperidge Farm American Collection, 1 cookie	130	7	2	0	100	16	<1
Bells and stars, Archway, 3 cookies	150	7	1.5	5	100	19	<1
Biarritz, Pepperidge Farm International Collection, 6 cookies	160	8	4	0	50	21	<1
Biscotti, almond, Pepperidge Farm, 1 cookie	90	4	1	5	65	12	<1
Biscotti, almond, 5½", Pepperidge Farm, 1 cookie	160	6	2	10	125	23	1
Biscotti, almond, chocolate dipped, Pepperidge Farm, 1 cookie	110	4	2	10	70	14	1
Biscotti, almond, chocolate dipped, 5½", Pepperidge Farm, 1 cookie	210	10	4	20	130	26	2
Biscotti, anise, Pepperidge Farm, 1 cookie	90	3	1	5	75	14	0
Biscotti, anise, 5½", Pepperidge Farm, 1 cookie	160	5	2	15	140	25	<1
Biscotti, Caruso, almond, Pepperidge Farm, 1 cookie	90	4	1	5	65	12	<1
Biscotti, chocolate hazelnut, 3½", Pepperidge Farm, 1 cookie	90	5	1	15	80	11	2
Biscotti, chocolate hazelnut, 5½", Pepperidge Farm, 1 cookie	160	9	2	25	135	19	3

COOKIES	CAL (g)	FAT (g)	SAT FAT (g)	CHOL (mg)	SODIUM (mg)	CARB (g)	FIBER (g)
Biscotti, cinnamon chip, 3½", Pepperidge Farm, 1 cookie	90	4	1	15	60	14	0
Biscotti, cinnamon chip, 5½", Pepperidge Farm, 1 cookie	160	6	2	25	100	24	2
Biscotti, cranberry pistachio, Pepperidge Farm, 1 cookie	90	3	1	5	65	13	<1
Biscotti, cranberry pistachio, 5½", Pepperidge Farm, 1 cookie	160	6	2	10	120	25	1
Biscotti, Figaro, chocolate dipped, Pepperidge Farm, 1 cookie	110	4	2	10	70	14	1
Biscotti, La Scala, anise, Pepperidge Farm, 1 cookie	90	3	1	5	75	14	0
Biscotti, orange, chocolate dipped, Pepperidge Farm, 1 cookie	110	5	2	10	70	15	<1
Biscotti, orange, chocolate dipped, 5½", Pepperidge Farm, 1 cookie	200	8	3	15	130	27	2
Biscotti, Tosca, cranberry pistachio, Pepperidge Farm, 1 cookie	90	3	1	5	65	13	<1
Black walnut ice box, Archway, 1 cookie	120	6	1.5	5	75	15	0
Blueberry filled, Archway, 1 cookie	110	4	1	5	115	19	<1
Bordeaux, Pepperidge Farm, 4 cookies	130	5	3	10	95	20	<1
Bordeaux, milk chocolate, Pepperidge Farm, 3 cookies	160	9	4	0	95	19	0
Brown edge wafers, Nabisco, 5 cookies	140	6	1.5	<5	90	21	<1
Brownie, all varieties, fat free, Health Valley, 1 bar	110	0	0	0	30	26	4
Brownie, fudge, Little Debbie, 1 pkg	270	13	2.5	15	170	40	1
Brownie, fudge, fat free, cholesterol free, Entenmann's, ¹⁄₁₀ strip	110	0	0	0	140	27	1

COOKIES	CAL (g)	FAT (g)	SAT FAT (g)	CHOL (mg)	SODIUM (mg)	CARB (g)	FIBER (g)
Brownie, fudge, with chocolate chip, Eagle, 1 cookie	260	11	4	20	120	36	3
Brownie, fudge walnut, Tastykake, 1 brownie	370	17	4	80	150	52	1
Brownie, individual pack, Dolly Madison, 1 brownie	340	11	4	40	190	55	1
Brownie, multipack, Dolly Madison, 1 brownie	180	6	2	25	100	30	1
Brownie Bites, Hostess, 5 brownies	260	14	4	50	125	32	2
Brownie Bites, walnut, Hostess, 5 brownies	270	15	4	50	140	31	2
Brownie chocolate nut, Pepperidge Farm, 3 cookies	160	9	3	15	115	18	2
Brownie Lights, low fat, Little Debbie, 1 pkg	190	3	0.5	0	200	39	1
Brussels, Pepperidge Farm, 3 cookies	150	7	3	5	80	20	1
Brussels, mint, Pepperidge Farm, 3 cookies	190	10	4	0	100	22	1
Butter, Salerno, 6 cookies	160	7	2.5	10	130	22	<1
Butter, dark chocolate, Carr's, 2 cookies	150	7	4	0	40	19	2
Butter, milk chocolate, Carr's, 2 cookies	140	7	4	<5	50	18	1
Butter, reduced fat, Salerno, 6 cookies	150	5	2	15	170	24	<1
Butter Chessmen, Pepperidge Farm, 3 cookies	120	5	3	20	80	18	<1
Butter flavored sandwich with fudge creme filling, Keebler E.L. Fudge, 3 cookies	170	8	2	<5	105	24	<1
Butter sugar, Otis Spunkmeyer, 1 cookie	170	7	2.5	15	135	23	0
Butterscotch oatmeal, Pepperidge Farm, 3 cookies	170	9	3	10	110	22	1
Caramel cookie bars, Little Debbie, 1 pkg	160	8	1.5	0	85	22	0
Caramel pecan, soft baked, Pepperidge Farm, 1 cookie	130	7	2	20	55	16	<1

COOKIES	CAL (g)	FAT (g)	SAT FAT (g)	CHOL (mg)	SODIUM (mg)	CARB (g)	FIBER (g)
Carrot cake, Archway, 1 cookie	120	5	1	<5	180	18	0
Chantilly hazelnut raspberry, Pepperidge Farm, 1 cookie	80	3	1	5	50	12	<1
Charleston, milk chocolate toffee pecan, Pepperidge Farm American Collection, 1 cookie	130	7	3	20	110	16	<1
Cherry cobbler, Pepperidge Farm, 1 cookie	70	3	1	<5	45	11	0
Cherry filled, Archway, 1 cookie	110	4	1	10	100	19	<1
Cherry nougat, Archway, 3 cookies	150	9	1.5	0	40	18	0
Chesapeake, chocolate chunk pecan, Pepperidge Farm American Collection, 1 cookie	140	8	2	10	100	15	<1
Chocolat a l'Orange, Pepperidge Farm International Collection, 2 cookies	150	6	2	<5	20	23	0
Chocolate, fat free, Archway, 1 cookie	90	0	0	0	105	19	<1
Chocolate brownie, fat free, cholesterol free, Entenmann's, 2 cookies	80	0	0	0	90	20	1
Chocolate chip, Archway, 1 cookie	130	6	1.5	<5	150	19	0
Chocolate chip, Dolly Madison, 1 cookie	140	4	1.5	5	130	24	0
Chocolate chip, Eagle, 1 cookie	190	8	2.5	15	170	26	1
Chocolate chip, Entenmann's, 3 cookies	140	7	2	10	90	20	<1
Chocolate chip, Famous Amos, 4 cookies	130	6	2	10	100	20	1
Chocolate chip, Keebler Bakery Crisp Chips Deluxe, 3 cookies	180	9	3	10	135	23	<1
Chocolate chip, Keebler Chips Deluxe, 1 cookie	80	4.5	1.5	0	60	9	0

COOKIES	CAL (g)	FAT (g)	SAT FAT (g)	CHOL (mg)	SODIUM (mg)	CARB (g)	FIBER (g)
Chocolate chip, Keebler Chocolate Lovers Chips Deluxe, 1 cookie	90	5	2.5	10	75	11	<1
Chocolate chip, Nabisco Chips Ahoy!, 3 cookies	160	8	2.5	0	105	21	1
Chocolate chip, Otis Spunkmeyer, 1 cookie	170	8	4	15	120	23	0
Chocolate chip, Pepperidge Farm, 3 cookies	140	7	3	10	65	18	<1
Chocolate chip, Sunshine Chip-A-Roos, 3 cookies	190	10	3.5	0	150	23	1
Chocolate chip, Weight Watchers Smart Snackers, 1.06 oz	140	5	2	0	90	22	1
Chocolate chip, bite size, Keebler Bite Size Chips Deluxe, 8 cookies	160	9	3	<5	110	20	<1
Chocolate chip, bite size, Nabisco Chips Ahoy!, 14 cookies	150	7	2.5	0	105	21	<1
Chocolate chip, chewy, Nabisco Chips Ahoy!, 3 cookies	170	8	2.5	<5	125	23	<1
Chocolate chip, chunky, Nabisco Chips Ahoy!, 1 cookie	80	4	3	10	60	11	<1
Chocolate chip, double, Otis Spunkmeyer, 1 cookie	170	9	4	15	140	22	<1
Chocolate chip, mini, Sunshine, 5 cookies	160	8	3	0	120	20	<1
Chocolate chip, ready-to-bake, Mrs. Goodcookie, 2 cookies	120	6	2	0	80	15	0
Chocolate chip, reduced fat, Keebler Reduced Fat Chips Deluxe, 1 cookie	70	3	1	0	70	11	0
Chocolate chip, reduced fat, Nabisco Chips Ahoy!, 3 cookies	150	6	1.5	0	150	23	1
Chocolate chip, reduced fat, SnackWell's, 13 cookies	130	3.5	1.5	0	170	22	1
Chocolate chip, soft, Keebler Soft Batch, 1 cookie	80	3.5	1	0	70	10	<1

COOKIES	CAL (g)	FAT (g)	SAT FAT (g)	CHOL (mg)	SODIUM (mg)	CARB (g)	FIBER (g)
Chocolate chip, soft & chewy, Tastykake, 2 cookies	350	14	4	15	260	52	2
Chocolate chip, sprinkled, Nabisco Chips Ahoy!, 3 cookies	170	8	2.5	0	120	24	<1
Chocolate chip, striped, Nabisco Chips Ahoy!, 1 cookie	80	4	1.5	0	45	10	<1
Chocolate chip and pecans, Famous Amos, 4 cookies	140	7	1.5	10	90	19	1
Chocolate chip and toffee, Archway, 1 cookie	140	7	1.5	<5	120	19	<1
Chocolate chip bar, Tastykake, 1 bar	200	8	2	5	85	30	1
Chocolate chip drop, Archway, 1 cookie	140	10	3	10	105	11	<1
Chocolate chip ice box, Archway, 1 cookie	140	7	2.5	5	80	19	0
Chocolate chip pecan, Otis Spunkmeyer, 1 cookie	180	9	4	15	110	22	<1
Chocolate chip snaps, Nabisco, 7 cookies	150	5	1.5	0	115	24	<1
Chocolate chip supreme, Archway, 1 cookie	120	4.5	1.5	<5	120	19	1
Chocolate chip walnut, Otis Spunkmeyer, 1 cookie	180	9	4	15	110	22	<1
Chocolate chip with chocolate frosting, Betty Crocker Dunkaroos, 1 tray	120	4.5	1	0	85	20	<1
Chocolate chocolate chip, soft & chewy, Tastykake, 2 cookies	350	13	4	5	160	54	2
Chocolate chocolate walnut, soft baked, Pepperidge Farm, 1 cookie	130	6	2	5	45	16	1
Chocolate chunk, soft baked, Pepperidge Farm, 1 cookie	130	6	3	10	35	16	2
Chocolate fudge brownie, Eagle, 1 cookie	330	16	5	15	120	42	3
Chocolate graham, Nabisco, 3 cookies	160	8	5	0	90	21	1

COOKIES	CAL (g)	FAT (g)	SAT FAT (g)	CHOL (mg)	SODIUM (mg)	CARB (g)	FIBER (g)
Chocolate graham with chocolate chip frosting, Betty Crocker Dunkaroos, 1 tray	130	5	1	0	70	20	0
Chocolate laced pirouette, Pepperidge Farm, 5 cookies	180	10	3	5	90	20	<1
Chocolate sandwich, Famous Amos, 3 cookies	150	8	2	0	105	21	1
Chocolate sandwich, Nabisco Oreo, 3 cookies	160	7	1.5	0	220	23	1
Chocolate sandwich, Nabisco Oreo Double Stuf, 2 cookies	140	7	1.5	0	150	19	<1
Chocolate sandwich, Sunshine Hydrox, 3 cookies	150	7	2	0	125	21	1
Chocolate sandwich, Sunshine Vienna Fingers, 2 cookies	120	3.5	1	0	115	22	<1
Chocolate sandwich, Ultra Slim Fast, 3 cookies	130	3	1	0	130	24	1
Chocolate sandwich, Weight Watchers Smart Snackers, 1.06 oz	140	3.5	1	0	160	23	1
Chocolate sandwich, fudge covered, Nabisco Oreo, 1 cookie	110	6	1.5	0	85	14	<1
Chocolate sandwich, reduced fat, Nabisco Oreo, 3 cookies	140	5	1	0	190	24	1
Chocolate sandwich, reduced fat, Sunshine Hydrox, 3 cookies	130	4	1	0	140	24	1
Chocolate sandwich, white fudge covered, Nabisco Oreo, 1 cookie	110	6	1.5	0	70	14	<1
Chocolate sandwich with chocolate creme, reduced fat, SnackWell's, 2 cookies	100	2.5	0.5	0	190	20	1
Chocolate sandwich with fudge creme, reduced fat, Keebler Elfin Delights, 2 cookies	110	2.5	0.5	0	100	19	<1
Chocolate sandwich with vanilla creme, Keebler E.L. Fudge, 3 cookies	170	8	2	0	125	23	1

COOKIES	CAL (g)	FAT (g)	SAT FAT (g)	CHOL (mg)	SODIUM (mg)	CARB (g)	FIBER (g)
Chocolate sandwich with vanilla creme, reduced fat, Keebler Elfin Delights, 2 cookies	110	2.5	0.5	0	120	19	<1
Chocolate snaps, Nabisco, 7 cookies	140	5	2	0	180	23	1
Chocolate wafers, Nabisco, 5 cookies	140	4	1.5	<5	230	24	1
Chocolate wafers, Sunshine Sugar Wafer, 3 wafers	130	7	2	0	30	17	<1
Chocolate with vanilla frosting, Betty Crocker Dunkaroos, 1 tray	120	4.5	1	0	110	20	0
Cinnamon apple, Archway, 1 cookie	110	3.5	0.5	5	135	20	<1
Cinnamon graham with vanilla frosting and sprinkles, Betty Crocker Dunkaroos, 1 tray	130	4.5	1.5	0	65	21	0
Cinnamon grahams, Ultra Slim Fast, 40 cookies	120	1.5	0	0	120	24	1
Cinnamon honey heart, fat free, Archway, 3 cookies	100	0	0	0	115	24	<1
Cinnamon snaps, Archway, 5 cookies	150	7	1.5	<5	120	20	0
Coconut macaroon, Archway, 1 cookie	90	5	4	0	55	14	2
Cookie Jar Hermits, Archway, 1 cookie	110	3	0.5	<5	160	19	<1
Cookies 'n creme, honey graham sticks and vanilla creme, MooTown Snackers, 1 package	140	7	1	0	60	19	0
Cookies 'n creme, vanilla sticks and chocolate fudge, MooTown Snackers, 1 package	140	7	2	0	65	20	0
Cranberry, low-fat, Sunshine, 1 cookie	70	1	0	0	55	15	<1
Cranberry bar, fat free, Archway, 1 cookie	70	0	0	0	25	16	<1
Cranberry Newtons, fat free, Nabisco, 2 cookies	100	0	0	0	95	23	1

COOKIES	CAL (g)	FAT (g)	SAT FAT (g)	CHOL (mg)	SODIUM (mg)	CARB (g)	FIBER (g)
Creme sandwich, reduced fat, Keebler Elfin Delights, 2 cookies	110	2.5	0.5	0	90	19	0
Danish, imported, Nabisco, 5 cookies	170	8	2	0	80	22	1
Danish wedding, Keebler, 4 cookies	120	5	2	0	80	20	<1
Dark chocolate, Carr's Home Wheat, 2 cookies	130	6	3	0	90	17	<1
Date delight, fat free, Health Valley, 3 cookies	100	0	0	0	50	24	3
Date granola, fat free, Health Valley, 3 cookies	100	0	0	0	50	24	3
Delice au Chocolat, Pepperidge Farm International Collection, 2 cookies	110	4	2	0	50	19	0
Deluxe grahams, fudge covered grahams, Keebler Fudge Shoppe, 3 cookies	140	7	4.5	0	105	19	<1
Devil's food cake, fat free, SnackWell's, 2 cookies	50	0	0	0	25	13	<1
Devils food, fat free, Keebler Elfin Delights, 1 cookie	70	0	0	0	80	14	0
Double chocolate fudge, fat free, Pepperidge Farm, 1 cookie	60	0	0	0	60	13	<1
Double fudge cake, fat free, SnackWell's, 1 cookie	50	0	0	0	70	12	<1
Dutch cocoa, Archway, 1 cookie	120	4	1	<5	110	19	0
Esprits Blanc, Pepperidge Farm International Collection, 1 cookie	80	5	3	10	50	10	0
Esprits Noir, Pepperidge Farm International Collection, 1 cookie	90	5	4	10	50	10	0
Fig, Ultra Slim Fast, 1 cookie	60	0.5	0	0	70	14	1
Fig bar, fat free, Archway, 1 cookie	80	0	0	0	40	15	<1
Fig bars, Famous Amos, 2 cookies	120	2.5	0.5	0	95	23	1

COOKIES	CAL (g)	FAT (g)	SAT FAT (g)	CHOL (mg)	SODIUM (mg)	CARB (g)	FIBER (g)
Fig bars, fat free, Famous Amos, 2 cookies	100	0	0	0	70	21	1
Fig Newtons, Nabisco, 2 cookies	110	2.5	1	0	120	20	1
Fig Newtons, fat free, Nabisco, 2 cookies	110	0	0	0	115	22	2
Figaroos, Little Debbie, 1 pkg	160	3.5	0.5	0	125	31	1
Figbars, Sunshine, 2 cookies	110	2.5	0.5	0	120	20	1
Fortune, La Choy, 4 cookies	110	0	0	0	10	26	<1
French vanilla creme filled, Keebler, 1 cookie	80	3.5	1	0	85	12	0
Fruit and honey bar, Archway, 1 cookie	110	4	0.5	5	120	18	<1
Fruit bar, fat free, Archway, 1 cookie	90	0	0	0	95	21	0
Fruit cake, Archway, 3 cookies	140	7	1.5	0	100	20	2
Fruit centers, all flavors, fat free, Health Valley, 1 cookie	70	0	0	0	20	18	2
Fruit centers, mini, all flavors, fat free, Health Valley, 1 cookie	70	0	0	0	25	19	2
Fruit filled, fig, Weight Watchers Smart Snackers, 0.7 oz	70	0	0	0	50	16	0
Fruit filled, raspberry, Weight Watchers Smart Snackers, 0.7 oz	70	0	0	0	45	16	0
Fudge, caramel, and peanut bars, Nabisco Heyday, 1 bar	110	5	1	0	180	13	1
Fudge 'N Caramel, fudge covered shortbread with caramel, Keebler Fudge Shoppe, 2 cookies	120	6	4	<5	55	16	<1
Fudge bar, Tastykake, 1 bar	190	7	2	5	100	29	1
Fudge covered graham, Nabisco Family Favorites, 3 cookies	140	7	1.5	0	125	19	1
Fudge creme wafers, Little Debbie, 1 pkg	130	8	1.5	0	40	15	0
Fudge dipped grahams, Sunshine, 4 cookies	170	9	6	0	75	21	1

COOKIES	CAL (g)	FAT (g)	SAT FAT (g)	CHOL (mg)	SODIUM (mg)	CARB (g)	FIBER (g)
Fudge dipped wafers, Sunshine Oh! Berry, 3 cookies	120	4.5	4	0	30	20	2
Fudge Macaroo, Little Debbie, 1 pkg	140	8	4	0	65	18	1
Fudge mint patties, Sunshine, 2 cookies	130	7	3.5	0	60	16	<1
Fudge nut bar, Archway, 1 cookie	110	4.5	1	<5	120	17	<1
Fudge rounds, Little Debbie, 1 pkg	140	6	1	5	85	23	1
Fudge sandwich with fudge creme, Keebler E.L. Fudge, 3 cookies	160	7	2	0	100	23	1
Fudge sticks, fudge covered creme wafers, Keebler Fudge Shoppe, 3 cookies	150	8	4.5	0	55	20	<1
Fudge stripe creme, Eagle, 1 cookie	310	12	4	5	180	47	2
Fudge striped shortbread, Nabisco Family Favorites, 3 cookies	160	8	1.5	0	140	22	1
Fudge striped shortbread, Sunshine, 3 cookies	160	9	5	0	85	20	1
Fudge Stripes, fudge covered shortbread, Keebler Fudge Shoppe, 3 cookies	160	8	4.5	0	140	21	<1
Geneva, Pepperidge Farm, 3 cookies	160	9	4	0	95	19	1
Ginger, Eagle, 1 cookie	240	3.5	1	20	180	49	0
Ginger, Little Debbie, 1 pkg	90	3	0.5	5	60	15	0
Gingerbread, iced, Archway, 3 cookies	140	5	1	5	130	23	0
Gingerbread, iced, Sunshine, 5 cookies	130	6	1.5	5	135	19	<1
Gingerman, Pepperidge Farm, 4 cookies	120	4	1	10	95	21	<1
Gingersnaps, Archway, 5 cookies	140	5	1	0	110	18	0
Gingersnaps, Sunshine, 7 cookies	130	4.5	1	0	150	22	<1

COOKIES	CAL (g)	FAT (g)	SAT FAT (g)	CHOL (mg)	SODIUM (mg)	CARB (g)	FIBER (g)
Gingersnaps, old fashion, Nabisco, 4 cookies	120	2.5	0.5	0	170	22	<1
Golden bars, Stella D'Oro, 1 bar	110	3.5	na	20	65	17	na
Goldfish, chocolate, Pepperidge Farm, 19 pieces	140	5	2	10	85	22	2
Goldfish, chocolate chunk, Pepperidge Farm, 19 pieces	150	7	3	20	50	21	1
Goldfish, cinnamon graham, Pepperidge Farm, 19 pieces	150	7	3	10	140	20	2
Goldfish, graham, Pepperidge Farm, 19 pieces	150	7	3	15	150	20	2
Goldfish, vanilla, Pepperidge Farm, 19 pieces	150	7	3	20	50	21	1
Graham, Carr's Home Wheat, 2 cookies	140	6	3	0	200	20	<1
Graham, Nabisco Bugs Bunny, 10 cookies	140	5	1	0	160	23	1
Graham, chocolate, Nabisco Bugs Bunny, 13 pieces	140	5	1	0	180	22	1
Graham, cinnamon, Nabisco Bugs Bunny, 13 pieces	140	4.5	0.5	0	160	23	<1
Graham snacks, chocolate, Nabisco Teddy Grahams, 24 pieces	140	5	1	0	150	22	1
Graham snacks, cinnamon, Nabisco Teddy Grahams, 24 pieces	140	4	1	0	150	23	1
Graham snacks, cinnamon, fat free, SnackWell's, 20 pieces	110	0	0	0	90	26	1
Graham snacks, honey, Nabisco Teddy Grahams, 24 pieces	140	4	1	0	150	22	1
Granola, fat free, Archway, 2 cookies	100	0	0	0	120	24	1
Grasshopper, chocolate fudge mint, Keebler Fudge Shoppe, 4 cookies	150	7	5	0	70	20	<1
Hawaiian fruit, fat free, Health Valley, 3 cookies	100	0	0	0	50	24	3
Hazelnut, Pepperidge Farm, 3 cookies	160	8	2	0	135	21	<1

COOKIES	CAL (g)	FAT (g)	SAT FAT (g)	CHOL (mg)	SODIUM (mg)	CARB (g)	FIBER (g)
Healthy Chips, all varieties, fat free, Health Valley Chips, 3 cookies	100	0	0	0	20	24	4
Healthy Chocolate, all varieties, fat free, Health Valley, 2 cookies	70	0	0	0	20	17	3
Highland shortbread, Pepperidge Farm International Collection, 2 cookies	140	7	5	17	0	5	2
Hob-Nobs, Carr's, 2 cookies	140	6	2.5	0	150	19	1
Irish oatmeal, Pepperidge Farm, 3 cookies	130	6	2	<5	70	19	2
Jingles, Sunshine, 6 cookies	150	5	1	0	115	22	<1
Kichel, low sodium, Stella D'Oro, 21 kichel	150	9	na	80	25	13	na
Ladyfingers, 1 cookie	40	1	0	40	15	7	na
Lemon, frosty, Archway, 1 cookie	120	5	1	0	110	19	0
Lemon coolers, Sunshine, 5 cookies	140	6	1.5	0	100	21	<1
Lemon creme filled, Keebler Opera Creme, 1 cookie	80	3.5	1	0	70	12	0
Lemon creme sandwich, Eagle, 6 cookies	260	11	2.5	0	190	37	0
Lemon creme wafers, Little Debbie, 1 pkg	100	5	0.5	0	25	14	0
Lemon drop, Archway, 1 cookie	110	3.5	0.5	5	120	18	0
Lemon nuggets, fat free, Archway, 5 cookies	100	0	0	0	130	22	0
Lemon nut crunch, Pepperidge Farm, 3 cookies	170	9	2	15	60	18	2
Lemon snaps, Archway, 5 cookies	150	7	1.5	<5	115	20	0
Lido, Pepperidge Farm, 1 cookie	90	5	2	5	45	11	0
Linzer, raspberry filled, Pepperidge Farm, 1 cookie	100	4	1	5	65	15	<1
Macadamia coconut, Eagle, 1 cookie	330	16	5	20	230	42	3

COOKIES	CAL (g)	FAT (g)	SAT FAT (g)	CHOL (mg)	SODIUM (mg)	CARB (g)	FIBER (g)
Madaillon au Beurre, Pepperidge Farm International Collection, 4 cookies	150	5	3	15	105	25	<1
Mallomars, Nabisco, 2 cookies	120	5	3	0	35	17	1
Mandel bread (almond toast), Stella D'Oro, 2 pieces	110	2.5	0.5	30	85	21	1
Marshmallow puffs, fudge, Nabisco, 1 cookie	90	4	1	0	45	14	0
Marshmallow twirls fudge cakes, Nabisco, 1 cookie	130	6	1.5	0	75	20	<1
Milano, Pepperidge Farm, 3 cookies	180	10	4	10	80	21	<1
Milano, double chocolate, Pepperidge Farm, 2 cookies	150	8	3	10	70	17	<1
Milano, hazelnut, Pepperidge Farm, 2 cookies	130	7	2	5	65	15	1
Milano, milk chocolate, Pepperidge Farm, 3 cookies	180	10	4	10	80	21	<1
Milano, mint, Pepperidge Farm, 2 cookies	140	8	4	<5	70	16	<1
Milano, orange, Pepperidge Farm, 2 cookies	140	8	3	5	70	16	<1
Milk chocolate, Carr's Home Wheat, 2 cookies	130	6	3	0	95	16	<1
Milk chocolate macadamia, soft baked, Pepperidge Farm, 1 cookie	130	6	3	10	55	16	1
Milk chocolate ripple, fat free, Pepperidge Farm, 1 cookie	60	0	0	0	60	13	<1
Milk chocolate wafers, Carr's, 2 cookies	180	12	4	0	30	17	1
Mint creme, Alyce's, Salerno, 2 cookies	130	7	3.5	0	60	16	<1
Mint creme wafers, Little Debbie, 1 pkg	150	9	1.5	0	40	18	1
Molasses, Archway, 1 cookie	110	3.5	0.5	10	150	20	<1
Molasses, Dolly Madison, 1 cookie	110	3.5	1	10	110	19	0

COOKIES	CAL (g)	FAT (g)	SAT FAT (g)	CHOL (mg)	SODIUM (mg)	CARB (g)	FIBER (g)
Molasses, iced, Archway, 1 cookie	110	3.5	1	0	170	19	<1
Molasses, low fat, Archway, 1 cookie	100	1	0	0	95	22	1
Molasses, old fashion, Archway, 1 cookie	120	3	1	5	150	20	0
Molasses, soft, drop, Archway, 1 cookie	110	3.5	1	<5	160	18	<1
Molasses crisps, Pepperidge Farm, 5 cookies	150	6	2	0	140	20	<1
Mud pie, Archway, 1 cookie	110	4	1	<5	110	18	2
Mystic Mint, Nabisco, 1 cookie	90	4	1	0	65	11	0
Nantucket, chocolate chunk, Pepperidge Farm American Collection, 1 cookie	130	7	3	10	75	16	<1
New Orleans cake, Archway, 1 cookie	110	4	1	<5	105	18	<1
Nutty Bars, Little Debbie, 1 pkg	290	17	3	0	115	34	1
Nutty nougat, Archway, 3 cookies	160	10	2	0	60	18	0
Oatmeal, Archway, 1 cookie	110	3	1	<5	95	19	<1
Oatmeal, Dolly Madison, 1 cookie	160	6	1.5	10	130	23	0
Oatmeal, Nabisco Family Favorites, 1 cookie	80	3	0.5	0	65	12	<1
Oatmeal, Sunshine, 2 cookies	120	5	1	0	90	18	<1
Oatmeal, apple filled, Archway, 1 cookie	110	3	0.5	<5	105	18	0
Oatmeal, country style, Sunshine, 3 cookies	170	7	1.5	0	160	24	1
Oatmeal, date filled, Archway, 1 cookie	110	4	1	<5	120	18	<1
Oatmeal, golden, Ruth's, Archway, 1 cookie	120	5	1	<5	135	19	<1
Oatmeal, iced, Archway, 1 cookie	120	5	1	<5	85	19	1
Oatmeal, iced, Eagle, 1 cookie	170	5	1	0	110	28	1

COOKIES	CAL (g)	FAT (g)	SAT FAT (g)	CHOL (mg)	SODIUM (mg)	CARB (g)	FIBER (g)
Oatmeal, Ruth's, Archway, 1 cookie	120	4.5	1	<5	135	19	<1
Oatmeal chocolate chip, Sunshine, 3 cookies	170	8	3	0	130	23	2
Oatmeal chocolaty chip, fat free, cholesterol free, Entenmann's, 2 cookies	80	0	0	0	110	19	1
Oatmeal cream pie, Eagle, 1 cookie	310	12	3	5	340	46	2
Oatmeal creme pies, Little Debbie, 1 pkg	170	8	1.5	0	190	25	1
Oatmeal lights, low fat, Little Debbie, 1 pkg	130	2.5	0	0	190	28	1
Oatmeal macaroon sandwich, Famous Amos, 3 cookies	150	7	2	0	70	21	1
Oatmeal pecan, Archway, 1 cookie	120	5	1.5	<5	100	18	1
Oatmeal raisin, Archway, 1 cookie	110	4	1	<5	115	19	<1
Oatmeal raisin, Eagle, 1 cookie	330	17	4	10	190	40	4
Oatmeal raisin, Otis Spunkmeyer, 1 cookie	160	6	2.5	15	130	24	1
Oatmeal raisin, Pepperidge Farm, 3 cookies	160	6	2	10	150	23	1
Oatmeal raisin, Weight Watchers Smart Snackers, 1.06 oz	120	2	0	0	90	22	1
Oatmeal raisin, fat free, Archway, 1 cookie	100	0	0	0	170	23	<1
Oatmeal raisin, fat free, cholesterol free, Entenmann's, 2 cookies	80	0	0	0	120	18	<1
Oatmeal raisin, soft, Keebler Soft Batch, 1 cookie	70	3	1	0	65	10	<1
Oatmeal raisin, soft and chewy, Tastykake, 2 cookies	350	14	2.5	10	290	52	2
Oatmeal raisin, soft baked, Pepperidge Farm, 1 cookie	110	4	1	15	60	17	1
Oatmeal raisin bar, Tastykake, 1 bar	190	7	1.5	15	180	28	1

COOKIES	CAL (g)	FAT (g)	SAT FAT (g)	CHOL (mg)	SODIUM (mg)	CARB (g)	FIBER (g)
Oatmeal raisin bran, Archway, 1 cookie	110	3.5	1	<5	100	19	<1
Oatmeal raisin cinnamon, Famous Amos, 4 cookies	130	5	1	10	140	19	1
Oatmeal raspberry, fat free, Archway, 1 cookie	100	0	0	0	170	24	<1
Oatmeal with raisins, reduced fat, SnackWell's, 2 cookies	50	0	0	0	70	12	<1
P.B. Fudgebutters, fudge covered shortbread with peanut butter, Keebler Fudge Shoppe, 2 cookies	130	7	4	<5	90	14	<1
Peach tart, Pepperidge Farm, 2 cookies	120	3	1	0	115	23	<1
Peanut butter, Archway, 1 cookie	140	7	1.5	10	125	16	<1
Peanut butter, Otis Spunkmeyer, 1 cookie	180	11	3	15	190	17	<1
Peanut butter, ol' fashion, Archway, 1 cookie	130	6	1	10	160	17	<1
Peanut butter and graham sandwich, Eagle, 6 cookies	250	10	2.5	0	200	36	1
Peanut butter and jelly, Little Debbie, 1 pkg	130	5	1	0	100	22	1
Peanut butter bar, Eagle, 1 bar	170	10	3	0	75	19	1
Peanut butter bar, Little Debbie, 1 pkg	270	15	2.5	0	200	33	1
Peanut butter bar, chunky, Tastykake, 1 bar	240	11	3	5	110	18	<1
Peanut butter chocolate chip, Eagle, 1 cookie	360	20	6	15	110	39	4
Peanut butter creme, Keebler Pitter Patter, 1 cookie	90	4	1	0	115	12	<1
Peanut butter n' chips, Archway, 1 cookie	140	7	1.5	5	115	16	<1
Peanut butter sandwich, Famous Amos, 3 cookies	150	7	1.5	0	115	19	1
Peanut butter sandwich, Nabisco Nutter Butter, 2 cookies	130	6	1	<5	110	19	1

COOKIES	CAL (g)	FAT (g)	SAT FAT (g)	CHOL (mg)	SODIUM (mg)	CARB (g)	FIBER (g)
Peanut butter sandwich, Nabisco Nutter Butter Bites, 10 cookies	150	7	1.5	<5	125	20	1
Peanut butter wafer, Sunshine Sugar Wafer, 4 wafers	170	9	2	0	75	19	1
Peanut creme patties, Nabisco Nutter Butter, 5 patties	160	9	1.5	0	80	17	1
Peanut jumble, Archway, 1 cookie	130	7	1.5	<5	90	17	1
Pecan crunch, Archway, 6 cookies	150	8	2	10	120	18	0
Pecan ice box, Archway, 1 cookie	140	8	1.5	10	100	17	0
Pecan malted nougat, Archway, 3 cookies	160	10	2	0	60	17	2
Pecan Sandies, Keebler, 1 cookie	80	5	1	<5	75	9	<1
Pecan Sandies, bite size, Keebler, 8 cookies	170	10	2	<5	95	18	<1
Pecan Sandies, reduced fat, Keebler, 1 cookie	70	3	0.5	0	50	10	0
Pecan Sandies sandwich with praline creme, Keebler, 1 cookie	80	6	1.5	0	35	9	0
Pecan shortbread, Nabisco Pecan Passion, 1 cookie	140	7	1.5	0	125	19	1
Pecan shortbread, Pepperidge Farm, 2 cookies	140	9	3	<5	85	14	1
Pfeffernusse, Archway, 2 cookies	140	1	0	0	100	32	<1
Pinwheels, Nabisco, 1 cookie	130	5	2.5	0	35	21	<1
Pound cake cookie, Aunt Bea's, Archway, 1 cookie	110	4	1	10	95	17	0
Rainbow Chips Deluxe, Keebler, 1 cookie	80	4	2	<5	45	10	<1
Rainbow Chips Deluxe, Keebler Bite Size, 7 cookies	140	7	2.5	<5	95	19	<1
Raisin, Sunshine Golden Fruit, 1 cookie	80	1.5	0	0	40	15	<1

COOKIES	CAL (g)	FAT (g)	SAT FAT (g)	CHOL (mg)	SODIUM (mg)	CARB (g)	FIBER (g)
Raisin creme pies, Little Debbie, 1 pkg	140	5	1	0	120	23	0
Raisin oatmeal, fat free, Health Valley, 3 cookies	100	0	0	0	50	24	3
Raspberry apple, fat free, Health Valley, 3 cookies	100	0	0	0	50	24	3
Raspberry filled, Archway, 1 cookie	110	4	1	5	90	18	<1
Raspberry Newtons, fat free, Nabisco, 2 cookies	100	0	0	0	115	23	<1
Raspberry oatmeal, no fat, Archway, 1 cookie	100	0	0	0	170	24	<1
Rocky road, Archway, 1 cookie	120	4.5	1	10	75	19	1
Santa Fe, oatmeal raisin, Pepperidge Farm American Collection, 1 cookie	120	5	1	<5	110	18	<1
Sausalito, milk chcolate macadamia, Pepperidge Farm American Collection, 1 cookie	140	7	2	10	110	16	<1
Shortbread, Nabisco Lorna Doone, 4 cookies	140	7	1	5	130	19	<1
Shortbread, Pepperidge Farm, 2 cookies	140	7	3	10	105	16	<1
Shortbread, Bonnie, Salerno, 4 cookies	160	7	1.5	0	140	22	<1
Shortbread, butter, Carr's, 2 cookies	170	9	5	25	45	22	<1
Strawberry, Pepperidge Farm, 3 cookies	140	5	2	10	105	22	<1
Strawberry filled, Archway, 1 cookie	100	3.5	0.5	<5	80	16	<1
Strawberry fruit, fat free, Little Debbie, 1 pkg	130	0	0	0	100	33	1
Strawberry fruit bars, fat free, Famous Amos, 2 cookies	100	0	0	0	60	21	1
Strawberry Newtons, fat free, Nabisco, 2 cookies	100	0	0	0	115	8	6
Strawberry wafer, fat free, Sunshine Oh! Berry, 8 cookies	100	0	0	0	40	20	0
Sugar, Archway, 1 cookie	120	4	1	<5	190	20	0

COOKIES	CAL (g)	FAT (g)	SAT FAT (g)	CHOL (mg)	SODIUM (mg)	CARB (g)	FIBER (g)
Sugar, Pepperidge Farm, 3 cookies	140	6	2	15	90	20	<1
Sugar, fat free, Archway, 1 cookie	70	0	0	0	85	17	0
Sugar, soft, Archway, 1 cookie	110	4	1	5	110	18	0
Sugar wafers, Keebler Krisp Kreem, 5 pieces	140	7	1.5	0	50	19	0
Sugar wafers, Nabisco Biscos, 8 cookies	140	6	1.5	0	40	21	<1
Sweet Spots, shortbread with chocolate, Keebler, 1 pkg	120	6	3	<5	80	17	<1
Swiss fudge, Stella D'Oro, 2 cookies	130	6	1.5	15	65	17	<1
Tahoe, white chunk macadamia, Pepperidge Farm American Collection, 1 cookie	130	7	3	15	110	16	<1
Tea biscuits, Nabisco Social Tea, 6 cookies	120	4	0.5	5	105	20	<1
Teddy Berries, blueberry, Little Debbie, 1 pkg	140	4.5	1	5	115	24	0
Toffee Sandies, Keebler, 1 cookie	80	4.5	1	<5	55	10	0
Vanilla creme sandwich, Eagle, 6 cookies	260	11	2.5	0	170	37	0
Vanilla creme sandwich, Nabisco Cameo, 2 cookies	130	5	1	0	105	21	<1
Vanilla raspberry tart, Pepperidge Farm, 2 cookies	120	3	1	0	115	23	<1
Vanilla sandwich, Famous Amos, 3 cookies	150	7	1.5	0	70	22	1
Vanilla sandwich, Nabisco Cookie Break, 3 cookies	160	6	1.5	0	115	23	<1
Vanilla sandwich, Nabisco Family Favorites, 3 cookies	170	8	1.5	0	120	25	0
Vanilla sandwich, Sunshine Vienna Fingers, 2 cookies	140	6	1.5	0	105	21	<1
Vanilla sandwich, Ultra Slim Fast, 3 cookies	130	3	1	0	120	24	0
Vanilla sandwich, Weight Watchers Smart Snackers, 1.06 oz	140	3	1	0	80	25	1

COOKIES	CAL (g)	FAT (g)	SAT FAT (g)	CHOL (mg)	SODIUM (mg)	CARB (g)	FIBER (g)
Vanilla sandwich, lowfat, Sunshine Vienna Fingers, 2 cookies	130	3.5	0.5	0	95	23	<1
Vanilla sandwich, reduced fat, SnackWell's, 2 cookies	130	3.5	1.5	0	170	22	1
Vanilla sugar wafers, Tastykake, 5 wafers	170	10	2	0	35	21	<1
Vanilla wafers, Archway, 5 cookies	130	4	1	<5	140	22	0
Vanilla wafers, Keebler, 8 cookies	150	7	2	0	120	20	<1
Vanilla wafers, Nabisco Nilla, 8 cookies	140	5	1	5	105	24	0
Vanilla wafers, Sunshine Sugar Wafer, 3 wafers	130	6	1.5	0	20	18	<1
Vanilla wafers, Sunshine Vanilla Wafers, 7 cookies	150	7	1.5	3	110	20	<1
Vanilla wafers, reduced fat, Keebler, 8 cookies	130	3.5	0.5	0	140	25	<1
Waffle cremes, Nabisco Biscos, 4 cookies	180	9	2	0	35	24	<1
Wedding cakes, Archway, 3 cookies	160	8	1.5	0	45	20	0
White chocolate macadamia, Otis Spunkmeyer, 1 cookie	180	10	3.5	15	115	21	0
Windmill, old fashion, Archway, 1 cookie	100	4	0.5	0	95	15	0

AT A GLANCE: COOKIES

Try fat free, cholesterol free cookies from Archway, Entenmann's, Famous Amos, Health Valley, Keebler, Little Debbie, Nabisco, Pepperidge Farm, Sunshine, SnackWell's, and Weight Watchers.
Lowest in Calories: Nabisco National Arrowroot biscuits

CRACKERS

	CAL (g)	FAT (g)	SAT FAT (g)	CHOL (mg)	SODIUM (mg)	CARB (g)	FIBER (g)
Bacon flavored, Nabisco, 15 crackers	160	8	1.5	0	460	19	<1
Butter flavor, Sunshine Hi Ho, 9 crackers	160	9	1.5	3	280	19	<1
Butter flavored thins, Pepperidge Farm, 4 crackers	70	3	1	10	95	10	0

CRACKERS	CAL (g)	FAT (g)	SAT FAT (g)	CHOL (mg)	SODIUM (mg)	CARB (g)	FIBER (g)
Cheddar, Nabisco Snorkels, 56 crackers	140	5	1.5	5	200	19	1
Cheddar cheese biscuits, Carr's, 4 biscuits	90	5	3	<5	115	8	<1
Cheese, Nabisco Cheese Nips, 29 crackers	150	6	1.5	0	310	18	<1
Cheese, Sunshine Cheez-It, 27 crackers	160	8	2	0	240	16	<1
Cheese, baked, Nabisco Better Cheddars, 22 crackers	150	8	2	<5	290	17	<1
Cheese, baked, Nabisco Cheese Tid-Bits, 32 crackers	150	8	1.5	0	420	17	<1
Cheese, baked, low sodium, Nabisco Better Cheddars, 22 crackers	150	7	1.5	<5	75	18	<1
Cheese, baked, reduced fat, Nabisco Better Cheddars, 24 crackers	140	6	1.5	<5	350	19	<1
Cheese, hot 'n spicy, Sunshine Cheez-It, 26 crackers	160	8	1.5	0	220	17	1
Cheese, low sodium, Sunshine Cheez-It, 27 crackers	160	8	2	0	70	16	<1
Cheese, reduced fat, SnackWell's, 38 crackers	130	2	0.5	0	340	23	1
Cheese, reduced fat, Sunshine Cheez-It, 30 crackers	130	4.5	1	0	280	19	<1
Cheese, white cheddar, Sunshine Cheez-It, 26 crackers	160	9	2	3	280	17	<1
Chicken flavored, Nabisco Chicken in a Biskit, 14 crackers	160	9	1.5	0	270	17	<1
Chocolate covered, Nabisco Ritz, 3 crackers	140	5	1	0	150	22	1
Classic golden, reduced fat, SnackWell's, 6 crackers	60	1	0	0	140	11	0
Club partners, Keebler, 4 crackers	70	3	1	0	160	9	<1
Club partners, 50% reduced sodium, Keebler, 4 crackers	70	3	1	0	80	9	<1
Cracked pepper, SnackWell's, 7 crackers	60	0	0	0	150	13	<1

CRACKERS	CAL (g)	FAT (g)	SAT FAT (g)	CHOL (mg)	SODIUM (mg)	CARB (g)	FIBER (g)
Cracked pepper, Sunshine Hi Ho, 9 crackers	160	9	1.5	0	280	18	<1
Crispbread, golden rye, Wasa, 1 slice	35	0	0	0	50	7	2
Crispbread, light rye, Wasa, 1 slice	25	0	0	0	40	5	1
Crispbread, sesame rye, Wasa, 1 slice	30	1	0	0	55	5	3
Crispbread, whole grain, crispy thin, Kavli, 3 pieces	60	0	0	0	40	13	2
Crispbread, whole grain, hearty thick, Kavli, 2 pieces	70	0.5	0	0	55	15	3
Croissant, Carr's, 3 crackers	70	3	0.5	<5	115	10	0
Croissant, mini, Carr's, 24 crackers	140	6	1	5	180	20	<1
Croissant, with sesame and onion, Carr's, 21 crackers	150	7	1	0	190	19	<1
Crown Pilot, Nabisco, 1 cracker	70	1.5	0	0	85	13	<1
Fire Crackers, all varieties, fat free, Health Valley, 6 crackers	50	0	0	0	80	11	2
Five grain, Nabisco Harvest Crisps, 13 crackers	130	3.5	0.5	0	300	23	1
Flat bread, classical, Real Torino, 1 cracker	120	5	1	0	190	16	1
Flat bread, sesame, Real Torino, ½ cracker	120	5	1	0	190	18	2
Garlic bread flavored, Keebler Club, 4 crackers	70	3	1	0	140	9	0
Goldfish, cheddar cheese, Pepperidge Farm, 55 pieces	140	6	2	10	200	19	<1
Goldfish, cheddar cheese, reduced sodium, Pepperidge Farm, 60 pieces	150	6	2	10	140	18	<1
Goldfish, original, Pepperidge Farm, 55 pieces	140	6	2	0	230	19	<1
Goldfish, Parmesan, Pepperidge Farm, 60 pieces	140	5	2	0	300	19	1
Goldfish, pizza, Pepperidge Farm, 55 pieces	140	6	2	0	160	19	1

CRACKERS	CAL	FAT (g)	SAT FAT (g)	CHOL (mg)	SODIUM (mg)	CARB (g)	FIBER (g)
Goldfish, pretzel, Pepperidge Farm, 45 pieces	120	3	1	0	430	22	<1
Graham, Nabisco, 8 crackers	120	3	0.5	0	180	22	1
Graham, all varieties, fat free, Health Valley, 8 crackers	100	0	0	0	30	23	3
Graham, apple cinnamon, Keebler Graham Selects, 8 crackers	130	4	1	0	200	22	<1
Graham, cinnamon, Nabisco Honey Maid, 8 crackers	140	3	0.5	0	210	26	1
Graham, cinnamon, Sunshine Cinnamon Graham, 2 crackers	140	6	1.5	0	150	22	<1
Graham, cinnamon crisp, low fat, Keebler Graham Selects, 8 crackers	110	1.5	0.5	0	190	24	1
Graham, honey, Nabisco Honey Maid, 8 crackers	120	3	0.5	0	180	22	1
Graham, honey, Sunshine Honey Grahams, 2 crackers	120	4	1	0	130	20	1
Graham, honey, low fat, Keebler Graham Selects, 8 crackers	120	1.5	0.5	0	210	25	1
Graham, honey, old fashioned, Keebler Graham Selects, 8 crackers	150	6	1.5	0	140	21	1
Graham, original, old fashioned, Keebler Graham Selects, 8 crackers	130	3	1	0	135	23	<1
Hearty wheat, Pepperidge Farm, 3 crackers	80	4	0	0	100	10	1
Hi Ho, Sunshine, 9 crackers	160	9	1.5	0	280	18	<1
Hi Ho, multigrain, Sunshine, 9 crackers	160	9	1.5	0	370	18	1
Hi Ho, reduced fat, Sunshine, 9 crackers	140	5	1	0	280	21	<1
Matzo, egg, 1 cracker	110	0.5	0	25	5	22	na
Matzo, egg & onion, 1 cracker	110	1	0	15	80	22	1
Matzo, plain, 1 cracker	110	0	0	0	0	24	<1
Matzo, whole-wheat, 1 cracker	100	0	0	0	0	22	3

CRACKERS	CAL (g)	FAT (g)	SAT FAT (g)	CHOL (mg)	SODIUM (mg)	CARB (g)	FIBER (g)
Melba toast, plain, 1 toast	20	0	0	0	40	4	0
Melba toast, plain, unsalted, 1 toast	20	0	0	0	0	4	0
Melba toast, rye or pumpernickel, 1 toast	20	0	0	0	45	4	0
Melba toast, wheat, 1 toast	20	0	0	0	40	4	0
Milk, Nabisco Royal Lunch, 1 cracker	50	2	0	0	65	8	0
Multi-grain, Nabisco Wheat Thins, 17 crackers	130	4	0.5	0	290	21	2
Munch'ems, cheddar, Keebler 28 crackers	140	6	1	0	370	19	<1
Munch'ems, ranch, Keebler, 28 crackers	130	5	1	0	340	20	<1
Munch'ems, seasoned original, Keebler, 30 crackers	130	5	1	0	350	20	<1
Munch'ems, sour cream & onion, Keebler, 28 crackers	140	6	1	0	330	19	<1
Oat, Nabisco Harvest Crisps, 13 crackers	140	4.5	1	0	300	22	
Oat, Nabisco Oat Thins, 18 crackers	140	6	1	0	190	20	
Onion, Keebler Toasteds Complements, 9 crackers	140	6	1	0	310	19	<
Pizza crackers, all varieties, fat free, Health Valley, 6 crackers	50	0	0	0	140	11	
Poppy and sesame seed, Carr's, 4 crackers	80	4	0.5	0	80	9	<
Quartet assortment, Pepperidge Farm, 3 crackers	60	3	0	<5	80	9	<
Rice crunch, cheese, Ka-Me, 16 crackers	120	1.5	0	0	180	24	
Rice crunch, onion, Ka-Me, 16 crackers	120	1	0	0	75	25	
Rice crunch, plain, Ka-Me, 16 crackers	120	1.5	0	0	15	25	
Rice crunch, seaweed, Ka-Me, 16 crackers	120	1.5	0	0	100	25	

CRACKERS	CAL (g)	FAT (g)	SAT FAT (g)	CHOL (mg)	SODIUM (mg)	CARB (g)	FIBER (g)
Rice crunch, sesame, Ka-Me, 16 crackers	120	1.5	0	0	85	24	0
Rice crunch, unsalted, Ka-Me, 16 crackers	120	0.5	0	0	0	26	0
Ritz, Nabisco, 5 crackers	80	4	0.5	0	135	10	<1
Ritz, low sodium, Nabisco, 5 crackers	80	4	0.5	0	35	10	<1
Ritz Bits, Nabisco, 48 crackers	160	9	1.5	0	250	18	1
Rusk toast, 1 cracker	40	1	0	<5	25	7	na
Rye, wafers, plain, 1 cracker	30	0	0	0	65	7	na
Rye, wafers, seasoned, 1 cracker	35	1	0	0	75	6	na
Saltines, 50% reduced sodium, Keebler Zesta, 5 crackers	60	2	0.5	0	95	11	<1
Saltines, cracked pepper, Sunshine Krispy, 5 crackers	60	1.5	0	0	180	10	<1
Saltines, fat free, Keebler Zesta, 5 crackers	50	0	0	0	90	11	<1
Saltines, fat free, Nabisco Premium, 5 crackers	50	0	0	0	130	11	0
Saltines, fat free, Sunshine Crispy, 5 crackers	60	0	0	0	135	12	<1
Saltines, low sodium, Nabisco Premium, 5 crackers	60	1	0	0	35	10	<1
Saltines, mild cheddar, Sunshine Krispy, 5 crackers	60	2	0.5	0	180	10	<1
Saltines, mini, Nabisco Premium Bits, 34 crackers	150	7	1	0	340	19	<1
Saltines, original, Keebler Zesta, 5 crackers	60	2	0.5	0	190	10	<1
Saltines, original, Nabisco Premium, 5 crackers	60	1.5	0	0	180	10	<1
Saltines, unsalted tops, Keebler Zesta, 5 crackers	70	2	0.5	0	90	10	<1
Saltines, unsalted tops, Nabisco Premium, 5 crackers	60	1.5	0	0	135	10	<1
Saltines, unsalted tops, Nabisco Uneeda Biscuits, 5 crackers	60	1.5	0	0	110	11	<1

CRACKERS	CAL (g)	FAT (g)	SAT FAT (g)	CHOL (mg)	SODIUM (mg)	CARB (g)	FIBER (g)
Saltines, unsalted tops, Sunshine Krispy, 5 crackers	60	1.5	0	0	120	10	<1
Saltines, whole wheat, Sunshine Krispy, 5 crackers	60	1.5	0	0	130	10	<1
Sesame, Keebler Toasteds Complements, 9 crackers	140	6	1	0	320	19	<1
Sesame, Pepperidge Farm, 3 crackers	70	3	0	0	95	9	2
Sociables, Nabisco, 7 crackers	80	4	0.5	0	150	9	<1
Soup & oyster, Keebler Zesta, 42 crackers	70	2.5	1	0	160	10	<1
Soup & oyster, Nabisco Oysterettes, 19 crackers	60	2.5	0.5	0	150	10	<1
Soup & oyster, Nabisco Premium, 23 crackers	60	1.5	0	0	230	11	1
Soup & oyster, Sunshine Krispy, 17 crackers	60	1.5	0	0	200	11	<1
Swiss cheese, naturally flavored, Nabisco, 15 crackers	140	7	1.5	0	350	18	<1
Table water, bite size, Carr's, 5 crackers	70	1.5	0	0	100	13	<1
Table water, king size, Carr's, 2 crackers	60	1	0	0	90	12	<1
Table water, with cracked pepper, Carr's, 5 crackers	70	1.5	0	0	100	13	<1
Table water, with sesame, Carr's, 5 crackers	70	1.5	0	0	95	13	<1
Teething toast, Zwieback, 1 toast	35	1	0.5	0	10	5	<1
Touch of Cheddar Club, Keebler Club, 4 crackers	70	2.5	1	<5	180	9	0
Town House, Keebler, 5 crackers	80	4.5	1	0	150	9	<1
Town House, 50% reduced sodium, Keebler, 5 crackers	80	4.5	1	0	75	10	<1
Triscuit, Nabisco, 7 wafers	140	5	1	0	170	21	4
Triscuit, garden herb, Nabisco, 6 wafers	130	4.5	1	0	130	20	3
Triscuit, low sodium, Nabisco, 7 wafers	150	6	1	0	50	21	4

CRACKERS	CAL (g)	FAT (g)	SAT FAT (g)	CHOL (mg)	SODIUM (mg)	CARB (g)	FIBER (g)
Triscuit, reduced fat, Nabisco, 8 wafers	130	3	0.5	0	180	24	4
Triscuit, whole wheat n' bran, Nabisco, 7 wafers	140	5	1	0	180	22	4
Triscuit, whole wheat 'n bran, deli style, Nabisco, 7 wafers	140	5	1	0	170	22	4
Vegetable, Nabisco Garden Crisps, 15 crackers	130	3.5	0.5	0	290	22	1
Vegetable, Nabisco Vegetable Thins, 14 crackers	160	9	1.5	0	310	19	1
Water biscuit, cracked pepper, Pepperidge Farm International Collection, 5 crackers	60	1	1	<5	90	12	<1
Water biscuit, original, Pepperidge Farm International Collection, 5 crackers	60	1	1	<5	100	11	<1
Waverly, 5 crackers	70	3.5	1	0	135	10	0
Wheat, Keebler Toasteds Complements, 9 crackers	140	6	1.5	0	270	19	<1
Wheat, Keebler Town House, 5 crackers	80	4	1	0	140	10	<1
Wheat, Keebler Wheatables, 26 crackers	150	7	2	0	320	18	1
Wheat, 50% reduced sodium, Keebler Wheatables, 25 crackers	150	7	2	0	160	18	1
Wheat, cracked, Pepperidge Farm, 2 crackers	70	3	1	0	150	9	<1
Wheat, fat free, SnackWell's, 5 crackers	60	0	0	0	170	12	1
Wheat, French onion, Keebler Wheatables, 25 crackers	150	7	2	0	340	18	1
Wheat, low salt, Nabisco Wheat Thins, 16 crackers	140	6	1	0	75	20	2
Wheat, original, Nabisco Wheat Thins, 16 crackers	140	6	1	0	170	19	2
Wheat, ranch, Keebler Wheatables, 25 crackers	150	7	2	0	310	16	1
Wheat, reduced fat, Keebler Wheatables, 29 crackers	130	3.5	1	0	320	21	1

CRACKERS	CAL (g)	FAT (g)	SAT FAT (g)	CHOL (mg)	SODIUM (mg)	CARB (g)	FIBER (g)
Wheat, reduced fat, Nabisco Wheat Thins, 18 crackers	120	4	0.5	0	220	21	2
Wheat, stoned ground, Wheatsworth, 5 crackers	80	3.5	0.5	0	170	10	1
Wheat, white cheddar flavor, Keebler Wheatables, 25 crackers	150	7	2	0	330	18	1
Wheatmeal, bite size, Carr's, 2 crackers	80	3.5	0.5	0	100	11	1
Wheatolo, Carr's, 1 cracker	70	3	1.5	0	100	10	<1
Whole wheat, Carr's, 2 crackers	80	3.5	0.5	0	100	11	1
Whole wheat, Sunshine Hi Ho, 9 crackers	160	8	1.5	9	280	18	2
Whole wheat, all varieties, fat free, Health Valley, 5 crackers	50	0	0	0	80	11	2

AT A GLANCE: CRACKERS
Lowest in Calories and Fat: Melba Toast; Wasa Crispbread

CRACKER SANDWICHES

	CAL (g)	FAT (g)	SAT FAT (g)	CHOL (mg)	SODIUM (mg)	CARB (g)	FIBER (g)
Cheese crackers & cheese, Eagle, 6 crackers	210	11	3	<5	390	24	<1
Cheese crackers & honey roast peanut butter, Eagle, 6 crackers	230	12	2	0	320	25	<1
Cheese crackers & peanut butter, Keebler, 1 pkg	190	9	2	<5	420	22	<1
Cheese crackers & peanut butter, Little Debbie, 1 pkg	140	7	1.5	0	290	16	1
Cheese peanut butter sandwiches, Planters, 1 pkg	190	10	2	0	390	24	1
Cheese toast & peanut butter, Nabisco Nabs, 6 sandwiches	190	10	2	0	390	24	1
Club & cheddar, Keebler Cracker Paks, 1 pkg	190	11	2.5	10	320	20	<1
Crackers & cheese, Handi-Snacks, 1 pkg	130	8	4.5	15	340	10	0
Crackers & cheese, Nabisco Ritz Bits, 13 sandwiches	160	10	2.5	5	300	17	1

CRACKER SANDWICHES	CAL (g)	FAT (g)	SAT FAT (g)	CHOL (mg)	SODIUM (mg)	CARB (g)	FIBER (g)
Crackers & peanut butter, Handi-Snacks, 1 pkg	180	12	3	0	150	12	1
Crackers & peanut butter, Nabisco Ritz Bits, 13 sandwiches	150	8	1.5	0	130	17	<1
Crackers with cheese, Nabisco Ritz, 1 package	210	12	3	5	450	21	1
Toast & peanut butter, Eagle, 6 crackers	210	10	2.5	0	430	23	1
Toast & peanut butter, Keebler Cracker Paks, 1 pkg	190	9	2	0	300	23	1
Toast & peanut butter, Nabisco Nabs, 6 sandwiches	190	10	2	0	380	24	1
Toasty Crackers & peanut butter, Little Debbie, 1 pkg	140	7	1.5	0	290	16	1
Town House & cheddar, Keebler Cracker Paks, 1 pkg	200	13	2.5	10	300	19	<1
Wheat crackers & cheddar, Eagle, 6 crackers	200	10	3	<5	400	24	<1
Wheat crackers & cheddar, Little Debbie, 1 pkg	140	7	2	5	270	16	0

COOKING & BAKING PRODUCTS

	CAL (g)	FAT (g)	SAT FAT (g)	CHOL (mg)	SODIUM (mg)	CARB (g)	FIBER (g)
BAKING CHIPS & CHOCOLATE							
Bar, semi-sweet, Baker's, 1 square	130	9	5	0	0	17	2
Bar, semi-sweet, Nestle Tollhouse, ½ oz	70	4	2.5	ns	0	9	2
Bar, sweet, Baker's German, 2 squares	60	3.5	2	0	0	8	<1
Bar, unsweetened, Baker's, 1 square	140	14	9	5	0	9	4
Bar, unsweetened, Nestle Tollhouse, ½ oz	80	7	2	ns	0	5	3
Bar, white, Nestle Tollhouse, ½ oz	80	5	3	<5	15	8	ns
Bar, white chocolate, Baker's, 1 square	160	9	6	0	25	17	0
Bits, milk chocolate, M & M's, ½ oz	70	3	2	5	0	10	0
Bits, semi-sweet, M & M's, ½ oz	70	3.5	2	0	0	9	1
Chips, butterscotch morsels, Nestle, 1 Tbsp	80	4	4	ns	15	10	ns
Chips, chocolate mint morsels, Nestle Tollhouse, 1 Tbsp	70	4	2	ns	0	9	2
Chips, milk chocolate, Baker's, ½ oz	70	4	2	0	10	9	0
Chips, milk chocolate, Hershey's, 1 Tbsp	80	4	2.5	<5	15	9	0
Chips, milk chocolate morsels, Nestle Tollhouse, 1 Tbsp	70	4	2	ns	0	10	ns
Chips, rainbow morsels, Nestle Tollhouse, 1 Tbsp	70	3	2	ns	0	10	1
Chips, semi-sweet, Baker's, ½ oz	60	3.5	2	0	0	9	<1
Chips, semi-sweet, Hershey's, 1 Tbsp	80	4	2.5	0	0	10	0

BAKING CHIPS & CHOCOLATE	CAL (g)	FAT (g)	SAT FAT (g)	CHOL (mg)	SODIUM (mg)	CARB (g)	FIBER (g)
Chips, semi-sweet flavor, Baker's, ½ oz	70	3	3	0	10	10	<1
Chips, semi-sweet mini morsels, Nestle Tollhouse, 1 Tbsp	70	4	2	ns	0	9	2
Chips, semi-sweet morsels, Nestle Tollhouse, 1 Tbsp	70	4	2	ns	0	9	2
Cocoa, Hershey's, 1 Tbsp	20	0.5	0	0	0	3	1
Cocoa, Nestle, 1 Tbsp	15	1	0	0	0	3	2
Liquid, unsweetened, Nestle Choco Bake, ½ oz	80	8	5	ns	0	5	3

BAKING MIX

Bisquick, ⅓ cup	170	6	1.5	0	490	25	<1
Bisquick, reduced fat, ⅓ cup	150	2.5	0.5	0	460	28	<1

BATTER & COATING MIX See also Seasoning Mix.

All purpose, Don's Chuck Wagon, ¼ cup	100	0	0	0	580	20	0
Chicken, barbecue glaze, Shake 'N Bake, ⅛ packet	45	1	0	0	410	9	0
Chicken, extra crispy recipe, Oven Fry, ⅛ packet	60	1	0	0	420	10	0
Chicken, home style flour recipe, Oven Fry, ⅛ packet	40	1	0	0	470	7	0
Chicken, hot & spicy, Shake 'N Bake, ⅛ packet	40	1	0	0	190	7	0
Chicken, original recipe, Shake 'N Bake, ⅛ packet	40	1	0	0	230	7	0
Country mild recipe, Shake 'N Bake, ⅛ packet	35	2	1	0	240	5	0
Fish, original recipe, Shake 'N Bake, ⅛ packet	70	1.5	0	0	420	14	1
Honey mustard glaze, Shake 'N Bake, ⅛ packet	45	1	0	0	290	9	0
Italian herb spice, Shake 'N Bake, ⅛ packet	40	0.5	0	0	300	7	0
Onion ring, Don's Chuck Wagon, ¼ cup	100	0	0	0	690	21	0
Pork, barbecue glaze, Shake 'N Bake, ⅛ packet	35	0	0	0	250	8	0

BATTER & COATING MIX	CAL (g)	FAT (g)	SAT FAT (g)	CHOL (mg)	SODIUM (mg)	CARB (g)	FIBER (g)
Pork, extra crispy recipe, Oven Fry, ⅛ packet	60	1.5	0	0	340	11	0
Pork, hot & spicy, Shake 'N Bake, ⅛ packet	45	0.5	0	0	220	8	0
Pork, original recipe, Shake 'N Bake, ⅛ packet	40	0	0	0	320	9	0
Tangy honey glaze, Shake 'N Bake, ⅛ packet	45	1	0	0	280	10	0
Tempura, Dynasty, ¼ cup	100	0.5	0	0	200	22	<1
Tempura, Ka-Me, 1 oz	100	0	0	0	5	22	0

BISCUIT MIX

Buttermilk, Jiffy, ⅓ cup	160	4	2	<5	380	29	<1
Plain, Arrowhead Mills, ¼ cup	120	1	0	0	200	23	3
Plain, Gold Medal, ⅓ cup	180	7	2	0	470	26	<1
Plain, Jiffy, ¼ cup	130	4.5	1	0	320	22	1

BREAD MIX

Apple cinnamon, Pillsbury, 1/12 mix	140	1.5	0	0	170	30	1
Banana, Pillsbury, 1/12 mix	130	1.5	0	0	190	26	<1
Blueberry, Pillsbury, 1/12 mix	140	1.5	0	0	160	29	<1
Carrot, Pillsbury, 1/12 mix	110	1	0	0	150	22	<1
Cheddar cheese, Dromedary, 1/9 pkg	140	2.5	1.5	2	280	25	1
Corn bread, Arrowhead Mills, ¼ cup	120	1	0	0	270	24	4
Corn bread, Aunt Jemima Easy Mix, ⅓ cup	150	4	1	0	450	26	1
Corn bread, Dromedary, 1/10 pkg	140	2.5	0	0	550	26	1
Corn bread, Pillsbury Ballard, 1/18 mix	110	1.5	0	0	500	21	<1
Cranberry, Pillsbury, 1/12 mix	140	1.5	0	0	150	30	<1
Date, Pillsbury, 1/12 mix	150	1.5	0	0	150	32	1
Date nut, Dromedary, 1/12 pkg	180	7	2	0	550	10	0.5
Date nut roll, Dromedary, ⅓ pkg	200	7	2.5	0	670	31	4
Italian herb, Dromedary, 1/9 pkg	140	2.5	1.5	0	250	25	1

BREAD MIX	CAL (g)	FAT (g)	SAT FAT (g)	CHOL (mg)	SODIUM (mg)	CARB (g)	FIBER (g)
Kamut, Arrowhead Mills, ⅓ cup	140	1	0	0	190	31	5
Multigrain, Arrowhead Mills, ⅓ cup	160	1	0	0	190	31	3
Nut, Pillsbury, 1/12 mix	150	3.5	0.5	0	180	27	1
Pumpkin, Pillsbury, 1/12 mix	130	1.5	0	0	190	26	<1
Rolls, Dromedary, 1/16 pkg	100	0.5	0	0	340	20	1
Rolls, Pillsbury, ¼ cup	110	1	0	0	200	21	<1
Rye, Arrowhead Mills, ⅓ cup	160	0.5	0	0	190	33	3
Rye, caraway, Hodgson Mill, ¼ cup	120	2	0.5	0	190	22	3
Sourdough, Dromedary, 1/9 pkg	140	2	1	0	210	27	1
Spelt, Arrowhead Mills, ⅓ cup	150	1	0	0	190	31	5
Wheat, cracked, for machine, Pillsbury, 1/12 mix	130	2	0	0	260	25	2
Wheat, stoneground, Dromedary, 1/9 pkg	140	2	1	0	200	26	2
Wheat, whole, Arrowhead Mills, ⅓ cup	150	1	0	0	190	31	5
Wheat, whole, honey, Hodgson Mill, ¼ cup	120	2	0.5	0	160	22	3
White, Arrowhead Mills, ⅓ cup	150	0.5	0	0	170	31	2
White, Hodgson Mill, ¼ cup	120	2	0.5	0	170	22	3
White, country, Dromedary, 1/9 pkg	140	1	0.5	0	230	28	1
White, crusty, for machine, Pillsbury, 1/12 mix	130	2	0	0	250	25	<1

BROWNIE MIX

	CAL (g)	FAT (g)	SAT FAT (g)	CHOL (mg)	SODIUM (mg)	CARB (g)	FIBER (g)
Caramel, Betty Crocker, 1/18 pkg	130	2	0.5	0	140	27	0
Chocolate, Pillsbury, 1/20 mix	140	3	0.5	0	110	28	<1
Chocolate chip, Betty Crocker, 1/18 pkg	140	3.5	2	0	95	26	0
Cookies and cream, Betty Crocker, 1/18 pkg	140	3	1	0	110	27	0
Cream cheese swirl, Pillsbury, 1/20 mix	140	5	2	<5	90	22	<1

BROWNIE MIX	CAL (g)	FAT (g)	SAT FAT (g)	CHOL (mg)	SODIUM (mg)	CARB (g)	FIBER (g)
Dark chocolate fudge, Betty Crocker, 1/18 pkg	130	2	0.5	0	110	26	1
Fudge, Betty Crocker, 1/12 pkg	140	2.5	1	0	125	29	1
Fudge, Jiffy, 1/5 cup	150	4	1	0	150	28	<1
Fudge, Martha White, 1/10 pkg	110	2	0.5	0	140	23	1
Fudge, Pillsbury Lovin' Lites, 1/16 mix	150	3	1	0	120	29	0
Fudge, 15 oz box, Pillsbury, 1/16 mix	110	2.5	0.5	0	90	22	<1
Fudge, 21.5 oz box, Pillsbury, 1/20 mix	130	2.5	0.5	0	105	25	<1
Fudge, low fat, Betty Crocker, 1/18 pkg	130	2.5	0.5	0	110	26	1
German chocolate, Betty Crocker, 1/18 pkg	160	3	1.5	0	110	32	1
Hot fudge, Betty Crocker, 1/18 pkg	140	4	2	0	120	25	0
Hot fudge, Pillsbury, 1/24 mix	130	3.5	1.5	0	100	24	<1
Peanut butter candies, with Reese's pieces, Betty Crocker, 1/18 pkg	150	3.5	2	0	95	27	0
Plain, Arrowhead Mills, 1 prepared brownie	110	0	0	0	100	27	2
Plain, Betty Crocker, 1/18 pkg	140	2	1	0	115	29	1
Plain, fat free, Arrowhead Mills, 1 prepared brownie	120	0	0	0	110	28	2
Plain, frosted, Betty Crocker, 1/18 pkg	170	3.5	1.5	0	130	33	1
Plain, wheat free, Arrowhead Mills, 1 prepared brownie	120	2	0	0	110	26	2
Walnut, Betty Crocker, 1/18 pkg	140	4	1	0	95	23	1
Walnut, Pillsbury, 1/18 mix	140	5	1	0	90	22	1
White chocolate swirl, Betty Crocker, 1/18 pkg	150	3.5	2	0	105	27	0

CAKE DECORATIONS

	CAL (g)	FAT (g)	SAT FAT (g)	CHOL (mg)	SODIUM (mg)	CARB (g)	FIBER (g)
Choco trims, Durkee, 1 tsp	15	0.5	0	0	10	2	0
Fun sprinkles, red/white/pink hearts, Durkee, 1 tsp	20	0	0	0	0	4	0

CAKE DECORATIONS	CAL (g)	FAT (g)	SAT FAT (g)	CHOL (mg)	SODIUM (mg)	CARB (g)	FIBER (g)
Harvest mix, Durkee, 1 tsp	15	0.5	0	0	10	3	0
Icing, chocolate, Durkee, 1 tsp	20	0.5	0	0	0	4	0
Icing, other flavors, Durkee, 1 tsp	25	0.5	0	0	0	5	0
Nonpareil, all sugar crystals, and confetti, Durkee, 1 tsp	15	0	0	0	0	3	0
Party imperials and fruit cocktail, Durkee, 9 pieces	15	0	0	0	0	4	0

CAKE MIX

	CAL (g)	FAT (g)	SAT FAT (g)	CHOL (mg)	SODIUM (mg)	CARB (g)	FIBER (g)
Angel food, Betty Crocker SuperMoist, 1/12 pkg	130	0	0	0	160	30	0
Angel food, Pillsbury Moist Supreme, 1/12 mix	140	0	0	0	330	31	0
Angel food, Pillsbury Plus, 1/10 mix	150	0	0	0	360	34	0
Angel food, chocolate swirl, Betty Crocker SuperMoist, 1/12 pkg	150	0	0	0	280	34	0
Angel food, confetti, Betty Crocker SuperMoist, 1/12 pkg	150	0	0	0	300	34	0
Angel food, lemon custard, Betty Crocker SuperMoist, 1/12 pkg	140	0	0	0	290	33	0
Angel food, one-step white, Betty Crocker SuperMoist, 1/12 pkg	140	0	0	0	280	32	0
Banana, Pillsbury Moist Supreme, 1/12 mix	180	4	1.5	0	260	35	0
Banana, Pillsbury Plus, 1/12 mix	180	4	1.5	0	270	35	0
Bundt, chocolate caramel nut, Pillsbury, 1/16 mix	180	7	2	0	200	28	<1
Bundt, double hot fudge, Pillsbury, 1/16 mix	180	5	3.5	0	210	32	<1
Bundt, strawberry cream cheese, Pillsbury, 1/16 mix	190	5	2.5	<5	180	34	0
Butter, Pillsbury Moist Supreme, 1/12 mix	170	3	1	0	270	35	0
Butter, Pillsbury Plus, 1/12 mix	170	3	1	0	270	35	0

CAKE MIX	CAL (g)	FAT (g)	SAT FAT (g)	CHOL (mg)	SODIUM (mg)	CARB (g)	FIBER (g)
Butter chocolate, Betty Crocker SuperMoist, 1/12 pkg	190	4.5	1.5	0	290	34	1
Butter chocolate, Pillsbury Moist Supreme, 1/12 mix	180	4	1.5	0	330	33	1
Butter chocolate, Pillsbury Plus, 1/12 mix	180	4	1.5	0	330	33	2
Butter pecan, Betty Crocker SuperMoist, 1/12 pkg	180	3.5	1.5	0	280	34	0
Butter yellow, Betty Crocker SuperMoist, 1/12 pkg	170	2	1	0	240	37	0
Carrot, Betty Crocker SuperMoist, 1/10 pkg	210	4	1.5	0	340	41	0
Carrot, Pillsbury Moist Supreme, 1/12 mix	180	4	1.5	0	280	35	<1
Carrot, Pillsbury Plus, 1/12 mix	190	4.5	1.5	0	280	35	<1
Cherry chip, Betty Crocker SuperMoist, 1/10 pkg	210	4.5	2	0	330	40	0
Chocolate, Pillsbury Moist Supreme, 1/12 mix	180	4	1.5	0	270	35	<1
Chocolate, Pillsbury Plus, 1/12 mix	180	4.5	1.5	0	320	34	<1
Chocolate, dark, Pillsbury Moist Supreme, 1/12 mix	180	4	1.5	0	320	34	1
Chocolate, dark, Pillsbury Plus, 1/12 mix	180	4.5	1.5	0	330	33	1
Chocolate, pudding, Betty Crocker, 1/8 pkg	160	3	1	0	170	33	<1
Chocolate chip, Betty Crocker SuperMoist, 1/12 pkg	180	4	1.5	0	270	34	0
Chocolate chip, Pillsbury Moist Supreme, 1/12 mix	190	5	2	0	270	35	<1
Chocolate chip, Pillsbury Plus, 1/12 mix	190	5	2	0	270	35	<1
Chocolate fudge, Betty Crocker SuperMoist, 1/12 pkg	180	4	1.5	0	410	34	1
Cinnamon streusel, Pillsbury Streusel Swirl, 1/16 mix	210	5	1.5	0	210	38	0
Coffee cake, Aunt Jemima Easy Mix, 1/3 cup	170	5	1	0	240	30	1

CAKE MIX	CAL	FAT (g)	SAT FAT (g)	CHOL (mg)	SODIUM (mg)	CARB (g)	FIBER (g)
Devil's food, Betty Crocker SuperMoist, 1/12 pkg	180	4.5	1.5	0	360	33	1
Devil's food, Jiffy, 1/5 pkg	220	5	1.5	0	520	40	1
Devil's food, Pillsbury Moist Supreme, 1/12 mix	180	4	1.5	0	330	33	1
Devil's food, Pillsbury Moist Supreme Lovin' Lites, 1/10 mix	210	4.5	1.5	0	410	41	2
Devil's food, Pillsbury Plus, 1/12 mix	180	4	1.5	0	320	33	1
Devil's food, Pillsbury Plus Lovin' Lites, 1/10 mix	210	4.5	1.5	0	410	41	2
Devil's food, Robin Hood Pouch, 1/5 pkg	190	5	2	0	420	36	1
Devil's food, light, Betty Crocker SuperMoist, 1/10 pkg	210	3	1.5	0	380	42	2
Double chocolate swirl, Betty Crocker SuperMoist, 1/12 pkg	180	4.5	2	0	370	33	1
French vanilla, Betty Crocker SuperMoist, 1/12 pkg	180	3	1	0	260	35	0
French vanilla, Pillsbury Moist Supreme, 1/10 mix	220	5	1.5	0	330	42	1
French vanilla, Pillsbury Plus, 1/10 mix	230	6	2	0	340	41	<1
Fudge marble, Betty Crocker SuperMoist, 1/12 pkg	180	3.5	1.5	0	250	35	0
Fudge swirl, Pillsbury Moist Supreme, 1/12 mix	200	4.5	1.5	0	280	37	1
Fudge swirl, Pillsbury Plus, 1/12 mix	200	5	1.5	0	280	37	<1
Funfetti, Pillsbury Plus, 1/12 mix	190	4.5	1.5	0	280	36	<1
German chocolate, Betty Crocker SuperMoist, 1/12 pkg	180	4	1.5	0	390	34	<1
German chocolate, Pillsbury Moist Supreme, 1/12 mix	180	4	1.5	0	270	34	<1
German chocolate, Pillsbury Plus, 1/12 mix	180	4	1.5	0	270	34	<1
Golden vanilla, Betty Crocker SuperMoist, 1/12 pkg	180	4	1.5	0	250	35	0
Lemon, Betty Crocker SuperMoist, 1/12 pkg	180	3.5	1.5	0	240	35	0

CAKE MIX	CAL (g)	FAT (g)	SAT FAT (g)	CHOL (mg)	SODIUM (mg)	CARB (g)	FIBER (g)
Lemon, Pillsbury Moist Supreme, 1/10 mix	210	4	1.5	0	330	42	1
Lemon, Pillsbury Plus, 1/10 mix	210	4	1.5	0	320	42	<1
Lemon chiffon, Betty Crocker, 1/16 pkg	140	2.5	0	0	135	26	0
Lemon pudding, Betty Crocker, 1/8 pkg	160	3	1	0	200	33	0
Milk chocolate, Betty Crocker SuperMoist, 1/12 pkg	180	4.5	1.5	0	310	33	1
Party swirl, Betty Crocker SuperMoist, 1/12 pkg	180	3.5	1	0	260	35	0
Peanut butter chocolate swirl, Betty Crocker SuperMoist, 1/12 pkg	180	4	1.5	0	310	34	0
Pineapple upside down, Betty Crocker, 1/6 pkg	350	10	3	0	300	63	<1
Pound cake, Dromedary, 1/8 pkg	260	10	3	0	270	38	0.5
Pound cake, golden, Betty Crocker, 1/8 pkg	270	11	3	0	230	40	0
Rainbow chip, Betty Crocker SuperMoist, 1/12 pkg	180	4	2	0	290	34	0
Sour cream white, Betty Crocker SuperMoist, 1/10 pkg	210	5	2	0	360	39	0
Spice, Betty Crocker SuperMoist, 1/12 pkg	180	4	1.5	0	300	34	0
Strawberry, Pillsbury Moist Supreme, 1/12 mix	180	4	1.5	0	280	36	<1
Strawberry, Pillsbury Plus, 1/12 mix	180	4	1.5	0	290	36	0
Strawberry swirl, Betty Crocker SuperMoist, 1/10 pkg	200	3	1.5	0	320	41	0
Sunshine vanilla, Pillsbury Moist Supreme, 1/12 mix	190	5	1.5	0	280	34	<1
Sunshine vanilla, Pillsbury Plus, 1/12 mix	190	5	1.5	0	280	34	<1
White, Betty Crocker SuperMoist, 1/12 pkg	180	4	1.5	0	290	34	0
White, Jiffy, 1/5 pkg	210	4.5	1	0	320	41	<1

CAKE MIX	CAL (g)	FAT (g)	SAT FAT (g)	CHOL (mg)	SODIUM (mg)	CARB (g)	FIBER (g)
White, Pillsbury Moist Supreme, 1/10 mix	220	5	1.5	0	330	41	<1
White, Pillsbury Moist Supreme Lovin' Lites, 1/10 mix	210	4	1.5	0	340	42	1
White, Pillsbury Plus, 1/10 mix	220	5	1.5	0	330	41	<1
White, Pillsbury Plus Lovin' Lites, 1/10 mix	210	4	1.5	0	340	42	1
White, light, Betty Crocker SuperMoist, 1/10 pkg	210	3.5	1.5	0	380	43	0
White 'n fudge swirl, Pillsbury Moist Supreme, 1/12 mix	200	4.5	1.5	0	280	37	<1
White 'n fudge swirl, Pillsbury Plus, 1/12 mix	200	4.5	1.5	0	270	37	<1
White chocolate swirl, Betty Crocker SuperMoist, 1/12 pkg	180	3.5	1.5	0	280	35	0
Yellow, Betty Crocker SuperMoist, 1/12 pkg	170	2.5	1	0	280	36	0
Yellow, Jiffy, 1/5 pkg	210	4.5	1	0	340	41	<1
Yellow, Pillsbury Moist Supreme, 1/12 mix	180	4	1.5	0	280	35	<1
Yellow, Pillsbury Moist Supreme Lovin' Lites, 1/10 mix	220	4	1.5	0	370	43	1
Yellow, Pillsbury Plus, 1/12 mix	180	4	1.5	0	290	35	<1
Yellow, Pillsbury Plus Lovin' Lites, 1/10 mix	220	4	1.5	0	370	43	1
Yellow, Robin Hood Pouch, 1/5 pkg	190	4	1.5	0	300	37	0
Yellow, light, Betty Crocker SuperMoist, 1/10 pkg	210	3	1.5	0	330	43	0

AT A GLANCE: CAKE MIX
Lowest in Fat: Angel Food

CHEESECAKE MIX

	CAL (g)	FAT (g)	SAT FAT (g)	CHOL (mg)	SODIUM (mg)	CARB (g)	FIBER (g)
Blueberry, no bake, Jell-O Brand, 1/8 pkg	220	4	2.5	0	300	43	<1
Cherry, no bake, Jell-O Brand, 1/8 pkg	230	4	2	0	300	45	<1
Homestyle, no bake, Jell-O Brand, 1/6 pkg	220	4	1	5	430	42	<1

CHEESECAKE MIX	CAL (g)	FAT (g)	SAT FAT (g)	CHOL (mg)	SODIUM (mg)	CARB (g)	FIBER (g)
Plain, no bake, Jell-O Brand, 1/6 pkg	220	5	3	0	380	39	1
Strawberry, no bake, Jell-O Brand, 1/8 pkg	240	4	2.5	0	310	47	<1

COCONUT

	CAL (g)	FAT (g)	SAT FAT (g)	CHOL (mg)	SODIUM (mg)	CARB (g)	FIBER (g)
Baking, Durkee, 2 Tbsp	80	6	6	0	25	6	2
Cream, 2 Tbsp	100	10	9	0	0	2	na
Cream, canned, 2 Tbsp	70	7	6	0	20	4	na
Flakes, Peter Paul Mounds, 2 Tbsp	70	4.5	3.5	0	45	8	1
Flakes, bag, Baker's Angel Flake, 2 Tbsp	70	4.5	4	0	45	7	1
Flakes, can, Baker's Angel Flake, 2 Tbsp	70	5	4.5	0	0	7	1
Milk, 1 Tbsp	35	3.5	3.5	0	0	<1	na
Milk, canned, 1 Tbsp	30	3.5	3	0	0	0	na
Milk, frozen, 1 Tbsp	30	3	3	0	0	<1	na
Shredded, Baker's Angel Flake, 2 Tbsp	60	4	4	0	35	6	1

CRUMBS See also Crust & Crust Mix.

	CAL (g)	FAT (g)	SAT FAT (g)	CHOL (mg)	SODIUM (mg)	CARB (g)	FIBER (g)
Corn Flake crumbs, Kellogg's, 2 Tbsp	40	0	0	0	120	9	0
Cracker crumbs, Nabisco Ritz, 1/3 cup	140	7	1	0	270	17	1
Cracker crumbs, fat free, Nabisco Premium, 1/4 cup	100	0	0	0	0	23	1

CRUST & CRUST MIX

	CAL (g)	FAT (g)	SAT FAT (g)	CHOL (mg)	SODIUM (mg)	CARB (g)	FIBER (g)
Chocolate pie crust, Nabisco Oreo, 1/6 crust	140	7	1.5	0	180	18	<1
Cookie crumbs, Nabisco Nilla, 2 Tbsp	70	2.5	0.5	<5	55	13	<1
Cookie crumbs, Nabisco Oreo, 2 Tbsp	80	3	0.5	0	140	13	1
Graham cracker crumbs, Nabisco Honey Maid, crumbs to make 1/8 pie crust	70	1.5	0	0	90	13	<

CRUST & CRUST MIX	CAL	FAT (g)	SAT FAT (g)	CHOL (mg)	SODIUM (mg)	CARB (g)	FIBER (g)
Graham cracker crumbs, Sunshine Graham Crumbs, 3 Tbsp	80	2	0.5	0	150	13	<1
Graham pie crust, Nabisco Honey Maid, ⅙ crust	140	7	1.5	0	125	18	<1
Graham pie crust, Oronoque, ⅛ crust	110	6	1.5	0	120	13	0
Graham pie crust, Pet-Ritz, ⅛ crust	110	6	1.5	0	120	13	0
Phyllo dough, frozen, 1 sheet	60	1	0	0	90	10	na
Pie crust, 3-inch tart, frozen, Oronoque/Pet-Ritz, 1 tart	140	9	2	0	130	11	0
Pie crust, all vegetable shortening, 9", frozen, Pet-Ritz, ⅛ crust	90	6	1.5	0	60	8	0
Pie crust, deep dish, 9", frozen, Oronoque, ⅛ crust	100	7	1.5	0	95	8	0
Pie crust, deep dish, 9", frozen, Pet-Ritz, ⅛ crust	100	6	2	5	70	10	0
Pie crust, deep dish, vegetable shortening, Pet-Ritz, ⅛ crust	100	7	2	0	65	9	0
Pie crust, refrigerated, Pillsbury, ⅛ wedge	110	7	3	5	140	12	0
Pie crust, regular, 9", frozen, Oronoque, ⅛ crust	90	6	1.5	0	80	7	0
Pie crust, regular, 9", frozen, Pet-Ritz, ⅛ crust	80	5	2	5	60	9	0
Pie crust mix, Betty Crocker, ⅛ of 9" crust	110	8	2	0	150	9	0
Pie crust mix, Flako, ¼ cup	130	8	3	5	170	13	1
Pie crust mix, Jiffy, ¼ cup	180	10	4	<5	250	19	<1
Pie crust mix, Pillsbury, 2 Tbsp	100	6	1.5	0	150	10	0
Pizza crust, refrigerated, Pillsbury, ¼ wedge	180	2.5	0.5	0	390	33	1
Pizza crust mix, Jiffy, ⅓ cup	160	2.5	1.5	0	280	31	2
Pizza crust mix, Ragu Pizza Quick, ⅕ of 12" crust	130	1	0	0	270	24	1
Pizza crust mix, Robin Hood, ¼ crust	160	2	0	0	340	32	1
Vanilla pie crust, Nabisco Nilla, ⅙ crust	140	12	1.5	<5	65	18	0

	CAL (g)	FAT (g)	SAT FAT (g)	CHOL (mg)	SODIUM (mg)	CARB (g)	FIBER (g)
DESSERT BAR MIX							
Apple streusel, Pillsbury, 1/24 mix	130	4.5	1	0	40	22	<1
Banana cream, Betty Crocker, 1/9 pkg	160	4	1	45	330	31	0
Caramel oatmeal, Betty Crocker, 1/20 pkg	160	6	1.5	0	90	24	<1
Chips Ahoy, Pillsbury, 1/18 mix	140	4	1.5	0	100	26	<1
Chocolate chunk, Betty Crocker, 1/20 pkg	150	5	2	0	125	24	0
Chocolate French silk, Betty Crocker, 1/8 pkg	180	4	2.5	0	150	35	1
Chocolate peanut butter, Betty Crocker, 1/20 pkg	150	5	1.5	0	150	23	1
Coconut cream, Betty Crocker, 1/9 pkg	200	7	3.5	50	380	33	1
Cookies and cream, Betty Crocker, 1/6 pkg	280	7	2	0	300	50	0
Date, Betty Crocker, 1/12 pkg	160	7	2	0	90	23	1
Easy layer, Betty Crocker, 1/20 pkg	150	5	3.5	0	100	24	0
Fudge swirl, Pillsbury, 1/20 mix	150	5	1	0	105	25	<1
Lemon, Betty Crocker-Sunkist, 1/24 pkg	130	3.5	1	0	75	23	0
Lemon cheesecake, Pillsbury, 1/24 mix	170	9	3	10	45	20	0
Lemon supreme, Betty Crocker-Sunkist, 1/9 pkg	270	7	2.5	30	75	51	0
M&M's cookie, Betty Crocker, 1/20 pkg	140	5	2	0	125	24	0
Nutter Butter, Pillsbury, 1/18 mix	150	4	0.5	0	140	26	0
Oreo, Pillsbury, 1/24 mix	130	4	1	0	125	22	<1
Raspberry, Betty Crocker, 1/20 pkg	150	4	1	0	130	26	0
Strawberry swirl cheese cake, Betty Crocker, 1/24 pkg	130	6	2	0	55	19	0

	CAL	FAT (g)	SAT FAT (g)	CHOL (mg)	SODIUM (mg)	CARB (g)	FIBER (g)
DESSERT TOPPING MIX							
Whipped topping, reduced calorie, D-Zerta, 2 Tbsp	10	1	0.5	0	10	1	0
Whipped topping, with 2% milk & vanilla, Dream Whip, 2 Tbsp	20	1	1	0	10	2	0
FATS & OILS							
Almond oil, 1 Tbsp	120	14	1	0	0	0	0
Apricot kernel oil, 1 Tbsp	120	14	1	0	0	0	0
Avocado oil, 1 Tbsp	120	14	1.5	na	0	0	0
Babassu oil, 1 Tbsp	120	14	11	0	0	0	0
Best Blend, Wesson, 1 Tbsp	120	14	1	0	0	0	0
Butter oil, 1 Tbsp	110	13	8	35	0	0	0
Canola oil, Crisco Puritan, 1 Tbsp	120	14	1	0	0	0	ns
Canola oil, Smart Beat, 1 Tbsp	120	14	1	0	0	0	na
Canola oil, Wesson, 1 Tbsp	120	14	1	0	0	0	0
Canola & corn oil, Fleischmann's Harvest Blend, 1 Tbsp	120	14	1.5	0	0	0	0
Canola & corn oil, Mazola Rightblend, 1 Tbsp	120	14	1	0	0	0	ns
Cocoa butter oil, 1 Tbsp	120	14	8	0	0	0	0
Coconut oil, 1 Tbsp	120	14	12	0	0	0	0
Cod liver oil, 1 Tbsp	120	14	3	80	0	0	0
Cooking spray, Weight Watchers, 0.33 g	0	0	0	0	0	0	0
Cooking spray, butter flavor, Wesson, <1 spray (⅓ second)	0	0	0	0	0	0	0
Cooking spray, corn oil, Mazola No Stick, 1½ second spray	0	0	0	0	0	0	ns
Cooking spray, no-stick, aerosol, Wesson, 1 spray	0	0	0	0	0	0	0
Cooking spray, no-stick, pump, Wesson, 1 spray	0	0	0	0	0	0	0
Corn oil, Mazola, 1 Tbsp	120	14	2	0	0	0	ns
Corn oil, Wesson, 1 Tbsp	120	14	2	0	0	0	0

FATS & OILS	CAL (g)	FAT (g)	SAT FAT (g)	CHOL (mg)	SODIUM (mg)	CARB (g)	FIBER (g)
Corn & canola oil, Crisco, 1 Tbsp	120	14	1.5	0	0	0	ns
Cottonseed oil, 1 Tbsp	120	14	3.5	0	0	0	0
Grapeseed oil, 1 Tbsp	120	14	1.5	0	0	0	0
Hazelnut oil, 1 Tbsp	120	14	1	0	0	0	0
Herring oil, 1 Tbsp	120	14	3	105	0	0	0
Lard, 1 Tbsp	120	13	5	10	0	0	0
Lard, Armour, ½ oz	130	14	6	15	0	0	0
Menhaden oil, 1 Tbsp	120	14	4	70	0	0	0
Menhaden oil, hydrogenated, 1 Tbsp	120	13	12	65	0	0	0
Mustard oil, 1 Tbsp	120	14	1.5	na	0	0	0
Nutmeg butter oil, 1 Tbsp	120	14	12	0	0	0	0
Oat oil, 1 Tbsp	120	14	3	0	0	0	0
Olive oil, Classico, 1 Tbsp	130	14	2	ns	0	0	0
Olive oil, Wesson, 1 Tbsp	120	14	1.5	0	0	0	0
Olive oil, all varieties, Filippo Berio, 1 Tbsp	120	14	2	0	0	0	0
Olive oil, all varieties, Progresso, 1 Tbsp	120	14	2	0	0	0	0
Olive oil, extra virgin or extra light, Bertolli, 1 Tbsp	130	14	2	ns	0	0	0
Palm oil, 1 Tbsp	120	14	7	0	0	0	0
Palm kernel oil, 1 Tbsp	120	14	11	0	0	0	0
Peanut oil, Planters, 1 Tbsp	120	14	2.5	ns	0	0	ns
Peanut oil, Wesson, 1 Tbsp	120	14	2.5	0	na	0	0
Popcorn oil, Planters, 1 Tbsp	120	14	2.5	0	0	0	ns
Popping & topping oil, Orville Redenbacher's, 1 Tbsp	120	14	2	0	0	0	0
Poppyseed oil, 1 Tbsp	120	14	2	0	0	0	0
Rice bran oil, 1 Tbsp	120	14	3	0	0	0	0
Safflower oil, 1 Tbsp	120	14	1.5	0	0	0	0
Salmon oil, 1 Tbsp	120	14	3	65	0	0	0
Sardine oil, 1 Tbsp	120	14	4	95	0	0	0
Sesame oil, Dynasty, 1 Tbsp	130	14	2	0	0	0	0

FATS & OILS	CAL (g)	FAT (g)	SAT FAT (g)	CHOL (mg)	SODIUM (mg)	CARB (g)	FIBER (g)
Sesame chili oil, Dynasty Rayu, ¼ tsp	10	1	0	0	0	0	0
Sheanut oil, 1 Tbsp	120	14	6	0	0	0	0
Shortening, Crisco, 1 Tbsp	110	12	3	0	0	0	ns
Shortening, Wesson, 1 Tbsp	110	12	3	0	na	0	0
Shortening, butter flavored, Crisco, 1 Tbsp	110	12	3	0	0	0	ns
Shortening, confectionery, 1 Tbsp	110	13	12	0	0	0	0
Shortening, soybean, 1 Tbsp	110	13	3.5	0	0	0	0
Soybean oil, 1 Tbsp	100	14	2	0	0	0	0
Stir fry oil, Wesson, 1 Tbsp	120	14	1.5	0	na	0	0
Sunflower oil, Wesson, 1 Tbsp	120	14	2	0	na	0	0
Teaseed oil, 1 Tbsp	120	14	3	0	0	0	0
Tomatoseed oil, 1 Tbsp	120	14	3	0	0	0	0
Ucuuba butter oil, 1 Tbsp	120	14	12	0	0	0	0
Vegetable oil, Crisco, 1 Tbsp	120	14	2	0	0	0	ns
Vegetable oil, Wesson, 1 Tbsp	120	14	2	0	0	0	0
Walnut oil, 1 Tbsp	120	14	1.5	0	0	0	0
Wheat germ oil, 1 Tbsp	120	14	2.5	0	0	0	0

AT A GLANCE: COOKING OILS
Lowest in Sat Fat: Mazola Rightblend Canola Oil, Crisco Puritan Canola Oil, Smart Beat Canola Oil, Wesson Canola Oil.

FILLING

	CAL	FAT	SAT FAT	CHOL	SODIUM	CARB	FIBER
Almond, Solo, 2 Tbsp	120	2.5	0.5	0	45	23	2
Almond paste, Solo, 2 Tbsp	180	11	1	0	0	19	1
Apple, Dutch, Solo, 2 Tbsp	80	0	0	0	45	20	1
Apricot, Solo, 2 Tbsp	80	0	0	0	20	17	1
Blueberry, wild, Solo, 2 Tbsp	80	0	0	0	25	17	1
Cherry, Solo, 2 Tbsp	80	0	0	0	25	20	1
Date, Solo, 2 Tbsp	100	0	0	0	40	22	3
Nut, fancy, Solo, 2 Tbsp	140	5	0.5	0	55	25	5
Pecan, Solo, 2 Tbsp	130	4	0	0	50	24	1
Pineapple, Solo, 2 Tbsp	80	0	0	0	20	19	1
Poppyseed, Solo, 2 Tbsp	140	4	0	0	30	24	3

FILLING	CAL (g)	FAT (g)	SAT FAT (g)	CHOL (mg)	SODIUM (mg)	CARB (g)	FIBER (g)
Prune plum, Solo, 2 Tbsp	70	0	0	0	25	18	1
Raspberry, red, Solo, 2 Tbsp	80	0	0	0	25	19	1
Strawberry, Solo, 2 Tbsp	70	0	0	0	20	18	1

FLOURS & CORNMEAL *See also Grains.*

FILLING	CAL (g)	FAT (g)	SAT FAT (g)	CHOL (mg)	SODIUM (mg)	CARB (g)	FIBER (g)
Acorn, full fat, ¼ cup	160	10	1	0	0	17	na
All purpose, Gold Medal, ¼ cup	100	0	0	0	0	22	<1
All purpose, Red Band, ¼ cup	100	0	0	0	0	23	<1
All purpose, Robin Hood, ¼ cup	100	0	0	0	0	22	<1
All purpose, bleached, Pillsbury, ¼ cup	100	0	0	0	0	23	<1
All purpose, unbleached, Pillsbury, ¼ cup	100	0	0	0	0	21	<1
All trump, General Mills, ¼ cup	100	0	0	0	0	22	<1
Amaranth, Arrowhead Mills, ¼ cup	110	1.5	0	0	0	19	2
Arrowroot, ¼ cup	120	0	0	0	0	29	1
Barley, Arrowhead Mills, ¼ cup	70	0.5	0	0	0	19	3
Bread, Gold Medal, ¼ cup	100	0	0	0	0	22	<1
Bread, Pillsbury, ¼ cup	100	0	0	0	0	22	<1
Buckwheat, Arrowhead Mills, ¼ cup	100	1	0	0	0	21	3
Buckwheat soba, Eden, 2 oz	200	1.5	0	0	30	41	3
Cake, Betty Crocker Softasilk Velvet, ¼ cup	100	0	0	0	0	23	<1
Carob, ¼ cup	120	0	0	0	10	29	13
Corn, whole grain, white, ¼ cup	100	1	0	0	0	23	3
Corn, whole grain, yellow, ¼ cup	100	1	0	0	0	23	4
Corn (masa), enriched, ¼ cup	110	1	0	0	0	22	3
Cornmeal, blue, Arrowhead Mills, ¼ cup	130	1.5	0	0	0	25	3

FLOURS & CORNMEAL	CAL (g)	FAT (g)	SAT FAT (g)	CHOL (mg)	SODIUM (mg)	CARB (g)	FIBER (g)
Cornmeal, hi-lysine, Arrowhead Mills, ¼ cup	120	1	0	0	0	25	3
Cornmeal, self-rising, white or yellow, enriched, ¼ cup	120	0.5	0	0	460	26	3
Cornmeal, white, Albers, 3 Tbsp	110	0	ns	ns	0	34	<1
Cornmeal, white, Arrowhead Mills, ¼ cup	120	1	0	0	0	23	3
Cornmeal, white or yellow, enriched, ¼ cup	120	0.5	0	0	1	27	3
Cornmeal, whole grain, yellow or white, ¼ cup	110	1	0	0	10	23	2
Cornmeal, yellow, Albers, 3 Tbsp	110	0	ns	ns	0	34	<1
Cornmeal, yellow, Arrowhead Mills, ¼ cup	120	1	0	0	0	27	3
Garbanzo, toasted, Arrowhead Mills, ¼ cup	90	1	0	0	0	15	3
Kamut, Arrowhead Mills, ¼ cup	110	0.5	0	0	0	25	4
La Pina, General Mills, ¼ cup	100	0	0	0	0	23	<1
Millet, Arrowhead Mills, ¼ cup	110	1	0	0	0	26	2
MultiBlend, Arrowhead Mills, ¼ cup	120	0.5	0	0	0	25	4
Oat, Arrowhead Mills, ⅓ cup	120	2	0	0	0	20	4
Pastry, Arrowhead Mills, ⅓ cup	100	0.5	0	0	0	22	3
Peanut, defatted, ¼ cup	100	0	0	0	60	11	na
Peanut, low fat, ¼ cup	140	1	1	0	0	10	na
Pecan, ¼ cup	100	0.5	0	0	0	16	na
Potato, ¼ cup	160	0.5	0	0	15	36	3
Rice, brown, Arrowhead Mills, ¼ cup	120	1	0	0	0	27	2
Rice, white, Arrowhead Mills, ¼ cup	130	0.5	0	0	0	28	1
Rye, Arrowhead Mills, ¼ cup	100	1	0	0	0	20	4
Rye, dark, ¼ cup	100	1	0	0	0	22	7
Rye, light, ¼ cup	100	0.5	0	0	0	21	4

FLOURS & CORNMEAL	CAL (g)	FAT (g)	SAT FAT (g)	CHOL (mg)	SODIUM (mg)	CARB (g)	FIBER (g)
Rye, medium, Pillsbury, ¼ cup	100	0	0	0	0	22	2
Rye-wheat Bohemian, Pillsbury, ¼ cup	100	0	0	0	0	22	2
Self-rising, Gold Medal, ¼ cup	100	0	0	0	400	22	<1
Self-rising, Red Band, ¼ cup	100	0	0	0	400	22	<1
Self-rising, Robin Hood, ¼ cup	100	0	0	0	400	22	<1
Self-rising, bleached, Pillsbury, ¼ cup	100	0	0	0	360	22	<1
Self-rising, enriched, Aunt Jemima, 3 Tbsp	90	0	0	0	310	20	1
Self-rising, unbleached, Pillsbury, ¼ cup	100	0	0	0	360	22	<1
Semolina mix, Arrowhead Mills, ½ cup	240	1	0	0	0	50	4
Sesame, high fat, ¼ cup	170	12	1.5	0	15	9	na
Sesame seed, lowfat, ¼ cup	110	0.5	0	0	10	11	na
Sesame seed, partially defatted, ¼ cup	120	4	0.5	0	15	11	na
Shake & blend, Pillsbury, ¼ cup	100	0	0	0	0	23	<1
Soft pastry, Arrowhead Mills, ¼ cup	100	0.5	0	0	0	23	4
Soy, Arrowhead Mills, ½ cup	200	9	1.5	0	0	16	8
Soy, defatted, ½ cup	160	0.5	0	0	10	19	9
Soy, lowfat, ½ cup	140	3	0	0	10	17	4
Spelt, Arrowhead Mills, ¼ cup	100	0.5	0	0	0	24	5
Sunflower seed, partially defatted, ½ cup	130	1	0	0	0	14	2
Supreme hygluten, General Mills, ¼ cup	100	0	0	0	0	22	<1
Triticale, whole grain, ¼ cup	110	0.5	0	0	0	24	5
Unbleached, Arrowhead Mills, ⅓ cup	160	0.5	0	0	0	33	0
Unbleached, Gold Medal, ¼ cup	100	0	0	0	0	22	<1

FLOURS & CORNMEAL	CAL (g)	FAT (g)	SAT FAT (g)	CHOL (mg)	SODIUM (mg)	CARB (g)	FIBER (g)
Unbleached, Robin Hood, ¼ cup	100	0	0	0	0	22	<1
Vital wheat, Arrowhead Mills, 3 Tbsp	35	0	0	0	0	3	0
Wheat, Hodgson Mill, 1 Tbsp	30	0	0	0	0	2	1
Whole grain, Arrowhead Mills, ¼ cup	110	0.5	0	0	0	24	4
Whole wheat, Gold Medal, ¼ cup	90	0.5	0	0	0	21	3
Whole wheat, Pillsbury, ¼ cup	120	1	0	0	0	22	4
Whole wheat, stone ground, Arrowhead Mills, ¼ cup	130	0.5	0	0	0	25	4
Whole wheat blend, Gold Medal, ¼ cup	100	0.5	0	0	0	21	2
Wondra, Gold Medal, ¼ cup	100	0	0	0	0	23	<1

AT A GLANCE: FLOUR
Highest in Fiber: Carob, Soy, Dark Rye, Spelt, Triticale

FROSTING, MIX

	CAL (g)	FAT (g)	SAT FAT (g)	CHOL (mg)	SODIUM (mg)	CARB (g)	FIBER (g)
Chocolate, Robin Hood, 2 Tbsp	110	1.5	0.5	0	0	24	<1
Chocolate fudge, Betty Crocker Creamy, 3 Tbsp mix	110	1.5	0.5	0	15	24	0
Coconut pecan, Betty Crocker Creamy, 3 Tbsp mix	120	4	2	0	5	21	<1
Fudge, Jiffy, ¼ cup mix	150	4	1.5	0	150	28	<1
Vanilla, creamy, Betty Crocker Creamy, 3 Tbsp mix	110	1.5	0.5	0	0	24	0
White, Betty Crocker Fluffy, 3 Tbsp mix	100	0	0	0	60	24	0
White, Jiffy, ¼ cup mix	150	4.5	1	0	150	27	0

FROSTING, READY-TO-SPREAD

	CAL (g)	FAT (g)	SAT FAT (g)	CHOL (mg)	SODIUM (mg)	CARB (g)	FIBER (g)
Butter cream, Betty Crocker Creamy Deluxe, 2 Tbsp	160	6	1.5	0	70	25	0
Butter pecan, Betty Crocker Creamy Deluxe, 2 Tbsp	150	6	1.5	0	45	25	0

FROSTING, READY-TO-SPREAD	CAL	FAT (g)	SAT FAT (g)	CHOL (mg)	SODIUM (mg)	CARB (g)	FIBER (g)
Caramel chocolate chip, Betty Crocker Creamy Deluxe, 2 Tbsp	140	6	1.5	0	55	21	0
Caramel pecan, Pillsbury Creamy Supreme/Frosting Supreme, 2 Tbsp	150	8	2	0	65	19	0
Cherry, Betty Crocker Creamy Deluxe, 2 Tbsp	140	5	1.5	0	40	24	0
Chocolate, Betty Crocker Creamy Deluxe, 2 Tbsp	150	6	1.5	0	45	23	0
Chocolate, Pillsbury Creamy Supreme, 2 Tbsp	140	6	1.5	0	80	21	0
Chocolate, Pillsbury Frosting Supreme, 2 Tbsp	140	6	1.5	0	75	21	0
Chocolate, dark, Betty Crocker Creamy Deluxe, 2 Tbsp	150	6	1.5	0	50	22	0
Chocolate, dark, Pillsbury Creamy Supreme/Frosting Supreme, 2 Tbsp	130	6	1.5	0	45	20	0
Chocolate, light, Betty Crocker Creamy Deluxe, 2 Tbsp	120	1	0.5	0	50	27	0
Chocolate chip, Betty Crocker Creamy Deluxe, 2 Tbsp	160	6	2.5	0	25	25	0
Chocolate chip cookie dough, Betty Crocker Creamy Deluxe, 2 Tbsp	160	6	1.5	0	25	25	0
Chocolate chocolate chip, Betty Crocker Creamy Deluxe, 2 Tbsp	150	7	2.5	0	45	23	0
Chocolate fudge, Pillsbury Creamy Supreme, 2 Tbsp	140	6	1.5	0	80	21	0
Chocolate fudge, Pillsbury Frosting Supreme, 2 Tbsp	140	6	1.5	0	75	21	0
Chocolate fudge, reduced fat, Pillsbury Creamy Supreme/Frosting Supreme, 2 Tbsp	140	3.5	1	0	85	26	0
Chocolate Swiss almond, Betty Crocker Creamy Deluxe, 2 Tbsp	150	6	1.5	0	50	25	0

FROSTING, READY-TO-SPREAD	CAL (g)	FAT (g)	SAT FAT (g)	CHOL (mg)	SODIUM (mg)	CARB (g)	FIBER (g)
Chocolate with dinosaurs, Betty Crocker Creamy Deluxe, 2 Tbsp	150	5	1.5	0	45	24	0
Coconut almond, Pillsbury Frosting Supreme, 2 Tbsp	160	9	4	0	60	18	<1
Coconut pecan, Betty Crocker Creamy Deluxe, 2 Tbsp	150	8	3.5	0	55	18	0
Coconut pecan, Pillsbury Creamy Supreme/Frosting Supreme, 2 Tbsp	160	10	4	0	60	17	<1
Cream cheese, Betty Crocker Creamy Deluxe, 2 Tbsp	140	5	1.5	0	65	24	0
Cream cheese, Betty Crocker Whipped Deluxe, 2 Tbsp	110	5	1.5	0	45	16	0
Cream cheese, Pillsbury Creamy Supreme/Frosting Supreme, 2 Tbsp	150	6	1.5	0	70	24	0
Creamy candy, Pillsbury Creamy Supreme/Frosting Supreme, 2 Tbsp	150	7	2	0	95	22	0
French vanilla, Betty Crocker Creamy Deluxe, 2 Tbsp	140	5	1.5	0	20	24	0
French vanilla, Pillsbury Creamy Supreme, 2 Tbsp	150	6	1.5	0	80	25	0
French vanilla, Pillsbury Frosting Supreme, 2 Tbsp	160	6	1.5	0	75	26	0
Funfetti chocolate, Pillsbury Creamy Supreme/Frosting Supreme, 2 Tbsp	140	6	1.5	0	80	22	0
Funfetti pink vanilla, Pillsbury Creamy Supreme/Frosting Supreme, 2 Tbsp	150	6	1.5	0	70	24	0
Funfetti vanilla, Pillsbury Creamy Supreme, 2 Tbsp	150	6	1.5	0	75	25	0
Funfetti vanilla, Pillsbury Frosting Supreme, 2 Tbsp	160	6	1.5	0	75	26	0
Lemon, Betty Crocker Creamy Deluxe, 2 Tbsp	140	5	1.5	0	65	24	0
Lemon, Betty Crocker Whipped Deluxe, 2 Tbsp	110	5	1.5	0	45	16	0

FROSTING, READY-TO-SPREAD	CAL (g)	FAT (g)	SAT FAT (g)	CHOL (mg)	SODIUM (mg)	CARB (g)	FIBER (g)
Lemon creme, Pillsbury Creamy Supreme/Frosting Supreme, 2 Tbsp	150	6	1.5	0	75	24	0
Milk chocolate, Betty Crocker Creamy Deluxe, 2 Tbsp	150	6	1.5	0	45	24	0
Milk chocolate, Pillsbury Creamy Supreme/Frosting Supreme, 2 Tbsp	140	6	1.5	0	60	21	<1
Milk chocolate, Pillsbury Creamy Supreme/Frosting Supreme Lovin' Lites, 2 Tbsp	130	3	1	0	85	25	<1
Milk chocolate, light, Betty Crocker Creamy Deluxe, 2 Tbsp	120	1	0.5	0	45	27	0
Milk chocolate swirl, with fudge glaze, Pillsbury Creamy Supreme/Frosting Supreme, 2 Tbsp	140	6	1.5	0	60	22	<1
Oreo, Pillsbury Creamy Supreme/Frosting Supreme, 2 Tbsp	150	6	1.5	0	75	23	0
Rainbow chip, Betty Crocker Creamy Deluxe, 2 Tbsp	160	6	3	0	25	25	0
Sour cream chocolate, Betty Crocker Creamy Deluxe, 2 Tbsp	150	6	1.5	0	85	23	0
Sour cream white, Betty Crocker Creamy Deluxe, 2 Tbsp	150	6	1.5	0	45	25	0
Strawberry, Betty Crocker Whipped Deluxe, 2 Tbsp	110	5	1.5	0	25	16	0
Strawberry cream cheese, Betty Crocker Creamy Deluxe, 2 Tbsp	150	6	1.5	0	70	25	0
Strawberry creme, Pillsbury Creamy Supreme/Frosting Supreme, 2 Tbsp	150	6	1.5	0	75	24	0
Vanilla, Betty Crocker Creamy Deluxe, 2 Tbsp	140	5	1.5	0	35	24	0
Vanilla, Pillsbury Creamy Supreme/Frosting Supreme, 2 Tbsp	150	6	1.5	0	70	23	0

FROSTING, READY-TO-SPREAD	CAL	FAT (g)	SAT FAT (g)	CHOL (mg)	SODIUM (mg)	CARB (g)	FIBER (g)
Vanilla, Pillsbury Creamy Supreme/Frosting Supreme Lovin' Lites, 2 Tbsp	140	3	1	0	70	29	0
Vanilla, light, Betty Crocker Creamy Deluxe, 2 Tbsp	120	0.5	0.5	0	25	28	0
Vanilla, with bears, Betty Crocker Creamy Deluxe, 2 Tbsp	140	5	1	0	35	24	0
Vanilla cream, Betty Crocker Whipped Deluxe, 2 Tbsp	110	5	1.5	0	25	16	0
Vanilla swirl, with fudge glaze, Pillsbury Creamy Supreme/Frosting Supreme, 2 Tbsp	150	6	1.5	0	75	25	0
White chocolate, Betty Crocker Creamy Deluxe, 2 Tbsp	140	5	1.5	0	45	24	0

AT A GLANCE: READY-TO-SPREAD FROSTING
Lowest in Fat: Betty Crocker Creamy Deluxe Vanilla, Light; Chocolate, Light; Milk Chocolate, Light.

FRUIT PROTECTOR

EverFresh, 1/4 tsp	5	0	0			1	0

GINGERBREAD MIX

Betty Crocker, 1/8 pkg	220	6	2	0	360	38	0
Dromedary, 1/6 pkg	260	4	1	10	420	52	3
Pillsbury, 1/8 mix	220	5	1.5	0	340	40	<1
Fun kit, Betty Crocker, mix to make 2 cookies	130	3	1	0	160	25	0
Whole wheat, Hodgson Mill, 1/4 cup	120	4	1	0	200	21	2

GRAINS See also Dried Foods & Mixes, Grains.

Barley flakes, rolled, Arrowhead Mills, 1/3 cup	110	1	0	0	0	28	5
Corn bran, raw, 1/4 cup	40	0	0	0	0	17	16
Kamut flakes, rolled, Arrowhead Mills, 1/3 cup	130	1	0	0	0	29	5
Oat bran, Arrowhead Mills, 1/3 cup	150	2.5	0	0	0	23	7

GRAINS	CAL	FAT (g)	SAT FAT (g)	CHOL (mg)	SODIUM (mg)	CARB (g)	FIBER (g)
Oat flakes, rolled, Arrowhead Mills, 1/3 cup	130	2.5	0.5	0	0	23	4
Rice bran, raw, 1/4 cup	70	4.5	1	0	0	11	4
Rye flakes, rolled, Arrowhead Mills, 1/3 cup	110	0.5	0	0	0	24	4
Semolina, enriched, 1/4 cup	150	0.5	0	0	0	31	2
Sorghum, 1/4 cup	160	1.5	0	0	0	36	7
Teff, Arrowhead Mills, 1/4 cup	160	1	0	0	5	32	6
Triticale, 1/4 cup	160	1	0	0	0	35	9
Wheat, durum, 1/4 cup	160	1	0	0	0	34	3
Wheat, hard red spring, 1/4 cup	160	1	0	0	0	33	6
Wheat, hard red winter, Arrowhead Mills, 1/4 cup	160	1	0	0	0	34	7
Wheat, hard white, 1/4 cup	160	1	0	0	0	37	2
Wheat, soft red winter, 1/4 cup	140	0.5	0	0	0	31	3
Wheat, soft white, 1/4 cup	180	1	0	0	0	32	2
Wheat bran, Arrowhead Mills, 1/4 cup	30	0.5	0	0	0	7	6
Wheat flakes, rolled, Arrowhead Mills, 1/3 cup	110	0.5	0	0	0	24	5
Wheat germ, raw, Arrowhead Mills, 3 Tbsp	50	0.5	0	0	0	10	2

LEAVENING & THICKENING AGENTS

	CAL	FAT (g)	SAT FAT (g)	CHOL (mg)	SODIUM (mg)	CARB (g)	FIBER (g)
Baking powder, Calmut, 1/4 tsp	0	0	0	0	100	0	0
Baking soda, Arm & Hammer, 1/8 tsp	0	0	0	0	120	0	0
Cornstarch, Argo/Kingsford's, 1 Tbsp	30	0	0	0	0	7	0
Cream of tartar, 1/4 tsp	0	0	0	0	0	0	0
Tapioca, Minute, 1 1/2 tsp	20	0	0	0	0	5	0
Yeast, baker's, active dry, 1 pkg	20	0	0	0	0	3	2
Yeast, baker's, compressed, 1 cake	20	0	0	0	5	3	2

	CAL (g)	FAT (g)	SAT FAT (g)	CHOL (mg)	SODIUM (mg)	CARB (g)	FIBER (g)

MILK

	CAL (g)	FAT (g)	SAT FAT (g)	CHOL (mg)	SODIUM (mg)	CARB (g)	FIBER (g)
Evaporated, Carnation, 2 Tbsp	40	2.5	1.5	10	35	3	ns
Evaporated, Pet, 2 Tbsp	40	2	1	5	30	3	0
Evaporated, lowfat, Carnation, 2 Tbsp	25	0.5	ns	5	35	3	ns
Evaporated, skimmed, Carnation, 2 Tbsp	25	0	ns	ns	40	4	ns
Evaporated, skimmed, Pet, 2 Tbsp	25	0	0	<5	35	3	0
Sweetened condensed, Carnation, 2 Tbsp	130	3	2	10	45	22	ns
Sweetened condensed, Eagle Brand, 2 Tbsp	130	3	2	10	40	23	0
Sweetened condensed, low fat, Eagle Brand, 2 Tbsp	120	1.5	1	5	40	23	0

MISO

	CAL (g)	FAT (g)	SAT FAT (g)	CHOL (mg)	SODIUM (mg)	CARB (g)	FIBER (g)
Miso, 2 Tbsp	70	2	0	0	1260	10	2

MOLASSES

	CAL (g)	FAT (g)	SAT FAT (g)	CHOL (mg)	SODIUM (mg)	CARB (g)	FIBER (g)
Bead, La Choy, 1 Tbsp	50	0	0	0	50	12	0
Blackstrap, Glorybee, 1 Tbsp	45	0	0	0	10	11	0
Sweet, Glorybee, 1 Tbsp	50	0	0	0	5	13	0

MUFFIN MIX

	CAL (g)	FAT (g)	SAT FAT (g)	CHOL (mg)	SODIUM (mg)	CARB (g)	FIBER (g)
Apple cinnamon, Betty Crocker, ¼ cup	110	1.5	0.5	0	190	24	0
Apple-cinnamon, Jiffy, ¼ cup	170	5	2.5	0	300	28	1
Apple cinnamon, Martha White, ⅓ cup	150	3	1	0	340	29	1
Apple cinnamon, Robin Hood, ¼ cup	130	4	1	0	200	22	0
Banana nut, Betty Crocker, 3 Tbsp	130	2.5	0.5	0	190	24	0
Banana nut, Jiffy, ¼ cup	160	5	2.5	0	300	25	2
Banana nut, Robin Hood/Gold Medal, ¼ cup	140	5	1	0	170	21	0

MUFFIN MIX	CAL (g)	FAT (g)	SAT FAT (g)	CHOL (mg)	SODIUM (mg)	CARB (g)	FIBER (g)
Blueberry, Betty Crocker Twice the Blueberry, ¼ cup	120	1.5	0.5	0	180	25	0
Blueberry, Jiffy, ¼ cup	160	5	2	0	270	28	1
Blueberry, Martha White, ⅓ cup	150	3	1	0	340	29	1
Blueberry, Robin Hood, ¼ cup	120	3	0.5	0	210	23	0
Blueberry, light, Betty Crocker, 3 Tbsp	120	0.5	0	0	190	27	0
Bran with dates, Jiffy, ¼ cup	150	4	1.5	0	240	26	3
Caramel nut, Gold Medal/Robin Hood, ¼ cup	120	3	1	0	210	23	0
Cinnamon streusel, Betty Crocker, ¼ cup	160	7	1.5	0	170	21	0
Corn, Flako, ⅓ cup	160	4	1	0	380	29	1
Corn, Gold Medal, ¼ cup	110	1	ns	0	210	24	0
Corn, Jiffy, ¼ cup	160	4	1.5	0	320	28	1
Honey date, Jiffy, ¼ cup	150	4	1.5	0	200	27	1
Lemon poppyseed, Betty Crocker, ¼ cup	140	2	0.5	0	220	29	0
Oat bran, wheat free, Arrowhead Mills, ⅓ cup	160	4	1.5	0	310	23	7
Oatmeal, Jiffy, ¼ cup	150	4	2	0	270	26	2
Wheat bran, Arrowhead Mills, ⅓ cup	150	2	0	0	160	29	7
Wild berry, Betty Crocker, ¼ cup	140	1.5	0.5	0	210	29	0

AT A GLANCE: MUFFIN MIX
Highest in Fiber: Arrowhead Mills Oat Bran, Wheat Free; Arrowhead Mills Wheat Bran.
Lowest in Sodium: Arrowhead Mills Wheat Bran.

PANCAKE & WAFFLE MIX

	CAL (g)	FAT (g)	SAT FAT (g)	CHOL (mg)	SODIUM (mg)	CARB (g)	FIBER (g)
Blue corn, Arrowhead Mills, ⅓ cup	150	2	0	0	130	28	3
Blueberry, Bisquick Shake 'N Pour, ½ cup	220	4	1	0	640	40	1
Buckwheat, Arrowhead Mills, ⅓ cup	140	1.5	0	0	220	25	5

PANCAKE & WAFFLE MIX	CAL (g)	FAT (g)	SAT FAT (g)	CHOL (mg)	SODIUM (mg)	CARB (g)	FIBER (g)
Buckwheat, Aunt Jemima, ¼ cup	120	1	0	0	560	28	4
Buckwheat, Hodgson Mill, ⅓ cup	160	1	0	0	590	36	5
Buttermilk, Arrowhead Mills, ¼ cup	120	0.5	0	<5	350	25	2
Buttermilk, Aunt Jemima, ⅓ cup	190	2	0.5	10	480	38	2
Buttermilk, Bisquick Shake 'N Pour, ½ cup	200	3	1	0	680	38	1
Buttermilk, Pillsbury Hungry Jack, ⅓ cup	160	1.5	0	0	650	33	<1
Buttermilk, Robin Hood, ⅓ cup	170	4	1	0	540	30	<1
Buttermilk, complete, Betty Crocker, ⅓ cup	200	3	0.5	10	540	39	1
Buttermilk, complete, Pillsbury Hungry Jack, ⅓ cup	160	1.5	0	<5	560	32	<1
Buttermilk, reduced calorie, Aunt Jemima, ⅓ cup	140	1.5	0.5	15	510	30	5
Complete, Betty Crocker, ⅓ cup	210	3	1	10	540	40	1
Gluten-free, Arrowhead Mills, ¼ cup	130	2	0	0	180	24	5
Kamut, Arrowhead Mills, ¼ cup	130	1	0	0	330	26	4
Multigrain, Arrowhead Mills, ¼ cup	120	0.5	0	0	260	24	3
Oat bran, Arrowhead Mills, ⅓ cup	140	1.5	0	0	160	25	6
Original, Aunt Jemima, ⅓ cup	150	0.5	0	0	620	34	1
Original, Pillsbury Hungry Jack, ⅓ cup	150	1.5	0	0	640	32	<1
Plain, Aunt Jemima, ⅓ cup	190	2	0.5	15	470	39	1
Plain, Bisquick Shake 'N Pour, ½ cup	210	4	1	0	710	39	<1
Plain, premeasured packets, Pillsbury Hungry Jack, ½ packet	200	3.5	1	0	780	38	1
Potato pancake, Knorr, ¼ pkg	150	0.5	0	0	680	34	4

PANCAKE & WAFFLE MIX	CAL (g)	FAT (g)	SAT FAT (g)	CHOL (mg)	SODIUM (mg)	CARB (g)	FIBER (g)
Whole grain, Arrowhead Mills, ¼ cup	120	0.5	0	0	260	24	4
Whole wheat, Aunt Jemima, ¼ cup	130	0.5	0	0	560	28	3
Wild rice, Arrowhead Mills, ⅓ cup	140	1	0	0	65	30	0

AT A GLANCE: PANCAKE & WAFFLE MIX
Highest in Fiber: Arrowhead Mills Oat Bran
Lowest in Sodium: Arrowhead Mills Wheat Bran

PASTA MIX

	CAL (g)	FAT (g)	SAT FAT (g)	CHOL (mg)	SODIUM (mg)	CARB (g)	FIBER (g)
Semolina flour, Arrowhead Mills, ½ cup	240	1	0	0	0	50	4

PECTIN

	CAL (g)	FAT (g)	SAT FAT (g)	CHOL (mg)	SODIUM (mg)	CARB (g)	FIBER (g)
Fruit, Sure-Jell, ¼ tsp	5	0	0	0	0	1	0
Fruit, for lower sugar recipes, Sure-Jell, ¼ tsp	5	0	0	0	0	1	0
Pectin mix, unsweetened, ¼ pkg	40	0	0	0	25	11	ns

PIE FILLING, CANNED

	CAL (g)	FAT (g)	SAT FAT (g)	CHOL (mg)	SODIUM (mg)	CARB (g)	FIBER (g)
Apple, Comstock/Wilderness/Thank You, ⅓ cup	100	0	0	0	10	25	2
Apple, Comstock/Wilderness/Thank You More Fruit, ⅓ cup	80	0	0	0	40	20	1
Apple, Musselman's, ⅓ cup	90	0	0	0	40	22	2
Apple, cinnamon & spice, Comstock/Wilderness/Thank You, ⅓ cup	100	0	0	0	60	26	1
Apple, cinnamon & spice, Comstock/Wilderness/Thank You More Fruit, ⅓ cup	110	0	0	0	60	27	1
Apple, French, Comstock/Wilderness/Thank You, ⅓ cup	100	0	0	0	30	23	1
Apple cranberry, Comstock/Wilderness/Thank You, ⅓ cup	90	0	0	0	50	22	1
Apricot, Comstock/Wilderness/Thank You, ⅓ cup	100	0	0	0	5	23	1
Blackberry, Comstock/Wilderness/Thank You, ⅓ cup	110	0	0	0	20	26	3

PIE FILLING, CANNED	CAL (g)	FAT (g)	SAT FAT (g)	CHOL (mg)	SODIUM (mg)	CARB (g)	FIBER (g)
Blueberry, Comstock/Wilderness/Thank You, ⅓ cup	100	0	0	0	15	25	1
Blueberry, Comstock/Wilderness/Thank You More Fruit, ⅓ cup	80	0	0	0	45	21	1
Blueberry, Musselman's, ⅓ cup	90	0	0	0	50	22	1
Blueberry-cranberry, Comstock/Wilderness/Thank You, ⅓ cup	100	0	0	0	15	25	1
Cherry, Comstock/Wilderness/Thank You, ⅓ cup	90	0	0	0	25	23	1
Cherry, Comstock/Wilderness/Thank You More Fruit, ⅓ cup	90	0	0	0	70	23	0
Cherry, Musselman's, ⅓ cup	100	0	0	0	40	24	0
Cherry, lite, Comstock/Wilderness/Thank You, ⅓ cup	60	0	0	0	15	15	1
Cherry, lite, Comstock/Wilderness/Thank You More Fruit, ⅓ cup	60	0	0	0	30	13	0
Cherry-cranberry, Comstock/Wilderness/Thank You, ⅓ cup	90	0	0	0	30	22	0
Lemon, Durkee, 1 Tbsp	50	0	0	0	70	12	0
Mincemeat, None Such, ⅓ cup	190	0.5	0	0	230	45	0
Mincemeat, with brandy & rum, None Such, ⅓ cup	200	1	0	0	250	47	0
Peach, Comstock/Wilderness/Thank You, ⅓ cup	100	0	0	0	15	26	1
Peach, Comstock/Wilderness/Thank You More Fruit, ⅓ cup	80	0	0	0	15	19	1
Pineapple, Comstock/Wilderness/Thank You, ⅓ cup	110	0	0	0	10	27	1
Pumpkin, solid pack, Libby's, ½ cup	60	0.5	0	ns	5	15	4
Raisin, Comstock/Wilderness/Thank You, ⅓ cup	120	0	0	0	25	29	3
Raspberry, Comstock/Wilderness/Thank You, ⅓ cup	100	0	0	0	45	25	3
Strawberry, Comstock/Wilderness/Thank You, ⅓ cup	100	0	0	0	25	23	1

AT A GLANCE: PIE FILLING, CANNED (READY-TO-USE TYPES)
Highest in Fiber: Comstock/Wilderness/Thank You Raspberry
Lowest in Sodium: Comstock/Wilderness/Thank You Apricot Fruit

	CAL (g)	FAT (g)	SAT FAT (g)	CHOL (mg)	SODIUM (mg)	CARB (g)	FIBER (g)
SEASONING MIX							

See also Condiments, Dips, Spreads & Sauces; Gravy & Gravy Mix; Marinades.

	CAL (g)	FAT (g)	SAT FAT (g)	CHOL (mg)	SODIUM (mg)	CARB (g)	FIBER (g)
Alfredo, Spice Islands, ½ pkg	45	2.5	1.5	10	610	3	0
Au jus roasting bag mix, Durkee/French's, ⅛ pkg	10	0	0	0	340	2	0
Beef & broccoli, Sun Bird, ¾ Tbsp	20	0	0	0	140	5	0
Beef fajita, Durkee, ⅙ pkg	15	0	0	0	550	4	0
Beef stew, Durkee, ⅑ pkg	0	0	0	0	660	3	0
Beef stew, French's, ⅑ pkg	5	0	0	0	560	3	0
Beef stew roasting bag mix, Durkee, ⅒ pkg	15	0	0	0	310	3	0
Beef teriyaki, Durkee, ⅕ pkg	30	1	0	0	700	6	0
Bourguignonne mix, Knorr, ⅙ pkg	40	1	0.5	0	430	6	0
Buffalo wings, hot, Durkee, ¼ pkg	35	1	0	0	950	6	0
Buffalo wings, mild, Durkee, ¼ pkg	35	1	0	0	950	6	0
Buffalo wings, Screaming Hot, Durkee, ¼ pkg	35	1	0	0	950	6	0
Burrito, Durkee, ⅒ pkg	35	1	0	0	240	5	2
Burrito, Old El Paso, 2 tsp	20	0	0	0	290	3	1
Chicken, barbecue, roasting bag mix, Durkee, ⅙ pkg	30	0	0	0	570	8	0.5
Chicken, country, roasting bag mix, Durkee, ⅙ pkg	35	1.5	1	0	360	5	0
Chicken, sweet and sour, Durkee, ⅑ pkg	20	0	0	0	70	5	0
Chicken cacciatore, Durkee, ⅒ pkg	10	0	0	0	110	3	0
Chicken Mexican salsa, Durkee, ⅒ pkg	10	0	0	0	120	3	0
Chicken mushroom, Durkee, ⅛ pkg	15	0	0	0	200	3	0
Chicken roasting bag mix, Durkee/French's, ⅙ pkg	20	0	0	0	500	4	0

SEASONING MIX	CAL (g)	FAT (g)	SAT FAT (g)	CHOL (mg)	SODIUM (mg)	CARB (g)	FIBER (g)
Chili, Durkee, ⅕ pkg	30	0	0	0	660	7	0
Chili, Old El Paso, 1 Tbsp	25	5	0.5	0	770	4	1
Chili, mild, Durkee/French's, ⅕ pkg	30	0.5	0	0	380	5	0
Chili, Pot-o-, Durkee, ⅛ pkg	30	0	0	0	680	7	0
Chili, Texas red, Durkee, ⅓ pkg	45	1	0	0	910	9	0
Chili-O, onion, French's, ⅕ pkg	40	0	0	0	810	8	0
Chili-O, original, French's, ⅕ pkg	30	0	0	0	820	6	0
Chili-O, Texas style, French's, ⅓ pkg	45	1	0	0	1040	9	0.5
Chinese barbecue, Sun Bird, ½ Tbsp	10	0	0	0	600	2	0
Chinese chicken salad, Sun Bird, ½ Tbsp	15	0	0	0	400	2	0
Chop suey, Sun Bird, 1 Tbsp	20	0	0	0	550	5	0
Chow mein, Sun Bird, 2 tsp	15	0	0	0	310	3	0
Enchilada, Durkee, ⅛ pkg	10	0	0	0	260	2	0
Enchilada, French's, ⅐ pkg	15	0	0	0	410	3	0
Enchilada, Old El Paso, 2 tsp	10	0	0	0	540	2	<1
Fajitas, French's, ⅛ pkg	10	0	0	0	280	2	0
Fish, lemon butter, roasting bag mix, Durkee/French's, ¼ pkg	30	0.5	0	0	380	6	0
Fish, lemon pepper dill, Durkee, ⅙ pkg	20	0.5	0	0	160	4	0
Fish, tomato basil, Durkee, ⅐ pkg	15	0	0	0	170	4	0
Fried rice, Durkee, ¼ pkg	15	0	0	0	840	2	0
Fried rice, Sun Bird, ½ Tbsp	10	0	0	0	380	3	0
Fried rice, hot and spicy, Sun Bird, ½ Tbsp	15	0	0	0	160	3	0
Garlic and herb, Spice Islands, ¼ pkg	15	0	0	0	380	3	0
Ground beef, Durkee, ¼ pkg	25	0	0	0	490	5	0

SEASONING MIX	CAL (g)	FAT (g)	SAT FAT (g)	CHOL (mg)	SODIUM (mg)	CARB (g)	FIBER (g)
Honey teriyaki, Sun Bird, 1 tsp	15	0	0	0	135	3	0
Hot and spicy, Szechwan, Sun Bird, 2 tsp	15	0	0	0	260	3	1
Italian meatball, Durkee, ⅕ pkg	20	0	0	0	360	3	0
Kung Pao chicken, Sun Bird, ¾ Tbsp	20	0	0	0	310	5	1
Lemon chicken, Sun Bird, ½ Tbsp	10	0	0	0	450	3	0
Marinade for beef, Durkee, 1/10 pkg	0	0	0	0	220	<1	0
Meat marinade, French's, 1/10 pkg	0	0	0	0	150	0	0
Meatloaf, Durkee, ⅑ pkg	20	0	0	0	360	3	0
Meatloaf, French's, ⅑ pkg	10	0	0	0	600	2	0
Meatloaf roasting bag mix, Durkee/French's, ⅛ pkg	15	0	0	0	500	2	0
Orange beef, Sun Bird, ½ Tbsp	15	0	0	0	290	3	0
Pasta, zesty, French's, ⅕ pkg	20	0	0	0	350	5	0
Pasta salad, Durkee, ⅙ pkg	10	0	0	0	200	2	0
Pesto, Spice Islands, ¼ pkg	15	0.5	0	0	260	1	0
Pork frying batter, House of Tsang, 4 Tbsp	140	4	0	0	1300	32	0
Pork roasting bag mix, Durkee/French's, ⅙ pkg	25	0	0	0	320	5	0
Pot roast roasting bag mix, Durkee, ⅙ pkg	15	0	0	0	350	4	0
Pot roast roasting bag mix, French's, ⅙ pkg	20	0	0	0	410	4	0
Pot roast, onion roasting bag mix, Durkee/French's, ⅙ pkg	25	0	0	0	350	4	0
Potatoes, Betty Crocker Potato Shakers, 3 tsp	25	0.5	0	<5	530	5	0
Potatoes, cheddar, savory, Lipton Recipe Secrets, 1 Tbsp	60	5	1	5	420	1	0
Potatoes, cheddar, zesty, Betty Crocker Potato Shakers, 3 tsp	30	1.5	0	<5	540	4	0

SEASONING MIX	CAL (g)	FAT (g)	SAT FAT (g)	CHOL (mg)	SODIUM (mg)	CARB (g)	FIBER (g)
Potatoes, crispy cheddar, Shake 'N Bake Perfect Potatoes, 1/6 packet	30	2	1.5	5	380	2	0
Potatoes, garlic herb, Lipton Recipe Secrets, 1 Tbsp	50	5	1	5	290	2	0
Potatoes, herb and garlic, Shake 'N Bake Perfect Potatoes, 1/6 packet	20	0	0	0	370	5	0
Potatoes, onion, California, Lipton Recipe Secrets, 1 Tbsp	60	5	1	5	340	2	0
Potatoes, Parmesan, Betty Crocker Potato Shakers, 3 tsp	30	1	0	5	540	4	0
Primavera, Spice Islands, 1/5 pkg	30	1.5	0	5	440	3	0
Season It, dried tomato, Timber Crest Farms, 2–3 tsp	20	0	0	0	25	3	1
Sloppy Joe, Durkee/French's, 1/6 pkg	20	0	0	0	540	5	0
Spaghetti, Durkee, 1/5 pkg	15	0	0	0	390	5	0
Spaghetti, all-American, French's, 1/5 pkg	20	0	0	0	200	7	0
Spaghetti, American style, Durkee, 1/6 pkg	15	0	0	0	170	6	0
Spaghetti, family, Durkee, 1/10 pkg	20	0	0	0	560	4	0
Spaghetti, Italian, French's, 1/5 pkg	15	0	0	0	390	5	0
Spaghetti, mushroom, French's, 1/5 pkg	20	1	0	2	760	4	0
Spaghetti, thick, French's, 1/6 pkg	10	0	0	0	630	4	0
Spaghetti, with mushrooms, Durkee, 1/5 pkg	15	0	0	0	520	4	0
Spaghetti, zesty, Durkee, 1/5 pkg	20	0	0	0	350	5	0
Spareribs roasting bag mix, Durkee, 1/2 pkg	25	0	0	0	430	5	0
Stir-fry, Sun Bird, 1/2 Tbsp	15	0	0	0	310	3	0
Stroganoff, Durkee, 1/8 pkg	10	0	0	0	360	3	0
Stroganoff, French's, 1/4 pkg	45	2	1	5	420	6	0

SEASONING MIX	CAL (g)	FAT (g)	SAT FAT (g)	CHOL (mg)	SODIUM (mg)	CARB (g)	FIBER (g)
Sweet and sour, Sun Bird, ½ Tbsp	15	0	0	0	110	4	0
Swiss steak roasting bag mix, Durkee/French's, ⅑ pkg	10	0	0	0	310	3	0
Taco, Durkee/French's, ⅛ pkg	15	0	0	0	350	2	0
Taco, Old El Paso, 2 tsp	20	0	0	0	550	5	0
Taco, Pancho Villa, 2 tsp	20	0	0	0	550	5	0
Taco, 40% less sodium, Old El Paso, 2 tsp	20	0	0	0	330	4	0
Taco, family, Durkee, 1/16 pkg	10	0	0	0	280	2	0
Taco, mild, Durkee/French's, ⅛ pkg	15	0	0	0	320	3	0
Taco, onion, French's, ⅛ pkg	20	0	0	0	200	4	0
Taco salad, Durkee, ⅙ pkg	20	0	0	0	320	4	0
Tempura, Sun Bird, ½ Tbsp	15	0	0	0	140	4	0
Teriyaki marinade, Sun Bird, ½ Tbsp	10	0	0	0	500	3	0
Tomato pesto, Spice Islands, ¼ pkg	15	0	0	0	320	3	0

SEASONINGS, SPICES & FLAVORINGS

Ac'cent, flavor enhancer, ⅛ tsp	0	0	0	0	80	0	0
Adobo, Durkee, ¼ tsp	0	0	0	0	320	0	0
All-purpose seasoning, Durkee Smart Seasoning, ½ tsp	0	0	0	0	0	<1	0
All-purpose seasoning, no salt, Spice Islands, ½ tsp	0	0	0	0	0	<1	0
Arrowroot, Spice Islands, 2 Tbsp	35	0	0	0	0	9	0
Barbecue, Durkee, ¼ tsp	0	0	0	0	70	0	0
Beau Monde, Spice Islands, ¼ tsp	0	0	0	0	150	0	0
Beef stock base, Spice Islands, 2 tsp	10	0	0	0	810	2	0
Blackened redfish, Chef Paul Prudhomme's Magic Seasoning Blends, ¼ tsp	0	0	0	0	95	0	0

SEASONINGS, SPICES & FLAVORINGS	CAL	FAT (g)	SAT FAT (g)	CHOL (mg)	SODIUM (mg)	CARB (g)	FIBER (g)
Blackened steak, Chef Paul Prudhomme's Magic Seasoning Blends, ¼ tsp	0	0	0	0	80	0	0
Broil 'n grill, Durkee, ¼ tsp	0	0	0	0	240	0	0
Butter salt, Durkee, ½ tsp	0	0	0	0	340	0	0
Butter sprinkles, Durkee Smart Seasoning, ¾ tsp	0	0	0	0	60	1	0
Butter substitute, Molly McButter, 1 tsp	5	0	0	0	180	1	0
Cajun for fish, Durkee, ¼ tsp	0	0	0	0	80	0	0
Cajun for meat, Durkee, ¼ tsp	0	0	0	0	70	0	0
Cajun for poultry, Durkee, ¼ tsp	0	0	0	0	60	0	0
Celery salt, Durkee, ¼ tsp	0	0	0	0	290	0	0
Celery salt, Spice Islands, ½ tsp	0	0	0	0	290	0	0
Charcoal, Durkee, ¼ tsp	0	0	0	0	180	0	0
Charcol-It, Milani, ½ tsp	5	ns	ns	0	150	<1	0
Cheese sprinkles, Durkee Smart Seasoning, ½ tsp	0	0	0	0	70	0	0
Cheese substitute, Molly McButter, 1 tsp	5	0	0	0	125	1	0
Chicken, fried, Durkee, ¼ tsp	0	0	0	0	290	0	0
Chicken stock base, Spice Islands, 2 tsp	25	0	0	3	840	3	0
Chili con carne, Spice Islands, ¼ tsp	0	0	0	0	0	0	0
Chili powder, Durkee/Spice Islands, ¼ tsp	0	0	0	0	10	0	0
Chili powder, Gebhardt, ¼ tsp	0	0	0	0	0	0	0
Chili powder, hot, Durkee, ¼ tsp	0	0	0	0	15	0	0
Chili powder, hot Mexican, Durkee, ¼ tsp	0	0	0	0	20	0	0
Chili quick, Gebhardt, 2 Tbsp	30	0.5	0	0	410	5	0
Chilis, whole red, Spice Islands, 2 pieces	0	0	0	0	0	0	0

SEASONINGS, SPICES & FLAVORINGS	CAL	FAT (g)	SAT FAT (g)	CHOL (mg)	SODIUM (mg)	CARB (g)	FIBER (g)
Curry powder, Durkee, ¼ tsp	0	0	0	0	20	0	0
Five spice powder, Ka-Me, ¼ tsp	0	0	0	0	0	1	1
Garlic & herb sprinkles, Molly McButter, 1 tsp	5	0	0	0	130	1	0
Garlic bread, Spice Islands, ½ tsp	0	0	0	0	10	0	0
Garlic bread sprinkle, Durkee, ½ tsp	0	0	0	0	30	0	0
Garlic pepper, Spice Islands, ¼ tsp	0	0	0	0	60	0	0
Garlic, chopped, Christopher Ranch, 1 tsp	10	1	0	0	0	1	0
Garlic, crushed, Christopher Ranch, 1 tsp	10	0	0	0	0	1	0
Garlic, with Italian herb, Durkee Smart Seasoning, ½ tsp	0	0	0	0	0	0	0
Garlic, with parsley, Durkee Smart Seasoning, ¼ tsp	0	0	0	0	350	0	0
Garlic salt, Durkee, ¼ tsp	0	0	0	0	360	0	0
Garlic salt, Spice Islands, ½ tsp	0	0	0	0	290	0	0
Garlic salt, California style, Durkee, ½ tsp	0	0	0	0	240	0	0
Garlic salt, parslied, Durkee, ¼ tsp	0	0	0	0	310	0	0
Garlic seasoning powder, Spice Islands, ¼ tsp	0	0	0	0	190	0	0
Ginger, chopped, Christopher Ranch, 1 tsp	15	0	0	0	0	3	0
Hamburger, Spice Islands, ¼ tsp	0	0	0	0	50	0	0
Herb pepper, Spice Islands, ¼ tsp	0	0	0	0	50	0	0
Hickory smoked salt, Durkee, ¼ tsp	0	0	0	0	270	0	0
Italian salad, Durkee, ¼ tsp	0	0	0	0	40	0	0
Lemon fish, Durkee, ¼ tsp	0	0	0	0	85	0	0

SEASONINGS, SPICES & FLAVORINGS	CAL	FAT (g)	SAT FAT (g)	CHOL (mg)	SODIUM (mg)	CARB (g)	FIBER (g)
Lemon herb, salt free, Spice Islands, ½ tsp	0	0	0	0	0	0	0
Lemon pepper, Durkee, ¼ tsp	0	0	0	0	190	0	0
Lemon pepper marinade, Spice Islands, ¼ tsp	0	0	0	0	35	0	0
Meat, Chef Paul Prudhomme's Magic Seasoning Blends, ¼ tsp	0	0	0	0	135	0	0
Meat tenderizer, Durkee/Spice Islands, ¼ tsp	0	0	0	0	350	0	0
Meat tenderizer, seasoned, Durkee/Spice Islands, ¼ tsp	0	0	0	0	270	0	0
Meat tenderizer, sodium-free, Adolph's, ¼ Tbsp	0	0	0	0	0	1	ns
Meat tenderizer, unseasoned, Adolph's, ¼ Tbsp	0	0	0	0	450	1	ns
Mei yen, Spice Islands, ¼ tsp	0	0	0	0	105	0	0
Menudo mix, Gebhardt, ¼ tsp	0	0	0	0	45	0	0
MSG, Durkee/Spice Islands, ¼ tsp	0	0	0	0	100	0	0
Mustard powder, hot, Ka-Me, ¼ tsp	5	0	0	0	0	1	1
No-salt blends, all varieties, Mrs. Dash, ½ tsp	0	0	0	0	0	1	0
Old Bay, 1 tsp	5	0	0	0	570	<1	0
Onion pepper, Spice Islands, ¼ tsp	0	0	0	0	50	0	0
Onion salt, Durkee, ½ tsp	0	0	0	0	300	0	0
Onion salt, Spice Islands, ½ tsp	0	0	0	0	290	0	0
Onion salt, California style, Durkee, ½ tsp	0	0	0	0	290	0	0
Original seasoning, salt free, Spice Islands, ½ tsp	0	0	0	0	0	0	0
Pepper, seasoned, Durkee, ¼ tsp	0	0	0	0	10	0	0
Pepper & herb, Durkee Smart Seasoning, ¾ tsp	0	0	0	0	0	0	0
Pepper mix, Spice Islands, ¼ tsp	0	0	0	0	35	0	0

SEASONINGS, SPICES & FLAVORINGS	CAL	FAT (g)	SAT FAT (g)	CHOL (mg)	SODIUM (mg)	CARB (g)	FIBER (g)
Pizza, Spice Islands, ¼ tsp	0	0	0	0	15	0	0
Pizza & pasta, herbal or hot & sweet, Chef Paul Prudhomme's Magic Seasoning Blends, ¼ tsp	0	0	0	0	0	0	0
Popcorn cheese, Spice Islands, ½ tsp	0	0	0	0	55	1	0
Pork & veal, Chef Paul Prudhomme's Magic Seasoning Blends, ¼ tsp	0	0	0	0	130	0	0
Poultry, Chef Paul Prudhomme's Magic Seasoning Blends, ¼ tsp	0	0	0	0	105	0	0
Sa-Son, original, Ac'cent, ¼ tsp	0	0	0	0	150	0	0
Sa-Son con Ajo Cebolla, Ac'cent, ¼ tsp	0	0	0	0	140	0	0
Sa-Son con Azafran, Ac'cent, ¼ tsp	0	0	0	0	125	0	0
Sa-Son con Culantro, Ac'cent, ¼ tsp	0	0	0	0	170	0	0
Salad, Spice Islands, ½ tsp	0	0	0	0	380	0	0
Salad, with vinaigrette, Spice Islands, ¼ tsp	0	0	0	0	210	0	0
Salad seasoning, Durkee, ½ tsp	0	0	0	0	70	0	0
Salad seasoning with cheese, Durkee, ½ tsp	0	0	0	0	70	0	0
Salt, Spice Islands, ¼ tsp	0	0	0	0	360	0	0
Salt, lite, Morton, ½ tsp	0	0	0	0	550	0	0
Salt, lite, Papa Dash Lite Salt, ½ tsp	0	0	0	0	170	1	0
Seafood, Chef Paul Prudhomme's Magic Seasoning Blends, ¼ tsp	0	0	0	0	115	0	0
Seasoned salt, Durkee, ½ tsp	0	0	0	0	310	0	0
Seasoned salt, Lawry's, ¼ tsp	0	0	0	0	380	0	0
Seasoned salt, lite, Durkee, ½ tsp	0	0	0	0	135	<1	0

SEASONINGS, SPICES & FLAVORINGS	CAL (g)	FAT (g)	SAT FAT (g)	CHOL (mg)	SODIUM (mg)	CARB (g)	FIBER (g)
Seasoned salt substitute, Durkee, ½ tsp	0	0	0	0	0	0	0
Smoked salt, old hickory, Spice Islands, ¼ tsp	0	0	0	0	270	0	0
Sour cream substitute, Molly McButter, 1 tsp	5	0	0	0	115	1	0
Spaghetti sauce, Spice Islands, ¼ tsp	0	0	0	0	45	0	0
Spicy pepper, salt free, Spice Islands, ½ tsp	0	0	0	0	0	0	0
Steak spice, Durkee, ½ tsp	0	0	0	0	240	0	0
Sugar ginger, Dynasty, 1 oz	100	0	0	0	20	24	<1
Vegetable seasoning, Chef Paul Prudhomme's Magic Seasoning Blends, ¼ tsp	0	0	0	0	135	0	0
Vegetable seasoning, Spice Islands, ¼ tsp	0	0	0	0	150	0	0
Wasabi powder, Ka-Me, ¼ tsp	0	0	0	0	0	1	0

AT A GLANCE: SEASONINGS, SPICES & FLAVORINGS

The following spices and herbs have no calories, fat, cholesterol, sodium, or carbohydrates: allspice, alum, anise seed, apple pie spice, arrowroot, basil (ground or fresh), bay leaves, black pepper, caraway seed, cardamon, cayenne pepper, celery flakes or seeds, chervil, chives, cinnamon, cloves, coriander (leaf or seed), cream of tartar, crushed red pepper, cumin, dill weed (dried or fresh), dill seed, extracts & flavorings, fennel seed, fenugreek seed, garlic (liquid, minced, or powder), ginger, Italian seasoning, mace, marjoram, mint, mustard, nutmeg, onion (liquid, chopped, flaked, or powder), oregano, paprika, parsley flakes, pickling spice, poppyseed, pot herbs, pumpkin pie spice, rosemary, saffron, sage, savory, sesame seed, tarragon, thyme, turmeric, white pepper.

SEEDS

Lotus seeds, dried, 1 oz	90	0.5	0	0	0	18	na
Lotus seeds, raw, 1 oz	25	0	0	0	0	5	na
Safflower seed kernels, dried, 1 oz	150	11	1	0	0	10	na
Safflower seed meal, partially defatted, 1 oz	100	1	0	0	0	14	na
Sesame seed kernels, dried, 1 oz	170	16	2.5	0	10	3	0
Sesame seed kernels, toasted, salted, 1 oz	160	14	2	0	170	7	5

SEEDS	CAL (g)	FAT (g)	SAT FAT (g)	CHOL (mg)	SODIUM (mg)	CARB (g)	FIBER (g)
Sesame seeds, hulled, Arrowhead Mills, ¼ cup	210	20	2.5	0	0	5	5
Sesame seeds, whole, dried, 1 oz	160	14	2	0	0	7	3
Sesame seeds, whole, roasted and toasted, 1 oz	160	14	2	0	0	7	4
Sesame seeds, whole brown, Arrowhead Mills, ¼ cup	200	20	2.5	0	20	8	5

SOY PRODUCTS

	CAL (g)	FAT (g)	SAT FAT (g)	CHOL (mg)	SODIUM (mg)	CARB (g)	FIBER (g)
Soy meal, defatted, raw, ½ cup	210	1.5	0	0	0	24	na
Soy protein concentrate, produced by acid wash, 1 oz	90	0	0	0	250	9	na
Soy protein concentrate, produced by alcohol extraction, 1 oz	90	0	0	0	0	9	na
Soy protein isolate, 1 oz	90	1	0	0	280	2	2
Soy protein isolate, potassium type, 1 oz	90	0	0	0	15	3	na

SUGAR & SUGAR SUBSTITUTES

	CAL (g)	FAT (g)	SAT FAT (g)	CHOL (mg)	SODIUM (mg)	CARB (g)	FIBER (g)
Brown sugar, dark, Domino, 1 tsp	15	0	0	0	0	4	0
Brown sugar, light, Domino, 1 tsp	15	0	0	0	0	4	0
Brownulated sugar, Domino, 1 tsp	10	0	0	0	0	3	0
Confectioners sugar 10x, Domino, ¼ cup	120	0	0	0	0	30	0
Granulated sugar, Domino, 1 tsp	15	0	0	0	0	4	0
Granulated sugar, superfine, Domino, 1 tsp	15	0	0	0	0	4	0
Hostess crystal tablets, Domino, 1 tablet	20	0	0	0	0	5	0
Maple sugar, 1 tsp	20	0	0	0	0	4	0
Sugar 'n cinnamon, Domino, 1 tsp	15	0	0	0	0	4	0
Sugar dots, Domino, 1 cube	10	0	0	0	0	3	0

SUGAR & SUGAR SUBSTITUTES	CAL (g)	FAT (g)	SAT FAT (g)	CHOL (mg)	SODIUM (mg)	CARB (g)	FIBER (g)
Sugar packets, handy pack, Domino, 1 packet	15	0	0	0	0	4	0
Sweetener, Equal, 1 packet	4	0	0	0	0	<1	0
Sweetener, Equal Measure, ¼ tsp	4	0	0	0	0	<1	0
Sweetener, SugarTwin Calorie Free Sweetener, 1 packet	0	0	0	0	0	<1	0
Sweetener, Weight Watchers, 1 g	5	0	0	0	30	1	0
Sweetener, saccharin-based, Sweet 'N Low, 1 packet	0	0	0	0	0	1	0
Sweetener, tablet, Equal, 1 tablet	0	0	0	0	0	0	0

SYRUPS

	CAL (g)	FAT (g)	SAT FAT (g)	CHOL (mg)	SODIUM (mg)	CARB (g)	FIBER (g)
Corn syrup, dark, Karo, 2 Tbsp	120	0	0	0	80	30	ns
Corn syrup, light, Karo, 2 Tbsp	120	0	0	0	35	30	ns
Malt extract, 2 Tbsp	150	0	0	0	20	34	na
Sorghum, 2 Tbsp	120	0	0	0	0	31	0

VINEGAR

	CAL (g)	FAT (g)	SAT FAT (g)	CHOL (mg)	SODIUM (mg)	CARB (g)	FIBER (g)
Apple cider flavor, Heinz, 1 Tbsp	0	0	0	0	0	0	0
Cider, ½ cup	20	0	0	0	0	7	0
Cider flavor, Heinz, 1 Tbsp	0	0	0	0	0	0	0
Red wine, Regina, 1 Tbsp	0	0	0	0	0	1	0
Red wine, with garlic flavor, Regina, 1 Tbsp	0	0	0	0	0	1	0
White distilled, Heinz, 1 Tbsp	0	0	0	0	0	0	0
White wine, Regina, 1 Tbsp	0	0	0	0	0	1	0

WRAPPERS

	CAL (g)	FAT (g)	SAT FAT (g)	CHOL (mg)	SODIUM (mg)	CARB (g)	FIBER (g)
Egg roll skin, Dynasty, 2 wrappers	130	0.5	0	5	140	27	0
Gyoza skin, Dynasty, 8 wrappers	120	0.5	0	<5	120	24	0
Wonton skin, Dynasty, 7 wrappers	120	1	0	5	130	26	0

DAIRY & REFRIGERATED ITEMS

	CAL (g)	FAT (g)	SAT FAT (g)	CHOL (mg)	SODIUM (mg)	CARB (g)	FIBER (g)
BISCUIT & ROLL DOUGH							
1869, all types, Pillsbury, 1 biscuit	100	5	1.5	0	300	12	0
Ballard, all types, Pillsbury, 3 biscuits	150	2	0	0	490	29	<1
Butter, Pillsbury, 3 biscuits	150	2.5	0	0	490	29	<1
Butter, Pillsbury Grands!, 1 biscuit	200	10	2.5	0	580	23	<1
Butter Tastin', Pillsbury Big Country, 1 biscuit	100	4	1	0	300	13	0
Butter Tastin', flaky, Pillsbury Hungry Jack, 2 biscuits	170	7	1.5	0	580	23	<1
Butterflake, refrigerated, Pillsbury, 1 roll	130	5	1	0	530	19	<1
Buttermilk, Pillsbury, 3 biscuits	150	2.5	0	0	490	29	<1
Buttermilk, Pillsbury Big Country, 1 biscuit	100	4	1	0	300	14	0
Buttermilk, Pillsbury Grands!, 1 biscuit	200	10	3	0	570	23	<1
Buttermilk, flaky, Pillsbury Hungry Jack, 2 biscuits	170	7	1.5	0	600	23	<1
Buttermilk, tender layer, Pillsbury, 3 biscuits	160	4.5	1	0	480	27	<1
Country, Pillsbury, 3 biscuits	150	2.5	0	0	490	29	<1
Crescents, Pillsbury, 1 crescent	200	11	2.5	0	430	22	<1
Crescents, cheese, Pillsbury, 1 crescent	210	12	3	<5	600	21	<1
Flaky, Pillsbury Grands!, 1 biscuit	190	9	2	0	550	24	<1
Flaky, Pillsbury Hungry Jack, 2 biscuits	170	7	1.5	0	600	23	<1
Fluffy, Pillsbury Hungry Jack, 2 biscuits	180	8	2	0	570	23	<1

BISCUIT & ROLL DOUGH	CAL (g)	FAT (g)	SAT FAT (g)	CHOL (mg)	SODIUM (mg)	CARB (g)	FIBER (g)
Homestyle, Pillsbury Grands!, 1 biscuit	190	9	2.5	0	600	24	<1
Honey Tastin', flaky, Pillsbury Hungry Jack, 2 biscuits	180	7	1.5	0	580	25	<1
Mixed grain, 1 biscuit	130	3	1	0	320	23	4
Southern style, Pillsbury Big Country, 1 biscuit	100	4	1	0	300	14	0
Southern style, Pillsbury Grands!, 1 biscuit	200	10	2.5	0	580	23	<1
Southern style flaky, Pillsbury Hungry Jack, 2 biscuits	170	7	1.5	0	600	23	<1
Sweet rolls, apple cinnamon, with icing, Pillsbury, 1 roll	140	5	1.5	0	310	21	<1
Sweet rolls, caramel, Pillsbury, 1 roll	170	7	1.5	0	330	25	<1
Sweet rolls, cinnamon raisin, Pillsbury Grands!, 1 roll	180	7	1.5	0	310	26	<1
Sweet rolls, cinnamon raisin, with icing, Pillsbury, 1 roll	140	5	1.5	0	330	21	0
Sweet rolls, orange, with icing, Pillsbury, 1 roll	170	7	1.5	0	330	25	<1

AT A GLANCE: BISCUITS & ROLLS
Lowest in Fat: Pillsbury Ballard biscuits
Lowest in Sat Fat: Pillsbury Ballard, Butter, Buttermilk, and Country biscuits.

BREAD DOUGH

Breadsticks, Pillsbury, 1 stick	110	2.5	0.5	0	290	18	<1
Breadsticks, cornbread twists, Pillsbury, 1 stick	130	6	1.5	0	320	17	0
Cheddar cheese bread, Rich's, 1/8 loaf	180	6	3	15	350	25	1
French bread, Pillsbury, 1/5 loaf	150	1	0	0	370	28	<1
French bread, Rich's, 1/8 loaf	180	2	0	0	500	34	1
French onion bread, Rich's, 1/8 loaf	190	4	0.5	0	320	33	1
Honey oatmeal bread, Rich's, 1/8 loaf	160	2	1	0	280	30	2
Honey wheat bread, Bridgford Foods, 2 oz	130	2.5	1	0	240	26	3

BREAD DOUGH	CAL	FAT (g)	SAT FAT (g)	CHOL (mg)	SODIUM (mg)	CARB (g)	FIBER (g)
Italian bread, Rich's, ⅛ loaf	160	2.5	0.5	0	400	30	1
Pumpernickel bread, Rich's, ⅛ loaf	150	1.5	0	0	420	29	2
Rye bread, light, Rich's, ⅛ loaf	160	1.5	0	0	410	30	2
Sunflower seed cracked wheat bread, Rich's, ⅛ loaf	200	6	1	0	260	29	2
Wheat bread, Rich's, ⅛ loaf	150	2	0.5	0	280	27	2
White bread, Pillsbury Pipin' Hot, ⅙ loaf	110	0.5	0	0	350	22	<1
White bread, Rich's, ⅛ loaf	150	2.5	0.5	0	330	29	1

AT A GLANCE: BREAD
Lowest in Fat: Pillsbury Pipin' Hot Loaf (White)
Highest in Fiber: Bridgford Foods Honey Wheat

BUTTER, MARGARINE & SPREADS

	CAL	FAT (g)	SAT FAT (g)	CHOL (mg)	SODIUM (mg)	CARB (g)	FIBER (g)
Butter, stick, light, Land O' Lakes, 1 Tbsp	50	6	4	20	70	ns	ns
Butter, stick, salted, Land O' Lakes, 1 Tbsp	100	11	7	30	85	ns	ns
Butter, stick, unsalted, Land O' Lakes, 1 Tbsp	100	11	7	30	0	ns	ns
Butter, stick, unsalted, light, Land O' Lakes, 1 Tbsp	50	6	4	15	5	ns	ns
Butter, whipped, Land O' Lakes, 1 Tbsp	60	7	5	20	55	ns	ns
Butter, whipped, light, Land O' Lakes, 1 Tbsp	35	4	2.5	10	45	ns	ns
Butter, whipped, unsalted, Land O' Lakes, 1 Tbsp	60	7	5	20	0	ns	ns
Buttery spray, Weight Watchers, 0.28 g	0	0	0	0	0	0	0
Margarine, Mazola, 1 Tbsp	100	11	2	0	100	0	na
Margarine, light, Smart Beat Super Light, 1 Tbsp	20	2	0	0	105	0	na
Margarine, light, Weight Watchers, 1 Tbsp	45	4	1	0	70	2	0
Margarine, reduced calorie, Mazola, 1 Tbsp	50	6	1	0	130	0	na

BUTTER, MARGARINE & SPREADS	CAL	FAT (g)	SAT FAT (g)	CHOL (mg)	SODIUM (mg)	CARB (g)	FIBER (g)
Margarine, sodium free, light, Weight Watchers, 1 Tbsp	45	4	1	0	0	2	0
Margarine, soft, Chiffon, 1 Tbsp	100	11	2	0	105	0	0
Margarine, soft, Parkay, 1 Tbsp	100	11	2	0	105	0	0
Margarine, soft, diet, Parkay, 1 Tbsp	50	6	1	0	110	0	0
Margarine, spray, I Can't Believe It's Not Butter!, 1 spray	0	0	0	0	15	0	ns
Margarine, spreadable stick, Shedd's Spread Country Crock, 1 Tbsp	80	9	1.5	0	120	0	ns
Margarine, stick, Fleischmann's, 1 Tbsp	100	11	2	0	105	0	ns
Margarine, stick, Land O' Lakes, 1 Tbsp	100	11	2	0	115	ns	ns
Margarine, stick, lower fat, Fleischmann's, 1 Tbsp	50	6	1	0	60	0	ns
Margarine, stick, reduced fat, Weight Watchers, 1 Tbsp	60	7	1.5	0	130	0	0
Margarine, sweet, stick, unsalted, Fleischmann's, 1 Tbsp	100	11	2	0	0	0	ns
Margarine, tub, Land O' Lakes, 1 Tbsp	100	11	2	0	100	ns	ns
Margarine, tub, fat free, Promise Ultra, 1 Tbsp	5	0	0	0	90	0	ns
Margarine, tub, lower fat, Blue Bonnet, 1 Tbsp	45	4.5	1	0	110	<1	ns
Margarine, tub, lower fat, Fleischmann's, 1 Tbsp	40	4.5	0	0	55	0	ns
Margarine, unsalted, Mazola, 1 Tbsp	100	11	2	0	0	0	na
Margarine, unsalted, light, Smart Beat, 1 Tbsp	25	3	0	0	0	0	na
Margarine, whipped, Chiffon, 1 Tbsp	70	7	1.5	0	70	0	0
Margarine, whipped, Parkay, 1 Tbsp	70	7	1.5	0	70	0	0

BUTTER, MARGARINE & SPREADS	CAL	FAT (g)	SAT FAT (g)	CHOL (mg)	SODIUM (mg)	CARB (g)	FIBER (g)
Margarine spread, Mazola Extra Light, 1 Tbsp	50	6	1	0	100	0	na
Margarine spread, soft, Smart Beat Nucanola, 1 Tbsp	70	7	<1	0	90	0	na
Margarine spread, soft, tub, Imperial, 1 Tbsp	90	10	2	0	100	0	ns
Margarine spread, soft, tub, Mrs. Filbert's Family, 1 Tbsp	60	7	1.5	0	130	0	ns
Margarine spread, soft, tub, Promise Ultra, 1 Tbsp	35	4	0	0	50	0	ns
Margarine spread, soft, tub, Willow Run, 1 Tbsp	90	10	2	0	150	0	ns
Margarine spread, squeezable, I Can't Believe It's Not Butter!, 1 Tbsp	90	10	2	0	90	0	ns
Margarine spread, stick, I Can't Believe It's Not Butter!, 1 Tbsp	90	10	2	0	95	0	ns
Margarine spread, stick, Imperial, 1 Tbsp	90	10	2	0	110	0	ns
Margarine spread, stick, Promise, 1 Tbsp	90	10	2	0	95	0	ns
Margarine spread, stick, Willow Run, 1 Tbsp	100	11	2.5	0	160	0	ns
Margarine spread, stick, light, Imperial Delight, 1 Tbsp	70	7	1.5	0	110	0	ns
Margarine spread, stick, light, Promise Extra, 1 Tbsp	50	6	1	0	50	0	ns
Margarine spread, tub, I Can't Believe It's Not Butter!, 1 Tbsp	90	10	2	0	95	0	ns
Margarine spread, tub, Promise, 1 Tbsp	90	10	1.5	0	95	0	ns
Margarine spread, tub, Shedd's Spread Country Crock, 1 Tbsp	60	7	1.5	0	110	0	ns
Margarine spread, tub, Shedd's Spread Country Crock Churn Style, 1 Tbsp	60	7	1.5	0	60	0	ns
Margarine spread, tub, light, I Can't Believe It's Not Butter!, 1 Tbsp	50	6	1	0	90	0	ns

BUTTER, MARGARINE & SPREADS	CAL	FAT (g)	SAT FAT (g)	CHOL (mg)	SODIUM (mg)	CARB (g)	FIBER (g)
Margarine spread, tub, light, Promise Extra, 1 Tbsp	50	6	1	0	50	0	ns
Spread, 48% vegetable oil, tub, Blue Bonnet, 1 Tbsp	60	7	1	0	120	0	ns
Spread, 68% vegetable oil, tub, Blue Bonnet, 1 Tbsp	80	10	1.5	0	80	0	ns
Spread, squeeze, Fleischmann's, 1 Tbsp	90	10	1.5	0	110	0	ns
Spread, squeeze, Kraft Touch of Butter, 1 Tbsp	80	9	1.5	0	115	0	0
Spread, squeeze, Parkay, 1 Tbsp	80	9	1.5	0	120	0	0
Spread, squeeze, fat free, Fleischmann's, 1 Tbsp	5	0	0	0	125	1	ns
Spread, stick, Blue Bonnet, 1 Tbsp	70	8	1.5	0	100	0	ns
Spread, stick, Kraft Touch of Butter, 1 Tbsp	90	10	2	0	110	0	0
Spread, stick, Land O' Lakes Country Morning, 1 Tbsp	100	11	2.5	0	90	ns	ns
Spread, stick, Move Over Butter, 1 Tbsp	90	10	2	0	100	0	ns
Spread, stick, Parkay, 1 Tbsp	90	10	2	0	110	0	0
Spread, stick, 1/3 less fat, Parkay, 1 Tbsp	70	7	1.5	0	120	0	0
Spread, stick, light, Land O' Lakes Country Morning, 1 Tbsp	50	6	3	10	110	ns	ns
Spread, stick, light taste, Blue Bonnet, 1 Tbsp	70	8	1.5	0	90	0	ns
Spread, stick, unsalted, Land O' Lakes Country Morning, 1 Tbsp	100	11	2.5	0	0	ns	ns
Spread, stick or tub, light taste, Fleischmann's, 1 Tbsp	70	8	1.5	0	90	0	ns
Spread, sweet, tub, unsalted, Fleischmann's, 1 Tbsp	80	10	1.5	0	0	0	ns
Spread, tub, Fleischmann's, 1 Tbsp	80	9	1.5	0	90	0	ns
Spread, tub, Kraft Touch of Butter, 1 Tbsp	60	7	1.5	0	110	0	0

BUTTER, MARGARINE & SPREADS	CAL	FAT (g)	SAT FAT (g)	CHOL (mg)	SODIUM (mg)	CARB (g)	FIBER (g)
Spread, tub, Land O' Lakes Country Morning, 1 Tbsp	100	11	2	0	80	ns	ns
Spread, tub, Parkay, 1 Tbsp	60	7	1.5	0	110	0	0
Spread, tub, Parkay Light, 1 Tbsp	50	6	1	0	120	0	0
Spread, tub, light, Land O' Lakes Country Morning, 1 Tbsp	50	6	2.5	5	90	ns	ns
Spread, whipped, tub, Move Over Butter, 1 Tbsp	60	7	1.5	0	75	0	ns
Spread, with sweet cream, stick, Land O' Lakes, 1 Tbsp	90	10	2	0	95	ns	ns
Spread, with sweet cream, stick, unsalted, Land O' Lakes, 1 Tbsp	90	10	2	0	0	ns	ns
Spread, with sweet cream, tub, Land O' Lakes, 1 Tbsp	80	8	2	0	70	ns	ns

AT A GLANCE: BUTTER, MARGARINE & SPREADS
Lowest in Fat & Sat Fat, Butter: Land O'Lakes Whipped Butter, Light
Lowest in Fat & Sat Fat, Margarine: Promise Ultra, Fat Free, Tub
Lowest in Fat & Sat Fat, Spread: Fleischmann's Spread, Fat Free, Squeeze
Other lowfat choices: Weight Watchers Buttery Spray; I Can't Believe It's Not Butter Margarine Spray

CHEESE   *This section includes nonrefrigerated cheese products.*

	CAL	FAT	SAT FAT	CHOL	SODIUM	CARB	FIBER
4 cheese Mexican blend, shredded, Sargento, ¼ cup	110	9	6	25	200	<1	0
6 cheese Italian blend, shredded, Sargento, ¼ cup	90	7	4	20	180	0	0
American, County Line Cheese, 1 oz	110	9	6	25	440	2	0
American, Deli USA, 1 oz	110	8	8.5	10	370	0	0
American, Land O' Lakes, 1 oz	110	9	6	30	430	<1	0
American, fat free, Alpine Lace, 1 oz	45	0	0	<5	280	2	0
American, less salt, Land O' Lakes, 1 oz	110	9	6	30	270	<1	0
American, light, County Line Cheese, 1 oz	80	5	3	15	400	3	0
American, light, reduced fat, Land O' Lakes, 1 oz	70	4.5	3	20	400	2	0

CHEESE	CAL (g)	FAT (g)	SAT FAT (g)	CHOL (mg)	SODIUM (mg)	CARB (g)	FIBER (g)
American, loaf, Kraft, 1 oz	100	9	6	25	430	<1	0
American, sharp, Land O' Lakes, 1 oz	110	9	6	30	360	<1	0
American, sharp, loaf, Old English, 1 oz	100	9	6	25	440	<1	0
American, sharp, slice, Old English, 1 oz	110	9	6	30	460	<1	0
American, shredded, Kraft, ¼ cup	110	9	6	30	440	<1	0
American, slice, Borden, ¾ oz	80	7	4	20	320	1	0
American, slice, Harvest Moon, ⅔ oz	70	6	4	20	320	0	0
American, slice, Kraft, 1 oz	110	9	6	25	460	<1	0
American, slice, fat free, Smart Beat, 1 slice	25	0	0	0	180	3	na
American, slice, light, Borden, ¾ oz	45	2.5	1.5	10	300	1	0
American, slice, reduced sodium, Weight Watchers, 0.75 oz	30	0	0	5	150	2	0
American, white or yellow, singles, Healthy Choice, 1 slice	30	0	0	<5	290	2	<1
American and Swiss, processed, Land O' Lakes, 1 oz	100	8	6	35	380	0	0
American cheese food, Heluva Good, 1 slice	70	5	3	15	390	2	0
American cheese food, grated, Kraft, 1 Tbsp	25	1.5	1	<5	135	1	0
American cheese food, singles, Kraft, ¾ oz	70	5	3.5	15	290	2	0
American cheese food, slice, Borden, ¾ oz	70	5	3	20	290	2	0
American cheese spread, Easy Cheese, 2 Tbsp	100	7	4	25	400	2	0
American flavor, Harvest Moon, ⅔ oz	50	3	2	10	280	1	0
American flavor, 25% less fat, Kraft, ¾ oz	70	5	3	15	350	1	0

CHEESE	CAL	FAT (g)	SAT FAT (g)	CHOL (mg)	SODIUM (mg)	CARB (g)	FIBER (g)
American flavor, 50% less fat, Light N' Lively, ¾ oz	50	2.5	1.5	10	280	2	0
American flavor, imitation cheese, Golden Image, ¾ oz	70	5	1.5	5	270	1	0
American flavor, imitation cheese, shredded, Harvest Moon, ¼ cup	120	9	2	0	500	3	0
American flavor, imitation cheese, slice, Lunchwagon, ¾ oz	70	5	1	0	230	1	0
American flavor, singles, ⅓ less fat, Kraft, ¾ oz	50	3	2	10	330	2	0
American flavor, slice, fat free, Borden, ¾ oz	30	0	0	0	310	2	0
American flavor, slice, lowfat, Borden, ¾ oz	35	1	1	<5	280	1	0
American flavor cheese spread, Harvest Moon, ¾ oz	60	4.5	3	15	300	2	0
Asiago, Auricchio, 1 oz	100	8	5	25	340	<1	0
Babybel, The Laughing Cow, 1 oz	90	7	5	10	230	0	0
Babybel, mini, The Laughing Cow, 1 piece (21g)	70	6	4	15	170	0	0
Bacon cheese spread, Kraft, 2 Tbsp	90	8	5	25	570	<1	0
Bel Paese, medallions, Classica, ¾ oz	60	5	4	15	200	1	0
Bel Paese, traditional, Classica, 1 oz	100	8	5	25	20	1	0
Bel Paese, with basil & sun-dried tomatoes, Classica, 1 oz	100	8	5	25	20	1	0
Belle pepper trio cheese spread, Deli Alouette, 2 Tbsp	70	7	4	25	120	1	0
Bermuda onion & chives cheese spread, Fleur de Lait, 2 Tbsp	90	8	5	30	130	2	0
Blue cheese, County Line Cheese, 1 oz	110	9	6	25	400	<1	0
Blue cheese, Salemville, 1 oz	100	8	5	25	260	0	0
Blue cheese, cold pack or crumbles, Kraft, 1 oz	100	8	6	30	390	<1	0

CHEESE	CAL (g)	FAT (g)	SAT FAT (g)	CHOL (mg)	SODIUM (mg)	CARB (g)	FIBER (g)
Blue cheese, crumbled, Sargento, ¼ cup	100	8	5	20	380	1	0
Blue cheese, natural, 1 oz	100	8	5	20	390	<1	0
Blue cheese spread, Kraft Roka, 2 Tbsp	80	7	4.5	20	340	2	0
Brick, County Line Cheese, 1 oz	110	9	6	30	180	<1	0
Brick, Kraft, 1 oz	110	9	6	30	190	0	0
Brick, Land O' Lakes, 1 oz	100	8	5	30	160	<1	0
Brie, Bresse Brie, 1 oz	110	9	5	30	180	2	0
Brie, Gerard, 1 oz	90	7	5	25	180	2	0
Brie, baby, Alouette, 1 oz	110	9	5	30	180	2	0
Brie, baby with herbs, Alouette, 1 oz	110	9	5	30	180	2	0
Brie, light, Bresse Brie, 1 oz	70	4	3	20	160	1	<1
Brie, party, Bresse Brie, 1 oz	110	9	5	30	180	2	0
Brie, party, with herbs, Bresse Brie, 1 oz	110	9	5	30	180	2	0
Butter kase, Danekas, 1 oz	112	9	5	20	213	1	na
Camembert, domestic, 1 oz	80	7	4	20	240	0	0
Caraway, 1 oz	110	8	5	25	190	<1	0
Chedarella, Land O' Lakes, 1 oz	100	8	5	25	200	0	0
Cheddar, County Line Cheese, 1 oz	120	10	6	30	190	<1	0
Cheddar, Kraft, 1 oz	110	9	6	30	180	<1	0
Cheddar, Sonoma Cheese Factory, 1 oz	100	8	5	25	180	0	0
Cheddar, all varieties, block, Heluva Good/Father Time, 1 oz	110	9	5	30	180	1	0
Cheddar, curds, Heluva Good, 1 oz	113	9	5	28	179	1	0
Cheddar, extra old, Black Diamond, 1 oz	120	10	6	30	190	<1	0
Cheddar, fat free, Alpine Lace, 1 oz	45	0	0	<5	280	2	0
Cheddar, light, Land O' Lakes, 1 oz	70	4	2.5	10	230	<1	0

CHEESE	CAL (g)	FAT (g)	SAT FAT (g)	CHOL (mg)	SODIUM (mg)	CARB (g)	FIBER (g)
Cheddar, low sodium, Heluva Good, 1 oz	110	9	6	25	10	0	0
Cheddar, low sodium, lowfat, County Line Cheese, 1 oz	70	3	2	10	90	<1	0
Cheddar, mellow, slices, fat free, Smart Beat, 1 slice	25	0	0	0	180	3	na
Cheddar, mild, low sodium, natural, Weight Watchers, 1 oz	80	5	3	15	70	1	0
Cheddar, mild, reduced fat, Heluva Good, 1 oz	80	6	3.5	15	200	1	0
Cheddar, mild, reduced fat, Kraft, 1 oz	80	5	3.5	20	220	0	0
Cheddar, mild, shredded, reduced fat, Kraft, ¼ cup	90	6	4	20	230	<1	0
Cheddar, mild or sharp, Weight Watchers, 1 oz	80	5	3	15	180	1	0
Cheddar, nacho blend, with peppers, Kraft, 1 oz	110	9	6	30	250	0	0
Cheddar, reduced fat, Alpine Lace, 1 oz	80	4.5	3	15	95	1	0
Cheddar, sharp, reduced fat, Cracker Barrel, 1 oz	80	5	3	20	220	<1	0
Cheddar, sharp, reduced fat, Kraft, 1 oz	80	5	3	20	220	<1	0
Cheddar, sharp, slices, fat free, Weight Watchers, 0.75 oz	30	0	0	0	310	2	0
Cheddar, shredded, Heluva Good, ¼ cup	110	9	5	30	180	1	0
Cheddar, shredded, Kraft, ¼ cup	120	10	6	30	190	<1	0
Cheddar, shredded, all varieties, Sargento, ¼ cup	110	9	6	30	160	1	0
Cheddar, shredded, fat free, Kraft, ¼ cup	45	0	0	<5	220	1	0
Cheddar, shredded, fat free, Kraft Healthy Favorites, ¼ cup	45	0	0	<5	220	1	0
Cheddar, shredded, light, Sargento, ¼ cup	70	4.5	3	10	200	<1	0
Cheddar, sliced, Sargento, 1 slice	110	9	6	30	160	1	0

CHEESE	CAL	FAT (g)	SAT FAT (g)	CHOL (mg)	SODIUM (mg)	CARB (g)	FIBER (g)
Cheddar cheese food, sharp, cold pack, Cracker Barrel, 2 Tbsp	100	8	5	25	290	4	0
Cheddar cheese product, sharp, slices, fat free, Smart Beat, 1 slice	25	0	0	0	230	3	na
Cheddar cheese product, sharp flavor, slice, lowfat, Borden, 2/3 oz	30	1	1	<5	260	1	0
Cheddar cheese snack, MooTown Snackers, 1 piece	100	8	5	25	130	1	0
Cheddar cheese snack, light, MooTown Snackers, 1 piece	60	4	2.5	10	170	<1	0
Cheddar cheese spread, pasteurized process, Easy Cheese, 2 Tbsp	100	7	4	25	410	3	0
Cheddar cheese spread, port wine, cup, WisPride, 2 Tbsp	100	7	4	20	230	4	0
Cheddar cheese spread, port wine, log, WisPride, 2 Tbsp	100	8	4	20	190	4	0
Cheddar cheese spread, sharp, Easy Cheese, 2 Tbsp	100	7	4	25	440	3	0
Cheddar cheese spread, sharp, WisPride, 2 Tbsp	100	7	4	20	230	4	0
Cheddar cheese spread, sharp, ball, WisPride, 2 Tbsp	100	8	4	20	190	4	0
Cheddar flavor, imitation cheese, shredded, County Line Cheese, 1 oz	90	6	2	5	410	2	<1
Cheddar flavor, imitation cheese, shredded, Harvest Moon, 1/4 cup	120	9	2	0	480	3	0
Cheddar flavor, imitation cheese, shredded, Sargento, 1 cup	90	6	1	0	470	2	0
Cheddar flavor, singles, 1/3 less fat, Kraft, 3/4 oz	50	3	2	10	300	2	0
Cheddar flavor, singles, nonfat, Kraft Free, 3/4 oz	30	0	0	<5	290	3	0
Cheddar Jack, shredded, County Line Cheese, 1 oz	120	10	6	30	190	<1	0

CHEESE	CAL	FAT (g)	SAT FAT (g)	CHOL (mg)	SODIUM (mg)	CARB (g)	FIBER (g)
Cheddar shreds, regular & fancy, Healthy Choice, ¼ cup	45	0	0	<5	200	2	na
Cheddar spread, all varieties, cold pack, Spreadery, 2 Tbsp	80	4.5	3	15	290	3	0
Cheese food, County Line Cheese, 1 oz	100	7	5	20	360	2	0
Cheese food, imitation cheese, singles, County Line Cheese, 1 oz	90	6	1.5	5	410	2	0
Cheese food, sharp, singles, Kraft, ¾ oz	70	6	4	20	300	<1	0
Cheese food, sharp, spread, Kaukauna, 2 Tbsp	90	7	3	20	210	3	0
Cheese food, shredded, Velveeta, ¼ cup	130	9	6	30	500	3	0
Cheese food, with pimento, singles, Kraft, ¾ oz	70	5	3.5	15	290	2	0
Cheese product, lactose free, slices, fat free, Smart Beat, 1 slice	25	0	0	0	180	3	na
Cheese product, processed, County Line Advantage, 1 oz	80	5	3	15	150	2	<1
Cheese product, singles, County Line Cheese Good Day Substitute, 1 oz	90	6	2	10	410	2	0
Cheese product, singles, nonfat, Kraft Free, ¾ oz	30	0	0	<5	320	3	0
Cheese snack, Arpin Squiggles, 1 oz	80	5	3	15	180	1	0
Cheese spread, County Line Cheese Munchee, 1 oz	100	8	5	20	400	2	0
Cheese spread, loaf or singles, County Line Cheese, 1 oz	90	7	5	20	430	2	0
Cheese spread, slice, Velveeta, ¾ oz	60	4.5	3	15	300	2	
Cheez Whiz, 2 Tbsp	90	7	5	20	560	2	
Cheez Whiz, squeezable, 2 Tbsp	100	8	4	15	470	4	
Cheez Whiz, with jalapeno peppers, 2 Tbsp	90	8	5	25	530	2	

CHEESE	CAL (g)	FAT (g)	SAT FAT (g)	CHOL (mg)	SODIUM (mg)	CARB (g)	FIBER (g)
Cheez Whiz Light, 2 Tbsp	80	3	2	15	540	6	0
Cheezbits, The Laughing Cow, 6 pieces (28g)	70	6	4	20	370	1	0
Cheshire, 1 oz	110	9	5	30	200	1	0
Cinnamon raisin cheese spread, Fleur de Lait, 2 Tbsp	90	8	4.5	25	90	6	0
Colby, County Line Cheese, 1 oz	120	10	6	30	190	<1	0
Colby, Kraft, 1 oz	110	9	6	30	180	<1	0
Colby, longhorn style, Heluva Good/Father Time, 1 oz	120	9	6	30	190	0	0
Colby, low sodium, lowfat, County Line Cheese, 1 oz	70	3	2	10	110	<1	0
Colby, reduced fat, Alpine Lace, 1 oz	80	5	3	15	115	1	0
Colby, reduced fat, Kraft, 1 oz	80	5	3.5	20	220	0	0
Colby, sliced, Sargento, 1 slice	110	9	6	30	190	0	0
Colby & Monterey Jack, Kraft, 1 oz	110	9	6	30	190	0	0
Colby & Monterey Jack, shredded, Kraft, ¼ cup	120	10	6	30	200	<1	0
Colby Jack, County Line Cheese, 1 oz	110	9	5	30	190	<1	0
Colby-Jack, Heluva Good, 1 oz	110	9	6	30	200	0	0
Colby-Jack, shredded, Sargento, ¼ cup	110	9	6	25	190	<1	0
Colby-Jack snack, MooTown Snackers, 1 piece	90	8	5	20	160	<1	0
Cottage cheese, Breakstone's/Sealtest, ½ cup	120	5	3.5	25	400	4	0
Cottage cheese, 1% milkfat, lowfat, Friendship, ½ cup	90	1	0.5	10	360	4	0
Cottage cheese, 1% milkfat, lowfat, Weight Watchers, ½ cup	90	1	0.5	5	460	4	0
Cottage cheese, 1% milkfat, no salt, lowfat, Friendship, ½ cup	90	1	0.5	10	40	4	0

CHEESE	CAL (g)	FAT (g)	SAT FAT (g)	CHOL (mg)	SODIUM (mg)	CARB (g)	FIBE (g)
Cottage cheese, 2% milkfat, Weight Watchers, ½ cup	90	2	1.5	15	460	4	0
Cottage cheese, California style, 4% milkfat, Friendship, ½ cup	115	5	3	25	380	4	0
Cottage cheese, creamed, large or small curd, ½ cup	120	5	3	15	460	3	
Cottage cheese, dry curd, Borden/Meadow Gold, ½ cup	35	0	0	<5	15	<1	na
Cottage cheese, dry curd, Breakstone's, ¼ cup	45	0	0	5	25	3	
Cottage cheese, fat free, Viva, ½ cup	70	0	0	5	430	5	
Cottage cheese, lowfat, Breakstone's, ½ cup	90	2.5	1.5	15	380	4	
Cottage cheese, lowfat, Knudsen, ½ cup	100	2.5	1.5	15	400	3	
Cottage cheese, lowfat, Light N' Lively, ½ cup	80	1.5	1	15	380	4	
Cottage cheese, lowfat, Sealtest, ½ cup	90	2.5	1.5	15	380	4	
Cottage cheese, nonfat, Friendship, ½ cup	80	0	0	0	380	5	
Cottage cheese, nonfat, Knudsen Free, ½ cup	80	0	0	10	370	4	
Cottage cheese, nonfat, Light N' Lively Free, ½ cup	80	0	0	10	440	5	
Cottage cheese, peach, lowfat, Knudsen, 4 oz	110	1.5	1	10	290	12	
Cottage cheese, peach, nonfat, Friendship, ½ cup	110	0	0	0	300	15	
Cottage cheese, pineapple, 1% milkfat, lowfat, Friendship, ½ cup	120	1	0.5	10	300	17	
Cottage cheese, pineapple, 4% milkfat, Friendship, ½ cup	140	4	2.5	15	310	16	
Cottage cheese, pineapple, lowfat, Knudsen, 4 oz	110	1.5	1	10	290	11	
Cottage cheese, pineapple, nonfat, Friendship, ½ cup	120	0	0	0	310	17	

CHEESE	CAL (g)	FAT (g)	SAT FAT (g)	CHOL (mg)	SODIUM (mg)	CARB (g)	FIBER (g)
Cottage cheese, pot style, 2% milkfat, Friendship, ½ cup	90	2.5	1.5	15	430	3	0
Cottage cheese, small curd, Breakstone's/Sealtest, ½ cup	120	5	3.5	25	400	2	0
Cottage cheese, small curd, 1% lowfat, Borden/Meadow Gold, ½ cup	80	1	0.5	10	430	5	0
Cottage cheese, small curd, fat free, Borden LiteLine, ½ cup	80	0	0	10	450	5	0
Cottage cheese, small curd, no salt, 2% lowfat, Borden/Meadow Gold, ½ cup	90	2	1.5	15	50	5	0
Cottage cheese, strawberry, lowfat, Knudsen, 4 oz	110	1.5	1	10	280	12	0
Cottage cheese, tropical fruit, lowfat, Knudsen, 4 oz	120	2	1.5	10	300	15	0
Cottage cheese, with garden salad, lowfat, Light N' Lively, ½ cup	90	1.5	1	15	410	5	0
Cottage cheese, with peach and pineapple, lowfat, Light N' Lively, ½ cup	120	1	1	10	350	14	0
Cream cheese, blackberries & cream, light, Fleur de Lait Gourmet, 2 Tbsp	70	4	3	20	70	5	1
Cream cheese, blueberries & cream, light, Fleur de Lait Gourmet, 2 Tbsp	70	4	3	20	70	5	1
Cream cheese, chive & onion, Fleur de Lait Gourmet, 2 Tbsp	60	4	3	20	130	2	1
Cream cheese, fat free, Philadelphia Brand Free, 1 oz	25	0	0	<5	135	2	0
Cream cheese, herbs & garlic, Healthy Choice, 2 Tbsp	25	0	0	<5	200	2	<1
Cream cheese, light, Friendship, 2 Tbsp	60	5	3	15	120	3	0
Cream cheese, light, Weight Watchers, 2 Tbsp	40	2.5	1.5	10	105	1	0
Cream cheese, nacho, light, Fleur de Lait Gourmet, 2 Tbsp	60	4	3	20	190	2	<1

CHEESE	CAL (g)	FAT (g)	SAT FAT (g)	CHOL (mg)	SODIUM (mg)	CARB (g)	FIBER (g)
Cream cheese, Neufchatel, Philadelphia Brand, 1 oz	70	6	4	20	120	<1	0
Cream cheese, plain, Healthy Choice, 2 Tbsp	25	0	0	<5	200	2	<1
Cream cheese, plain, Philadelphia Brand, 1 oz	100	10	6	30	90	<1	0
Cream cheese, reduced fat, Friendship, 2 Tbsp	50	2.5	1.5	10	120	0	0
Cream cheese, soft, Friendship, 2 Tbsp	100	10	6	30	100	2	0
Cream cheese, soft, fat free, Philadelphia Brand Free, 2 Tbsp	30	0	0	<5	160	2	0
Cream cheese, soft, light, Philadelphia Brand Light, 2 Tbsp	70	5	3.5	15	150	2	0
Cream cheese, soft, plain, Philadelphia Brand, 2 Tbsp	100	10	7	30	100	1	0
Cream cheese, soft, with chives & onion, Philadelphia Brand, 2 Tbsp	110	10	7	30	110	2	0
Cream cheese, soft, with herb & garlic, Philadelphia Brand, 2 Tbsp	110	10	7	30	180	2	0
Cream cheese, soft, with olive & pimento, Philadelphia Brand, 2 Tbsp	100	9	6	30	170	2	0
Cream cheese, soft, with pineapple, Philadelphia Brand, 2 Tbsp	100	9	6	30	100	4	0
Cream cheese, soft, with smoked salmon, Philadelphia Brand, 2 Tbsp	100	9	6	30	200	1	0
Cream cheese, soft, with strawberries, Philadelphia Brand, 2 Tbsp	100	9	6	30	65	5	0
Cream cheese, strawberry, Healthy Choice, 2 Tbsp	35	0	0	<5	200	5	na
Cream cheese, strawberry, light, Fleur de Lait Gourmet, 2 Tbsp	60	4	3	20	80	4	1

CHEESE	CAL (g)	FAT (g)	SAT FAT (g)	CHOL (mg)	SODIUM (mg)	CARB (g)	FIBER (g)
Cream cheese, whipped, Breakstone's Temp-Tee, 3 Tbsp	110	10	7	30	115	1	0
Cream cheese, whipped, plain, Philadelphia Brand, 3 Tbsp	110	11	7	35	95	1	0
Cream cheese, whipped, with smoked salmon, Philadelphia Brand, 3 Tbsp	100	9	6	30	200	2	0
Cream cheese, white, Fleur de Lait, 2 Tbsp	100	10	6	35	60	1	0
Cream cheese, with chives or pimentos, Philadelphia Brand, 1 oz	90	9	6	30	150	<1	0
Creme de Brie, Delico, 2 Tbsp	90	8	5	25	220	<1	0
Creme Fraiche, Delico, 2 Tbsp	100	11	7	40	10	<1	0
Cucumber dill crudite cheese spread, Alouette Light, 2 Tbsp	50	4	2.5	20	130	2	0
Date, nut & rum cheese spread, Fleur de Lait, 2 Tbsp	90	8	4.5	30	90	4	0
Delice de France, Delico, 1 oz	110	9	5	30	180	2	0
Dijon moutarde et honey cheese spread, Alouette, 2 Tbsp	80	7	4.5	25	100	2	0
Edam, County Line Cheese, 1 oz	100	8	5	25	280	0	0
Farmer, Friendship, 1 oz	50	2.5	1.5	10	120	0	0
Farmer, hoop, Friendship, 1 oz	20	0	0	0	10	0	0
Farmer, no salt, Friendship, 1 oz	50	2.5	1.5	10	10	0	0
Farmers, Kraft, 1 oz	100	8	6	25	190	<1	0
Feta, all varieties, Feta Classika, 1 oz	90	7	5	20	270	<1	<1
Feta, cup, Delico, 1 oz	90	7	5	18	380	<1	0
Feta, wedge, Delico, 1 oz	90	7	5	18	380	<1	0
Fontina, Auricchio, 1 oz	100	8	4	25	170	<1	0
Fontina, Classica, 1 oz	110	9	5	25	160	<1	0

CHEESE	CAL (g)	FAT (g)	SAT FAT (g)	CHOL (mg)	SODIUM (mg)	CARB (g)	FIBER (g)
French onion cheese spread, La Cheeserie, 2 Tbsp	70	7	4.5	30	160	1	0
French onion melange cheese spread, Alouette, 2 Tbsp	80	7	4.5	25	95	1	0
Garlic cheese spread, La Cheeserie, 2 Tbsp	70	7	4.5	30	135	1	0
Garlic cheese spread, New Holland, 1 oz	90	7	4.5	30	105	<1	0
Garlic & herbs cheese spread, Alouette, 2 Tbsp	70	7	4.5	30	135	1	0
Garlic & spice cheese spread, Fleur de Lait, 2 Tbsp	90	9	6	30	160	1	0
Garlic et herbs classique cheese spread, Alouette Light, 2 Tbsp	50	4	3	20	120	1	<1
Ginger apple epice cheese spread, Deli Alouette, 2 Tbsp	80	6	4	25	80	4	0
Gjetost, 1 oz	130	8	5	25	170	12	0
Goat, Chavrie, 2 Tbsp	40	3	2	15	110	<1	0
Goat, Montrachet Classic, 1 oz	70	6	4	30	130	<1	0
Goat, hard, 1 oz	130	10	7	30	100	<1	0
Goat, plain, Montrachet, 1 oz	70	6	4	30	135	<1	0
Goat, semisoft, 1 oz	100	8	6	20	150	<1	0
Goat, soft, 1 oz	80	6	4	15	105	0	0
Goat, with chive, Montrachet, 1 oz	70	6	4	30	135	<1	0
Goat, with herbs, Montrachet Classic, 1 oz	70	6	4	30	150	<1	0
Gorgonzola, Auricchio, 1 oz	100	8	5	30	280	<1	0
Gorgonzola, Salemville, 1 oz	100	8	5	25	260	0	0
Gorgonzola dolcelatte, Galbani, 1 oz	90	8	4	20	230	<1	0
Gouda, County Line Cheese, 1 oz	110	9	6	30	260	0	0
Gouda, Kraft, 1 oz	110	9	6	25	160	<1	0
Grana Padano, Galbani, 1 oz	110	8	6	40	450	0	0
Gruyere, 1 oz	120	9	5	30	95	0	0
Havarti, Kraft, 1 oz	120	11	7	35	240	0	0

CHEESE	CAL	FAT (g)	SAT FAT (g)	CHOL (mg)	SODIUM (mg)	CARB (g)	FIBER (g)
Havarti, Sonoma Cheese Factory, 1 oz	120	10	6	35	150	0	0
Havarti, vegetable, Danekas, 1 oz	112	9	5	20	210	1	na
Herb & spice cheese spread, Fleur de Lait, 2 Tbsp	90	9	6	30	190	2	0
Herbs & garlic cheese spread, Alouette Light, 2 Tbsp	50	4	3	20	120	1	<1
Italian, grated, 1/3 less fat, Kraft, 2 tsp	25	1	0.5	<5	115	1	0
Italian, sharp, Auricchio, 1 oz	110	9	5	30	270	<1	0
Italian blend, grated, Kraft, 2 tsp	25	1.5	1	<5	95	0	0
Italico, Classica, 1 oz	110	10	3	10	90	1	0
Jack, Sonoma Cheese Factory, 1 oz	100	8	5	25	180	0	0
Jack, light, Sonoma Cheese Factory, 1 oz	70	4	2.5	15	180	0	0
Jalapeno, Deli USA, 1 oz	90	7	4	20	390	<1	0
Jalapeno cheese product, light, Land O' Lakes, 1 oz	70	4	2.5	15	400	1	0
Jalapeno cheese spread, New Holland, 1 oz	80	6	4	25	140	<1	0
Jalapeno pepper cheese spread, loaf, Kraft, 1 oz	80	6	4	20	470	2	0
Jarlsberg, semi-soft, loaf, Norwegian Dairies, 1 oz	100	8	4	25	130	0	0
Jarlsberg, semi-soft, wheel, Norwegian Dairies, 1 oz	100	8	5	20	180	0	0
Jarlsberg, sliced, Sargento, 1 slice	120	9	5	20	50	1	0
Jarlsberg, smoked, semi-soft, Norwegian Dairies, 1 oz	110	8	4	25	130	0	0
Jarlsberg Lite, reduced fat, Norwegian Dairies, 1 oz	70	3.5	2	10	130	0	0
Kasseri, Auricchio, 1 oz	110	9	5	30	270	<1	0
The Laughing Cow, wedge, piece (28g)	70	6	4	20	370	1	0
The Laughing Cow, wedge, light, 1 piece (28g)	50	3	2	10	370	1	0

CHEESE	CAL (g)	FAT (g)	SAT FAT (g)	CHOL (mg)	SODIUM (mg)	CARB (g)	FIBER (g)
Limburger, Kraft, 1 oz	90	8	5	25	240	0	0
Limburger cheese spread, Mohawk Valley, 2 Tbsp	80	7	4.5	20	500	0	0
Lox cheese spread, Fleur de Lait, 2 Tbsp	90	8	5	30	125	1	0
Mandarin orange cheese spread, Fleur de Lait, 2 Tbsp	90	7	5	30	90	3	0
Mascarpone, Auricchio, 1 oz	120	13	8	35	15	<1	0
Mascarpone, domestic, Classica, 1 oz	120	12	8	25	15	1	<1
Mascarpone, imported, Galbani, 1 oz	140	14	9	31	10	1	0
Mexican cheese food with jalapeno peppers, mild, shredded, Velveeta, ¼ cup	130	9	6	30	520	3	0
Mexican cheese food with jalapeno peppers, singles, Kraft, ¾ oz	70	5	3.5	15	330	2	0
Mexican cheese spread, hot, with jalapeno peppers, Velveeta, 1 oz	80	6	4	20	520	2	0
Mexican cheese spread, mild, with jalapeno peppers, Velveeta, 1 oz	80	6	4	20	440	3	0
Mexican shreds, Healthy Choice, ¼ cup	45	0	0	<5	200	2	na
Monterey cheese food, singles, Kraft, ¾ oz	70	5	3.5	15	290	2	0
Monterey Jack, County Line Cheese, 1 oz	110	9	5	30	180	<1	0
Monterey Jack, Heluva Good, 1 oz	100	8	6	25	180	0	0
Monterey Jack, Kraft, 1 oz	110	9	6	30	190	0	0
Monterey Jack, Land O' Lakes, 1 oz	110	9	5	30	160	<1	0
Monterey Jack, Weight Watchers, 1 oz	80	5	3	15	180	1	0
Monterey Jack, low sodium, lowfat, County Line Cheese, 1 oz	70	2.5	2	10	110	<1	0

CHEESE	CAL (g)	FAT (g)	SAT FAT (g)	CHOL (mg)	SODIUM (mg)	CARB (g)	FIBER (g)
Monterey Jack, reduced fat, Alpine Lace, 1 oz	70	4.5	3	15	170	1	0
Monterey Jack, reduced fat, Kraft, 1 oz	80	5	3.5	20	220	0	0
Monterey Jack, shredded, Heluva Good, ¼ cup	100	8	5	30	170	1	0
Monterey Jack, shredded, Kraft, ¼ cup	110	9	6	30	200	<1	0
Monterey Jack, shredded, Sargento, ¼ cup	100	9	5	30	190	0	0
Monterey Jack, sliced, Sargento, 1 slice	100	9	5	30	190	0	0
Monterey Jack, with jalapeno, Heluva Good, 1 oz	100	8	6	25	180	0	0
Monterey Jack, with jalapeno peppers, Kraft, 1 oz	110	9	6	30	190	<1	0
Monterey Jack, with peppers, County Line Cheese, 1 oz	110	9	6	25	200	<1	0
Monterey Jack, with peppers, reduced fat, Kraft, 1 oz	80	5	3.5	20	220	<1	0
Mozzarella, Land O' Lakes, 1 oz	80	6	3.5	15	190	<1	0
Mozzarella, Polly-O Fior Di Latte, 1 oz	80	7	5	20	15	0	0
Mozzarella, fat free, Polly-O, 1 oz	35	0	0	<5	220	<1	0
Mozzarella, fresh, Auricchio, 1 oz	80	6	4	25	40	<1	0
Mozzarella, light, Polly-O, 1 oz	60	2.5	2	10	230	<1	0
Mozzarella, low sodium, lowfat, County Line Cheese, 1 oz	70	3	2	10	95	<1	0
Mozzarella, part skim, County Line Cheese, 1 oz	80	5	3	15	180	<1	0
Mozzarella, part-skim, Heluva Good, 1 oz	70	5	3	15	220	<1	0
Mozzarella, part-skim, Kraft, 1 oz	80	5	4	15	200	<1	0
Mozzarella, part skim, Polly-O, 1 oz	80	5	4	20	220	<1	0

CHEESE	CAL	FAT (g)	SAT FAT (g)	CHOL (mg)	SODIUM (mg)	CARB (g)	FIBER (g)
Mozzarella, part skim, reduced sodium, Alpine Lace, 1 oz	70	5	3	15	75	1	0
Mozzarella, part-skim, shredded, reduced fat, Kraft, ¼ cup	80	5	3	15	210	<1	0
Mozzarella, shredded, Heluva Good, ¼ cup	80	5	3	15	170	1	0
Mozzarella, shredded, all varieties, Sargento, ¼ cup	80	6	3.5	15	150	1	0
Mozzarella, shredded, fat free, Kraft, ¼ cup	50	0	0	<5	280	2	<1
Mozzarella, shredded, fat free, Kraft Healthy Favorites, ¼ cup	50	0	0	<5	280	2	<1
Mozzarella, shredded, fat free, Polly-O, ¼ cup	45	0	0	<5	270	1	<1
Mozzarella, shredded, light, Polly-O, ¼ cup	60	3	2	15	220	1	0
Mozzarella, shredded, light, Sargento, ¼ cup	70	3	2	10	140	<1	0
Mozzarella, shredded, part-skim, Kraft, ¼ cup	90	6	4	20	210	<1	0
Mozzarella, shredded, whole milk, Kraft, ¼ cup	90	7	5	25	210	<1	0
Mozzarella, sliced, Sargento, 1 slice	130	9	6	25	230	2	0
Mozzarella, sliced, light, Sargento, 1 slice	100	5	3	15	210	0	0
Mozzarella, whole milk, County Line Cheese, 1 oz	80	6	4	20	200	<1	0
Mozzarella, whole milk, Heluva Good, 1 oz	80	6	4	20	220	<1	0
Mozzarella cheese product, fat free, Alpine Lace, 1 oz	45	0	0	<5	280	2	0
Mozzarella flavor, imitation cheese, shredded, Georgio's, ¼ cup	90	7	1	0	350	1	0
Mozzarella flavor, imitation cheese, shredded, Sargento, ¼ cup	80	6	1	0	320	<1	0
Mozzarella flavor, imitation, shredded, County Line Cheese, 1 oz	90	7	1.5	0	410	1	<1

CHEESE	CAL (g)	FAT (g)	SAT FAT (g)	CHOL (mg)	SODIUM (mg)	CARB (g)	FIBER (g)
Mozzarella flavor, imitation, shredded, Harvest Moon, ¼ cup	110	8	1.5	0	430	1	0
Mozzarella shreds, regular & fancy, Healthy Choice, ¼ cup	45	0	0	<5	200	2	na
Muenster, County Line Cheese, 1 oz	110	9	5	30	200	0	0
Muenster, Kraft, 1 oz	110	9	6	30	190	0	0
Muenster, Land O' Lakes, 1 oz	100	8	5	25	220	0	0
Muenster, New York style, Heluva Good, 1 oz	100	8	6	25	180	0	0
Muenster, sliced, Sargento, 1 slice	100	9	6	25	200	<1	0
Nacho cheese spread, Easy Cheese, 2 Tbsp	100	7	4	25	390	3	0
Nachos & tacos, shredded, Sargento, ¼ cup	110	9	5	25	240	1	0
Neufchatel, 1 oz	70	7	4	20	110	<1	0
Neufchatel cheese spread, garden vegetables, Spreadery, 2 Tbsp	70	6	4	20	230	2	0
Neufchatel cheese spread, garlic & herb, Spreadery, 2 Tbsp	80	7	5	20	180	1	0
Neufchatel cheese spread, ranch flavor, Spreadery, 2 Tbsp	80	7	5	20	210	1	0
Olive & pimento cheese spread, Kraft, 2 Tbsp	70	6	4	20	220	3	0
Onion, toasted, cheese spread, Fleur de Lait, 2 Tbsp	90	9	6	30	190	2	0
Parmesan, Auricchio, 1 oz	110	7	4	25	260	<1	0
Parmesan, Di Giorno, 2 tsp	20	1	1	5	55	0	0
Parmesan, 100%, grated, Di Giorno, 2 tsp	20	1.5	1	5	85	0	0
Parmesan, 100%, grated, Kraft, 2 tsp	20	1.5	1	5	85	0	0
Parmesan, 100%, shredded, Di Giorno, 2 tsp	20	1.5	1	<5	75	0	0
Parmesan, 100%, shredded, Kraft, 2 tsp	20	1.5	1	<5	75	0	0

CHEESE	CAL (g)	FAT (g)	SAT FAT (g)	CHOL (mg)	SODIUM (mg)	CARB (g)	FIBER (g)
Parmesan, grated, Classica, 1 Tbsp	25	2	0	5	65	0	0
Parmesan, grated, County Line Cheese, 1 oz	25	1.5	1	5	100	0	0
Parmesan, grated, Polly-O, 2 tsp	25	1.5	1	5	80	0	0
Parmesan, Italian topping, fat free, grated, Weight Watchers, 1 Tbsp	15	0	0	5	45	2	0
Parmesan, piece, 1 oz	110	7	4.5	20	450	<1	0
Parmesan, shredded, 1 Tbsp	20	1.5	1	<5	85	0	0
Parmesan, shredded, Classica, 1 Tbsp	20	1	1	0	35	0	0
Parmesan, shredded, Sargento, ¼ cup	110	7	5	25	300	1	0
Parmesan/Romano, grated, County Line Cheese, 1 oz	25	1.5	1	5	100	0	0
Parmesan/Romano blend, shredded, Sargento, ¼ cup	110	7	5	25	340	1	0
Peach cheese spread, Fleur de Lait, 2 Tbsp	90	7	4.5	25	90	3	0
Pecorino Romano, block, Fulvi, 1 Tbsp grated	25	2	na	na	140	0	0
Pecorino Romano, grated, Classica, 1 Tbsp	20	2	1.5	0	100	0	0
Pecorino Romano, shredded, Classica, 1 Tbsp	20	2	1.5	0	100	0	0
Pimento, slice, Kraft, 1 oz	100	8	6	25	430	<1	0
Pimiento, 1 oz	110	9	6	25	400	0	0
Pimento cheese spread, Kraft, 2 Tbsp	80	6	4	20	170	3	0
Pimento cheese spread, Spreadery, 2 Tbsp	100	8	5	20	320	3	0
Pineapple cheese spread, Fleur de Lait, 2 Tbsp	90	8	5	30	95	3	0
Pineapple cheese spread, Kraft, 2 Tbsp	70	5	3.5	15	120	4	0
Pizza, cheddar, mild, & whole milk mozzarella, shredded, Kraft, ¼ cup	90	7	5	20	170	<1	0

CHEESE	CAL (g)	FAT (g)	SAT FAT (g)	CHOL (mg)	SODIUM (mg)	CARB (g)	FIBER (g)
Pizza, double cheese, shredded, Sargento, ¼ cup	90	6	4.5	20	150	1	0
Pizza, four cheese, shredded, Kraft, ¼ cup	90	7	4.5	20	230	<1	0
Pizza, mozzarella & cheddar, shredded, Kraft, ¼ cup	100	8	5	25	190	<1	0
Pizza, mozzarella & provolone, shredded, Kraft, ¼ cup	90	7	4.5	20	210	<1	0
Pizza, shredded, Sargento, ¼ cup	90	6	4	20	210	0	0
Pizza shreds, Healthy Choice, ¼ cup	45	0	0	<5	200	2	na
Plain cheese spread, New Holland, 1 oz	90	7	4.5	30	105	0	0
Port de salut, 1 oz	100	8	5	35	150	0	0
Port wine cheese food, spread, Kaukauna, 2 Tbsp	90	7	3	20	210	3	0
Provolone, County Line Cheese, 1 oz	110	8	5	25	260	<1	0
Provolone, Land O' Lakes, 1 oz	100	8	4.5	20	240	<1	0
Provolone, imported, Auricchio, 1 oz	110	9	5	30	390	<1	0
Provolone, lightly smoked, reduced fat, Alpine Lace, 1 oz	70	5	3	15	120	1	0
Provolone, medium, Auricchio, 1 oz	100	8	5	25	220	<1	0
Provolone, mild, Auricchio, 1 oz	100	8	5	25	120	<1	0
Provolone, sharp, Auricchio, 1 oz	110	9	5	30	320	<1	0
Provolone, sliced, Sargento, 1 slice	100	8	5	25	190	0	0
Provolone, with smoke flavor, Kraft, 1 oz	100	7	5	25	240	<1	0
Ricotta, Breakstone's, ¼ cup	110	8	5	25	90	3	0
Ricotta, fat free, Polly-O, ¼ cup	50	0	0	<5	80	2	0
Ricotta, light, Polly-O, ¼ cup	70	3	2	10	80	3	0

CHEESE	CAL (g)	FAT (g)	SAT FAT (g)	CHOL (mg)	SODIUM (mg)	CARB (g)	FIBER (g)
Ricotta, light, Sargento, ¼ cup	60	2.5	1.5	15	55	3	0
Ricotta, old fashioned, Sargento, ¼ cup	90	6	4	25	75	3	0
Ricotta, part skim, Polly-O, ¼ cup	90	6	4	20	65	2	0
Ricotta, part skim, Sargento, ¼ cup	80	5	3	20	75	2	0
Ricotta, whole milk, Polly-O, ¼ cup	110	8	5	25	60	2	0
Romano, Auricchio, 1 oz	100	7	4	25	330	<1	0
Romano, Di Giorno, 2 tsp	20	1.5	1	5	75	0	0
Romano, 100%, grated, Di Giorno, 2 tsp	25	1.5	1	5	90	0	0
Romano, 100%, grated, Kraft, 2 tsp	25	1.5	1	5	90	0	0
Romano, 100%, shredded, Di Giorno, 2 tsp	20	1.5	1	5	70	0	0
Romano, grated, County Line Cheese, 1 oz	25	1.5	1	5	100	0	0
Romano & Parmesan, grated, Polly-O, 2 tsp	25	1.5	1	5	80	0	0
Roquefort, 1 oz	100	9	5	25	510	<1	0
Salmon cheese spread, La Cheeserie, 2 Tbsp	60	5	3	15	95	<1	0
Salmon fume et capers cheese spread, Deli Alouette, 2 Tbsp	70	7	4	25	110	1	0
Salsa cheese spread, hot, Cheez Whiz, 2 Tbsp	90	7	5	25	540	2	0
Salsa cheese spread, light, Fleur de Lait Gourmet, 2 Tbsp	60	4	3	20	140	2	1
Salsa cheese spread, mild, Cheez Whiz, 2 Tbsp	90	7	5	25	530	2	0
Scallion variete cheese spread, Alouette Light, 2 Tbsp	50	4	2.5	20	130	2	0
Sharp cheese product, slice, fat free, Borden, ¾ oz	30	0	0	0	310	2	0
Sharp cheese spread, Old English, 2 Tbsp	90	8	5	25	520	<1	0

CHEESE	CAL (g)	FAT (g)	SAT FAT (g)	CHOL (mg)	SODIUM (mg)	CARB (g)	FIBER (g)
Sharp cheese spread, Squeez-A-Snak, 2 Tbsp	90	8	5	25	440	<1	0
Spinach cheese spread, La Cheeserie, 2 Tbsp	60	6	3.5	25	85	1	0
Spinach Florentine cheese spread, Alouette, 2 Tbsp	60	6	3.5	25	85	1	0
Strawberry cheese spread, Fleur de Lait, 2 Tbsp	90	8	5	30	90	3	0
String cheese, MooTown Snackers, 1 piece	70	5	3	15	170	<1	0
String cheese, all varieties, Healthy Choice, 1 oz	45	0	0	<5	200	1	na
String cheese, cheddar, Polly-O, 1 oz	80	6	4	20	220	<1	0
String cheese, light, MooTown Snackers, 1 piece	60	3	2	10	200	<1	0
String cheese, mozzarella, Handi-Snacks, 1 stick	80	6	4	20	240	<1	0
String cheese, mozzarella, part-skim, Kraft, 1 stick	80	6	3.5	20	240	<1	0
Sundried tomatoes et basil cheese spread, Deli Alouette, 2 Tbsp	70	7	4.5	25	100	1	0
Swiss, County Line Cheese, 1 oz	110	8	5	30	60	<1	0
Swiss, Kraft, 1 oz	110	9	6	30	50	0	0
Swiss, Land O' Lakes, 1 oz	110	8	6	25	75	<1	0
Swiss, baby, Delico, 1 oz	110	8	5	30	150	1	0
Swiss, baby, Kraft, 1 oz	110	9	6	25	110	0	0
Swiss, baby, Land O' Lakes, 1 oz	110	8	5	25	125	0	0
Swiss, baby, part-skim, Zivney, 1 oz	109	9	5	15	180	1	na
Swiss, baby, smoked, Delico, 1 oz	110	8	5	30	150	1	0
Swiss, fat free, slices, Weight Watchers, 0.75 oz	30	0	0	0	280	2	0
Swiss, light, Delico, 1 oz	90	6	3	15	140	0	0
Swiss, light, Land O' Lakes, 1 oz	80	4	3	15	60	<1	0

CHEESE	CAL	FAT (g)	SAT FAT (g)	CHOL (mg)	SODIUM (mg)	CARB (g)	FIBER (g)
Swiss, low sodium, lowfat, County Line Cheese, 1 oz	80	4	3	15	50	<1	0
Swiss, petite, part-skim, Danekas, 1 oz	109	9	5	15	180	1	na
Swiss, processed, County Line Cheese, 1 oz	110	9	6	25	390	1	0
Swiss, processed, slices, Kraft, 1 oz	90	7	5	25	420	<1	0
Swiss, reduced fat, Alpine Lace, 1 oz	90	6	4	20	35	1	0
Swiss, shredded, Kraft, ¼ cup	110	9	6	30	45	<1	0
Swiss, shredded, Sargento, ¼ cup	110	8	5	30	40	0	0
Swiss, sliced, Sargento, 1 slice	80	6	4	20	30	0	0
Swiss, sliced, Sargento Wafer Thin, 1 slice	110	9	5	25	40	0	0
Swiss, sliced, light, Sargento, 1 cup	80	4	2.5	15	50	<1	0
Swiss American, processed, County Line Cheese, 1 oz	110	9	6	25	350	1	0
Swiss cheese food, County Line Cheese, 1 oz	100	7	5	20	370	2	0
Swiss cheese food, singles, Kraft, ¾ oz	70	5	3.5	15	320	1	0
Swiss flavor, singles, ⅓ less fat, Kraft, ¾ oz	50	2.5	1.5	10	270	2	0
Swiss flavor, singles, nonfat, Kraft Free, ¾ oz slice	30	0	0	<5	290	3	0
Swiss flavor, slice, fat free, Borden, ¾ oz	30	0	0	0	310	2	0
Swiss flavor, slice, lowfat, Borden, ⅔ oz	30	1	1	<5	260	1	0
Swiss-style, semisoft, Saxony Lace, 1 oz	90	6	3	10	35	0	0
Taco, cheddar & Monterey Jack, shredded, Kraft, ¼ cup	100	8	6	25	180	<1	0
Taco, shredded, Sargento, ¼ cup	110	9	6	25	220	1	0
Taco, shredded, light, Sargento, ¼ cup	70	4.5	2.5	15	240	<1	0

CHEESE	CAL (g)	FAT (g)	SAT FAT (g)	CHOL (mg)	SODIUM (mg)	CARB (g)	FIBER (g)
Taleggio, Tal-Fino, 1 oz	110	9	4	5	90	2	1
Teleme, Sonoma Cheese Factory, 1 oz	90	7	4	25	180	0	0
Tilsit, whole milk, 1 oz	100	7	4.5	30	210	<1	0
Toscanello, Auricchio, 1 oz	110	9	5	30	270	<1	0
Vegetable, garden, cheese spread, Fleur de Lait, 2 Tbsp	80	8	5	30	200	1	0
Vegetable, garden, cheese spread, La Cheeserie, 2 Tbsp	60	6	4	30	130	1	0
Vegetable, garden, cheese spread, light, Fleur de Lait Gourmet, 2 Tbsp	50	4	3	20	150	2	1
Vegetable, spring, cheese spread, Alouette Light, 2 Tbsp	50	4	2.5	20	110	1	<1
Vegetable cheese spread, New Holland, 1 oz	80	6	4	25	110	0	0
Vegetable jardin cheese spread, Deli Alouette, 2 Tbsp	60	6	4	25	130	1	0
Velveeta, 1 oz	80	6	4	20	420	3	0
Velveeta Italiana, 1 oz	80	6	4	20	430	2	0
Velveeta Light, 1 oz	60	3	2	10	420	3	0
Wildberry cheese spread, Fleur de Lait, 2 Tbsp	90	7	4.5	25	90	4	0

AT A GLANCE: CHEESE

Choose from among the many fat free cheese products from such names as Alpine Lace, Borden, Breakstone's, Friendship, Healthy Choice, Kraft, Knudsen, Polly-O, Smart Beat, and Weight Watchers.

COOKIE DOUGH

	CAL (g)	FAT (g)	SAT FAT (g)	CHOL (mg)	SODIUM (mg)	CARB (g)	FIBER (g)
Chocolate chip, Pillsbury, 1 oz	130	6	1.5	<5	85	17	<1
Chocolate chocolate chip, Pillsbury, 1 oz	130	6	1.5	0	65	17	<1
Dinosaurs, Pillsbury, 2 oz	120	5	1.5	<5	95	17	<1
Oatmeal chocolate chip, Pillsbury, 1 oz	120	6	1.5	<5	95	16	<1
Peanut butter, Pillsbury, 1 oz	110	5	1	<5	135	15	0
Sugar, Pillsbury, 2 oz	130	5	1.5	<5	125	19	0
Teddy bears, Pillsbury, 2 oz	120	5	1	<5	105	18	0
With candy, Pillsbury, 1 oz	130	6	2	<5	80	18	<1

	CAL	FAT (g)	SAT FAT (g)	CHOL (mg)	SODIUM (mg)	CARB (g)	FIBER (g)

CREAM & NONDAIRY CREAMERS

	CAL	FAT (g)	SAT FAT (g)	CHOL (mg)	SODIUM (mg)	CARB (g)	FIBER (g)
Cream, light, coffee or table, 1 Tbsp	30	3	2	10	5	<1	0
Cream, medium, 25% fat, 1 Tbsp	40	4	2.5	15	5	<1	0
Creamer, amaretto, International Delight, 1 Tbsp	45	1.5	0	0	5	7	0
Creamer, nondairy, Avoset, 1 container	10	1	0	0	0	1	0
Creamer, nondairy, Coffee Companion, ⅜ fl oz	15	1	0	0	0	1	0
Creamer, nondairy, fat free, Carnation Coffee-Mate, 1 Tbsp	10	0	0	0	0	2	0
Creamer, nondairy, flavored, all flavors, Carnation Coffee-Mate, 1 Tbsp	40	2	0	0	5	5	0
Creamer, nondairy, lite, Carnation Coffee-Mate, 1 Tbsp	10	0.5	0	0	5	1	0
Creamer, nondairy, regular, Carnation Coffee-Mate, 1 Tbsp	20	1	0	0	0	2	0
Creamer, Suisse chocolate mocha, International Delight, 1 Tbsp	45	1.5	0	0	10	7	0
Devon cream, double, Somerdale, 1 Tbsp	70	7	5	20	5	1	0
Half & half (cream & milk), 2 Tbsp	40	4	2	10	10	<1	0
Half & half, sour, cultured, 1 Tbsp	20	2	1	5	5	<1	0
Whipping cream, heavy, liquid, 2 Tbsp	100	12	7	40	10	0	0
Whipping cream, light, liquid, 2 Tbsp	90	9	6	35	10	0	0

AT A GLANCE: CREAM & NONDAIRY CREAMERS
Lowest in Fat: Carnation Coffee-Mate Fat Free Nondairy Creamer

	CAL	FAT (g)	SAT FAT (g)	CHOL (mg)	SODIUM (mg)	CARB (g)	FIBER (g)
EGGNOG							
Eggnog, 4 fl oz	170	10	6	75	70	17	0
Eggnog, light, Meadow Gold/Viva, ½ cup	150	4	2.5	20	65	23	0
Eggnog flavor mix, 2 tsp	110	0	0	5	45	28	<1
EGGS & EGG SUBSTITUTES							
Duck egg, whole, fresh, raw, 1 egg	130	10	2.5	620	100	1	0
Egg, liquid, scrambled, Simply Eggs, ½ cup	80	2.5	1	95	350	3	3
Egg, whole, cooked, poached, 1 large egg	70	5	1.5	210	140	<1	0
Egg, whole, dried, 1 Tbsp	30	2	0.5	100	25	0	0
Egg, whole, fresh, 1 large egg	70	5	1.5	215	65	<1	0
Egg, whole, hard-boiled, 1 large egg	80	5	1.5	210	60	<1	0
Egg product, cholesterol free, Healthy Choice, ¼ cup	25	0	0	0	95	<1	0
Egg product, real, Egg Beaters, ¼ cup	30	0	0	0	100	1	0
Egg substitute, Better 'n Eggs, ¼ cup	30	0	0	0	100	1	0
Egg substitute, nonfat, Second Nature, ¼ cup	40	0	0	0	115	3	0
Egg white, dried, flakes, 1 oz	100	0	0	0	330	1	0
Egg white, dried, powder, ¼ cup sifted	100	0	0	0	330	1	0
Egg white, fresh, raw, 1 large egg white	20	0	0	0	55	0	0
Egg yolk, dried, 1 Tbsp	30	2.5	1	115	0	0	0
Egg yolk, fresh, raw, 1 large egg yolk	60	5	1.5	215	5	0	0
Goose egg, whole, fresh, raw, 1 egg	270	19	5	1230	200	2	0
Quail egg, whole, fresh, raw, 1 egg	15	1	0	75	15	0	0

EGGS & EGG SUBSTITUTES	CAL (g)	FAT (g)	SAT FAT (g)	CHOL (mg)	SODIUM (mg)	CARB (g)	FIBER (g)
Turkey egg, whole, fresh, raw, 1 egg	140	9	3	735	120	<1	0

AT A GLANCE: EGGS & EGG SUBSTITUTES

Lowest in Cholesterol: Egg Beaters Real Egg Product, Healthy Choice Egg product, Better 'n Eggs Egg Substitute

MILK

See also Dried Foods & Mixes, Milk, Milk Alternatives & Creamers.

	CAL (g)	FAT (g)	SAT FAT (g)	CHOL (mg)	SODIUM (mg)	CARB (g)	FIBER (g)
0.5% lowfat milk, vitamin A & D fortified, Borden/Meadow Gold, 8 fl oz	90	1	0.5	5	125	12	0
1% fat, lowfat, 8 fl oz	100	3	1.5	10	125	12	0
1% fat, protein fortified, vitamin A added, lowfat, 8 fl oz	110	2.5	1.5	10	130	12	0
1% lowfat acidophilus milk, vitamin A & D fortified, Borden/Meadow Gold, 8 fl oz	100	2.5	1.5	10	125	12	0
2% fat, lowfat, Hershey's, 8 fl oz juice box	130	5	3	20	130	13	0
2% fat, protein fortified, lowfat, 8 fl oz	140	5	3	20	140	13	0
2% fat, protein fortified, vitamin A added, lowfat, 8 fl oz	120	5	3	20	130	12	0
2% fat, vitamin A added, lowfat, 8 fl oz	120	4.5	3	20	120	12	0
Banana flavored, vitamin A & D fortified, lowfat, Nestle Quik, 8 fl oz	200	5	3	20	95	30	0
Blueberry Blast flavored milk, lowfat, Borden Crazy Milk, 8 fl oz	200	5	3	20	90	31	0
Butterfinger flavored, vitamin A & D fortified, lowfat, Nestle Quik, 8 fl oz	200	5	3	20	120	30	1
Buttermilk, cultured, 1% lowfat, Meadow Gold, 8 fl oz	100	2.5	1.5	10	290	12	0
Buttermilk, dried, 1 Tbsp	25	0	0	<5	35	3	0
Buttermilk, lowfat, Friendship, 8 fl oz	120	4	2.5	15	125	12	0

MILK	CAL (g)	FAT (g)	SAT FAT (g)	CHOL (mg)	SODIUM (mg)	CARB (g)	FIBER (g)
Chocolate, 1% milkfat, lowfat, Dean Foods, 8 fl oz	170	2.5	1.5	15	210	29	1
Chocolate, 1% milkfat, lowfat, Dean Foods, 10 oz carton	200	3	2	15	270	32	<1
Chocolate, 2%, lowfat, Hershey's, 8 fl oz juice box	200	4.5	2.5	15	120	31	<1
Chocolate, vitamin A & D fortified, 1% lowfat, Borden/Meadow Gold, 8 fl oz	170	2.5	1.5	15	180	29	0
Chocolate, vitamin A & D fortified, lowfat, Nestle Quik, 8 fl oz	190	5	3	20	150	29	0
Chocolate, whole, unfortified, Nestle Quik, 8 fl oz	230	9	5	30	120	31	0
Chocolate drink mix, chocolate malt flavor, traditional, Ovaltine, 4 Tbsp	80	0	0	0	115	18	1
Chocolate peanut butter flavored milk, lowfat, Borden Crazy Milk, 8 fl oz	210	5	3	20	140	33	0
Chocolate Smash flavored milk, lowfat, Borden Crazy Milk, 8 fl oz	200	5	3	20	170	31	0
Evaporated, Carnation, 2 Tbsp	40	2.5	1.5	10	35	3	ns
Evaporated, Pet, 2 Tbsp	40	2	1	5	30	3	0
Evaporated, lowfat, Carnation, 2 Tbsp	25	0.5	ns	5	35	3	ns
Evaporated, skimmed, Carnation, 2 Tbsp	25	0	ns	ns	40	4	ns
Evaporated, skimmed, Pet, 2 Tbsp	25	0	0	<5	35	3	0
Goat, 8 fl oz	170	10	7	25	120	11	0
Indian buffalo, whole, 8 fl oz	240	17	11	45	130	13	0
Malted milk mix, chocolate, Carnation, 3 Tbsp	90	1	0.5	0	40	18	<1
Malted milk mix, chocolate, Kraft, 3 Tbsp	80	1	0	0	40	17	<1
Malted milk mix, natural, Kraft, 3 Tbsp	90	2	1	5	85	15	0

MILK	CAL (g)	FAT (g)	SAT FAT (g)	CHOL (mg)	SODIUM (mg)	CARB (g)	FIBER (g)
Malted milk mix, original, Carnation, 3 Tbsp	90	2	1	5	85	15	<1
Milk shake, Bananaberry, Killer Shakes, 14 fl oz	450	15	9	70	240	66	3
Milk shake, chocolate, Killer Shakes, 14 fl oz	470	17	10	60	320	65	6
Milk shake, chocolate, Nestle Quik, 9 fl oz	300	11	6	40	200	41	4
Milk shake, root beer, Killer Shakes, 14 fl oz	460	15	9	70	220	67	4
Milk shake, strawberry, Killer Shakes, 14 fl oz	420	14	8	55	250	62	5
Milk shake, strawberry, Nestle Quik, 9 fl oz	270	9	5	35	160	40	3
Milk shake, vanilla, Killer Shakes, 14 fl oz	430	14	8	55	330	65	4
Milk shake, vanilla, Nestle Quik, 9 fl oz	280	9	5	35	210	42	3
Rootbeer flavored milk, lowfat, Borden Crazy Milk, 8 fl oz	200	5	3	20	115	31	0
Sheep, whole, 8 fl oz	260	17	11	65	110	13	0
Skim, 8 fl oz	90	0	0	<5	130	12	0
Skim, protein fortified, vitamin A added, 8 fl oz	90	1	0	<5	130	12	0
Skim, vitamin A added, 8 fl oz	90	0	0	<5	130	12	0
Skim, vitamin A & D fortified, Borden/Meadow Gold, 8 fl oz	80	0	0	5	125	12	0
Skim, vitamin A & D and protein fortified, Borden/Meadow Gold, 8 fl oz	110	1	0.5	5	125	14	0
Strawberry, vitamin A & D fortified, lowfat, Nestle Quik, 8 fl oz	200	5	3	20	120	32	0
Strawberry, whole, unfortified, Nestle Quik, 8 fl oz	230	9	5	30	100	31	0
Strawberry-banana, vitamin A & D fortified, lowfat, Nestle Quik, 8 fl oz	200	5	3	20	110	31	0

MILK	CAL (g)	FAT (g)	SAT FAT (g)	CHOL (mg)	SODIUM (mg)	CARB (g)	FIBER (g)
Strawberry Surprise flavored milk, lowfat, Borden Crazy Milk, 8 fl oz	200	5	3	20	85	31	0
Sweetened condensed, Eagle Brand, 2 Tbsp	130	3	2	10	40	23	0
Sweetened condensed, lowfat, Eagle Brand, 2 Tbsp	120	1.5	1	5	40	23	0
Whey, acid, dried, 1 Tbsp	10	0	0	0	30	2	0
Whey, acid, fluid, 8 fl oz	60	0	0	<5	120	13	0
Whey, sweet, dried, 1 Tbsp	25	0	0	0	80	6	0
Whey, sweet, fluid, 8 fl oz	70	1	0.5	<5	130	13	0
Whole, 3.3% fat, 8 fl oz	150	8	5	35	120	11	0
Whole, 3.7% fat, 8 fl oz	160	9	6	35	120	11	0
Whole, low sodium, 8 fl oz	150	9	5	35	5	11	0

AT A GLANCE: MILK
Lowest in Fat, Sat Fat, & Cholesterol: Skim Milk

MILK ALTERNATIVES

	CAL (g)	FAT (g)	SAT FAT (g)	CHOL (mg)	SODIUM (mg)	CARB (g)	FIBER (g)
Nondairy, chocolate, enriched, Rice Dream, 8 fl oz	160	2.5	0	0	100	35	0
Nondairy, original, enriched, Rice Dream, 8 fl oz	120	2	0	0	90	25	0
Nondairy, vanilla, enriched, Rice Dream, 8 fl oz	130	2	0	0	90	28	0
Nondairy soy drink, Edensoy, 8 fl oz	130	4	0.5	0	105	13	0
Nondairy soy drink, carob, Edensoy, 8 fl oz	150	4	0.5	0	105	23	0
Nondairy soy drink, fat free, Health Valley Soy Moo, 8 fl oz	110	0	0	0	60	22	1
Nondairy soy drink, vanilla, Edensoy, 8 fl oz	150	3	0	0	90	23	0
Nondairy soy drink, vanilla, vitamin fortified, Edensoy Extra, 8 fl oz	140	3	0	0	90	23	0
Nondairy soy drink, vitamin fortified, Edensoy Extra, 8 fl oz	130	5	0.5	0	100	12	0
Nondairy soy & rice drink, EdenBlend, 8 fl oz	120	3	0.5	0	85	16	0

	CAL (g)	FAT (g)	SAT FAT (g)	CHOL (mg)	SODIUM (mg)	CARB (g)	FIBER (g)
PASTA							
Angel hair, Contadina, 1¼ cups	240	3	1	90	30	43	2
Angel's hair, Di Giorno, 2 oz	160	1	0	0	190	31	1
Egg noodles, veggie, Di Giorno, 2 oz	200	2	1	35	25	37	2
Fettucine, Di Giorno, 2.5 oz	190	1.5	0	0	125	39	2
Fettucine, spinach, Di Giorno, 2.5 oz	190	1.5	0	0	140	38	2
Fettucini, Contadina, 1¼ cups	250	3.5	1	85	30	45	2
Fettucini, cholesterol free, Contadina, 1 cup	240	2.5	ns	ns	16	46	2
Linguine, Contadina, 1¼ cups	260	4	1	95	30	47	2
Linguine, Di Giorno, 2.5 oz	190	1.5	0	0	125	39	2
Linguine, herb, Di Giorno, 2.5 oz	190	1.5	0	0	125	39	2
Linguini, cholesterol free, Contadina, 1¼ cups	250	2.5	ns	ns	20	49	2
Linguini, tomato & herb, Contadina, 1¼ cups	250	3.5	1	85	30	45	2
Ravioli, beef & garlic, Contadina, 1¼ cups	350	14	5	110	350	39	3
Ravioli, cheese, Contadina, 1 cup	280	12	6	85	350	31	2
Ravioli, cheese, light, Contadina, 1 cup	240	5	2	60	340	35	2
Ravioli, cheese & garlic, Di Giorno Light Varieties, 1 cup	270	2	1	5	580	45	1
Ravioli, chicken & rosemary, Contadina, 1¼ cups	330	12	4	85	420	43	3
Ravioli, Gorgonzola cheese & walnut, Contadina, 1¼ cups	380	15	5	80	390	46	3
Ravioli, Italian herb cheese, Di Giorno, 1 cup	350	13	8	45	610	44	2
Ravioli, Italian sausage, Di Giorno, ¾ cup	340	12	5	50	630	41	2
Ravioli, light garden vegetable, Contadina, 1 cup	240	5	3	65	320	36	2

PASTA	CAL (g)	FAT (g)	SAT FAT (g)	CHOL (mg)	SODIUM (mg)	CARB (g)	FIBER (g)
Ravioli, tomato & cheese, Di Giorno Light Varieties, 1 cup	280	3	1.5	10	490	49	2
Tagliatelle, spinach, Contadina, 1¼ cup	270	4	1	105	110	46	4
Tortellini, cheese, Contadina, ¾ cup	260	6	2.5	45	330	39	3
Tortellini, cheese, Di Giorno, ¾ cup	260	6	3.5	30	230	37	1
Tortellini, cheese & basil, Contadina, 1 cup	360	11	4	65	380	49	3
Tortellini, chicken & herbs, Di Giorno, 1 cup	260	5	2.5	35	290	40	1
Tortellini, chicken & prosciutto, Contadina, 1 cup	360	13	4	75	440	46	3
Tortellini, chicken & vegetable, Contadina, ¾ cup	260	7	2	45	220	39	2
Tortellini, hot red peppers, cheese, Di Giorno, 1 cup	310	9	5	40	310	41	3
Tortellini, light garlic & cheese, Contadina, 1 cup	280	5	2.5	55	380	50	3
Tortellini, meat, Di Giorno, ¾ cup	290	9	4.5	40	380	40	1
Tortellini, mozzarella, garlic, Di Giorno, 1 cup	300	9	5	45	440	40	1
Tortellini, mushroom, Contadina, 1 cup	310	8	2.5	45	250	49	2
Tortellini, mushrooms, Di Giorno, 1 cup	290	7	4.5	30	510	42	2
Tortellini, spinach three cheese, Contadina, ¾ cup	260	6	3	55	390	39	3
Tortellini, sweet Italian sausage, Contadina, 1 cup	330	10	3	50	350	48	3

AT A GLANCE: PASTA
Lowest in Fat: Di Giorno Angel's Hair
Highest in Fiber: Contadina Spinach Tagliatelle

POLENTA

	CAL (g)	FAT (g)	SAT FAT (g)	CHOL (mg)	SODIUM (mg)	CARB (g)	FIBER (g)
Mite Foods, 4 oz	100	0	0	0	440	21	3

	CAL	FAT (g)	SAT FAT (g)	CHOL (mg)	SODIUM (mg)	CARB (g)	FIBER (g)
SOUR CREAM							
Breakstone's, 2 Tbsp	60	5	4	25	15	1	0
Friendship, 2 Tbsp	60	5	3.5	20	15	2	0
Knudsen Hampshire, 2 Tbsp	60	6	4	25	15	1	0
Sealtest, 2 Tbsp	60	5	3.5	20	15	1	0
Fat free, Borden, 2 Tbsp	20	0	0	0	45	3	0
Fat free, Breakstone's Free, 2 Tbsp	35	0	0	<5	25	6	0
Fat free, Sealtest Free, 2 Tbsp	35	0	0	<5	25	6	0
Half and half sour cream, Breakstone's, 2 Tbsp	45	3.5	2.5	15	20	2	0
Light, Friendship, 2 Tbsp	35	2.5	1.5	10	30	2	0
Light, Land O' Lakes, 2 Tbsp	35	2	1.5	10	30	4	0
Light, Sealtest Light/Knudsen, 2 Tbsp	40	2.5	2	10	20	2	0
Lite, Viva, 2 Tbsp	40	2.5	1.5	10	35	3	0
No fat, Land O' Lakes, 2 Tbsp	30	0	0	<5	40	5	0
Nondairy, imitation, cultured, 2 Tbsp	60	5	4.5	0	30	2	0
Nonfat, Friendship, 2 Tbsp	20	0	0	0	25	3	0
Thick, fat free, Knudsen Free, 2 Tbsp	35	0	0	0	25	6	0
With chives, light, Land O' Lakes, 2 Tbsp	40	2	1.5	10	95	4	0

AT A GLANCE: SOUR CREAM

Lowest in Fat: Fat free varieties, including Borden Fat Free, Breakstone's Free, Knudsen Free, Land O'Lakes No Fat, Sealtest Free

TEMPEH							
Five grain, White Wave, 1/3 block	140	4	0.5	0	0	15	4
Original soy, White Wave, 1/3 block	150	6	1	0	0	10	6
Tempeh burger, Barbecue Marinated Grilles, Lightlife, 1 patty	120	3.5	1.5	0	180	11	0

TEMPEH	CAL (g)	FAT (g)	SAT FAT (g)	CHOL (mg)	SODIUM (mg)	CARB (g)	FIBER (g)
Tempeh burger, Lemon Marinated Grilles, Lightlife, 1 patty	140	6	2	0	280	11	0
Tempeh burger, Tamari Marinated Grilles, Lightlife, 1 patty	120	5	2	0	260	9	0

TOFU

	CAL (g)	FAT (g)	SAT FAT (g)	CHOL (mg)	SODIUM (mg)	CARB (g)	FIBER (g)
5 Spice, Nasoya, ¼ block	70	4	0.5	0	70	0	0
Extra firm, Nasoya, ⅕ block	90	5	0.5	0	10	1	0
Firm, Nasoya, ⅕ block	80	4	0.5	0	10	2	0
French country, Nasoya, ⅕ block	70	4	0.5	0	130	0	0
Okara, ½ cup	50	1	0	0	5	8	na
Salted and fermented (fuyu), 1 block	15	1	0	0	320	<1	0
Silken, Nasoya, ⅙ block	50	2	0	0	10	2	0
Soft, Nasoya, ⅕ block	60	3	0	0	5	2	0

WHIPPED TOPPINGS

	CAL (g)	FAT (g)	SAT FAT (g)	CHOL (mg)	SODIUM (mg)	CARB (g)	FIBER (g)
Nondairy, pressurized, 2 Tbsp	20	2	2	0	0	<1	0
Whipped cream topping, pressurized, 2 Tbsp	20	2	0	<5	0	0	0
Whipped topping, Avoset, 2 Tbsp	20	1.5	1.5	0	0	1	0
Whipped topping, Kraft, 2 tbsp	20	1.5	1	0	0	1	0
Whipped topping, lite, Pet Whip, 2 Tbsp	30	2	2	0	0	2	0
Whipped topping, nonfat, Avoset, 2 Tbsp	15	0	0	0	10	2	0
Whipped topping, real cream, Kraft, 2 Tbsp	20	1.5	1	5	0	1	0

YOGURT

	CAL (g)	FAT (g)	SAT FAT (g)	CHOL (mg)	SODIUM (mg)	CARB (g)	FIBER (g)
Apple cinnamon, lowfat, fruit on the bottom, Dannon, 8 oz	240	3	1.5	15	140	46	1
Banana, 99% fat free, Yoplait, 6 oz	180	1.5	1	10	105	33	0

YOGURT	CAL (g)	FAT (g)	SAT FAT (g)	CHOL (mg)	SODIUM (mg)	CARB (g)	FIBER (g)
Banana, lowfat, Dannon Sprinkl'ins, 4.1 oz	140	2.5	1.5	10	85	24	0
Banana, nonfat, Dannon Tropifruta, 6 oz	150	0	0	5	105	31	0
Banana cream pie, nonfat, Dannon Light, 8 oz	100	0	0	<5	150	17	0
Banana creme with strawberry topping, lowfat, Dannon Double Delights, 6 oz	170	2.5	1.5	10	90	30	1
Bavarian creme with raspberry topping, lowfat, Dannon Double Delights, 6 oz	170	2.5	1.5	10	115	31	0
Black cherry, lowfat, Breyers, 8 oz	260	2.5	1.5	15	110	50	0
Black cherry, nonfat, Knudsen Cal 70, 6 oz	170	0	0	5	85	12	0
Black cherry, nonfat, Light N' Lively Free 70 Calories, 6 oz	70	0	0	<5	85	11	0
Blueberries 'n creme, Weight Watchers Ultimate 90, 1 cup	90	0	0	5	140	14	3
Blueberry, 99% fat free, Yoplait, 6 oz	180	1.5	1	10	105	33	0
Blueberry, fat free, fruit on the bottom, Yoplait, 6 oz	160	0	0	<5	105	33	0
Blueberry, lowfat, Breyers, 8 oz	250	2.5	1.5	15	110	48	0
Blueberry, lowfat, Dannon Danimals, 4.4 oz	140	2	1	10	90	25	0
Blueberry, lowfat, fruit on the bottom, Dannon, 8 oz	240	3	1.5	15	140	46	1
Blueberry, nonfat, Dannon, 6 oz	160	0	0	<5	105	33	0
Blueberry, nonfat, Dannon Light, 8 oz	100	0	0	<5	140	20	0
Blueberry, nonfat, Knudsen Cal 70, 6 oz	70	0	0	5	80	12	0
Blueberry, nonfat, Light N' Lively, 6 oz	190	0	0	5	105	38	0
Blueberry, nonfat, Light N' Lively Free 70 Calories, 6 oz	70	0	0	<5	80	11	0
Blueberry or strawberry banana, Friendship Fruit Crunch, 1 container	190	3.5	1.5	10	125	32	0

YOGURT	CAL (g)	FAT (g)	SAT FAT (g)	CHOL (mg)	SODIUM (mg)	CARB (g)	FIBER (g)
Borden, 1% lowfat, all flavors, Borden, 1 container	230	2.5	1.5	15	150	42	0
Boysenberry, lowfat, fruit on the bottom, Dannon, 8 oz	240	3	1.5	15	150	45	1
Cappuccino, Weight Watchers Ultimate 90, 1 cup	90	0	0	5	140	14	0
Cappuccino, nonfat, Dannon Light, 8 oz	100	0	0	<5	140	17	0
Cappuccino, with chocolate nuggets, Yoplait, 7 oz	130	1.5	0	<5	150	22	0
Cappuccino with chocolate, nonfat, Dannon Light 'N Crunchy, 8 oz	150	0	0	<5	170	27	0
Caramel apple crunch, nonfat, Dannon Light 'N Crunchy, 8 oz	150	0	0	<5	180	28	0
Cheesecake with cherry topping, lowfat, Dannon Double Delights, 6 oz	170	2.5	1.5	10	90	31	0
Cheesecake with strawberry topping, lowfat, Dannon Double Delights, 6 oz	170	2.5	1.5	10	90	30	1
Cherries jubilee, Weight Watchers Ultimate 90, 1 cup	90	0	0	5	140	14	0
Cherry, 99% fat free, Yoplait, 6 oz	180	1.5	1	10	105	33	0
Cherry, fat free, fruit on the bottom, Yoplait, 6 oz	160	0	0	<5	105	33	0
Cherry, lowfat, fruit on the bottom, Dannon, 8 oz	240	3	1.5	15	135	46	1
Cherry, with honey grahams, lowfat, Dannon Sprinkl'ins Crazy Crunch, 4.4 oz	170	3	1.5	10	150	30	0
Cherry cheesecake, with graham crunch, Yoplait, 7 oz	130	1	0	<5	115	23	0
Cherry vanilla, lowfat, Dannon Sprinkl'ins, 4.1 oz	140	2.5	1.5	10	95	24	0
Cherry vanilla, nonfat, Dannon Light, 8 oz	100	0	0	<5	140	17	0
Chocolate cappuccino, nonfat, SnackWell's, ¾ cup	190	0	0	<5	230	40	2
Coffee, Friendship, 1 cup	210	3	1.5	20	170	30	0

YOGURT	CAL (g)	FAT (g)	SAT FAT (g)	CHOL (mg)	SODIUM (mg)	CARB (g)	FIBER (g)
Coffee, lowfat, Breyers, 8 oz	220	3	2	20	135	38	0
Coffee, lowfat, Dannon, 8 oz	210	3	2	15	160	36	0
Cranberry raspberry, Weight Watchers Ultimate 90, 1 cup	90	0	0	5	140	14	0
Cranberry-raspberry, lowfat, Dannon, 8 oz	210	3	2	15	160	36	0
Creme caramel, nonfat, Dannon Light, 8 oz	100	0	0	<5	125	15	0
Custard style, all flavors, light, Yoplait, 6 oz	90	0	0	0	85	14	0
Custard style, all fruit flavors, Yoplait, 6 oz	170	2.5	1.5	10	105	29	0
Custard style, vanilla, Yoplait, 6 oz	170	2.5	1.5	10	115	28	0
French vanilla, nonfat, Dannon, 6 oz	160	0	0	<5	100	31	0
Grape, with chocolate grahams, lowfat, Dannon Sprinkl'ins Crazy Crunch, 4.4 oz	160	2.5	1.5	10	170	29	0
Grape lemonade, lowfat, Dannon Danimals, 4.4 oz	130	2	1	10	80	23	0
Guava, nonfat, Dannon Tropifruta, 6 oz	150	0	0	5	105	29	0
Lemon, 1.5% lowfat, Meadow Gold, 1 container	200	3.5	2	15	135	35	0
Lemon, 99% fat free, Yoplait, 6 oz	180	1.5	1	10	105	33	0
Lemon, lowfat, Breyers, 8 oz	220	3	2	20	140	38	0
Lemon, lowfat, Dannon, 8 oz	210	3	2	15	160	36	0
Lemon, nonfat, Dannon Light, 8 oz	100	0	0	<5	140	17	0
Lemon, nonfat, Knudsen Cal 70, 6 oz	70	0	0	5	100	11	0
Lemon, nonfat, Knudsen Free, 6 oz	160	0	0	5	105	33	0
Lemon, nonfat, Light N' Lively Free 70 Calories, 6 oz	70	0	0	<5	120	12	0
Lemon chiffon, Weight Watchers Ultimate 90, 1 cup	90	0	0	5	140	14	1

YOGURT	CAL (g)	FAT (g)	SAT FAT (g)	CHOL (mg)	SODIUM (mg)	CARB (g)	FIBER (g)
Lemon chiffon, nonfat, Dannon, 6 oz	150	0	0	<5	110	31	0
Lemon chiffon with blueberry, nonfat, Dannon Light 'N Crunchy, 8 oz	140	0	0	<5	150	26	0
Lemon flavored, nonfat, Light N' Lively, 6 oz	170	0	0	5	105	35	0
Lemon ice, lowfat, Dannon Danimals, 4.4 oz	130	2	1	10	90	22	0
Light N' Lively Free 50 Calories, nonfat, all flavors, 4.4 oz	50	0	0	<5	60	8	0
Mandarin orange, 1.5% lowfat, Meadow Gold, 1 container	200	3.5	2	15	120	35	0
Mango, nonfat, Dannon Tropifruta, 6 oz	150	0	0	5	105	31	0
Mixed berries, lowfat, fruit on the bottom, Dannon, 8 oz	240	3	1.5	15	150	45	1
Mixed berry, Breyers, 8 oz	250	2.5	1.5	15	110	48	0
Mixed berry, 99% fat free, Yoplait, 6 oz	180	1.5	1	10	105	33	0
Mixed berry, lowfat, Yoplait, 6 oz	200	2	1	10	125	40	2
Mixed berry, nonfat, Knudsen Free, 6 oz	170	0	0	5	105	33	0
Mixed berry, nonfat, Light N' Lively, 6 oz	170	0	0	5	105	34	0
Orange, lowfat, fruit on the bottom, Dannon, 8 oz	240	3	1.5	15	135	45	0
Orange-banana, lowfat, Dannon Danimals, 4.4 oz	140	2	1	10	80	24	0
Papaya-pineapple, nonfat, Dannon Tropifruta, 6 oz	150	0	0	5	105	30	0
Peach, Friendship Fruit Crunch, 1 container	190	4.5	1.5	10	125	31	0
Peach, Knudsen Free, 6 oz	170	0	0	5	105	33	0
Peach, Light N' Lively, 6 oz	170	0	0	5	105	35	0
Peach, Weight Watchers Ultimate 90, 1 cup	90	0	0	5	140	14	0

YOGURT	CAL (g)	FAT (g)	SAT FAT (g)	CHOL (mg)	SODIUM (mg)	CARB (g)	FIBER (g)
Peach, fat free, fruit on the bottom, Yoplait, 6 oz	160	0	0	<5	105	33	0
Peach, lowfat, Breyers, 8 oz	250	2.5	1.5	15	110	48	0
Peach, lowfat, fruit on the bottom, Dannon, 8 oz	240	3	1.5	15	140	45	1
Peach, nonfat, Dannon, 6 oz	150	0	0	<5	100	31	0
Peach, nonfat, Dannon Light, 8 oz	100	0	0	<5	140	18	0
Peach, nonfat, Knudsen Cal 70, 6 oz	70	0	0	5	80	11	0
Peach, nonfat, Light N' Lively Free 70 Calories, 6 oz	70	0	0	<5	80	12	0
Peach, with granola, Yoplait, 7 oz	220	1.5	0	<5	115	43	<1
Pear, lowfat, fruit on the bottom, Dannon, 8 oz	240	3	1.5	15	135	45	0
Pina colada, 1.5% lowfat, Meadow Gold, 1 container	200	3.5	2	15	135	35	0
Pina colada, nonfat, Dannon Tropifruta, 6 oz	150	0	0	5	105	30	0
Pineapple, lowfat, Breyers, 8 oz	250	2.5	1.5	15	110	49	0
Pineapple, nonfat, Knudsen Cal 70, 6 oz	70	0	0	5	80	11	0
Plain, Friendship, 1 cup	150	3	1.5	20	190	13	0
Plain, Weight Watchers Ultimate 90, 1 cup	90	0	0	5	140	14	0
Plain, 1.5% lowfat, Meadow Gold, 1 container	160	3.5	2	20	135	20	0
Plain, extra creamy, nonfat, Yoplait, 1 cup	140	0	0	10	190	21	0
Plain, lowfat, Breyers, 8 oz	130	3	2	20	150	15	0
Plain, lowfat, Dannon, 8 oz	140	4	2	20	150	16	0
Plain, nonfat, Dannon, 8 oz	110	0	0	5	150	16	0
Plain, nonfat, Yoplait, 6 oz	100	0	0	5	140	16	0
Plum, lowfat, fruit on the bottom, Dannon, 8 oz	240	3	1.5	15	160	45	0
Raspberries 'n creme, Weight Watchers Ultimate 90, 1 cup	90	0	0	5	140	14	0

YOGURT	CAL (g)	FAT (g)	SAT FAT (g)	CHOL (mg)	SODIUM (mg)	CARB (g)	FIBER (g)
Raspberry, 99% fat free, Yoplait, 6 oz	180	1.5	1	10	105	33	0
Raspberry, fat free, fruit on the bottom, Yoplait, 6 oz	160	0	0	<5	105	33	0
Raspberry, lowfat, fruit on the bottom, Dannon, 8 oz	240	3	1.5	15	150	45	1
Raspberry, nonfat, Dannon, 6 oz	160	0	0	<5	100	32	0
Raspberry, nonfat, Dannon Light, 8 oz	100	0	0	<5	150	18	0
Raspberry, red, Light N' Lively Free 70 Calories, 6 oz	70	0	0	<5	80	11	0
Raspberry, red, lowfat, Breyers, 8 oz	250	2.5	1.5	15	110	48	2
Raspberry, red, nonfat, Knudsen Cal 70, 6 oz	70	0	0	5	75	11	0
Raspberry, red, nonfat, Knudsen Free, 6 oz	160	0	0	5	105	31	0
Raspberry, red, nonfat, Light N' Lively, 6 oz	180	0	0	5	105	36	0
Raspberry, wild, lowfat, Dannon Danimals, 4.4 oz	130	2	1	10	80	22	0
Raspberry, with granola, Light, Yoplait, 7 oz	130	1	0	<5	115	25	4
Raspberry, with granola, nonfat, Dannon Light 'N Crunchy, 8 oz	150	0	0	<5	135	17	0
Strawberry, Friendship Fruit Crunch, 1 container	190	4.5	1.5	10	125	31	0
Strawberry, Weight Watchers Ultimate 90, 1 cup	90	0	0	5	140	14	2
Strawberry, 99% fat free, Yoplait, 6 oz	180	1.5	1	10	105	33	0
Strawberry, fat free, fruit on the bottom, Yoplait, 6 oz	160	0	0	<5	105	33	0
Strawberry, lowfat, Breyers, 8 oz	250	2.5	1.5	15	110	47	0
Strawberry, lowfat, Dannon Danimals, 4.4 oz	140	2	1	10	85	24	0
Strawberry, lowfat, Dannon Sprinkl'ins, 4.1 oz	140	2.5	1.5	10	95	24	0

YOGURT	CAL (g)	FAT (g)	SAT FAT (g)	CHOL (mg)	SODIUM (mg)	CARB (g)	FIBER (g)
Strawberry, lowfat, fruit on the bottom, Dannon, 8 oz	240	3	1.5	15	135	46	1
Strawberry, nonfat, Dannon, 6 oz	150	0	0	<5	105	31	0
Strawberry, nonfat, Dannon Light, 8 oz	100	0	0	<5	140	18	0
Strawberry, nonfat, Dannon Tropifruta, 6 oz	150	0	0	5	105	31	0
Strawberry, nonfat, Knudsen Cal 70, 6 oz	70	0	0	5	85	11	0
Strawberry, nonfat, Knudsen Free, 6 oz	160	0	0	5	105	32	0
Strawberry, nonfat, Light N' Lively, 6 oz	180	0	0	5	105	36	0
Strawberry, nonfat, Light N' Lively Free 70 Calories, 6 oz	70	0	0	<5	85	11	0
Strawberry, with cereal nuggets, Yoplait, 7 oz	200	0.5	0	<5	160	42	2
Strawberry, with granola, Yoplait, 7 oz	220	1.5	0	<5	115	42	<1
Strawberry, with granola, light, Yoplait, 7 oz	130	1	0	<5	115	25	4
Strawberry banana, Weight Watchers Ultimate 90, 1 cup	90	0	0	5	140	14	2
Strawberry banana, 99% fat free, Yoplait, 6 oz	180	1.5	1	10	105	33	0
Strawberry banana, fat free, fruit on the bottom, Yoplait, 6 oz	160	0	0	<5	105	33	0
Strawberry banana, lowfat, Yoplait, 6 oz	200	2	1	10	115	41	2
Strawberry banana, lowfat, Breyers, 8 oz	250	2.5	1.5	15	115	50	<1
Strawberry banana, lowfat, Dannon Sprinkl'ins, 4.1 oz	140	2.5	1.5	10	95	24	0
Strawberry banana, lowfat, fruit on the bottom, Dannon, 8 oz	240	3	1.5	15	140	43	1
Strawberry banana, nonfat, Dannon, 6 oz	150	0	0	<5	105	31	0

YOGURT	CAL (g)	FAT (g)	SAT FAT (g)	CHOL (mg)	SODIUM (mg)	CARB (g)	FIBER (g)
Strawberry banana, nonfat, Dannon Light, 8 oz	100	0	0	<5	140	18	0
Strawberry banana, nonfat, Dannon Tropifruta, 6 oz	150	0	0	5	105	31	0
Strawberry banana, nonfat, Knudsen Cal 70, 6 oz	70	0	0	5	85	11	0
Strawberry banana, nonfat, Light N' Lively Free 70 Calories, 6 oz	70	0	0	<5	85	11	0
Strawberry fruit basket, nonfat, Knudsen Cal 70, 6 oz	70	0	0	5	90	11	0
Strawberry fruit cup, nonfat, Dannon Light, 8 oz	100	0	0	<5	140	18	0
Strawberry fruit cup, nonfat, Light N' Lively, 6 oz	170	0	0	5	105	35	0
Strawberry fruit cup, nonfat, Light N' Lively Free 70 Calories, 6 oz	70	0	0	<5	80	11	0
Strawberry-kiwi, nonfat, Dannon Tropifruta, 6 oz	150	0	0	5	105	30	0
Sundae style, all flavors, 1.5% lowfat, fruit on the bottom, Meadow Gold, 1 container	220	3.5	2	15	120	40	0
Swiss style, all flavors, 2% lowfat, Viva, 1 container	200	3	2	15	120	36	0
Swiss style, all flavors, fat free, Borden/Meadow Gold/Viva, 1 container	100	0	0	5	105	17	0
Trix, all flavors, Yoplait, 6 oz	180	3	1.5	10	110	30	0
Tropical fruit, lowfat, Yoplait, 6 oz	210	2.5	1	10	125	42	2
Tropical fruit, nonfat, Dannon Light, 8 oz	100	0	0	<5	140	19	0
Tropical punch, lowfat, Dannon Danimals, 4.4 oz	140	2	1	10	85	25	0
Vanilla, Weight Watchers Ultimate 90, 1 cup	90	0	0	5	140	14	0
Vanilla, 1.5% lowfat, Meadow Gold, 1 container	190	3.5	2	20	135	30	0
Vanilla, 99% fat free, Yoplait, 6 oz	170	2	1	10	140	30	0

YOGURT	CAL	FAT (g)	SAT FAT (g)	CHOL (mg)	SODIUM (mg)	CARB (g)	FIBER (g)
Vanilla, extra creamy, nonfat, Yoplait, 1 cup	210	0	0	10	160	41	0
Vanilla, lowfat, Breyers, 8 oz	220	3	2	20	135	38	0
Vanilla, lowfat, Dannon, 8 oz	210	3	2	15	160	36	0
Vanilla, lowfat, Dannon Danimals, 4.4 oz	140	2	1	10	80	24	0
Vanilla, nonfat, Dannon Light, 8 oz	100	0	0	<5	140	17	0
Vanilla, nonfat, Knudsen Cal 70, 6 oz	70	0	0	5	80	11	0
Vanilla, nonfat, Knudsen Free, 6 oz	170	0	0	5	100	32	0
Vanilla, nonfat, Light N' Lively, 6 oz	160	0	0	5	105	32	0
Vanilla, with chocolate, nonfat, Dannon Light 'N Crunchy, 8 oz	150	0	0	<5	170	26	1
Vanilla, with chocolate crunchies, Yoplait, 7 oz	220	1.5	0.5	<5	180	42	<1
Vanilla, with chocolate grahams, lowfat, Dannon Sprinkl'ins Crazy Crunch, 4.4 oz	160	2.5	1.5	10	140	29	0
Vanilla, with granola, Yoplait, 7 oz	220	1.5	0	<5	120	42	<1
Vanilla, with honey grahams, lowfat, Dannon Sprinkl'ins Crazy Crunch, 4.4 oz.	170	3	1.5	10	135	30	0
Vanilla, with peach or apricot topping, lowfat, Dannon Double Delights, 6 oz	170	2.5	1.5	10	90	30	0
Vanilla, with strawberry topping, lowfat, Dannon Double Delights, 6 oz	170	2.5	1.5	10	90	30	1
Yoplait Light, all fruit flavors, 6 oz	90	0	0	<5	85	16	0

AT A GLANCE: YOGURT

Choose from among the dozens of fat free yogurts from Dannon, Knudsen, Light N' Lively, SnackWells, Weight Watchers, and Yoplait, many with 100 calories or less.

Highest in Fiber: Yoplait Raspberry with Granola and Yoplait Strawberry with Granola

DELI & PACKAGED MEATS

	CAL (g)	FAT (g)	SAT FAT (g)	CHOL (mg)	SODIUM (mg)	CARB (g)	FIBER (g)
BACON							

Nutrient values are for cooked bacon, except where noted.

	CAL (g)	FAT (g)	SAT FAT (g)	CHOL (mg)	SODIUM (mg)	CARB (g)	FIBER (g)
Hormel Black Label/Hormel Red Label, 2 slices	80	7	2.5	15	330	0	0
Hormel Layout Pack, 2 slices	80	7	2.5	15	330	0	0
Hormel Old Smokehouse, slices	80	7	2.5	15	280	0	0
Hormel Range Brand, 2 slices	100	9	3.5	20	460	0	0
Oscar Mayer, 2 slices	60	5	1.5	10	250	0	0
⅛" thick cut, Oscar Mayer, slice	60	5	1.5	10	250	0	0
bulk deli, Hormel Red Label/Hormel Black Label, 2 slices	80	7	2.5	15	330	0	0
Canadian style, Hormel, 2 oz	70	3	1.5	30	610	0	0
Canadian-style, Oscar Mayer, slices	50	2	1	25	600	0	0
center cut, Hormel Black Label, 3 slices	70	6	2.5	15	240	0	0
center cut, Oscar Mayer, slices	90	7	2.5	20	380	0	0
low salt, Hormel Black Label, slices	80	7	2.5	15	210	0	0
low salt, Hormel Layout Pack, slices	80	7	2.5	15	210	0	0
lower sodium, Oscar Mayer, slices	60	4	1.5	10	170	0	0
microwave, Hormel, slices	70	5	2	15	230	0	0
precooked, Hormel Fast 'N Easy, 2 slices	80	7	2.5	15	290	0	0
turkey, Louis Rich, 1 slice	30	2.5	0.5	10	190	0	0
turkey, smoked, Butterball, slices	70	5	1.5	20	360	1	0

BACON	CAL (g)	FAT (g)	SAT FAT (g)	CHOL (mg)	SODIUM (mg)	CARB (g)	FIBER (g)
Wide shingle, Hormel Old Smokehouse, 2 slices	80	7	2.5	15	280	0	0
Wide shingle, raw, Hormel Griddlemaster, 2 slices	140	14	6	20	190	1	0

AT A GLANCE: BACON
Lowest in Fat: Oscar Mayer Canadian-style Bacon
Lowest in Sat Fat: Louis Rich Turkey Bacon
Lowest in Cholesterol: Louis Rich Turkey Bacon
Lowest in Sodium: Oscar Mayer Bacon, Low Sodium

BACON ALTERNATIVES

	CAL (g)	FAT (g)	SAT FAT (g)	CHOL (mg)	SODIUM (mg)	CARB (g)	FIBER (g)
Bacon, meatless, smoked, Worthington Stripples, 2 strips	60	5	0.5	0	260	2	0
Canadian bacon, meatless, Yves Veggie Cuisine, 3 slices	80	0	0	0	550	3	<1

BREAKFAST SAUSAGE

Nutrient values are for cooked sausage, except where noted.

	CAL (g)	FAT (g)	SAT FAT (g)	CHOL (mg)	SODIUM (mg)	CARB (g)	FIBER (g)
Apple cinnamon sausage, links, Johnsonville, 3 links	200	18	6	40	600	1	ns
Beef sausage, links, fully cooked, Swift Premium Brown 'N Serve, 3 links	260	25	10	45	440	1	0
Beef sausage, patty, fully cooked, Swift Premium Brown 'N Serve, 2 patties	210	21	9	40	370	1	0
Browned sausage, mild, links, fully cooked, Jones Golden Brown, 2 links	190	18	6	35	300	1	ns
Browned sausage, patty, fully cooked, Jones Golden Brown, 1 patty	150	14	5	30	240	1	ns
Browned sausage & rice, links, fully cooked, Jones Golden Brown, 2 links	110	9	3	30	230	1	ns
Country sausage, original or maple syrup, links, fresh, Johnsonville, 3 links	200	18	6	40	600	1	ns
Maple sausage, links, fully cooked, Swift Premium Brown 'N Serve, 2 links	140	12	4.5	35	300	1	0

BREAKFAST SAUSAGE	CAL (g)	FAT (g)	SAT FAT (g)	CHOL (mg)	SODIUM (mg)	CARB (g)	FIBER (g)
Original sausage, links, fully cooked, lite, Swift Premium Brown 'N Serve, 3 links	120	8	3	45	410	3	0
Original sausage, links, prebrowned, Swift Premium Brown 'N Serve, 2 links	140	12	4.5	35	300	1	0
Original sausage, patties, fully cooked, Swift Premium Brown 'N Serve, 2 patties	150	12	5	40	340	2	0
Pork sausage, Cantipalos, 2 oz	130	10	3.5	40	550	1	1
Pork sausage, Corte's Linguica, 2 oz	160	12	4	45	700	1	1
Pork sausage, hot, Corte's Chourico, 2 oz	160	11	4	40	670	1	1
Pork sausage, links, Hormel Little Sizzlers, 3 links	210	20	7	45	570	0	0
Pork sausage, links, Hormel Special Recipe, 2 links	110	10	4	20	210	1	0
Pork sausage, links, Oscar Mayer, 2 links	170	15	5	40	410	1	0
Pork sausage, links, brown 'n serve, Hormel Little Sizzlers, 8 links	230	22	8	45	670	1	0
Pork sausage, original recipe, mild, Bob Evans Farms, 2 oz	210	19	7	25	440	0	0
Pork sausage, patties, Hormel Little Sizzlers, 2 patties	250	23	8	50	680	0	0
Pork sausage, patties, Hormel Special Recipe, 2 patties	110	10	4	20	210	1	0
Pork sausage, patties, brown 'n serve, Hormel Little Sizzlers, 2 patties	190	18	6	40	560	1	0
Pork sausage, patties, Bob Evans Farms, 2 patties	210	19	6	20	450	1	0
Pork sausage, regular or hot, fresh, Jimmy Dean, 2 oz	250	24	8	50	540	0	ns
Pork sausage, regular or hot, fully cooked, links, Jimmy Dean Heat 'N Serve, 3 links	200	19	6	45	430	0	ns
Pork sausage, ring, Mentejana, 2 oz	160	11	4	45	700	1	1

BREAKFAST SAUSAGE	CAL	FAT (g)	SAT FAT (g)	CHOL (mg)	SODIUM (mg)	CARB (g)	FIBER (g)
Pork sausage, sage, fresh, Jimmy Dean, 2 oz	250	24	8	50	540	0	ns
Pork sausage, zesty hot, Bob Evans Farms, 2 oz	230	20	7	20	480	0	0
Pork sausage & rice, links, fresh, Jones, 2 links	130	11	4	20	420	1	ns
Sausage biscuits, Jimmy Dean, 2 sandwiches	330	21	7	30	910	25	2
Turkey sausage, hot or original, Louis Rich, 2.5 oz	120	8	2.5	55	430	1	0
Turkey sausage, links, Louis Rich, 2 links	90	6	1.5	45	470	0	0
Turkey sausage, links, fully cooked, Swift Premium Brown 'N Serve, 3 links	140	11	3	50	370	1	0
Turkey sausage, links, hot or mild, The Turkey Store, 2 oz	80	6	1.5	15	200	0	ns
Turkey sausage, patties, hot, The Turkey Store, 2.3 oz	90	7	2	20	230	0	ns
Turkey sausage, patties, mild, The Turkey Store, 2.3 oz	90	7	2	20	240	0	ns
Turkey & pork sausage, fresh, lite, Jimmy Dean, 2.5 oz	180	14	1	55	500	0	ns

AT A GLANCE: BREAKFAST SAUSAGE

Lowest in Fat: Louis Rich Turkey Sausage, Links; The Turkey Store Turkey Sausage, Links
Lowest in Sat Fat: Jimmy Dean Turkey & Pork Sausage, Links
Lowest in Cholesterol and Sodium: The Turkey Store Turkey Sausage, Links

BREAKFAST SAUSAGE ALTERNATIVES

See also Canned & Bottled Foods, Meat & Poultry Alternatives.

	CAL	FAT (g)	SAT FAT (g)	CHOL (mg)	SODIUM (mg)	CARB (g)	FIBER (g)
Sausage, meatless, links, frozen, Green Giant Harvest Burgers, 3 links	110	5	0.5	0	340	5	4
Sausage, meatless, links, frozen, Worthington Prosage, 2 links	120	9	1.5	0	290	2	2
Sausage, meatless, lowfat, frozen, GardenSausage, 2.5 oz	240	2.5	0.5	5	160	45	4
Sausage, meatless, patties, frozen, Green Giant, 2 patties	100	4	0.5	0	280	5	3

BREAKFAST SAUSAGE ALTERNATIVES	CAL (g)	FAT (g)	SAT FAT (g)	CHOL (mg)	SODIUM (mg)	CARB (g)	FIBER (g)
Sausage, meatless, patties, frozen, Worthington Prosage, 1 pattie	100	7	2	0	370	1	1
Sausage, meatless, roll, frozen, Worthington Prosage, ⅝" slice	140	10	2	0	390	2	2

FRANKFURTERS

See also Sausage in this chapter.

	CAL (g)	FAT (g)	SAT FAT (g)	CHOL (mg)	SODIUM (mg)	CARB (g)	FIBER (g)
Beef, Ball Park, 1 frank	180	16	7	35	670	2	0
Beef, Healthy Choice, 1 frank	60	1.5	0.5	20	480	5	0
Beef, Hebrew National, 1 frank	150	14	5	30	370	1	0
Beef, Oscar Mayer, 1 frank	140	13	6	25	450	1	0
Beef, Bun-Length brand, Oscar Mayer, 1 frank	190	17	7	35	570	2	0
Beef, deli style, Oscar Mayer Big & Juicy, 1 frank	230	22	10	50	680	1	0
Beef, jumbo, Ekrich, 1 frank	200	17	8	30	510	5	0
Beef, light, Oscar Mayer, 1 frank	110	9	3.5	25	620	2	0
Beef, original, Oscar Mayer Big & Juicy, 1 frank	240	22	9	45	700	1	0
Beef, quarter pound, Oscar Mayer Big & Juicy, 1 frank	350	33	13	65	1050	2	0
Beef, reduced fat, lite, Hebrew National, 1 frank	120	10	4	25	350	1	0
Beef cocktail, Hebrew National, 1 frank	160	15	na	35	410	0	0
Beef dinner, Hebrew National, 1 frank	350	34	12	75	890	1	0
Beef knocks, Hebrew National, 1 frank	260	25	9	55	670	1	0
Bun-Length brand, made with turkey & chicken, Louis Rich, 1 frank	110	8	2.5	50	630	3	0
Bunsize, Ball Park, 1 frank	180	16	6	40	660	2	0
Bunsize, Healthy Choice, 1 frank	70	1.5	0.5	20	590	5	0

FRANKFURTERS	CAL	FAT (g)	SAT FAT (g)	CHOL (mg)	SODIUM (mg)	CARB (g)	FIBER (g)
Cheese, made with turkey & chicken, Louis Rich, 1 frank	90	7	2.5	40	420	2	0
Chicken, Wampler-Longacre, 1 frank	120	11	3	60	480	0	0
Corn dogs, Ball Park, 1 frank	220	13	3	20	840	21	1
Fat free, Ball Park, 1 frank	40	0	0	15	560	4	0
Fat free, Ekrich, 1 frank	50	0	0	15	550	5	0
Franks, Healthy Choice, 1 frank	50	1.5	0.5	20	420	4	0
Fun franks, Ball Park, 2 franks	350	21	6	45	900	29	3
Hot dogs, cheese, made with pork, turkey & beef, Oscar Mayer, 1 hot dog	140	13	5	35	520	1	0
Hot dogs, Spanish, Corte's, 1 hot dog	220	18	6	50	880	2	2
Hot dogs, turkey & beef, fat free, Oscar Mayer, 1 hot dog	40	0	0	15	460	2	0
Jumbo, Ekrich, 1 frank	190	17	6	40	520	2	0
Jumbo, Healthy Choice, 1 frank	70	1.5	0.5	30	530	5	0
Turkey, Butterball, 1 frank	45	0	0	15	480	4	0
Turkey, Wampler-Longacre, 1 frank	90	8	2.5	35	430	0	2
Turkey & chicken, 8-count pkg, Louis Rich, 1 frank	80	6	2	40	480	1	0
Turkey & chicken, 10-count pkg, Louis Rich, 1 frank	80	6	2	40	500	1	0
Wieners, Bun-Length brand, pork & turkey, Oscar Mayer, 1 link	190	17	6	35	570	1	0
Wieners, hot 'n spicy, Oscar Mayer Big & Juicy, 1 link	220	20	8	45	750	1	0
Wieners, light, pork, turkey & beef, Oscar Mayer, 1 link	110	9	3	35	590	1	0
Wieners, little, Oscar Mayer, 6 links	180	17	6	30	610	1	0
Wieners, original, Oscar Mayer Big & Juicy, 1 link	240	22	9	45	690	1	0
Wieners, pork & turkey, Oscar Mayer, 1 link	150	13	4.5	30	450	1	0

FRANKFURTERS	CAL (g)	FAT (g)	SAT FAT (g)	CHOL (mg)	SODIUM (mg)	CARB (g)	FIBER (g)
Wieners, smokie links, Oscar Mayer Big & Juicy, 1 link	220	19	7	50	770	1	0

AT A GLANCE: FRANKS
Lowest in Fat: Ball Park Franks, Fat Free; Ekrich Franks, Fat Free; Oscar Mayer Hot Dogs, Fat Free; Butterball Turkey Franks
Lowest in Sodium: Hebrew National Beef Franks, Reduced Fat, Lite

FRANKFURTER ALTERNATIVES

	CAL (g)	FAT (g)	SAT FAT (g)	CHOL (mg)	SODIUM (mg)	CARB (g)	FIBER (g)
Corn dogs, meatless, frozen, Loma Linda, 1 dog	200	9	1.5	0	240	18	3
Hot dogs, meatless, Lightlife Wonderdogs, 1 link	55	1	0	0	170	1	0
Hot dogs, meatless, Yves Veggie Cuisine, 1 link	60	0	0	0	350	4	1
Hot dogs, meatless, frozen, GardenDog, 1 link	90	2	0.5	0	250	4	1
Hot dogs, meatless, frozen, Worthington Leanies, 1 link	110	8	1.5	0	430	2	1
Smart Dogs, fat free, Lightlife, 1 link	45	0	0	0	170	1	0

LUNCHEON MEATS

	CAL (g)	FAT (g)	SAT FAT (g)	CHOL (mg)	SODIUM (mg)	CARB (g)	FIBER (g)
Beef, Buddig, 1 pkg	100	5	2	50	1020	<1	ns
Beef, cured, oven roasted, Hillshire Farm Deli Select, 6 slices	50	0.5	0	25	570	1	ns
Bologna, beef, Healthy Choice, 1 slice	35	1	0	10	280	3	0
Bologna, beef, Hebrew National, 2 oz	180	16	na	40	440	0	0
Bologna, beef, Oscar Mayer, 1 slice	90	8	4	15	300	1	0
Bologna, beef, light, Oscar Mayer, 1 slice	60	4	1.5	10	310	2	0
Bologna, beef, reduced fat/lite, Hebrew National, 2 oz	130	12	na	35	320	0	0
Bologna, garlic, pork, chicken beef, Oscar Mayer, 1 slice	130	12	4.5	30	400	1	0
Bologna, lean, Hebrew National, 2 oz	90	6	na	25	430	0	0

LUNCHEON MEATS	CAL (g)	FAT (g)	SAT FAT (g)	CHOL (mg)	SODIUM (mg)	CARB (g)	FIBER (g)
Bologna, Lebanon, beef, 1 oz	60	4	2	20	380	<1	0
Bologna, pork, chicken & beef, Oscar Mayer, 1 slice	90	8	3	20	270	0	0
Bologna, pork, chicken & beef, light, Oscar Mayer, 1 slice	50	4	1.5	15	310	1	0
Bologna, turkey, Louis Rich, 1 slice	50	4	1	20	250	1	0
Bologna, turkey, beef & pork, fat free, Oscar Mayer, 2 slices	35	0	0	15	480	2	0
Bologna, turkey, pork & beef, Healthy Choice, 1 slice	30	1	0	15	290	1	0
Bologna, turkey, pork & beef, Healthy Choice Deli Thin Sliced, 4 slices	60	1.5	0.5	30	580	3	0
Chicken, oven roasted, deli thin, National Foods, 5 slices	45	0.5	0	20	460	0	0
Chicken, white, oven roasted, Louis Rich, 1 slice	40	2.5	0.5	15	350	1	0
Chicken breast, honey glazed, Oscar Mayer Deli-Thin, 4 slices	60	1	0	25	740	2	0
Chicken breast, oven roasted, Butterball Sliced Deli, 6 slices	50	0	0	25	480	2	0
Chicken breast, oven roasted, Healthy Choice, 1 slice	35	1	0.5	15	310	0	0
Chicken breast, oven roasted, Healthy Choice Deli Thin Sliced, 6 slices	50	0	0	25	480	2	0
Chicken breast, oven roasted, Healthy Choice Fresh-Trak, 1 slice	30	1	0	15	290	0	0
Chicken breast, oven roasted, Hillshire Farm Deli Select, 6 slices	50	0	0	15	690	1	ns
Chicken breast, oven roasted, Louis Rich, 1 slice	30	1	0	15	330	1	0

LUNCHEON MEATS	CAL (g)	FAT (g)	SAT FAT (g)	CHOL (mg)	SODIUM (mg)	CARB (g)	FIBER (g)
Chicken breast, oven roasted, Louis Rich Deli-Thin, 4 slices	60	1.5	0.5	25	620	1	0
Chicken breast, oven roasted, fat free, Oscar Mayer, 4 slices	45	0	0	25	650	1	0
Chicken breast, skinless, bulk deli, Healthy Choice, 2 oz	45	0	0	25	460	0	0
Chicken breast, smoked, Healthy Choice, 1 slice	35	1	0	15	220	0	0
Chicken breast, smoked, Healthy Choice Deli Thin Sliced, 6 slices	60	1.5	0.5	25	400	1	0
Corned beef, Buddig, 1 pkg	100	5	2	50	950	<1	ns
Corned beef, Healthy Choice Deli Thin Sliced, 6 slices	60	1.5	0.5	25	470	1	0
Corned beef, Hillshire Farm Deli Select, 6 slices	60	1	0	15	590	1	ns
Corned beef, bulk deli, Healthy Choice, 2 oz	60	1.5	1	30	460	0	0
Dutch brand loaf, 1 oz	70	5	2	15	350	2	0
Ham, Buddig, 1 pkg	120	7	2.5	50	980	<1	ns
Ham, Healthy Choice Deli Thin Sliced, 6 slices	60	1.5	0.5	25	500	1	0
Ham, Healthy Choice Fresh-Trak, 1 slice	30	1	0	10	250	1	0
Ham, baked, Healthy Choice, slices	70	2	0.5	30	580	1	0
Ham, baked, Healthy Choice Deli Thin Sliced, 6 slices	60	1.5	0.5	30	520	2	0
Ham, baked, Oscar Mayer, slices	60	1	0.5	30	720	2	0
Ham, baked, Oscar Mayer Healthy Favorites, 4 slices	50	1	0	25	600	1	0
Ham, boiled, Oscar Mayer, slices	60	2.5	1	30	820	0	0
Ham, boiled, Oscar Mayer Deli-Thin, 4 slices	50	2	0.5	25	680	0	0
Ham, brown sugar baked, Hillshire Farm Deli Select, slices	60	1.5	0.5	20	570	2	ns

LUNCHEON MEATS	CAL (g)	FAT (g)	SAT FAT (g)	CHOL (mg)	SODIUM (mg)	CARB (g)	FIBER (g)
Ham, bulk deli, Healthy Choice, 2 oz	60	1.5	0.5	25	460	1	0
Ham, chopped, Oscar Mayer, 1 slice	45	3	1	15	340	1	0
Ham, honey, Buddig, 1 pkg	120	7	2.5	50	760	3	ns
Ham, honey, Buddig Lean Slices, 1 pkg	90	2	1	35	850	4	ns
Ham, honey, Healthy Choice, 1 slice	30	1	0.5	15	250	1	0
Ham, honey, Healthy Choice Deli Thin Sliced, 6 slices	60	1.5	0.5	30	500	2	0
Ham, honey, Healthy Choice Fresh-Trak, 1 slice	30	1	0	15	250	1	0
Ham, honey, Hillshire Farm Deli Select, 6 slices	60	1.5	0	20	600	2	ns
Ham, honey, Oscar Mayer, 3 slices	70	2.5	1	30	760	2	0
Ham, honey, Oscar Mayer Deli-Thin, 4 slices	60	2	0.5	25	630	2	0
Ham, honey, Oscar Mayer Healthy Favorites, 4 slices	50	1.5	0.5	25	630	2	0
Ham, honey, bulk deli, Healthy Choice, 2 oz	60	1.5	0.5	25	580	2	0
Ham, honey glazed with natural juices, thin carved, Louis Rich Carving Board, 6 slices	70	2	1	35	760	2	0
Ham, honey glazed with natural juices, traditional carved, Louis Rich Carving Board, 2 slices	50	1.5	0.5	25	530	1	0
Ham, lower sodium, Oscar Mayer, 3 slices	70	2.5	1	30	520	2	0
Ham, minced, 1 oz	70	6	2	20	350	<1	0
Ham, smoked, Buddig Lean Slices, 1 pkg	80	2	1	35	850	1	ns
Ham, smoked, Healthy Choice, 3 slices	70	2	0.5	30	560	1	0
Ham, smoked, Healthy Choice Deli Thin Sliced, 6 slices	60	1.5	0.5	25	500	1	0

LUNCHEON MEATS	CAL (g)	FAT (g)	SAT FAT (g)	CHOL (mg)	SODIUM (mg)	CARB (g)	FIBER (g)
Ham, smoked, Hillshire Farm Deli Select, 6 slices	60	1.5	0	20	580	1	ns
Ham, smoked, Oscar Mayer, 3 slices	60	2.5	1	30	750	0	0
Ham, smoked, Oscar Mayer Deli-Thin, 4 slices	50	2	0.5	25	620	0	0
Ham, smoked, Oscar Mayer Healthy Favorites, 4 slices	50	1.5	0.5	25	620	0	0
Ham, smoked, bulk deli, Healthy Choice, 2 oz	60	1.5	1	30	390	1	0
Ham, smoked, with natural juices, Louis Rich Carving Board, 2 slices	50	1.5	0.5	25	560	0	0
Ham, turkey, Healthy Choice, 1 slice	30	1	0.5	20	250	0	0
Ham, turkey, Louis Rich Deli-Thin, 4 slices	60	1.5	0.5	35	580	0	0
Ham, turkey, chopped, Louis Rich, 1 slice	45	2.5	1	20	300	0	0
Ham, turkey, honey cured, Louis Rich, 3 slices	70	2	0.5	45	660	2	0
Ham, turkey, round, Louis Rich, 1 slice	35	1	0	20	300	0	0
Ham, turkey, square, Louis Rich, 3 slices	70	2.5	0.5	45	710	1	0
Ham, turkey, thin sliced, Healthy Choice, 6 slices	60	1.5	0.5	40	500	1	0
Ham, Virginia brand, bulk deli, Healthy Choice, 2 oz	60	1.5	0.5	25	510	1	0
Ham & cheese loaf, Oscar Mayer, 1 slice	70	5	2.5	20	350	1	0
Ham & Swiss, twin-pack, Eagle, 1 oz	100	7	4	20	380	2	0
Head cheese, Oscar Mayer, 1 slice	50	4	1.5	25	360	0	0
Honey loaf, Oscar Mayer, 1 slice	35	1	0	15	380	1	0
Liver cheese, pork fat wrapped, Oscar Mayer, 1 slice	120	10	4	80	420	1	0
Liverwurst spread, Hormel, 4 Tbsp	130	10	3.5	70	650	2	0

LUNCHEON MEATS	CAL	FAT (g)	SAT FAT (g)	CHOL (mg)	SODIUM (mg)	CARB (g)	FIBER (g)
Lunch 'N Munch, bologna, American, Snickers, Hi-C, Hillshire Farm, 1 pkg	590	31	14	50	1270	64	1
Lunch 'N Munch, honey ham, cheddar, Snickers, Hi-C, Hillshire Farm, 1 pkg	520	22	11	50	1200	62	1
Lunch 'N Munch, smoked turkey, cheddar, with brownie, Hi-C, Hillshire Farm, 1 pkg	590	31	14	50	1270	64	1
Lunchables, bologna & Kraft American, Oscar Mayer, 1 pkg	470	35	16	85	1580	22	<1
Lunchables, bologna & wild cherry drink, Oscar Mayer, 1 pkg	530	28	13	60	1120	60	<1
Lunchables, ham & Kraft cheddar, Oscar Mayer, 1 pkg	360	21	11	75	1760	21	<1
Lunchables, ham & Kraft Swiss, Oscar Mayer, 1 pkg	340	20	10	70	1790	20	<1
Lunchables, ham, with fruit punch, Oscar Mayer, 1 pkg	440	20	9	50	1270	54	<1
Lunchables, ham, with fruit punch, low fat, Oscar Mayer, 1 pkg	360	10	4.5	35	1150	52	0
Lunchables, ham, with Surfer Cooler, low fat, Oscar Mayer, 1 pkg	380	10	4.5	35	1380	57	<1
Lunchables, pizza, with Kraft mozzarella & cheddar, Oscar Mayer, 1 pkg	330	14	8	35	870	33	2
Lunchables, pizza, with Kraft mozzarella & fruit punch, Oscar Mayer, 1 pkg	480	17	10	35	900	65	2
Lunchables, pizza, with pepperoni & Kraft mozzarella, Oscar Mayer, 1 pkg	330	15	7	35	850	32	2
Lunchables, pizza, with pepperoni & orange drink, Oscar Mayer, 1 pkg	480	17	8	35	900	65	2
Lunchables, salami & American, Oscar Mayer, 1 pkg	420	29	14	80	1690	21	<1

LUNCHEON MEATS	CAL (g)	FAT (g)	SAT FAT (g)	CHOL (mg)	SODIUM (mg)	CARB (g)	FIBER (g)
Lunchables, turkey & Kraft cheddar, Oscar Mayer, 1 pkg	350	20	11	70	1750	22	1
Lunchables, turkey & Kraft Monterey Jack, Oscar Mayer, 1 pkg	350	21	11	75	1700	19	1
Lunchables, turkey & Pacific Cooler, Oscar Mayer, 1 pkg	450	20	10	50	1330	53	1
Lunchables, turkey & Pacific Cooler, low fat, Oscar Mayer, 1 pkg	360	9	4	30	1280	55	<1
Lunchables, turkey & Surfer Cooler, Oscar Mayer, 1 pkg	430	15	8	45	1240	61	0
Luncheon loaf, spiced, Oscar Mayer, 1 slice	70	5	1.5	20	340	2	0
Luxury loaf, pork, 1 oz	40	1.5	0	10	350	1	0
Mother's loaf, 1 oz	80	6	2.5	15	320	2	0
Old fashioned loaf, Oscar Mayer, 1 slice	60	5	1.5	15	340	2	0
Olive loaf, Oscar Mayer, 1 slice	70	5	1.5	20	370	2	0
Peppered loaf, 1 oz	40	2	1	15	430	1	0
Pickle & pimiento loaf, Oscar Mayer, 1 slice	70	6	2	20	360	2	0
Picnic loaf, 1 oz	70	5	2	10	330	1	0
Roast beef, Healthy Choice Deli Thin Sliced, 6 slices	60	1.5	0.5	25	520	1	0
Roast beef, Healthy Choice Fresh-Trak, 1 slice	30	1	0	10	260	0	0
Roast beef, Oscar Mayer Deli-Thin, 4 slices	60	1.5	0.5	25	530	1	0
Roast beef, bulk deli, Healthy Choice, 2 oz	60	1.5	1	25	450	1	0
Roast beef, bulk deli, Hormel, 2 oz	60	2	1	30	620	0	0
Roast beef, bulk deli, Hormel Light & Lean 97, 2 oz	60	2	1	25	600	0	0
Roast beef, with gravy, bulk deli, Hormel, 2 oz	60	2	1	30	280	1	0
Turkey, Buddig, 1 pkg	110	7	2.5	40	710	<1	ns

LUNCHEON MEATS	CAL	FAT (g)	SAT FAT (g)	CHOL (mg)	SODIUM (mg)	CARB (g)	FIBER (g)
Turkey, hickory smoked, deli thin, National Foods, 5 slices	55	0.5	0	25	310	0	0
Turkey, honey roasted, Buddig, 1 pkg	110	6	2	40	780	3	ns
Turkey, lemon garlic, deli thin, National Foods, 5 slices	50	0.5	0	20	400	0	0
Turkey, oven roasted, deli thin, National Foods, 5 slices	50	0.5	0	20	420	0	0
Turkey, white, smoked, Louis Rich, 1 slice	30	1	0	15	280	0	0
Turkey breast, bulk deli, Hormel Light & Lean 97, 2 oz	50	0.5	0	20	420	1	0
Turkey breast, bulk deli, Hormel Sandwich Maker, 2 oz	45	0.5	0	15	390	2	0
Turkey breast, hickory smoked, Louis Rich, 1 slice	25	0.5	0	10	260	0	0
Turkey breast, hickory smoked, Louis Rich Deli-Thin, 4 slices	50	1	0	20	560	1	0
Turkey breast, hickory smoked, fat free, Louis Rich, 1 slice	25	0	0	10	300	1	0
Turkey breast, honey, bulk deli, Hormel Light & Lean 97, 2 oz	50	0.5	0	20	530	1	0
Turkey breast, honey roasted, Louis Rich, 1 slice	30	1	0	10	320	1	0
Turkey breast, honey roasted & smoked, Butterball Sliced Deli, 6 slices	50	0	0	20	400	3	0
Turkey breast, honey roasted & smoked, Healthy Choice, 1 slice	35	1	0	15	220	1	0
Turkey breast, honey roasted & smoked, Healthy Choice Deli Thin Sliced, 6 slices	70	1.5	0.5	25	410	2	0
Turkey breast, honey roasted & smoked, Healthy Choice Fresh-Trak, 1 slice	35	1	0	10	200	1	0
Turkey breast, honey roasted & smoked, bulk deli, Healthy Choice, 2 oz	60	0	0	25	410	2	0

LUNCHEON MEATS	CAL (g)	FAT (g)	SAT FAT (g)	CHOL (mg)	SODIUM (mg)	CARB (g)	FIBER (g)
Turkey breast, no salt, bulk deli, Hormel, 2 oz	60	0.5	0	30	35	0	0
Turkey breast, oven roasted, Buddig Lean Slices, 1 pkg	70	1	0.5	30	980	1	ns
Turkey breast, oven roasted, Butterball Sliced Deli, 6 slices	50	0	0	20	480	2	0
Turkey breast, oven roasted, Healthy Choice, 1 slice	35	1	0	15	270	1	0
Turkey breast, oven roasted, Healthy Choice Deli Thin Sliced, 6 slices	60	1.5	0.5	20	480	2	0
Turkey breast, oven roasted, Healthy Choice Fresh-Trak, 1 slice	35	1	0	15	270	1	0
Turkey breast, oven roasted, Hillshire Farm Deli Select, 6 slices	50	0	0	5	620	2	ns
Turkey breast, oven roasted, Louis Rich, 1 slice	30	0.5	0	10	310	1	0
Turkey breast, oven roasted, Louis Rich Deli-Thin, 4 slices	50	1	0	20	580	2	0
Turkey breast, oven roasted, Oscar Mayer, 1 slice	25	0.5	0	10	310	1	0
Turkey breast, oven roasted, fat free, Louis Rich, 1 slice	25	0	0	10	310	1	0
Turkey breast, oven roasted, fat free, Oscar Mayer, 4 slices	40	0	0	15	610	2	0
Turkey breast, oven roasted, thin carved, Louis Rich Carving Board, 6 slices	60	0.5	0	25	740	0	0
Turkey breast, oven roasted, traditional carved, Louis Rich Carving Board, 2 slices	40	0.5	0	20	560	0	0
Turkey breast, peppered, Healthy Choice Deli Thin Sliced, 6 slices	60	1.5	0.5	25	480	1	0
Turkey breast, roasted, Oscar Mayer Deli-Thin, 4 slices	50	1	0	20	580	2	0
Turkey breast, skin-on, premium, bulk deli, Hormel, oz	50	1	0.5	25	460	0	0

LUNCHEON MEATS	CAL	FAT (g)	SAT FAT (g)	CHOL (mg)	SODIUM (mg)	CARB (g)	FIBER (g)
Turkey breast, smoked, Buddig Lean Slices, 1 pkg	70	1	0.5	30	880	1	ns
Turkey breast, smoked, Butterball Sliced Deli, 6 slices	50	0	0	25	400	1	0
Turkey breast, smoked, Healthy Choice, 1 slice	30	1	0	10	230	0	0
Turkey breast, smoked, Healthy Choice Deli Thin Sliced, 6 slices	60	1.5	0.5	25	420	1	0
Turkey breast, smoked, Hillshire Farm Deli Select, 6 slices	60	1	0	25	600	2	ns
Turkey breast, smoked, Louis Rich Carving Board, 2 slices	40	0.5	0	20	490	0	0
Turkey breast, smoked, fat free, Oscar Mayer, 4 slices	40	0	0	15	550	2	0
Turkey breast, smoked, honey roasted, Oscar Mayer Deli-Thin, 4 slices	60	1	0	20	520	2	0

AT A GLANCE: LUNCHEON MEATS

Lowest in Sodium: Hormel Turkey Breast, No Salt (bulk deli)

Choose products with less than 2 grams of fat and saturated fat. Fat free luncheon meats are available from Butterball, Healthy Choice, Hillshire Farm, Louis Rich, and Oscar Mayer.

LUNCHEON MEAT ALTERNATIVES

	CAL	FAT	SAT FAT	CHOL	SODIUM	CARB	FIBER
Beef, meatless, smoked, frozen, Worthington, ⅜" slice	120	6	1	0	700	5	3
Bologna, meatless, frozen, Worthington Bolono, ⅜" slice	80	3	0.5	0	690	2	2
Chicken, meatless, sliced, Worthington, 2 slices	80	4.5	1	0	370	1	<1
Corned beef, meatless, sliced, frozen, Worthington, 4 slices	140	9	2	0	520	5	2
Turkey, meatless, smoked, sliced, frozen, Worthington, ⅜" slice	140	10	2	0	600	3	2
Wham, meatless, slices, frozen, Worthington, ⅜" slice	100	6	1	0	520	2	0

	CAL (g)	FAT (g)	SAT FAT (g)	CHOL (mg)	SODIUM (mg)	CARB (g)	FIBER (g)

SAUSAGE

See also Canned & Bottled Foods, Meat & Poultry Alternatives.

	CAL (g)	FAT (g)	SAT FAT (g)	CHOL (mg)	SODIUM (mg)	CARB (g)	FIBER (g)
Beef, smoked, Hillshire Farm Flavorseal, 2 oz	190	17	8	40	460	1	ns
Berliner, 1 oz	70	5	2	15	370	<1	0
Blood sausage or blood pudding, 1 oz	110	10	4	35	190	0	0
Bockwurst, 1 oz	90	8	3	15	310	0	0
Bratwurst, cooked, Johnsonville, 1 link	250	22	8	50	770	2	ns
Bratwurst, fresh, Johnsonville, 1 link	300	27	10	70	800	1	ns
Bratwurst, fully cooked, link, Hillshire Farm, 1 link	230	21	10	45	460	0	0
Bratwurst, smoked, Johnsonville, 1 link	240	22	9	60	650	2	ns
Bratwurst, turkey, lean, The Turkey Store, 3 oz	160	10	3	45	530	2	ns
Bratwurst, with beer, fresh, Johnsonville Beer 'n Bratwurst, 1 link	300	27	10	70	800	1	ns
Braunschweiger, Hillshire Farm, 2 oz	180	16	9	80	360	3	0
Braunschweiger liver sausage, Oscar Mayer, 1 slice	100	9	3	50	320	1	0
Braunschweiger liver sausage, spread, Oscar Mayer, 2 oz	190	17	6	90	630	2	0
CheddarWurst, link, Hillshire Farm, 1 link	260	23	12	50	900	3	0
Chorizo, hot, Corte's Special, link	270	21	9	75	1060	1	ns
Chorizo, pork, Corte's Special, link	260	20	9	75	920	2	ns
Chorizo, pork & beef, Baturo, 1 link	210	17	6	45	630	3	2
Hot link, Hillshire Farm, link	250	23	11	35	620	3	0
Italian, fresh, 3 oz	270	22	8	65	780	1	0

SAUSAGE	CAL	FAT (g)	SAT FAT (g)	CHOL (mg)	SODIUM (mg)	CARB (g)	FIBER (g)
Italian, turkey, hot, The Turkey Store, 3 oz	140	9	2.5	45	680	2	ns
Italian, turkey, sweet, The Turkey Store, 3 oz	140	9	2.5	45	550	2	ns
Knockwurst, 1 oz	90	8	3	15	290	<1	0
Liverwurst, pork, 1 oz	90	8	3	45	240	<1	0
Morcilla (blood pudding), Corte's, 2 oz	200	15	6	50	710	8	2
Mortadella, 1 oz	90	7	3	15	350	<1	0
New England brand sausage, Oscar Mayer, 2 slices	60	2.5	1	25	570	1	0
Pastrami, bulk deli, Healthy Choice, 2 oz	60	1.5	0.5	30	500	1	0
Pastrami, deli, Hebrew National, 2 oz	80	3	na	30	510	0	0
Pastrami, turkey, Louis Rich, 2 oz	70	2	1	40	590	1	0
Pastrami, turkey, square, Louis Rich, 2 slices	45	1.5	0	30	520	0	0
Pepperoni, Hormel/Hormel Pillow Pack, 1 oz	140	13	6	35	470	0	0
Pepperoni, Oscar Mayer, 15 slices	140	13	5	25	550	0	0
Pickled sausage, smoked or hot, Hormel, 6 links	140	11	5	40	380	1	0
Polish, Hillshire Farm, 1 link	250	23	11	35	620	3	0
Polish, Johnsonville, 1 link	240	22	9	60	650	2	ns
Polish, beef, Hebrew National, 1 link	240	22	na	50	680	1	0
Polish, skinless, Thorn Apple Valley, 1 link	190	21	7	80	810	5	0
Polish, skinless, fully cooked, Thorn Apple Valley, 1 link	240	21	7	80	810	5	0
Polska kielbasa, Eckrich, 2 oz	180	17	7	40	460	1	0
Polska kielbasa, Healthy Choice, 2 oz	70	1.5	0.5	25	590	4	1
Polska kielbasa, Hillshire Farm Flavorseal, 2 oz	190	17	8	25	460	2	0
Polska kielbasa, turkey, Louis Rich, 2 oz	80	4.5	1.5	35	500	1	0

SAUSAGE	CAL (g)	FAT (g)	SAT FAT (g)	CHOL (mg)	SODIUM (mg)	CARB (g)	FIBER (g)
Salami, beef, Hebrew National, 2 oz	170	14	6	40	420	0	0
Salami, beef, Machiach brand, Oscar Mayer, 2 slices	120	10	5	30	510	1	0
Salami, beef, reduced fat, lite, Hebrew National, 2 oz	110	8	4	30	380	0	0
Salami, beer, beef, 1 oz	90	8	4	15	290	0	0
Salami, beer, pork, 1 oz	70	5	2	15	350	<1	0
Salami, cotto, beef, Oscar Mayer, 2 slices	90	7	3	35	590	1	0
Salami, cotto, beef, pork & chicken, Oscar Mayer, 2 slices	110	9	4	35	500	0	0
Salami, cotto, turkey, Louis Rich, 1 slice	40	2.5	1	25	290	0	0
Salami, Genoa, Hormel Pillow Pack, 4 slices	120	10	4	30	540	0	0
Salami, Genoa, Oscar Mayer, 3 slices	100	9	3	25	490	0	0
Salami, hard, Oscar Mayer, 3 slices	100	9	3	25	510	0	0
Salami, hard, Oscar Mayer Deli-Thin, 4 slices	130	11	4	30	620	0	0
Salami, lean, Hebrew National, 2 oz	90	6	na	30	340	0	0
Salami, turkey, Louis Rich, 2 oz	120	9	2.5	50	500	1	0
Salami, turkey, Wampler-Longacre, 2 oz	90	6	1.5	55	560	1	ns
Salami, turkey, presliced, Louis Rich, 1 slice	45	2.5	1	20	290	0	0
Salami for beer, Oscar Mayer, 2 slices	110	9	3	30	580	1	0
Smoked, Armour, 1 link	270	23	8	70	870	40	0
Smoked, Eckrich, 2 oz	180	17	7	40	460	1	0
Smoked, Healthy Choice, 2 oz	70	1.5	0.5	25	590	4	1
Smoked, Hillshire Farm, 2 oz	190	17	8	25	460	2	0
Smoked, beef, Eckrich, 2 oz	180	16	6	40	460	2	0
Smoked, lite, Hillshire Farm, 2 oz	120	8	4.5	25	510	2	0

SAUSAGE	CAL	FAT (g)	SAT FAT (g)	CHOL (mg)	SODIUM (mg)	CARB (g)	FIBER (g)
Smoked, reduced fat, Eckrich, 2 oz	120	9	3	35	570	3	0
Smoked, skinless, Eckrich, 2 oz	180	16	6	35	430	2	0
Smoked, skinless, Thorn Apple Valley, 1 link	190	21	7	80	810	5	0
Smoked, skinless, fully cooked, Thorn Apple Valley, 1 link	240	21	7	80	810	5	0
Smoked, turkey, Butterball, 2 oz	90	5	1.5	40	510	2	0
Smoked, turkey, Eckrich, 2 oz	120	9	3.5	40	540	2	0
Smoked, turkey, Hillshire Farm, 2 oz	80	4.5	2.5	30	790	2	ns
Smoked, turkey, Louis Rich, 2 oz	80	5	1.5	35	500	2	0
Smoked, turkey, fat free, Butterball, 2 oz	60	0	0	25	630	5	0
Smoked, turkey, with cheese, Louis Rich, 2 oz	90	5	2	35	540	2	0
Smoked, with cheese, Johnsonville Beddar with Cheddar, 1 link	240	22	8	50	650	2	ns
Smokie links, Oscar Mayer, 1 link	130	12	4	25	430	1	0
Smokies, Hillshire Farm Lit'l Smokies, 6 links	180	17	8	15	620	2	ns
Smokies, beef, Oscar Mayer, 1 link	120	11	5	30	420	1	0
Smokies, cheddar, Hillshire Farm Lit'l Smokies, 6 links	180	16	8	30	610	2	ns
Smokies, cheese, Oscar Mayer, 1 link	130	12	4.5	30	450	1	0
Smokies, little, Oscar Mayer, 6 links	170	16	6	35	580	1	0
Smokies, little cheese, Oscar Mayer, 6 links	180	16	6	35	600	1	0
Summer sausage, Old Dutch, 1 pkg	110	10	4	20	370	0	0

SAUSAGE	CAL (g)	FAT (g)	SAT FAT (g)	CHOL (mg)	SODIUM (mg)	CARB (g)	FIBER (g)
Summer sausage (thuringer Cervelat), Oscar Mayer, 2 slices	140	13	5	40	650	0	0
Summer sausage, beef, Hillshire Farm, 2 oz	190	17	10	30	400	<1	ns
Summer sausage, beef (thuringer Cervelat), Oscar Mayer, 2 slices	140	12	5	35	640	1	0
Thuringer, 1 oz	90	8	3.5	20	350	0	0
Vienna sausage, Hormel, 2 oz	140	13	4	45	420	1	0
Vienna sausage, chicken, Hormel, 2 oz	110	10	3	55	420	1	0

AT A GLANCE: SAUSAGE

Lowest in Fat: Butterball Smoked Turkey Sausage, Fat Free
Other low fat choices: Healthy Choice Pastrami; Healthy Choice Smoked Sausage or Polska Kielbasa; Louis Rich Turkey Pastrami

SAUSAGE ALTERNATIVE

	CAL (g)	FAT (g)	SAT FAT (g)	CHOL (mg)	SODIUM (mg)	CARB (g)	FIBER (g)
Salami, meatless, Worthington, ⅜" slice	120	8	1	0	900	2	2

DRIED FOODS & MIXES

	CAL (g)	FAT (g)	SAT FAT (g)	CHOL (mg)	SODIUM (mg)	CARB (g)	FIBER (g)
FRUIT							
Apples, Timber Crest Farms, 10–12 pieces	110	0	0	0	0	29	4
Apples, dehydrated, sulfered, ½ cup	100	0	0	0	40	28	4
Apples, sliced, Del Monte, ⅓ cup	80	0	0	0	310	23	5
Apples, sulfured, 10 rings	160	0	0	0	55	42	6
Apricots, Timber Crest Farms, 10 pieces	120	0	0	0	0	31	1
Apricots, dehydrated, sulfered, ½ cup	190	0	0	0	10	50	1
Apricots, sulfured, 10 halves	80	0	0	0	0	22	3
Apricots, sun dried, Del Monte, ⅓ cup	80	0	0	0	5	25	6
Apricots, Turkish, Dole Sun Giant, 6 pieces	90	0	0	0	0	22	2
Bananas, Timber Crest Farms, 2 pieces	140	0	0	0	0	33	1
Bananas, dehydrated, or banana powder, 1 Tbsp	20	0	0	0	0	5	0
Cherries, Bing, Melissa's, 1 oz	80	0	0	0	0	21	2
Cherries, Rainier, Melissa's, 1 oz	70	0	0	0	5	17	2
Cherries, tart, Melissa's, 1 oz	100	0	0	0	0	23	1
Coconut, unsweetened, 1 oz	190	18	16	0	10	7	5
Currants, Zante, ½ cup	200	0	0	0	5	53	5
Dates, Timber Crest Farms, 5–6 dates	110	0	0	0	15	30	5
Dates, chopped, Del Monte, ¼ cup	120	0	0	0	10	33	3
Dates, chopped, Dole, ½ cup	230	0	0	0	5	56	na
Dates, dehydrated, coarse or fine ground, Dole, 1 oz	110	0	0	0	0	27	2

FRUIT	CAL (g)	FAT (g)	SAT FAT (g)	CHOL (mg)	SODIUM (mg)	CARB (g)	FIBER (g)
Dates, pitted, Del Monte, 5–6 dates	120	0	0	0	50	31	3
Dates, pitted, Dole, ½ cup	280	0	0	0	0	62	na
Figs, 5 fruits	240	1	0	0	10	61	9
Jujube (Chinese date), 3.5 oz	290	1	0	0	10	74	3
Longans, 3.5 oz	290	0	0	0	50	74	5
Mango, Timber Crest Farms, 8 pieces	180	1	0	0	50	44	0
Mixed fruits, Del Monte, ⅓ cup	110	0	0	0	50	30	5
Mixed fruits, Dole Sun Giant, 1½ oz	100	0	0	0	35	24	3
Peaches, dehydrated, sulfered, ½ cup	190	0.5	0	0	5	48	na
Peaches, sulfured, 4 halves	120	0.5	0	0	5	32	4
Peaches, sun dried, Del Monte, ⅓ cup	90	0	0	0	0	26	5
Pears, sulfured, 4 halves	180	0.5	0	0	5	49	5
Persimmons, Japanese, 1 fruit	90	0	0	0	0	25	5
Prunes, Dole, 2 oz	140	1	ns	ns	<10	36	na
Prunes, pitted, Del Monte, ¼ cup	120	0	0	0	5	29	3
Prunes, pitted, Timber Crest Farms, ¼ cup	120	0	0	0	5	29	3
Prunes, unpitted, Del Monte, ¼ cup	120	0	0	0	5	29	3
Raisins, golden, Sun Maid, ¼ cup	130	0	0	0	10	31	2
Raisins, natural, Del Monte, 1½ oz	130	0.5	0	0	20	36	5
Raisins, natural or golden, Del Monte, ¼ cup	120	0	0	0	20	33	5
Raisins, seeded, ¼ cup	110	0	0	0	10	29	2

GELATIN

	CAL (g)	FAT (g)	SAT FAT (g)	CHOL (mg)	SODIUM (mg)	CARB (g)	FIBER (g)
Apricot, Jell-O Brand, ½ cup	80	0	0	0	50	19	0
Berry blue, Jell-O Brand, ½ cup	80	0	0	0	50	19	0

GELATIN	CAL (g)	FAT (g)	SAT FAT (g)	CHOL (mg)	SODIUM (mg)	CARB (g)	FIBER (g)
Berry blue, sugar free, low calorie, Jell-O Brand, ½ cup	10	0	0	0	60	0	0
Blackberry, Jell-O Brand, ½ cup	80	0	0	0	50	19	0
Black cherry, Jell-O Brand, ½ cup	80	0	0	0	50	19	0
Black raspberry, Jell-O Brand, ½ cup	80	0	0	0	35	20	0
Cherry, Jell-O Brand, ½ cup	80	0	0	0	70	19	0
Cherry, Royal, ½ cup	80	0	0	0	105	19	0
Cherry, sugar free, low calorie, Jell-O Brand, ½ cup	10	0	0	0	70	0	0
Cranberry, Jell-O Brand, ½ cup	80	0	0	0	70	19	0
Fruit punch, Royal, ½ cup	80	0	0	0	80	19	0
Grape, Jell-O Brand, ½ cup	80	0	0	0	45	19	0
Grape, Concord, Royal, ½ cup	80	0	0	0	100	19	0
Grape, sugar free, low calorie, Jell-O Brand, ½ cup	10	0	0	0	50	0	0
Lemon, Jell-O Brand, ½ cup	80	0	0	0	75	19	0
Lemon, Royal, ½ cup	80	0	0	0	115	19	0
Lemon, sugar free, low calorie, Jell-O Brand, ½ cup	10	0	0	0	55	0	0
Lime, Jell-O Brand, ½ cup	80	0	0	0	60	19	0
Lime, Royal, ½ cup	80	0	0	0	105	19	0
Lime, sugar free, low calorie, Jell-O Brand, ½ cup	10	0	0	0	60	0	0
Mango, Jell-O Brand, ½ cup	80	0	0	0	45	19	0
Mixed berry, Royal, ½ cup	80	0	0	0	80	19	0
Mixed fruit, Jell-O Brand, ½ cup	80	0	0	0	50	19	0
Mixed fruit, sugar free, low calorie, Jell-O Brand, ½ cup	10	0	0	0	50	0	0
Orange, Jell-O Brand, ½ cup	80	0	0	0	50	19	0
Orange, Royal, ½ cup	80	0	0	0	100	19	0
Orange, sugar free, low calorie, Jell-O Brand, ½ cup	10	0	0	0	65	0	0

GELATIN	CAL (g)	FAT (g)	SAT FAT (g)	CHOL (mg)	SODIUM (mg)	CARB (g)	FIBER (g)
Orange pineapple, Jell-O Brand, ½ cup	80	0	0	0	65	19	0
Peach, Jell-O Brand, ½ cup	80	0	0	0	50	19	0
Pectin mix, unsweetened, ¼ pkg	40	0	0	0	25	11	ns
Pineapple, Jell-O Brand, ½ cup	80	0	0	0	45	19	0
Pineapple, Hawaiian, sugar free, low calorie, Jell-O Brand, ½ cup	10	0	0	0	50	0	0
Raspberry, Jell-O Brand, ½ cup	80	0	0	0	50	19	0
Raspberry, Royal, ½ cup	80	0	0	0	110	19	0
Raspberry, sugar free, low calorie, Jell-O Brand, ½ cup	10	0	0	0	55	0	0
Strawberry, Jell-O 1-2-3 Brand, ½ cup	130	1.5	1	0	45	26	0
Strawberry, Jell-O Brand, ½ cup	80	0	0	0	50	19	0
Strawberry, Royal, ½ cup	80	0	0	0	110	19	0
Strawberry, low calorie, D-Zerta, ½ cup	10	0	0	0	5	0	0
Strawberry, sugar free, low calorie, Jell-O Brand, ½ cup	10	0	0	0	55	0	0
Strawberry, wild, Jell-O Brand, ½ cup	80	0	0	0	75	19	0
Strawberry banana, Jell-O Brand, ½ cup	80	0	0	0	50	19	0
Strawberry banana, Royal, ½ cup	80	0	0	0	110	19	0
Strawberry banana, sugar free, low calorie, Jell-O Brand, ½ cup	10	0	0	0	50	0	0
Triple berry, sugar free, low calorie, Jell-O Brand, ½ cup	10	0	0	0	50	0	0
Tropical punch, Jell-O Brand, ½ cup	80	0	0	0	45	19	0
Unflavored, Knox, 1 envelope	25	0	0	0	15	0	0
Watermelon, Jell-O Brand, ½ cup	80	0	0	0	50	19	0

GELATIN	CAL (g)	FAT (g)	SAT FAT (g)	CHOL (mg)	SODIUM (mg)	CARB (g)	FIBER (g)
Watermelon, sugar free, low calorie, Jell-O Brand, ½ cup	10	0	0	0	55	0	0
Gelatin snack, all flavors, Del Monte, 1 snack	100	0	0	0	80	25	<1
Gelatin snack, all flavors, Hunt's Snack Pack Juicy Gels, 1 snack	100	0	0	0	40	25	0
Gelatin snack, all flavors but strawberry, Kraft Handi-Snacks, 1 snack	80	0	0	0	40	20	0
Gelatin snack, all flavors, refrigerated, Jell-O Brand, 1 snack	80	0	0	0	45	18	0
Gelatin snack, all flavors, refrigerated, Swiss Miss Gels, 1 snack	80	0	0	0	40	18	0
Gelatin snack, all flavors, sugar free, low calorie, refrigerated, Jell-O Brand, 1 snack	10	0	0	0	50	0	0
Gelatin snack, strawberry, Kraft Handi-Snacks, 1 snack	80	0	0	0	45	20	0

AT A GLANCE: GELATIN
Lowest in Calories: Jell-O Sugar-Free varieties

GRAINS

See also Cooking & Baking Products, Grains. Serving sizes are for dry product unless indicated otherwise.

	CAL (g)	FAT (g)	SAT FAT (g)	CHOL (mg)	SODIUM (mg)	CARB (g)	FIBER (g)
Amaranth, Arrowhead Mills, ¼ cup	170	2	0.5	0	0	29	3
Barley, hulless, Arrowhead Mills, ¼ cup	140	1	0	0	0	35	6
Barley, pearled, Arrowhead Mills, ¼ cup	170	0.5	0	0	0	37	6
Buckwheat groats, brown, Arrowhead Mills, ¼ cup	140	1	0	0	0	30	3
Bulgur, ¼ cup	120	0	0	0	5	27	6
Couscous, Arrowhead Mills, ¼ cup	170	0	0	0	0	35	2
Couscous, Fantastic Foods, ¼ cup	210	0	0	0	5	43	3

GRAINS	CAL (g)	FAT (g)	SAT FAT (g)	CHOL (mg)	SODIUM (mg)	CARB (g)	FIBER (g)
Couscous, whole wheat, Fantastic Foods, ¼ cup	180	0.5	0	0	10	42	5
Flax, Arrowhead Mills, 2 Tbsp	140	10	1	0	0	11	6
Kamut, Arrowhead Mills, ¼ cup	140	1	0	0	0	32	5
Millet, hulled, Arrowhead Mills, ¼ cup	150	1.5	0	0	0	34	3
Oat bran, Arrowhead Mills, ⅓ cup	150	2.5	0	0	0	23	7
Oat groats, Arrowhead Mills, ¼ cup	160	3	0.5	0	0	29	4
Quinoa, Arrowhead Mills, ¼ cup	140	2	0	0	0	25	4
Quinoa, Eden, ¼ cup	170	2.5	0	0	0	31	3
Rice, arborio, Fantastic Foods, ¼ cup	210	0	0	0	0	45	1
Rice, basmati, Fantastic Foods, ¼ cup	180	0	0	0	0	38	1
Rice, basmati, long grain, Arrowhead Mills, ¼ cup	150	1	0	0	0	33	2
Rice, boil-in-bag, Minute Rice, ½ bag (1 cup cooked)	190	0	0	0	10	42	0
Rice, brown, Mahatma, ¼ cup	150	1	0	0	0	32	1
Rice, brown, Success, ½ cup	350	2	0	0	20	77	5
Rice, brown, basmati, Fantastic Foods, ¼ cup	170	1.5	0	0	0	36	1
Rice, brown, jasmine, Fantastic Foods, ¼ cup	170	1.5	0	0	0	36	1
Rice, brown, long grain, Arrowhead Mills, ¼ cup	150	1	0	0	0	33	2
Rice, brown, long grain, Carolina, ¼ cup	150	1	0	0	0	32	1
Rice, brown, medium grain, Arrowhead Mills, ¼ cup	160	1	0	0	0	35	2
Rice, brown, quick, Arrowhead Mills, ⅓ cup	150	1	0	0	0	32	2
Rice, brown, quick, wild, Arrowhead Mills, ⅓ cup	140	1	0	0	220	28	3
Rice, brown, short grain, Arrowhead Mills, ¼ cup	170	1	0	0	0	36	2

GRAINS	CAL	FAT (g)	SAT FAT (g)	CHOL (mg)	SODIUM (mg)	CARB (g)	FIBER (g)
Rice, brown, whole grain, instant, Minute Rice, ½ cup (⅔ cup cooked)	170	1.5	0	0	10	34	2
Rice, jasmine, Fantastic Foods, ¼ cup	170	0	0	0	0	38	1
Rice, long grain, premium, Minute Rice, ½ cup (1 cup cooked)	170	0	0	0	5	36	0
Rice, multigrain, Uncle Ben's, 1 cup	160	1	0	0	0	35	1
Rice, original, Minute Rice, ½ cup (¾ cup cooked)	170	0	0	0	5	37	0
Rice, white, Mahatma, ¼ cup	150	0	0	0	0	35	0
Rice, white, Success, ½ cup	190	0	0	0	5	44	<1
Rice, white, extra long-grain, Carolina, ¼ cup	150	1	0	0	0	35	1
Rice, white, medium-grain, enriched, ¼ cup	180	0	0	0	0	39	<1
Rice, white, short-grain, ¼ cup	180	0	0	0	0	40	1
Rice, wild, Fantastic Foods, ¼ cup	140	0	0	0	0	28	2
Rice, wild blend, prepared, Uncle Ben's, 1 cup	160	0.5	0	0	0	36	1
Rice trio, prepared, Uncle Ben's, 1 cup	160	1	0	0	0	35	1
Rye, whole, Arrowhead Mills, ¼ cup	160	1	0	0	0	34	6
Teff, Arrowhead Mills, ¼ cup	160	1	0	0	5	32	6
Triticale, dry, ¼ cup	160	1	0	0	0	35	9

AT A GLANCE: GRAINS
Highest in Fiber: Triticale

MEALS & SIDE DISHES

Serving sizes are for dry product unless indicated otherwise. Prepared products are made according to package directions.

	CAL	FAT (g)	SAT FAT (g)	CHOL (mg)	SODIUM (mg)	CARB (g)	FIBER (g)
Almond chicken vegetarian, Casbah, 1 pkg	160	1.5	0	0	470	29	<1
Asparagus au gratin, Casbah, 1 pkg	150	2	0	<5	420	28	1

MEALS & SIDE DISHES	CAL	FAT (g)	SAT FAT (g)	CHOL (mg)	SODIUM (mg)	CARB (g)	FIBER (g)
Beans, black, & rice, prepared, Carolina, 1 cup	200	1.5	0	0	850	39	6
Beans, black, & rice, prepared, Mahatma, 1 cup	200	1.5	0	0	850	39	6
Beans, Italian, Knorr, 1 pkg	230	2	0	0	920	50	8
Beans, mixed, & radiatore pasta, Napoli, prepared, Terrazza, ½ cup	140	3	0	0	135	24	2
Beans, pinto, & rice, prepared, Mahatma, 1 cup	190	0.5	0	0	280	40	4
Beans, red, & fusilli, Florentine, prepared, Terrazza, ½ cup	150	3	0	0	150	24	2
Beans, red, & rice, prepared, Carolina, 1 cup	190	1	0	0	790	40	7
Beans, red, & rice, prepared, Mahatma, 1 cup	190	1	0	0	790	40	7
Beans, red, & rice, prepared, Rice-A-Roni, 1 cup	280	7	1	0	1200	51	5
Beans, white, & gemelli pasta, Tuscan, prepared, Terrazza, ½ cup	150	3	0	0	160	25	2
Burger, meatless, BBQ, Fantastic Foods Nature's Burger, ⅓ cup	170	3	0	0	330	30	5
Burger, meatless, original, Fantastic Foods Nature's Burger, ¼ cup	170	1.5	0	20	580	34	5
Burger, meatless, patty, dehydrated, Loma Linda, ⅓ cup	90	1	0	0	480	7	5
Burrito, Old El Paso, 1 burrito	190	3.5	0.5	0	770	35	2
Cheddar broccoli, Casbah, pkg	130	2	1	<5	470	23	<1
Chicken, stir fried, Betty Crocker Skillet Chicken Helper, ¼ cup	140	0.5	0	0	690	30	1
Chicken alternative, Loma Linda Chicken Supreme, ⅓ cup	90	1	0	0	720	6	4
Chicken dijonnne, Knorr, ⅙ pkg	30	1	1	0	360	5	0
Chili, 7 spice, original, Tabasco, ½ cup	50	0.5	ns	ns	115	8	3

MEALS & SIDE DISHES	CAL (g)	FAT (g)	SAT FAT (g)	CHOL (mg)	SODIUM (mg)	CARB (g)	FIBER (g)
Chili, 7 spice, spicy, Tabasco, ½ cup	60	0.5	ns	ns	115	10	2
Chili, cha-cha, Fantastic Foods, 1 pkg	200	1.5	0	0	470	40	14
Chili, four bean, Knorr, 1 pkg	230	1.5	0	0	970	53	7
Chili, three bean, spicy, Spice Islands, 1 pkg	180	1.5	0	0	670	34	9
Chili, vegetarian, Fantastic Foods, ⅛ cup	50	0	0	0	280	10	3
Chili, vegetarian, Spice Islands, 1 pkg	110	1.5	0	0	230	19	2
Chili, with beans, Old El Paso, 1 cup	200	11	1.5	30	420	15	6
Couscous, lentil curry, Marrakesh Express, ½ cup	200	0.5	0	0	160	42	3
Couscous, lucky 7 vegetable, Marrakesh Express, ½ cup	210	0.5	0	0	180	42	3
Couscous, Moroccan pasta, prepared, Near East, 1¼ cups	260	6	1.5	0	65	46	2
Couscous, spicy, Knorr, ¼ pkg	150	1	0	0	340	30	1
Couscous, sun-dried tomatoes, Marrakesh Express, ½ cup	210	1	0	0	170	41	3
Couscous, wild mushroom, Marrakesh Express, ¼ cup	200	0	0	0	180	42	3
Dinner loaf, meatless, Loma Linda Savory, ⅓ cup	90	1.5	0	0	560	7	5
Etouffee dinner, prepared, Luzianne Cajun Creole, 1 cup	200	1	0	0	1030	42	<1
Falafel, prepared, Casbah, 5 falafel balls	130	3	0	0	530	20	2
Falafel vegetable burger, prepared, Near East, 2½ patties	230	15	2	0	560	18	5
Falafil, fantastic, Fantastic Foods, ½ cup	250	4	0.5	0	610	42	11
Fish alternative, Loma Linda Ocean Platter, ⅓ cup	90	1	0	0	450	8	4
Goulash, Knorr, ⅙ pkg	40	1	0.5	<5	470	6	0
Gumbo dinner, prepared, Luzianne Cajun Creole, 1 cup	160	1	0	0	760	33	1

MEALS & SIDE DISHES	CAL	FAT (g)	SAT FAT (g)	CHOL (mg)	SODIUM (mg)	CARB (g)	FIBER (g)
Gyro, natural burger mix, Casbah, 1/10 pkg	50	0	0	0	470	12	0
Hamburger Helper, beef noodle, Betty Crocker, 2/3 cup	120	1.5	0	25	870	23	<1
Hamburger Helper, beef Romanoff, Betty Crocker, 2/3 cup	150	1.5	0.5	<5	890	28	<1
Hamburger Helper, beef stew, Betty Crocker, 1/2 cup	110	0.5	0	0	710	26	2
Hamburger Helper, beef taco, Betty Crocker, 1/2 cup	160	2	0	0	870	30	1
Hamburger Helper, beef teriyaki, Betty Crocker, 1/3 cup	170	1	0	0	1010	37	<1
Hamburger Helper, cheddar 'n bacon, Betty Crocker, 2/3 cup	170	5	1.5	10	810	25	<1
Hamburger Helper, cheeseburger macaroni, Betty Crocker, 1/3 cup	170	4	1	5	960	30	1
Hamburger Helper, cheesy shells, Betty Crocker, 1/2 cup	180	6	1.5	5	780	27	1
Hamburger Helper, chili macaroni, Betty Crocker, 1/3 cup	140	1	0	0	820	30	<1
Hamburger Helper, fettuccini Alfredo, Betty Crocker, 1/2 cup	150	4	2	10	940	22	<1
Hamburger Helper, hamburger stew, Betty Crocker, 2/3 cup	100	0.5	0	0	870	22	3
Hamburger Helper, Italian, cheesy, Betty Crocker, 1/2 cup	150	3	1	<5	850	26	<1
Hamburger Helper, Italian, zesty, Betty Crocker, 1/3 cup	160	1	0	0	840	34	<1
Hamburger Helper, Italian rigatoni, Betty Crocker, 1/3 cup	150	1	0	0	740	32	1
Hamburger Helper, Lasagna, Betty Crocker, 2/3 cup	140	0.5	0	0	920	30	1
Hamburger Helper, meat loaf, Betty Crocker, 1 1/2 Tbsp	50	0.5	0	0	510	10	0
Hamburger Helper, mushroom & wild rice, Betty Crocker, 1/4 cup	170	2.5	0.5	0	890	33	<1
Hamburger Helper, nacho cheese, Betty Crocker, 1/2 cup	160	3	1	<5	870	27	<1

MEALS & SIDE DISHES	CAL (g)	FAT (g)	SAT FAT (g)	CHOL (mg)	SODIUM (mg)	CARB (g)	FIBER (g)
Hamburger Helper, Oriental rice, Betty Crocker, ¼ cup	160	0.5	0	0	1000	35	0
Hamburger Helper, pizza pasta with cheese topping, Betty Crocker, ½ cup	150	2	0	0	620	29	1
Hamburger Helper, pizzabake, Betty Crocker, ⅓ cup	140	1.5	0	0	670	28	<1
Hamburger Helper, potato stroganoff, Betty Crocker, ⅔ cup	120	2	0.5	0	810	24	2
Hamburger Helper, potatoes au gratin, Betty Crocker, ⅔ cup	120	2.5	0.5	<5	740	23	2
Hamburger Helper, salisbury, Betty Crocker, ⅔ cup	140	1	0	0	780	28	1
Hamburger Helper, spaghetti, Betty Crocker, ½ cup	150	1	0	0	890	29	<1
Hamburger Helper, stroganoff, Betty Crocker, ⅔ cup	170	3	0.5	<5	880	30	<1
Hamburger Helper, Swedish meatballs, Betty Crocker, ⅔ cup	170	7	2	20	750	24	<1
Hamburger Helper, three cheese, Betty Crocker, ½ cup	180	6	2	10	760	28	<1
Hearty Harvest, Casbah, 10 fl oz	180	1	0	0	460	36	2
Jambalaya, Casbah, 10 fl oz	120	0	0	0	490	27	2
Jambalaya, prepared, Luzianne Cajun Creole, 1 cup	200	1	0	0	690	43	1
Jambalaya, prepared, Mahatma, 1 cup	190	1	0	0	700	43	<1
La Presta, Casbah, 10 fl oz	170	1	0	0	400	34	4
Lentils, hearty, & wild rice, Spice Islands, 1 pkg	200	2.5	0	0	720	39	6
Lentils, red, & bow tie pasta, Sicilian, prepared, Terrazza, ½ cup	150	4	0	25	135	22	3
Macaroni & cheese, Kraft, 1 cup	390	17	4	10	730	48	1
Macaroni & cheese, Kraft Super Mario Bros., 1 cup	390	17	4.5	10	770	48	1

MEALS & SIDE DISHES	CAL	FAT (g)	SAT FAT (g)	CHOL (mg)	SODIUM (mg)	CARB (g)	FIBER (g)
Macaroni & cheese, Kraft The Flintstones, 1 cup	390	17	4.5	10	770	48	1
Macaroni & cheese, Kraft Thick 'N Creamy, 1 cup	320	10	6	25	730	50	2
Macaroni & cheese, cheddar, Fantastic Foods, 3/8 cup	200	1.5	0	0	550	40	5
Macaroni & cheese, deluxe original, Kraft, 1 cup	320	10	6	25	730	44	1
Macaroni & cheese, dinosaurs, Kraft, 1 cup	390	17	4.5	10	770	48	1
Macaroni & cheese, mild white cheddar, Kraft, 1 cup	390	17	4	10	730	48	1
Macaroni & cheese, Parmesan, Fantastic Foods, 3/8 cup	200	1.5	0	0	550	40	5
Macaroni & cheese, Santa Mac, Kraft, 1 cup	390	17	4.5	10	770	48	1
Macaroni & cheese, spirals, Kraft, 1 cup	390	17	4.5	10	770	48	1
Macaroni & cheese, teddy bears, Kraft, 1 cup	390	17	4.5	10	770	48	1
Noodles, egg, cheddar cheese, Kraft, 1 cup	430	21	6	70	780	46	1
Noodles, egg, chicken, Kraft, 1 cup	330	12	3.5	60	1430	45	1
Noodles, Japanese style, beef flavor, Sapporo Ichiban, 3.5 oz	480	23	9	0	2100	58	10
Noodles, Japanese style, chicken flavor, Sapporo Ichiban, 3.5 oz	480	23	10	0	1600	59	11
Noodles, Japanese style, chow mein, Sapporo Ichiban, 3.6 oz	510	24	9	<5	940	64	14
Noodles, Japanese style, kitsune udon, Sapporo Ichiban, 3.78 oz	490	20	9	0	1940	67	10
Noodles, Japanese style, miso flavor, Sapporo Ichiban, 3.55 oz	460	20	10	0	1990	60	10
Noodles, Japanese style, original flavor, Sapporo Ichiban, 3.5 oz	480	22	11	0	2060	61	12

MEALS & SIDE DISHES	CAL (g)	FAT (g)	SAT FAT (g)	CHOL (mg)	SODIUM (mg)	CARB (g)	FIBER (g)
Noodles, Japanese style, shrimp flavor, Sapporo Ichiban, 3.5 oz	500	22	11	0	2500	60	11
Noodles, Oriental, Knorr, 1 pkg	210	3	0.5	20	830	39	2
Pasta, Alfredo broccoli, Lipton Noodles & Sauce, 2/3 cup	260	7	3.5	75	940	39	2
Pasta, Alfredo carbonara, Lipton Noodles & Sauce, 2/3 cup	260	7	3	85	890	38	2
Pasta, Alfredo sauce, Lipton Noodles & Sauce, 2/3 cup	250	7	3.5	75	940	38	1
Pasta, angel hair, with herbs, prepared, Noodle Roni, 1 cup	320	14	2.5	5	840	42	2
Pasta, angel hair chicken broccoli, Lipton Golden Saute, 1/2 cup	210	1.5	0.5	0	850	44	2
Pasta, angel hair Parmesan, Lipton Golden Saute, 1/2 cup	240	5	2	10	890	42	2
Pasta, angel hair Parmesan, prepared, Noodle Roni, 1 cup	320	15	3	5	900	40	2
Pasta, beef, Lipton Noodles & Sauce, 2/3 cup	220	3.5	1	60	930	42	2
Pasta, bow tie, Italian cheese, Lipton Pasta & Sauce, 3/4 cup	230	5	2.5	10	790	37	1
Pasta, butter, Lipton Noodles & Sauce, 2/3 cup	260	8	3.5	65	910	40	2
Pasta, butter & herb, Lipton Noodles & Sauce, 2/3 cup	250	7	2.5	65	860	41	2
Pasta, cheddar bacon, Lipton Noodles & Sauce, 2/3 cup	230	4.5	2	65	930	38	2
Pasta, cheddar broccoli, Lipton Pasta & Sauce, 1/2 cup	260	3.5	1.5	10	870	46	1
Pasta, cheese, Lipton Noodles & Sauce, 2/3 cup	250	4.5	2	65	850	44	1
Pasta, cheese, Lipton Pasta & Sauce, 1/2 cup	240	5	2.5	10	870	41	1
Pasta, chicken, creamy, Lipton Noodles & Sauce, 2/3 cup	230	6	2.5	65	710	39	2
Pasta, chicken broccoli, Lipton Noodles & Sauce, 2/3 cup	220	4	1.5	60	750	40	2

MEALS & SIDE DISHES	CAL	FAT (g)	SAT FAT (g)	CHOL (mg)	SODIUM (mg)	CARB (g)	FIBER (g)
Pasta, chicken flavor, Lipton Noodles & Sauce, ⅔ cup	230	4.5	1.5	60	760	41	2
Pasta, chicken herb Parmesan, Lipton Golden Saute, ½ cup	230	3	1.5	<5	830	45	3
Pasta, chicken primavera, Lipton Pasta & Sauce, ¾ cup	220	3	1.5	5	730	40	1
Pasta, chicken stir fry, Lipton Golden Saute, ½ cup	220	2	0	0	850	45	2
Pasta, chicken Tetrazzini, Lipton Noodles & Sauce, ⅔ cup	220	5	2	65	850	37	2
Pasta, corkscrew, with creamy garlic sauce, prepared, Noodle Roni, 1 cup	420	25	5	5	1010	40	2
Pasta, corkscrew, with four cheese sauce, prepared, Noodle Roni, 1 cup	410	18	5	10	1040	49	2
Pasta, fettuccini, with Alfredo sauce, prepared, Noodle Roni, 1 cup	470	25	6	10	1110	47	2
Pasta, fettuccini, with broccoli au gratin, prepared, Noodle Roni, 1 cup	290	10	3.5	10	850	39	2
Pasta, fettuccini, with chicken sauce, prepared, Noodle Roni, 1 cup	320	14	2.5	5	1020	41	2
Pasta, fettuccini, with mild cheddar sauce, prepared, Noodle Roni, 1 cup	300	11	3.5	10	890	40	2
Pasta, fettuccini, with Romanoff sauce, prepared, Noodle Roni, 1 cup	410	19	6	10	1070	47	2
Pasta, fettuccini, with stroganoff sauce, prepared, Noodle Roni, 1 cup	370	14	3.5	10	1030	48	2
Pasta, garlic, creamy, Lipton Pasta & Sauce, ⅔ cup	260	6	2.5	10	840	45	1
Pasta, garlic & herb, Spice Islands, 1 pkg	160	1	0	0	660	32	1
Pasta, garlic butter, Lipton Golden Saute, ½ cup	230	3	2	<5	790	43	2
Pasta, herb tomato, Lipton Pasta & Sauce, ⅔ cup	240	2	<1	0	690	48	3

MEALS & SIDE DISHES	CAL	FAT (g)	SAT FAT (g)	CHOL (mg)	SODIUM (mg)	CARB (g)	FIBER (g)
Pasta, linguine, with chicken & broccoli, prepared, Noodle Roni, 1 cup	370	16	4	5	1000	50	3
Pasta, linguine, with creamy chicken Parmesan, prepared, Noodle Roni, 1 cup	410	19	4.5	5	1100	46	2
Pasta, Oriental style, with stir fry sauce, prepared, Noodle Roni, 1 cup	290	12	1	0	1000	38	2
Pasta, Parmesan, Lipton Noodles & Sauce, 2/3 cup	250	8	3.5	70	750	37	2
Pasta, penne, herb & butter, prepared, Noodle Roni, 1 cup	430	25	6	0	750	42	2
Pasta, penne, herb & garlic, Lipton Golden Saute, 1/2 cup	230	3	2	5	810	44	2
Pasta, rigatoni, with tomato basil, prepared, Noodle Roni, 1 cup	240	9	1	0	700	34	2
Pasta, rigatoni, with white cheddar & broccoli sauce, prepared, Noodle Roni, 1 cup	400	19	5	10	920	48	2
Pasta, Romanoff, Lipton Noodles & Sauce, 2/3 cup	260	7	3.5	70	920	41	2
Pasta, sour cream & chive, Lipton Noodles & Sauce, 2/3 cup	260	8	3.5	70	800	41	2
Pasta, spinach & mushroom, Spice Islands, 1 pkg	160	1.5	0.5	3	460	29	1
Pasta, stroganoff, Lipton Noodles & Sauce, 2/3 cup	210	4	2	65	850	37	2
Pasta, tenderthin broccoli & mushroom, prepared, Noodle Roni, 1 cup	460	24	5	5	1140	49	2
Pasta, tenderthin Parmesan, prepared, Noodle Roni, 1 cup	400	17	4.5	10	950	49	2
Pasta, tomato basil, creamy, Spice Islands, 1 pkg	200	2	0	0	510	40	2
Pasta, vermicelli, garlic & olive oil, prepared, Noodle Roni, 1 cup	360	16	2.5	0	1010	48	2
Pasta primavera, Spice Islands, 1 pkg	170	2	0.5	5	470	30	1

MEALS & SIDE DISHES	CAL (g)	FAT (g)	SAT FAT (g)	CHOL (mg)	SODIUM (mg)	CARB (g)	FIBER (g)
Pasta salad, classic, Betty Crocker Suddenly Salad, ¾ cup	170	1	0	0	830	34	1
Pasta salad, classic ranch with bacon, Kraft, ¾ cup	360	23	4	15	500	30	2
Pasta salad, creamy Caesar, Kraft, ¾ cup	350	22	4	15	650	30	2
Pasta salad, garden primavera, Kraft, ¾ cup	280	12	2.5	<5	730	34	2
Pasta salad, Italian, light, Kraft, ¾ cup	190	2	1	<5	660	34	2
Pasta salad, Italian1 herb, Fantastic Foods, ⅔ cup	170	1.5	0.5	0	380	34	2
Pasta salad, macaroni, creamy, Betty Crocker Suddenly Salad, ⅓ cup	140	1	0	0	400	29	2
Pasta salad, Parmesan peppercorn, Kraft, ¾ cup	360	4.5	4.5	20	610	28	2
Pasta salad, spicy Oriental, Fantastic Foods, ⅔ cup	200	3	0	0	420	37	3
Pilaf, barley, prepared, Near East, 1 cup	220	4	1	0	620	41	5
Pilaf, basmati, Knorr, ¼ pkg	150	0.5	0	0	390	33	1
Pilaf, beef flavor, prepared, Near East, 1 cup	220	4.5	1	0	850	42	1
Pilaf, brown rice, prepared, Near East, 1 cup	220	5	1	0	710	41	2
Pilaf, brown rice with miso, Fantastic Foods, ½ cup	250	3	0	0	570	55	1
Pilaf, bulgar, prepared, Casbah, ½ cup	100	0	0	0	270	21	2
Pilaf, chicken flavor, prepared, Near East, 1 cup	220	4.5	1	0	940	42	1
Pilaf, couscous, prepared, Casbah, ½ cup	100	0	0	0	280	20	<1
Pilaf, couscous, savory, Fantastic Foods, ⅓ cup	240	1	0	0	450	50	4
Pilaf, curry rice, prepared, Near East, 1 cup	220	4	1	0	660	42	1

MEALS & SIDE DISHES	CAL	FAT (g)	SAT FAT (g)	CHOL (mg)	SODIUM (mg)	CARB (g)	FIBER (g)
Pilaf, garden vegetable bean & rice, prepared, Near East, 1 cup	270	5	1	0	1120	52	5
Pilaf, harvest, Knorr, ¼ pkg	90	0.5	0	0	360	20	<1
Pilaf, jasmine, Knorr, ¼ pkg	130	1	0	0	130	28	<1
Pilaf, lentil, prepared, Casbah, ½ cup	100	0	0	0	230	19	1
Pilaf, lentil, prepared, Near East, 1 cup	210	4	1	0	650	37	5
Pilaf, long grain & wild rice, prepared, Near East, 1 cup	220	4.5	1	0	810	42	2
Pilaf, long grain & wild rice, prepared, Rice-A-Roni, 1 cup	240	6	1	0	910	43	1
Pilaf, Mediterranean black bean & rice, prepared, Near East, 1 cup	270	5	1	0	990	52	5
Pilaf, Mediterranean chicken with wild rice, prepared, Near East, 1 cup	220	4	1	0	910	43	1
Pilaf, nutted, prepared, Casbah, ½ cup	110	2	0	0	290	20	<1
Pilaf, red beans & rice, prepared, Near East, 1 cup	220	3.5	1	0	730	41	4
Pilaf, rice, Lipton Rice & Sauce, ½ cup	230	1	0	0	850	46	1
Pilaf, rice, Success, ½ cup	200	0	0	0	630	44	2
Pilaf, rice, chicken, Spice Islands, 1 pkg	180	1.5	0	0	710	34	1
Pilaf, rice, prepared, Casbah, ½ cup	100	0	0	0	220	22	<1
Pilaf, rice, prepared, Mahatma, 1 cup	190	0	0	0	820	43	<1
Pilaf, rice, prepared, Near East, 1 cup	220	4.5	1	0	870	42	1
Pilaf, rice, prepared, Rice-A-Roni, 1 cup	310	9	1	0	1100	53	1
Pilaf, Spanish, prepared, Casbah, ½ cup	100	0	0	0	310	22	<1
Pilaf, Spanish brown, Fantastic Foods, ½ cup	240	2	0	0	650	55	2

MEALS & SIDE DISHES	CAL	FAT (g)	SAT FAT (g)	CHOL (mg)	SODIUM (mg)	CARB (g)	FIBER (g)
Pilaf, Spanish rice, prepared, Near East, 1 cup	230	6	1	0	990	42	1
Pilaf, three grains with herbs, Fantastic Foods, 1/3 cup	240	2	0	0	570	49	8
Pilaf, toasted almond, prepared, Near East, 1 cup	230	6	1	0	730	41	2
Pilaf, tomato herb bean & rice, prepared, Near East, 1 cup	270	5	1	0	950	52	5
Pilaf, wheat, prepared, Near East, 1 cup	220	4.5	1	0	690	42	5
Polenta Fantastica, Fantastic Foods, 3/8 cup	260	5	1.5	5	550	46	4
Potatoes, American cheese, Betty Crocker Homestyle, 2/3 cup	100	1.5	0.5	0	530	19	1
Potatoes, au gratin, Betty Crocker Specialty, 1/2 cup	100	1.5	0	0	550	20	1
Potatoes, au gratin, 9 oz, Betty Crocker Specialty, 1/2 cup	110	1.5	0	<5	590	22	1
Potatoes, broccoli au gratin, Betty Crocker Homestyle, 2/3 cup	100	1.5	0	0	520	19	1
Potatoes, broccoli au gratin, Betty Crocker Potatoes Express, 1/2 cup	100	1	0.5	<5	520	21	1
Potatoes, cheddar, Betty Crocker Homestyle, 2/3 cup	100	2	0.5	0	450	19	1
Potatoes, cheddar, Betty Crocker Potato Buds, 1/3 cup	120	3	0.5	0	490	22	1
Potatoes, cheddar, Betty Crocker Potatoes Express, 1/2 cup	100	1	0.5	<5	630	22	1
Potatoes, cheddar, smokey, Betty Crocker Specialty, 1/2 cup	100	1	0	0	540	21	1
Potatoes, cheddar & bacon, Betty Crocker Cheddar Classics, 2/3 cup	110	2	0.5	<5	640	20	1
Potatoes, cheddar 'n bacon, Betty Crocker Specialty, 1/2 cup	100	1.5	0	<5	500	21	1

MEALS & SIDE DISHES	CAL (g)	FAT (g)	SAT FAT (g)	CHOL (mg)	SODIUM (mg)	CARB (g)	FIBER (g)
Potatoes, cheddar & sour cream, Betty Crocker Cheddar Classics, ⅔ cup	120	1.5	0.5	<5	560	25	1
Potatoes, hash brown, Betty Crocker Specialty, ½ cup	130	0	0	0	30	30	2
Potatoes, julienne, Betty Crocker Specialty, ½ cup	90	1	0.5	0	550	18	1
Potatoes, scalloped, Betty Crocker Specialty, ½ cup	100	1.5	0	0	600	21	1
Potatoes, scalloped, cheesy, Betty Crocker Homestyle, ⅔ cup	100	1.5	0.5	0	500	19	1
Potatoes, scalloped, creamy, Betty Crocker Potatoes Express, ½ cup	110	2	0.5	0	560	23	1
Potatoes, scalloped potatoes 'n ham, Betty Crocker Specialty, ½ cup	100	1.5	0	0	510	19	1
Potatoes, sour cream 'n chive, Betty Crocker Potato Buds, ⅓ cup	120	3.5	1	<5	470	21	1
Potatoes, sour cream 'n chive, Betty Crocker Specialty, ½ cup	100	1.5	0.5	0	480	21	1
Potatoes, three cheese, Betty Crocker Cheddar Classics, ½ cup	100	1.5	0.5	<5	540	21	1
Potatoes, twice baked, cheddar & bacon, Betty Crocker, ⅓ cup	110	2.5	1	0	490	20	1
Potatoes, twice baked, mild cheddar & onion, Betty Crocker, ⅓ cup	110	3	1	0	570	19	1
Potatoes, twice baked, sour cream & chive, Betty Crocker, ⅓ cup	100	2.5	1	<5	430	19	1
Potatoes, white cheddar, Betty Crocker Cheddar Classics, ½ cup	110	2	0.5	<5	580	21	1
Rice, Alfredo broccoli, Lipton Rice & Sauce, ½ cup	250	4.5	2	10	860	44	1
Rice, beef, Lipton Golden Saute, ½ cup	230	4	1.5	0	930	43	1

MEALS & SIDE DISHES	CAL (g)	FAT (g)	SAT FAT (g)	CHOL (mg)	SODIUM (mg)	CARB (g)	FIBER (g)
Rice, beef, Lipton Rice & Sauce, ½ cup	230	1	0	0	940	47	2
Rice, beef and mushroom, prepared, Rice-A-Roni, 1 cup	290	6	1	0	1270	51	2
Rice, beef broccoli, Lipton Rice & Sauce, ½ cup	230	1	0	0	940	46	2
Rice, beef flavor, ⅓ less salt, prepared, Rice-A-Roni, 1 cup	280	5	1	0	750	53	2
Rice, beef flavor, prepared, Rice-A-Roni, 1 cup	320	10	1	0	1170	51	2
Rice, beef Oriental, Success, ½ cup	190	0.5	0	0	920	43	2
Rice, broccoli & cheese, Success, ½ cup	200	2	1	10	690	41	2
Rice, broccoli & cheese, prepared, Mahatma, 1 cup	200	1.5	0.5	5	620	41	2
Rice, broccoli almondine, Uncle Ben's Country Inn Recipes, mix to make 1 cup	260	3.5	0.5	0	690	50	2
Rice, broccoli au gratin, ⅓ less salt, prepared, Rice-A-Roni, 1 cup	320	11	2.5	5	590	49	2
Rice, broccoli au gratin, prepared, Rice-A-Roni, 1 cup	370	17	4	5	890	47	2
Rice, broccoli cheese, prepared, Rice-A-Roni Fast Cook, 1 cup	300	12	2.5	5	730	41	1
Rice, brown & wild, Success, ½ cup	190	1	0	0	830	40	3
Rice, brown & wild, mushroom recipe, Uncle Ben's, mix to make 1 cup	190	1.5	0	0	600	40	2
Rice, Cajun, Lipton Rice & Beans, ½ cup	260	1	0	0	540	53	7
Rice, Cajun, Lipton Rice & Sauce, ½ cup	230	1	0	0	930	49	2
Rice, cheddar broccoli, Lipton Rice & Sauce, ½ cup	250	3	1	<5	940	48	1
Rice, chicken, Lipton Golden Saute, ½ cup	240	5	2	0	920	44	1
Rice, chicken, Lipton Rice & Sauce, ½ cup	240	2	0.5	<5	900	48	1

MEALS & SIDE DISHES	CAL (g)	FAT (g)	SAT FAT (g)	CHOL (mg)	SODIUM (mg)	CARB (g)	FIBER (g)
Rice, chicken, classic, Success, ½ cup	150	1	0	0	720	32	1
Rice, chicken, creamy, Lipton Rice & Sauce, ½ cup	260	5	1	0	770	46	2
Rice, chicken, prepared, Mahatma, 1 cup	190	0.5	0	0	970	41	1
Rice, chicken and broccoli, prepared, Rice-A-Roni, 1 cup	290	8	1	0	1410	51	2
Rice, chicken and mushroom, prepared, Rice-A-Roni, 1 cup	360	14	2.5	0	1480	52	2
Rice, chicken and vegetables, prepared, Rice-A-Roni, 1 cup	290	7	1	0	1470	52	2
Rice, chicken broccoli, Lipton Golden Saute, ½ cup	260	4.5	1.5	0	800	47	2
Rice, chicken broccoli, Lipton Rice & Sauce, ½ cup	250	2	1	<5	940	48	2
Rice, chicken flavor, ⅓ less salt, prepared, Rice-A-Roni, 1 cup	280	5	1	0	690	53	1
Rice, chicken flavor, prepared, Rice-A-Roni, 1 cup	320	10	1	0	1100	51	1
Rice, chicken flavor, prepared, Rice-A-Roni Fast Cook, 1 cup	250	7	1.5	5	920	41	1
Rice, curry, Spice Islands, 1 pkg	190	2.5	0	0	340	35	3
Rice, fried, La Choy, 1 cup	240	1	0	0	1020	53	2
Rice, fried, Lipton Golden Saute, ½ cup	240	1	0	0	900	47	1
Rice, fried, ⅓ less salt, prepared, Rice-A-Roni, 1 cup	260	3.5	0.5	0	930	52	2
Rice, fried, prepared, Rice-A-Roni, 1 cup	320	11	2	0	1600	51	2
Rice, gumbo, prepared, Mahatma, 1 cup	160	2.5	0.5	0	720	31	1
Rice, herb and butter, Lipton Golden Saute, ½ cup	240	5	2	<5	870	42	1
Rice, herb and butter, Lipton Rice & Sauce, ½ cup	240	4	2	10	920	43	1
Rice, herb and butter, prepared, Rice-A-Roni, 1 cup	310	9	1.5	5	1160	53	1

MEALS & SIDE DISHES	CAL	FAT (g)	SAT FAT (g)	CHOL (mg)	SODIUM (mg)	CARB (g)	FIBER (g)
Rice, herbed, au gratin, Uncle Ben's Country Inn Recipes, mix to make 1 cup	260	3.5	1.5	5	770	51	2
Rice, long grain, Lipton Rice & Sauce, ½ cup	250	1	0	0	890	51	2
Rice, long grain & wild, Minute Rice, ⅓ box (1 cup cooked)	230	0.5	0	0	950	50	1
Rice, long grain & wild, Success, ½ cup	190	0	0	0	890	42	1
Rice, long grain & wild, Uncle Ben's, mix to make 1 cup	190	0.5	0	0	630	42	1
Rice, long grain & wild, prepared, Mahatma, 1 cup	190	0.5	0	0	710	41	2
Rice, long grain & wild, prepared, Rice-A-Roni, 1 cup	290	9	1.5	0	1240	50	3
Rice, long grain & wild, with chicken & almonds, prepared, Rice-A-Roni, 1 cup	290	9	1.5	0	1240	50	3
Rice, long grain mushroom, Lipton Rice & Sauce, ½ cup	250	1.5	0.5	0	550	50	1
Rice, Mexican, Old El Paso, ½ cup	410	2	0.5	0	1350	90	3
Rice, mushroom, Lipton Rice & Sauce, ½ cup	220	1	1	0	890	45	1
Rice, mushroom and wild, Uncle Ben's Country Inn Recipes, mix to make 1 cup	260	4	1.5	5	810	50	1
Rice, onion mushroom, Lipton Golden Saute, ½ cup	240	4	1.5	0	850	45	2
Rice, Oriental, Lipton Golden Saute, ½ cup	240	4.5	1.5	0	910	43	1
Rice, Oriental, Lipton Rice & Sauce, ½ cup	230	1	0	<5	750	46	1
Rice, Oriental, & vegetables, Spice Islands, 1 pkg	180	2.5	0	0	600	33	1
Rice, Oriental stir fry, prepared, Rice-A-Roni, 1 cup	290	6	1	0	1080	53	1
Rice, Oriental style, prepared, Rice-A-Roni Fast Cook, 1 cup	290	10	2	0	930	43	1
Rice, saffron yellow, prepared, Carolina, 1 cup	190	0	0	0	970	43	<1

MEALS & SIDE DISHES	CAL (g)	FAT (g)	SAT FAT (g)	CHOL (mg)	SODIUM (mg)	CARB (g)	FIBER (g)
Rice, savory herb, Lipton Golden Saute, ½ cup	240	4.5	1.5	0	900	43	1
Rice, Spanish, Lipton Golden Saute, ½ cup	250	4.5	1.5	0	910	46	2
Rice, Spanish, Lipton Rice & Sauce, ½ cup	230	1	0	0	940	47	2
Rice, Spanish, Old El Paso, 1 cup	130	1	na	0	1340	28	2
Rice, Spanish, Success, ½ cup	190	0.5	0	0	780	43	1
Rice, Spanish, prepared, Mahatma, 1 cup	180	0.5	0	0	760	42	2
Rice, Spanish, prepared, Rice-A-Roni, 1 cup	270	8	1	0	1210	46	3
Rice, Spanish, prepared, Rice-A-Roni Fast Cook, 1 cup	250	6	1	0	1010	44	2
Rice, Spanish, quick brown, Arrowhead Mills, ⅓ cup	150	1	0	0	250	30	2
Rice, stroganoff, prepared, Rice-A-Roni, 1 cup	360	15	3.5	5	1040	50	1
Rice, vegetable, quick brown, Arrowhead Mills, ⅓ cup	150	1	0	0	160	30	3
Rice, white cheddar & herbs, prepared, Rice-A-Roni, 1 cup	340	14	4	5	980	49	1
Rice, wild, and vegetables, Spice Islands, 1 pkg	160	0	0	0	360	32	1
Rice, yellow, prepared, Mahatma, 1 cup	190	0	0	0	970	43	<1
Rice & beans, Bombay curry, Fantastic Foods, 1 pkg	230	3	1.5	0	470	47	8
Rice & beans, cajun, Fantastic Foods, 1 pkg	210	2	0	0	480	47	9
Rice & beans, Caribbean, Fantastic Foods, 1 pkg	190	1.5	0	0	490	44	8
Rice & beans, northern Italian, Fantastic Foods, 1 pkg	210	1.5	0	0	530	48	6
Rice & beans, Spanish, Fantastic Foods, 1 pkg	210	1.5	0	0	140	49	8
Rice & beans, spicy black, Spice Islands, 1 pkg	100	0	0	0	300	20	2

MEALS & SIDE DISHES	CAL	FAT (g)	SAT FAT (g)	CHOL (mg)	SODIUM (mg)	CARB (g)	FIBER (g)
Rice & beans, spicy red, Spice Islands, 1 pkg	110	0.5	0	0	480	23	2
Rice & beans, Szechuan, Fantastic Foods, 1 pkg	190	2	0	0	480	42	4
Rice & beans, Tex-Mex, Fantastic Foods, 1 pkg	230	2	0	0	540	53	9
Rice & country vegetables, Spice Islands, 1 pkg	170	0.5	0	0	610	38	1
Rice medley, Lipton Rice & Sauce, ½ cup	240	2	0.5	<5	810	46	2
Risotto, chicken, Lipton Rice & Sauce, ½ cup	230	2	0.5	5	740	44	1
Risotto, Milanese, Knorr, ¼ pkg	130	0.5	ns	ns	530	29	ns
Risotto, primavera, Knorr, ¼ pkg	140	0.5	ns	ns	530	30	ns
Risotto, with mushrooms, Knorr, ¼ pkg	140	0.5	ns	ns	570	31	ns
Risotto, with onions and herbs, Knorr, ¼ pkg	150	0.5	ns	ns	670	33	ns
Rotini primavera, Lipton Pasta & Sauce, ½ cup	240	5	2	10	880	42	2
Rotini & cheese, broccoli, Kraft Velveeta, 1 cup	400	16	10	45	1240	46	2
Salad, Caesar, Betty Crocker Suddenly Salad, ⅔ cup	170	1	0	0	650	33	1
Salad, garden Italian, 98% fat-free, Betty Crocker Suddenly Salad, ½ cup	130	1	0	0	520	28	2
Salad, ranch & bacon, Betty Crocker Suddenly Salad, ¾ cup	150	1	0.5	<5	320	31	1
Sauerbraten, Knorr, ⅙ pkg	35	1	0.5	2	430	5	0
Shells & cheese, bacon, Kraft Velveeta, 1 cup	360	14	8	40	1140	43	1
Shells & cheese, original, Kraft Velveeta, 1 cup	360	13	8	40	1030	44	1
Shells & cheese, salsa, Kraft Velveeta, 1 cup	380	14	9	40	1180	47	2

MEALS & SIDE DISHES	CAL	FAT (g)	SAT FAT (g)	CHOL (mg)	SODIUM (mg)	CARB (g)	FIBER (g)
Shells with white cheddar sauce, prepared, Noodle Roni, 1 cup	390	16	4.5	15	1150	47	2
Shrimp creole, prepared, Luzianne Cajun Creole, 1 cup	150	0.5	0	<5	810	34	<1
Spaghetti, American, mild, Kraft, 1 cup	270	4.5	1	<5	690	48	3
Spaghetti, tangy Italian, Kraft, 1 cup	270	4	1	<5	780	46	3
Spaghetti with meat sauce, Kraft, 1 cup	330	11	4	15	830	46	3
Stew, beef, Borden Stew Starter, ½ pkg	80	0	0	0	850	17	2
Stew, Moroccan, Casbah, 10 fl oz	180	0	0	0	460	38	2
Stew, vegetable, Knorr, 1 pkg	160	2	0	0	760	32	2
Taboule salad, prepared, Near East, ⅔ cup	120	3	0.5	0	340	23	3
Tabouli salad, Fantastic Foods, ¼ cup	120	0.5	0	0	450	26	6
Tabouli salad, prepared, Casbah, ⅔ cup	90	0.5	0	0	350	20	1
Taco, Old El Paso, 2 tacos	140	7	1	0	860	19	2
Taco, soft, Old El Paso, 2 tacos	210	3.5	1	0	1220	40	1
Taco dinner, Pancho Villa, 2 shells	150	8	1.5	0	790	20	2
Tamale, Old El Paso, 3 tamales	330	19	7	30	590	31	5
Tofu, breakfast scramble, NewMenu TofuMate, ¼ pkg	15	0	0	0	320	3	0
Tofu, eggless salad, NewMenu TofuMate, ¼ pkg	15	0	0	0	290	3	0
Tofu, Mandarin chow mein, Fantastic Foods, ⅝ cup	170	1.5	0	0	720	33	3
Tofu, Mandarin stirfry, NewMenu TofuMate, ¼ pkg	25	0	0	0	290	5	0
Tofu, Mediterranean herb, NewMenu TofuMate, ¼ pkg	15	0	0	0	310	3	0
Tofu, shells 'n curry, Fantastic Foods, ½ cup	200	1.5	0	0	500	40	5

MEALS & SIDE DISHES	CAL (g)	FAT (g)	SAT FAT (g)	CHOL (mg)	SODIUM (mg)	CARB (g)	FIBER (g)
Tofu, stroganoff, Fantastic Foods, ½ cup	190	5	3	5	660	35	3
Tofu, Szechwan stir fry, NewMenu TofuMate, ¼ pkg	20	0	0	0	280	4	0
Tofu, Texas taco, NewMenu TofuMate, ¼ pkg	15	0	0	0	360	3	0
Tofu Burger, Fantastic Foods, ⅛ cup	70	1.5	0	0	320	12	2
Tofu Scrambler, Fantastic Foods, 2½ tsp	60	0	0	0	430	12	3
Tomato Parmesan, Casbah, 1 package	170	1.5	0	<5	490	34	2
Tuna Helper, au gratin, Betty Crocker, ½ cup	190	4	1	<5	740	34	1
Tuna Helper, cheesy noodles, Betty Crocker, ⅔ cup	170	4	1	35	770	28	<1
Tuna Helper, creamy broccoli, Betty Crocker, ⅔ cup	190	5	1.5	<5	720	32	1
Tuna Helper, creamy noodles, Betty Crocker, ¾ cup	190	6	2	35	760	29	1
Tuna Helper, fettuccini Alfredo, Betty Crocker, 1 cup	180	4	2	10	790	30	<1
Tuna Helper, garden cheddar, Betty Crocker, ⅔ cup	190	4	1	<5	850	33	1
Tuna Helper, pasta salad, Betty Crocker, ⅓ cup	120	0.5	0	0	480	25	1
Tuna Helper, pasta salad, low fat, Betty Crocker, ⅔ cup	230	1.5	0	10	790	46	1
Tuna Helper, Tetrazzini, Betty Crocker, ⅔ cup	180	3	1.5	5	790	32	1
Tuna Helper, tuna pot pie, Betty Crocker, ½ cup	340	20	5	0	920	35	1
Tuna Helper, tuna Romanoff, Betty Crocker, ⅔ cup	210	3	1	5	650	38	1

AT A GLANCE: MEALS & SIDE DISHES

Lowest in Fat: La Choy Fried Rice; Fantastic Foods Cha Cha Chili
Lowest in Sodium, Meal: Tabasco 7-Spice Chili
Lowest in Sodium, Side Dish: Betty Crocker Specialty Hash Brown Potatoes

	CAL (g)	FAT (g)	SAT FAT (g)	CHOL (mg)	SODIUM (mg)	CARB (g)	FIBER (g)

MILK DRINKS, MILK ALTERNATIVES & CREAMERS

	CAL (g)	FAT (g)	SAT FAT (g)	CHOL (mg)	SODIUM (mg)	CARB (g)	FIBER (g)
Banana drink mix, Nestle Quik, 2 Tbsp	90	0	0	0	0	22	0
Buttermilk, dried, 1 Tbsp	25	0	0	<5	35	3	0
Chocolate drink mix, Nestle Quik, 2 Tbsp	90	0.5	0.5	0	30	19	1
Chocolate drink mix, no sugar added, Nestle Quik, 2 Tbsp	40	1	0.5	0	45	7	2
Chocolate malt flavor drink mix, traditional, Ovaltine, 4 Tbsp	80	0	0	0	115	18	1
Creamer, nondairy powder, Cremora, 1 tsp	10	1	0.5	ns	0	1	ns
Creamer, nondairy powder, all flavors, Carnation Coffee-Mate, 1⅓ Tbsp	60	3	2.5	0	15	9	0
Creamer, nondairy powder, lite, Cremora, 1 tsp	10	0	0	0	0	2	ns
Creamer, nondairy powder, lite or fat free, Carnation Coffee-Mate, 1 tsp	10	0	0	0	0	2	0
Creamer, nondairy powder, regular, Carnation Coffee-Mate, 1 tsp	10	0.5	0.5	0	0	1	0
Eggnog flavor mix, 2 tsp	110	0	0	5	45	28	<1
Malted milk mix, chocolate, Carnation, 3 Tbsp	90	1	0.5	0	40	18	<1
Malted milk mix, chocolate, Kraft, 3 Tbsp	80	1	0	0	40	17	<1
Malted milk mix, natural, Kraft, 3 Tbsp	90	2	1	5	85	15	0
Malted milk mix, original flavor, Carnation, 3 Tbsp	90	2	1	5	85	15	<1
Nondairy soy drink mix, all purpose, Loma Linda Soyagen, ¼ cup	130	6	1	0	150	12	3
Nondairy soy drink mix, carob, Loma Linda Soyagen, ¼ cup	130	6	1	0	170	13	2

MILK DRINKS, MILK ALTERNATIVES & CREAMERS	CAL	FAT (g)	SAT FAT (g)	CHOL (mg)	SODIUM (mg)	CARB (g)	FIBER (g)
Nondairy soy drink mix, no sucrose, Loma Linda Soyagen, ¼ cup	130	6	1	0	160	12	3
Nonfat, instant dry milk, Carnation, ⅓ cup	80	0	0	<5	125	12	na
Nonfat, instant dry milk, Sanalac, ¼ cup	90	0	0	5	120	13	0
Strawberry drink mix, Nestle Quik, 2 Tbsp	90	0	0	0	0	22	0
Whey, acid, dried, 1 Tbsp	10	0	0	0	30	2	0
Whey, sweet, dried, 1 Tbsp	25	0	0	0	80	6	0
Whole dry milk, ¼ cup	160	9	5	30	120	12	0

PASTA

Serving sizes are for dry product, unless indicated otherwise.

	CAL	FAT (g)	SAT FAT (g)	CHOL (mg)	SODIUM (mg)	CARB (g)	FIBER (g)
All varieties, Mueller's, 2 oz	210	1	0	0	0	42	na
All varieties, Napolina, 2 oz	210	1	0	0	0	43	na
All varieties, San Giorgio, 2 oz	210	1	0	0	0	40	2
All varieties with egg, Borden, 2 oz	220	3	1	55	15	40	1
All varieties with egg, enriched, Creamette, 2 oz	220	3	1	55	15	40	1
All varieties with egg and spinach, Borden, 2 oz	220	3	1	55	35	40	2
All varieties without egg, Borden/No Yolks, 2 oz	210	1	0	0	0	42	2
All varieties without egg, enriched, Creamette, ½ cup	210	1	0	0	0	42	2
All varieties without egg, with spinach, Borden, 2 oz	210	1	0	0	25	42	2
All varieties without egg, with tomato, Borden, 2 oz	210	1	0	0	20	42	1
Bows, veggie, Hodgson Mill, 2 oz	190	1	0	0	15	41	1
Fettucine, whole wheat, Hodgson Mill, 2 oz	190	1	1	0	10	34	6
Lasagna, whole wheat, Hodgson Mill, 2 oz	190	1	1	0	10	34	6

PASTA	CAL (g)	FAT (g)	SAT FAT (g)	CHOL (mg)	SODIUM (mg)	CARB (g)	FIBER (g)
Mung bean pasta, Eden, 2 oz	190	0	0	0	5	47	0
Noodles, bean thread, Dynasty, 1 bundle	170	0	0	0	10	42	0
Noodles, bean thread, Ka-Me, 1 cup	190	0	0	0	0	50	1
Noodles, chow mein, La Choy, ½ cup	140	6	1	0	220	19	1
Noodles, crispy, wide, La Choy, ½ cup	150	8	1.5	0	290	16	1
Noodles, egg, Kluski, 1 cup	220	3	1	55	210	40	1
Noodles, egg, Mueller's, 2 oz	220	3	0.5	60	10	38	na
Noodles, egg, enriched, 2 oz	220	2.5	0.5	55	15	41	2
Noodles, egg, enriched, cooked, ½ cup	110	1	0	25	5	20	<1
Noodles, egg, spinach, enriched, 2 oz	220	2.5	0.5	55	40	40	4
Noodles, egg, spinach, enriched, cooked, ½ cup	110	1	0	25	10	19	2
Noodles, Japanese, soba, 2 oz	190	0	0	0	450	43	na
Noodles, Japanese, soba, cooked, ½ cup	60	0	0	0	35	12	<1
Noodles, Japanese, somen, 2 oz	200	0	0	0	1050	42	2
Noodles, Japanese, somen, cooked, ½ cup	120	0	0	0	140	24	1
Noodles, rice, La Choy, ½ cup	120	3	0.5	0	380	21	0
Noodles, rice stick, Dynasty, 2 oz	200	0.5	0	0	90	48	0
Noodles, rice stick, Ka-Me, 2 oz	190	0	0	0	100	48	0
Noodles, somen, Ka-Me, 2 oz	190	1	0	0	670	41	1
Noodles, yolk free, cholesterol free, Mueller's, 2 oz	210	1	0	0	10	42	na
Ribbons, pesto, Eden, 2 oz	220	1	0	0	0	44	3
Ribbons, spinach, whole grain, Eden, 2 oz	200	1.5	0	0	10	40	7
Rice pasta, Eden, 2 oz	200	0.5	0	0	5	44	0

PASTA	CAL (g)	FAT (g)	SAT FAT (g)	CHOL (mg)	SODIUM (mg)	CARB (g)	FIBER (g)
Spaghetti, parsley garlic, Eden, 2 oz	210	1	0	0	10	42	2
Spaghetti, spinach, whole wheat, Hodgson Mill, 2 oz	190	2	1	0	25	35	5
Spaghetti, whole grain, Eden, 2 oz	210	1.5	0	0	0	39	6
Spaghetti, whole grain kamut, Eden, 2 oz	210	1.5	0	0	0	38	6
Spaghetti, whole wheat, Hodgson Mill, 2 oz	190	1	1	0	10	34	6
Spirals, vegetable, whole grain, Eden, 2 oz	210	1.5	0	0	0	39	6
Tri-color, Mueller's, 2 oz	210	1	0	0	10	42	na
Tricolor, without egg, with vegetables, all types, Borden, 2 oz	210	1	0	0	20	42	1

AT A GLANCE: PASTA
Highest in Fiber: Eden Whole Grain Spinach Ribbons

PUDDING DESSERTS

	CAL (g)	FAT (g)	SAT FAT (g)	CHOL (mg)	SODIUM (mg)	CARB (g)	FIBER (g)
Banana, instant, fat free, sugar free, reduced calorie, made with skim milk, Jell-O Brand, ½ cup	70	0	0	0	410	12	0
Banana cream, cook & serve, made with 2% milk, Jell-O Brand, ½ cup	140	2.5	1.5	10	240	26	0
Banana cream, instant, made with 2% milk, Jell-O Brand, ½ cup	150	2.5	1.5	10	410	29	0
Butter pecan, instant, made with 2% milk, Jell-O Brand, ½ cup	160	3	1.5	10	410	29	0
Butterscotch, cook & serve, made with 2% milk, Jell-O Brand, ½ cup	160	2.5	1.5	10	190	30	0
Butterscotch, instant, fat free, sugar free, reduced calorie, made with skim milk, Jell-O Brand, ½ cup	70	0	0	0	400	12	0

PUDDING DESSERTS	CAL (g)	FAT (g)	SAT FAT (g)	CHOL (mg)	SODIUM (mg)	CARB (g)	FIBER (g)
Butterscotch, instant, made with 2% milk, Jell-O Brand, ½ cup	150	2.5	1.5	10	450	29	0
Chocolate, cook & serve, Royal, mix to make ½ cup	90	0	0	0	80	22	<1
Chocolate, cook & serve, made with 2% milk, Jell-O Brand, ½ cup	150	2.5	1.5	10	170	28	<1
Chocolate, cook & serve, sugar free, reduced calorie, made with 2% milk, Jell-O Brand, ½ cup	90	2.5	1.5	10	170	23	<1
Chocolate, instant, fat free, sugar free, reduced calorie, made with skim milk, Jell-O Brand, ½ cup	80	0	0	0	390	14	<1
Chocolate, instant, made with 2% milk, Jell-O Brand, ½ cup	160	2.5	1.5	10	470	31	<1
Chocolate, reduced calorie, made with skim milk, D-Zerta, ½ cup	60	0	0	0	65	11	<1
Chocolate fudge, cook & serve, made with 2% milk, Jell-O Brand, ½ cup	150	2.5	1.5	10	170	28	1
Chocolate fudge, instant, fat free, sugar free, reduced calorie, made with skim milk, Jell-O Brand, ½ cup	80	0	0	0	390	14	<1
Chocolate fudge, instant, made with 2% milk, Jell-O Brand, ½ cup	160	3	1.5	10	440	31	<1
Coconut cream, cook & serve, made with 2% milk, Jell-O Brand, ½ cup	150	5	4	10	210	24	<1
Coconut cream, instant, made with 2% milk, Jell-O Brand, ½ cup	160	4.5	3.5	10	320	27	<1
Custard, made with 2% milk, Jell-O Americana, ½ cup	140	2.5	1.5	10	190	25	0
Custard, egg, made with 2% milk, ½ cup	150	4	2	75	200	24	ns
Danish dessert, all flavors, Junket, ½ cup	130	0	0	0	5	32	0

PUDDING DESSERTS	CAL	FAT (g)	SAT FAT (g)	CHOL (mg)	SODIUM (mg)	CARB (g)	FIBER (g)
Flan, cook & serve, made with 2% milk, Jell-O Brand, ½ cup	140	2.5	1.5	10	65	26	0
Flan, caramel custard, made with 2% milk, ½ cup	140	2.5	1.5	10	70	26	ns
Flan, creme caramel, Alsa, ¼ pkg	110	0	0	5	15	27	na
French vanilla, instant, made with 2% milk, Jell-O Brand, ½ cup	150	2.5	1.5	10	410	29	0
Key lime, cook & serve, Royal, ⅙ box	50	0	0	0	120	13	0
Lemon, cook & serve, made with sugar, egg yolks & water, Jell-O Brand, ½ cup	140	2	0.5	75	75	29	0
Lemon, instant, made with 2% milk, Jell-O Brand, ½ cup	150	2.5	1.5	10	360	29	0
Milk chocolate, cook & serve, made with 2% milk, Jell-O Brand, ½ cup	150	2.5	1.5	10	170	28	<1
Milk chocolate, instant, made with 2% milk, Jell-O Brand, ½ cup	160	3	2	10	460	31	<1
Mousse, dark chocolate, Alsa, ¼ pkg	80	4	4	na	40	8	na
Mousse, milk chocolate, Alsa, ¼ pkg	80	4	4	na	40	10	na
Mousse, white chocolate, Alsa, ¼ pkg	70	3.5	3	na	40	8	na
Pistachio, instant, Royal, mix to make ½ cup	90	0.5	0	0	350	22	0
Pistachio, instant, fat free, sugar free, reduced calorie, made with skim milk, Jell-O Brand, ½ cup	70	0	0	0	380	12	0
Pistachio, instant, made with 2% milk, Jell-O Brand, ½ cup	160	3	1.5	10	410	29	0
Rice, made with 2% milk, Jell-O Americana, ½ cup	160	2.5	1.5	10	160	30	0
Tapioca, Minute, 1½ tsp	20	0	0	0	0	5	0
Tapioca, made with 2% milk, Jell-O Americana, ½ cup	140	2.5	1.5	10	170	26	0

PUDDING DESSERTS	CAL (g)	FAT (g)	SAT FAT (g)	CHOL (mg)	SODIUM (mg)	CARB (g)	FIBER (g)
Vanilla, cook & serve, Royal, mix to make ½ cup	80	0	0	0	160	20	<1
Vanilla, cook & serve, made with 2% milk, Jell-O Brand, ½ cup	140	2.5	1.5	10	200	26	0
Vanilla, cook & serve, made with 2% milk, sugar free, reduced calorie, Jell-O Brand, ½ cup	80	2.5	1.5	10	170	11	0
Vanilla, instant, Royal, mix to make ½ cup	90	0	0	0	330	23	0
Vanilla, instant, fat free, sugar free, reduced calorie, made with skim milk, Jell-O Brand, ½ cup	70	0	0	0	400	12	0
Vanilla, instant, made with 2% milk, Jell-O Brand, ½ cup	150	2.5	1.5	10	410	29	0
Pudding snack, banana, Del Monte, 4 oz	140	4	1	0	190	25	0
Pudding snack, banana, Hunt's Snack Pack, 1 snack	160	6	2	0	160	25	0
Pudding snack, banana, refrigerated, Jell-O Brand, 1 snack	170	7	2	0	170	25	0
Pudding snack, butterscotch, Del Monte, 1 snack	140	4	1	0	170	25	0
Pudding snack, butterscotch, Hunt's Snack Pack, 1 snack	150	6	2	0	210	24	0
Pudding snack, butterscotch, refrigerated, Swiss Miss, 1 snack	160	6	1.5	0	180	24	0
Pudding snack, chocolate, Del Monte, 1 snack	160	4	1	0	130	27	0
Pudding snack, chocolate, Hunt's Snack Pack, 1 snack	170	6	1.5	0	170	25	0
Pudding snack, chocolate, fat free, Hunt's Snack Pack, 1 snack	100	0	0	0	210	21	0
Pudding snack, chocolate, fat free, Jell-O Brand, 1 snack	100	0	0	0	190	23	0
Pudding snack, chocolate, fat free, refrigerated, Swiss Miss, 1 snack	100	0	0	0	150	22	0

PUDDING DESSERTS	CAL	FAT (g)	SAT FAT (g)	CHOL (mg)	SODIUM (mg)	CARB (g)	FIBER (g)
Pudding snack, chocolate, lite, Del Monte, 1 snack	100	1	0	0	140	19	0
Pudding snack, chocolate, refrigerated, Jell-O Brand, 1 snack	160	5	2	0	190	28	0
Pudding snack, chocolate, refrigerated, Swiss Miss, 1 snack	170	6	1.5	0	180	26	0
Pudding snack, chocolate caramel swirl, Hunt's Snack Pack, 1 snack	170	6	1.5	0	180	26	0
Pudding snack, chocolate-caramel swirl, refrigerated, Jell-O Brand, 1 snack	160	5	2	0	180	27	0
Pudding snack, chocolate caramel swirl, refrigerated, Swiss Miss, 1 snack	170	6	1.5	0	180	26	0
Pudding snack, chocolate-chocolate fudge parfait, refrigerated, Swiss Miss, 1 snack	160	6	1.5	0	200	25	0
Pudding snack, chocolate fudge, Del Monte, 1 snack	150	4	1	0	190	25	0
Pudding snack, chocolate fudge, Hunt's Snack Pack, 1 snack	170	6	1.5	0	190	26	0
Pudding snack, chocolate fudge, fat free, refrigerated, Swiss Miss, 1 snack	100	0	0	0	150	23	0
Pudding snack, chocolate fudge, refrigerated, Swiss Miss, 1 snack	180	6	1.5	0	210	28	0
Pudding snack, chocolate marshmallow, Hunt's Snack Pack, 1 snack	160	6	2	0	125	23	0
Pudding snack, chocolate peanut butter swirl, Hunt's Snack Pack, 1 snack	170	6	1.5	0	170	25	0
Pudding snack, chocolate vanilla parfait, refrigerated, Swiss Miss, 1 snack	160	6	1.5	0	200	25	0

PUDDING DESSERTS	CAL (g)	FAT (g)	SAT FAT (g)	CHOL (mg)	SODIUM (mg)	CARB (g)	FIBER (g)
Pudding snack, chocolate-vanilla swirl, fat free, refrigerated, Jell-O Brand, 1 snack	100	0	0	0	210	23	0
Pudding snack, chocolate-vanilla swirl, refrigerated, Jell-O Brand, 1 snack	160	5	2	0	180	27	0
Pudding snack, chocolate vanilla swirl, refrigerated, Swiss Miss, 1 snack	170	6	1.5	0	160	26	0
Pudding snack, lemon, Hunt's Snack Pack, 1 snack	160	3.5	1	0	100	33	0
Pudding snack, milk chocolate swirl, Hunt's Snack Pack, 1 snack	160	6	1.5	0	180	26	0
Pudding snack, milk chocolate-chocolate fudge parfait, refrigerated, Swiss Miss, 1 snack	160	6	1.5	0	200	25	0
Pudding snack, s'mores swirl, Hunt's Snack Pack, 1 snack	150	6	1.5	0	130	25	0
Pudding snack, tapioca, Del Monte, 1 snack	140	4	1	0	110	23	0
Pudding snack, tapioca, Hunt's Snack Pack, 1 snack	150	6	1	0	135	23	0
Pudding snack, tapioca, fat free, Hunt's Snack Pack, 1 snack	90	0	0	0	190	21	0
Pudding snack, tapioca, fat free, refrigerated, Swiss Miss, 1 snack	100	0	0	0	150	22	0
Pudding snack, tapioca, refrigerated, Jell-O Brand, 1 snack	140	4	1.5	0	160	26	0
Pudding snack, tapioca, refrigerated, Swiss Miss, 1 snack	140	3.5	1	0	180	24	0
Pudding snack, vanilla, Del Monte, 1 snack	150	4	1	0	150	26	0
Pudding snack, vanilla, Hunt's Snack Pack, 1 snack	160	6	1.5	0	170	25	0

PUDDING DESSERTS	CAL (g)	FAT (g)	SAT FAT (g)	CHOL (mg)	SODIUM (mg)	CARB (g)	FIBER (g)
Pudding snack, vanilla, fat free, Hunt's Snack Pack, 1 snack	90	0	0	0	170	21	0
Pudding snack, vanilla, fat free, refrigerated, Jell-O Brand, 1 snack	100	0	0	0	240	23	0
Pudding snack, vanilla, fat free, refrigerated, Swiss Miss, 1 snack	100	0	0	0	160	22	0
Pudding snack, vanilla, lite, Del Monte, 1 snack	90	1	0	0	190	18	0
Pudding snack, vanilla, refrigerated, Jell-O Brand, 1 snack	160	5	2	0	170	25	0
Pudding snack, vanilla, refrigerated, Swiss Miss, 1 snack	160	6	1.5	0	180	24	0
Pudding snack, vanilla-chocolate parfait, fat free, refrigerated, Swiss Miss, 1 snack	100	0	0	0	170	23	0
Pudding snack, vanilla-chocolate parfait, refrigerated, Swiss Miss, 1 snack	160	6	1.5	0	200	25	0
Pudding snack, vanilla-chocolate swirl, fat free, refrigerated, Jell-O Brand, 1 snack	100	0	0	0	220	23	0
Pudding snack, vanilla-chocolate swirl, refrigerated, Jell-O Brand, 1 snack	160	5	2	0	180	26	0

AT A GLANCE: PUDDING DESSERTS

Lowest in Calories: Minute Tapioca, D-Zerta Chocolate Pudding, Reduced Calorie; Jell-O Brand Pistachio or Vanilla, Fat Free, Sugar Free, Reduced Calorie

RENNET

Rennet, chocolate, 1 Tbsp	35	0	0	0	5	8	ns
Rennet, chocolate, made with 2% milk, ½ cup	110	3	2	10	70	18	ns
Rennet, strawberry or raspberry custard mix, Junket, mix to make ½ cup	40	0	0	0	0	10	0

RENNET	CAL (g)	FAT (g)	SAT FAT (g)	CHOL (mg)	SODIUM (mg)	CARB (g)	FIBER (g)
Rennet, vanilla, 1 Tbsp	40	0	0	0	0	11	ns
Rennet, vanilla, made with 2% milk, ½ cup	100	2.5	1.5	10	60	16	ns
Rennet, vanilla or chocolate custard mix, Junket, mix to make ½ cup	40	0	0	0	5	10	0

VEGETABLES

	CAL (g)	FAT (g)	SAT FAT (g)	CHOL (mg)	SODIUM (mg)	CARB (g)	FIBER (g)
Beans, adzuki, Arrowhead Mills, ¼ cup	160	0.5	0	0	0	29	6
Beans, Anasazis, Arrowhead Mills, ¼ cup	150	0.5	0	0	0	27	9
Beans, black, ¼ cup	170	0.5	0	0	0	30	7
Beans, black, boiled, ½ cup	110	0	0	0	0	20	7
Beans, black, instant, Fantastic Foods, ⅓ cup	120	0.5	0	0	370	29	11
Beans, black turtle, Arrowhead Mills, ¼ cup	150	0.5	0	0	10	28	9
Beans, black turtle, boiled, ½ cup	120	0	0	0	0	22	5
Beans, blackeye peas, Allen/East Texas Fair, ½ cup	110	1	0.5	0	340	18	4
Beans, chickpeas (garbanzo beans), ¼ cup	180	3	0	0	15	30	9
Beans, chickpeas (garbanzo beans), boiled, ½ cup	130	2	0	0	5	22	4
Beans, cowpeas (black-eyed, crowder, Southern), ¼ cup	140	1	0	0	25	25	4
Beans, cowpeas (black-eyed, crowder, Southern), boiled, ½ cup	100	0	0	0	0	18	6
Beans, cowpeas, catjang, ¼ cup	140	1	0	0	25	25	na
Beans, cowpeas, catjang, boiled, ½ cup	100	0.5	0	0	15	17	na
Beans, cranberry (Roman), ¼ cup	160	0.5	0	0	0	30	na
Beans, cranberry (Roman), boiled, ½ cup	120	0	0	0	0	22	7

VEGETABLES	CAL (g)	FAT (g)	SAT FAT (g)	CHOL (mg)	SODIUM (mg)	CARB (g)	FIBER (g)
Beans, fava (broadbeans), ¼ cup	130	0.5	0	0	5	22	9
Beans, fava (broadbeans), boiled, ½ cup	90	0	0	0	0	17	5
Beans, French, ¼ cup	160	1	0	0	10	30	na
Beans, French, boiled, ½ cup	110	0.5	0	0	5	21	na
Beans, garbanzo, Arrowhead Mills, ¼ cup	170	2	0	0	10	29	6
Beans, great Northern, ¼ cup	150	0.5	0	0	5	29	na
Beans, great Northern, boiled, ½ cup	100	0	0	0	0	19	6
Beans, hyacinth, ¼ cup	180	1	0	0	10	32	4
Beans, hyacinth, boiled, ½ cup	110	0.5	0	0	10	20	0
Beans, kidney, Arrowhead Mills, ¼ cup	160	0.5	0	0	0	29	10
Beans, kidney, California red, ¼ cup	150	0	0	0	5	28	11
Beans, kidney, California red, boiled, ½ cup	110	0	0	0	0	20	0
Beans, kidney, royal red, ¼ cup	150	0	0	0	5	27	5
Beans, kidney, royal red, boiled, ½ cup	110	0	0	0	0	19	7
Beans, lentils, green, Arrowhead Mills, ¼ cup	150	0	0	0	15	27	7
Beans, lentils, red, Arrowhead Mills, ¼ cup	150	0	0	0	15	27	7
Beans, lima, baby, ¼ cup	170	0	0	0	10	32	9
Beans, lima, baby, boiled, ½ cup	120	0	0	0	0	21	7
Beans, lima, large, ¼ cup	150	0	0	0	10	28	8
Beans, lima, large, boiled, ½ cup	110	0	0	0	0	20	7
Beans, lupins, ¼ cup	170	4.5	0.5	0	10	18	na
Beans, lupins, boiled, ½ cup	100	2.5	0	0	0	8	2
Beans, moth, ¼ cup	170	1	0	0	15	30	na

VEGETABLES	CAL	FAT (g)	SAT FAT (g)	CHOL (mg)	SODIUM (mg)	CARB (g)	FIBER (g)
Beans, moth, boiled, ½ cup	100	0.5	0	0	10	18	na
Beans, mung, Arrowhead Mills, ¼ cup	160	0.5	0	0	0	28	9
Beans, mung, boiled, ½ cup	110	0	0	0	0	19	8
Beans, mungo, ¼ cup	180	1	0	0	15	32	na
Beans, mungo, boiled, ½ cup	90	0.5	0	0	5	16	6
Beans, navy, ¼ cup	170	1	0	0	10	32	13
Beans, navy, boiled, ½ cup	130	0.5	0	0	0	24	8
Beans, pink, ¼ cup	180	0.5	0	0	0	34	7
Beans, pink, boiled, ½ cup	130	0	0	0	0	23	4
Beans, pinto, Arrowhead Mills, ¼ cup	150	0.5	0	0	0	27	8
Beans, refried, instant, Fantastic Foods, ⅓ cup	120	0.5	0	0	380	30	12
Beans, small white, ¼ cup	180	1	0	0	10	34	10
Beans, small white, boiled, ½ cup	130	0.5	0	0	0	23	7
Beans, soybeans, Arrowhead Mills, ¼ cup	170	8	1	0	0	14	10
Beans, white, ¼ cup	170	0	0	0	10	31	8
Beans, white, boiled, ½ cup	130	0	0	0	5	23	6
Beans, winged, ½ cup	370	15	2	0	35	38	6
Beans, winged, boiled, ½ cup	130	5	1	0	10	13	2
Beans, yard-long, ½ cup	290	1	0	0	15	52	
Beans, yard-long, boiled, ½ cup	100	0	0	0	0	18	
Beans, yellow, ¼ cup	170	1.5	0	0	5	30	na
Beans, yellow, boiled, ½ cup	130	1	0	0	0	22	
Chiles, De Arbol, Don Enrique, ½ oz (24 pieces)	50	0	0	0	5	8	
Chiles, Habanero, Don Enrique, ½ pkg	25	0	0	0	0	4	<
Chiles, New Mexico, Don Enrique, ½ oz (2 pieces)	50	0	0	0	5	8	
Corn, dry, 2 oz	200	1.5	0	0	0	45	

VEGETABLES	CAL (g)	FAT (g)	SAT FAT (g)	CHOL (mg)	SODIUM (mg)	CARB (g)	FIBER (g)
Kanpyo (dried gourd strips), 3 strips	50	0	0	0	0	12	na
Leeks, bulb & lower leaf, freeze-dried, 1 Tbsp	0	0	0	0	0	0	na
Mushrooms, porcini (truffles), Urbani, ½ oz	35	0	0	0	25	6	6
Mushrooms, Shiitake, Seneca, ½ cup	25	0	0	0	540	5	3
Onions, dehydrated flakes, 1 Tbsp	15	0	0	0	0	4	0
Parsley, freeze-dried, 1 Tbsp	0	0	0	0	0	0	0
Peas, pigeon, ½ cup	100	0	0	0	0	20	na
Peas, split, boiled, ½ cup	120	0	0	0	0	21	8
Peas, split, green, Arrowhead Mills, ¼ cup	170	0.5	0	0	20	31	7
Peppers, sweet, green, freeze-dried, 1 Tbsp	0	0	0	0	0	0	7
Peppers, sweet, red, freeze-dried, 1 Tbsp	0	0	0	0	0	0	7
Potato mix, Betty Crocker Potato Buds, ⅓ cup	80	0	0	0	20	18	1
Potatoes, flakes, Idahoan, ⅓ cup	80	0	0	0	15	18	2
Radishes, Oriental, dried, ½ cup	160	0	0	0	160	37	na
Seaweed, agar, 1 sheet	5	0	0	0	0	2	0
Seaweed, spirulina, 1 sheet	5	0	0	0	20	0	0
Shallots, 1 Tbsp	0	0	0	0	0	<1	na
Tomato, halves, Timber Crest Farms, 2–3 halves	15	0	0	0	5	3	1

AT A GLANCE: VEGETABLES

Highest in Fiber: Arrowhead Mills Anasazi, Black Turtle, and Mung Beans

FROZEN FOODS

	CAL (g)	FAT (g)	SAT FAT (g)	CHOL (mg)	SODIUM (mg)	CARB (g)	FIBE (g)
BREADS & ROLLS							
Bagels, blueberry, Brooklyn Bagel Boys, 1 bagel	200	1	0	0	360	40	2
Bagels, blueberry, Lender's Bagels, 1 bagel	200	2	0	0	330	38	1
Bagels, cinnamon raisin, Brooklyn Bagel Boys, 1 bagel	200	1	0	0	250	42	*
Bagels, cinnamon raisin, Lender's Bagels, 1 bagel	200	1.5	0	0	290	39	2
Bagels, egg, Brooklyn Bagel Boys, 1 bagel	200	1	0	0	240	40	
Bagels, egg, Lender's Bagels, 1 bagel	160	1.5	0	10	320	30	
Bagels, garlic, Lender's Bagels, 1 bagel	150	1	0	0	280	29	
Bagels, oat bran, Lender's Bagels, 1 bagel	190	1.5	0	0	300	36	
Bagels, onion, Brooklyn Bagel Boys, 1 bagel	200	1	0	0	300	40	
Bagels, onion, Lender's Bagels, 1 bagel	160	1.5	0	0	300	30	
Bagels, plain, Brooklyn Bagel Boys, 1 bagel	200	1	0	0	340	40	<
Bagels, plain, Lender's Bagels, 1 bagel	160	1	0	0	320	30	
Bagels, plain, mini, Brooklyn Bagel Boys, 1 bagel	100	0	0	0	160	22	
Bagels, poppy, Lender's Bagels, 1 bagel	150	1	0	0	290	30	
Bagels, pumpernickel, Lender's Bagels, 1 bagel	150	1	0	0	340	31	
Bagels, rye, Lender's Bagels, 1 bagel	150	1	0	0	320	30	
Bagels, sesame, Lender's Bagels, 1 bagel	150	1.5	0	0	290	29	
Garlic & cheese biscuits, Pepperidge Farm, 1 biscuit	170	6	3	10	510	24	

BREADS & ROLLS	CAL (g)	FAT (g)	SAT FAT (g)	CHOL (mg)	SODIUM (mg)	CARB (g)	FIBER (g)
Garlic & cheese rolls, Pepperidge Farm, 1 roll	130	5	2	15	280	16	2
Garlic bread, Pepperidge Farm, 1/6 loaf	160	10	3	30	250	14	1
Garlic bread, cheddar cheese, Pepperidge Farm, 1/6 loaf	210	11	5	50	280	21	1
Garlic bread, Monterey Jack w/ jalapeno cheese, Pepperidge Farm, 1/6 loaf	200	10	4	40	280	22	1
Garlic bread, mozzarella, Pepperidge Farm, 1/6 loaf	200	10	5	40	280	21	1
Garlic bread, Parmesan, Pepperidge Farm, 1/6 loaf	160	7	2	10	260	19	2
Garlic bread, sourdough, Pepperidge Farm, 1/6 loaf	180	9	3	10	220	20	2
White bread, Bridgford Foods, 2 oz	160	3	0.5	0	290	29	1
White rolls, Bridgford Foods, 1.5 oz	120	2	0.5	0	220	22	1

BREAKFAST ITEMS

	CAL (g)	FAT (g)	SAT FAT (g)	CHOL (mg)	SODIUM (mg)	CARB (g)	FIBER (g)
Bagel sandwich, ham & cheese, Weight Watchers Breakfast On-The-Go, 3 oz	200	5	2	15	470	27	1
Burrito, bacon & scrambled eggs, Swanson Great Starts, 1 pkg	250	11	4	90	540	27	1
Burrito, breakfast sausage, Swanson Great Starts, 1 pkg	240	12	4	90	500	24	1
Burrito, ham & cheese flavor, Swanson Great Starts, 1 pkg	210	6	2	60	440	29	2
Burrito, hot & spicy, Swanson Great Starts, 1 pkg	220	7	3	55	490	30	3
Burrito, pizza with cheese & pepperoni, Swanson Great Starts, 1 pkg	240	9	3	60	410	28	2
Burrito, scrambled eggs, Swanson Great Starts, 1 pkg	200	8	3	60	510	25	2
Coffee cake, cinnamon streudel, Weight Watchers, 2.25 oz	190	3.5	1	0	190	35	2

BREAKFAST ITEMS	CAL	FAT (g)	SAT FAT (g)	CHOL (mg)	SODIUM (mg)	CARB (g)	FIBER (g)
Egg, cheese & bacon on a biscuit, Swanson Great Starts, 1 pkg	360	19	8	170	950	35	1
Egg product, real, Egg Beaters, ¼ cup	30	0	0	0	100	1	0
Eggs, bacon & cheese on a muffin, Swanson Great Starts, 1 pkg	290	15	6	95	750	25	2
Eggs, scrambled, Swanson Great Starts Budget, 1 pkg	200	12	8	190	390	15	2
Eggs, scrambled, & bacon, Swanson Great Starts, 1 pkg	290	19	9	240	700	17	1
Eggs, scrambled, & sausage, Swanson Great Starts, 1 pkg	360	26	10	280	800	21	3
Eggs and silver dollar pancakes, Swanson Great Starts Budget, 1 pkg	250	14	6	290	540	22	1
English muffin sandwich, Weight Watchers Breakfast On-The-Go, 4 oz	220	7	2	20	380	31	3
French toast, Downyflake, 2 slices	260	6	1.5	50	540	43	2
French toast, cinnamon swirl, Downyflake, 2 slices	270	6	1.5	40	520	45	1
French toast, cinnamon swirl, Swanson Great Starts, 1 pkg	440	28	12	150	580	34	2
French toast, with sausage, Swanson Great Starts, 1 pkg	410	26	9	110	580	33	3
French toast sticks, Rich-SeaPak, 5 pieces	400	20	3.5	25	330	48	3
French toast sticks, mini, Swanson Kids Breakfast Blast, 1 pkg	310	14	4	45	300	41	2
French toast sticks, with syrup, Swanson Great Starts, 1 pkg	320	10	5	25	260	50	2
Muffins, apple oatmeal, Pepperidge Farm, 1 muffin	160	4	1	0	190	28	3
Muffins, banana nut, Weight Watchers, 2.5 oz	190	5	1.5	5	280	32	3
Muffins, blueberry, Pepperidge Farm, 1 muffin	140	3	0	0	190	27	2

BREAKFAST ITEMS	CAL	FAT (g)	SAT FAT (g)	CHOL (mg)	SODIUM (mg)	CARB (g)	FIBER (g)
Muffins, blueberry, Weight Watchers, 2.5 oz	250	5	1	45	380	46	4
Muffins, bran, with raisins, Pepperidge Farm, 1 muffin	150	3	1	0	260	30	4
Muffins, chocolate chocolate chip, Weight Watchers, 2.5 oz	200	4	1.5	5	250	39	1
Muffins, corn, Pepperidge Farm, 1 muffin	150	3	0	0	190	27	1
Muffins, harvest honey bran, Weight Watchers, 2.5 oz	220	4	1	0	150	43	10
Omelet, ham & cheese, Weight Watchers Breakfast On-The-Go, 4 oz	230	6	3	35	470	30	3
Omelet sandwich, classic, Weight Watchers Breakfast On-The-Go, 3.84 oz	220	5	1	0	410	28	1
Omelet sandwich, garden, Weight Watchers Breakfast On-The-Go, 3.60 oz	220	6	2	15	440	31	2
Pancakes, Downyflake, 3 pancakes	270	7	2	5	700	47	2
Pancakes, 6 mini, Swanson Kids Breakfast Blast, 1 pkg	320	8	4	45	640	54	2
Pancakes, 6 silver dollar, Swanson Great Starts Budget, 1 pkg	340	18	9	70	670	36	1
Pancakes, all flavors, microwave, Act II, 1 box	370	15	3	5	690	53	1
Pancakes, blueberry, microwave, Pillsbury Hungry Jack, 3 pancakes	230	3.5	0.5	10	550	45	1
Pancakes, buttermilk, microwave, Pillsbury Hungry Jack, 3 pancakes	240	4	1	10	580	46	1
Pancakes, buttermilk, minis, microwave, Pillsbury Hungry Jack, 11 pancakes	230	4	1	10	550	44	1
Pancakes, original, microwave, Pillsbury Hungry Jack, 3 pancakes	240	4	1	10	550	47	1
Pancakes with bacon, Swanson Great Starts, 1 pkg	400	20	7	100	1030	42	1

BREAKFAST ITEMS	CAL (g)	FAT (g)	SAT FAT (g)	CHOL (mg)	SODIUM (mg)	CARB (g)	FIBER (g)
Pancakes with sausage, Swanson Great Starts, 1 pkg	490	25	11	90	950	52	3
Pastries, apple, Pillsbury Toaster Strudel, 1 pastry	180	7	1.5	5	190	27	<1
Pastries, blueberry, Pillsbury Toaster Strudel, 1 pastry	180	7	1.5	5	200	26	<1
Pastries, cherry, Pillsbury Toaster Strudel, 1 pastry	180	7	1.5	5	200	27	<1
Pastries, cinnamon, Pillsbury Toaster Strudel, 1 pastry	190	8	1.5	5	200	26	<1
Pastries, cream cheese, Pillsbury Toaster Strudel, 1 pastry	190	10	3.5	15	230	23	0
Pastries, cream cheese & fruit, all flavors, Pillsbury Toaster Strudel, 1 pastry	190	9	3	10	220	24	<1
Pastries, French toast flavor, Pillsbury Toaster Strudel, 1 pastry	190	7	1.5	5	200	28	<1
Pastries, raspberry, Pillsbury Toaster Strudel, 1 pastry	180	7	1.5	5	200	26	<1
Pastries, strawberry, Pillsbury Toaster Strudel, 1 pastry	180	7	1.5	5	200	26	<1
Sausage biscuit, Weight Watchers Breakfast On-The-Go, 3 oz	230	11	3.5	25	560	20	4
Sausage, egg & cheese, on a biscuit, Swanson Great Starts, 1 pkg	490	30	12	145	1110	36	3
Sweet rolls, apple Danish, Pepperidge Farm, 1 Danish	210	9	3	15	190	29	2
Sweet rolls, cheese Danish, Pepperidge Farm, 1 Danish	230	11	4	55	230	25	1
Sweet rolls, cinnamon roll, Pepperidge Farm, 1 roll	250	12	3	15	220	33	2
Sweet rolls, glazed cinnamon roll, Weight Watchers, 2.1 oz	200	5	1.5	5	200	33	1
Sweet rolls, raspberry Danish, Pepperidge Farm, 1 Danish	210	9	3	15	190	29	2
Waffles, apple cinnamon, Downyflake Crisp & Healthy, 2 waffles	180	2	0.5	0	360	36	2

BREAKFAST ITEMS	CAL (g)	FAT (g)	SAT FAT (g)	CHOL (mg)	SODIUM (mg)	CARB (g)	FIBER (g)
Waffles, apple cinnamon, Kellogg's Eggo, 2 waffles	220	8	1.5	20	450	33	0
Waffles, blueberry, Aunt Jemima, 2 waffles	190	6	1	10	640	29	1
Waffles, blueberry, Downyflake, 2 waffles	180	4	1	0	480	31	1
Waffles, blueberry, Kellogg's Eggo, 2 waffles	220	8	1.5	20	450	33	0
Waffles, blueberry, Kellogg's Eggo Minis, 3 sets of 4 waffles	240	8	1.5	25	510	37	0
Waffles, butter & syrup, Downyflake, 2 waffles	150	4	1	0	470	30	2
Waffles, buttermilk, Downyflake, 2 waffles	160	4	1	<5	480	28	1
Waffles, buttermilk, Kellogg's Eggo, 2 waffles	220	8	1.5	25	480	30	0
Waffles, cinnamon toast, Kellogg's Eggo Minis, 3 sets of 4 waffles	280	9	2	25	470	44	0
Waffles, homestyle, Downyflake, 4 waffles	230	5	1.5	0	620	40	2
Waffles, homestyle, Kellogg's Eggo, 2 waffles	220	8	1.5	25	470	30	0
Waffles, homestyle, Kellogg's Eggo Minis, 3 sets of 4 waffles	240	8	1.5	25	520	34	0
Waffles, hot 'n buttery, Downyflake, 4 waffles	180	6	1.5	<5	490	28	2
Waffles, nut & honey, Kellogg's Eggo, 2 waffles	240	10	2	25	480	32	0
Waffles, Nutri-Grain, Kellogg's Eggo, 2 waffles	190	6	1	0	430	30	4
Waffles, Nutri-Grain, multi-bran, Kellogg's Eggo, 2 waffles	80	6	1	0	400	32	6
Waffles, Nutri-Grain, raisin and bran, Kellogg's Eggo, 2 waffles	210	6	1	0	390	36	5
Waffles, oat bran, Kellogg's Eggo Common Sense, 2 waffles	200	7	1.5	0	350	27	3

BREAKFAST ITEMS	CAL	FAT (g)	SAT FAT (g)	CHOL (mg)	SODIUM (mg)	CARB (g)	FIBER (g)
Waffles, oat bran, with fruit & nut, Kellogg's Eggo Common Sense, 2 waffles	220	8	1.5	0	340	32	4
Waffles, original, Aunt Jemima, 2 waffles	190	7	2	15	570	29	1
Waffles, plain, Downyflake Crisp & Healthy, 2 waffles	170	2	0.5	0	340	34	2
Waffles, Special K, Kellogg's Eggo, 2 waffles	140	0	0	0	250	29	0
Waffles, strawberry, Kellogg's Eggo, 2 waffles	220	8	1.5	20	460	32	0
Waffle sticks, Swanson Kids Breakfast Blast, 1 pkg	330	17	7	75	250	39	1

AT A GLANCE: BREAKFAST ITEMS
Highest in Fiber: Egg Beaters Real Egg Product, Kellogg's Eggo Special K Waffles

DESSERTS

	CAL	FAT (g)	SAT FAT (g)	CHOL (mg)	SODIUM (mg)	CARB (g)	FIBER (g)
Cake, Boston creme, Pepperidge Farm Special Recipe, 1/8 cake	260	9	3	45	120	42	<1
Cake, carrot, deluxe, Pepperidge Farm Special Recipe, 1/8 cake	310	16	4	40	320	39	1
Cake, chocolate fudge, Pepperidge Farm, 1/6 cake	300	16	5	35	230	38	2
Cake, chocolate fudge stripe, Pepperidge Farm, 1/6 cake	290	14	3	35	150	38	2
Cake, chocolate mousse, Pepperidge Farm Special Recipe, 1/8 cake	250	10	3	25	120	35	2
Cake, coconut, Pepperidge Farm, 1/6 cake	300	14	4	40	200	41	1
Cake, devil's food, Pepperidge Farm, 1/6 cake	290	14	5	35	220	40	2
Cake, German chocolate, Pepperidge Farm, 1/6 cake	300	16	4	35	280	37	2
Cake, golden, Pepperidge Farm, 1/6 cake	290	14	3	50	230	40	23
Cake, lemon mousse, Pepperidge Farm Special Recipe, 1/8 cake	250	12	4	40	100	34	<1

DESSERTS	CAL (g)	FAT (g)	SAT FAT (g)	CHOL (mg)	SODIUM (mg)	CARB (g)	FIBER (g)
Cake, pineapple cream, Pepperidge Farm Special Recipe, 1/9 cake	240	10	3	30	120	38	<1
Cake, pound, all-butter, Pepperidge Farm, 1/5 cake	290	13	7	110	280	39	<1
Cake, strawberry stripe, Pepperidge Farm, 1/6 cake	310	13	4	65	150	47	<1
Cake, vanilla, Pepperidge Farm, 1/6 cake	290	13	3	45	190	41	<1
Cobbler, apple, Pet-Ritz, 1/6 cobbler	280	12	5	5	380	41	0
Cobbler, apple crumb, Pet-Ritz, 1/6 cobbler	280	9	4	5	270	49	0
Cobbler, blackberry, Pet-Ritz, 1/6 cobbler	260	11	4	5	230	38	1
Cobbler, blackberry crumb, Pet-Ritz, 1/6 cobbler	260	8	3	5	170	45	1
Cobbler, blueberry, Pet-Ritz, 1/6 cobbler	280	11	5	5	240	42	0
Cobbler, cherry, Pet-Ritz, 1/6 cobbler	300	11	4	5	300	48	1
Cobbler, cherry crumb, Pet-Ritz, 1/6 cobbler	280	6	2.5	5	330	54	0
Cobbler, peach, Pet-Ritz, 1/6 cobbler	230	9	3	5	220	37	1
Cobbler, peach crumb, Pet-Ritz, 1/6 cobbler	230	7	3	5	170	38	1
Cobbler, strawberry, Pet-Ritz, 1/6 cobbler	260	9	3	5	330	41	1
Dumplings, apple, Pepperidge Farm, 1 dumpling	290	11	3	0	160	44	3
Dumplings, cherry, Pepperidge Farm, 1 dumpling	280	9	2	0	280	47	2
Dumplings, peach, Pepperidge Farm, 1 dumpling	300	11	3	0	150	47	6
Fritters, apple, Mrs. Paul's, 2 fritters	260	11	4	5	570	36	2
Pie, apple, Banquet, 1/5 pie	300	13	6	5	370	41	2
Pie, apple, 8", Mrs. Smith's, 1/6 pie	270	11	2	0	300	41	1

DESSERTS	CAL (g)	FAT (g)	SAT FAT (g)	CHOL (mg)	SODIUM (mg)	CARB (g)	FIBER (g)
Pie, apple, Dutch, 8", Mrs. Smith's, 1/6 pie	320	13	2.5	0	260	48	1
Pie, apple cranberry, 8", Mrs. Smith's, 1/6 pie	280	11	2	0	300	43	1
Pie, apple lattice, 8", ready-to-serve, Mrs. Smith's, 1/5 pie	310	13	2.5	0	350	46	2
Pie, banana cream, Banquet, 1/3 pie	350	21	5	<5	290	39	1
Pie, banana cream, Pet-Ritz, 1/4 pie	270	13	8	5	250	37	1
Pie, banana cream, 8", Mrs. Smith's, 1/4 pie	280	14	4	0	170	37	1
Pie, berry, 8", Mrs. Smith's, 1/6 pie	280	11	2	0	340	44	0
Pie, blackberry, Banquet, 1/5 pie	300	12	5	5	430	15	3
Pie, blackberry, 8", Mrs. Smith's, 1/6 pie	280	11	2	0	320	43	0
Pie, blueberry, Banquet, 1/5 pie	260	12	5	5	400	36	2
Pie, blueberry, 8", Mrs. Smith's, 1/6 pie	260	11	2	0	320	39	1
Pie, Boston cream, 8", Mrs. Smith's, 1/8 pie	170	5	1.5	25	140	29	0
Pie, cherry, Banquet, 1/5 pie	290	14	6	5	310	39	2
Pie, cherry, 8", Mrs. Smith's, 1/6 pie	270	11	2	0	320	41	1
Pie, cherry lattice, 8", ready-to-serve, Mrs. Smith's, 1/5 pie	320	13	2.5	0	340	47	1
Pie, chocolate cream, Banquet, 1/3 pie	360	20	5	<5	240	43	3
Pie, chocolate cream, Pet-Ritz, 1/4 pie	290	13	8	5	270	39	2
Pie, chocolate cream, 8", Mrs. Smith's, 1/4 pie	330	17	4	0	200	42	1
Pie, coconut cream, Banquet, 1/3 pie	350	20	6	<5	250	39	2
Pie, coconut cream, Pet-Ritz, 1/4 pie	270	13	8	5	250	37	1
Pie, coconut cream, 8", Mrs. Smith's, 1/4 pie	340	19	5	0	260	40	0

DESSERTS	CAL (g)	FAT (g)	SAT FAT (g)	CHOL (mg)	SODIUM (mg)	CARB (g)	FIBER (g)
Pie, coconut custard, 8", Mrs. Smith's, ⅕ pie	280	12	5	75	350	35	0
Pie, French silk chocolate, 8", Mrs. Smith's, ⅕ pie	410	21	6	5	250	55	1
Pie, fudge vanilla cream, Pet-Ritz, ¼ pie	300	15	9	5	190	40	1
Pie, lemon cream, Banquet, ⅓ pie	360	20	5	<5	240	43	2
Pie, lemon cream, Pet-Ritz, ¼ pie	270	13	8	5	250	37	1
Pie, lemon cream, 8", Mrs. Smith's, ¼ pie	300	15	4	0	160	40	0
Pie, lemon meringue, 8", Mrs. Smith's, ⅕ pie	300	8	2	65	220	55	0
Pie, mince, 8", Mrs. Smith's, ⅙ pie	300	11	2	0	400	48	2
Pie, mincemeat, Banquet, ⅕ pie	310	13	6	10	430	46	2
Pie, peach, Banquet, ⅕ pie	260	12	5	5	340	36	2
Pie, peach, 8", Mrs. Smith's, ⅙ pie	260	11	2	0	310	38	1
Pie, peanut butter chocolate, Pet-Ritz, ¼ pie	300	15	8	5	180	37	2
Pie, pecan, 8", Mrs. Smith's, ⅙ pie	520	23	4	70	450	73	1
Pie, pumpkin, Banquet, ⅕ pie	250	8	3	20	340	40	3
Pie, pumpkin, hearty, 8", Mrs. Smith's, ⅕ pie	250	8	1.5	50	320	42	2
Pie, pumpkin cream, Pet-Ritz, ¼ pie	270	13	8	5	250	37	1
Pie, pumpkin custard, 8", Mrs. Smith's, ⅕ pie	270	8	2	45	350	44	1
Pie, raspberry, red, 8", Mrs. Smith's, ⅙ pie	280	11	2	0	320	43	0
Pie, strawberry, 8", Mrs. Smith's, ⅕ pie	280	11	2.5	0	190	45	1
Pie, strawberry cream, Banquet, ⅓ pie	340	17	4	<5	240	44	2
Pie, strawberry rhubarb, 8", Mrs. Smith's, ⅙ pie	280	11	2	0	380	44	0

DESSERTS	CAL (g)	FAT (g)	SAT FAT (g)	CHOL (mg)	SODIUM (mg)	CARB (g)	FIBER (g)
Turnovers, apple, Pepperidge Farm, 1 turnover	330	14	3	0	180	48	6
Turnovers, apple, mini, Pepperidge Farm, 1 turnover	140	8	2	0	80	15	1
Turnovers, apple, with vanilla icing, Pepperidge Farm, 1 turnover	360	14	3	0	190	53	2
Turnovers, blueberry, Pepperidge Farm, 1 turnover	340	16	3	0	200	45	6
Turnovers, cherry, Pepperidge Farm, 1 turnover	320	13	3	0	190	46	6
Turnovers, cherry, mini, Pepperidge Farm, 1 turnover	140	8	2	0	70	16	1
Turnovers, cherry, with vanilla icing, Pepperidge Farm, 1 turnover	340	13	3	0	200	51	3
Turnovers, peach, Pepperidge Farm, 1 turnover	340	15	3	0	180	47	6
Turnovers, peach, mini, Pepperidge Farm, 1 turnover	160	8	2	<5	45	21	<1
Turnovers, raspberry, Pepperidge Farm, 1 turnover	330	14	3	0	190	47	6
Turnovers, raspberry, with vanilla icing, Pepperidge Farm, 1 turnover	360	14	3	0	190	53	3
Turnovers, strawberry, mini, Pepperidge Farm, 1 turnover	140	7	2	0	100	18	<1
Whipped cream, La Creme, 2 Tbsp	15	1	1	0	10	2	0
Whipped topping, Cool Whip, 2 Tbsp	25	1.5	1.5	0	0	2	0
Whipped topping, extra creamy, Cool Whip, 2 Tbsp	30	2	2	0	5	2	0
Whipped topping, lite, Cool Whip, 2 Tbsp	20	1	1	0	0	2	0

AT A GLANCE: DESSERTS
Lowest in Fat: Prepared Desserts: Mrs. Smith's Boston Creme Pie

	CAL	FAT (g)	SAT FAT (g)	CHOL (mg)	SODIUM (mg)	CARB (g)	FIBER (g)

DESSERTS, SPECIALTY

	CAL	FAT (g)	SAT FAT (g)	CHOL (mg)	SODIUM (mg)	CARB (g)	FIBER (g)
Brownie a la mode, Weight Watchers Sweet Celebrations, 6.42 oz	190	4	1	5	160	35	4
Brownie cheesecake, Weight Watchers Sweet Celebrations, 3.5 oz	200	6	2	5	220	33	4
Caramel fudge a la mode, Weight Watchers Sweet Celebrations, 6.07 oz	180	3	1	0	170	34	0
Chocolate chip cookie dough sundae, Weight Watchers Sweet Celebrations, 5.43 oz	180	4	1.5	5	120	34	2
Chocolate eclair, Weight Watchers Sweet Celebrations, 2.1 oz	150	5	1.5	0	150	24	2
Chocolate frosted brownie, Weight Watchers Sweet Celebrations, 1.25 oz	100	2.5	1	0	135	22	3
Chocolate mocha pie, Weight Watchers Sweet Celebrations, 2.75 oz	170	4	1	5	125	31	2
Chocolate mousse, Weight Watchers Sweet Celebrations, 2.75 oz	190	4	1.5	5	150	33	3
Double fudge brownie parfait, Weight Watchers Sweet Celebrations, 5.3 fl oz	190	2.5	2	5	170	39	2
Double fudge cake, Weight Watchers Sweet Celebrations, 2.75 oz	190	4.5	1	0	200	36	2
Milk chocolate or dark chocolate clouds, Pepperidge Farm, 2 pastries	580	38	15	55	400	54	3
Mississippi mud pie, Weight Watchers Sweet Celebrations, 5.04 oz	180	5	1.5	5	120	30	2
Peanut butter fudge brownie, Weight Watchers Sweet Celebrations, 1.23 oz	110	2.5	0.5	0	140	21	3
Praline pecan mousse, Weight Watchers Sweet Celebrations, 2.71 oz	170	3.5	1	0	140	31	0

DESSERTS, SPECIALTY	CAL	FAT (g)	SAT FAT (g)	CHOL (mg)	SODIUM (mg)	CARB (g)	FIBER (g)
Praline toffee crunch parfait, Weight Watchers Sweet Celebrations, 5.10 fl oz	190	3	2	5	140	40	2
Strawberry cheesecake, Weight Watchers Sweet Celebrations, 3.9 oz	180	5	2	15	230	28	2
Strawberry shortcake a la mode, Weight Watchers Sweet Celebrations, 6.49 oz	180	1.5	0.5	5	160	39	1
Toasted almond amaretto cheesecake, Weight Watchers Sweet Celebrations, 3 oz	170	5	2.5	5	160	24	3
Triple chocolate caramel mousse, Weight Watchers Sweet Celebrations, 2.75 oz	200	4	1	5	120	34	2
Triple chocolate cheesecake, Weight Watchers Sweet Celebrations, 3.15 oz	200	5	2.5	10	200	32	1

AT A GLANCE: SPECIALTY DESSERTS
Lowest in Fat: Weight Watchers Strawberry Shortcake a la Mode

FROZEN NOVELTIES

	CAL	FAT (g)	SAT FAT (g)	CHOL (mg)	SODIUM (mg)	CARB (g)	FIBER (g)
Berries 'n creme mousse bar, Weight Watchers, 2 bars	70	1.5	0	0	75	17	1
Chocolate milkshake, Good Humor, 1 cup	230	5	3	15	105	38	2
Chocolate malt milk shake, lowfat, Milky Way, 1 cup	220	3	2	10	135	44	2
Chocolate mousse bar, Weight Watchers, 2 bars	70	1	0.5	5	80	18	4
Chocolate Treat, Weight Watchers, 1 bar	100	1	0	10	150	21	1
Frozen yogurt bar, cherry chocolate fudge, Haagen-Dazs, 1 bar	240	13	8	35	45	26	1
Frozen yogurt bar, Cherry Garcia, Ben & Jerry's, 1 pop	290	16	10	20	60	34	2
Frozen yogurt bar, Creamsicle, Popsicle, 1 bar	100	1	1	<5	20	23	0
Frozen yogurt bar, peach, Haagen-Dazs, 1 bar	90	1	0.5	15	20	19	0

FROZEN NOVELTIES	CAL (g)	FAT (g)	SAT FAT (g)	CHOL (mg)	SODIUM (mg)	CARB (g)	FIBER (g)
Frozen yogurt bar, pina colada, Haagen-Dazs, 1 bar	100	1	0.5	15	45	19	0
Frozen yogurt bar, raspberry/vanilla, Haagen-Dazs, 1 bar	90	1	0	15	25	19	0
Frozen yogurt bar, Starburst, all flavors, lowfat, 1 bar	70	1	0.5	<5	25	13	0
Frozen yogurt bar, strawberry daiquiri, Haagen-Dazs, 1 bar	90	1	0.5	15	20	18	0
Frozen yogurt bar, Tropical Orange Passion, Haagen-Dazs, 1 bar	100	1	0.5	15	20	20	0
Fruit 'n juice bar, peach passion, Dole, 1 bar	70	0	0	0	5	17	0
Fruit 'n juice bar, pine-orange-banana, Dole, 1 bar	70	0	0	0	5	16	0
Fruit 'n juice bar, raspberry, Dole, 1 bar	70	0	0	0	5	16	0
Fruit 'n juice bar, strawberry, Dole, 1 bar	70	0	0	0	5	17	0
Fruit juice bar, Starburst, 1 bar	50	0	0	0	0	12	0
Fruit juice bar, coconut, Good Humor Snowfruit, 1 bar	150	4	3	10	35	27	<1
Fruit juice bar, grape, Dole, 1 bar	45	0	0	0	5	11	0
Fruit juice bar, grape, sugar free, Dole, 1 bar	25	0	0	0	5	6	0
Fruit juice bar, Minute Maid, all flavors, Good Humor, 1 bar	60	0.5	0	0	0	14	0
Fruit juice bar, orange, Good Humor Snowfruit, 1 bar	140	0	0	0	10	34	<1
Fruit juice bar, raspberry, Dole, 1 bar	45	0	0	0	5	11	0
Fruit juice bar, raspberry, sugar free, Dole, 1 bar	25	0	0	0	5	6	0
Fruit juice bar, strawberry, Dole, 1 bar	45	0	0	0	5	11	0
Fruit juice bar, strawberry, Good Humor Snowfruit, 1 bar	120	0	0	0	15	31	<1

FROZEN NOVELTIES	CAL (g)	FAT (g)	SAT FAT (g)	CHOL (mg)	SODIUM (mg)	CARB (g)	FIBER (g)
Fruit juice bar, strawberry, sugar free, Dole, 1 bar	25	0	0	0	5	6	0
Fruit juice bar, tropical fruit, Good Humor Snowfruit, 1 bar	110	0	0	0	10	28	0
Fruit juice bar, Welch's, all flavors, 1 bar	45	0	0	0	0	11	ns
Fruit juice bar, Welch's, all flavors, light, 1 bar	25	0	0	0	0	6	ns
Fudgsicle, Popsicle, 1 bar	50	0	0	0	0	13	0
Ice cream bar, 3 Musketeers, chocolate, 6-pack, 1 bar	140	8	4	10	30	16	0
Ice cream bar, 3 Musketeers, chocolate, single, 1 bar	190	11	6	20	40	22	0
Ice cream bar, 3 Musketeers, vanilla, 6-pack, 1 bar	140	7	4	10	30	16	0
Ice cream bar, 3 Musketeers, vanilla, single, 1 bar	190	10	6	20	40	21	0
Ice cream bar, Arctic D'Lites, Weight Watchers, 1 bar	130	7	3.5	5	20	4	0
Ice cream bar, Butterfinger, Nestle, 1 bar	170	12	7	15	40	14	0
Ice cream bar, candy center crunch, Good Humor Classic, 1 bar	280	21	17	15	75	21	0
Ice cream bar, Caramel Cone Explosion, Haagen-Dazs Extraas, 1 bar	330	22	13	60	150	30	<1
Ice cream bar, caramel nut, Weight Watchers, 1 bar	130	8	3.5	5	25	14	0
Ice cream bar, Choco Taco, Good Humor, 1 taco	320	17	11	20	100	38	1
Ice cream bar, chocolate chip cookie dough, Ben & Jerry's, 1 pop	450	28	15	60	150	48	1
Ice cream bar, chocolate dip, Weight Watchers, 1 bar	100	6	3	5	15	11	0
Ice cream bar, chocolate eclair, Good Humor Classic, 1 bar	220	10	7	10	80	28	2
Ice cream bar, chocolate eclair, Sealtest Colonel Crunch, 1 bar	160	7	4	10	60	21	1

FROZEN NOVELTIES	CAL (g)	FAT (g)	SAT FAT (g)	CHOL (mg)	SODIUM (mg)	CARB (g)	FIBER (g)
Ice cream bar, chocolate mint, Breyers, 1 bar	230	15	11	50	45	20	0
Ice cream bar, chocolate/dark chocolate, Haagen-Dazs, 1 bar	320	22	15	70	70	27	3
Ice cream bar, coffee/almond crunch, Haagen-Dazs, 1 bar	290	21	12	80	70	22	<1
Ice cream bar, cookie dough, Breyers, 1 bar	280	17	9	30	80	27	<1
Ice cream bar, Cool Cream, Flintstones, 1 bar	90	2	1	5	30	18	0
Ice cream bar, Creamsicle, Popsicle, 1 bar	110	3	2	10	30	20	0
Ice cream bar, crispy pralines 'n creme, Weight Watchers, 1 bar	130	7	3.5	5	40	15	0
Ice cream bar, double fudge bar, Popsicle Supersicle, 1 bar	150	2	1	10	95	29	<1
Ice cream bar, Dove Bite Size, double chocolate, 5 bars	360	23	15	30	40	37	1
Ice cream bar, Dove Bite Size, French vanilla, 5 bars	370	23	15	60	45	37	0
Ice cream bar, Dove Bite Size, vanilla, 5 bars	360	24	16	40	60	34	0
Ice cream bar, DoveBar, almond, 4-pack, 1 bar	280	19	11	30	110	23	1
Ice cream bar, DoveBar, almond, single, 1 bar	350	24	14	40	140	29	1
Ice cream bar, DoveBar, caramel creme swirl & toffee chips, 1 bar	280	16	11	30	100	31	0
Ice cream bar, DoveBar, chocolate & dark chocolate, 4-pack, 1 bar	260	17	10	25	30	27	1
Ice cream bar, DoveBar, chocolate & dark chocolate, single, 1 bar	330	21	13	30	40	34	1
Ice cream bar, DoveBar, mocha cashew crunch, 1 bar	260	17	10	30	55	25	0
Ice cream bar, DoveBar, vanilla & dark chocolate, 4-pack, 1 bar	260	17	11	30	30	26	0

FROZEN NOVELTIES	CAL (g)	FAT (g)	SAT FAT (g)	CHOL (mg)	SODIUM (mg)	CARB (g)	FIBER (g)
Ice cream bar, DoveBar, vanilla & dark chocolate, single, 1 bar	330	21	14	35	40	32	0
Ice cream bar, DoveBar, vanilla & milk chocolate, 4-pack, 1 bar	260	17	11	30	45	25	0
Ice cream bar, DoveBar, vanilla & milk chocolate, single, 1 bar	330	21	15	40	55	31	0
Ice cream bar, DoveBar, vanilla & white coating, 1 bar	270	17	11	30	50	26	0
Ice cream bar, English toffee crunch, Ben & Jerry's, 1 pop	340	23	15	75	140	35	0
Ice cream bar, English toffee crunch, Weight Watchers, 1 bar	120	7	3.5	5	25	12	0
Ice cream bar, Heath, Nestle, 1 bar	160	12	8	15	35	13	0
Ice cream bar, iced cappuccino, Haagen-Dazs Extraas, 1 bar	290	21	12	70	60	21	<1
Ice cream bar, Klondike, almond, 1 bar	310	21	14	25	90	26	3
Ice cream bar, Klondike, caramel crunch, 1 bar	300	18	13	30	95	31	<1
Ice cream bar, Klondike, chocolate-chocolate, 1 bar	280	20	14	20	50	22	4
Ice cream bar, Klondike, coffee, 1 piece	290	20	14	15	65	24	0
Ice cream bar, Klondike, dark chocolate, 1 piece	290	20	14	30	75	24	<1
Ice cream bar, Klondike, original, 1 bar	290	20	14	15	65	24	0
Ice cream bar, Klondike Krispy, 1 bar	300	20	13	25	85	28	0
Ice cream bar, Klondike Krunch, 1 bar	200	13	8	20	55	19	<1
Ice cream bar, Mickey Mouse, Nestle Cool Creations, 1 bar	110	7	3	10	25	12	0
Ice cream bar, Milky Way, chocolate & milk chocolate, reduced fat, 1 bar	140	7	3	5	50	19	0

FROZEN NOVELTIES	CAL (g)	FAT (g)	SAT FAT (g)	CHOL (mg)	SODIUM (mg)	CARB (g)	FIBER (g)
Ice cream bar, Milky Way, vanilla & dark chocolate, reduced fat, 1 bar	140	7	3	5	50	19	0
Ice cream bar, Nestle Crunch, reduced fat, 1 bar	130	7	5	5	40	14	0
Ice cream bar, New York super fudge chunk, Ben & Jerry's, 1 pop	390	31	13	30	55	27	4
Ice cream bar, Orange Vanilla Treat, Weight Watchers, 2 bars	70	1	0.5	5	80	17	3
Ice cream bar, Snickers, full size, 1 bar	190	12	4	15	50	18	0
Ice cream bar, Snickers, fun size, 4 bars	390	25	9	25	105	38	0
Ice cream bar, Snoopy, Good Humor Specialty, 1 bar	150	8	7	20	50	18	0
Ice cream bar, strawberry, Sealtest Colonel Crunch, 1 bar	170	8	6	10	45	22	0
Ice cream bar, strawberry shortcake, Good Humor Classic, 1 bar	210	11	7	15	80	26	1
Ice cream bar, sundae twist, Good Humor Specialty, 1 cup	160	3	2	10	100	33	0
Ice cream bar, toasted almond, Good Humor Classic, 1 bar	230	11	4	15	30	31	1
Ice cream bar, Triple Brownie Overload, Haagen-Dazs Extraas, 1 bar	320	23	12	80	95	23	1
Ice cream bar, vanilla, Ben & Jerry's, 1 pop	360	28	15	75	75	30	0
Ice cream bar, vanilla, Breyers, 1 bar	230	15	11	50	45	20	0
Ice cream bar, vanilla, Popsicle, 1 bar	160	11	9	15	35	15	1
Ice cream bar, vanilla/almonds, Haagen-Dazs, 1 bar	300	22	12	70	65	21	1
Ice cream bar, vanilla/dark chocolate, Haagen-Dazs, 1 bar	320	22	15	70	50	27	4

FROZEN NOVELTIES	CAL (g)	FAT (g)	SAT FAT (g)	CHOL (mg)	SODIUM (mg)	CARB (g)	FIBER (g)
Ice cream bar, vanilla/milk chocolate, 1 bar, Haagen-Dazs, 1 bar	280	20	12	75	65	20	0
Ice cream bar, vanilla/milk chocolate, original, Good Humor, 1 bar	230	13	10	20	45	28	1
Ice cream bar, vanilla with almonds, Breyers, 1 bar	250	17	11	50	45	21	<1
Ice cream bar, WWF, Good Humor Specialty, 1 bar	200	10	8	15	100	24	<1
Ice cream bar, X-Men, Good Humor Specialty, 1 bar	140	5	2	<5	100	22	<1
Ice cream cone, butter pecan, Breyers, 1 cone	300	17	7	45	200	31	1
Ice cream cone, chocolate mint, Breyers, 1 cone	280	14	8	40	105	35	1
Ice cream cone, Drumstick, chocolate, Nestle, 1 cone	340	19	10	25	95	37	2
Ice cream cone, Drumstick, chocolate dipped, Nestle, 1 cone	340	17	10	25	95	41	1
Ice cream cone, Drumstick, vanilla, Nestle, 1 cone	350	20	11	20	95	36	2
Ice cream cone, Drumstick, vanilla caramel, Nestle, 1 cone	360	20	12	25	100	39	2
Ice cream cone, Drumstick, vanilla fudge, Nestle, 1 cone	370	21	11	20	105	40	2
Ice cream cone, King Cone, vanilla, Good Humor, 1 cone	300	10	6	20	110	48	1
Ice cream cone, Klondike Kone, 1 cone	310	17	7	20	100	34	2
Ice cream cone, Lion King, Nestle Cool Creations, 1 cone	280	14	9	15	90	36	1
Ice cream cone, Nestle Crunch, 1 cone	300	16	10	25	95	36	2
Ice cream cone, Olde Nut Sundae, Sealtest, 1 cone	230	9	6	5	100	32	2
Ice cream cup, Breyers, 1 cup	90	10	7	35	65	25	1
Ice cream cup, chocolate, Sealtest, 1 cup	140	7	4	25	50	19	<1

FROZEN NOVELTIES	CAL (g)	FAT (g)	SAT FAT (g)	CHOL (mg)	SODIUM (mg)	CARB (g)	FIBER (g)
Ice cream cup, strawberry, Sealtest, 1 cup	130	6	4	25	45	19	0
Ice cream cup, strawberry sundae, Carnation, 1 cup	200	8	5	30	55	29	0
Ice cream cup, vanilla, Sealtest, 1 cup	140	7	5	30	55	16	0
Ice cream nuggets, Nestle Crunch, 8 pack	300	20	10	20	50	25	0
Ice cream nuggets, Nestle Bon Bons, dark chocolate, 9 bon bons	350	24	15	25	60	30	0
Ice cream nuggets, Nestle Bon Bons, milk chocolate, 9 bon bons	370	26	15	25	65	30	0
Ice cream sandwich, Breyers, 1 sandwich	250	11	4	35	170	34	2
Ice cream sandwich, Chip Burrrger, Sealtest, 1 sandwich	320	15	9	20	190	44	1
Ice cream sandwich, chocolate chip cookie, Good Humor, 1 sandwich	320	15	9	20	190	44	1
Ice cream sandwich, cookies & cream, Nestle Cool Creations, 1 sandwich	240	11	4	15	250	34	1
Ice cream sandwich, Creameee Burrrger, Sealtest, 1 sandwich	310	17	12	20	150	40	1
Ice cream sandwich, mini, Nestle Cool Creations, 1 sandwich	110	5	2	10	70	16	0
Ice cream sandwich, neapolitan, Good Humor, 1 sandwich	260	10	7	20	150	39	1
Ice cream sandwich, sidewalk sundae, Good Humor, 1 sandwich	190	8	4	15	120	28	1
Ice cream sandwich, vanilla, Popsicle, 1 sandwich	190	8	4	15	120	28	1
Ice cream sandwich, vanilla, Weight Watchers, 1 bar	160	3.5	2	5	180	30	1
Ice cream sandwich, vanilla, giant, Good Humor, 1 sandwich	240	10	6	20	160	35	1

FROZEN NOVELTIES	CAL (g)	FAT (g)	SAT FAT (g)	CHOL (mg)	SODIUM (mg)	CARB (g)	FIBER (g)
Ices, Bubble Gum Swirl, Popsicle, 1 bar	50	0	0	0	0	13	0
Ices, Bubble Play sports bar, Good Humor, 1 bar	110	1	1	0	5	25	0
Ices, cherry, Good Humor Calippo, 1 bar	100	0	0	0	5	23	0
Ices, cherry/pineapple, Popsicle Big Stick, 1 bar	50	0	0	0	5	12	0
Ices, cotton candy, Popsicle, 1 bar	90	1	1	5	55	17	<1
Ices, dinosaur, Good Humor, 1 bar	110	2	1	0	5	25	0
Ices, Firecracker Jr., Popsicle, 1 bar	40	0	0	0	0	10	0
Ices, First 'N' Goal sports bar, Good Humor, 1 bar	90	0	0	0	0	22	0
Ices, Free Kick sports bar, Good Humor, 1 bar	90	0	0	0	0	23	0
Ices, Freeza Pizza, Good Humor, 1 bar	140	5	2.5	0	0	23	0
Ices, Garfield, Good Humor Specialty, 1 unit	90	0	0	0	0	22	0
Ices, grape/lemon, Good Humor Calippo, 1 bar	90	0	0	0	0	22	0
Ices, The Great White, Good Humor Specialty, 1 bar	70	0	0	0	0	18	0
Ices, Hyper Stripe, Good Humor, 1 bar	80	0	0	0	0	21	0
Ices, Italian, cherry, Luigi's, 1 cup	120	0	0	0	10	28	0
Ices, Italian, chocolate fudge, Luigi's, 1 cup	150	0	0	0	10	38	0
Ices, Italian, grape, Luigi's, 1 cup	110	0	0	0	10	26	0
Ices, Italian, lemon, Luigi's, 1 cup	110	0	0	0	10	25	0
Ices, Italian, lemon, Mazzone's, 1 cup	30	0	0	0	15	7	0
Ices, Italian, strawberry, Luigi's, 1 cup	110	0	0	0	10	26	0

FROZEN NOVELTIES	CAL (g)	FAT (g)	SAT FAT (g)	CHOL (mg)	SODIUM (mg)	CARB (g)	FIBER (g)
Ices, Jumbo Jet Star, Good Humor, 1 bar	80	0	0	0	0	20	0
Ices, Laser Blazer, Popsicle, 1 bar	70	0	0	0	5	16	0
Ices, Lick-A-Color, Popsicle, 1 bar	90	0	0	0	0	22	0
Ices, LifeSavers, all flavors, 1 bar	35	0	0	0	0	9	0
Ices, LifeSavers, sugar free, all flavors, 1 bar	15	0	0	0	0	0	1
Ices, Nestle Cool Creations, all flavors, 1 pop	50	0	0	0	5	13	0
Ices, rainbow, Good Humor, 1 bar	90	0	0	0	0	22	0
Ices, Screwball cup, Good Humor Specialty, 1 cone	100	1	0	0	5	22	0
Ices, Shoot Hoops sports bar, Good Humor, 1 bar	90	0	0	0	0	23	0
Ices, snow cone, all flavors, Good Humor Specialty, 1 cone	60	0	0	0	5	14	0
Ices, Super Mario, Good Humor Specialty, 1 bar	120	1	1	0	10	27	0
Ices, Supersicle, all varieties, Popsicle, 1 bar	80	0	0	0	0	20	0
Ices, super twin, Good Humor, 1 bar	70	0	0	0	5	16	0
Ices, surprise pops, all flavors, Nestle Cool Creations, 1 pop	60	0	0	0	5	14	0
Ices, watermelon, Good Humor, 1 bar	80	0	0	0	0	20	0
Pop-up, orange, Popsicle, 1 pop-up	80	1	0	<5	15	19	0
Pop-up, rainbow, Popsicle, 1 pop-up	90	1	0	<5	15	19	0
Pudding pops, chocolate, 1 pop	70	2.5	na	0	80	12	0
Pudding pops, vanilla, 1 pop	70	2	na	0	50	13	0
Push-up, Flintstones Pebbles Treats, 1 push-up	120	6	4	20	25	15	0
Push-up, sherbet, Flintstones, 1 push-up	100	2	1	5	25	20	0

FROZEN NOVELTIES	CAL	FAT (g)	SAT FAT (g)	CHOL (mg)	SODIUM (mg)	CARB (g)	FIBER (g)
Reese's peanut butter cup, Good Humor, 1 cup	220	16	8	10	65	20	0
Vanilla slices, Sealtest, 1 slice	130	7	3	20	40	16	0
Viennetta, cappuccino/vanilla, mini, Breyers, 1 dessert	220	14	10	40	40	20	0
Viennetta, chocolate ice cream, Breyers, ½ cup	190	12	8	25	40	18	0
Viennetta, mint ice cream, Breyers, ½ cup	190	11	7	40	40	19	0
Viennetta, strawberry frozen yogurt, Breyers, ½ cup	170	8	5	25	35	23	0
Viennetta, strawberry frozen yogurt, mini, Breyers, 1 dessert	185	10	7	25	30	22	0
Viennetta, vanilla ice cream, Breyers, ½ cup	190	11	7	40	40	19	0
Viennetta, vanilla ice cream, mini, Breyers, 1 unit	220	14	10	40	40	20	0

AT A GLANCE: FROZEN NOVELTIES
Choose from the many Fruit Juice bars, Ices, and Frozen Yogurt bars with 1 gram or less of fat.

FROZEN YOGURT

	CAL	FAT (g)	SAT FAT (g)	CHOL (mg)	SODIUM (mg)	CARB (g)	FIBER (g)
Apple pie, Ben & Jerry's, ½ cup	170	3	2	10	90	32	0
Banana cream pie, Dannon Light 'N Crunchy, ½ cup	110	1	0	0	65	24	0
Banana strawberry, Ben & Jerry's, ½ cup	160	2	1	5	60	32	1
Berry Berry Strawberry, fat free, Borden/Meadow Gold, ½ cup	100	0	0	0	45	21	0
Black cherry, Borden Premium, ½ cup	110	3	2	10	40	19	0
Black cherry, lowfat, Breyers, ½ cup	140	3	2.5	15	45	25	0
Black cherry, nonfat, Sealtest, ½ cup	110	0	0	<5	45	23	0
Blueberry, Borden Premium, ½ cup	110	2.5	1.5	10	40	19	0

FROZEN YOGURT	CAL (g)	FAT (g)	SAT FAT (g)	CHOL (mg)	SODIUM (mg)	CARB (g)	FIBER (g)
Bluesberry, Ben & Jerry's, ½ cup	160	2	1	5	60	32	1
Brownie Nut Blast, Haagen-Dazs Extraas, ½ cup	220	8	3.5	40	65	29	1
Butter pecan, Breyers, ½ cup	170	7	2	10	105	26	0
Cappuccino, Dannon Light, ½ cup	80	0	0	0	70	19	0
Cappuccino, no fat, Ben & Jerry's, ½ cup	140	0	0	0	85	32	0
Caramel toffee crunch, fat free, Borden/Meadow Gold, ½ cup	120	0	0	0	70	27	0
Cherry chocolate cherry, Dannon Pure Indulgence, ½ cup	150	3	1	15	85	26	0
Cherry chocolate cordial, lowfat, Sealtest, ½ cup	140	2.5	1.5	5	45	26	2
Cherry Garcia, Ben & Jerry's, ½ cup	170	3	2	10	70	31	0
Cherry vanilla swirl, Dannon Light, ½ cup	90	0	0	0	65	21	0
Chocolate, Borden Premium, ½ cup	110	3	2	10	55	18	0
Chocolate, Dannon Light, ½ cup	80	0	0	0	60	21	1
Chocolate, Haagen-Dazs, ½ cup	160	2.5	1.5	30	60	26	<1
Chocolate, fat free, Borden/Meadow Gold, ½ cup	100	0	0	0	50	22	0
Chocolate, lowfat, Breyers, ½ cup	150	3	2	15	50	26	1
Chocolate, lowfat, Sealtest, ½ cup	120	1.5	1	5	45	24	<1
Chocolate chip cookie dough, lowfat, Breyers, ½ cup	160	3	2	10	80	29	0
Chocolate cookie, fat free, Borden/Meadow Gold, ½ cup	110	0	0	0	65	25	0
Chocolate fudge brownie, Ben & Jerry's, ½ cup	190	4	2	10	130	35	2
Chocolate fudge brownie, lowfat, Breyers, ½ cup	160	3	2	20	50	29	1

FROZEN YOGURT	CAL (g)	FAT (g)	SAT FAT (g)	CHOL (mg)	SODIUM (mg)	CARB (g)	FIBER (g)
Chocolate raspberry swirl, Ben & Jerry's, ½ cup	200	2.5	1.5	5	75	40	1
Chunky chocolate nut, Dannon Pure Indulgence, ½ cup	150	3	0	0	65	25	0
Coco-nut fudge, Dannon Pure Indulgence, ½ cup	160	3	1.5	15	70	28	0
Coffee, Haagen-Dazs, ½ cup	160	2.5	1.5	45	55	26	0
Coffee almond fudge, Ben & Jerry's, ½ cup	200	7	2	15	85	30	1
Columbo, all flavors, lowfat, ½ cup	110	1.5	1	5	55	20	0
Columbo, all flavors, nonfat, ½ cup	100	0	0	0	50	21	0
Cookies 'n cream, Dannon Pure Indulgence, ½ cup	150	3	2	0	105	24	0
Cookies in cream, fat free, Breyers, ½ cup	110	0	0	<5	80	25	0
Crunchy espresso, Dannon Pure Indulgence, ½ cup	150	3	2	15	85	26	0
English toffee crunch, Ben & Jerry's, ½ cup	190	6	2.5	10	110	32	0
Fudge twirl, fat free, Breyers, ½ cup	100	0	0	0	50	24	0
Heath toffee crunch, Dannon Pure Indulgence, ½ cup	150	3	1.5	5	105	25	0
Lemon chiffon, Dannon Light, ½ cup	90	0	0	0	65	22	0
Mint chocolate chip, lowfat, Breyers, ½ cup	150	3	2	10	55	28	1
Mint cookies and cream, lowfat, Sealtest, ½ cup	140	2	1	10	85	27	1
Mocha chocolate chunk, Dannon Light 'N Crunchy, ½ cup	110	1	0	0	60	26	0
Mocha fudge, lowfat, Sealtest, ½ cup	130	2	1.5	10	45	25	<1
Orange Tango, Haagen-Dazs, ½ cup	130	1	0.5	20	25	26	0
Peach, Borden Premium, ½ cup	110	2.5	1.5	10	40	18	0

FROZEN YOGURT	CAL (g)	FAT (g)	SAT FAT (g)	CHOL (mg)	SODIUM (mg)	CARB (g)	FIBER (g)
Peach, lowfat, Breyers, ½ cup	140	3	2	15	45	24	0
Peach, nonfat, Sealtest, ½ cup	100	0	0	<5	35	22	0
Peach raspberry melba, Dannon Light, ½ cup	90	0	0	0	65	21	0
Peachy, fat free, Borden/Meadow Gold, ½ cup	100	0	0	0	50	22	0
Peanut chocolate crunch, Dannon Light 'N Crunchy, ½ cup	110	0	0	0	65	29	0
Pina colada, Haagen-Dazs, ½ cup	130	1.5	1	25	25	26	0
Raspberry, Borden Premium, ½ cup	110	3	2	10	40	18	0
Raspberry Rendezvous, Haagen-Dazs, ½ cup	130	1.5	0.5	20	25	26	1
Starburst, all flavors, lowfat, 1 cup	80	1.5	1	5	35	14	0
Strawberry, Borden Premium, ½ cup	100	2.5	1.5	10	40	18	0
Strawberry, fat free, Breyers, ½ cup	90	0	0	0	40	22	0
Strawberry, lowfat, Breyers, ½ cup	130	3	2	15	45	23	0
Strawberry, no fat, Ben & Jerry's, ½ cup	140	0	0	0	60	31	0
Strawberry, nonfat, Sealtest, ½ cup	100	0	0	0	40	22	0
Strawberry cheesecake, Dannon Light, ½ cup	90	0	0	0	60	22	0
Strawberry cheesecake, lowfat, Breyers, ½ cup	140	3	2	20	65	26	0
Strawberry Cheesecake Craze, Haagen-Dazs Extraas, ½ cup	220	8	4	65	140	31	0
Strawberry Duet, Haagen-Dazs, ½ cup	130	2	1	25	25	26	<1
Toffee bar crunch, lowfat, Breyers, ½ cup	150	3	2	15	60	26	0
Triple chocolate, Dannon Light 'N Crunchy, ½ cup	110	0	0	0	60	28	0

FROZEN YOGURT	CAL	FAT (g)	SAT FAT (g)	CHOL (mg)	SODIUM (mg)	CARB (g)	FIBER (g)
Vanilla, Borden Premium, ½ cup	110	3	2	10	55	18	0
Vanilla, Dannon Light, ½ cup	80	0	0	0	65	21	0
Vanilla, Dreyer's/Edy's, ½ cup	100	2.5	1.5	10	30	17	0
Vanilla, Haagen-Dazs, ½ cup	160	2.5	1.5	45	55	26	0
Vanilla, fat free, Borden/Meadow Gold Premium, ½ cup	100	0	0	0	55	21	0
Vanilla, fat free, Breyers, ½ cup	100	0	0	<5	50	21	0
Vanilla, fat free, Dreyer's/Edy's, ½ cup	90	0	0	0	65	18	0
Vanilla, lowfat, Breyers, ½ cup	140	3	2	10	50	24	0
Vanilla, lowfat, Sealtest, ½ cup	120	1.5	1	10	45	24	0
Vanilla, no sugar added, Breyers, ½ cup	100	5	3	25	45	12	0
Vanilla, reduced fat, no sugar added, Dreyer's/Edy's, ½ cup	100	4	2.5	15	45	13	na
Vanilla blueberry swirl, Dannon Light 'N Crunchy, ½ cup	110	1	0	0	65	26	0
Vanilla/chocolate, fat free, Breyers, ½ cup	100	0	0	<5	45	21	0
Vanilla/chocolate/strawberry, lowfat, Breyers, ½ cup	140	3	2	15	50	24	0
Vanilla fudge sundae, fat free, Borden/Meadow Gold, ½ cup	110	0	0	0	55	24	0
Vanilla fudge swirl, no fat, Ben & Jerry's, ½ cup	150	0	0	5	80	32	0
Vanilla fudge twirl, lowfat, Breyers, ½ cup	140	3	2	15	50	25	1
Vanilla raspberry truffle, Dannon Pure Indulgence, ½ cup	150	3	2	15	70	25	1
Vanilla raspberry twirl, lowfat, Breyers, ½ cup	130	3	2	15	50	24	0

AT A GLANCE: FROZEN YOGURT

Choose from the dozens of fat free frozen yogurt products from Borden/Meadow Gold, Ben & Jerry's, Breyers, Dannon, Dreyer's/Edy's, and Sealtest.

FROZEN YOGURT	CAL (g)	FAT (g)	SAT FAT (g)	CHOL (mg)	SODIUM (mg)	CARB (g)	FIBER (g)

FRUIT

	CAL (g)	FAT (g)	SAT FAT (g)	CHOL (mg)	SODIUM (mg)	CARB (g)	FIBER (g)
Apples, escalloped, Stouffer's, ⅔ cup	180	3	0	0	70	37	3
Apples, unsweetened, heated, ½ cup slices	50	0	0	0	0	12	2
Apples, unsweetened, unheated, ½ cup slices	40	0	0	0	0	11	1
Apricots, sweetened, ½ cup	120	0	0	0	0	30	2
Blackberries, unsweetened, ½ cup	50	0	0	0	0	12	4
Blueberries, sweetened, ½ cup	90	0	0	0	0	25	2
Blueberries, unsweetened, ½ cup	40	0	0	0	0	9	2
Boysenberries, unsweetened, ½ cup	35	0	0	0	0	8	3
Cherries, sour, red, unsweetened, ½ cup	35	0	0	0	0	9	<1
Cherries, sweet, sweetened, ½ cup	100	0	0	0	0	25	1
Loganberries, 1 cup	80	0	0	0	0	19	7
Melon balls, ½ cup	30	0	0	0	30	7	<1
Mixed fruit, in syrup, Birds Eye, ½ cup	90	0	0	0	5	23	0
Peaches, sliced, sweetened, ½ cup	120	0	0	0	10	30	2
Pineapple, chunks, sweetened, ½ cup	100	0	0	0	0	27	1
Raspberries, red, in syrup, Birds Eye, ½ cup	90	0	0	0	5	22	5
Raspberries, red, sweetened, ½ cup	130	0	0	0	0	33	6
Rhubarb, cooked, with sugar, ½ cup	140	0	0	0	0	37	2
Strawberries, halved, in syrup, Birds Eye, ½ cup	120	0	0	0	0	31	1
Strawberries, halved, in syrup, lite, Birds Eye, ½ cup	70	0	0	0	0	17	1
Strawberries, unsweetened, ½ cup	25	0	0	0	0	7	2

FRUIT	CAL (g)	FAT (g)	SAT FAT (g)	CHOL (mg)	SODIUM (mg)	CARB (g)	FIBER (g)
Strawberries, whole, Birds Eye, ½ cup	100	0	0	0	0	25	1

AT A GLANCE: FRUIT
Choose unsweetened fruits for lowest calories and flavor most like that of fresh fruit.

ICE CREAM

	CAL (g)	FAT (g)	SAT FAT (g)	CHOL (mg)	SODIUM (mg)	CARB (g)	FIBER (g)
Aztec Harvest, smooth, Ben & Jerry's, ½ cup	230	16	10	90	55	22	0
Bailey's Original Irish Cream, Haagen-Dazs, ½ cup	280	18	11	110	100	23	0
Banana walnut, Ben & Jerry's, ½ cup	290	21	9	75	50	26	1
Bananas Foster, low-fat, Healthy Choice, ½ cup	110	1.5	1	5	60	21	1
Black cherry, fat free, Borden/Meadow Gold, ½ cup	90	0	0	0	45	19	0
Black forest, low-fat, Healthy Choice, ½ cup	120	2	1	5	50	23	1
Bordeaux cherry chocolate chip, low-fat, Healthy Choice, ½ cup	110	2	1.5	<5	55	19	<1
Brownie marble fudge, reduced fat, Breyers Light, ½ cup	150	5	3	30	55	23	<1
Brownie sundae, fat free, Borden/Meadow Gold, ½ cup	100	0	0	0	45	21	0
Brownies a la Mode, Haagen-Dazs Extraas, ½ cup	280	18	11	100	130	25	0
Butter almond, Breyers, ½ cup	170	11	6	35	120	15	0
Butter pecan, Ben & Jerry's, ½ cup	310	26	11	100	160	20	1
Butter pecan, Breyers, ½ cup	180	12	6	35	125	15	0
Butter pecan, Haagen-Dazs, ½ cup	320	24	11	105	140	20	<1
Butter pecan, Sealtest, ½ cup	160	9	5	30	115	16	0
Butter pecan crunch, low-fat, Healthy Choice, ½ cup	120	2	1	<5	60	22	1

ICE CREAM	CAL (g)	FAT (g)	SAT FAT (g)	CHOL (mg)	SODIUM (mg)	CARB (g)	FIBER (g)
Cappuccino, Sealtest Gold, ½ cup	140	7	4	25	40	15	0
Cappuccino chocolate chunk, low-fat, Healthy Choice, ½ cup	120	2	1	10	60	22	1
Cappuccino Commotion, Haagen-Dazs Extraas, ½ cup	310	21	12	100	105	25	1
Cappuccino mocha fudge, low-fat, Healthy Choice, ½ cup	120	2	1	<5	50	23	1
Caramel Cone Explosion, Haagen-Dazs Extraas, ½ cup	310	20	12	95	130	27	<1
Caramel praline almond, Sealtest Gold, ½ cup	150	7	3.5	<5	55	19	0
Caramel praline crunch, fat free, Breyers, ½ cup	120	0	0	5	70	27	0
Cherry cheesecake, fat free, Borden, ½ cup	90	0	0	0	45	20	0
Cherry chocolate chunk, Sealtest Gold, ½ cup	140	7	4	0	35	17	0
Cherry chocolate chunk, low-fat, Healthy Choice, ½ cup	110	2	1	<5	55	19	<1
Cherry Garcia, Ben & Jerry's, ½ cup	240	16	10	80	60	25	0
Cherry vanilla, Ben & Jerry's, ½ cup	240	15	9	85	60	26	0
Cherry vanilla, Breyers, ½ cup	150	7	5	30	40	17	0
Cherry vanilla, low fat, Borden, ½ cup	110	2	1	10	40	20	0
Chocolate, Breyers, ½ cup	160	8	6	30	30	19	1
Chocolate, Haagen-Dazs, ½ cup	270	18	11	115	75	22	1
Chocolate, Sealtest, ½ cup	140	7	4	25	50	19	<1
Chocolate, fat free, Borden/Meadow Gold, ½ cup	90	0	0	0	45	19	0
Chocolate, fat free, Breyers Free, ½ cup	90	0	0	<5	45	20	<1
Chocolate, fat free, Sealtest, ½ cup	100	0	0	0	45	21	<1

ICE CREAM	CAL	FAT (g)	SAT FAT (g)	CHOL (mg)	SODIUM (mg)	CARB (g)	FIBER (g)
Chocolate, low fat, Borden, ½ cup	110	2	1	10	50	21	0
Chocolate, reduced fat, Viva, ½ cup	120	4	2.5	15	60	18	0
Chocolate chip, Breyers, ½ cup	170	10	6	35	40	18	0
Chocolate chip, Sealtest, ½ cup	150	8	5	30	50	18	0
Chocolate chip cookie dough, Ben & Jerry's, ½ cup	270	17	9	80	95	30	0
Chocolate chip cookie dough, Breyers, ½ cup	170	9	5	25	50	20	1
Chocolate chip cookie dough, Sealtest, ½ cup	160	8	4	25	70	20	1
Chocolate chip cookie dough, low fat, Borden, ½ cup	120	2.5	1.5	10	60	23	0
Chocolate chocolate chip, Haagen-Dazs, ½ cup	300	20	12	100	70	26	2
Chocolate chocolate chip, reduced fat, Breyers Light, ½ cup	150	5	3.5	25	50	21	<1
Chocolate fudge brownie, Ben & Jerry's, ½ cup	250	14	9	50	100	31	2
Chocolate fudge brownie, Sealtest Gold, ½ cup	160	7	4	20	45	20	1
Chocolate fudge twirl, reduced fat, Breyers Light, ½ cup	140	4	2.5	25	55	22	1
Chocolate swirl, low fat, Borden, ½ cup	110	2	1	10	45	20	0
Chocolate marshmallow swirl, low fat, Borden, ½ cup	110	2	1.5	10	50	21	0
Chubby Hubby, Ben & Jerry's, ½ cup	350	23	11	75	160	31	2
Chunky Monkey, Ben & Jerry's, ½ cup	280	19	10	70	50	29	1
Coconut almond, Ben & Jerry's, ½ cup	260	20	9	80	80	19	1
Coconut almond fudge chip, Ben & Jerry's, ½ cup	320	25	14	75	85	24	2
Coffee, Breyers, ½ cup	150	8	5	35	45	15	0

ICE CREAM	CAL (g)	FAT (g)	SAT FAT (g)	CHOL (mg)	SODIUM (mg)	CARB (g)	FIBER (g)
Coffee, Haagen-Dazs, ½ cup	270	18	11	120	85	21	0
Coffee, Sealtest, ½ cup	140	7	4	30	55	16	0
Coffee almond fudge, Ben & Jerry's, ½ cup	290	20	9	75	85	24	2
Coffee toffee crunch, Ben & Jerry's, ½ cup	280	19	10	80	120	28	0
Cookie Dough Craze, light, Weight Watchers, ½ cup	140	3.5	2	5	85	24	1
Cookie Dough Dynamo, Haagen-Dazs Extraas, ½ cup	300	19	12	95	140	29	0
Cookies and cream, Haagen-Dazs, ½ cup	270	17	11	110	115	23	0
Cookies in cream, Breyers, ½ cup	170	9	6	30	45	19	0
Cookies 'n cream, low fat, Borden, ½ cup	110	2	1	5	55	20	0
Cookies n' cream, low-fat, Healthy Choice, ½ cup	120	2	1.5	<5	90	21	<1
Cookies n' cream, reduced fat, Viva, ½ cup	130	5	3	15	95	19	0
Cubic scoops, vanilla/orange, Sealtest, ½ cup	130	4	3	20	45	22	0
Deep dark chocolate, smooth, Ben & Jerry's, ½ cup	260	15	9	55	55	32	2
DiSaronno Amaretto, Haagen-Dazs, ½ cup	260	15	9	95	80	26	0
Double chocolate fudge, smooth, Ben & Jerry's, ½ cup	280	16	9	55	60	35	3
Double fudge swirl, low-fat, Healthy Choice, ½ cup	120	2	1.5	<5	50	21	1
English toffee crunch, Ben & Jerry's, ½ cup	310	21	12	90	130	30	0
French vanilla, Breyers, ½ cup	170	10	6	105	45	15	0
French vanilla, Sealtest, ½ cup	140	8	5	60	50	16	0
Fudge brownie, low-fat, Healthy Choice, ½ cup	120	2	1	5	55	22	2
Fudge royale, Sealtest, ½ cup	150	7	4	25	55	19	0
Fudge toffee parfait, reduced fat, Breyers Light, ½ cup	150	5	3.5	35	55	23	<1

ICE CREAM	CAL (g)	FAT (g)	SAT FAT (g)	CHOL (mg)	SODIUM (mg)	CARB (g)	FIBER (g)
Fudge twirl, Breyers, ½ cup	160	8	5	35	50	19	1
Fudge twirl, fat free, Breyers Free, ½ cup	100	0	0	0	50	24	0
Heavenly hash, Sealtest, ½ cup	150	7	4	25	50	20	<1
Heavenly hash, reduced fat, Breyers Light, ½ cup	150	5	3	25	55	22	<1
Macadamia brittle, Haagen-Dazs, ½ cup	300	20	11	110	120	25	0
Malt caramel cone, low-fat, Healthy Choice, ½ cup	120	2	1	10	60	22	1
Maple walnut, Sealtest, ½ cup	160	9	5	30	50	16	0
Mint chocolate chip, Breyers, ½ cup	170	10	6	35	40	18	0
Mint chocolate chip, Sealtest, ½ cup	150	8	4	25	45	17	1
Mint chocolate chip, low-fat, Healthy Choice, ½ cup	120	2	1	<5	50	21	<1
Mint chocolate chip, no sugar added, Breyers, ½ cup	110	6	3	20	50	15	0
Mint cookies in cream, reduced fat, Breyers Light, ½ cup	140	5	2	30	80	21	1
Mint with chocolate cookie, Ben & Jerry's, ½ cup	260	17	10	80	120	27	1
Mocha almond fudge, reduced fat, Breyers Light, ½ cup	160	6	3	30	55	20	<1
Mocha fudge, smooth, Ben & Jerry's, ½ cup	270	18	10	85	65	30	1
Neapolitan, Sealtest Gold, ½ cup	110	6	3	5	30	13	0
Neapolitan, fat free, Borden/Meadow Gold, ½ cup	90	0	0	0	45	18	0
Neapolitan, low fat, Borden, ½ cup	110	2	1	10	40	20	0
Neapolitan, reduced fat, Viva, ½ cup	110	4	2.5	15	60	17	0
New York super fudge chunk, Ben & Jerry's, ½ cup	290	20	11	50	55	28	2

ICE CREAM	CAL (g)	FAT (g)	SAT FAT (g)	CHOL (mg)	SODIUM (mg)	CARB (g)	FIBER (g)
Oh So Very Vanilla, light, Weight Watchers, ½ cup	120	2.5	1.5	5	65	20	1
Orange sherbet n' cream, low fat, Borden, ½ cup	100	2	1	10	35	19	0
Orange sorbet and cream, low-fat, Healthy Choice, ½ cup	90	2	1	<5	50	17	1
Peach, Breyers, ½ cup	130	6	4	25	30	18	0
Peach, fat free, Borden/Meadow Gold, ½ cup	90	0	0	0	45	19	0
Peanut Butter Burst, Haagen-Dazs Extraas, ½ cup	330	22	11	95	150	26	1
Peanut butter cookie dough and fudge, low-fat, Healthy Choice, ½ cup	120	2	1	<5	60	22	<1
Peanut butter cup, Ben & Jerry's, ½ cup	370	26	12	75	140	30	2
Positively Praline Crunch, light, Weight Watchers, ½ cup	140	3	1.5	5	105	25	0
Praline almond, Breyers, ½ cup	170	8	4	25	70	21	0
Praline almond crunch, reduced fat, Breyers Light, ½ cup	140	5	3	35	70	20	0
Praline and caramel, low-fat, Healthy Choice, ½ cup	130	2	0.5	<5	70	25	<1
Rainbow, Sealtest, ½ cup	140	7	5	30	55	16	0
Rainforest Crunch, Ben & Jerry's, ½ cup	300	23	11	85	140	24	0
Raspberry sorbet and cream, low-fat, Healthy Choice, ½ cup	90	2	1	<5	50	17	1
Reckless Rocky Road, light, Weight Watchers, ½ cup	140	3	1.5	5	75	23	1
Rocky road, Breyers, ½ cup	190	9	5	25	30	24	1
Rocky road, low-fat, Healthy Choice, ½ cup	140	2	1	<5	60	28	2
Rum raisin, Haagen-Dazs, ½ cup	270	17	10	110	75	22	0
Strawberry, Breyers, ½ cup	130	6	4	25	35	15	0

ICE CREAM	CAL	FAT (g)	SAT FAT (g)	CHOL (mg)	SODIUM (mg)	CARB (g)	FIBER (g)
Strawberry, Haagen-Dazs, ½ cup	250	16	10	95	80	23	<1
Strawberry, Sealtest, ½ cup	130	6	4	25	45	19	0
Strawberry, fat free, Borden, ½ cup	80	0	0	0	45	18	0
Strawberry, low fat, Borden, ½ cup	100	2	1	10	40	19	0
Strawberry, reduced fat, Breyers Light, ½ cup	120	4	2.5	30	45	18	0
Strawberry Cheesecake Craze, Haagen-Dazs Extraas, ½ cup	290	18	10	100	160	28	<1
Strawberry sorbet and cream, low-fat, Healthy Choice, ½ cup	90	2	1	<5	50	17	1
Swiss almond fudge, reduced fat, Breyers Light, ½ cup	160	6	3.5	30	55	22	<1
Toffee bar crunch, Breyers, ½ cup	170	9	4	30	60	18	1
Triple Brownie Overload, Haagen-Dazs Extraas, ½ cup	300	20	11	90	100	26	1
Triple chocolate chunk, low-fat, Healthy Choice, ½ cup	110	2	1	<5	60	21	1
Triple Chocolate Tornado, light, Weight Watchers, ½ cup	150	3.5	1.5	5	80	26	1
Turtle fudge cake, low-fat, Healthy Choice, ½ cup	130	2	1	<5	60	25	2
Vanilla, Ben & Jerry's, ½ cup	230	17	10	95	55	21	0
Vanilla, Breyers, ½ cup	150	8	6	35	45	15	0
Vanilla, Dreyer's/Edy's Grand, ½ cup	150	10	6	35	30	14	0
Vanilla, Dreyer's/Edy's Grand Light, ½ cup	100	4	2.5	25	35	14	0
Vanilla, Haagen-Dazs, ½ cup	270	18	11	120	85	21	0
Vanilla, Sealtest, ½ cup	140	7	5	30	55	16	0
Vanilla, Sealtest Gold, ½ cup	130	7	3.5	0	35	14	0
Vanilla, fat free, Borden, ½ cup	80	0	0	0	45	18	0
Vanilla, fat free, Breyers Free, ½ cup	100	0	0	<5	50	21	0

ICE CREAM	CAL (g)	FAT (g)	SAT FAT (g)	CHOL (mg)	SODIUM (mg)	CARB (g)	FIBER (g)
Vanilla, fat free, Dreyer's/Edy's, ½ cup	90	0	0	0	65	20	0
Vanilla, fat free, Sealtest, ½ cup	100	0	0	0	40	22	0
Vanilla, fat free, no sugar added, Dreyer's/Edy's, ½ cup	80	0	0	0	45	18	0
Vanilla, low fat, Borden, ½ cup	100	2	1	10	40	18	0
Vanilla, lowfat, Dreyer's/Edy's, ½ cup	100	2	1	5	35	19	0
Vanilla, lowfat, Healthy Choice, ½ cup	100	2	1.5	5	50	18	1
Vanilla, no sugar added, Breyers, ½ cup	90	5	2	20	45	12	0
Vanilla, no sugar added, reduced fat, Sealtest, 1 cup	90	4.5	2	20	45	12	0
Vanilla, nondairy dessert, Rice Dream, ½ cup	130	5	na	0	70	19	na
Vanilla, reduced fat, Breyers Light, ½ cup	130	4.5	3	35	55	18	0
Vanilla, reduced fat, Viva, ½ cup	110	4	2.5	15	65	17	0
Vanilla bean, smooth, Ben & Jerry's, ½ cup	230	17	10	95	55	21	0
Vanilla/black cherry, Breyers, ½ cup	150	8	6	35	45	16	0
Vanilla caramel fudge, smooth, Ben & Jerry's, ½ cup	280	17	10	95	75	33	1
Vanilla/chocolate, Breyers, ½ cup	160	8	6	35	35	17	0
Vanilla/chocolate/strawberry, Breyers, ½ cup	150	8	5	30	35	16	0
Vanilla/chocolate/strawberry, Sealtest, ½ cup	140	6	4	25	50	18	0
Vanilla/chocolate/strawberry, fat free, Sealtest, ½ cup	100	0	0	0	40	21	0
Vanilla/chocolate/strawberry, no sugar added, Breyers, ½ cup	100	5	2.5	20	50	13	0

ICE CREAM	CAL (g)	FAT (g)	SAT FAT (g)	CHOL (mg)	SODIUM (mg)	CARB (g)	FIBER (g)
Vanilla/chocolate/strawberry, reduced fat, Breyers Light, ½ cup	120	4	2.5	30	50	18	0
Vanilla fudge, Haagen-Dazs, ½ cup	280	18	11	105	105	25	0
Vanilla fudge royale, fat free, Sealtest, ½ cup	100	0	0	5	45	22	0
Vanilla fudge twirl, no sugar added, Breyers, ½ cup	100	4	2	20	55	16	0
Vanilla/orange sherbet, Breyers, ½ cup	140	5	3	25	35	21	0
Vanilla/strawberry, fat free, Breyers Free, ½ cup	90	0	0	0	40	21	0
Vanilla Swiss almond, Haagen-Dazs, ½ cup	310	21	11	105	80	23	1
Wavy Gravy, Ben & Jerry's, ½ cup	330	24	10	80	95	29	2
White Russian, smooth, Ben & Jerry's, ½ cup	240	16	10	90	55	23	0

AT A GLANCE: ICE CREAM

Choose from the dozens of fat free ice cream products from Borden/Meadow Gold, Breyers, Dreyer's/Edy's, and Sealtest.

MEALS & SIDE DISHES

See also Pizza and Vegetables in this chapter.

	CAL (g)	FAT (g)	SAT FAT (g)	CHOL (mg)	SODIUM (mg)	CARB (g)	FIBER (g)
Angel hair pasta, Stouffer's Lean Cuisine, 1 pkg	210	4	1	0	420	35	4
Angel hair pasta, Weight Watchers Smart Ones, 9 oz	180	2	0.5	0	230	33	7
Beef, creamed chipped, Banquet Hot Sandwich Toppers, 1 bag	100	3	1.5	25	700	8	0
Beef, creamed chipped, Stouffer's, ½ cup	150	11	3	40	690	6	1
Beef, creamed chipped, over country biscuit, Stouffer's, 1 pkg	510	29	8	40	1630	45	2
Beef, Oriental, The Budget Gourmet Light and Healthy, 10 oz	270	8	4	35	1070	35	3

MEALS & SIDE DISHES	CAL	FAT (g)	SAT FAT (g)	CHOL (mg)	SODIUM (mg)	CARB (g)	FIBER (g)
Beef, Oriental, Stouffer's Lean Cuisine, 1 pkg	250	8	3	30	480	30	4
Beef, Oriental, Stouffer's Lunch Express, 1 pkg	260	8	1.5	20	1220	34	4
Beef, sliced, & gravy, Banquet Hot Sandwich Toppers, 1 bag	70	2	1	25	440	5	<1
Beef, teriyaki, The Budget Gourmet Light and Healthy, 10.75 oz	310	6	2	45	600	46	7
Beef & gravy dinner, Swanson, 1 pkg	330	9	5	40	660	37	5
Beef & macaroni, family size, Banquet, 1 cup	230	7	3	25	810	31	3
Beef & noodles, family size, Banquet, 1 cup	150	4	2	40	1200	17	2
Beef & peppers Cantonese, Healthy Choice, 1 meal	270	5	2.5	35	560	40	5
Beef and broccoli dinner, Swanson, 1 pkg	350	11	5	30	760	51	4
Beef barbecue, mesquite, Healthy Choice, 1 meal	310	4	1.5	45	490	45	6
Beef broccoli Beijing, Healthy Choice, 1 meal	330	3	1	20	500	55	5
Beef Cantonese, The Budget Gourmet, 9.1 oz	280	8	3	30	1670	36	3
Beef macaroni casserole, Healthy Choice, 1 meal	200	1	0.5	15	450	34	5
Beef patties, belly bustin', Swanson Kids Fun Feast, 1 pkg	470	19	7	40	490	54	5
Beef patty sandwich with cheese, Kids Cuisine, 1 meal	270	7	4	20	330	40	5
Beef patty with gravy dinner, Banquet, 1 meal	300	20	8	35	1060	21	3
Beef pepper steak, Chun King, 1 meal	300	4	1	10	1610	50	5
Beef pepper steak, lite, Armour Classics, 1 meal	210	4	1.5	60	870	29	5
Beef pepper steak Oriental, Healthy Choice, 1 meal	250	4	1.5	35	470	34	3
Beef pie, Stouffer's, 1 pkg	450	26	9	65	1140	36	3

MEALS & SIDE DISHES	CAL	FAT (g)	SAT FAT (g)	CHOL (mg)	SODIUM (mg)	CARB (g)	FIBER (g)
Beef pie, Swanson Hungry-Man, 1 pkg	670	32	14	55	1480	71	6
Beef pie, family size, Banquet, 8 oz	450	25	11	30	930	44	4
Beef pot pie, Banquet, 1 pie	330	15	7	25	1000	38	3
Beef pot pie, Morton, 7 oz	310	17	8	15	1380	34	2
Beef pot pie, Swanson, 1 pkg	380	19	8	30	850	39	3
Beef pot pie, meatless, Worthington, 1 pie	410	24	4	0	1340	40	6
Beef pot pie, supreme, Banquet, 1 pie	270	12	5	30	1280	38	3
Beef pot roast, with browned potatoes, Stouffer's, 1 pkg	270	10	3	40	640	25	4
Beef pot roast & whipped potatoes, Stouffer's Lean Cuisine, 1 pkg	210	7	1.5	40	570	21	3
Beef sirloin meatballs & gravy, The Budget Gourmet Light and Healthy, 11 oz	310	8	3	35	540	37	5
Beef stew, family size, Banquet, 1 cup	160	4	2	25	1110	16	4
Beef stroganoff, The Budget Gourmet Light and Healthy, 8.75 oz	290	7	4	35	580	32	3
Beef stroganoff, Pepperidge Farm, 1 filled shell	420	29	12	40	500	27	5
Beef stroganoff, Stouffer's, 1 pkg	380	20	7	85	1100	30	2
Beef tips, traditional, Healthy Choice, 1 meal	260	5	2	40	390	32	6
Beef tips Francais, Healthy Choice, 1 meal	280	5	1.5	30	520	40	4
Beef tips with sauce, Healthy Choice, 1 meal	290	6	2.5	40	270	40	5
Bow tie pasta and chicken, Stouffer's Lean Cuisine Cafe Classics, 1 pkg	270	6	1.5	60	550	34	5
Britos, beef & bean, Patio, 10 britos	420	19	7	20	800	51	7
Britos, nacho beef, Patio, 10 britos	410	18	18	20	520	48	5

MEALS & SIDE DISHES	CAL (g)	FAT (g)	SAT FAT (g)	CHOL (mg)	SODIUM (mg)	CARB (g)	FIBER (g)
Britos, nacho cheese, Patio, 10 britos	360	13	4	15	500	52	3
Britos, spicy chicken, Patio, 10 britos	400	16	4	25	640	52	3
Burrito, bean & cheese, Old El Paso, 1 burrito	290	9	4.5	15	840	44	3
Burrito, bean & cheese, Patio, 1 burrito	270	5	2	5	530	46	7
Burrito, bean & cheese, Tina's, 1 burrito	340	9	3	<5	600	52	8
Burrito, beef & bean, Patio, 1 burrito	280	7	3	15	860	45	7
Burrito, beef & bean, hot, Old El Paso, 1 burrito	320	10	4	15	850	45	3
Burrito, beef & bean, medium, Old El Paso, 1 burrito	320	10	4	15	800	46	3
Burrito, beef & bean, mild, Old El Paso, 1 burrito	330	9	3	15	690	48	4
Burrito, beef & bean, with green chili, Patio, 1 burrito	260	5	1.5	10	890	44	7
Burrito, beef & bean, with red chili, Patio, 1 burrito	260	5	2	10	640	42	7
Burrito, chicken, Patio, 1 burrito	260	4	1.5	15	740	44	3
Burrito, chicken con queso, Healthy Choice, 1 burrito	280	6	1.5	10	600	43	5
Burrito, pizza, cheese, Old El Paso, 1 burrito	320	9	4	20	430	27	0
Burrito, pizza, pepperoni, Old El Paso, 1 burrito	260	10	5	20	510	31	0
Burrito, pizza, sausage, Old El Paso, 1 burrito	260	9	4	10	420	32	0
Burrito, red chili, Patio, 1 burrito	270	6	2	10	850	42	6
Burrito ranchero, beef, medium, Healthy Choice, 1 burrito	290	7	2.5	15	500	44	6
Burrito ranchero, beef, mild, Healthy Choice, 1 burrito	300	7	2.5	15	480	45	7

MEALS & SIDE DISHES	CAL (g)	FAT (g)	SAT FAT (g)	CHOL (mg)	SODIUM (mg)	CARB (g)	FIBER (g)
Cabbage, stuffed, with whipped potatoes, Stouffer's Lean Cuisine, 1 pkg	220	7	1.5	25	460	27	5
Cannelloni, cheese, Stouffer's Lean Cuisine, 1 pkg	270	8	3.5	30	500	28	3
Cheddar bake, with pasta, Stouffer's Lean Cuisine, 1 pkg	220	6	2	20	560	29	3
Chicken, baked, with gravy & whipped potatoes, Stouffer's, 1 pkg	270	12	3	75	750	19	2
Chicken, baked, with whipped potatoes & stuffing, Stouffer's Lean Cuisine, 1 pkg	240	5	0.5	35	480	31	3
Chicken, barbecue glazed, Weight Watchers, 7.4 oz	190	3.5	1	20	340	22	1
Chicken, barbecue style, dinner, Banquet, 1 meal	320	12	2.5	60	800	36	3
Chicken, boneless, dinner, Swanson Hungry-Man, 1 pkg	700	28	11	105	1380	76	7
Chicken, broccoli & cheddar pocket sandwich, Weight Watchers, 5 oz	250	6	2.5	25	310	40	1
Chicken, cacciatore, Healthy Choice, 1 meal	260	3	0.5	25	510	36	6
Chicken, Calypso, Stouffer's Lean Cuisine Cafe Classics, 1 pkg	280	6	2	40	590	42	3
Chicken, country fried, Banquet, 3 oz	270	18	5	65	620	13	1
Chicken, country glazed, Healthy Choice, 1 meal	200	1.5	0.5	30	480	30	3
Chicken, country herb, Healthy Choice, 1 meal	270	4	1.5	35	340	40	6
Chicken, creamed, Stouffer's, 1 pkg	280	20	7	80	720	8	1
Chicken, escalloped, and noodles, Stouffer's, 1 pkg	440	29	6	80	880	28	2
Chicken, fiesta, Weight Watchers Smart Ones, 8.5 oz	220	2	0.5	25	480	38	5
Chicken, frazzlin' fried, Swanson Kids Fun Feast, 1 pkg	660	36	13	90	1100	58	4

MEALS & SIDE DISHES	CAL	FAT (g)	SAT FAT (g)	CHOL (mg)	SODIUM (mg)	CARB (g)	FIBER (g)
Chicken, French recipe, The Budget Gourmet Light and Healthy, 10 oz	200	8	3	30	950	19	4
Chicken, fried, Banquet, 3 oz	270	18	5	65	620	13	1
Chicken, fried, Kids Cuisine, 1 meal	440	20	6	65	710	48	6
Chicken, fried (dark portions), Swanson, 1 pkg	570	30	7	110	1430	50	4
Chicken, fried (dark portions), Swanson Budget, 1 pkg	420	22	8	100	1040	36	4
Chicken, fried (dark portions), Swanson Hungry-Man, 1 pkg	810	41	14	120	1710	76	9
Chicken, fried (mostly white) dinner, Swanson Hungry-Man, 1 pkg	810	40	14	120	2060	77	7
Chicken, fried (white portions), Swanson, 1 pkg	580	28	7	70	1610	54	5
Chicken, fried, and whipped potatoes, Swanson, 1 pkg	400	21	8	80	1120	34	2
Chicken, fried, breast, Banquet, 1 piece	410	26	13	85	600	18	4
Chicken, fried, dinner, Banquet Extra Helping, 1 meal	790	39	9	110	1820	72	8
Chicken, fried, drums & thighs, Banquet, 3 oz	260	18	5	65	540	10	2
Chicken, fried, hot & spicy, Banquet, 3 oz	260	18	5	65	590	13	1
Chicken, fried, meal, Banquet, 1 meal	470	27	9	105	980	35	6
Chicken, fried, meal, Morton, 1 meal	420	25	8	85	1000	30	4
Chicken, fried, skinless, Banquet, 3 oz	210	13	3	55	480	7	2
Chicken, fried, with whipped potatoes, Stouffer's, 1 pkg	330	16	4	55	780	29	3
Chicken, garlic, Milano, Healthy Choice, 1 meal	240	4	2	35	510	34	3
Chicken, ginger, Hunan, Healthy Choice, 1 meal	350	2.5	0.5	25	430	59	5

MEALS & SIDE DISHES	CAL (g)	FAT (g)	SAT FAT (g)	CHOL (mg)	SODIUM (mg)	CARB (g)	FIBER (g)
Chicken, glazed, Armour Classics, 1 meal	280	14	4	55	740	20	4
Chicken, glazed, with vegetable rice, Stouffer's Lean Cuisine, 1 pkg	240	6	1	60	460	24	2
Chicken, grilled, salsa, Stouffer's Lean Cuisine Cafe Classics, 1 pkg	240	6	1.5	40	550	32	4
Chicken, grilled, white meat in garlic sauce, Swanson, 1 pkg	270	7	3	30	640	35	5
Chicken, grilled, with angel hair pasta, Stouffer's Lunch Express, 1 pkg	340	13	3	50	650	35	3
Chicken, herb roasted, Stouffer's Lean Cuisine Cafe Classics, 1 pkg	210	5	1	40	430	25	4
Chicken, honey mustard, Healthy Choice, 1 meal	260	2	0	30	550	40	4
Chicken, honey mustard, Weight Watchers Smart Ones, 8.5 oz	200	2	0.5	30	340	33	6
Chicken, honey mustard, with vegetable rice, Stouffer's Lean Cuisine, 1 pkg	250	4.5	1	50	460	32	4
Chicken, hot & spicy snackin', Banquet, 4 pieces	240	16	4	45	480	11	2
Chicken, hot popcorn, Banquet, 3 oz	290	19	4	35	790	18	2
Chicken, imperial, Chun King, 1 meal	460	10	3	25	1670	59	5
Chicken, in honey barbecue sauce, Stouffer's Lean Cuisine, 1 pkg	250	4.5	1	50	560	35	6
Chicken, in peanut sauce, Stouffer's Lean Cuisine, 1 pkg	280	6	1	45	590	33	3
Chicken, Mandarin, The Budget Gourmet Light and Healthy, 10 oz	250	5	1	45	850	37	4
Chicken, Mandarin, Healthy Choice, 1 meal	280	2.5	0	25	520	44	4

MEALS & SIDE DISHES	CAL	FAT (g)	SAT FAT (g)	CHOL (mg)	SODIUM (mg)	CARB (g)	FIBER (g)
Chicken, Mandarin, Stouffer's Lean Cuisine Lunch Express, 1 pkg	270	6	1	30	520	41	2
Chicken, mesquite, Armour Classics, 1 meal	280	13	4	65	630	39	5
Chicken, Oriental, Stouffer's Lunch Express, 1 pkg	320	9	1.5	40	930	45	2
Chicken, Oriental, with vegetables and vermicelli, Stouffer's Lean Cuisine, 1 pkg	260	6	1	45	530	30	3
Chicken, Oriental style, dinner, Banquet, 1 meal	260	9	2.5	40	610	34	4
Chicken, roast glazed, Weight Watchers, 8.9 oz	200	5	2.5	15	510	25	4
Chicken, sesame, Healthy Choice, 1 meal	240	3	0.5	30	600	38	3
Chicken, sesame, Shanghai, Healthy Choice, 1 meal	310	5	1	30	460	42	5
Chicken, Southern fried, Banquet Extra Helping, 1 meal	750	37	9	120	2140	67	9
Chicken, Southern fried, Weight Watchers Smart Ones, 8 oz	280	11	4.5	65	590	25	1
Chicken, Southwestern glazed, Healthy Choice, 1 meal	300	3	1	45	430	48	6
Chicken, sweet & sour, The Budget Gourmet, 10 oz	330	5	1	40	700	55	4
Chicken, sweet & sour, Healthy Choice, 1 meal	310	5	1	50	250	42	5
Chicken, sweet & sour, with vegetables & rice, Stouffer's Lean Cuisine, 1 pkg	260	2.5	1	45	440	43	3
Chicken, Tex-Mex, Weight Watchers, 8.3 oz	260	4	1.5	35	430	35	1
Chicken, white meat, dinner, Banquet Extra Helping, 1 meal	820	41	9	95	1890	72	8
Chicken, with garden vegetables & rice, Stouffer's Lunch Express, 1 pkg	340	11	3	30	750	45	2

MEALS & SIDE DISHES	CAL (g)	FAT (g)	SAT FAT (g)	CHOL (mg)	SODIUM (mg)	CARB (g)	FIBER (g)
Chicken, with linguini, Stouffer's Lunch Express, 1 pkg	300	11	2	40	680	36	5
Chicken, with wine & mushrooms, Armour Classics, 1 meal	260	11	5	50	540	20	4
Chicken & broccoli, creamy, Stouffer's, 1 pkg	320	15	5	60	820	26	2
Chicken & cheddar nuggets, Banquet, 2.5 oz	280	19	6	25	560	13	1
Chicken & dumplings, Banquet, 1 meal	260	8	2.5	35	780	35	3
Chicken & dumplings, family size, Banquet, 1 cup	310	15	5	40	1360	32	2
Chicken & egg noodles, The Budget Gourmet, 10 oz	410	23	12	110	930	30	3
Chicken & noodle casserole, Swanson Homestyle, 1 pkg	290	9	3	40	1000	33	2
Chicken & noodles, Armour Classics, 1 meal	280	9	5	60	550	30	6
Chicken & noodles, Stouffer's, 1 pkg	310	14	5	80	1030	23	2
Chicken & noodles, family size, Banquet, 1 cup	210	9	3	40	810	24	2
Chicken & noodles with vegetables, Swanson Homestyle, 1 pkg	320	15	8	50	980	32	4
Chicken & rice stir fry casserole, Swanson Homestyle, 1 pkg	240	3	1	20	1200	40	2
Chicken & vegetables, Stouffer's Lean Cuisine, 1 pkg	240	5	1	35	520	30	5
Chicken a la king, Banquet Hot Sandwich Toppers, 1 bag	100	4	1.5	40	480	7	1
Chicken a la king, Pepperidge Farm, 1 filled shell	400	26	10	35	590	28	5
Chicken a la king, Stouffer's, 1 pkg	320	10	3	55	750	43	3
Chicken a l'orange, Stouffer's Lean Cuisine, 1 pkg	260	2.5	0.5	40	260	40	1
Chicken Alfredo, Stouffer's Lunch Express, 1 pkg	360	17	6	60	620	34	3

MEALS & SIDE DISHES	CAL	FAT (g)	SAT FAT (g)	CHOL (mg)	SODIUM (mg)	CARB (g)	FIBER (g)
Chicken and rice, Mexican style, Stouffer's Lunch Express, 1 pkg	280	8	1	40	540	40	4
Chicken and vegetables Marsala, Healthy Choice, 1 meal	220	1	0	30	440	32	3
Chicken au gratin, The Budget Gourmet Light and Healthy, 9.1 oz	250	8	5	45	820	26	3
Chicken Bangkok, Healthy Choice, 1 meal	270	4	0.5	45	390	35	5
Chicken barbecue, mesquite, Healthy Choice, 1 meal	320	2	0.5	35	290	55	6
Chicken barbecue, smoky, Healthy Choice, 1 meal	380	5	1.5	50	450	57	7
Chicken breast, herbed, with fettucini, The Budget Gourmet Light and Healthy, 11 oz	300	8	3	65	620	34	5
Chicken breast, honey mustard, The Budget Gourmet Light and Healthy, 11 oz	310	6	1.5	50	540	46	6
Chicken breast, orange glazed, The Budget Gourmet Light and Healthy, 9 oz	300	2	1	30	920	56	1
Chicken breast, roast, with herb gravy, The Budget Gourmet Light and Healthy, 11 oz	240	7	2	35	660	29	4
Chicken breast, teriyaki, with Oriental style vegetables, The Budget Gourmet Light and Healthy, 11 oz	290	6	1	35	800	42	3
Chicken broccoli Alfredo, Healthy Choice, 1 meal	370	8	3	45	470	53	6
Chicken Burgundy, lite, Armour Classics, 1 meal	210	5	1.5	45	760	20	4
Chicken Cantonese, Healthy Choice, 1 meal	210	0.5	0	30	360	31	5
Chicken carbonara, Stouffer's Lean Cuisine Cafe Classics, 1 pkg	290	8	2	40	540	32	4

MEALS & SIDE DISHES	CAL	FAT (g)	SAT FAT (g)	CHOL (mg)	SODIUM (mg)	CARB (g)	FIBER (g)
Chicken chow mein, Banquet, 1 meal	210	7	2	30	850	28	3
Chicken chow mein, Chun King, 1 meal	370	14	5	45	2010	45	4
Chicken chow mein, Weight Watchers Smart Ones, 9 oz	200	2	0.5	25	430	34	3
Chicken chow mein with rice, Stouffer's Lean Cuisine, 1 pkg	210	5	1	35	510	28	2
Chicken chow mein with rice, Stouffer's Lunch Express, 1 pkg	260	4	1	30	940	43	3
Chicken cordon bleu, Weight Watchers, 9 oz	220	6	2	20	500	27	3
Chicken dijon, Healthy Choice, 1 meal	280	4	1.5	30	410	41	9
Chicken drumlets, chompin', Swanson Kids Fun Feast, 1 pkg	490	25	10	60	1010	50	3
Chicken fajitas, fiesta, Healthy Choice, 1 meal	260	4	1	30	410	36	5
Chicken fettucini, Armour Classics, 1 meal	230	8	4	25	520	25	6
Chicken fettucini, Stouffer's, 1 pkg	380	15	4	65	1250	32	3
Chicken fettucini, Stouffer's Lean Cuisine, 1 pkg	270	6	2.5	45	580	33	2
Chicken fettucini, Weight Watchers, 8.25 oz	280	9	3	40	590	25	2
Chicken fettucini Alfredo, Healthy Choice, 1 meal	250	3	1	30	370	34	3
Chicken fettucini with broccoli, Stouffer's Lean Cuisine Lunch Express, 1 pkg	290	8	3.5	40	570	38	3
Chicken fiesta with rice and vegetables, Stouffer's Lean Cuisine, 1 pkg	240	5	1	45	590	31	3
Chicken filets, breaded, and potato rounds, Stouffer's, 1 pkg	380	18	3	50	1060	33	4
Chicken Francesca, Healthy Choice, 1 meal	360	5	2	30	500	51	5

MEALS & SIDE DISHES	CAL (g)	FAT (g)	SAT FAT (g)	CHOL (mg)	SODIUM (mg)	CARB (g)	FIBER (g)
Chicken fried steak dinner, Banquet Extra Helping, 1 meal	800	44	14	55	2050	73	6
Chicken imperial, Healthy Choice, 1 meal	230	4	1	40	470	31	3
Chicken in mesquite barbecue sauce, The Budget Gourmet Light and Healthy, 11 oz	280	6	2	40	480	37	6
Chicken Italiano, with fettucini & vegetables, Stouffer's Lean Cuisine, 1 pkg	270	6	1.5	40	560	31	3
Chicken Marsala, The Budget Gourmet, 9 oz	270	7	4	80	750	34	1
Chicken Marsala, Weight Watchers Smart Ones, 9 oz	150	2	0.5	25	500	22	6
Chicken Marsala & vegetables, Stouffer's Lean Cuisine, 1 pkg	180	4	1	60	470	13	5
Chicken Mediterranean, Stouffer's Lean Cuisine Cafe Classics, 1 pkg	250	4	1	30	570	35	4
Chicken mirabella, Weight Watchers Smart Ones, 9.2 oz	170	2	0.5	20	410	26	6
Chicken Monterey, with Mexican-style rice, Stouffer's, 1 pkg	410	20	9	75	700	35	4
Chicken nibbles, Swanson Homestyle, 3 oz	340	20	9	90	730	31	2
Chicken nugget dinner, Morton, 1 meal	320	17	4	30	460	30	3
Chicken nuggets, Kids Cuisine, 1 meal	360	13	3	30	500	46	6
Chicken nuggets, Swanson, 1 pkg	450	21	7	35	890	48	4
Chicken nuggets dinner, Banquet, 1 meal	410	21	5	45	650	38	4
Chicken Oriental, The Budget Gourmet Light and Healthy, 9 oz	300	6	2	20	700	44	6
Chicken Parmesan, Banquet, 1 meal	290	15	4	50	900	27	3

MEALS & SIDE DISHES	CAL	FAT (g)	SAT FAT (g)	CHOL (mg)	SODIUM (mg)	CARB (g)	FIBER (g)
Chicken Parmesan, Banquet Extra Helping, 1 meal	650	33	8	65	1770	64	9
Chicken Parmesan, Banquet Family Entrees, 1 patty with sauce	240	13	5	20	690	18	2
Chicken Parmesan and pasta, Stouffer's Lean Cuisine, 1 pkg	220	5	1.5	50	530	22	5
Chicken parmigian, Armour Classics, 1 meal	360	18	6	45	1020	25	7
Chicken parmigiana, The Budget Gourmet Light and Healthy, 11 oz	300	10	3	45	480	32	5
Chicken parmigiana, Healthy Choice, 1 meal	300	1.5	0.5	35	490	47	6
Chicken parmigiana, Swanson, 1 pkg	400	19	7	35	1150	43	4
Chicken parmigiana, Swanson Budget, 1 pkg	340	18	8	40	760	33	4
Chicken parmigiana, Weight Watchers, 9.1 oz	230	6	3	50	470	25	2
Chicken parmigiana, with spaghetti, Stouffer's, 1 pkg	320	10	2	75	890	30	4
Chicken pattie, breaded, dinner, Morton, 1 meal	280	15	3	20	840	24	4
Chicken patties, grilled, dinner, Swanson Hungry-Man, 1 pkg	580	19	8	90	1350	67	13
Chicken patty strips, breaded, Swanson Homestyle, 1 pkg	340	19	4	30	560	31	3
Chicken picante, Healthy Choice, 1 meal	220	2	1.5	35	330	30	6
Chicken piccata, Stouffer's Lean Cuisine Cafe Classics, 1 pkg	290	6	1.5	30	540	45	1
Chicken piccata, lemon herb, Weight Watchers Smart Ones, 8.5 oz	190	2	0.5	25	590	32	3
Chicken pie, Stouffer's, 1 pkg	520	33	8	70	1000	37	3
Chicken pie, Stouffer's Lean Cuisine, 1 pkg	320	10	2.5	35	590	39	3
Chicken pie, Swanson, 1 pkg	410	22	8	45	1010	39	5

MEALS & SIDE DISHES	CAL (g)	FAT (g)	SAT FAT (g)	CHOL (mg)	SODIUM (mg)	CARB (g)	FIBER (g)
Chicken pie, 16 oz, Stouffer's, 1 cup	460	30	10	65	850	35	3
Chicken pie, deluxe, Swanson, 1 pkg	410	22	8	45	1010	39	5
Chicken pie, family size, Banquet, 8 oz	450	30	12	35	1010	39	6
Chicken pot pie, Banquet, 1 pie	350	18	7	40	950	36	3
Chicken pot pie, Morton, 7 oz	320	18	7	25	1020	32	3
Chicken pot pie, Swanson, 1 pkg	410	22	8	30	810	45	3
Chicken pot pie, Swanson Hungry-Man, 1 pkg	650	35	14	65	1470	64	3
Chicken pot pie, meatless, Worthington, 1 pie	450	27	6	0	1080	44	8
Chicken pot pie, supreme, Banquet, 1 pie	330	15	5	30	1320	38	3
Chicken sandwich, Kids Cuisine, 1 meal	440	14	3	20	680	63	4
Chicken sandwich, grilled, Weight Watchers, 4 oz	210	5	2	20	420	24	2
Chicken tenders, Swanson, 1 pkg	320	12	3	25	790	39	3
Chicken teriyaki, Healthy Choice, 1 meal	270	2	0.5	40	420	42	5
Chicken walnut, Chun King, 1 meal	460	19	5	35	1820	56	5
Chicken with fettucini, The Budget Gourmet, 10 oz	380	19	10	85	810	33	3
Chili, three bean, with rice, Stouffer's Lean Cuisine, 1 pkg	210	6	2	10	460	32	7
Chili, vegetarian, Tabatchnick, 7.5 oz	210	6	1	0	530	28	10
Chili, with beans, Stouffer's, 1 pkg	270	10	4	35	1130	29	8
Chimichanga, beef, Old El Paso, 1 chimichanga	370	20	5	10	470	37	3
Chimichanga, chicken, Old El Paso, 1 chimichanga	350	16	4	20	540	39	2
Chimichanga meal, Banquet, 1 meal	470	23	7	15	1180	56	9

MEALS & SIDE DISHES	CAL	FAT (g)	SAT FAT (g)	CHOL (mg)	SODIUM (mg)	CARB (g)	FIBER (g)
Crab Delights, stir fry kit, Tyson, 1 cup	240	8	2	15	650	34	8
Egg roll, beef steak teriyaki, Lo-An, 1 egg roll	140	4	1	10	380	20	1
Egg roll, cabbage & meatless ham, Worthington, 1 egg roll	180	8	1.5	0	380	20	2
Egg roll, chicken, Chun King, 6 egg rolls	210	7	1.5	10	260	30	3
Egg roll, chicken, mini, La Choy, 7 egg rolls	220	6	1.5	5	460	35	3
Egg roll, chicken, restaurant style, La Choy, 1 egg roll	170	5	2.5	10	450	25	4
Egg roll, chicken, white meat, Lo-An, 1 egg roll	140	4	1	10	400	20	1
Egg roll, chicken & shrimp, Lo-An, 1 egg roll	140	4	1	20	430	20	1
Egg roll, chicken teriyaki, Lo-An, 1 egg roll	140	4	1	10	420	19	1
Egg roll, lobster, La Choy, 7 egg rolls	210	6	1	0	360	34	5
Egg roll, lobster, Lo-An, 1 egg roll	150	4	1	15	450	21	1
Egg roll, meat & shrimp, La Choy, 15 egg rolls	240	9	2	10	350	31	3
Egg roll, mu sho pork, restaurant style, La Choy, 1 egg roll	190	7	1.5	15	330	25	2
Egg roll, pork, Lo-An, 1 egg roll	150	5	2	20	450	19	1
Egg roll, pork, restaurant style, La Choy, 1 egg roll	170	6	1.5	5	390	23	3
Egg roll, pork & shrimp, Chun King, 6 egg rolls	220	8	2	10	260	29	3
Egg roll, pork & shrimp, Lo-An, 1 egg roll	150	5	2	25	450	17	1
Egg roll, pork & shrimp, mini, La Choy, 7 egg rolls	220	6	1.5	10	460	33	3
Egg roll, shrimp, Chun King, 6 egg rolls	190	6	1	10	360	29	3
Egg roll, shrimp, mini, La Choy, 7 egg rolls	210	4	1	5	510	35	3

MEALS & SIDE DISHES	CAL (g)	FAT (g)	SAT FAT (g)	CHOL (mg)	SODIUM (mg)	CARB (g)	FIBER (g)
Egg roll, shrimp, restaurant style, La Choy, 1 egg roll	150	4	0.5	10	420	24	3
Egg roll, sweet & sour, restaurant style, La Choy, 1 egg roll	180	4	1	5	300	29	3
Eggplant parmigiana, Mrs. Paul's, ½ cup	220	14	4	10	530	19	3
Enchilada, beef, dinner, Banquet, 1 meal	380	12	5	15	1330	54	10
Enchilada, beef, dinner, Patio, 1 meal	320	8	3	15	1810	52	9
Enchilada, beef, dinner, Swanson, 1 pkg	480	21	12	40	1350	56	7
Enchilada, beef, family entree, Patio, 2 enchiladas with cheese	250	7	2.5	15	1350	35	8
Enchilada, beef, family entree, 6 count, Patio, 2 enchiladas with sour cream	170	4	1.5	10	940	27	5
Enchilada, beef, with cheese, family size, Banquet, 1 enchilada with cheese	130	4	1.5	5	690	19	3
Enchilada, beef & cheese, family entree, Patio, 2 enchiladas with cheese	250	6	2.5	20	1130	35	9
Enchilada, cheese, and Mexican-style rice, Stouffer's, 1 pkg	370	14	5	25	890	48	5
Enchilada, cheese, dinner, Banquet, 1 meal	340	6	2.5	15	1500	56	9
Enchilada, cheese, dinner, Patio, 1 meal	330	8	3	15	1570	52	10
Enchilada, cheese, family entree, 6 pack, Patio, 2 enchiladas with sour cream	170	4	2	10	880	26	4
Enchilada, chicken, dinner, Banquet, 1 meal	360	10	3	20	1580	54	9
Enchilada, chicken, dinner, Patio, 1 meal	380	9	3	25	1470	58	9
Enchilada, chicken, nacho grande, Weight Watchers, 9 oz	290	8	2.5	20	560	42	4

MEALS & SIDE DISHES	CAL (g)	FAT (g)	SAT FAT (g)	CHOL (mg)	SODIUM (mg)	CARB (g)	FIBER (g)
Enchilada, chicken, suprema, Healthy Choice, 1 meal	390	9	5	30	390	60	8
Enchilada, chicken, and Mexican-style rice, Stouffer's, 1 pkg	370	14	3.5	30	970	45	3
Enchilada Rio Grande, beef, Healthy Choice, 1 meal	410	8	3	15	480	70	9
Enchilada suiza, chicken, Healthy Choice, 1 meal	270	4	2	25	440	43	5
Enchilada suiza, chicken, Weight Watchers, 9 oz	250	8	3	25	570	28	4
Enchiliada suiza, chicken, with Mexican-style rice, Stouffer's Lean Cuisine, 1 pkg	290	5	2	25	530	48	5
Fettucini Alfredo, Healthy Choice, 1 meal	240	5	2	10	430	39	3
Fettucini Alfredo, Stouffer's, 1 pkg	580	39	21	120	810	42	4
Fettucini Alfredo, Stouffer's Lean Cuisine, 1 pkg	270	7	3	15	590	38	2
Fettucini Alfredo with broccoli, Weight Watchers, 8.5 oz	220	6	2.5	15	540	24	6
Fettucini Alfredo with four cheeses, The Budget Gourmet Special Selections, 11.5 oz	480	24	13	55	1120	48	3
Fettucini primavera, Stouffer's Lean Cuisine, 1 pkg	260	8	2.5	35	580	33	4
Fettucini primavera, Stouffer's Lunch Express, 1 pkg	420	25	12	95	690	33	4
Fiesta dinner, Patio, 1 meal	340	9	4	15	1760	51	11
Fish, lemon pepper, Healthy Choice, 1 meal	290	5	1	25	360	47	7
Fish & mac and cheese, Swanson Homestyle, 1 pkg	350	15	5	30	930	38	4
Fish 'n chips, Swanson, 1 pkg	480	20	4	45	1040	55	5
Fish 'n chips, Swanson Homestyle, 1 pkg	310	12	5	35	620	38	4
Fish divan, Stouffer's Lean Cuisine, 1 pkg	210	6	1	65	490	15	3

MEALS & SIDE DISHES	CAL (g)	FAT (g)	SAT FAT (g)	CHOL (mg)	SODIUM (mg)	CARB (g)	FIBER (g)
Fish fillet, with macaroni & cheese, Stouffer's, 1 pkg	430	21	5	70	930	37	2
Fish fillet sandwich with cheese, Mrs. Paul's, 1 sandwich	330	15	5	25	630	38	3
Fish n' fries, Van de Kamp's, 1 pkg	380	18	3	25	370	41	2
Fish sticks, frenzied, Swanson Kids Fun Feast, 1 pkg	360	14	5	25	650	47	4
Fish sticks meal, breaded, Swanson Budget, 1 pkg	370	13	6	25	610	51	3
Flounder fillet, crab meat stuffing, Triton, 1 pkg	190	2	1	20	680	33	5
Flounder fillet, spinach florentine, Triton, 1 pkg	170	2	1	25	620	26	5
Flounder Provencal with pasta, Mrs. Paul's, 1 fillet with sauce	310	13	7	50	990	34	2
Fried rice, with chicken, Chun King, 1 meal	270	6	1.5	25	1330	44	4
Fried rice, with pork, Chun King, 1 meal	290	6	2	25	1310	48	5
Green pepper steak, Stouffer's, 1 pkg	330	9	3	35	650	45	3
Grilled cheese, growlin', Swanson Kids Fun Feast, 1 pkg	460	20	8	30	760	56	5
Ham, hickory smoked, & cheddar pretzel sandwich, Weight Watchers On-The-Go, 4 oz	260	8	3	10	580	33	3
Ham and asparagus au gratin, The Budget Gourmet Light and Healthy, 8.7 oz	290	13	5	50	870	26	3
Ham and asparagus bake, Stouffer's, 1 pkg	520	36	14	75	1040	32	2
Ham and cheese pocket sandwich, Weight Watchers, 5 oz	240	7	2.5	10	480	32	5
Hot dog on a bun, Swanson Kids Fun Feast, 1 pkg	350	12	5	35	800	47	3

MEALS & SIDE DISHES	CAL (g)	FAT (g)	SAT FAT (g)	CHOL (mg)	SODIUM (mg)	CARB (g)	FIBER (g)
Lasagna, cheese, Stouffer's Lean Cuisine, 1 pkg	290	6	3	30	560	38	5
Lasagna, cheese, with chicken scaloppini, Stouffer's Lean Cuisine Cafe Classics, 1 pkg	290	8	2.5	40	560	34	4
Lasagna, four cheese, Stouffer's, 1 pkg	410	19	10	55	840	37	3
Lasagna, garden, Weight Watchers, 11 oz	230	5	1	5	460	30	6
Lasagna, Italian cheese, Weight Watchers, 11 oz	300	8	3	25	560	28	7
Lasagna, Italian sausage, The Budget Gourmet, 10.5 oz	430	21	9	60	730	40	4
Lasagna, meat, Rich's, 1 cup	400	23	11	70	760	29	1
Lasagna, three cheese, The Budget Gourmet, 10.5 oz	370	16	10	60	870	38	5
Lasagna, vegetable, The Budget Gourmet Light and Healthy, 10.5 oz	290	10	5	20	770	29	5
Lasagna, vegetable, Rich's, 1 cup	360	15	9	65	640	37	4
Lasagna, vegetable, Stouffer's, 1 pkg	370	19	5	35	820	31	3
Lasagna, with meat sauce, The Budget Gourmet Light and Healthy, 9.4 oz	250	7	3	30	690	31	3
Lasagna, with meat sauce, Stouffer's, 1 pkg	410	15	7	65	1080	45	5
Lasagna, with meat sauce, Stouffer's Lean Cuisine, 1 pkg	270	6	2.5	25	560	34	5
Lasagna, with meat sauce, Stouffer's Lunch Express, 1 pkg	330	10	5	40	910	42	5
Lasagna, with meat sauce, Swanson, 1 pkg	410	15	7	65	1080	45	5
Lasagna, with meat sauce, Weight Watchers, 10.25 oz	290	7	2.5	15	580	34	7
Lasagna, with meat sauce, 21- or 40-oz pkg, Stouffer's, 1 cup	260	10	4	35	560	24	4
Lasagna, with meat sauce, 28-oz pkg, family size, Banquet, 1 cup	250	8	4	40	570	31	3

MEALS & SIDE DISHES	CAL (g)	FAT (g)	SAT FAT (g)	CHOL (mg)	SODIUM (mg)	CARB (g)	FIBER (g)
Lasagna, with meat sauce, 48-oz pkg, family size, Banquet, 1 cup	240	7	3	15	650	32	5
Lasagna, with meat sauce, 96-oz pkg, Stouffer's, 1 cup	290	12	6	35	710	26	3
Lasagna, with meat sauce casserole, Swanson Homestyle, 1 pkg	330	9	5	25	1050	41	3
Lasagna, zucchini, Healthy Choice, 1 meal	330	1.5	1	10	310	58	11
Lasagna, zucchini, Stouffer's Lean Cuisine, 1 pkg	240	4	1.5	15	470	33	4
Lasagna casserole, cheese, Stouffer's Lean Cuisine Lunch Express, 1 pkg	270	7	2.5	15	590	38	5
Lasagna casserole, cheesy vegetable, Swanson, 1 pkg	350	13	7	20	1360	40	3
Lasagna curls with Italian vegetables, Weight Watchers Smart Ones, 9.5 oz	170	2	0.5	5	390	33	7
Lasagna Florentine, Weight Watchers Smart Ones, 10 oz	210	2	0.5	10	420	37	5
Lasagna Roma, Healthy Choice, 1 meal	390	5	2	15	580	60	9
Linguini with bay shrimp & clams marinara, The Budget Gourmet, 10 oz	300	11	6	55	760	37	4
Linguini with shrimp & clams, The Budget Gourmet Light and Healthy, 9.5 oz	280	8	5	70	800	38	3
Linguini with tomato sauce & Italian sausage, The Budget Gourmet Special Selections, 10.25 oz	360	14	4	25	610	43	5
Mac & cheese, family size, Banquet, 1 cup	220	5	2.5	10	1380	35	4
Mac & cheese pot pie, Morton, 1 container	160	3	1.5	10	640	30	3
Macaroni & beef, Stouffer's, 1 pkg	340	12	5	50	1530	40	4
Macaroni & beef, Stouffer's Lean Cuisine, 1 pkg	280	8	2	25	550	40	3

MEALS & SIDE DISHES	CAL	FAT (g)	SAT FAT (g)	CHOL (mg)	SODIUM (mg)	CARB (g)	FIBER (g)
Macaroni & beef, Weight Watchers Smart Ones, 9.5 oz	220	4.5	1.5	10	560	32	4
Macaroni & beef casserole with tomato sauce, Swanson Homestyle, 1 pkg	270	5	5	35	1060	39	2
Macaroni & cheese, The Budget Gourmet, 6 oz	270	13	8	40	600	27	1
Macaroni & cheese, The Budget Gourmet Special Selections, 10 oz	400	20	12	45	1320	38	4
Macaroni & cheese, Healthy Choice, 1 meal	290	5	2	15	580	45	4
Macaroni & cheese, Kids Cuisine, 1 meal	310	7	2.5	15	710	54	6
Macaroni & cheese, Stouffer's Lean Cuisine, 1 pkg	270	7	3.5	20	550	39	2
Macaroni & cheese, Swanson, 1 pkg	240	9	4	20	800	30	2
Macaroni & cheese, Swanson Budget, 1 pkg	320	11	7	20	960	43	6
Macaroni & cheese, Swanson Mac and More, 1 pkg	180	5	3	15	480	25	2
Macaroni & cheese, Tabatchnick, 7.5 oz	280	12	6	25	840	30	2
Macaroni & cheese, Weight Watchers, 9 oz	260	6	2	20	550	43	7
Macaroni & cheese, 12-, 20- & 40-oz pkgs, Stouffer's, 1 cup	310	16	6	30	970	29	2
Macaroni & cheese, family size, Banquet, 1 cup	300	10	5	25	1190	39	2
Macaroni & cheese, with broccoli, Stouffer's Lean Cuisine Lunch Express, 1 pkg	240	6	3	15	460	35	5
Macaroni & cheese, with broccoli, Stouffer's Lunch Express, 1 pkg	360	19	5	30	900	32	3
Macaroni & cheese and salsa pot pie, Swanson Mac and More, 1 pkg	210	8	3	15	870	27	2
Macaroni & cheese casserole, Morton, 1 cup	230	4	2	5	1000	40	3

MEALS & SIDE DISHES	CAL (g)	FAT (g)	SAT FAT (g)	CHOL (mg)	SODIUM (mg)	CARB (g)	FIBER (g)
Macaroni & cheese entree, Swanson, 1 pkg	280	10	5	20	1050	36	2
Macaroni & cheese pot pie, Banquet, 1 pie	200	3	1.5	10	600	35	2
Macaroni & cheese with cheddar & Parmesan, The Budget Gourmet Light and Healthy, 10 oz	340	8	5	25	760	48	2
Macaroni bake casserole, three cheese, Swanson Homestyle, 1 pkg	400	14	6	20	1580	53	3
Manicotti, cheese, Stouffer's, 1 manicotti	150	7	3	15	480	15	2
Manicotti, cheese, Stouffer's, 1 pkg	340	16	7	50	810	32	7
Manicotti, cheese, Weight Watchers, 9.25 oz	290	9	3.5	20	600	34	4
Manicotti, cheese, with meat sauce, The Budget Gourmet, 10 oz	420	22	11	85	810	38	4
Manicotti, three cheese, Healthy Choice, 1 meal	310	9	5	20	450	41	7
Marinara twist, Stouffer's Lean Cuisine, 1 pkg	240	3	1	5	440	42	4
Meatloaf, Armour Classics, 1 meal	300	10	5	65	600	33	7
Meatloaf, Banquet Extra Helping, 1 meal	650	38	16	85	2140	49	10
Meatloaf, traditional, Healthy Choice, 1 meal	320	8	4	35	460	46	7
Meatloaf, with whipped potatoes, Stouffer's, 1 pkg	380	24	8	80	910	24	3
Meatloaf & tomato sauce, Swanson Homestyle, 1 pkg	270	13	6	50	850	20	7
Meatloaf & whipped potatoes, Stouffer's Lean Cuisine, 1 pkg	250	7	2	45	570	25	5
Meatloaf dinner, Banquet, 1 meal	280	17	7	40	1100	23	4
Meatloaf dinner, Morton, 1 meal	250	13	4	20	1110	24	5

MEALS & SIDE DISHES	CAL (g)	FAT (g)	SAT FAT (g)	CHOL (mg)	SODIUM (mg)	CARB (g)	FIBER (g)
Meatloaf dinner, Swanson, 1 pkg	410	18	9	35	1060	44	5
Meatloaf dinner, Swanson Hungry-Man, 1 pkg	620	31	16	60	1640	57	9
Meatloaf meal, Swanson Budget, 1 pkg	350	21	10	25	870	29	4
Mexican combo meal, Banquet, 1 meal	380	11	5	15	1370	55	9
Mexican dinner, Morton, 1 meal	260	7	3	5	1000	40	8
Mexican dinner, Patio, 1 meal	440	15	6	20	1840	59	13
Mexican style combination dinner, Swanson, 1 pkg	410	18	9	35	1060	44	5
Mexican style dinner, Banquet Extra Helping, 1 meal	820	34	14	50	2060	100	20
Mexican style dinner, Swanson Hungry-Man, 1 pkg	780	36	16	60	2120	86	12
Mexican style meal, Banquet, 1 meal	400	13	5	15	1520	56	10
Mexican style meal, Swanson Budget, 1 pkg	400	16	7	20	1350	52	7
Mexican style rice with chicken, Stouffer's Lean Cuisine Lunch Express, 1 pkg	270	8	1.5	20	590	39	3
Mozzarella cheese sticks, Rich-SeaPak, 4 sticks	240	16	4	20	580	15	<1
Mozzarella nuggets, Banquet, 1.25 oz	110	6	2.5	10	200	8	1
Noodles, escalloped, and turkey, The Budget Gourmet Special Selections, 10.75 oz	440	20	10	115	840	44	2
Noodles Romanoff, Stouffer's, 1 pkg	460	25	6	60	1400	48	4
Pasta, penne, with chunky tomato sauce & Italian sausage, The Budget Gourmet Light and Healthy Special Selections, 10 oz	330	8	2.5	10	530	49	6
Pasta, penne, with sun-dried tomatoes, Weight Watchers, 10 oz	290	9	2.5	15	550	48	8

MEALS & SIDE DISHES	CAL	FAT (g)	SAT FAT (g)	CHOL (mg)	SODIUM (mg)	CARB (g)	FIBER (g)
Pasta, wide ribbon with ricotta & chunky tomato sauce, The Budget Gourmet Special Selections, 10.25 oz	420	22	8	65	620	41	2
Pasta Alfredo with broccoli, The Budget Gourmet, 5.8 oz	230	11	7	30	670	23	1
Pasta and chicken marinara, Stouffer's Lean Cuisine Lunch Express, 1 pkg	270	6	1.5	20	540	38	4
Pasta and chicken meal, Swanson Budget, 1 pkg	250	11	6	40	660	30	5
Pasta and tuna casserole, Stouffer's Lean Cuisine Lunch Express, 1 pkg	280	6	2	20	590	39	4
Pasta and turkey Dijon, Stouffer's Lean Cuisine Lunch Express, 1 pkg	270	6	1.5	30	570	37	6
Pasta shells marinara, Healthy Choice, 1 meal	370	4	2	25	390	59	5
Pepper steak with rice, The Budget Gourmet, 10 oz	290	8	3	40	1060	38	4
Pollock fillet, grilled, Italian herb glaze, Triton, 1 pkg	210	2	0	35	560	32	4
Pollock fillet, grilled, lemon pepper glaze, Triton, 1 pkg	240	3	1	30	600	35	4
Pork, sweet & sour, Chun King, 1 meal	450	6	2.5	20	1180	86	4
Pork patty, rib shaped, dinner, Swanson, 1 pkg	510	23	8	50	1140	57	6
Pork rib shaped patty with barbecue sauce, Swanson Homestyle, 1 pkg	460	22	7	45	1060	48	6
Pot roast, Yankee, The Budget Gourmet Light and Healthy, 10.5 oz	270	7	2.5	30	430	32	8
Pot roast, Yankee, Healthy Choice, 1 meal	280	5	2	45	460	38	5
Pot roast, Yankee, Swanson, 1 pkg	270	7	4	50	660	36	6
Pot roast, Yankee, Swanson Hungry-Man, 1 pkg	400	11	3	45	910	47	10

MEALS & SIDE DISHES	CAL	FAT (g)	SAT FAT (g)	CHOL (mg)	SODIUM (mg)	CARB (g)	FIBER (g)
Potato, baked, with broccoli & cheddar cheese sauce, Stouffer's Lean Cuisine Lunch Express, 1 pkg	250	9	4	25	490	28	6
Potato, baked, with broccoli & cheese, The Budget Gourmet Light and Healthy, 10.5 oz	270	8	5	25	580	38	5
Potato, baked, with broccoli & cheese, Ore Ida, ½ potato	150	4	1.5	10	410	24	4
Potato, baked, with broccoli & cheese, Weight Watchers Smart Ones, 10 oz	230	7	2	10	510	34	6
Potato, baked, with salsa & cheese, Ore Ida, ½ potato	160	4.5	1.5	10	430	25	3
Potato, deluxe cheddar, Stouffer's Lean Cuisine, 1 pkg	270	10	3.5	30	550	30	3
Potato, twice baked, butter flavor, Ore Ida, 1 potato	200	9	3	0	350	27	4
Potato, twice baked, cheddar cheese, Ore Ida, 1 potato	190	8	2.5	0	460	27	3
Potato, twice baked, ranch flavor, Ore Ida, 1 potato	180	6	2	0	400	27	3
Potato, twice baked, sour cream & chives, Ore Ida, 1 potato	180	6	1.5	0	370	28	3
Potato casserole, garden, Healthy Choice, 1 meal	200	4	1.5	10	520	30	6
Potatoes, cheddar broccoli, Healthy Choice, 1 meal	310	5	2	10	550	53	8
Potatoes, cheddared, The Budget Gourmet, 5.5 oz	260	17	9	40	740	21	4
Potatoes, cheddared, and broccoli, The Budget Gourmet, 5.25 oz	170	8	6	25	440	17	2
Potatoes, scalloped, & ham, Swanson Homestyle, 1 pkg	290	12	8	45	1020	29	4
Potatoes, stuffed, with onion, sour cream & chives, Oh Boy!, 1 potato	140	2.5	0.5	<5	310	26	3
Potatoes au gratin, Stouffer's, ½ cup	130	6	2.5	15	590	15	1

MEALS & SIDE DISHES	CAL	FAT (g)	SAT FAT (g)	CHOL (mg)	SODIUM (mg)	CARB (g)	FIBER (g)
Ranchera dinner, Patio, 1 meal	410	15	6	25	2400	55	14
Ravioli, beef, Stouffer's, 1 pkg	370	14	4	80	680	43	5
Ravioli, cheese, The Budget Gourmet Light and Healthy, 9.5 oz	310	13	9	45	720	36	3
Ravioli, cheese, Stouffer's Lean Cuisine, 1 pkg	240	7	3	50	590	34	4
Ravioli, cheese, Stouffer's Lunch Express, 1 pkg	360	14	5	60	700	43	7
Ravioli, cheese, mini, Kids Cuisine, 1 meal	310	4	1	10	750	61	5
Ravioli, cheese, with tomato sauce, Stouffer's, 1 pkg	360	14	5	85	720	42	4
Ravioli, roarin', Swanson Kids Fun Feast, 1 pkg	440	10	4	25	530	73	8
Ravioli Florentine, Weight Watchers Smart Ones, 8.5 oz	200	2	0.5	5	480	12	4
Ravioli parmigiana, cheese, Healthy Choice, 1 meal	250	4	2	20	290	44	6
Razzlin' Rings, Swanson Kids Fun Feast, 1 pkg	380	12	6	25	770	57	4
Reuben pocket sandwich, Weight Watchers, 5 oz	250	6	2	20	400	42	5
Rice, Oriental, with vegetables, The Budget Gourmet, 5.75 oz	220	12	5	15	560	25	2
Rice, Oriental style with mixed vegetables, Green Giant, 8 oz	180	0.5	0	0	980	37	4
Rice, white and wild, Green Giant, 1 pkg	250	5	0.5	0	1000	45	3
Rice, with broccoli, Green Giant, 1 pkg	320	12	3.5	15	1000	44	2
Rice and chicken stir-fry, Stouffer's Lean Cuisine Lunch Express, 1 pkg	280	9	1	15	590	39	3
Rice medley, Green Giant, 1 pkg	240	3	1.5	5	880	46	3
Rice pilaf, Green Giant, 1 pkg	230	3	1.5	5	1020	44	3

MEALS & SIDE DISHES	CAL (g)	FAT (g)	SAT FAT (g)	CHOL (mg)	SODIUM (mg)	CARB (g)	FIBER (g)
Rice pilaf with green beans, The Budget Gourmet, 5.62 oz	230	12	3	10	570	28	1
Rigatoni, Stouffer's Lean Cuisine, 1 pkg	180	4	1.5	20	560	25	4
Rigatoni in cream sauce with broccoli & chicken, The Budget Gourmet Light and Healthy Special Selections, 10.8 oz	310	6	2.5	15	670	46	5
Roast beef, open faced, with mashed potatoes & gravy, The Budget Gourmet, 9 oz	340	17	6	40	890	33	3
Roast beef sandwich, hot, smothered, Swanson, 1 pkg	380	13	4	30	500	46	5
Roast sirloin supreme, The Budget Gourmet, 9 oz	300	13	7	65	850	32	3
Salisbury con queso dinner, Patio, 1 meal	390	20	11	40	1570	33	10
Salisbury steak, Armour Classics, 1 meal	330	18	8	50	1310	20	4
Salisbury steak, Banquet, 1 meal	310	16	7	35	910	28	5
Salisbury steak, Banquet Extra Helping, 1 meal	740	46	19	75	1860	52	11
Salisbury steak, Banquet Hot Sandwich Toppers, 1 bag	220	16	7	25	790	8	2
Salisbury steak, Healthy Choice, 1 meal	260	6	2.5	30	500	32	5
Salisbury steak, Morton, 1 meal	210	9	4	20	950	23	3
Salisbury steak, Swanson, 1 pkg	420	20	8	60	980	40	5
Salisbury steak, Swanson Hungry-Man, 1 pkg	610	34	17	80	1460	45	11
Salisbury steak, beef sirloin, The Budget Gourmet Light and Healthy, 9 oz	240	5	2	40	550	28	2
Salisbury steak, beef sirloin, with red skinned potatoes, The Budget Gourmet Light and Healthy, 11 oz	260	8	3	35	430	31	6

MEALS & SIDE DISHES	CAL (g)	FAT (g)	SAT FAT (g)	CHOL (mg)	SODIUM (mg)	CARB (g)	FIBER (g)
Salisbury steak, grilled, Weight Watchers, 8.5 oz	250	9	3	30	590	24	4
Salisbury steak, lite, Armour Classics, 1 meal	260	7	4	55	860	26	6
Salisbury steak, traditional, Healthy Choice, 1 meal	320	6	3	45	470	48	7
Salisbury steak, with macaroni & cheese, Stouffer's Lean Cuisine, 1 pkg	280	9	3.5	60	590	27	4
Salisbury steak & gravy, with macaroni & cheese, Stouffer's, 1 pkg	370	19	6	50	1220	26	0
Salisbury steak in gravy with mashed potatoes, Swanson Homestyle, 1 pkg	330	19	11	30	920	23	2
Shells, cheese, with tomato sauce, Stouffer's, 1 pkg	340	16	7	50	920	29	5
Shrimp, sweet & sour, stir fry kit, Gorton's, 10 oz	280	1.5	0	45	540	56	2
Shrimp, teriyaki, stir fry kit, Gorton's, 10 oz	300	1.5	0	55	1280	59	1
Shrimp and vegetables Maria, Healthy Choice, 1 meal	270	3	1	35	540	46	5
Shrimp Creole, lite, Armour Classics, 1 meal	220	0.5	0	20	720	49	16
Shrimp marinara, Healthy Choice, 1 meal	220	0.5	0	50	220	44	5
Shrimp marinara, Weight Watchers Smart Ones, 9 oz	190	2	0.5	40	400	35	4
Shrimp mariner, The Budget Gourmet Light and Healthy, 11 oz	260	6	2	60	540	39	5
Shrimp Newburg, Pepperidge Farm, 1 filled shell	340	20	7	60	670	31	4
Shrimp scampi, stir fry kit, Gorton's, 10 oz	320	14	8	70	880	34	2
Shrimp stir fry dinner, Contessa, 1¾ cups	140	0	0	40	460	26	3
Sirloin beef, chopped, with gravy dinner, Swanson, 1 pkg	350	17	11	60	730	30	4

MEALS & SIDE DISHES	CAL (g)	FAT (g)	SAT FAT (g)	CHOL (mg)	SODIUM (mg)	CARB (g)	FIBER (g)
Sirloin beef peppercorn, Stouffer's Lean Cuisine Cafe Classics, 1 pkg	210	7	1.5	25	480	24	4
Sirloin beef tips, Swanson Hungry-Man, 1 pkg	450	16	6	120	870	49	9
Sirloin beef tips and noodles with gravy, Swanson Homestyle, 1 pkg	200	8	3	35	380	20	2
Sirloin beef tips with noodles & beef gravy, Swanson, 1 pkg	290	11	5	50	490	32	5
Sirloin cheddar melt, The Budget Gourmet, 9.4 oz	370	21	10	85	800	29	3
Sirloin of beef, special recipe, The Budget Gourmet Light and Healthy, 11 oz	310	7	3	25	550	42	5
Sirloin of beef in herb sauce, The Budget Gourmet Light and Healthy, 9.5 oz	260	7	4	30	850	30	5
Sirloin of beef in wine sauce, The Budget Gourmet Light and Healthy, 11 oz	270	6	2	40	460	36	5
Sirloin tips with country style vegetables, The Budget Gourmet, 10 oz	250	13	6	40	1060	20	4
Sloppy Joe, Banquet Hot Sandwich Toppers, 1 bag	140	7	3	25	530	12	1
Sloppy Joe, slammin', Swanson Kids Fun Feast, 1 pkg	290	10	4	70	530	41	3
Southern fried meal, Banquet, 1 meal	530	30	8	85	1610	44	4
Spaghetti, with chunky tomato & meat sauce, The Budget Gourmet Light and Healthy Special Selections, 10 oz	320	7	2.5	5	470	49	4
Spaghetti, with meat sauce, Stouffer's Lean Cuisine, 1 pkg	290	6	1.5	20	550	45	4
Spaghetti, with meat sauce, Stouffer's Lunch Express, 1 pkg	320	10	3.5	30	580	43	5

MEALS & SIDE DISHES	CAL (g)	FAT (g)	SAT FAT (g)	CHOL (mg)	SODIUM (mg)	CARB (g)	FIBER (g)
Spaghetti, with meat sauce, Weight Watchers Smart Ones, 10 oz	250	6	2	10	470	24	6
Spaghetti, with meatballs, Stouffer's, 1 pkg	420	15	4	45	680	51	5
Spaghetti, with meatballs, Stouffer's Lean Cuisine, 1 pkg	290	7	2	30	520	40	4
Spaghetti and meatballs, Swanson Budget, 1 pkg	300	13	6	20	1040	36	5
Spaghetti Bolognese, Healthy Choice, 1 meal	260	3	1	15	470	43	5
Spaghetti dinner, Morton, 1 meal	170	3	1	<5	600	30	4
Stuffed peppers, Stouffer's, 1 pepper	180	7	1	20	590	20	3
Stuffed peppers, Stouffer's, 1 pkg	200	8	1.5	25	900	24	1
Swedish meatballs, Armour Classics, 1 meal	300	17	7	40	940	20	4
Swedish meatballs, The Budget Gourmet, 10 oz	550	34	16	150	1050	40	3
Swedish meatballs, Stouffer's, 1 pkg	440	23	8	85	840	36	3
Swedish meatballs, Weight Watchers, 9 oz	280	8	3	30	510	35	3
Swedish meatballs, traditional, Healthy Choice, 1 meal	320	9	3	65	600	37	5
Swedish meatballs, with pasta, Stouffer's Lean Cuisine, 1 pkg	290	8	3	55	590	32	3
Swedish meatballs, with pasta, Stouffer's Lunch Express, 1 pkg	530	32	11	65	1010	41	3
Sweet & sour, lite, Armour Classics, 1 meal	220	1	0	30	520	38	4
Sweet & sour nuggets, Banquet, 6 nuggets	320	18	4	45	670	25	2
Teriyaki stir fry, Birds Eye Easy Recipe, 2 cups	210	2.5	0.5	0	1680	27	2

MEALS & SIDE DISHES	CAL	FAT (g)	SAT FAT (g)	CHOL (mg)	SODIUM (mg)	CARB (g)	FIBER (g)
Teriyaki stir-fry, Stouffer's Lean Cuisine Lunch Express, 1 pkg	260	5	1	30	550	39	4
Tortellini, cheese, The Budget Gourmet, 6.25 oz	190	8	2	10	800	24	3
Tortellini, cheese, with Alfredo sauce, Stouffer's, 1 pkg	550	33	18	160	720	38	5
Tortellini, cheese, with tomato sauce, Stouffer's, 1 pkg	290	6	5	105	740	40	4
Tuna noodle casserole, Stouffer's, 1 pkg	330	14	2	40	1130	31	3
Tuna noodle casserole, Swanson Homestyle, 1 pkg	320	11	6	25	800	38	1
Tuna noodle casserole, Weight Watchers Smart Ones, 9.5 oz	240	7	2.5	15	580	30	5
Turkey, country inn roast, Healthy Choice, 1 meal	250	4	1	30	530	29	6
Turkey, country, and pasta, Healthy Choice, 1 meal	300	4	2	35	450	42	6
Turkey, country roast, with mushroom, Healthy Choice, 1 meal	220	4	1	25	440	28	3
Turkey, glazed, The Budget Gourmet Light and Healthy, 9 oz	250	4	2	30	730	38	2
Turkey, homestyle, Stouffer's Lean Cuisine, 1 pkg	230	6	1.5	50	590	26	3
Turkey, homestyle, with vegetables, Healthy Choice, 1 meal	260	2	0.5	35	490	24	3
Turkey, honey dijon, pretzel sandwich, Weight Watchers On-The-Go, 4 oz	230	4	1.5	25	500	36	3
Turkey, mostly white meat, Swanson, 1 pkg	320	8	3	35	1030	42	4
Turkey, mostly white meat, Swanson Hungry-Man, 1 pkg	490	13	8	45	1420	59	9
Turkey, open faced, with gravy & mashed potatoes, The Budget Gourmet, 9 oz	330	15	4	40	1010	32	3

MEALS & SIDE DISHES	CAL	FAT (g)	SAT FAT (g)	CHOL (mg)	SODIUM (mg)	CARB (g)	FIBER (g)
Turkey, roast, medallions, Weight Watchers Smart Ones, 8.5 oz	190	2	0.5	20	530	34	4
Turkey, roast, with stuffing, Stouffer's, 1 pkg	280	11	2.5	40	950	25	1
Turkey, sliced, and gravy, Banquet Hot Sandwich Toppers, 1 bag	90	4	1.5	30	670	7	<1
Turkey, mostly white, in gravy with dressing, Swanson Homestyle, 1 pkg	240	7	2	30	890	30	3
Turkey and dressing, Armour Classics, 1 meal	270	7	4	60	1020	34	5
Turkey breast, roasted, with stuffing & cinnamon apples, Stouffer's Lean Cuisine, 1 pkg	290	4	1	25	530	48	3
Turkey breast, stuffed, The Budget Gourmet Light and Healthy, 11 oz	260	6	2	35	660	29	7
Turkey breast, stuffed, Weight Watchers, 8.75 oz	240	8	3	20	590	26	1
Turkey breast, traditional, Healthy Choice, 1 meal	280	3	1	45	460	40	7
Turkey breast meat with pasta dinner, Swanson, 1 pkg	290	8	4	35	700	31	6
Turkey dinner, Banquet, 1 meal	270	10	3	45	1100	31	3
Turkey dinner, Banquet Extra Helping, 1 meal	560	20	5	75	1910	63	7
Turkey fettuccine alla crema, Healthy Choice, 1 meal	350	4	1.5	30	370	50	5
Turkey meal, Morton, 1 meal	230	8	3	35	1090	27	5
Turkey pie, Stouffer's, 1 cup	500	31	8	55	910	36	3
Turkey pie, Stouffer's, 1 pkg	530	33	9	65	1040	36	3
Turkey pie, Stouffer's Lean Cuisine, 1 pkg	300	9	2	50	590	34	3
Turkey pie, Swanson, 1 pkg	440	24	9	20	750	44	2
Turkey pie, Swanson Hungry-Man, 1 pkg	650	34	13	45	1450	65	5
Turkey pot pie, Banquet, pie	370	20	8	45	850	38	3

MEALS & SIDE DISHES	CAL (g)	FAT (g)	SAT FAT (g)	CHOL (mg)	SODIUM (mg)	CARB (g)	FIBER (g)
Turkey pot pie, Morton, 7 oz	300	18	9	25	1060	29	2
Turkey pot pie, supreme, Banquet, 1 pie	330	13	5	25	1280	39	3
Turkey tetrazzini, Stouffer's, 1 pkg	360	19	3	40	1140	28	2
Veal Parmesan, Morton, 1 meal	280	13	4	20	950	30	4
Veal parmigian, Banquet Family Entrees, 1 patty with sauce	230	14	4	20	740	19	2
Veal parmigiana, Armour Classics, 1 meal	400	22	11	65	1050	35	5
Veal parmigiana, Banquet, 1 meal	320	14	5	25	960	35	7
Veal parmigiana, Swanson, 1 pkg	400	18	8	85	1060	40	5
Veal parmigiana, Swanson Homestyle, 1 pkg	310	12	5	60	970	33	4
Veal parmigiana, Swanson Hungry-Man, 1 pkg	590	25	14	95	1750	58	12
Veal parmigiana with spaghetti, Stouffer's, 1 pkg	420	19	4	75	1200	43	6
Vegetable and cheese pot pie, Banquet, 1 pie	390	18	8	15	1000	49	3
Vegetable pasta Italiano, Healthy Choice, 1 meal	220	1	0	0	340	44	6
Vegetables and chicken, Chinese style, The Budget Gourmet Light and Healthy Special Selections, 10 oz	290	9	1.5	15	720	42	4
Vegetables and chicken, Italian style, The Budget Gourmet Light and Healthy Special Selections, 10 oz	280	7	2	25	660	44	3
Vegetables and chicken, spicy Szechwan style, The Budget Gourmet Special Selections, 10 oz	300	9	1.5	10	710	41	5
Welsh rarebit, Stouffer's Side Dishes, ¼ cup	120	9	4	20	280	5	na
Western meal, Morton, 1 meal	290	16	7	25	1210	26	6

MEALS & SIDE DISHES	CAL	FAT (g)	SAT FAT (g)	CHOL (mg)	SODIUM (mg)	CARB (g)	FIBER (g)
Western style meal, Banquet, 1 meal	350	20	9	30	1400	28	5
White meat meal, Banquet, 1 meal	470	28	11	100	1100	33	6
Wobblin' Wheels & Cheese, Swanson Kids Fun Feast, 1 pkg	380	11	5	20	570	58	9
Ziti in marinara sauce, The Budget Gourmet, 6.25 oz	220	10	4	15	720	25	2

AT A GLANCE: MEALS & SIDE DISHES

Choose from the dozens of dinners with 2 grams or less of total fat from Armour Classics, The Budget Gourmet Light & Healthy, Healthy Choice, Stouffer's Lean Cuisine, and Weight Watchers.
Lowest in Fat: Contessa Shrimp Stir Fry Dinner.

PASTA, PLAIN

	CAL	FAT (g)	SAT FAT (g)	CHOL (mg)	SODIUM (mg)	CARB (g)	FIBER (g)
Angel hair, La Pace, ¼ pkg	210	2	0	25	20	39	2
Manicotti, Rich's, 2 manicotti	320	15	10	65	270	27	1
Ravioli, cheese, Rich's, 5 oz	290	10	6	45	160	36	2
Ravioli, mini, La Pace, 1 cup	320	9	5	50	530	42	2
Shells, stuffed, Rich's, 3 shells	300	15	9	60	230	29	2
Shells, stuffed, Rosetto, 2 shells	250	12	7	60	660	22	1
Tortellini, cheese, La Pace, 1 cup	310	8	4	55	420	44	2
Tortellini, cheese, Rich's, 1 cup	410	12	7	70	840	55	4

PIZZA

	CAL	FAT (g)	SAT FAT (g)	CHOL (mg)	SODIUM (mg)	CARB (g)	FIBER (g)
Bacon burger, Totino's Party, ½ pie	370	20	4.5	15	880	33	2
Canadian style bacon, Jeno's Crisp 'N Tasty, 1 pie	430	18	3.5	10	1150	49	2
Canadian style bacon, Totino's Party, ½ pie	320	15	2.5	10	900	33	2
Canadian style bacon, 12", Tombstone, ¼ pizza	360	15	7	40	920	36	2
Cheese, Jeno's Crisp 'N Tasty, 1 pie	450	19	6	20	870	51	2
Cheese, Kids Cuisine, 1 meal	320	8	3	25	470	53	5
Cheese, Totino's Party, ½ pie	320	14	5	20	630	33	2

PIZZA	CAL (g)	FAT (g)	SAT FAT (g)	CHOL (mg)	SODIUM (mg)	CARB (g)	FIBER (g)
Cheese, ½ less fat, Tombstone for One, 1 pizza	360	10	4.5	15	920	45	3
Cheese, family size, Totino's Party, ⅓ pie	360	16	6	20	720	38	2
Cheese, naturally rising, Jack's, ⅙ of pizza	290	10	6	25	500	35	2
Cheese, sausage & mushroom, 12", Tombstone, ⅕ pizza	320	16	7	30	630	29	2
Cheese, single serving, microwave-ready, Jeno's, 1 pie	240	11	3.5	15	530	25	1
Cheese, single serving, microwave-ready, Totino's, 1 pie	240	11	3.5	15	530	25	1
Cheese & hamburger, 9", Tombstone, ⅓ pizza	310	16	7	30	620	28	2
Cheese & hamburger, 12", Tombstone, ⅕ pizza	320	16	8	30	660	29	2
Cheese & pepperoni, Tombstone for One, 1 pizza	580	35	15	50	1170	41	3
Cheese & pepperoni, 9", Tombstone, ⅓ pizza	340	19	8	30	740	28	2
Cheese & pepperoni, 12", Tombstone, ⅕ pizza	340	18	8	35	750	29	2
Cheese & sausage, 9", Tombstone, ⅓ pizza	310	16	7	30	610	28	2
Cheese & sausage, 12", Tombstone, ⅕ pizza	320	16	8	30	650	29	2
Combination, Jeno's Crisp 'N Tasty, 1 pie	520	28	7	25	1120	49	3
Combination, Totino's Party, ½ pie	390	21	4.5	20	910	34	2
Combination, Totino's Pizza Rolls, 10 rolls	370	17	5	40	410	38	2
Combination, family size, Totino's Party, ¼ pie	300	16	3.5	15	740	28	1
Combination, single serving, microwave-ready, Jeno's, 1 pie	310	18	4.5	15	720	25	1

PIZZA	CAL (g)	FAT (g)	SAT FAT (g)	CHOL (mg)	SODIUM (mg)	CARB (g)	FIBER (g)
Combination, single serving, microwave-ready, Totino's, 1 pie	310	18	4.5	15	720	25	1
Deluxe, Stouffer's Lunch Express, 1 pkg	470	25	8	45	1000	40	4
Deluxe, 9", Tombstone, ⅓ pizza	320	16	7	30	620	28	2
Deluxe, 12", Tombstone, ⅕ pizza	320	16	7	30	640	29	2
Deluxe combo, Weight Watchers, 6.57 oz	380	11	3.5	40	550	47	6
Extra cheese, Tombstone for One, 1 pizza	540	30	14	45	910	41	3
Extra cheese, Weight Watchers, 5.74 oz	390	12	4	35	590	49	6
Extra cheese, 9", Tombstone, ½ pizza	420	19	9	30	730	42	3
Extra cheese, 12", Tombstone, ¼ pizza	370	17	9	30	680	36	2
Four cheese, 12", Tombstone Special Order, ⅕ pizza	400	19	10	40	760	37	2
Four meat, 9", Tombstone Special Order, ⅓ pizza	400	20	10	45	910	35	2
Four meat, 12", Tombstone Special Order, ⅙ pizza	350	18	8	40	810	31	2
French bread, bacon cheddar, Stouffer's French Bread Pizza, pizza	440	22	7	30	940	44	4
French bread, cheese, Healthy Choice, 1 pizza	310	4	2	10	470	49	6
French bread, cheese, Stouffer's French Bread Pizza, pizza	350	14	5	15	660	42	3
French bread, cheese, Stouffer's Lean Cuisine French Bread Pizza, 1 pkg	350	8	4	20	400	48	4
French bread, cheeseburger, Stouffer's French Bread Pizza, pizza	440	26	9	55	1110	31	5
French bread, deluxe, Stouffer's French Bread Pizza, pizza	440	22	7	35	980	42	5

PIZZA	CAL (g)	FAT (g)	SAT FAT (g)	CHOL (mg)	SODIUM (mg)	CARB (g)	FIBER (g)
French bread, deluxe, Stouffer's Lean Cuisine French Bread Pizza, 1 pkg	330	6	2.5	30	560	45	5
French bread, double cheese, Stouffer's French Bread Pizza, 1 pizza	420	19	7	30	790	44	5
French bread, garden vegetable, Stouffer's French Bread Pizza, 1 pizza	370	14	5	15	990	45	6
French bread, pepperoni, Healthy Choice, 1 pizza	360	9	4	25	580	48	5
French bread, pepperoni, Stouffer's French Bread Pizza, 1 pizza	420	20	6	35	930	42	3
French bread, pepperoni, Stouffer's Lean Cuisine French Bread Pizza, 1 pkg	330	7	3	25	590	46	4
French bread, pepperoni & mushroom, Stouffer's French Bread Pizza, 1 pizza	430	21	6	30	1000	43	3
French bread, sausage, Healthy Choice, 1 pizza	330	4	1.5	20	470	52	6
French bread, sausage, Stouffer's French Bread Pizza, 1 pizza	420	20	5	35	900	41	4
French bread, sausage & pepperoni, Stouffer's French Bread Pizza, 1 pizza	490	25	7	40	1130	45	4
French bread, supreme, Healthy Choice, 1 meal	340	6	2	25	510	49	5
French bread, vegetable deluxe, Stouffer's French Bread Pizza, 1 pizza	380	17	6	25	830	43	5
French bread, white, Stouffer's French Bread Pizza, 1 pizza	490	28	8	25	760	43	5
Hamburger, Jeno's Crisp 'N Tasty, 1 pie	480	23	5	25	1100	49	3
Hamburger, Kids Cuisine, 1 meal	330	9	2.5	20	440	50	5
Hamburger, Totino's Party, ½ pie	350	18	4	20	860	33	2

PIZZA	CAL (g)	FAT (g)	SAT FAT (g)	CHOL (mg)	SODIUM (mg)	CARB (g)	FIBER (g)
Hamburger & cheese, Totino's Pizza Rolls, 10 rolls	350	14	4.5	35	570	40	2
Italian sausage, Tombstone for One, 1 pizza	560	33	14	55	1130	40	3
Italian sausage, Totino's Pizza Pops, 1 pop	310	15	6	20	680	30	2
Italian sausage & pepperoni, Totino's Pizza Pops, 1 pop	320	17	6	20	680	28	2
Nacho cheese & beef, Totino's Pizza Rolls, 10 rolls	340	16	6	40	730	37	2
Pepperoni, Jeno's Crisp 'N Tasty, 1 pie	500	26	6	25	1170	49	2
Pepperoni, Stouffer's Lunch Express, 1 pkg	440	23	8	40	960	39	4
Pepperoni, Totino's Party, ½ pie	380	21	5	20	920	33	2
Pepperoni, Totino's Pizza Pops, 1 pop	320	16	6	25	790	30	2
Pepperoni, Weight Watchers, 5.56 oz	390	12	4	45	650	46	4
Pepperoni, ½ less fat, Tombstone for One, 1 pizza	400	13	5	35	1040	45	4
Pepperoni, 9", Tombstone Special Order, ⅓ pizza	400	21	10	45	880	35	2
Pepperoni, 12", Tombstone Special Order, ⅙ pizza	360	19	9	40	790	31	2
Pepperoni, deep dish, Pappalo's, ⅕ pie	340	14	6	30	720	37	2
Pepperoni, deep dish, single serving, Pappalo's, 1 pie	600	26	12	55	1300	62	3
Pepperoni, family size, Totino's Party, ⅓ pie	410	22	5	20	1000	37	2
Pepperoni, pizzeria style crust, 9", Pappalo's, ½ pie	440	19	9	40	950	45	2
Pepperoni, pizzeria style crust, 12", Pappalo's, ¼ pie	380	17	8	40	840	38	2
Pepperoni, single serving, Pappalo's, 1 pie	570	27	13	60	1280	52	3
Pepperoni, single serving, microwave-ready, Jeno's, 1 pie	280	16	3.5	15	710	25	1

PIZZA	CAL (g)	FAT (g)	SAT FAT (g)	CHOL (mg)	SODIUM (mg)	CARB (g)	FIBER (g)
Pepperoni, single serving, microwave-ready, Totino's, 1 pie	280	16	3.5	15	710	25	1
Pepperoni & cheese, Totino's Pizza Rolls, 10 rolls	360	17	5	35	580	37	2
Pepperoni with double cheese, Tombstone Double Top, ⅙ pizza	350	20	10	45	850	25	2
Pizza, chillin' cheese, Swanson Kids Fun Feast, 1 pkg	350	9	4	15	500	57	7
Pizza crust, Totino's, ¼ pie	180	7	1	0	190	25	1
Pizza pocket, Act II, 1 pocket	410	20	9	25	850	40	4
Pizza pocket sandwich, Weight Watchers, 5 oz	300	7	2.5	15	490	46	4
Sausage, Jeno's Crisp 'N Tasty, 1 pie	510	27	6	20	1070	49	3
Sausage, Totino's Party, ½ pie	380	20	4.5	15	870	34	2
Sausage, deep dish, Pappalo's, ⅕ pie	330	13	8	25	600	36	2
Sausage, family size, Totino's Party, ⅓ pie	300	16	3.5	10	720	28	2
Sausage, pizzeria style crust, 9", Pappalo's, ½ pie	420	18	11	35	800	45	2
Sausage, pizzeria style crust, 12", Pappalo's, ¼ pie	370	16	10	30	710	38	2
Sausage, single serving, microwave-ready, Jeno's, 1 pie	280	16	4	10	650	25	1
Sausage, single serving, microwave-ready, Totino's, 1 pie	280	16	4	10	650	25	1
Sausage, with double cheese, Tombstone Double Top, ⅙ pizza	350	19	10	40	740	25	2
Sausage & cheese, Totino's Pizza Rolls, 10 rolls	350	15	4	30	580	39	2
Sausage & mushroom, Totino's Pizza Rolls, 10 rolls	330	14	4	30	570	38	2
Sausage & pepperoni, Tombstone for One, 1 pizza	590	37	15	55	1200	40	3

PIZZA	CAL (g)	FAT (g)	SAT FAT (g)	CHOL (mg)	SODIUM (mg)	CARB (g)	FIBER (g)
Sausage & pepperoni, Totino's, ⅓ pie	360	19	7	30	760	30	2
Sausage & pepperoni, 9", Tombstone, ⅓ pizza	360	21	9	35	820	28	2
Sausage & pepperoni, 12", Tombstone, ⅕ pizza	340	18	8	35	740	29	2
Sausage & pepperoni, deep dish, Pappalo's, ⅕ pie	330	14	8	25	650	36	2
Sausage & pepperoni, deep dish, single serving, Pappalo's, 1 pie	610	27	15	50	1180	61	3
Sausage & pepperoni, pizzeria style crust, 9", Pappalo's, ½ pie	430	19	11	35	870	44	2
Sausage & pepperoni, pizzeria style crust, 12", Pappalo's, ¼ pie	380	17	9	35	780	39	2
Sausage & pepperoni, single serving, Pappalo's, 1 pie	570	27	16	55	1170	51	3
Sausage & pepperoni, with double cheese, Tombstone Double Top, ⅙ pizza	360	20	10	45	800	25	2
Spicy Italian style, Totino's Pizza Rolls, 10 rolls	370	18	5	40	370	37	2
Super supreme, 9", Tombstone Special Order, ⅓ pizza	400	21	10	45	900	36	2
Super supreme, 12", Tombstone Special Order, ⅙ pizza	350	18	9	40	800	31	2
Supreme, Jeno's Crisp 'N Tasty, 1 pie	520	28	7	25	1120	49	3
Supreme, Tombstone for One, 1 pizza	570	34	14	50	1130	41	3
Supreme, Tombstone Light, ⅕ pizza	270	9	3.5	20	710	30	2
Supreme, Totino's, ⅓ pie	340	18	7	30	770	29	2
Supreme, Totino's Party, ½ pie	380	20	4.5	20	890	34	2
Supreme, Totino's Pizza Pops, 1 pop	300	15	5	20	680	30	2

PIZZA	CAL (g)	FAT (g)	SAT FAT (g)	CHOL (mg)	SODIUM (mg)	CARB (g)	FIBER (g)
Supreme, ½ less fat, Tombstone for One, 1 pizza	400	13	5	35	1090	45	4
Supreme, 12", Tombstone, ⅕ pizza	330	17	8	35	720	29	2
Supreme, deep dish, Pappalo's, ⅕ pie	340	14	8	25	680	37	2
Supreme, deep dish, single serving, Pappalo's, 1 pie	610	27	16	50	1230	62	4
Supreme, pizzeria style crust, 9", Pappalo's, ½ pie	290	13	7	25	610	30	2
Supreme, pizzeria style crust, 12", Pappalo's, ¼ pie	380	16	9	30	790	40	2
Supreme, single serving, Pappalo's, 1 pie	560	27	16	55	1170	50	3
Supreme, single serving, microwave-ready, Totino's, 1 pie	290	17	4	15	680	25	2
Thin crust, Italian style, four meat combo, Tombstone, ¼ pizza	410	25	12	50	940	25	2
Thin crust, Italian style, Italian sausage, Tombstone, ¼ pizza	400	24	11	50	880	25	2
Thin crust, Italian style, pepperoni, Tombstone, ¼ pizza	420	27	13	55	950	25	2
Thin crust, Italian style, supreme, Tombstone, ¼ pizza	400	24	11	45	880	26	2
Thin crust, Italian style, three cheese, Tombstone, ¼ pizza	380	22	12	45	730	25	2
Thin crust, Mexican style, supreme taco, Tombstone, ¼ pizza	380	23	11	50	850	26	2
Three cheese, Totino's, ⅓ pie	300	14	6	20	590	29	1
Three cheese, Totino's Pizza Rolls, 10 rolls	360	15	6	35	610	42	2
Three cheese, deep dish, Pappalo's, ⅕ pie	370	12	6	25	670	46	2
Three cheese, deep dish, single serving, Pappalo's, 1 pie	540	20	10	45	1000	61	3

PIZZA	CAL (g)	FAT (g)	SAT FAT (g)	CHOL (mg)	SODIUM (mg)	CARB (g)	FIBER (g)
Three cheese, pizzeria style crust, 9", Pappalo's, ½ pie	400	15	8	35	760	44	2
Three cheese, pizzeria style crust, 12", Pappalo's, ¼ pie	340	12	6	30	770	39	2
Three cheese, single serving, Pappalo's, 1 pie	500	20	10	45	960	50	3
Three meat, Jeno's Crisp 'N Tasty, 1 pie	500	26	6	25	1180	48	2
Three meat, Totino's Party, ½ pie	360	19	4	15	910	33	2
Three meat, Totino's Pizza Rolls, 10 rolls	340	15	4.5	35	630	37	2
Three sausage, 9", Tombstone Special Order, ⅓ pizza	390	19	9	40	830	35	2
Three sausage, 12", Tombstone Special Order, ⅙ pizza	340	17	8	35	740	31	2
Two cheese & Canadian style bacon, Totino's, ⅓ pie	310	14	5	25	790	30	1
Two cheese & pepperoni, Totino's, ⅓ pie	360	20	8	35	820	30	1
Two cheese & sausage, Totino's, ⅓ pie	360	19	7	30	760	31	2
Vegetable, Tombstone Light, ⅕ pizza	240	7	2.5	10	500	31	3
Vegetable, ½ less fat, Tombstone for One, 1 pizza	360	10	4	15	730	46	5
Zesty Italian, Totino's Party, ½ pie	390	21	4.5	20	900	35	2
Zesty Mexican, single serving, microwave-ready, Totino's, 1 pie	280	16	4	15	560	25	2
Zesty Mexican style, Totino's Party, ½ pie	370	19	4.5	15	750	34	2

AT A GLANCE: PIZZA

Lowest in Fat, Individual Serving: Healthy Choice French Bread Cheese and French Bread Sausage
Lowest in Fat, Large: Tombstone Light Vegetable

SHERBETS & SORBETS

	CAL (g)	FAT (g)	SAT FAT (g)	CHOL (mg)	SODIUM (mg)	CARB (g)	FIBER (g)
Sherbet, all flavors, Borden, ½ cup	130	2	1	5	30	27	0

SHERBETS & SORBETS	CAL (g)	FAT (g)	SAT FAT (g)	CHOL (mg)	SODIUM (mg)	CARB (g)	FIBER (g)
Sherbet, orange, Breyers, ½ cup	120	1	0.5	<5	25	26	0
Sherbet, orange, Sealtest, ½ cup	130	1	0.5	5	25	28	0
Sherbet, orange, cup, Sealtest, 1 cup	130	1	1	5	25	28	0
Sherbet, rainbow, Breyers, ½ cup	120	1	0	<5	25	26	0
Sherbet, rainbow, Sealtest, ½ cup	130	1	0.5	5	25	28	0
Sherbet, raspberry, Breyers, ½ cup	120	1	0.5	<5	25	27	0
Sherbet, strawberry kiwi, Dreyer's/Edy's, ½ cup	120	2	1	<5	25	27	na
Sherbet, tropical, Breyers, ½ cup	120	1	0	<5	25	26	0
Sorbet and cream, orange, Haagen-Dazs, ½ cup	200	9	5	60	45	27	0
Sorbet and cream, raspberry, Haagen-Dazs, ½ cup	190	9	5	60	45	23	<1

VEGETABLES

	CAL (g)	FAT (g)	SAT FAT (g)	CHOL (mg)	SODIUM (mg)	CARB (g)	FIBER (g)
Artichoke hearts, Birds Eye, ½ cup	40	0	0	0	45	8	6
Artichokes (globe or French), boiled, ½ cup	40	0	0	0	45	8	4
Artichokes (globe or French), unprepared, ½ cup	35	0	0	0	40	7	3
Asparagus, cuts, Birds Eye, ½ cup	25	0	0	0	5	4	2
Asparagus, cuts, Green Giant Harvest Fresh, ⅔ cup	25	0	0	0	85	4	1
Asparagus, spears, Birds Eye, 3 oz (8 spears)	20	0	0	0	5	4	1
Austrian brand, Birds Eye International Recipe, ½ cup	110	6	3	15	370	9	2
Bavarian style, Birds Eye International Recipe, 1 cup	160	8	4.5	50	430	18	2
Bean sprouts, baby lima, in butter sauce, Green Giant, ⅔ cup	120	2.5	2	<5	330	18	6

VEGETABLES	CAL	FAT (g)	SAT FAT (g)	CHOL (mg)	SODIUM (mg)	CARB (g)	FIBER (g)
Beans, green, cut, Birds Eye, ½ cup	25	0	0	0	0	6	2
Beans, green, cut, Green Giant, ¾ cup	25	0	0	0	0	5	2
Beans, green, cut, Green Giant Harvest Fresh, ⅔ cup	25	0	0	0	95	5	2
Beans, green, French cut, Birds Eye, ½ cup	25	0	0	0	0	6	2
Beans, green, French, with toasted almonds, Birds Eye, ½ cup	70	3.5	0	0	480	8	3
Beans, green, Italian, Birds Eye, ½ cup	35	0	0	0	0	8	3
Beans, green, whole, Birds Eye, 3 oz	20	0	0	0	0	5	2
Beans, green, with almonds, Green Giant Harvest Fresh, ⅔ cup	60	3	0	0	95	5	2
Beans, green bean mushroom casserole, Stouffer's, ½ cup	130	8	2	10	530	13	2
Beans, lima, Green Giant Harvest Fresh, ½ cup	80	0	0	0	130	15	4
Beans, lima, baby, Birds Eye, ½ cup	130	0	0	0	115	24	6
Beans, lima, Fordhook, Birds Eye, ½ cup	100	0	0	0	10	19	5
Beans, yellow, snap, ½ cup	20	0	0	0	0	5	1
Broccoli, carrots & water chestnuts, Birds Eye, ½ cup	30	0	0	0	30	7	3
Broccoli, cauliflower & carrots, Birds Eye, ½ cup	25	0	0	0	30	5	2
Broccoli, cauliflower & carrots, in butter sauce, Birds Eye, ½ cup	50	2.5	1.5	5	250	8	2
Broccoli, cauliflower & carrots, in cheese sauce, Birds Eye, ½ cup	60	2.5	1	5	310	8	2
Broccoli, cauliflower & red peppers, Birds Eye, ½ cup	20	0	0	0	20	5	2
Broccoli, chopped, Birds Eye, ⅓ cup	25	0	0	0	15	5	2

VEGETABLES	CAL (g)	FAT (g)	SAT FAT (g)	CHOL (mg)	SODIUM (mg)	CARB (g)	FIBER (g)
Broccoli, chopped, Green Giant, ¾ cup	25	0	0	0	25	4	2
Broccoli, corn & red peppers, Birds Eye, ½ cup	50	0	0	0	15	12	3
Broccoli, cuts, Birds Eye, ½ cup	25	0	0	0	30	5	3
Broccoli, cuts, Green Giant, 1 cup	25	0	0	0	25	4	2
Broccoli, cuts, Green Giant Harvest Fresh, ⅔ cup	25	0	0	0	150	4	2
Broccoli, florets, Birds Eye, 3 oz	25	0	0	0	35	4	2
Broccoli, florets, Green Giant, 1⅓ cups	25	0	0	0	25	4	2
Broccoli, green beans, pearl onions & red peppers, Birds Eye, ½ cup	25	0	0	0	15	6	2
Broccoli, in cheese flavored sauce, Green Giant, ⅔ cup	70	2.5	1	<5	520	9	2
Broccoli, red peppers, onions & mushrooms, Birds Eye, ½ cup	25	0	0	0	20	5	2
Broccoli, spears, Birds Eye, 3 oz	25	0	0	0	20	4	2
Broccoli, spears, Green Giant, 3 oz	25	0	0	0	25	4	2
Broccoli, spears, Green Giant Harvest Fresh, 3.5 oz	25	0	0	0	125	4	2
Broccoli, spears, baby, Birds Eye, 3 oz	25	0	0	0	10	4	3
Broccoli, spears, boiled, ½ cup	25	0	0	0	25	5	3
Broccoli, spears, in butter sauce, Green Giant, 4 oz	50	1.5	1	<5	330	7	2
Broccoli, stir fry, Birds Eye, ½ cup	30	0	0	0	30	5	2
Broccoli, with cheese sauce, Birds Eye, ½ cup	70	3	1.5	10	430	7	2
Broccoli & cauliflower, Birds Eye, ½ cup	20	0	0	0	20	4	2

VEGETABLES	CAL (g)	FAT (g)	SAT FAT (g)	CHOL (mg)	SODIUM (mg)	CARB (g)	FIBER (g)
Broccoli and mixed vegetables, stir fry, Green Giant Create A Meal!, 2⅓ cups as packaged	120	3.5	0.5	0	1100	16	4
Broccoli with cheese in pastry, Pepperidge Farm, 1 pastry	240	14	5	50	430	24	3
Brussels sprouts, ½ cup	35	0	0	0	10	6	3
Brussels sprouts, Birds Eye, 3 oz	35	0	0	0	15	7	3
Brussels sprouts, baby, in butter sauce, Green Giant, ⅔ cup	60	1.5	1.5	<5	270	9	4
Brussels sprouts, cauliflower & carrots, Birds Eye, ½ cup	30	0	0	0	20	7	3
Cacciatore, with vegetables, Birds Eye Easy Recipe, 2 cups	180	2.5	0.5	0	690	22	1
California style, Birds Eye International Recipe, ½ cup	120	6	3	10	310	12	4
Carrots, sliced, Birds Eye, ½ cup	35	0	0	0	45	9	3
Carrots, baby, cut, Green Giant, ¾ cup	30	0	0	0	40	7	3
Carrots, baby, cut, Green Giant Harvest Fresh, ⅔ cup	20	0	0	0	70	5	2
Carrots, baby, whole, Birds Eye, ½ cup	40	0	0	0	45	9	2
Cauliflower, Birds Eye, ½ cup	20	0	0	0	15	4	2
Cauliflower, florets, Green Giant, 1 cup	25	0	0	0	25	4	2
Cauliflower, in cheese flavored sauce, Green Giant, ½ cup	60	2.5	0.5	<5	510	8	2
Cauliflower, in cheese sauce, Birds Eye, ½ cup	60	3	1.5	5	390	7	2
Cauliflower nuggets, carrots & snow pea pods, Birds Eye, ½ cup	30	0	0	0	25	6	2
Chinese stir fry, Birds Eye International Recipe, ½ cup	45	0	0	0	310	9	3
Collards, chopped, ½ cup	30	0	0	0	40	6	2

VEGETABLES	CAL	FAT (g)	SAT FAT (g)	CHOL (mg)	SODIUM (mg)	CARB (g)	FIBER (g)
Corn, cream style, Green Giant, ½ cup	110	1	0	0	330	23	2
Corn, cut, Birds Eye, ⅓ cup	70	0.5	0	0	0	17	2
Corn, extra sweet, Green Giant Niblets, ⅔ cup	70	1	0	0	0	13	2
Corn, in butter sauce, Green Giant Niblets, ⅔ cup	130	3	1.5	<5	350	23	3
Corn, regular, Green Giant Harvest Fresh Niblets, ⅔ cup	80	0.5	0	0	60	17	3
Corn, regular, Green Giant Niblets, ⅔ cup	80	0.5	0	0	5	17	2
Corn, sweet, bag, Birds Eye, ⅓ cup	70	0.5	0	0	0	17	2
Corn, sweet, box, Birds Eye, ⅓ cup	60	1	0	0	0	14	2
Corn, sweet, in butter sauce, Birds Eye, ½ cup	110	3	1.5	5	230	23	2
Corn, white, extra sweet, Green Giant, ⅔ cup	50	0.5	0	0	0	10	3
Corn, white shoepeg, Green Giant Harvest Fresh, ½ cup	70	0.5	0	0	45	14	2
Corn, white shoepeg, Green Giant LeSueur, ¾ cup	100	1	0	0	0	20	3
Corn, white shoepeg, in butter sauce, Green Giant, ¾ cup	120	2.5	1.5	<5	320	21	3
Corn on the cob, Green Giant Nibblers, 1 ear	70	0.5	0	0	5	5	1
Corn on the cob, Green Giant Niblets, 1 ear	160	1.5	0	0	10	32	3
Corn on the cob, Ore Ida, 1 ear	180	2.5	0	0	5	33	4
Corn on the cob, big ears, Birds Eye, 1 ear	120	1	0	0	0	28	3
Corn on the cob, extra sweet, Green Giant, 1 ear	120	2	0	0	0	22	3
Corn on the cob, little ears, Birds Eye, 2 ears	110	1	0	0	0	26	3
Corn on the cob, mini-gold, Ore Ida, 1 ear	90	1	0	0	0	16	2

VEGETABLES	CAL (g)	FAT (g)	SAT FAT (g)	CHOL (mg)	SODIUM (mg)	CARB (g)	FIBER (g)
Corn souffle, Stouffer's, ½ cup	170	7	1.5	65	490	21	1
French country style, Birds Eye International Recipe, ½ cup	100	6	3	10	250	10	2
Italian style, Birds Eye International Recipe, 1 cup	140	9	3.5	15	380	13	3
Japanese stir fry, Birds Eye International Recipe, ½ cup	35	0	0	0	450	7	2
Japanese style, Birds Eye International Recipe, ½ cup	80	4.5	3	10	330	8	2
Kale, boiled, ½ cup	20	0	0	0	10	3	1
Mixed vegetables, Birds Eye, ⅓ cup	50	0	0	0	35	12	3
Mixed vegetables, Green Giant, ¾ cup	50	0	0	0	35	11	3
Mixed vegetables, Green Giant Harvest Fresh, ⅔ cup	50	0	0	0	125	10	3
Mixed vegetables, broccoli, cauliflower & carrots, Green Giant Harvest Fresh, 1 cup	30	0	0	0	125	5	3
Mixed vegetables, broccoli, cauliflower & carrots, in cheese flavored sauce, Green Giant, ⅔ cup	80	2.5	1.5	<5	560	11	2
Mixed vegetables, broccoli, cauliflower, carrots, corn & sweet peas, in butter sauce, Green Giant, ¾ cup	60	2	1.5	<5	300	8	2
Mixed vegetables, broccoli, pasta, sweet peas, corn & red peppers, in butter sauce, Green Giant, ¾ cup	70	2	1.5	<5	280	11	2
Mixed vegetables, California style, Green Giant American Mixtures, ¾ cup	25	0	0	0	15	5	2
Mixed vegetables, English style cheddar, Green Giant, 4 oz	120	5	2	5	390	15	3
Mixed vegetables, for soup, Birds Eye, ⅔ cup	45	0	0	0	45	9	2

VEGETABLES	CAL	FAT (g)	SAT FAT (g)	CHOL (mg)	SODIUM (mg)	CARB (g)	FIBER (g)
Mixed vegetables, French style garlic Dijon, Green Giant, 4 oz	60	3	2	10	380	6	2
Mixed vegetables, Heartland style, Green Giant American Mixtures, 1 cup	30	0	0	0	35	6	3
Mixed vegetables, in butter sauce, Green Giant, ¾ cup	70	2	1	<5	240	11	3
Mixed vegetables, Italian style Parmesan, Green Giant, 4 oz	70	2.5	1.5	5	250	8	3
Mixed vegetables, Japanese style teriyaki, Green Giant, 4 oz	50	0	0	0	400	9	2
Mixed vegetables, lo mein stir fry, Green Giant Create A Meal!, 2⅓ cups as packaged	160	0.5	0	0	1070	32	5
Mixed vegetables, Manhattan style, Green Giant American Mixtures, 1 cup	25	0	0	0	15	4	2
Mixed vegetables, New England style, Green Giant American Mixtures, ¾ cup	70	1.5	0	0	70	13	3
Mixed vegetables, Normandy style mushroom, Green Giant, 4 oz	80	3	2	10	270	11	2
Mixed vegetables, San Francisco style, Green Giant American Mixtures, ¾ cup	30	0	0	0	20	6	2
Mixed vegetables, Santa Fe style, Green Giant American Mixtures, ¾ cup	60	0	0	0	10	13	2
Mixed vegetables, Seattle style, Green Giant American Mixtures, ¾ cup	25	0	0	0	15	5	2
Mixed vegetables, stir fry, with almonds, Green Giant Create A Meal!, 1¾ cups as packaged	150	4.5	0	0	1110	22	6
Mixed vegetables, sweet and sour stir fry, Green Giant Create A Meal!, 1¾ cups as packaged	130	0	0	0	390	29	5

VEGETABLES	CAL (g)	FAT (g)	SAT FAT (g)	CHOL (mg)	SODIUM (mg)	CARB (g)	FIBER (g)
Mixed vegetables, Szechwan stir fry, Green Giant Create A Meal!, 1¾ cups as packaged	150	5	0.5	0	1220	21	5
Mixed vegetables, teriyaki stir fry, Green Giant Create A Meal!, 1¾ cups as packaged	100	0	0	0	870	19	4
Mixed vegetables, western style, Green Giant American Mixtures, ¾ cup	50	1.5	0	0	10	9	2
Mixed vegetables, with pasta, Alfredo, Green Giant Pasta Accents, 2 cups	210	8	2.5	15	480	25	4
Mixed vegetables, with pasta, creamy cheddar, Green Giant Pasta Accents, 2⅓ cups	250	8	3	15	700	36	5
Mixed vegetables, with pasta, Florentine, Green Giant Pasta Accents, 2 cups	310	9	3	20	910	44	5
Mixed vegetables, with pasta, garden herb, Green Giant Pasta Accents, 2 cups	230	7	4	15	750	32	7
Mixed vegetables, with pasta, garlic seasoning, Green Giant Pasta Accents, 2 cups	260	10	5	15	640	36	5
Mixed vegetables, with pasta, primavera, Green Giant Pasta Accents, 2¼ cups	320	12	5	20	500	40	7
Mixed vegetables, with pasta, white cheddar sauce, Green Giant Pasta Accents, 1¾ cups	300	12	3.5	20	570	38	4
Mustard greens, ½ cup	15	0	0	0	20	2	1
New England style, Birds Eye International Recipe, 1 cup	190	11	4	15	380	21	3
Onion rings, Mrs. Paul's, 7 rings	230	12	3	0	45	29	1
Onion rings, Ore Ida, 6 rings	240	14	2.5	0	250	26	2
Onions, chopped, Ore Ida, ¼ cup	25	0	0	0	20	6	1
Onions, small, in cream sauce, Birds Eye, ½ cup	60	1.5	1	5	340	10	2
Onions, small, whole, Birds Eye, 17 pieces	30	0	0	0	10	7	1

VEGETABLES	CAL (g)	FAT (g)	SAT FAT (g)	CHOL (mg)	SODIUM (mg)	CARB (g)	FIBER (g)
Orange glaze, with vegetables, Birds Eye Easy Recipe, 2⅓ cups	210	2.5	0.5	0	450	27	3
Oriental stir fry, Birds Eye Easy Recipe, 2¼ cups	210	4	0.5	0	1400	23	2
Pasta Alfredo, with vegetables, Birds Eye Easy Recipe, 2¼ cups	370	25	11	30	590	27	2
Pasta Primavera, Birds Eye Easy Recipe, 1¾ cups	180	5	1	0	610	17	3
Peas, baby, early, Green Giant Harvest Fresh LeSueur, ⅔ cup	70	0	0	0	220	13	4
Peas, baby, early, in butter sauce, Green Giant, ¾ cup	100	2	1.5	<5	370	16	4
Peas, baby, sweet, Green Giant LeSueur, ⅔ cup	60	0	0	0	150	11	5
Peas, early June, Green Giant LeSueur, ¾ cup	60	0	0	0	150	11	5
Peas, early June, with mushrooms, Green Giant LeSueur, ¾ cup	60	0	0	0	105	10	4
Peas, green, Birds Eye, ½ cup	70	0	0	0	125	13	5
Peas, snap, Birds Eye, ½ cup	40	0	0	0	10	7	2
Peas, sugar snap, Green Giant, ¾ cup	35	0	0	0	0	7	3
Peas, sugar snap, Green Giant Harvest Fresh, ⅔ cup	50	0	0	0	95	10	3
Peas, sugar snap stir fry, Birds Eye, ¾ cup	35	0	0	0	20	5	1
Peas, sweet, Green Giant, ⅔ cup	70	0	0	0	135	13	4
Peas, sweet, Green Giant Harvest Fresh, ⅔ cup	60	0	0	0	200	12	4
Peas, sweet, in butter sauce, Birds Eye, ½ cup	90	2	1	5	210	15	6
Peas, sweet, in butter sauce, Green Giant, ¾ cup	100	2	1.5	<5	400	16	5
Peas, sweet, with pearl onions, Green Giant, ⅔ cup	60	0	0	0	125	12	4

VEGETABLES	CAL (g)	FAT (g)	SAT FAT (g)	CHOL (mg)	SODIUM (mg)	CARB (g)	FIBER (g)
Peas, sweet, with pearl onions, Green Giant Harvest Fresh, ½ cup	50	0	0	0	170	10	3
Peas, tiny, tender, Birds Eye, ½ cup	60	0	0	0	110	10	5
Peas & carrots, boiled, ½ cup	40	0	0	0	55	8	3
Peas & pearl onions, Birds Eye, ½ cup	80	0	0	0	430	15	5
Peas & potatoes, in cream sauce, Birds Eye, ½ cup	70	2	1	5	390	12	3
Pepper stir fry, Birds Eye, 1 cup	25	0	0	0	15	5	2
Peppers, sweet, green, ½ cup	20	0	0	0	5	5	2
Peppers, sweet, red, ½ cup	15	0	0	0	0	3	1
Potato crisp, fillets, Gorton's, 2 fillets	300	19	1.5	30	320	20	0
Potato crisp, sticks, Gorton's, 6 sticks	270	16	4	25	270	22	0
Potatoes, Crispers!, Ore Ida, 3 oz	220	13	2	0	510	24	2
Potatoes, Crispy Crunchies!, Ore Ida, 3 oz	160	9	1.5	0	370	18	2
Potatoes, french fries, microwave, Act II, 1 box	220	12	2.5	0	105	30	5
Potatoes, french fries, sour cream & chive flavor, microwave, Act II, 1 box	240	12	2.5	0	120	30	3
Potatoes, french fries, zesty flavor, microwave, Act II, 1 box	240	12	2.5	0	160	30	3
Potatoes, fried, cottage, Ore Ida, 3 oz	130	4	1	0	20	21	1
Potatoes, fried, crinkle cuts, MicroMagic, 1 box	220	10	2.5	0	45	27	2
Potatoes, fried, crinkle cuts, microwave, Ore Ida, 3.5 oz	180	8	1.5	0	10	26	2
Potatoes, fried, Crispy Crowns!, Ore Ida, 3 oz	190	11	2	0	450	21	2
Potatoes, fried, deep fries, Ore Ida, 3 oz	160	7	1	0	20	22	2

VEGETABLES	CAL (g)	FAT (g)	SAT FAT (g)	CHOL (mg)	SODIUM (mg)	CARB (g)	FIBER (g)
Potatoes, fried, deep fries, crinkle cut, Ore Ida, 3 oz	160	7	1	0	15	23	2
Potatoes, fried, dinner fries, country style, Ore Ida, 3 oz	110	3	1	0	20	19	1
Potatoes, fried, fast fries, ranch flavor, Ore Ida, 3 oz	150	7	1.5	0	430	21	1
Potatoes, fried, Golden Crinkles, Ore Ida, 3 oz	120	3.5	1	0	25	20	2
Potatoes, fried, Golden Fries, Ore Ida, 3 oz	120	4	0.5	0	25	20	1
Potatoes, fried, Golden Twirls, Ore Ida, 3 oz	160	7	1	0	25	22	2
Potatoes, fried, Pixie Crinkles, Ore Ida, 3 oz	140	5	1	0	25	21	3
Potatoes, fried, Shoestrings, Ore Ida, 3 oz	150	5	1	0	20	22	2
Potatoes, fried, Snackin' fries, Ore Ida, 5 oz	340	20	3.5	0	590	36	3
Potatoes, fried, Snackin' fries, extra zesty, Ore Ida, 3 oz	340	20	3.5	0	510	35	4
Potatoes, fried, waffle, Ore Ida, 3 oz	140	5	1.5	0	35	22	2
Potatoes, fried, wedges with skin, Ore Ida, 3 oz	110	2.5	1	0	15	19	2
Potatoes, Golden Patties, Ore Ida, 1 patty	140	7	1.5	0	280	16	1
Potatoes, hash browns, Simplot Okray, 1 patty	60	0	0	0	25	14	2
Potatoes, hash browns, cheddar browns, Ore Ida, 1 patty	90	2.5	1	<5	350	14	1
Potatoes, hash browns, country style, Ore Ida, 1 cup	60	0	0	0	10	13	1
Potatoes, hash browns, microwave, Ore Ida, 1 patty	110	6	1.5	0	150	13	<1
Potatoes, hash browns, shredded, Ore Ida, 1 patty	70	0	0	0	25	15	1
Potatoes, hash browns, Southern style, Ore Ida, ¾ cup	70	0	0	0	25	17	2

VEGETABLES	CAL (g)	FAT (g)	SAT FAT (g)	CHOL (mg)	SODIUM (mg)	CARB (g)	FIBER (g)
Potatoes, hash browns, toaster, Ore Ida, 2 patties	190	12	2	0	550	24	1
Potatoes, Hot Tots, Ore Ida, 3 oz	150	6	1	0	380	21	2
Potatoes, mashed, natural butter flavor, Ore Ida, ½ cup	80	2	0.5	<5	140	14	<1
Potatoes, O'Brien, Ore Ida, ¾ cup	60	0	0	0	15	13	2
Potatoes, scalloped, Stouffer's, ½ cup	130	6	1	5	450	17	2
Potatoes, Tater ABC's, Ore Ida, 3 oz	190	11	4.5	0	310	20	2
Potatoes, Tater Tots, Ore Ida, 3 oz	160	8	1.5	0	340	21	2
Potatoes, Tater Tots, bacon flavor, Ore Ida, 3 oz	150	7	1.5	0	490	20	1
Potatoes, Tater Tots, microwave, Ore Ida, 3.75 oz	190	10	2.5	0	420	26	2
Potatoes, Tater Tots, onion, Ore Ida, 3 oz	150	7	1.5	0	370	20	2
Potatoes, Texas Crispers!, Ore Ida, 3 oz	170	10	2.5	0	270	19	2
Potatoes, three cheese, The Budget Gourmet, 6.125 oz	230	12	7	35	530	22	3
Potatoes, Zesties, Ore Ida, 3 oz	160	9	1.5	0	370	21	1
Spinach, chopped, Birds Eye, ⅓ cup	20	0	0	0	80	3	2
Spinach, cream style, Green Giant, ½ cup	80	3	1.5	0	520	10	2
Spinach, creamed, Birds Eye, ½ cup	110	8	4.5	20	580	7	1
Spinach, creamed, Stouffer's, ½ cup	150	12	4	15	380	8	2
Spinach, creamed, Tabatchnick, 7.5 oz	60	2	1	5	270	8	2
Spinach, cut leaf, Green Giant, ¾ cup	25	0	0	0	65	3	3
Spinach, cut leaf, in butter sauce, Green Giant, ½ cup	40	1.5	1	<5	280	5	2

VEGETABLES	CAL (g)	FAT (g)	SAT FAT (g)	CHOL (mg)	SODIUM (mg)	CARB (g)	FIBER (g)
Spinach, leaf, Green Giant Harvest Fresh, ½ cup	25	0	0	0	240	3	2
Spinach, whole leaf, Birds Eye, ⅓ cup	20	0	0	0	75	3	2
Spinach au gratin, The Budget Gourmet, 5.5 oz	150	11	7	30	730	9	1
Spinach souffle, Stouffer's, ½ cup	150	10	2	120	480	9	0
Squash, summer, crookneck & straightneck, ½ cup	15	0	0	0	0	3	<1
Squash, summer, zucchini with skin, ½ cup	15	0	0	0	0	3	1
Squash, winter, cooked, Birds Eye, ½ cup	50	0	0	0	0	12	4
Stew vegetables, Ore Ida, ⅔ cup	50	0	0	0	50	11	<1
Succotash, ½ cup	70	1	0	0	35	16	na
Sweet potatoes, baked, ½ cup	90	0	0	0	10	21	3
Sweet potatoes, candied, Mrs. Paul's, 5 fl oz	300	1	1	0	130	73	3
Sweet potatoes, candied, and apples, Mrs. Paul's, 1 cup	270	0	0	5	90	66	3
Turnip greens, ½ cup	20	0	0	0	10	3	2
Turnips, ½ cup	15	0	0	0	20	2	1
Turnips & greens, ½ cup	20	0	0	0	15	3	2

AT A GLANCE: VEGETABLES
Highest in Fiber: Green Giant Pasta Accents, Primavera or Garden Herb

MEAT & POULTRY

	CAL (g)	FAT (g)	SAT FAT (g)	CHOL (mg)	SODIUM (mg)	CARB (g)	FIBER (g)
BEEF							

Serving size is 3 ounces cooked. Start with 4 ounces of raw beef to yield a 3 ounce cooked serving. See also Veal.

	CAL (g)	FAT (g)	SAT FAT (g)	CHOL (mg)	SODIUM (mg)	CARB (g)	FIBER (g)
Brain, pan-fried, 3 oz	170	13	3.5	1700	135	0	0
Brain, simmered, 3 oz	140	11	2.5	1750	100	0	0
Brisket, flat half, all grades, marbled fat, fat trimmed, 3 oz	180	8	3	80	50	0	0
Brisket, flat half, all grades, no marbling, braised, fat trimmed, 3 oz	160	5	1.5	80	55	0	0
Brisket, point half, all grades, marbled fat, braised, fat trimmed, 3 oz	300	24	10	80	60	0	0
Brisket, point half, all grades, no marbling, braised, fat trimmed, 3 oz	210	12	4.5	75	70	0	0
Brisket, whole, all grades, marbled fat, braised, fat trimmed, 3 oz	250	17	6	80	60	0	0
Brisket, whole, all grades, no marbling, braised, fat trimmed, 3 oz	190	9	3	80	60	0	0
Charbroiled, with gravy, family size, frozen, Banquet, 1 patty with gravy	180	13	6	25	640	7	2
Chuck, arm pot roast, choice, marbled fat, braised, fat trimmed, 3 oz	250	16	6	85	55	0	0
Chuck, arm pot roast, choice, no marbling, braised, fat trimmed, 3 oz	190	7	3	85	55	0	0
Chuck, arm pot roast, prime, marbled fat, braised, 1/2" edge fat, 3 oz	330	26	11	85	50	0	0
Chuck, arm pot roast, prime, no marbling, braised, 1/2" edge fat, 3 oz	220	11	4.5	85	55	0	0

BEEF	CAL (g)	FAT (g)	SAT FAT (g)	CHOL (mg)	SODIUM (mg)	CARB (g)	FIBER (g)
Chuck, arm pot roast, select, marbled fat, braised, fat trimmed, 3 oz	220	12	5	85	55	0	0
Chuck, arm pot roast, select, no marbling, braised, fat trimmed, 3 oz	170	5	2	85	55	0	0
Chuck, blade roast, choice, marbled fat, braised, fat trimmed, 3 oz	300	22	9	90	55	0	0
Chuck, blade roast, choice, no marbling, braised, fat trimmed, 3 oz	230	13	5	90	60	0	0
Chuck, blade roast, prime, marbled fat, braised, ½" edge fat, 3 oz	350	29	12	90	55	0	0
Chuck, blade roast, prime, no marbling, braised, ½" edge fat, 3 oz	270	17	7	90	60	0	0
Chuck, blade roast, select, marbled fat, braised, fat trimmed, 3 oz	270	18	7	90	55	0	0
Chuck, blade roast, select, no marbling, braised, fat trimmed, 3 oz	200	10	4	90	60	0	0
Corned beef, Hormel, 2 oz	120	7	3	50	490	0	0
Corned beef, brisket, cured, cooked, 1 oz	70	5	2	30	320	0	0
Corned beef, canned, 1 oz	70	4	2	25	290	0	0
Corned beef, sliced, Hebrew National Deli Express, 2 oz	80	3	na	35	450	0	0
Cured, dried, 1 oz	50	1	0	10	980	0	0
Cured, smoked, chopped, 1 oz	35	1.5	0.5	15	360	<1	0
Flank, choice, marbled fat, braised, fat trimmed, 3 oz	220	14	6	60	60	0	0
Flank, choice, marbled fat, broiled, fat trimmed, 3 oz	190	11	4.5	60	70	0	0
Flank, choice, no marbling, braised, fat trimmed, 3 oz	200	11	5	60	60	0	0
Flank, choice, no marbling, broiled, fat trimmed, 3 oz	180	9	4	60	70	0	0

BEEF	CAL (g)	FAT (g)	SAT FAT (g)	CHOL (mg)	SODIUM (mg)	CARB (g)	FIBER (g)
Ground, extra lean, baked, medium, 3 oz	210	14	5	70	40	0	0
Ground, extra lean, baked, well done, 3 oz	230	14	5	90	55	0	0
Ground, extra lean, broiled, medium, 3 oz	220	14	5	70	60	0	0
Ground, extra lean, broiled, well done, 3 oz	230	13	5	85	70	0	0
Ground, extra lean, pan-fried, medium, 3 oz	220	14	5	70	60	0	0
Ground, extra lean, pan-fried, well done, 3 oz	220	14	5	80	70	0	0
Ground, lean, baked, medium, 3 oz	230	16	6	65	50	0	0
Ground, lean, baked, well done, 3 oz	250	16	6	85	60	0	0
Ground, lean, broiled, medium, 3 oz	230	16	6	75	65	0	0
Ground, lean, broiled, well done, 3 oz	240	15	6	85	75	0	0
Ground, lean, pan-fried, medium, 3 oz	230	16	6	70	65	0	0
Ground, lean, pan-fried, well done, 3 oz	240	15	6	80	75	0	0
Ground, regular, baked, medium, 3 oz	240	18	7	75	50	0	0
Ground, regular, baked, well done, 3 oz	270	18	7	90	65	0	0
Ground, regular, broiled, medium, 3 oz	250	18	7	80	70	0	0
Ground, regular, broiled, well done, 3 oz	250	17	7	85	80	0	0
Ground, regular, pan-fried, medium, 3 oz	260	19	8	75	70	0	0
Ground, regular, pan-fried, well done, 3 oz	240	16	6	85	80	0	0
Heart, simmered, 3 oz	150	5	1.5	165	55	0	0
Kidneys, simmered, 3 oz	120	3	1	330	115	<1	0
Liver, braised, 3 oz	140	4	1.5	330	60	3	0
Liver, pan-fried, 3 oz	180	7	2.5	410	90	7	0

BEEF	CAL	FAT (g)	SAT FAT (g)	CHOL (mg)	SODIUM (mg)	CARB (g)	FIBER (g)
Lungs, braised, 3 oz	100	3.5	1	235	90	0	0
Pancreas, braised, 3 oz	230	15	5	225	50	0	0
Porterhouse steak, choice, marbled fat, broiled, ¼" edge fat, 3 oz	260	19	8	70	50	0	0
Porterhouse steak, choice, no marbling, broiled, ¼" edge fat, 3 oz	190	9	4	70	55	0	0
Rib, large end (ribs 6–9), choice, marbled fat, broiled, ¼" edge fat, 3 oz	310	26	11	70	55	0	0
Rib, large end (ribs 6–9), choice, marbled fat, roasted, ¼" edge fat, 3 oz	330	27	11	70	55	0	0
Rib, large end (ribs 6–9), choice, marbled fat, roasted, fat trimmed, 3 oz	320	26	10	70	55	0	0
Rib, large end (ribs 6–9), choice, no marbling, broiled, ¼" edge fat, 3 oz	200	13	5	65	60	0	0
Rib, large end (ribs 6–9), choice, no marbling, roasted, ½" edge fat, 3 oz	210	12	5	70	60	0	0
Rib, large end (ribs 6–9), choice, no marbling, roasted, fat trimmed, 3 oz	220	13	5	70	60	0	0
Rib, large end (ribs 6–9), prime, marbled fat, broiled, ¼" edge fat, 3 oz	350	31	13	75	50	0	0
Rib, large end (ribs 6–9), prime, marbled fat, roasted, ¼" edge fat, 3 oz	340	29	12	70	55	0	0
Rib, large end (ribs 6–9), prime, no marbling, broiled, ¼" edge fat, 3 oz	250	18	8	70	60	0	0
Rib, large end (ribs 6–9), prime, no marbling, roasted, ¼" edge fat, 3 oz	240	16	7	70	60	0	0
Rib, large end (ribs 6–9), select, marbled fat, broiled, ¼" edge fat, 3 oz	280	22	9	70	55	0	0

BEEF	CAL (g)	FAT (g)	SAT FAT (g)	CHOL (mg)	SODIUM (mg)	CARB (g)	FIBER (g)
Rib, large end (ribs 6–9), select, marbled fat, roasted, ¼" edge fat, 3 oz	290	23	9	70	55	0	0
Rib, large end (ribs 6–9), select, marbled fat, roasted, fat trimmed, 3 oz	280	22	9	70	55	0	0
Rib, large end (ribs 6–9), select, no marbling, broiled, ¼" edge fat, 3 oz	180	9	4	65	60	0	0
Rib, large end (ribs 6–9), select, no marbling, roasted, fat trimmed, 3 oz	190	10	4	70	60	0	0
Rib, shortribs, choice, marbled fat, braised, 3 oz	400	36	15	80	45	0	0
Rib, shortribs, choice, no marbling, braised, 3 oz	250	15	7	80	50	0	0
Rib, small end (ribs 10–12), choice, marbled fat, broiled, fat trimmed, 3 oz	270	19	8	70	55	0	0
Rib, small end (ribs 10–12), choice, marbled fat, roasted, ¼" edge fat, 3 oz	310	26	10	70	55	0	0
Rib, small end (ribs 10–12), choice, no marbling, broiled, fat trimmed, 3 oz	190	10	4	70	60	0	0
Rib, small end (ribs 10–12), choice, no marbling, roasted, ¼" edge fat, 3 oz	200	11	4.5	65	60	0	0
Rib, small end (ribs 10–12), prime, marbled fat, broiled, ¼" edge fat, 3 oz	310	24	10	70	55	0	0
Rib, small end (ribs 10–12), prime, marbled fat, roasted, ½" edge fat, 3 oz	360	31	13	70	55	0	0
Rib, small end (ribs 10–12), prime, marbled fat, roasted, ¼" edge fat, 3 oz	350	31	13	70	55	0	0
Rib, small end (ribs 10–12), prime, no marbling, broiled, ¼" edge fat, 3 oz	220	13	6	70	60	0	0
Rib, small end (ribs 10–12), prime, no marbling, roasted, ¼" edge fat, 3 oz	260	18	8	70	65	0	0

BEEF	CAL (g)	FAT (g)	SAT FAT (g)	CHOL (mg)	SODIUM (mg)	CARB (g)	FIBER (g)
Rib, small end (ribs 10–12), select, marbled fat, broiled, ¼" edge fat, 3 oz	270	21	8	70	55	0	0
Rib, small end (ribs 10–12), select, marbled fat, broiled, fat trimmed, 3 oz	240	17	7	70	55	0	0
Rib, small end (ribs 10–12), select, marbled fat, roasted, ¼" edge fat, 3 oz	280	22	9	70	55	0	0
Rib, small end (ribs 10–12), select, no marbling, broiled, fat trimmed, 3 oz	170	7	3	70	60	0	0
Rib, small end (ribs 10–12), select, no marbling, roasted, ¼" edge fat, 3 oz	170	8	3.5	65	60	0	0
Rib, whole (ribs 6–12), choice, marbled fat, broiled, ¼" edge fat, 3 oz	310	25	10	70	55	0	0
Rib, whole (ribs 6–12), choice, marbled fat, roasted, ¼" edge fat, 3 oz	320	27	11	70	55	0	0
Rib, whole (ribs 6–12), choice, no marbling, broiled, ¼" edge fat, 3 oz	200	12	5	65	60	0	0
Rib, whole (ribs 6–12), choice, no marbling, roasted, ¼" edge fat, 3 oz	210	12	5	70	60	0	0
Rib, whole (ribs 6–12), prime, marbled fat, broiled, ¼" edge fat, 3 oz	330	28	12	70	55	0	0
Rib, whole (ribs 6–12), prime, marbled fat, roasted, ¼" edge fat, 3 oz	350	30	12	70	55	0	0
Rib, whole (ribs 6–12), prime, no marbling, broiled, ¼" edge fat, 3 oz	240	16	7	70	60	0	0
Rib, whole (ribs 6–12), prime, no marbling, roasted, ¼" edge fat, 3 oz	250	17	7	70	65	0	0
Rib, whole (ribs 6–12), select, marbled fat, broiled, ¼" edge fat, 3 oz	270	21	9	70	55	0	0

BEEF	CAL	FAT (g)	SAT FAT (g)	CHOL (mg)	SODIUM (mg)	CARB (g)	FIBER (g)
Rib, whole (ribs 6–12), select, marbled fat, roasted, ¼" edge fat, 3 oz	290	23	9	70	55	0	0
Rib, whole (ribs 6–12), select, no marbling, broiled, ¼" edge fat, 3 oz	180	9	3.5	65	60	0	0
Rib, whole (ribs 6–12), select, no marbling, roasted, ¼" edge fat, 3 oz	180	9	3.5	70	60	0	0
Ribeye, small end (ribs 10–12), choice, marbled fat, broiled, fat trimmed, 3 oz	260	19	8	70	55	0	0
Ribeye, small end (ribs 10–12), choice, no marbling, broiled, fat trimmed, 3 oz	190	10	4	70	60	0	0
Round, bottom round, choice, marbled fat, braised, fat trimmed, 3 oz	190	9	3	80	45	0	0
Round, bottom round, choice, marbled fat, roasted, ¼" edge fat, 3 oz	220	14	5	70	55	0	0
Round, bottom round, choice, marbled fat, roasted, fat trimmed, 3 oz	170	8	3	65	55	0	0
Round, bottom round, choice, no marbling, braised, fat trimmed, 3 oz	180	7	2.5	80	45	0	0
Round, bottom round, choice, no marbling, roasted, fat trimmed, 3 oz	160	7	2	80	55	0	0
Round, bottom round, prime, marbled fat, braised, ½" edge fat, 3 oz	250	16	6	80	45	0	0
Round, bottom round, prime, no marbling, braised, ½" edge fat, 3 oz	210	11	4	80	45	0	0
Round, bottom round, select, marbled fat, braised, fat trimmed, 3 oz	170	6	2	80	45	0	0
Round, bottom round, select, marbled fat, roasted, fat trimmed, 3 oz	150	5	2	65	55	0	0

BEEF	CAL (g)	FAT (g)	SAT FAT (g)	CHOL (mg)	SODIUM (mg)	CARB (g)	FIBER (g)
Round, bottom round, select, no marbling, braised, fat trimmed, 3 oz	160	5	2	80	45	0	0
Round, bottom round, select, no marbling, roasted, fat trimmed, 3 oz	150	4.5	1.5	65	55	0	0
Round, eye of round, choice, marbled fat, roasted, fat trimmed, 3 oz	150	5	2	60	55	0	0
Round, eye of round, choice, no marbling, roasted, fat trimmed, 3 oz	150	5	2	60	55	0	0
Round, eye of round, prime, marbled fat, roasted, ½" edge fat, 3 oz	210	13	5	60	50	0	0
Round, eye of round, prime, no marbling, roasted, ½" edge fat, 3 oz	170	7	3	60	55	0	0
Round, eye of round, select, marbled fat, roasted, fat trimmed, 3 oz	140	3.5	1.5	60	55	0	0
Round, eye of round, select, no marbling, roasted, fat trimmed, 3 oz	130	3	1	60	55	0	0
Round, full cut, choice, marbled fat, broiled, ¼" edge fat, 3 oz	200	12	4.5	70	50	0	0
Round, full cut, choice, no marbling, broiled, ¼" edge fat, 3 oz	160	6	2	65	55	0	0
Round, full cut, select, marbled fat, broiled, ¼" edge fat, 3 oz	190	10	3.5	45	55	0	0
Round, full cut, select, no marbling, broiled, ¼" edge fat, 3 oz	150	4.5	1.5	65	55	0	0
Round, tip round, choice, marbled fat, roasted, fat trimmed, 3 oz	170	8	3	70	55	0	0
Round, tip round, choice, no marbling, roasted, fat trimmed, 3 oz	150	5	2	70	55	0	0

BEEF	CAL (g)	FAT (g)	SAT FAT (g)	CHOL (mg)	SODIUM (mg)	CARB (g)	FIBER (g)
Round, tip round, prime, marbled fat, roasted, ¼" edge fat, 3 oz	230	15	6	70	55	0	0
Round, tip round, prime, no marbling, roasted, ¼" edge fat, 3 oz	180	9	3	70	55	0	0
Round, tip round, select, marbled fat, roasted, fat trimmed, 3 oz	160	6	2.5	70	55	0	0
Round, tip round, select, no marbling, roasted, fat trimmed, 3 oz	140	4.5	1.5	70	55	0	0
Round, top round, choice, marbled fat, braised, fat trimmed, 3 oz	180	6	2	75	40	0	0
Round, top round, choice, marbled fat, broiled, ¼" edge fat, 3 oz	190	9	3.5	70	50	0	0
Round, top round, choice, marbled fat, pan-fried, ¼" edge fat, 3 oz	240	13	4.5	80	60	0	0
Round, top round, choice, no marbling, braised, fat trimmed, 3 oz	180	5	1.5	75	40	0	0
Round, top round, choice, no marbling, broiled, ¼" edge fat, 3 oz	160	5	2	70	50	0	0
Round, top round, choice, no marbling, pan-fried, ¼" edge fat, 3 oz	190	7	2	80	60	0	0
Round, top round, prime, marbled fat, broiled, ¼" edge fat, 3 oz	190	9	3	70	50	0	0
Round, top round, prime, no marbling, broiled, ¼" edge fat, 3 oz	180	8	2.5	70	50	0	0
Round, top round, select, marbled fat, braised, fat trimmed, 3 oz	170	4.5	1.5	75	40	0	0
Round, top round, select, marbled fat, broiled, ¼" edge fat, 3 oz	180	7	3	70	50	0	0

BEEF	CAL (g)	FAT (g)	SAT FAT (g)	CHOL (mg)	SODIUM (mg)	CARB (g)	FIBER (g)
Round, top round, select, no marbling, braised, fat trimmed, 3 oz	160	3.5	1	75	40	0	0
Round, top round, select, no marbling, broiled, ¼" edge fat, 3 oz	140	3.5	1	70	50	0	0
Salisbury steak, family size, frozen, Banquet, 1 patty with gravy	200	14	6	25	610	7	2
Shank crosscuts, choice, marbled fat, simmered, ¼" edge fat, 3 oz	220	13	5	70	50	0	0
Shank crosscuts, choice, no marbling, simmered, ¼" edge fat, 3 oz	170	5	2	65	55	0	0
Short loin, tenderloin, choice, marbled fat, broiled, fat trimmed, 3 oz	210	12	5	70	50	0	0
Short loin, tenderloin, choice, marbled fat, roasted, ¼" edge fat, 3 oz	290	22	9	75	55	0	0
Short loin, tenderloin, choice, no marbling, broiled, fat trimmed, 3 oz	180	9	3	70	55	0	0
Short loin, tenderloin, choice, no marbling, roasted, ¼" edge fat, 3 oz	200	11	4	70	60	0	0
Short loin, tenderloin, prime, marbled fat, broiled, ¼" edge fat, 3 oz	270	20	8	75	50	0	0
Short loin, tenderloin, prime, marbled fat, roasted, ¼" edge fat, 3 oz	300	24	9	75	50	0	0
Short loin, tenderloin, prime, no marbling, broiled, ¼" edge fat, 3 oz	200	11	4	70	55	0	0
Short loin, tenderloin, prime, no marbling, roasted, ¼" edge fat, 3 oz	220	13	5	75	50	0	0
Short loin, tenderloin, select, marbled fat, broiled, fat trimmed, 3 oz	190	11	4	70	55	0	0

BEEF	CAL (g)	FAT (g)	SAT FAT (g)	CHOL (mg)	SODIUM (mg)	CARB (g)	FIBER (g)
Short loin, tenderloin, select, marbled fat, roasted, ¼" edge fat, 3 oz	280	21	8	75	50	0	0
Short loin, tenderloin, select, no marbling, broiled, fat trimmed, 3 oz	170	7	3	70	55	0	0
Short loin, tenderloin, select, no marbling, roasted, ¼" edge fat, 3 oz	180	9	3.5	70	50	0	0
Short loin, top loin, choice, marbled fat, broiled, ¼" edge fat, 3 oz	250	18	7	65	55	0	0
Short loin, top loin, choice, marbled fat, broiled, fat trimmed, 3 oz	190	10	4	65	60	0	0
Short loin, top loin, choice, no marbling, broiled, ¼" edge fat, 3 oz	180	9	3	65	60	0	0
Short loin, top loin, choice, no marbling, broiled, fat trimmed, 3 oz	180	8	3	65	60	0	0
Short loin, top loin, prime, marbled fat, broiled, ¼" edge fat, 3 oz	270	20	8	65	55	0	0
Short loin, top loin, prime, no marbling, broiled, ½" edge fat, 3 oz	210	12	4.5	65	60	0	0
Short loin, top loin, prime, no marbling, broiled, ¼" edge fat, 3 oz	210	12	4.5	65	60	0	0
Short loin, top loin, select, marbled fat, broiled, fat trimmed, 3 oz	170	7	3	65	60	0	0
Short loin, top loin, select, no marbling, broiled, fat trimmed, 3 oz	160	6	2	65	60	0	0
Short loin, top sirloin, choice, marbled fat, broiled, fat trimmed, 3 oz	190	10	4	75	55	0	0
Short loin, top sirloin, choice, marbled fat, pan-fried, ¼" edge fat, 3 oz	280	19	8	85	60	0	0

BEEF	CAL (g)	FAT (g)	SAT FAT (g)	CHOL (mg)	SODIUM (mg)	CARB (g)	FIBER (g)
Short loin, top sirloin, choice, no marbling, broiled, fat trimmed, 3 oz	170	7	2.5	75	55	0	0
Short loin, top sirloin, choice, no marbling, pan-fried, ¼" edge fat, 3 oz	200	9	3.5	85	65	0	0
Short loin, top sirloin, prime, marbled fat, broiled, ½" edge fat, 3 oz	270	19	8	75	55	0	0
Short loin, top sirloin, prime, no marbling, broiled, ½" edge fat, 3 oz	200	10	4	75	55	0	0
Short loin, top sirloin, select, marbled fat, broiled, fat trimmed, 3 oz	170	6	2.5	75	55	0	0
Short loin, top sirloin, select, no marbling, broiled, fat trimmed, 3 oz	150	5	2	75	55	0	0
Sliced beef & gravy, family size, frozen, Banquet, 2 slices with gravy	100	3	1.5	40	850	7	<1
Spleen, braised, 3 oz	120	3.5	1.5	295	50	0	0
Swedish meatballs, precooked, frozen, Rich's, 6 meatballs	260	20	9	45	490	7	1
T-bone steak, choice, marbled fat, broiled, ¼" edge fat, 3 oz	250	18	7	70	50	0	0
T-bone steak, choice, no marbling, broiled, ¼" edge fat, 3 oz	180	9	3.5	70	55	0	0
Thymus, braised, 3 oz	270	21	7	250	100	0	0
Tongue, simmered, 3 oz	240	18	8	90	50	0	0
Tongue, sliced, Hebrew National Deli Express, 2 oz	120	9	na	50	330	0	0

AT A GLANCE: BEEF

Choose cuts of beef with less than 9 grams of total fat, 4 grams of saturated fat, and 80 milligrams of cholesterol. Beef cuts labeled "loin/round"—round tip, top round, eye of round, top loin, tenderloin, and sirloin—are lean choices when trimmed.

	CAL (g)	FAT (g)	SAT FAT (g)	CHOL (mg)	SODIUM (mg)	CARB (g)	FIBER (g)

BEEF ALTERNATIVES

	CAL (g)	FAT (g)	SAT FAT (g)	CHOL (mg)	SODIUM (mg)	CARB (g)	FIBER (g)
Burger, meatless, fat free, frozen, Gardenburger Veggie, 1 patty	190	0	0	0	180	40	8
Burger, meatless, fat free, frozen, Natural Touch Vegan Burger, 1 patty	70	0	0	0	370	6	3
Burger, meatless, frozen, Gardenburger Mexi, 1 patty	215	2.5	1.5	5	160	36	10
Burger, meatless, frozen, GardenVegan, 1 patty	140	0	0	0	250	23	4
Burger, meatless, frozen, Ken and Robert's, 1 patty	110	2	0	0	390	19	na
Burger, meatless, frozen, Loma Linda Sizzle Burger, 1 patty	200	12	1.5	<5	540	10	6
Burger, meatless, frozen, Morningstar Farms Garden Vege Patties, 1 patty	110	4	0.5	0	350	150	8
Burger, meatless, frozen, Worthington FriPats, 1 patty	130	6	1	0	320	4	3
Burger, meatless, Italian style, frozen, Green Giant Harvest Burgers, 1 burger	140	4.5	1.5	0	370	8	5
Burger, meatless, lowfat, frozen, Gardenburger, 1 patty	140	2.5	0.5	5	180	21	5
Burger, meatless, original, frozen, Green Giant Harvest Burgers, 1 burger	140	4	1.5	0	380	8	5
Burger, meatless, Southwestern style, frozen, Green Giant Harvest Burgers, 1 burger	140	4	1.5	0	370	9	5
Dinner roast, meatless, frozen, Worthington, ¾" slice	180	12	2	<5	580	5	3
Steak, cubed, meatless, frozen, Worthington Stakelets, 1 piece	140	8	1.5	0	480	6	2
Steak, meatless, frozen, Loma Linda Griddle Steaks, 1 piece	130	7	1	0	410	4	4

	CAL (g)	FAT (g)	SAT FAT (g)	CHOL (mg)	SODIUM (mg)	CARB (g)	FIBER (g)

CHICKEN

Serving size is 3 ounces cooked. Start with 4 ounces of raw chicken to yield a 3 ounce cooked serving.

	CAL (g)	FAT (g)	SAT FAT (g)	CHOL (mg)	SODIUM (mg)	CARB (g)	FIBER (g)
Breast, boneless, skinless, roasted, Perdue, 3 oz	130	2	0.5	70	10	0	ns
Breast, Cajun, Chicken By George, 1 breast	130	4	1	60	700	3	0
Breast, chunk, Hormel, 2 oz	60	1.5	0.5	25	100	0	0
Breast, cooked, Wampler-Longacre, 2 oz	90	5	1.5	30	550	2	ns
Breast, Italian, skinless, boneless, Butterball, 1 breast fillet	120	2	0	25	690	3	0
Breast, lemon herb, Chicken By George, 1 breast	120	3	1	60	800	3	0
Breast, mesquite BBQ, Chicken By George, 1 breast	130	3	1	60	700	5	0
Breast, no salt, Hormel, 2 oz	60	1.5	0.5	30	20	0	0
Breast, roaster, Chicken By George, 1 breast	110	3	1	55	500	1	0
Breast, split, roasted, Perdue, 1 breast	370	19	6	175	80	0	0
Breast, tenders, roasted, Perdue, 3 oz	110	1	0.5	65	30	0	ns
Breast, teriyaki, Chicken By George, 1 breast	130	3	3	60	650	6	0
Breast, teriyaki, skinless, boneless, Butterball, 1 breast fillet	120	1	0	25	440	3	0
Breast, tomato herb, Chicken By George, 1 breast	140	5	1	60	630	5	0
Broiler-fryer, back, meat & skin, roasted, 3 oz	260	18	5	75	75	0	0
Broiler-fryer, back, meat & skin, stewed, 3 oz	220	15	4	65	55	0	0
Broiler-fryer, back, meat only, roasted, 3 oz	200	11	3	75	80	0	0
Broiler-fryer, back, meat only, stewed, 3 oz	180	10	2.5	70	60	0	0

CHICKEN	CAL (g)	FAT (g)	SAT FAT (g)	CHOL (mg)	SODIUM (mg)	CARB (g)	FIBER (g)
Broiler-fryer, breast, meat & skin, roasted, 3 oz	170	7	2	70	60	0	0
Broiler-fryer, breast, meat & skin, stewed, 3 oz	160	6	2	65	55	0	0
Broiler-fryer, breast, meat only, roasted, 3 oz	140	3	1	70	65	0	0
Broiler-fryer, breast, meat only, stewed, 3 oz	130	2.5	0.5	65	55	0	0
Broiler-fryer, dark meat, meat & skin, roasted, 3 oz	220	13	4	75	75	0	0
Broiler-fryer, dark meat, meat & skin, stewed, 3 oz	200	13	3.5	70	60	0	0
Broiler-fryer, dark meat, meat only, roasted, 3 oz	170	8	2	80	80	0	0
Broiler-fryer, dark meat, meat only, stewed, 3 oz	160	8	2	75	65	0	0
Broiler-fryer, drumstick, meat & skin, roasted, 3 oz	180	10	2.5	75	80	0	0
Broiler-fryer, drumstick, meat & skin, stewed, 3 oz	170	9	2.5	70	65	0	0
Broiler-fryer, drumstick, meat only, roasted, 3 oz	150	5	1	80	80	0	0
Broiler-fryer, drumstick, meat only, stewed, 3 oz	140	5	1	75	70	0	0
Broiler-fryer, giblets, simmered, 3 oz	130	4	1	335	50	<1	0
Broiler-fryer, leg, meat & skin, roasted, 3 oz	200	11	3	80	75	0	0
Broiler-fryer, leg, meat & skin, stewed, 3 oz	190	11	3	70	60	0	0
Broiler-fryer, leg, meat only, roasted, 3 oz	160	7	2	80	80	0	0
Broiler-fryer, leg, meat only, stewed, 3 oz	160	7	2	75	65	0	0
Broiler-fryer, light meat, meat & skin, roasted, 3 oz	190	9	2.5	70	65	0	0
Broiler-fryer, light meat, meat & skin, stewed, 3 oz	170	9	2.5	60	55	0	0
Broiler-fryer, light meat, meat only, roasted, 3 oz	150	4	1	70	65	0	0

CHICKEN	CAL (g)	FAT (g)	SAT FAT (g)	CHOL (mg)	SODIUM (mg)	CARB (g)	FIBER (g)
Broiler-fryer, light meat, meat only, stewed, 3 oz	140	3.5	1	65	55	0	0
Broiler-fryer, neck, meat & skin, simmered, 3 oz	210	15	4	60	45	0	0
Broiler-fryer, neck, meat only, simmered, 3 oz	150	7	2	65	55	0	0
Broiler-fryer, skin only, roasted, 3 oz	390	35	10	70	55	0	0
Broiler-fryer, skin only, stewed, 3 oz	310	28	8	55	50	0	0
Broiler-fryer, thigh, meat & skin, roasted, 3 oz	210	13	4	80	70	0	0
Broiler-fryer, thigh, meat & skin, stewed, 3 oz	200	13	3.5	70	60	0	0
Broiler-fryer, thigh, meat only, roasted, 3 oz	180	9	2.5	80	75	0	0
Broiler-fryer, thigh, meat only, stewed, 3 oz	170	8	2.5	75	65	0	0
Broiler-fryer, whole, meat & skin, roasted, 3 oz	200	12	3	75	70	0	0
Broiler-fryer, whole, meat & skin, stewed, 3 oz	190	11	3	65	60	0	0
Broiler-fryer, whole, meat only, roasted, 3 oz	160	6	2	75	75	0	0
Broiler-fryer, whole, meat only, stewed, 3 oz	150	6	1.5	70	60	0	0
Broiler-fryer, whole, meat, skin, giblets & neck, roasted, 3 oz	200	11	3	90	70	0	0
Broiler-fryer, whole, meat, skin, giblets & neck, stewed, 3 oz	180	11	3	80	55	0	0
Broiler-fryer, wing, meat & skin, roasted, 3 oz	250	17	4.5	70	70	0	0
Broiler-fryer, wing, meat & skin, stewed, 3 oz	210	14	4	60	60	0	0
Broiler-fryer, wing, meat only, roasted, 3 oz	170	7	2	70	80	0	0
Broiler-fryer, wing, meat only, stewed, 3 oz	150	6	2	65	60	0	0

CHICKEN	CAL (g)	FAT (g)	SAT FAT (g)	CHOL (mg)	SODIUM (mg)	CARB (g)	FIBER (g)
Capon, giblets, simmered, 3 oz	140	4.5	1.5	370	50	<1	0
Capon, meat & skin, roasted, 3 oz	190	10	3	75	40	0	0
Capon, meat, skin, giblets & neck, roasted, 3 oz	190	10	3	90	45	0	0
Chunk, Southern fried, frozen, Country Skillet, 5 chunks	250	15	3	20	550	16	1
Chunks, frozen, Country Skillet, 5 chunks	270	17	3	20	720	18	1
Drumstick, roasted, Perdue, 1 drumstick	110	6	1.5	85	50	0	ns
Fried, Southern, frozen, Banquet, 3 oz	270	18	5	65	590	13	1
Fryer-roaster, dark meat, roasted, Perdue, 3 oz	210	15	4	110	55	0	ns
Fryer-roaster, white meat, roasted, Perdue, 3 oz	160	9	2.5	85	40	0	ns
Gizzard, simmered, 3 oz	130	3.5	1	165	60	<1	0
Ground, cooked, Pederson's, 3 oz	150	8	na	55	55	na	na
Ground, cooked, Perdue, 3 oz	180	12	3.5	145	55	0	ns
Heart, simmered, 3 oz	160	7	2	205	40	0	0
Liver, simmered, 3 oz	130	4.5	1.5	535	45	<1	0
Nuggets, frozen, Banquet, 9 nuggets	240	15	3	35	540	12	1
Nuggets, frozen, Country Skillet, 10 nuggets	280	18	4	25	620	16	1
Nuggets, Southern fried, frozen, Banquet, 6 nuggets	340	20	4	45	840	22	2
Nuggets, Southern fried, frozen, Banquet, 9 nuggets	230	15	3	30	500	14	1
Patties, frozen, Banquet, 1 pattie	200	12	25	25	400	11	1
Patties, frozen, Country Skillet, 1 patty	190	12	2.5	20	500	12	1
Patties, Southern fried, frozen, Banquet, 2.5 oz	190	12	3	25	480	12	<1
Patties, Southern fried, frozen, Country Skillet, 1 patty	190	12	2.5	20	450	12	1

CHICKEN	CAL (g)	FAT (g)	SAT FAT (g)	CHOL (mg)	SODIUM (mg)	CARB (g)	FIBER (g)
Roasting, dark meat, meat only, roasted, 3 oz	150	7	2	65	80	0	0
Roasting, giblets, simmered, 3 oz	140	4.5	1.5	300	50	<1	0
Roasting, light meat, meat only, roasted, 3 oz	130	3.5	1	65	45	0	0
Roasting, whole, meat & skin, roasted, 3 oz	190	11	3	65	60	0	0
Roasting, whole, meat only, roasted, 3 oz	140	6	1.5	65	65	0	0
Roasting, whole, meat, skin & giblets, roasted, 3 oz	190	11	3	80	60	0	0
Stewing, dark meat, meat only, stewed, 3 oz	220	13	3.5	80	80	0	0
Stewing, giblets, simmered, 3 oz	160	8	2	300	50	0	0
Stewing, light meat, meat only, stewed, 3 oz	180	7	2	60	50	0	0
Stewing, whole, meat & skin, stewed, 3 oz	240	16	4.5	65	60	0	0
Stewing, whole, meat only, stewed, 3 oz	200	10	2.5	70	65	0	0
Stewing, whole, meat, skin & giblets, stewed, 3 oz	230	15	4	85	60	0	0
Sweet & sour, Wampler-Longacre, 1 cup	250	4	0.5	55	510	35	1
Tenders, frozen, Banquet, 3 tenders	210	10	2	25	470	13	1
Tenders, Southern fried, frozen, Banquet, 3 tenders	210	10	2	20	490	14	2
Thigh, boneless, skinless, roasted, Perdue, 2 thighs	200	11	3	130	60	0	ns
Wings, barbecue, frozen, Banquet Game Time, 4 pieces	190	12	4	70	540	5	1
Wings, hot & spicy, frozen, Banquet Game Time, 4 pieces	230	16	5	85	280	5	1

AT A GLANCE: CHICKEN

Choose chicken portions with less than 8 grams of total fat, 3.5 grams of saturated fat, and 80 milligrams of cholesterol. Skinless breast, wing, and leg are lean choices.

	CAL (g)	FAT (g)	SAT FAT (g)	CHOL (mg)	SODIUM (mg)	CARB (g)	FIBER (g)
CHICKEN ALTERNATIVES							
Chik-Nuggets, meatless, frozen, Loma Linda, 5 pieces	240	16	2.5	0	710	13	5
ChikStiks, meatless, frozen, Worthington, 1 piece	120	8	2	0	360	3	2
CrispyChik patties, meatless, frozen, Worthington, 1 patty	170	9	1.5	0	600	15	4
Fried Chik'n, meatless, frozen, Loma Linda, 1 piece	180	15	2	<5	500	<1	<1
Ground, meatless, roll, frozen, Worthington Chic-Ketts, 2 slices, ⅜" each	120	7	1	0	390	2	2
DEER							
Roasted, 3 oz	130	3	1	95	45	0	0
DUCK							
Meat & skin, roasted, 3 oz	290	24	8	70	50	0	0
Meat only, roasted, 3 oz	170	10	3.5	75	55	0	0
FAT							
Chicken, 1 Tbsp	120	13	4	10	0	0	0
Duck, 1 Tbsp	120	13	4	15	0	0	0
Goose, 1 Tbsp	120	13	3.5	15	0	0	0
Turkey, 1 Tbsp	120	13	4	15	0	0	0
GOOSE							
Meat & skin, roasted, 3 oz	260	19	6	75	60	0	0
Meat only, roasted, 3 oz	200	11	4	80	65	0	0
HAM							

Serving size is 3 ounces cooked. Start with 4 ounces of raw ham to yield a 3 ounce cooked serving.

	CAL (g)	FAT (g)	SAT FAT (g)	CHOL (mg)	SODIUM (mg)	CARB (g)	FIBER (g)
Baked, dinner sliced, Louis Rich, 1 slice	80	1.5	0.5	40	1150	1	0
Boneless, extra lean, cured, roasted, 3 oz	120	5	1.5	45	1020	1	0

HAM	CAL	FAT (g)	SAT FAT (g)	CHOL (mg)	SODIUM (mg)	CARB (g)	FIBER (g)
Boneless, extra lean, cured, unheated, 3 oz	110	4.5	1.5	40	1210	<1	0
Boneless, regular (about 11% fat), cured, roasted, 3 oz	150	8	3	50	1280	0	0
Boneless, regular (about 11% fat), cured, unheated, 3 oz	150	9	3	50	1120	3	0
Canned, Hormel Supreme Cut, 1 oz	30	1	1	15	300	1	1
Canned, extra lean, cured, roasted, 3 oz	120	4	1.5	25	960	0	0
Canned, extra lean, cured, unheated, 3 oz	100	4	1.5	30	1070	0	0
Canned, premium boneless, Armour, 3 oz	100	4	1.5	40	1020	1	0
Canned, refrigerated, Hormel Black Label, 3 oz	100	5	2	40	960	0	0
Canned, regular (about 13% fat), cured, roasted, 3 oz	190	13	4	55	800	0	0
Canned, regular (about 13% fat), cured, unheated, 3 oz	160	11	3.5	35	1050	0	0
Canned, shelf stable, Hormel Black Label, 3 oz	110	5	2	45	900	0	0
Center slice, marbled fat, cured, unheated, 3 oz	170	11	4	45	1180	0	0
Chopped, cured, 3 oz	190	15	5	45	1170	0	0
Dinner slice, Oscar Mayer, 3 oz	80	3	1	40	1010	0	0
Half, Hormel Cure 81, 3 oz	100	5	1.5	45	890	0	0
Ham steak, boneless, extra lean, cured, unheated, 3 oz	100	4	1	40	1080	0	0
Ham steak, dinner, Oscar Mayer, 1 steak	60	2	0.5	30	750	0	0
Minced, cured, 3 oz	220	18	6	60	1060	2	0
Patties, Hormel, 1 patty	180	17	6	35	550	1	0
Patties, grilled, 1 oz	100	9	3	20	300	0	0
Patties, with cheese, Hormel, 1 patty	190	17	6	45	470	0	0
Proscuitti, Hormel Primissimo, 1 oz	70	4.5	1.5	25	540	0	0
Rump half, marbled fat, fresh, roasted, 3 oz	210	12	4.5	80	55	0	0

HAM	CAL (g)	FAT (g)	SAT FAT (g)	CHOL (mg)	SODIUM (mg)	CARB (g)	FIBER (g)
Rump half, no marbling, fresh, roasted, 3 oz	180	7	2.5	80	55	0	0
Shank half, marbled fat, fresh, roasted, 3 oz	250	17	6	80	50	0	0
Shank half, no marbling, fresh, roasted, 3 oz	180	9	3	80	55	0	0
Turkey ham, Louis Rich, 2 oz	70	2.5	1	40	620	1	0
Turkey ham, chunk, Hormel, 2 oz	70	4	1.5	40	600	0	0
Turkey ham, smoked, Wampler-Longacre, 2 oz	60	2.5	1	30	590	1	na
Turkey ham, water added, Louis Rich, 2 oz	70	3	1	45	640	1	0
Whole, Hormel Curemaster, 3 oz	80	3	1	40	940	0	0
Whole, Hormel Light & Lean, 3 oz	90	2.5	1	35	950	2	0
Whole, fully cooked, marbled fat, cured, roasted, 3 oz	210	14	5	55	1010	0	0
Whole, fully cooked, marbled fat, cured, unheated, 3 oz	210	16	6	50	1090	0	0
Whole, fully cooked, no marbling, cured, roasted, 3 oz	130	5	1.5	45	1130	0	0
Whole, fully cooked, no marbling, cured, unheated, 3 oz	120	5	1.5	45	1290	0	0
Whole, marbled fat, fresh, roasted, 3 oz	230	15	6	80	50	0	0
Whole, no marbling, fresh, roasted, 3 oz	180	8	3	80	55	0	0

AT A GLANCE: HAM

Choose hams with less than 9 grams of total fat, 4 grams of saturated fat, and 80 milligrams or less of cholesterol. Boneless cured ham is a lean choice.

LAMB

Serving size is 3 ounces cooked. Start with 4 ounces of raw meat to yield a 3 ounce cooked serving.

	CAL (g)	FAT (g)	SAT FAT (g)	CHOL (mg)	SODIUM (mg)	CARB (g)	FIBER (g)
Arm, domestic, choice, marbled fat, braised, 3 oz	290	20	8	100	60	0	0
Arm, domestic, choice, marbled fat, broiled, 3 oz	240	17	7	80	65	0	0

LAMB	CAL (g)	FAT (g)	SAT FAT (g)	CHOL (mg)	SODIUM (mg)	CARB (g)	FIBER (g)
Arm, domestic, choice, marbled fat, roasted, 3 oz	240	17	7	80	55	0	0
Arm, domestic, choice, no marbling, braised, 3 oz	240	12	4	100	65	0	0
Arm, domestic, choice, no marbling, broiled, 3 oz	170	8	3	80	70	0	0
Arm, domestic, choice, no marbling, roasted, 3 oz	160	8	3	75	60	0	0
Blade, domestic, choice, marbled fat, braised, 3 oz	290	21	9	100	65	0	0
Blade, domestic, choice, marbled fat, broiled, 3 oz	240	17	7	80	70	0	0
Blade, domestic, choice, marbled fat, roasted, 3 oz	240	18	7	80	55	0	0
Blade, domestic, choice, no marbling, braised, 3 oz	240	14	5	100	70	0	0
Blade, domestic, choice, no marbling, broiled, 3 oz	180	10	3.5	75	75	0	0
Blade, domestic, choice, no marbling, roasted, 3 oz	180	10	4	75	60	0	0
Foreshank, domestic, choice, marbled fat, braised, 3 oz	210	11	5	90	60	0	0
Foreshank, domestic, choice, no marbling, braised, 3 oz	160	5	2	90	65	0	0
Foreshank, New Zealand, marbled fat, braised, 3 oz	220	13	7	85	40	0	0
Foreshank, New Zealand, no marbling, braised, 3 oz	160	5	2	85	40	0	0
Leg, shank, domestic, choice, marbled fat, roasted, 3 oz	190	11	4.5	75	55	0	0
Leg, shank, domestic, choice, no marbling, roasted, 3 oz	150	6	2	75	55	0	0
Leg, sirloin, domestic, choice, marbled fat, roasted, 3 oz	250	18	7	80	60	0	0
Leg, sirloin, domestic, choice, no marbling, roasted, 3 oz	170	8	3	80	60	0	0
Leg, whole, domestic, choice, marbled fat, roasted, 3 oz	220	14	6	80	55	0	0
Leg, whole, domestic, choice, no marbling, roasted, 3 oz	160	7	2.5	75	60	0	0

LAMB	CAL (g)	FAT (g)	SAT FAT (g)	CHOL (mg)	SODIUM (mg)	CARB (g)	FIBER (g)
Leg, whole, New Zealand, marbled fat, roasted, 3 oz	210	13	6	85	40	0	0
Leg, whole, New Zealand, no marbling, roasted, 3 oz	150	6	2.5	85	40	0	0
Loin, domestic, choice, marbled fat, broiled, 3 oz	270	20	8	85	65	0	0
Loin, domestic, choice, marbled fat, roasted, 3 oz	260	20	9	80	55	0	0
Loin, domestic, choice, no marbling, broiled, 3 oz	180	8	3	80	70	0	0
Loin, domestic, choice, no marbling, roasted, 3 oz	170	8	3	75	55	0	0
Loin, New Zealand, marbled fat, broiled, 3 oz	270	20	10	95	40	0	0
Loin, New Zealand, no marbling, roasted, 3 oz	170	7	3	95	50	0	0
Rib, domestic, choice, marbled fat, broiled, 3 oz	310	25	11	85	65	0	0
Rib, domestic, choice, marbled fat, roasted, 3 oz	310	25	11	80	60	0	0
Rib, domestic, choice, no marbling, broiled, 3 oz	200	11	4	75	70	0	0
Rib, domestic, choice, no marbling, roasted, 3 oz	200	11	4	75	70	0	0
Rib, New Zealand, marbled fat, roasted, 3 oz	290	24	12	85	40	0	0
Rib, New Zealand, no marbling, roasted, 3 oz	170	9	4	80	40	0	0
Shoulder, domestic, choice, marbled fat, braised, 3 oz	290	21	9	100	65	0	0
Shoulder, domestic, choice, marbled fat, broiled, 3 oz	240	16	7	80	65	0	0
Shoulder, domestic, choice, marbled fat, roasted, 3 oz	230	17	7	80	55	0	0
Shoulder, domestic, choice, no marbling, braised, 3 oz	240	14	5	100	70	0	0
Shoulder, domestic, choice, no marbling, broiled, 3 oz	180	9	3.5	80	70	0	0
Shoulder, domestic, choice, no marbling, roasted, 3 oz	170	9	3.5	75	60	0	0

LAMB	CAL (g)	FAT (g)	SAT FAT (g)	CHOL (mg)	SODIUM (mg)	CARB (g)	FIBER (g)
Shoulder, whole (arm and blade), New Zealand, marbled fat, braised, 3 oz	300	22	11	105	45	0	0
Shoulder, whole (arm and blade), New Zealand, no marbling, braised, 3 oz	240	13	6	110	50	0	0
Stew or kabob cuts, domestic, choice, no marbling, braised, 3 oz	190	7	3	90	60	0	0
Stew or kabob cuts, domestic, choice, no marbling, broiled, 3 oz	160	6	2	75	65	0	0

AT A GLANCE: LAMB

Choose lamb cuts with less than 9 grams of total fat, 4 grams of saturated fat, and 80 milligrams or less of cholesterol. Lamb cuts labeled "loin/leg"— such as loin chop or leg—are lean choices.

PORK

Serving size is 3 ounces cooked. Start with 4 ounces of raw pork to yield a 3 ounce cooked serving.

	CAL (g)	FAT (g)	SAT FAT (g)	CHOL (mg)	SODIUM (mg)	CARB (g)	FIBER (g)
Backribs, marbled fat, roasted, 3 oz	310	25	9	100	90	0	0
Blade roll, boneless, marbled fat, cured, roasted, 3 oz	240	20	7	55	830	0	0
Blade roll, boneless, marbled fat, cured, unheated, 3 oz	230	19	7	45	1060	0	0
Brains, braised, 3 oz	120	8	2	2170	80	0	0
Chitterlings, simmered, 3 oz	260	24	9	120	30	0	0
Ears, simmered, 3 oz	140	9	3	75	140	0	0
Feet, cured, pickled, 1 oz	60	4.5	1.5	25	260	0	0
Feet, simmered, 3 oz	160	11	3.5	85	25	0	0
Ground, cooked, 3 oz	250	18	7	80	60	0	0
Heart, braised, 3 oz	130	4.5	1	190	30	0	0
Kidneys, braised, 3 oz	130	4	1	410	70	0	0
Liver, braised, 3 oz	140	4	1	300	40	3	0
Loin, blade, marbled fat, braised, 3 oz	270	22	8	70	50	0	0
Loin, blade, marbled fat, broiled, 3 oz	270	21	8	75	60	0	0

PORK	CAL (g)	FAT (g)	SAT FAT (g)	CHOL (mg)	SODIUM (mg)	CARB (g)	FIBER (g)
Loin, blade, marbled fat, pan-fried, 3 oz	290	24	9	70	60	0	0
Loin, blade, marbled fat, roasted, 3 oz	270	21	8	80	25	0	0
Loin, blade, no marbling, braised, 3 oz	190	11	4	70	55	0	0
Loin, blade, no marbling, broiled, 3 oz	200	12	4.5	70	70	0	0
Loin, blade, no marbling, pan-fried, 3 oz	200	13	4.5	70	65	0	0
Loin, blade, no marbling, roasted, 3 oz	210	13	4.5	80	25	0	0
Loin, center loin, marbled fat, braised, 3 oz	210	12	4.5	75	50	0	0
Loin, center loin, marbled fat, broiled, 3 oz	200	11	4	70	50	0	0
Loin, center loin, marbled fat, pan-fried, 3 oz	240	14	5	80	70	0	0
Loin, center loin, marbled fat, roasted, 3 oz	200	11	4.5	70	55	0	0
Loin, center loin, no marbling, braised, 3 oz	170	7	2.5	70	55	0	0
Loin, center loin, no marbling, broiled, 3 oz	170	7	2.5	70	50	0	0
Loin, center loin, no marbling, pan-fried, 3 oz	200	9	3	80	75	0	0
Loin, center loin, no marbling, roasted, 3 oz	170	8	3	65	55	0	0
Loin, center rib, boneless, marbled fat braised, 3 oz	220	13	5	60	35	0	0
Loin, center rib, boneless, marbled fat, broiled, 3 oz	220	13	5	70	55	0	0
Loin, center rib, boneless, marbled fat, pan-fried, 3 oz	190	10	4	60	45	0	0
Loin, center rib, boneless, marbled fat, roasted, 3 oz	210	13	4.5	70	40	0	0
Loin, center rib, boneless, no marbling, braised, 3 oz	180	9	3.5	60	35	0	0
Loin, center rib, boneless, no marbling, broiled, 3 oz	180	9	3	70	55	0	0

PORK	CAL (g)	FAT (g)	SAT FAT (g)	CHOL (mg)	SODIUM (mg)	CARB (g)	FIBER (g)
Loin, center rib, boneless, no marbling, pan-fried, 3 oz	190	10	4	60	45	0	0
Loin, center rib, boneless, no marbling, roasted, 3 oz	180	9	3	70	45	0	0
Loin, center rib, marbled fat, braised, 3 oz	210	13	5	60	35	0	0
Loin, center rib, marbled fat, broiled, 3 oz	220	13	5	70	55	0	0
Loin, center rib, marbled fat, pan-fried, 3 oz	230	14	5	60	45	0	0
Loin, center rib, marbled fat, roasted, 3 oz	220	13	5	60	40	0	0
Loin, center rib, no marbling, braised, 3 oz	180	8	3	60	35	0	0
Loin, center rib, no marbling, broiled, 3 oz	190	8	3	70	55	0	0
Loin, center rib, no marbling, pan-fried, 3 oz	190	9	3.5	60	45	0	0
Loin, center rib, no marbling, roasted, 3 oz	190	10	4	60	40	0	0
Loin, country-style ribs, marbled fat, braised, 3 oz	250	18	7	75	50	0	0
Loin, country-style ribs, marbled fat, roasted, 3 oz	280	22	8	80	45	0	0
Loin, country-style ribs, no marbling, braised, 3 oz	200	12	4	75	55	0	0
Loin, country-style ribs, no marbling, roasted, 3 oz	210	13	4.5	80	25	0	0
Loin, sirloin, boneless, marbled fat, braised, 3 oz	160	7	2.5	70	40	0	0
Loin, sirloin, boneless, marbled fat, broiled, 3 oz	180	7	2.5	75	50	0	0
Loin, sirloin, boneless, marbled fat, roasted, 3 oz	180	8	3	75	50	0	0
Loin, sirloin, boneless, no marbling, braised, 3 oz	150	6	2	70	40	0	0
Loin, sirloin, boneless, no marbling, broiled, 3 oz	160	6	2	80	50	0	0
Loin, sirloin, boneless, no marbling, roasted, 3 oz	170	7	2.5	75	50	0	0

PORK	CAL (g)	FAT (g)	SAT FAT (g)	CHOL (mg)	SODIUM (mg)	CARB (g)	FIBER (g)
Loin, sirloin, marbled fat, braised, 3 oz	210	13	4.5	70	45	0	0
Loin, sirloin, marbled fat, broiled, 3 oz	220	14	5	75	60	0	0
Loin, sirloin, marbled fat, roasted, 3 oz	220	14	5	75	50	0	0
Loin, sirloin, no marbling, braised, 3 oz	170	8	2.5	70	45	0	0
Loin, sirloin, no marbling, broiled, 3 oz	180	9	3	70	60	0	0
Loin, sirloin, no marbling, roasted, 3 oz	180	9	3	75	55	0	0
Loin, tenderloin, no marbling, roasted, 3 oz	140	4	1.5	65	50	0	0
Loin, top loin, marbled fat, braised, 3 oz	200	11	4	65	35	0	0
Loin, top loin, marbled fat, broiled, 3 oz	190	10	3.5	70	55	0	0
Loin, top loin, marbled fat, pan-fried, 3 oz	220	13	4.5	65	50	0	0
Loin, top loin, marbled fat, roasted, 3 oz	190	10	3.5	65	40	0	0
Loin, top loin, no marbling, braised, 3 oz	170	7	3	60	35	0	0
Loin, top loin, no marbling, broiled, 3 oz	170	7	2.5	70	55	0	0
Loin, top loin, no marbling, pan-fried, 3 oz	190	9	3	65	50	0	0
Loin, top loin, no marbling, roasted, 3 oz	160	6	2	65	40	0	0
Loin, whole, marbled fat, braised, 3 oz	200	12	4.5	70	40	0	0
Loin, whole, marbled fat, broiled, 3 oz	210	12	4.5	70	55	0	0
Loin, whole, marbled fat, roasted, 3 oz	210	13	4.5	70	50	0	0
Loin, whole, no marbling, braised, 3 oz	170	8	3	65	45	0	0
Loin, whole, no marbling, broiled, 3 oz	180	8	3	65	55	0	0

PORK	CAL (g)	FAT (g)	SAT FAT (g)	CHOL (mg)	SODIUM (mg)	CARB (g)	FIBER (g)
Loin, whole, no marbling, roasted, 3 oz	180	8	3	70	50	0	0
Lungs, braised, 3 oz	80	2.5	1	330	70	0	0
Pancreas, braised, 3 oz	190	9	3	270	35	0	0
Pigs feet, pickled, Hormel, 2 oz	80	6	2	45	530	0	0
Pork hocks, pickled, Hormel, 2 oz	110	8	3	45	530	0	0
Pork tidbits, pickled, Hormel, 2 oz	100	8	2.5	45	530	0	0
Shoulder, arm picnic, marbled fat, cured, roasted, 3 oz	240	18	7	50	910	0	0
Shoulder, arm picnic, marbled fat, fresh, braised, 3 oz	280	20	7	95	75	0	0
Shoulder, arm picnic, marbled fat, fresh, roasted, 3 oz	270	20	7	80	60	0	0
Shoulder, arm picnic, no marbling, cured, roasted, 3 oz	140	6	2	40	1050	0	0
Shoulder, arm picnic, no marbling, fresh, braised, 3 oz	210	10	3.5	95	90	0	0
Shoulder, arm picnic, no marbling, fresh, roasted, 3 oz	190	11	3.5	80	70	0	0
Shoulder, blade, Boston, marbled fat, braised, 3 oz	270	18	7	95	60	0	0
Shoulder, blade, Boston, marbled fat, broiled, 3 oz	220	14	5	80	60	0	0
Shoulder, blade, Boston, marbled fat, roasted, 3 oz	230	16	6	75	60	0	0
Shoulder, blade, Boston, no marbling, braised, 3 oz	230	13	5	100	65	0	0
Shoulder, blade, Boston, no marbling, broiled, 3 oz	190	11	4	80	65	0	0
Shoulder, blade, Boston, no marbling, roasted, 3 oz	200	12	4.5	70	75	0	0
Shoulder, whole, marbled fat, roasted, 3 oz	250	18	7	75	60	0	0
Shoulder, whole, no marbling, roasted, 3 oz	200	11	4	75	65	0	0
Shoulder butt, smoked, boneless, Oscar Mayer, 3 oz	180	15	5	50	990	0	0

PORK	CAL (g)	FAT (g)	SAT FAT (g)	CHOL (mg)	SODIUM (mg)	CARB (g)	FIBER (g)
Spareribs, marbled fat, braised, 3 oz	340	26	9	105	80	0	0
Spleen, braised, 3 oz	130	3	1	430	90	0	0
Tail, simmered, 3 oz	340	30	11	110	20	0	0
Tenderloin, marbled fat, broiled, 3 oz	170	7	2.5	80	55	0	0
Tenderloin, marbled fat, roasted, 3 oz	150	5	2	65	50	0	0
Tenderloin, no marbling, broiled, 3 oz	160	5	2	80	55	0	0
Tongue, braised, 3 oz	230	16	5	120	95	0	0

AT A GLANCE: PORK

Choose cuts of pork with less than 9 grams of total fat, 4 grams of saturated fat, and 80 milligrams of cholesterol. Pork cuts labeled "loin/leg"—tenderloin, boneless top loin chop, and center loin chop—are lean choices.

RABBIT

	CAL (g)	FAT (g)	SAT FAT (g)	CHOL (mg)	SODIUM (mg)	CARB (g)	FIBER (g)
Domesticated, roasted, 3 oz	170	7	2	70	40	0	0
Domesticated, stewed, 3 oz	180	7	2	75	30	0	0
Wild, stewed, 3 oz	150	3	1	105	40	0	0

TURKEY

Serving size is 3 ounces cooked. Start with 4 ounces of raw turkey to yield a 3 ounce cooked serving.

	CAL (g)	FAT (g)	SAT FAT (g)	CHOL (mg)	SODIUM (mg)	CARB (g)	FIBER (g)
Breast, Falls Gourmet, 3 oz	80	1	na	35	320	0	0
Breast, Falls Premium, 3 oz	100	2	na	40	240	0	0
Breast, Louis Rich, 2 oz	60	1	0.5	20	630	2	0
Breast, barbecued, skinless, Louis Rich, 2 oz	60	1	0	25	630	2	0
Breast, browned, Healthy Choice, 2 oz	50	0.5	0	25	420	0	0
Breast, fat free, skinless, Wampler-Longacre, 2 oz	45	0	0	20	440	1	0
Breast, ground, extra lean, The Turkey Store, 4 oz	120	1.5	0.5	55	75	0	0
Breast, hickory smoked, Butterball, 3 oz	80	1	0	35	710	1	0
Breast, hickory smoked, inner slice, Louis Rich, 1 slice	80	1	0	35	1050	2	0

TURKEY	CAL (g)	FAT (g)	SAT FAT (g)	CHOL (mg)	SODIUM (mg)	CARB (g)	FIBER (g)
Breast, hickory smoked, skinless, Louis Rich, 2 oz	60	0.5	0	25	740	1	0
Breast, honey roasted, dinner slice, Louis Rich, 1 slice	80	1	0.5	35	940	3	0
Breast, honey roasted, skinless, Louis Rich, 2 oz	60	0.5	0	25	660	2	0
Breast, no salt, Hormel, 2 oz	60	0.5	0	30	35	0	0
Breast, oven roasted, Butterball, 3 oz	80	1	0	30	750	2	0
Breast, oven roasted, dinner slice, Louis Rich, 1 slice	70	1	0	35	890	1	0
Breast, oven roasted, skinless, Louis Rich, 2 oz	50	0.5	0	25	620	1	0
Breast, roast, The Turkey Store, 3 oz	130	6	1.5	40	60	0	0
Breast, skinless, Healthy Choice, 2 oz	45	0	0	20	380	1	0
Breast, skinless, premium, Hormel, 2 oz	50	0.5	0	20	480	0	0
Breast, slices, The Turkey Store, 3 oz	90	1	ns	40	65	0	0
Breast, smoked, Healthy Choice, 2 oz	50	0	0	25	400	1	0
Breast, strips, The Turkey Store, 3 oz	90	1	ns	40	60	0	0
Breast, tenderloins, The Turkey Store, 3 oz	90	1	ns	40	65	0	0
Burger, Wampler-Longacre, 5.33 oz	270	20	4	140	40	0	0
Burger, patties, breaded, Louis Rich, 1 pattie	220	13	2.5	35	550	13	0
Burger, patties, lean, The Turkey Store, 4 oz	160	8	2	70	80	1	0
Burger, patties, seasoned, lean, The Turkey Store, 4 oz	160	8	2	70	680	5	0
Chunk, Hormel, 2 oz	70	3	1	35	340	0	0
Dark meat, fresh, roasted, Perdue, 3 oz	200	14	5	95	55	0	ns
Drumstick, Perdue, 3 oz	150	7	2	100	70	0	ns

TURKEY	CAL (g)	FAT (g)	SAT FAT (g)	CHOL (mg)	SODIUM (mg)	CARB (g)	FIBER (g)
Fryer-roaster, back, meat & skin, roasted, 3 oz	170	9	2.5	90	60	0	0
Fryer-roaster, back, meat only, roasted, 3 oz	140	5	1.5	80	60	0	0
Fryer-roaster, breast, meat & skin, roasted, 3 oz	130	3	1	75	45	0	0
Fryer-roaster, breast, meat only, roasted, 3 oz	110	0.5	0	70	45	0	0
Fryer-roaster, dark meat, meat & skin, roasted, 3 oz	150	6	2	100	65	0	0
Fryer-roaster, dark meat, meat only, roasted, 3 oz	140	4	1	95	70	0	0
Fryer-roaster, leg, meat & skin, roasted, 3 oz	140	4.5	1.5	60	70	0	0
Fryer-roaster, leg, meat only, roasted, 3 oz	140	3	1	100	70	0	0
Fryer-roaster, light meat, meat & skin, roasted, 3 oz	140	4	1	80	50	0	0
Fryer-roaster, light meat, meat only, roasted, 3 oz	120	1	0	75	50	0	0
Fryer-roaster, skin only, roasted, 3 oz	250	20	5	120	50	0	0
Fryer-roaster, whole, meat & skin, roasted, 3 oz	150	5	1.5	90	55	0	0
Fryer-roaster, whole, meat only, roasted, 3 oz	130	2	1	85	60	0	0
Fryer-roaster, whole, meat, skin, giblets & neck, roasted, 3 oz	150	5	1.5	100	55	0	0
Fryer-roasters, wing, meat & skin, roasted, 3 oz	180	8	2.5	100	60	0	0
Fryer-roasters, wing, meat only, roasted, 3 oz	140	3	1	85	65	0	0
Giblets, simmered, some giblet fat, 3 oz	140	4.5	1.5	355	50	2	0
Gizzard, simmered, 3 oz	140	3.5	1	200	45	<1	0
Ground, Louis Rich, 4 oz	190	12	3.5	90	140	0	0
Ground, Wampler-Longacre, 4 oz	210	15	3	100	30	0	na
Ground, 93% lean, roasted, Perdue, 3 oz	170	9	3	110	65	0	ns

TURKEY	CAL	FAT (g)	SAT FAT (g)	CHOL (mg)	SODIUM (mg)	CARB (g)	FIBER (g)
Ground, extra lean, white meat, Butterball, 4 oz	130	3	1	70	65	0	0
Ground, lean, Butterball, 4 oz	180	10	3.5	95	90	0	0
Ground, lean, The Turkey Store, 4 oz	160	8	2	70	80	0	0
Heart, simmered, 3 oz	150	5	1.5	190	50	2	0
Leg, meat & skin, roasted, 3 oz	180	8	2.5	70	65	0	0
Liver, simmered, 3 oz	140	5	1.5	530	55	3	0
Neck, meat only, simmered, 3 oz	150	6	2	105	50	0	0
Nuggets, breaded, Louis Rich, 4 nuggets	260	16	3	35	640	15	0
Sliced turkey with gravy, family size, frozen, Banquet, 2 slices with gravy	100	5	1.5	25	590	5	<1
Sticks, breaded, Louis Rich, 3 sticks	230	15	3	35	580	12	0
Thigh, prebasted, meat & skin, roasted, 3 oz	130	7	2	55	370	0	0
White meat, chunk, Hormel, 2 oz	60	1	0.5	25	320	0	0
White meat, fresh, roasted, Perdue, 3 oz	70	9	3	70	35	0	ns
Whole, meat, skin, giblets & neck, roasted, 3 oz	170	8	2.5	80	60	0	0
Whole, young, frozen, Butterball, 4 oz	150	6	2	65	55	1	0
Wings, Perdue, 3 oz	170	8	2.5	65	35	0	ns
Young hen, back, meat & skin, roasted, 3 oz	220	13	4	70	60	0	0
Young hen, breast, meat & skin, roasted, 3 oz	160	7	2	60	50	0	0
Young hen, dark meat, meat & skin, roasted, 3 oz	200	11	3	70	60	0	0
Young hen, dark meat, meat only, roasted, 3 oz	160	7	2	70	65	0	0
Young hen, leg, meat & skin, roasted, 3 oz	180	9	3	70	60	0	0
Young hen, light meat, meat & skin, roasted, 3 oz	180	8	2	65	50	0	0

TURKEY	CAL (g)	FAT (g)	SAT FAT (g)	CHOL (mg)	SODIUM (mg)	CARB (g)	FIBER (g)
Young hen, light meat, meat only, roasted, 3 oz	140	3.5	1	60	50	0	0
Young hen, skin only, roasted, 3 oz	410	38	10	90	40	0	0
Young hen, whole, meat & skin, roasted, 3 oz	190	9	2.5	80	55	0	0
Young hen, whole, meat only, roasted, 3 oz	150	5	1.5	60	60	0	0
Young hen, whole, meat, skin, giblets & neck, roasted, 3 oz	180	9	2.5	80	55	0	0
Young hen, wing, meat & skin, roasted, 3 oz	200	11	3	65	50	0	0
Young tom, back, meat & skin, roasted, 3 oz	200	12	3.5	80	65	0	0
Young tom, breast, meat & skin, roasted, 3 oz	160	6	2	65	60	0	0
Young tom, dark meat, meat & skin, roasted, 3 oz	180	9	3	75	70	0	0
Young tom, dark meat, meat only, roasted, 3 oz	160	6	2	75	70	0	0
Young tom, leg, meat & skin, roasted, 3 oz	180	8	2.5	75	70	0	0
Young tom, light meat, meat & skin, roasted, 3 oz	160	7	2	65	60	0	0
Young tom, light meat, meat only, roasted, 3 oz	130	2.5	1	60	60	0	0
Young tom, skin only, roasted, 3 oz	360	32	8	100	50	0	0
Young tom, whole, meat & skin, roasted, 3 oz	170	8	2	70	60	0	0
Young tom, whole, meat only, roasted, 3 oz	140	4	1.5	65	65	0	0
Young tom, whole, meat, skin, giblets & neck, roasted, 3 oz	170	7	2.5	80	60	0	0
Young tom, wing, meat & skin, roasted, 3 oz	190	10	3	70	55	0	0

AT A GLANCE: TURKEY

Choose turkey portions with less than 8 grams of total fat, 3.5 grams of saturated fat, and 80 milligrams of cholesterol. Most skinless cuts fit into these guidelines.

	CAL (g)	FAT (g)	SAT FAT (g)	CHOL (mg)	SODIUM (mg)	CARB (g)	FIBER (g)

VEAL

Serving size is 3 ounces cooked. Start with 4 ounces of raw meat to yield a 3 ounce cooked serving.

	CAL (g)	FAT (g)	SAT FAT (g)	CHOL (mg)	SODIUM (mg)	CARB (g)	FIBER (g)
Arm, marbled fat, braised, 3 oz	200	9	3.5	125	75	0	0
Arm, marbled fat, roasted, 3 oz	160	7	3	90	80	0	0
Arm, no marbling, braised, 3 oz	170	4.5	1	130	80	0	0
Arm, no marbling, roasted, 3 oz	140	5	2	95	80	0	0
Blade, marbled fat, braised, 3 oz	190	9	3	130	85	0	0
Blade, marbled fat, roasted, 3 oz	160	7	3	100	85	0	0
Blade, no marbling, braised, 3 oz	170	6	1.5	135	90	0	0
Blade, no marbling, roasted, 3 oz	150	6	2	100	90	0	0
Ground, broiled, 3 oz	150	6	2.5	90	70	0	0
Leg, marbled fat, braised, 3 oz	180	5	2	115	60	0	0
Leg, marbled fat, pan-fried, 3 oz	180	7	3	90	65	0	0
Leg, marbled fat, roasted, 3 oz	140	4	1.5	90	60	0	0
Leg, no marbling, braised, 3 oz	170	4.5	1.5	115	60	0	0
Leg, no marbling, pan-fried, 3 oz	160	4	1	90	65	0	0
Leg, no marbling, roasted, 3 oz	130	3	1	90	60	0	0
Leg and shoulder, cubed, no marbling, braised, 3 oz	160	4	1	125	80	0	0
Loin, marbled fat, braised, 3 oz	240	15	6	100	70	0	0
Loin, marbled fat, roasted, 3 oz	180	10	4.5	90	80	0	0
Loin, no marbling, braised, 3 oz	190	8	2	105	70	0	0

VEAL	CAL (g)	FAT (g)	SAT FAT (g)	CHOL (mg)	SODIUM (mg)	CARB (g)	FIBER (g)
Loin, no marbling, roasted, 3 oz	150	6	2	90	80	0	0
Rib, marbled fat, braised, 3 oz	210	11	4	120	80	0	0
Rib, marbled fat, roasted, 3 oz	190	12	4.5	95	80	0	0
Rib, no marbling, braised, 3 oz	190	7	2	120	85	0	0
Rib, no marbling, roasted, 3 oz	150	6	2	100	80	0	0
Shoulder, whole, marbled fat, braised, 3 oz	190	9	3	105	80	0	0
Shoulder, whole, marbled fat, roasted, 3 oz	160	7	3	95	80	0	0
Shoulder, whole, no marbling, braised, 3 oz	170	5	1.5	110	80	0	0
Shoulder, whole, no marbling, roasted, 3 oz	140	6	2	95	80	0	0
Sirloin, marbled fat, braised, 3 oz	210	11	4.5	90	70	0	0
Sirloin, marbled fat, roasted, 3 oz	170	9	4	85	70	0	0
Sirloin, no marbling, braised, 3 oz	170	6	1.5	95	70	0	0
Sirloin, no marbling, roasted, 3 oz	140	5	2	90	70	0	0

AT A GLANCE: VEAL

Choose cuts of veal with less than 9 grams of total fat, 4 grams of saturated fat, and 80 milligrams of cholesterol. Cuts labeled "loin/leg" are lean choices when trimmed.

VEAL ALTERNATIVE

	CAL (g)	FAT (g)	SAT FAT (g)	CHOL (mg)	SODIUM (mg)	CARB (g)	FIBER (g)
Veelets, frozen, Worthington, pattie	180	9	1.5	0	390	10	5

PRODUCE

	CAL (g)	FAT (g)	SAT FAT (g)	CHOL (mg)	SODIUM (mg)	CARB (g)	FIBER (g)
FRUIT *See also Dried Foods & Mixes, Fruit.*							
Apple, with skin, 1 medium	80	0.5	0	0	0	21	4
Apple, without skin, 1 medium	70	0	0	0	0	19	2
Apple, without skin, boiled, ½ cup slices	45	0	0	0	0	12	2
Apple, without skin, microwaved, ½ cup slices	50	0	0	0	0	12	2
Apricot, 1 fruit	20	0	0	0	0	4	<1
Avocado, California, ½ avocado	150	15	2.5	0	10	6	3
Avocado, Florida, ¼ avocado	90	7	1.5	0	0	7	4
Banana, 1 fruit	100	0.5	0	0	0	27	3
Blackberry, ¾ cup	60	0	0	0	0	14	5
Blueberry, ¾ cup	60	0	0	0	10	15	3
Carambola (starfruit), 1 fruit	40	0.5	0	0	0	10	3
Carissa (natal plum), 1 fruit	15	0	0	0	0	3	na
Cherimoya, ¼ fruit	130	0.5	0	0	na	33	3
Cherry, sour, red, 1 cup whole	50	0	0	0	0	13	1
Cherry, sweet, 20 fruits	100	1.5	0	0	0	22	3
Coconut, 1 oz	100	10	8	0	5	4	3
Crabapple, ½ cup	40	0	0	0	0	11	<1
Cranberry, ½ cup whole	25	0	0	0	0	6	2
Currant, European, black, ½ cup	35	0	0	0	0	9	4
Currant, red or white, ½ cup	35	0	0	0	0	8	2
Custard apple (bullock's heart), 5 oz	140	1	0	0	5	35	5
Elderberry, ½ cup	50	0	0	0	na	14	5
Feijoa (pineapple guava), 1 fruit	25	0	0	0	0	5	
Fig, 1 cup	110	0	0	0	0	28	5
Gooseberry, ½ cup	35	0	0	0	0	8	
Grape, American (slip skin variety), 20 fruits	30	0	0	0	0	8	

FRUIT	CAL (g)	FAT (g)	SAT FAT (g)	CHOL (mg)	SODIUM (mg)	CARB (g)	FIBER (g)
Grape, European (adherent skin variety), 20 fruits	70	0.5	0	0	0	18	1
Grapefruit, pink or red, California or Arizona, ½ fruit	50	0	0	0	0	14	2
Grapefruit, pink or red, Florida, ½ fruit	40	0	0	0	0	11	2
Grapefruit, white, California, ½ fruit	50	0	0	0	0	14	2
Grapefruit, white, Florida, ½ fruit	45	0	0	0	0	12	2
Ground-cherry (cape gooseberry), ½ cup	40	0	0	0	na	8	<1
Guava, 1 fruit	45	0.5	0	0	0	11	5
Guava, strawberry, 1 fruit	0	0	0	0	0	1	na
Jackfruit, 5 oz	130	0	0	0	0	34	2
Java-plum (jambolan), 1 fruit	0	0	0	0	0	0	0
Jujube (Chinese date), 5 oz	110	0	0	0	0	28	2
Kiwifruit (Chinese gooseberry), 1 medium	45	0	0	0	0	11	3
Kumquat, 1 fruit	15	0	0	0	0	3	1
Lemon, without peel, 1 medium	20	0	0	0	0	5	2
Lemon peel, 1 tsp	0	0	0	0	0	0	0
Lime, 1 fruit	20	0	0	0	0	7	2
Litchi, 1 fruit	5	0	0	0	0	2	0
Longan (dragon's eye), 31 fruits	60	0	0	0	0	15	1
Loquat (Japanese medlar, Japanse plum), 1 fruit	0	0	0	0	0	1	0
Mango, 1 fruit	130	0.5	0	0	0	35	4
Melon, cantaloupe, 1 cup	60	0	0	0	15	13	1
Melon, casaba, 1 cup	45	0	0	0	20	11	1
Melon, honeydew, 1 cup	60	0	0	0	20	16	1
Mulberry, 20 fruits	10	0	0	0	0	2	<1
Nectarine, 1 fruit	70	1	0	0	0	16	2
Orange, California, navel, medium	60	0	0	0	0	16	2

FRUIT	CAL (g)	FAT (g)	SAT FAT (g)	CHOL (mg)	SODIUM (mg)	CARB (g)	FIBER (g)
Orange, California, Valencia, 1 medium	60	0	0	0	0	14	2
Orange, Florida, 1 medium	70	0	0	0	0	17	4
Orange peel, 1 tsp	0	0	0	0	0	<1	0
Papaya, ½ fruit	60	0	0	0	5	15	3
Passion fruit (granadilla), purple, 1 fruit	20	0	0	0	5	4	2
Peach, 1 fruit	40	0	0	0	0	10	2
Pear, 1 fruit	100	1	0	0	0	25	4
Pear, Asian, 1 fruit	50	0	0	0	0	13	4
Persimmon, Fuyu, 1 fruit	35	0	0	0	0	8	0
Persimmon, Japanese (Hachiya), 1 fruit	120	0	0	0	0	31	6
Pineapple, diced, 1 cup	80	0.5	0	0	0	19	2
Pitanga (surinam cherry), 1 fruit	0	0	0	0	0	<1	0
Plantain, 1 fruit	220	1	0	0	10	57	4
Plum, 1 fruit	35	0	0	0	0	9	<1
Pomegranate, 1 fruit	100	0	0	0	0	26	<1
Pomelo (pummelo), ½ fruit	120	0	0	0	0	29	3
Prickly pear (cactus pear), 1 fruit	40	0.5	0	0	5	10	4
Quince, 1 fruit	50	0	0	0	0	14	2
Raspberry, ½ cup	30	0	0	0	0	7	4
Rhubarb, diced, ½ cup	10	0	0	0	0	2	<1
Sapodilla, ½ fruit	70	1	0	0	10	17	5
Sapote (marmalade plum), ½ fruit	150	0.5	0	0	10	38	3
Soursop, ¼ fruit	100	0.5	0	0	20	26	5
Strawberry, 1 cup	45	0.5	0	0	0	10	3
Sweetsop (sugar apple), ½ fruit	70	0	0	0	5	19	3
Tamarind (Indian date), 1 fruit	0	0	0	0	0	1	0
Tangerine, 1 fruit	40	0	0	0	0	9	2
Watermelon, 1 cup	50	0.5	0	0	0	12	<1

	CAL (g)	FAT (g)	SAT FAT (g)	CHOL (mg)	SODIUM (mg)	CARB (g)	FIBER (g)
SPROUTS							
Alfalfa, Arrowhead Mills, 1 cup	30	0.5	0	0	5	4	2
Kidney bean, 1 cup	50	1	0	0	10	8	na
Kidney bean, cooked, ½ cup	30	0.5	0	0	5	4	na
Lentil, raw, 1 cup	80	0	0	0	10	17	na
Mung bean, 1 cup	30	0	0	0	5	6	2
Mung bean, boiled, ½ cup	15	0	0	0	5	3	<1
Navy bean, 1 cup	70	1	0	0	15	14	na
Navy bean, boiled, ½ cup	70	1	0	0	15	14	na
Pea, ½ cup	80	0	0	0	15	17	na
Pea, boiled, ½ cup	90	0	0	0	0	18	na
Pinto bean, 1 cup	120	2	0	0	300	22	na
Pinto bean, boiled, ½ cup	20	0	0	0	45	4	na
Radish, 1 cup	15	1	0	0	0	1	0
Soybean, 10 sprouts	15	1	0	0	0	<1	0
Soybean, steamed, ½ cup	40	2	0	0	0	3	0
VEGETABLES							
Amaranth greens, 1 cup	10	0	0	0	5	1	<1
Amaranth greens, boiled, ½ cup	15	0	0	0	15	3	1
Arrowhead, 1 medium corm	15	0	0	0	0	2	na
Arrowhead, boiled, 1 medium corm	10	0	0	0	0	2	na
Artichoke (globe or French), 1 medium	60	0	0	0	120	13	7
Artichoke (globe or French), boiled, 1 medium	60	0	0	0	115	13	6
Artichoke, Jerusalem, ½ cup	60	0	0	0	0	13	1
Arugula, 1 leaf	0	0	0	0	0	0	na
Asparagus, 1 cup	30	0	0	0	0	6	3
Asparagus, boiled, ½ cup	25	0	0	0	10	4	2
Balsam pear, leafy tips, ½ cup	10	0	0	0	0	1	<1
Balsam pear, leafy tips, boiled, ½ cup	10	0	0	0	0	2	<1

VEGETABLES	CAL (g)	FAT (g)	SAT FAT (g)	CHOL (mg)	SODIUM (mg)	CARB (g)	FIBER (g)
Balsam pear, pods, 1 cup	15	0	0	0	0	3	3
Balsam pear, pods, boiled, ½ cup	5	0	0	0	0	1	<1
Bamboo shoot, ½ cup	20	0	0	0	0	4	2
Bamboo shoot, boiled, ½ cup	10	0	0	0	0	1	<1
Bean, cowpea, ½ cup	70	0	0	0	0	14	4
Bean, cowpea, boiled, ½ cup	80	0	0	0	0	17	4
Bean, cowpea, leafy tips, 1 cup chopped	10	0	0	0	0	2	na
Bean, cowpea, leafy tips, boiled, ½ cup	5	0	0	0	0	<1	0
Bean, cowpea, pods with seeds, ½ cup	20	0	0	0	0	10	0
Bean, cowpea, pods with seeds, boiled, ½ cup	15	0	0	0	0	3	na
Bean, fava (broadbean), ½ cup	40	0	0	0	0	6	2
Bean, fava (broadbean), boiled, ½ cup	50	0	0	0	35	9	na
Bean, green, snap, ½ cup	15	0	0	0	0	4	2
Bean, green, snap, boiled, ½ cup	20	0	0	0	0	5	2
Bean, lima, ½ cup	90	0.5	0	0	5	16	4
Bean, lima, boiled, ½ cup	110	0	0	0	15	20	5
Bean, soybean, green, ½ cup	190	9	1	0	20	14	5
Bean, soybean, green, boiled, ½ cup	130	6	0.5	0	15	10	4
Bean, winged, ½ cup	10	0	0	0	0	<1	0
Bean, winged, boiled, ½ cup	25	0	0	0	0	2	na
Bean, winged, leaves, 3.5 oz	70	1	0	0	10	14	2
Bean, winged, tuber, 3.5 oz	160	1	0	0	35	28	7
Bean, yambean, 1 slice	0	0	0	0	0	<1	0
Bean, yambean, boiled, ½ cup	25	0	0	0	0	6	<1
Bean, yard-long, ½ cup	20	0	0	0	0	4	na
Bean, yard-long, boiled, ½ cup	25	0	0	0	0	5	na
Bean, yellow, snap, ½ cup	15	0	0	0	0	4	<1

VEGETABLES	CAL (g)	FAT (g)	SAT FAT (g)	CHOL (mg)	SODIUM (mg)	CARB (g)	FIBER (g)
Bean, yellow, snap, boiled, ½ cup	20	0	0	0	0	5	<1
Beet, ½ cup	30	0	0	0	50	7	2
Beet, boiled, ½ cup	40	0	0	0	65	9	1
Beet greens, 1 cup	10	0	0	0	75	2	1
Beet greens, boiled, ½ cup	20	0	0	0	170	4	2
Borage, ½ cup	10	0	0	0	35	2	0
Borage, boiled, 3.5 oz	25	1	0	0	90	4	1
Breadfruit, ¼ breadfruit	100	0	0	0	0	26	5
Broccoli, ½ cup	10	0	0	0	10	3	2
Broccoli, boiled, ½ cup	25	0	0	0	20	4	2
Brussels sprout, boiled, ½ cup	30	0	0	0	15	7	3
Burdock root, ½ cup	45	0	0	0	0	11	2
Burdock root, boiled, ½ cup	60	0	0	0	0	13	1
Butterbur (fuki), 1 petiole	0	0	0	0	0	0	1
Butterbur (fuki), boiled, 3.5 oz	10	0	0	0	0	2	1
Cabbage, 1 cup	20	0	0	0	15	4	2
Cabbage, boiled, ½ cup	20	0	0	0	5	3	2
Cabbage, Chinese (bok choy), 1 cup	10	0	0	0	45	2	<1
Cabbage, Chinese (bok choy), boiled, ½ cup	10	0	0	0	30	2	1
Cabbage, Chinese (pe-tsai), 1 cup	15	0	0	0	10	2	<1
Cabbage, Chinese (pe-tsai), boiled, ½ cup	10	0	0	0	5	1	1
Cabbage, red, 1 cup	20	0	0	0	10	4	1
Cabbage, red, boiled, ½ cup	15	0	0	0	5	3	2
Cabbage, savoy, 1 cup	20	0	0	0	20	4	2
Cabbage, savoy, boiled, ½ cup	20	0	0	0	20	4	2
Cardoon, ½ cup	20	0	0	0	150	5	1
Cardoon, boiled, 3.5 oz	25	0	0	0	180	5	na
Carrot, ½ cup	25	0	0	0	20	6	2
Carrot, baby, 1 medium	0	0	0	0	0	<1	0

VEGETABLES	CAL (g)	FAT (g)	SAT FAT (g)	CHOL (mg)	SODIUM (mg)	CARB (g)	FIBER (g)
Carrot, boiled, ½ cup	35	0	0	0	50	8	3
Cassava, 3.5 oz	120	0	0	0	10	27	2
Cauliflower, ½ cup	5	0	0	0	10	1	<1
Cauliflower, boiled, ½ cup	10	0	0	0	0	1	<1
Celeriac, ½ cup	30	0	0	0	80	7	1
Celeriac, boiled, 3.5 oz	25	0	0	0	60	6	4
Celery, 1 stalk	5	0	0	0	35	1	<1
Celery, boiled, ½ cup	15	0	0	0	70	3	1
Chard, Swiss, 1 cup	10	0	0	0	80	1	<1
Chard, Swiss, ½ cup	20	0	0	0	160	4	2
Chayote, 1 cup	35	0	0	0	5	7	4
Chayote, boiled, ½ cup	10	0	0	0	0	2	<1
Chicory, greens, 1 cup	40	0.5	0	0	80	8	7
Chicory, roots, 1 cup	35	0	0	0	25	8	<1
Chicory, witloof, 1 cup	15	0	0	0	0	4	3
Chives, 1 tsp	0	0	0	0	0	0	0
Collard, 1 cup	10	0	0	0	10	3	1
Collard, boiled, ½ cup	20	0	0	0	10	4	1
Coriander, ¼ cup	0	0	0	0	0	0	0
Corn, sweet, white, ½ cup	70	1	0	0	15	15	2
Corn, sweet, white, boiled, ½ cup	90	1	0	0	15	21	5
Corn, sweet, yellow, ½ cup	70	1	0	0	15	15	2
Corn, sweet, yellow, boiled, ½ cup	90	1	0	0	15	21	2
Cornsalad, 1 cup	15	0	0	0	0	2	na
Cress, garden, 1 sprig	0	0	0	0	0	0	0
Cress, garden, boiled, ½ cup	15	0	0	0	5	3	0
Cucumber, ½ cup	10	0	0	0	0	2	0
Dandelion greens, 1 cup	25	0	0	0	45	5	2
Dandelion greens, boiled, ½ cup	20	0	0	0	25	3	2
Dock, 1 cup	30	1	0	0	5	4	4
Dock, boiled, 3.5 oz	20	0.5	0	0	0	3	na
Eggplant, ½ cup	5	0	0	0	0	2	<1

VEGETABLES	CAL (g)	FAT (g)	SAT FAT (g)	CHOL (mg)	SODIUM (mg)	CARB (g)	FIBER (g)
Eggplant, boiled, ½ cup	10	0	0	0	0	2	<1
Endive, 1 cup chopped	10	0	0	0	10	2	2
Eppaw, ½ cup	80	1	na	0	5	16	na
Fennel, bulb, ½ cup	15	0	0	0	25	3	2
Garlic, 1 clove	0	0	0	0	0	<1	0
Ginger root, ¼ cup	20	0	0	0	0	4	0
Gourd, dishcloth (towelgourd), ½ cup	10	0	0	0	0	2	na
Gourd, dishcloth (towelgourd), boiled, ½ cup	25	0	0	0	10	6	na
Gourd, white-flowered (calabash), ½ cup	0	0	0	0	0	1	0
Gourd, white-flowered (calabash), boiled, ½ cup	5	0	0	0	0	1	0
Horseradish tree, leafy tips, ½ cup	10	0	0	0	0	1	0
Horseradish tree, leafy tips, boiled, ½ cup	15	0	0	0	0	2	0
Horseradish tree, pods, 1 pod	0	0	0	0	0	<1	0
Horseradish tree, pods, boiled, ½ cup	20	0	0	0	25	5	2
Kale, 1 cup	35	0	0	0	30	7	1
Kale, boiled, ½ cup	20	0	0	0	15	4	1
Kale, Scotch, 1 cup	30	0	0	0	50	6	na
Kale, Scotch, boiled, ½ cup	20	0	0	0	30	4	1
Kohlrabi (bulblike stem), ½ cup	20	0	0	0	15	5	3
Kohlrabi (bulblike stem), boiled, ½ cup	25	0	0	0	20	5	<1
Lambsquarter, 3.5 oz	45	1	0	0	45	7	4
Lambsquarter, boiled, ½ cup	30	0.5	0	0	25	5	2
Leek (bulb and lower leaf portion), ½ cup	35	0	0	0	10	8	<1
Leek (bulb and lower leaf portion), boiled, ½ cup	15	0	0	0	5	4	2
Lettuce, Boston or bibb types, leaves	0	0	0	0	0	0	0

VEGETABLES	CAL (g)	FAT (g)	SAT FAT (g)	CHOL (mg)	SODIUM (mg)	CARB (g)	FIBER (g)
Lettuce, butter, 1 head	20	0	0	0	10	4	2
Lettuce, iceberg, ⅙ head	20	0	0	0	10	4	1
Lettuce, leaf, 1½ cups shredded	10	0	0	0	40	1	1
Lettuce, romaine (cos), 1½ cups shredded	20	1	0	0	40	2	1
Lotus root, 10 slices	45	0	0	0	35	14	4
Lotus root, boiled, 10 slices	60	0	0	0	40	14	3
Mountain yam, Hawaii, ½ cup	45	0	0	0	10	11	na
Mountain yam, Hawaii, steamed, ½ cup	60	0	0	0	10	14	2
Mushroom, ½ cup	10	0	0	0	0	2	0
Mushroom, boiled, ½ cup	20	0	0	0	0	4	2
Mushroom, enoki (enokitake), 1 medium	0	0	0	0	0	0	0
Mushroom, Shiitake, 4 mushrooms	40	0	0	0	0	10	2
Mustard greens, 1 cup	15	0	0	0	15	3	1
Mustard greens, boiled, ½ cup	10	0	0	0	10	1	1
Okra, ½ cup	20	0	0	0	0	4	1
Okra, boiled, ½ cup	25	0	0	0	0	6	2
Onion, ½ cup	30	0	0	0	0	7	1
Onion, boiled, ½ cup	45	0	0	0	0	11	1
Onion, spring (includes tops and bulb), ½ cup	15	0	0	0	10	4	1
Onion, Welsh, 3.5 oz	35	0	0	0	20	7	1
Parsley, 10 sprigs	0	0	0	0	5	<1	0
Parsnip, ½ cup	50	0	0	0	10	12	3
Parsnip, boiled, ½ cup	60	0	0	0	10	15	3
Pea, green, ½ cup	60	0	0	0	0	11	4
Pea, green, boiled, ½ cup	70	0	0	0	0	12	4
Pea, snow & sugar snap, boiled, ½ cup	35	0	0	0	0	6	2
Pepper, chili, green, hot, 1 pepper	20	0	0	0	0	4	<

VEGETABLES	CAL	FAT (g)	SAT FAT (g)	CHOL (mg)	SODIUM (mg)	CARB (g)	FIBER (g)
Pepper, chili, red, hot, 1 pepper	20	0	0	0	0	4	<1
Pepper, sweet, green, 1 pepper	20	0	0	0	0	5	1
Pepper, sweet, green, boiled, 1 pepper	20	0	0	0	0	5	<1
Pepper, sweet, red, 1 pepper	20	0	0	0	0	5	1
Pepper, sweet, red, boiled, 1 pepper	20	0	0	0	0	5	<1
Pepper, sweet, yellow, 1 large pepper	50	0	0	0	0	12	4
Pokeberry shoot (poke), ½ cup	20	0	0	0	20	3	1
Pokeberry shoot (poke), boiled, ½ cup	15	0	0	0	15	3	1
Potato, baked, flesh & skin, 1 potato	220	0	0	0	15	51	5
Potato, baked, flesh only, ½ cup	60	0	0	0	0	13	<1
Potato, baked, skin only, 1 potato	110	0	0	0	15	27	2
Potato, boiled in skin, flesh only, ½ cup	70	0	0	0	0	16	1
Potato, boiled in skin, skin only, 1 potato	30	0	0	0	0	6	na
Potato, boiled without skin, ½ cup	70	0	0	0	0	16	1
Potato, microwaved, flesh & skin, 1 potato	210	0	0	0	15	49	na
Potato, microwaved with skin, flesh only, ½ cup	80	0	0	0	5	18	na
Potato, microwaved with skin, skin only, 1 potato	80	0	0	0	10	17	na
Potato, raw, flesh, 1 cup	120	0	0	0	10	27	2
Potato, raw, skin, 1 potato	25	0	0	0	0	5	na
Potherb (Jute), 1 cup	10	0	0	0	0	2	0
Potherb (Jute), boiled, ½ cup	15	0	0	0	0	3	<1
Pumpkin, ½ cup	10	0	0	0	0	2	<1

VEGETABLES	CAL	FAT (g)	SAT FAT (g)	CHOL (mg)	SODIUM (mg)	CARB (g)	FIBER (g)
Pumpkin, boiled, ½ cup mashed	25	0	0	0	0	6	1
Pumpkin, flowers, 1 cup	0	0	0	0	0	1	0
Pumpkin, flowers, boiled, ½ cup	10	0	0	0	0	2	<1
Pumpkin, leaves, 1 cup	10	0	0	0	0	<1	0
Pumpkin, leaves, boiled, ½ cup	10	0	0	0	0	1	<1
Purslane, 1 cup	10	0	0	0	20	1	0
Purslane, boiled, ½ cup	10	0	0	0	25	2	0
Radicchio, 1 medium head	0	0	0	0	0	0	0
Radish, 1 medium	10	0	0	0	10	2	<1
Radish, Oriental, 1 long	60	0	0	0	70	14	5
Radish, Oriental, boiled, ½ cup slices	15	0	0	0	10	3	1
Radish, white icicle, 1 radish	0	0	0	0	0	0	0
Rutabaga, ½ cup	25	0	0	0	15	6	2
Rutabaga, boiled, ½ cup cubes	35	0	0	0	20	7	2
Salsify (oyster plant), ½ cup	60	0	0	0	15	13	2
Salsify (oyster plant), boiled, ½ cup slices	45	0	0	0	10	10	2
Seaweed, agar, ½ cup	10	0	0	0	0	3	0
Seaweed, Irishmoss, ½ cup	20	0	0	0	30	5	<1
Seaweed, kelp, ½ cup	20	0	0	0	95	4	<1
Seaweed, laver, ½ cup	15	0	0	0	20	2	0
Seaweed, spirulina, ½ cup	10	0	0	0	40	1	0
Seaweed, wakame, 1 oz	15	0	0	0	250	3	0
Sesbania flower, 1 flower	0	0	0	0	0	0	
Sesbania flower, steamed, ½ cup	10	0	0	0	5	3	
Shallot, 1 Tbsp	10	0	0	0	0	2	
Spinach, 1 cup	15	0	0	0	45	2	
Spinach, boiled, ½ cup	20	0	0	0	65	3	

VEGETABLES	CAL (g)	FAT (g)	SAT FAT (g)	CHOL (mg)	SODIUM (mg)	CARB (g)	FIBER (g)
Spinach, mustard (tendergreen), 1 cup	35	0	0	0	35	6	0
Spinach, mustard (tendergreen), boiled, ½ cup	15	0	0	0	15	3	0
Spinach, New Zealand, 1 cup	10	0	0	0	75	1	0
Spinach, New Zealand, boiled, ½ cup	10	0	0	0	100	2	0
Squash, summer, crookneck or straightneck, ½ cup	15	0	0	0	0	3	1
Squash, summer, crookneck or straightneck, boiled, ½ cup	20	0	0	0	0	4	1
Squash, summer, scallop, ½ cup	15	0	0	0	0	3	<1
Squash, summer, scallop, boiled, ½ cup	15	0	0	0	0	3	1
Squash, summer, zucchini with skin, ½ cup	10	0	0	0	0	2	<1
Squash, summer, zucchini with skin, boiled, ½ cup	15	0	0	0	0	4	1
Squash, winter, acorn, ½ cup	30	0	0	0	0	8	na
Squash, winter, acorn, baked, ½ cup	60	0	0	0	0	15	4
Squash, winter, acorn, boiled, mashed, ½ cup	40	0	0	0	0	11	3
Squash, winter, butternut, ½ cup	35	0	0	0	0	8	na
Squash, winter, butternut, baked, ½ cup	40	0	0	0	0	11	3
Squash, winter, hubbard, ½ cup	25	0	0	0	0	5	na
Squash, winter, hubbard, baked, ½ cup	50	0.5	0	0	10	11	3
Squash, winter, hubbard, boiled, mashed, ½ cup	35	0	0	0	5	8	3
Squash, winter, spaghetti, ½ cup	20	0	0	0	10	4	na
Squash, winter, spaghetti, boiled or baked, ½ cup	25	0	0	0	15	5	1

VEGETABLES	CAL (g)	FAT (g)	SAT FAT (g)	CHOL (mg)	SODIUM (mg)	CARB (g)	FIBER (g)
Succotash, 3.5 oz	100	1	0	0	0	20	na
Succotash, boiled, ½ cup	110	1	0	0	15	23	5
Swamp cabbage (skunk cabbage), 1 shoot	0	0	0	0	15	0	0
Swamp cabbage (skunk cabbage), boiled, ½ cup	10	0	0	0	60	2	<1
Sweet potato, baked in skin, ½ cup	100	0	0	0	10	24	3
Sweet potato, boiled without skin, ½ cup	170	0	0	0	20	40	4
Sweet potato, raw, 1 medium	15	0	0	0	0	3	0
Sweet potato leaves, 1 leaf	5	0	0	0	0	1	0
Sweet potato leaves, steamed, ½ cup	10	0	0	0	0	2	<1
Taro, ½ cup	60	0	0	0	5	14	2
Taro, leaves, 1 leaf	0	0	0	0	0	<1	0
Taro, leaves, steamed, ½ cup	20	0	0	0	0	3	na
Taro, root (poi), ½ cup	130	0	0	0	15	33	0
Taro, shoots, 1 cup	10	0	0	0	0	2	na
Taro, shoots, cooked, ½ cup	10	0	0	0	0	2	na
Taro, Tahitian, ½ cup	25	0.5	0	0	30	5	na
Taro, Tahitian, cooked, ½ cup	30	0	0	0	40	5	na
Tomatillo, 1 medium	10	0	0	0	0	2	<1
Tomato, boiled, ½ cup	35	0	0	0	15	7	1
Tomato, green, 1 tomato	30	0	0	0	15	6	2
Tomato, red, 1 tomato	25	0	0	0	10	6	1
Tomato, sun-dried, ¼ cup	35	0	0	0	280	8	2
Tomato, sun-dried, packed in oil, drained, ¼ cup	60	4	0.5	0	75	6	2
Tree fern, cooked, ½ cup	30	0	0	0	0	8	3
Turnip, ½ cup	20	0	0	0	45	4	1
Turnip greens, 1 cup	15	0	0	0	25	3	1
Turnip greens, boiled, ½ cup	15	0	0	0	20	3	2

VEGETABLES	CAL (g)	FAT (g)	SAT FAT (g)	CHOL (mg)	SODIUM (mg)	CARB (g)	FIBER (g)
Turnip, boiled, ½ cup	15	0	0	0	40	4	2
Vinespinach (basella), 1 cup	20	0	0	0	25	3	na
Water chestnut, Chinese (matai), 4 waterchestnuts	40	0	0	0	5	9	1
Watercress, 1 sprig	0	0	0	0	0	0	0
Waxgourd (Chinese preserving melon), ½ cup	10	0	0	0	75	2	2
Waxgourd (Chinese preserving melon), boiled, ½ cup	10	0	0	0	95	3	<1
Yam, ½ cup	90	0	0	0	10	21	3
Yam, boiled or baked, ½ cup	80	0	0	0	5	19	3

VEGETABLE MIX

	CAL	FAT	SAT FAT	CHOL	SODIUM	CARB	FIBER
California style, Dole, 3 oz	30	1	0	0	190	5	2
Garden style, Dole, 3 oz	30	0.5	0	0	40	4	2
Italian style, Dole, 3 oz	25	0.5	0	0	280	3	3
New England mix, Dole, 3 oz	50	0.5	0	0	30	9	2
Oriental style, Dole, 3 oz	30	0.5	0	0	45	4	2

VEGETABLES, SALAD MIX

	CAL	FAT	SAT FAT	CHOL	SODIUM	CARB	FIBER
Caesar Salad-In-A-Minute, Dole, 3.5 oz	170	14	1.5	5	480	9	1
Classic blend salad mix, Dole, 3.5 oz	25	1	0	0	20	4	1
Coleslaw blend salad mix, Dole, 3.5 oz	30	0.5	0	0	35	5	2
French blend salad mix, Dole, 3.5 oz	25	0.5	0	0	15	4	1
Italian blend salad mix, Dole, 3.5 oz	25	1	0	0	45	3	1
Oriental Salad-In-A-Minute, Dole, 3.5 oz	110	7	1	0	290	12	2
Spinach Salad-In-A-Minute, Dole, 3.5 oz	180	9	1.5	0	660	19	3

SEAFOOD

	CAL (g)	FAT (g)	SAT FAT (g)	CHOL (mg)	SODIUM (mg)	CARB (g)	FIBER (g)
FRESHWATER & SALTWATER FISH							

Dry heat cooking methods are broiling, grilling, baking, or microwaving without added salt or fat.

	CAL (g)	FAT (g)	SAT FAT (g)	CHOL (mg)	SODIUM (mg)	CARB (g)	FIBER (g)
Ahi (bigeye tuna), raw, 3 oz	90	1	0	40	30	0	0
Anchovy, raw, 3 oz	110	4	na	na	90	0	0
Bass, freshwater, mixed species, cooked, dry heat, 3 oz	120	4	1	75	80	0	0
Bass, striped, cooked, dry heat, 3 oz	110	2.5	0.5	90	75	0	0
Bluefish, cooked, dry heat, 3 oz	140	4.5	1	65	65	0	0
Burbot, cooked, dry heat, 3 oz	100	1	0	65	105	0	0
Butterfish, cooked, dry heat, 3 oz	160	9	na	70	100	0	0
Carp, cooked, dry heat, 3 oz	140	6	1	70	55	0	0
Catfish, channel, farmed, cooked, dry heat, 3 oz	130	7	1.5	55	70	0	0
Catfish, channel, wild, cooked, dry heat, 3 oz	90	2.5	0.5	60	45	0	0
Caviar, black or red, granular, 3 oz	210	15	3.5	500	1280	3	0
Cisco, smoked, 3 oz	150	10	1.5	25	410	0	0
Cod, Atlantic, cooked, dry heat, 3 oz	90	1	0	45	65	0	0
Cod, Atlantic, dried & salted, 3 oz	250	2	0	130	5970	0	0
Cod, cakes, frozen, Gorton's, 4 oz	100	0.5	0	15	640	16	0
Cod, fillet, Mrs. Paul's Premium Fillets, 1 fillet	250	11	3	40	510	24	2
Cod, fillet, lightly breaded, frozen, Van de Kamp's, 1 fillet	220	10	1.5	35	410	19	0
Cod, Pacific, cooked, dry heat, 3 oz	90	1	0	40	80	0	0

FRESHWATER & SALTWATER FISH	CAL (g)	FAT (g)	SAT FAT (g)	CHOL (mg)	SODIUM (mg)	CARB (g)	FIBER (g)
Cusk, cooked, dry heat, 3 oz	100	1	0	45	35	0	0
Dolphinfish, cooked, dry heat, 3 oz	90	1	0	80	100	0	0
Drum, freshwater, cooked, dry heat, 3 oz	130	5	1	70	80	0	0
Eel, cooked, dry heat, 3 oz	200	13	2.5	135	55	0	0
Fish fillet, batter dipped, frozen, Fisher Boy, 1 fillet	170	9	2	20	310	15	0
Fish fillet, batter dipped, frozen, Mrs. Paul's, 1 fillet	170	11	3	15	460	13	1
Fish fillet, battered, frozen, Van de Kamp's, 1 fillet	180	11	1.5	20	340	12	0
Fish fillet, breaded, frozen, Mrs. Paul's Healthy Treasures, 3 oz fillet	130	3	1	25	220	16	1
Fish fillet, breaded, frozen, Mrs. Paul's Healthy Treasures, 4 oz fillet	170	3	2	30	290	21	2
Fish fillet, breaded, frozen, Van de Kamp's, 2 fillets	280	19	3	35	270	17	0
Fish fillet, breaded, frozen, Van de Kamp's Crisp & Healthy, 2 fillets	150	2.5	0.5	30	380	20	0
Fish fillet, crispy batter, frozen, Gorton's, 2 fillets	290	21	4	25	550	16	0
Fish fillet, crispy batter, lemon pepper, frozen, Gorton's, 2 fillets	250	16	2	35	630	18	0
Fish fillet, crispy crunchy batter, frozen, Mrs. Paul's, 2 fillets	220	10	3	35	490	21	2
Fish fillet, crispy crunchy breaded, frozen, Mrs. Paul's, 2 fillets	220	10	3	35	490	21	2
Fish fillet, crunchy batter, frozen, Mrs. Paul's, 2 fillets	250	13	3	25	680	23	2
Fish fillet, crunchy breaded, frozen, Gorton's, 2 fillets	250	14	1.5	35	490	21	0
Fish fillet, crunchy breaded, garlic 'n herb, frozen, Gorton's, 2 fillets	250	14	1.5	35	720	20	0

FRESHWATER & SALTWATER FISH	CAL	FAT (g)	SAT FAT (g)	CHOL (mg)	SODIUM (mg)	CARB (g)	FIBER (g)
Fish fillet, crunchy breaded, hot 'n spicy, frozen, Gorton's, 2 fillets	250	14	1.5	30	620	19	0
Fish fillet, crunchy breaded, Southern fried country style, frozen, Gorton's, 2 fillets	270	16	2	30	660	20	0
Fish fillet, fried, frozen, Weight Watchers, 7.7 oz	230	8	2.5	25	450	25	2
Fish fillet, grilled, Italian herb, frozen, Gorton's, 1 fillet	130	6	1	60	310	1	0
Fish fillet, grilled, lemon pepper, frozen, Gorton's, 1 fillet	120	6	1	60	160	1	0
Fish nuggets, battered, frozen, Van de Kamp's, 8 pieces	280	18	2.5	25	600	20	0
Fish portions, batter dipped, frozen, Gorton's Value Pack, 1 portion	160	10	2	20	400	12	0
Fish portions, battered, frozen, Van de Kamp's, 2 pieces	350	22	3.5	35	710	26	0
Fish portions, breaded, frozen, Van de Kamp's, 3 pieces	330	21	3	35	410	23	0
Fish portions, crunchy breaded, frozen, Gorton's Value Pack, 1 portion	180	12	3	15	350	11	0
Fish portions, frozen, Fisher Boy, 2 portions	250	13	3	15	590	21	1
Fish shapes, breaded, frozen, Mrs. Paul's Sea Pals, 5 pieces	190	9	3	20	320	18	1
Fish sticks, 0.5 oz stick, frozen, Fisher Boy, 6 sticks	170	8	2	15	400	14	1
Fish sticks, 0.8 oz stick, frozen, Fisher Boy, 5 sticks	230	11	3	15	530	19	2
Fish sticks, battered, frozen, Mrs. Paul's, 6 sticks	240	15	4	25	720	19	1
Fish sticks, battered, frozen, Van de Kamp's, 6 sticks	260	16	3	30	540	18	0
Fish sticks, breaded, frozen, Gorton's Value Pack, 6 sticks	220	12	1	25	380	18	0

FRESHWATER & SALTWATER FISH	CAL	FAT (g)	SAT FAT (g)	CHOL (mg)	SODIUM (mg)	CARB (g)	FIBER (g)
Fish sticks, breaded, 20-count pkg, frozen, Gorton's Value Pack, 5 sticks	220	8	2	20	470	25	0
Fish sticks, breaded, frozen, Mrs. Paul's Healthy Treasures, 4 sticks	170	3	2	20	350	20	2
Fish sticks, breaded, frozen, Van de Kamp's, 6 sticks	290	17	2.5	35	390	23	0
Fish sticks, breaded, frozen, Van de Kamp's Crisp & Healthy, 6 sticks	180	3	0.5	25	440	26	0
Fish sticks, breaded, mini, frozen, Van de Kamp's, 13 sticks	250	14	2	30	330	19	0
Fish sticks, crispy, frozen, Booth, 6 sticks	220	11	2.5	25	380	19	1
Fish sticks, crispy batter, frozen, Gorton's, 5 sticks	290	20	5	20	600	18	0
Fish sticks, crispy crunchy breaded, frozen, Mrs. Paul's, 5 sticks	210	9	3	20	570	20	2
Fish sticks, crunchy breaded, frozen, Gorton's, 6 sticks	260	15	1.5	30	470	21	0
Fish sticks, mini, 18-count package, frozen, Gorton's Value Pack, 13 sticks	230	13	4	25	440	18	0
Fish sticks, mini, frozen, Gorton's Value Pack, 13 sticks	230	14	1.5	25	390	17	0
Fish sticks, minis, frozen, Mrs. Paul's, 12 minis	220	11	3	30	330	20	2
Fish sticks, with bread crumb coating, frozen, Mrs. Paul's, 6 sticks	200	9	3	20	510	20	2
Flounder, cooked, dry heat, 3 oz	100	1	0	60	90	0	0
Flounder, fillet, crunchy batter, frozen, Mrs. Paul's, 2 fillets	260	14	3	30	540	24	2
Flounder, fillet, frozen, Mrs. Paul's Premium Fillets, 1 fillet	170	8	3	25	370	16	1
Flounder, fillet, frozen, Van de Kamp's, 1 fillet	110	2	0	45	105	0	0

FRESHWATER & SALTWATER FISH	CAL	FAT (g)	SAT FAT (g)	CHOL (mg)	SODIUM (mg)	CARB (g)	FIBER (g)
Flounder, fillet, lightly breaded, frozen, Van de Kamp's, 1 fillet	230	11	1.5	40	400	19	0
Gefiltefish, sweet recipe, 3 oz	70	1.5	0	25	450	6	0
Grouper, cooked, dry heat, 3 oz	100	1	0	40	45	0	0
Haddock, cooked, dry heat, 3 oz	100	1	0	65	75	0	0
Haddock, fillet, battered, frozen, Van de Kamp's, 2 fillets	260	16	2.5	30	530	18	0
Haddock, fillet, breaded, frozen, Van de Kamp's, 2 fillets	280	17	3	25	310	19	0
Haddock, fillet, crispy batter, frozen, Gorton's, 2 fillets	270	19	4	30	610	14	0
Haddock, fillet, crunchy batter, frozen, Mrs. Paul's, 2 fillets	250	12	3	25	630	25	2
Haddock, fillet, frozen, Mrs. Paul's Premium Fillets, 1 fillet	230	11	3	35	390	17	2
Haddock, fillet, lightly breaded, frozen, Van de Kamp's, 1 fillet	220	10	1.5	30	410	19	0
Haddock, smoked, 3 oz	100	1	0	65	650	0	0
Halibut, Atlantic or Pacific, cooked, dry heat, 3 oz	120	2.5	0	35	60	0	0
Halibut, fillet, battered, frozen, Van de Kamp's, 3 fillets	300	21	3	20	520	16	0
Halibut, Greenland, cooked, dry heat, 3 oz	200	15	2.5	50	90	0	0
Herring, Atlantic, cooked, dry heat, 3 oz	170	10	2	65	100	0	0
Herring, Atlantic, kippered, 3 oz	180	11	2.5	70	780	0	0
Herring, Atlantic, pickled, 3 oz	220	15	2	10	740	8	0
Herring, Pacific, cooked, dry heat, 3 oz	210	15	3.5	85	80	0	0
Ling, cooked, dry heat, 3 oz	90	1	0	45	150	0	0

FRESHWATER & SALTWATER FISH	CAL (g)	FAT (g)	SAT FAT (g)	CHOL (mg)	SODIUM (mg)	CARB (g)	FIBER (g)
Lingcod, cooked, dry heat, 3 oz	90	1.5	0	55	65	0	0
Mackerel, Atlantic, cooked, dry heat, 3 oz	220	15	3.5	65	70	0	0
Mackerel, King, cooked, dry heat, 3 oz	110	2.5	0	60	170	0	0
Mackerel, Pacific or Jack, cooked, dry heat, 3 oz	170	9	2.5	50	95	0	0
Mackerel, Spanish, cooked, dry heat, 3 oz	130	5	1.5	60	55	0	0
Milkfish, cooked, dry heat, 3 oz	160	7	na	60	80	0	0
Monkfish, cooked, dry heat, 3 oz	80	2	na	30	20	0	0
Mullet, striped, cooked, dry heat, 3 oz	130	4	1.5	55	60	0	0
Ocean perch, Atlantic, cooked, dry heat, 3 oz	100	2	0	45	80	0	0
Orange roughy, cooked, dry heat, 3 oz	80	1	0	20	70	0	0
Perch, cooked, dry heat, 3 oz	100	1	0	100	70	0	0
Perch, fillet, battered, frozen, Van de Kamp's, 2 fillets	300	20	2.5	25	480	19	0
Pike, Northern, cooked, dry heat, 3 oz	100	1	0	45	40	0	0
Pike, Walleye, cooked, dry heat, 3 oz	100	1.5	0	95	55	0	0
Pollock, Atlantic, cooked, dry heat, 3 oz	100	1	0	75	95	0	0
Pollock, fillet, baked garlic herb, Triton, 1 pkg	210	2	1	40	710	30	6
Pollock, fillet, crispy batter, frozen, Gorton's, 2 fillets	280	19	5	20	630	16	0
Pollock, Walleye, cooked, dry heat, 3 oz	100	1	0	80	100	0	0
Pompano, Florida, cooked, dry heat, 3 oz	180	10	4	55	65	0	0
Pout, Ocean, cooked, dry heat, 3 oz	90	1	0	55	65	0	0
Rockfish, Pacific, cooked, dry heat, 3 oz	100	2	0	35	65	0	0

FRESHWATER & SALTWATER FISH	CAL (g)	FAT (g)	SAT FAT (g)	CHOL (mg)	SODIUM (mg)	CARB (g)	FIBER (g)
Roe, cooked, dry heat, 3 oz	170	7	1.5	405	100	2	0
Sablefish, cooked, dry heat, 3 oz	210	17	3.5	55	60	0	0
Sablefish, smoked, 3 oz	220	17	3.5	55	630	0	0
Salmon, Atlantic, farmed, cooked, dry heat, 3 oz	180	11	2	55	50	0	0
Salmon, Atlantic, wild, cooked, dry heat, 3 oz	150	7	1	60	50	0	0
Salmon, Chinook, cooked, dry heat, 3 oz	200	11	3	70	50	0	0
Salmon, Chinook, smoked, 3 oz	100	3.5	0.5	20	670	0	0
Salmon, Chinook, smoked (lox), 3 oz	100	3.5	0.5	20	1700	0	0
Salmon, chum, cooked, dry heat, 3 oz	130	4	1	80	55	0	0
Salmon, coho, farmed, cooked, dry heat, 3 oz	150	7	1.5	55	45	0	0
Salmon, coho, wild, cooked, dry heat, 3 oz	120	3.5	1	45	50	0	0
Salmon, coho, wild, steamed or boiled, 3 oz	160	6	1.5	50	45	0	0
Salmon, pink, cooked, dry heat, 3 oz	130	4	0.5	55	75	0	0
Salmon, sockeye, cooked, dry heat, 3 oz	180	9	1.5	75	55	0	0
Salmon burger, frozen, Ocean Beauty, 1 burger	80	0.5	0	35	70	1	0
Scup, cooked, dry heat, 3 oz	110	3	na	55	45	0	0
Sea bass, cooked, dry heat, 3 oz	110	2.5	0.5	45	75	0	0
Seatrout, cooked, dry heat, 3 oz	110	4	1	90	65	0	0
Shad, American, cooked, dry heat, 3 oz	210	15	na	80	55	0	0
Shark, mixed species, raw, 3 oz	110	4	na	40	65	0	0
Sheepshead, cooked, dry heat, 3 oz	110	1.5	0	55	60	0	0

FRESHWATER & SALTWATER FISH	CAL (g)	FAT (g)	SAT FAT (g)	CHOL (mg)	SODIUM (mg)	CARB (g)	FIBER (g)
Smelt, rainbow, cooked, dry heat, 3 oz	110	2.5	0	75	65	0	0
Snapper, cooked, dry heat, 3 oz	110	1.5	0	40	50	0	0
Sole, cooked, dry heat, 3 oz	100	1	0	60	90	0	0
Sole, fillet, frozen, Mrs. Paul's Premium Fillets, 1 fillet	250	13	4	40	510	22	2
Sole, fillet, frozen, Van de Kamp's, 1 fillet	110	1.5	0	50	125	0	0
Sole, fillet, lightly breaded, frozen, Van de Kamp's, 1 fillet	220	11	2	40	410	17	0
Spot, cooked, dry heat, 3 oz	130	5	1.5	65	30	0	0
Sturgeon, cooked, dry heat, 3 oz	110	4.5	1	65	60	0	0
Sturgeon, smoked, 3 oz	150	3.5	1	70	630	0	0
Sucker, white, cooked, dry heat, 3 oz	100	2.5	0	45	45	0	0
Sunfish, pumpkinseed, cooked, dry heat, 3 oz	100	1	0	75	90	0	0
Swordfish, cooked, dry heat, 3 oz	130	4.5	1	45	100	0	0
Tilefish, cooked, dry heat, 3 oz	120	4	1	55	50	0	0
Trout, mixed species, cooked, dry heat, 3 oz	160	7	1	65	60	0	0
Trout, rainbow, farmed, cooked, dry heat, 3 oz	140	6	1.5	60	35	0	0
Trout, rainbow, wild, cooked, dry heat, 3 oz	130	5	1.5	60	50	0	0
Tuna, fresh, bluefin, cooked, dry heat, 3 oz	160	5	1.5	40	45	0	0
Tuna, skipjack, fresh, cooked, dry heat, 3 oz	110	1	0	50	40	0	0
Tuna, yellowfin, fresh, cooked, dry heat, 3 oz	120	1	0	50	40	0	0
Tuna burger, frozen, Ocean Beauty, 3.2 oz	100	3	1	30	100	<1	na
Turbot, European, cooked, dry heat, 3 oz	100	3	na	55	160	0	0

FRESHWATER & SALTWATER FISH	CAL	FAT (g)	SAT FAT (g)	CHOL (mg)	SODIUM (mg)	CARB (g)	FIBER (g)
Whitefish, cooked, dry heat, 3 oz	150	6	1	65	55	0	0
Whitefish, smoked, 3 oz	90	0.5	0	30	870	0	0
Whiting, cooked, dry heat, 3 oz	100	1.5	0	70	110	0	0
Wolffish, Atlantic, cooked, dry heat, 3 oz	100	2.5	0	50	95	0	0
Yellowtail, cooked, dry heat, 3 oz	160	6	na	60	45	0	0

AT A GLANCE: FRESH FISH

Naturally low in calories, total fat, saturated fat, and cholesterol, just about any fish fits well into a low fat diet when prepared without added fat. Most of the more than 90 types of fresh fish listed here contain 4 grams or less of fat, 1 gram or less of saturated fat, and 80 milligrams or less of cholesterol.
Lowest in Fat, Prepared Frozen Fish: Gorton's Cod Cakes; Ocean Beauty Salmon Burger; Van de Kamp's Fillet of Sole

SEAFOOD ALTERNATIVE

	CAL	FAT (g)	SAT FAT (g)	CHOL (mg)	SODIUM (mg)	CARB (g)	FIBER (g)
Fishless fillets, frozen, Worthington, 2 pieces	180	10	2	0	750	8	4

SHELLFISH

Unless otherwise indicated, serving size is cooked and with shell removed, without added salt or fat.

	CAL	FAT (g)	SAT FAT (g)	CHOL (mg)	SODIUM (mg)	CARB (g)	FIBER (g)
Abalone, raw, 3 oz	90	1	0	70	260	5	0
Clams, crunchy fried, frozen, Gorton's, 3 oz	260	17	4	10	300	17	0
Clams, fried, frozen, Mrs. Paul's, 3 oz	280	15	3	10	480	28	1
Clams, raw, 3 oz	60	1	0	30	50	2	0
Clams, steamed or boiled, 3 oz (12 small)	130	2	0	55	95	4	0
Clam strips, oven crunchy, frozen, Rich-SeaPak, 1 pkg	240	16	4	20	580	15	<1
Crab, Alaska king, imitation, made from surimi, 3 oz	90	1	0	15	710	9	0
Crab, Alaska king, steamed or boiled, 3 oz	80	1	0	45	910	0	0
Crab, blue, crab cakes, 3 oz	130	6	1	130	280	0	0

SHELLFISH	CAL	FAT (g)	SAT FAT (g)	CHOL (mg)	SODIUM (mg)	CARB (g)	FIBER (g)
Crab, blue, steamed or boiled, 3 oz	90	1.5	0	85	240	0	0
Crab, deviled, Mrs. Paul's, 1 cake	180	9	2	25	520	17	1
Crab, deviled, miniatures, Mrs. Paul's, 6 minis	230	11	3	15	620	25	2
Crab, Dungeness, steamed or boiled, 3 oz	90	1	0	65	320	<1	0
Crab, queen, steamed or boiled, 3 oz	100	1.5	0	60	590	0	0
Crayfish, farmed, steamed or boiled, 3 oz	70	1	0	115	80	0	0
Crayfish, wild, steamed or boiled, 3 oz	70	1	0	115	80	0	0
Cuttlefish, steamed or boiled, 3 oz	130	1.5	0	190	630	1	0
Lobster, Northern, steamed or boiled, 3 oz	80	0.5	0	60	320	1	0
Lobster, spiny, steamed or boiled, 3 oz	120	1.5	0	75	190	3	0
Mussels, blue, raw, 3 oz	70	2	0	25	240	3	0
Mussels, blue, steamed or boiled, 3 oz	150	4	1	50	310	6	0
Octopus, steamed or boiled, 3 oz	140	2	0	80	390	4	0
Oysters, Eastern, farmed, cooked, dry heat, 3 oz	70	2	0.5	30	140	6	0
Oysters, Eastern, farmed, raw, 3 oz	50	1.5	0	20	150	5	0
Oysters, Eastern, wild, cooked, dry heat, 3 oz	60	1.5	0	40	210	4	0
Oysters, Eastern, wild, raw, 3 oz	60	2	0.5	45	180	3	0
Oysters, Eastern, wild, steamed or boiled, 3 oz	120	4	1.5	90	360	7	0
Oysters, Pacific, raw, 3 oz	70	2	0	45	90	4	0
Oysters, Pacific, steamed or boiled, 3 oz	140	4	1	85	180	8	0
Scallops, bay style, imitation, frozen, Louis Kemp, ½ cup	80	0	0	10	560	11	0

SHELLFISH	CAL (g)	FAT (g)	SAT FAT (g)	CHOL (mg)	SODIUM (mg)	CARB (g)	FIBER (g)
Scallops, broiled, 3 oz (6 large or 14 small)	150	1	0	60	275	2	0
Scallops, fried, frozen, Mrs. Paul's, 12 scallops	200	8	2	10	360	20	1
Scallops, imitation, made from surimi, 3 oz	80	0	0	20	680	9	0
Shrimp, beer batter, frozen, Gorton's, 6 pieces	250	15	2.5	70	630	19	0
Shrimp, boiled, 3 oz	110	2	0	160	160	22	na
Shrimp, breaded, garlic & herb, Mrs. Paul's, 1 pkg	340	15	3	110	910	33	3
Shrimp, breaded, special recipe, Mrs. Paul's, 1 pkg	350	16	3	95	720	32	2
Shrimp, butterfly, breaded, frozen, Van de Kamp's, 7 shrimp	280	14	2.5	55	580	28	2
Shrimp, butterfly, oven crunchy, frozen, Rich-SeaPak, about 4 shrimp	200	9	1	60	770	20	<1
Shrimp, fantail, breaded, frozen, Booth, about 8 shrimp	300	17	4	50	580	27	1
Shrimp, imitation, made from surimi, 3 oz	90	1	0	30	600	8	0
Shrimp, marinated & breaded, original seasoning, frozen, Gorton's, 6 pieces	230	13	2.5	80	550	18	0
Shrimp, microwave crunchy, frozen, Gorton's, 1 pkg	300	16	2.5	100	810	27	0
Shrimp, mini, frozen, Fisher Boy, 18 shrimp	170	7	1.5	45	320	20	1
Shrimp, popcorn, breaded, frozen, Booth, about 29 shrimp	300	15	4	65	520	31	1
Shrimp, popcorn, breaded, frozen, Van de Kamp's, 20 shrimp	270	13	2	35	610	28	1
Shrimp, popcorn, frozen, Fisher Boy, about 23 shrimp	300	15	4	65	520	31	1
Shrimp, popcorn, frozen, Gorton's, 1 cup	260	16	3	60	600	21	0

SHELLFISH	CAL (g)	FAT (g)	SAT FAT (g)	CHOL (mg)	SODIUM (mg)	CARB (g)	FIBER (g)
Shrimp, popcorn, garlic & herb, Gorton's, 1¼ cups	270	13	3	100	500	26	0
Shrimp, popcorn, oven crunchy, Rich-SeaPak, about 15 shrimp	210	12	2	50	720	18	<1
Shrimp, poppers, Rich-SeaPak, about 25 poppers	290	17	na	70	770	26	na
Shrimp, round, breaded, Booth, about 10 shrimp	300	15	3	50	580	31	1
Shrimp, scampi, baked, Gorton's, 6 pieces	250	16	3	70	410	18	0
Shrimp, steamed or boiled, 3 oz	80	1	0	165	190	0	0
Shrimp, whole, breaded, Van de Kamp's, 7 shrimp	240	10	1.5	50	520	26	2
Snails (whelk), steamed or boiled, 3 oz	230	0.5	0	110	350	13	0
Squid, raw, 3 oz	80	1	0	200	35	0	0
Surimi, imitation crabmeat, 3 oz	80	1	0	25	120	6	0

AT A GLANCE: SHELLFISH

Shellfish is low in calories, total fat, and saturated fat. Of the more than 30 types of fresh shellfish listed here, all but four contain 2 grams or less of fat and 0.5 gram or less of saturated fat. Most also contain less than 80 milligrams of cholesterol.

SOUPS

	CAL (g)	FAT (g)	SAT FAT (g)	CHOL (mg)	SODIUM (mg)	CARB (g)	FIBER (g)
CONDENSED							
Serving size is for condensed product (equivalent to 1 cup prepared with water).							
Bean with bacon, Campbell's, ½ cup	180	5	2	<5	890	25	7
Bean with bacon, Campbell's Healthy Request, ½ cup	180	5	2	5	480	25	7
Bean with frankfurters, ½ cup	190	7	2	15	1090	22	6
Beef broth, Campbell's, ½ cup	15	0	0	<5	900	1	0
Beef noodle, Campbell's, ½ cup	70	3	1	15	920	8	1
Beef stew, old fashioned, Campbell's Homestyle, ½ cup	220	7	3	40	950	20	6
Beef with vegetables & barley, Campbell's, ½ cup	80	2	1	15	920	11	2
Beefy mushroom, Campbell's, ½ cup	70	3	1	10	1000	6	1
Black bean, Campbell's, ½ cup	120	2	1	0	1030	19	
Broccoli cheese, Campbell's, ½ cup	110	7	3	10	860	9	
Cheddar cheese, Campbell's, ½ cup	150	10	5	20	1120	10	
Chicken alphabet with vegetables, Campbell's, ½ cup	80	2	1	10	880	11	
Chicken and stars, Campbell's, ½ cup	70	2	1	0	1010	9	
Chicken broth, Campbell's, ½ cup	30	2	1	<5	770	2	
Chicken dumplings, Campbell's, ½ cup	80	3	1	25	1050	10	
Chicken gumbo, Campbell's, ½ cup	60	2	1	10	990	9	

CONDENSED	CAL (g)	FAT (g)	SAT FAT (g)	CHOL (mg)	SODIUM (mg)	CARB (g)	FIBER (g)
Chicken mushroom, ½ cup	130	9	2.5	10	940	9	0
Chicken noodle, Campbell's, ½ cup	60	2	1	15	950	8	1
Chicken noodle, Campbell's Healthy Request, ½ cup	70	3	1	15	480	8	1
Chicken NoodleO's, Campbell's, ½ cup	80	3	1	15	980	10	1
Chicken rice, Campbell's Healthy Request, ½ cup	70	3	1	10	480	9	<1
Chicken vegetable, Campbell's, ½ cup	80	2	1	10	940	12	2
Chicken vegetable, Campbell's Healthy Request, ½ cup	80	2	1	5	480	12	1
Chicken vegetable, Southwestern style, Campbell's, ½ cup	110	2	1	10	900	18	4
Chicken with dumplings, ½ cup	100	6	1.5	35	860	6	<1
Chicken with rice, Campbell's, ½ cup	70	3	1	<5	830	9	0
Chicken with wild rice, Campbell's, ½ cup	70	2	1	10	900	9	1
Chicken won ton, Campbell's, ½ cup	45	1	0	15	940	5	1
Chili beef with beans, Campbell's, ½ cup	170	5	3	15	910	24	4
Clam chowder, Manhattan, Campbell's, ½ cup	60	1	0	<5	910	12	2
Clam chowder, New England, Campbell's, ½ cup	100	3	1	<5	980	15	1
Consomme, beef, Campbell's, ½ cup	25	0	0	5	820	2	0
Corn, golden, Campbell's, ½ cup	120	4	1	<5	730	20	2
Cream of asparagus, Campbell's, ½ cup	110	7	2	<5	910	9	1
Cream of broccoli, Campbell's, ½ cup	100	6	3	5	770	9	1
Cream of broccoli, Campbell's Healthy Request, ½ cup	70	2	1	<5	480	9	1

CONDENSED	CAL	FAT (g)	SAT FAT (g)	CHOL (mg)	SODIUM (mg)	CARB (g)	FIBER (g)
Cream of celery, Campbell's, ½ cup	110	7	3	<5	900	9	1
Cream of celery, Campbell's Healthy Request, ½ cup	70	2	1	<5	480	11	1
Cream of celery, reduced fat, Campbell's, ½ cup	80	4	2	5	900	11	1
Cream of chicken, Campbell's, ½ cup	130	8	3	10	890	11	1
Cream of chicken, Campbell's Healthy Request, ½ cup	80	3	1	10	480	11	0
Cream of chicken, reduced fat, Campbell's, ½ cup	80	4	2	15	950	9	1
Cream of chicken & broccoli, Campbell's, ½ cup	120	8	3	15	860	9	1
Cream of chicken & broccoli, Campbell's Healthy Request, ½ cup	80	3	1	5	480	10	1
Cream of Mexican pepper, Campbell's, ½ cup	110	7	2	<5	860	10	2
Cream of mushroom, Campbell's, ½ cup	110	7	3	<5	870	9	1
Cream of mushroom, Campbell's Healthy Request, ½ cup	70	3	1	10	480	9	1
Cream of mushroom, reduced fat, Campbell's, ½ cup	70	4	1	5	940	10	1
Cream of onion, ½ cup	110	5	1.5	15	930	13	<1
Cream of potato, Campbell's, ½ cup	100	3	2	10	890	16	1
Cream of shrimp, Campbell's, ½ cup	100	7	2	20	890	8	1
Cream of tomato, Campbell's Homestyle, ½ cup	110	3	1	5	860	21	1
Creamy chicken mushroom, Campbell's, ½ cup	130	9	3	15	1000	9	1
Creamy chicken noodle, Campbell's, ½ cup	130	7	2	15	880	12	2
Creamy onion, Campbell's, ½ cup	110	6	2	20	910	13	1
Curly noodle, with chicken broth, Campbell's, ½ cup	80	3	1	15	840	12	1

CONDENSED	CAL (g)	FAT (g)	SAT FAT (g)	CHOL (mg)	SODIUM (mg)	CARB (g)	FIBER (g)
Double noodle in chicken broth, Campbell's, ½ cup	100	3	1	15	810	15	2
French onion, Campbell's, ½ cup	70	3	0	<5	980	10	1
Green pea, Campbell's, ½ cup	180	3	1	5	890	29	5
Minestrone, Campbell's, ½ cup	100	2	0.5	<5	960	16	4
Minestrone, Campbell's Healthy Request, ½ cup	90	1	1	0	480	17	2
Mushroom, golden, Campbell's, ½ cup	80	3	1	5	930	10	1
Mushroom barley, ½ cup	70	2	0	0	890	12	<1
Mushroom with beef stock, ½ cup	90	4	1.5	5	970	9	<1
Nacho cheese, Campbell's, ½ cup	140	8	4	15	810	11	2
Noodles & ground beef, Campbell's, ½ cup	100	4	2	25	900	11	2
Oyster stew, Campbell's, ½ cup	90	6	4	20	940	6	0
Pepper pot, Campbell's, ½ cup	100	5	2	15	1020	9	1
Scotch broth, Campbell's, ½ cup	80	3	2	10	870	9	1
Split pea, with ham & bacon, Campbell's, ½ cup	180	4	2	<5	860	28	5
Stockpot, ½ cup	100	4	1	5	1050	12	na
Teddy bear pasta, Campbell's, ½ cup	80	2	1	5	840	12	2
Tomato, Campbell's, ½ cup	100	2	0	0	730	18	2
Tomato, Campbell's Healthy Request, ½ cup	90	2	1	0	460	18	1
Tomato, fiesta, Campbell's, ½ cup	60	0	0	0	720	13	1
Tomato, Italian, Campbell's, ½ cup	100	1	0	0	820	23	2
Tomato bisque, Campbell's, ½ cup	130	3	2	5	900	24	2
Tomato rice, old fashioned, Campbell's, ½ cup	120	2	1	5	790	23	1

CONDENSED	CAL (g)	FAT (g)	SAT FAT (g)	CHOL (mg)	SODIUM (mg)	CARB (g)	FIBER (g)
Turkey noodle, Campbell's, ½ cup	80	3	1	15	970	10	1
Turkey vegetable, Campbell's, ½ cup	80	3	1	10	840	11	2
Vegetable, Campbell's, ½ cup	90	1	0	0	750	17	2
Vegetable, Campbell's Healthy Request, ½ cup	90	2	1	0	480	15	2
Vegetable, Campbell's Homestyle, ½ cup	70	2	1	0	970	10	2
Vegetable, California style, Campbell's, ½ cup	60	1	0	0	850	10	2
Vegetable, hearty, Campbell's Healthy Request, ½ cup	70	3	1	10	480	9	1
Vegetable, hearty, with pasta, Campbell's, ½ cup	90	1	0	0	830	18	2
Vegetable, old fashioned, Campbell's, ½ cup	70	3	1	<5	950	10	2
Vegetable, vegetarian, Campbell's, ½ cup	70	1	0	0	770	14	2
Vegetable beef, Campbell's, ½ cup	80	2	1	10	810	10	2
Vegetable beef, Campbell's Healthy Request, ½ cup	80	2	1	5	480	11	2

AT A GLANCE: CONDENSED SOUPS

Lowest in Sodium: Campbell's Healthy Request Tomato
Highest in Fiber: Campbell's Bean with Bacon original and Healthy Request varieties
Lowest in Fat: Campbell's Beef Broth, Beef Consomme, Fiesta Tomato

READY-TO-SERVE

	CAL (g)	FAT (g)	SAT FAT (g)	CHOL (mg)	SODIUM (mg)	CARB (g)	FIBER (g)
Bacon, lettuce & tomato, Pepperidge Farm, ⅔ cup	130	7	2	5	1130	14	1
Barley mushroom, frozen, Tabatchnick, 7.5 oz	70	0	0	0	540	13	3
Barley mushroom, no salt added, frozen, Tabatchnick, 7.5 oz	70	0	0	0	100	13	3
Bean, Yankee, frozen, Tabatchnick, 7.5 oz	160	1.5	0	0	570	27	11
Bean 'n ham, Campbell's Chunky, 1 cup	190	2	1	15	880	29	9

READY-TO-SERVE	CAL (g)	FAT (g)	SAT FAT (g)	CHOL (mg)	SODIUM (mg)	CARB (g)	FIBER (g)
Bean & ham, microwave cup, Hormel, 1 cup	190	4	1.5	25	650	28	7
Bean and ham, Campbell's Home Cookin', 1 cup	180	2	1	5	720	33	9
Bean and ham, Healthy Choice, 1 cup	180	3	1	5	460	34	10
Bean and ham, Progresso, 1 cup	160	2	0.5	10	870	25	8
Bean with bacon, Grandma Brown's, 1 cup	190	3.5	1	0	700	31	10
Bean with bacon, microwave cup, Campbell's, 1 container	280	6	2	15	1300	40	11
Beef, chunky, microwave cup, Campbell's, 1 container	210	5	1	35	1120	24	3
Beef, hearty, Old El Paso, 1 cup	120	2.5	1.5	25	690	14	0
Beef & potato, Healthy Choice, 1 cup	120	1	0.5	5	450	16	0
Beef barley, Progresso, 1 cup	130	4	1.5	25	780	13	3
Beef barley, Progresso Healthy Classics, 1 cup	140	2	1	20	490	20	3
Beef broth, College Inn, 1 cup	20	0	0	0	1140	0	0
Beef broth, Swanson, 1 cup	20	1	0.5	0	820	1	0
Beef broth, fat free, Health Valley, 1 cup	20	0	0	0	160	0	0
Beef broth, low sodium, College Inn, 1 cup	20	0	0	0	620	0	0
Beef minestrone, Progresso, 1 cup	140	4	1.5	25	850	14	3
Beef noodle, Progresso, 1 cup	140	3.5	1.5	30	950	15	1
Beef pasta, Campbell's Chunky, 1 cup	150	3	1	20	970	18	2
Beef vegetable, Progresso Healthy Classics, 1 cup	150	1.5	0.5	15	410	25	6
Beef vegetable, microwave cup, Hormel, 1 cup	90	1	0	10	740	14	2
Beef vegetable and rotini, Progresso Pasta Soups, 1 cup	120	3.5	1.5	20	830	10	3
Beef with country vegetables, Campbell's Chunky, 1 cup	160	4	1	25	900	18	3

READY-TO-SERVE	CAL (g)	FAT (g)	SAT FAT (g)	CHOL (mg)	SODIUM (mg)	CARB (g)	FIBER (g)
Black bean, hearty, Progresso, 1 cup	170	1.5	0	<5	730	30	10
Black bean, with bacon, Old El Paso, 1 cup	160	1.5	0.5	5	960	26	7
Black bean, with sherry, Pepperidge Farm, ⅔ cup	120	3	1	0	1050	19	4
Black bean and vegetable, fat free, Health Valley, 1 cup	110	0	0	0	280	24	12
Broccoli, plus carotene, fat free, Health Valley, 1 cup	70	0	0	0	240	16	7
Broccoli and shells, Progresso Pasta Soups, 1 cup	70	1	0	<5	720	14	3
Broccoli cheese, with ham, microwave cup, Hormel, 1 cup	170	13	5	60	700	10	1
Cabbage, frozen, Tabatchnick, 7.5 oz	60	0	0	0	160	14	2
Chickarina, Progresso, 1 cup	120	5	2	20	710	10	1
Chicken, hearty, Healthy Choice, 1 cup	130	2.5	1	20	460	20	1
Chicken, hearty, Progresso, 1 can	120	2.5	0.5	25	1070	10	0
Chicken, New York, frozen, Tabatchnick, 7.5 oz	35	0	0	0	850	6	0
Chicken, old fashioned, Campbell's Chunky, 1 cup	130	3	2	20	950	12	3
Chicken & rice, microwave cup, Hormel, 1 cup	110	3	1	10	900	17	1
Chicken and rice, Weight Watchers, 10.5 oz	110	1.5	0	10	720	17	4
Chicken and rotini, hearty, Progresso Pasta Soups, 1 cup	90	2	0.5	20	860	8	0
Chicken and wild rice, Progresso, 1 cup	100	2	0.5	20	820	15	2
Chicken barley, Progresso, 1 cup	110	2.5	0.5	15	720	14	3
Chicken broccoli cheese, Campbell's Chunky, 1 cup	200	12	5	25	1120	14	1
Chicken broth, Campbell's Healthy Request, 1 cup	20	0	0	0	400	1	0

READY-TO-SERVE	CAL	FAT (g)	SAT FAT (g)	CHOL (mg)	SODIUM (mg)	CARB (g)	FIBER (g)
Chicken broth, College Inn, 1 cup	25	1.5	0.5	<5	1050	1	0
Chicken broth, Progresso, 1 cup	20	0.5	0	5	860	1	0
Chicken broth, Swanson, 1 cup	30	2	0.5	0	1000	1	0
Chicken broth, 1/3 less salt, Swanson, 1 cup	15	0	0	0	560	1	0
Chicken broth, fat free, Health Valley, 1 cup	30	0	0	0	170	0	0
Chicken broth, low sodium, Campbell's, 1 cup	25	2	1	5	110	1	<1
Chicken broth, low sodium, College Inn, 1 cup	25	1.5	0.5	<5	640	1	ns
Chicken corn chowder, Campbell's Chunky, 1 cup	250	15	7	25	870	18	3
Chicken corn chowder, Campbell's Healthy Request, 1 cup	140	3	1	15	480	7	2
Chicken corn chowder, Healthy Choice, 1 cup	150	3	1	10	430	27	7
Chicken curry, Pepperidge Farm, 2/3 cup	170	8	4	25	1030	16	2
Chicken minestrone, Progresso, 1 cup	120	3.5	1	20	790	12	2
Chicken mushroom chowder, Campbell's Chunky, 1 cup	210	12	4	10	970	15	3
Chicken noodle, Campbell's Home Cookin', 1 cup	100	4	1	15	980	11	1
Chicken noodle, Healthy Choice, 1 cup	140	3	1	10	400	20	<1
Chicken noodle, Progresso, 1 cup	80	2	0.5	20	730	8	1
Chicken noodle, Progresso Healthy Classics, 1 cup	80	2	0.5	20	480	10	1
Chicken noodle, Weight Watchers, 10.5 oz	150	2	0.5	30	740	25	4
Chicken noodle, chunky, microwave cup, Campbell's, 1 container	160	5	2	35	1060	17	3

READY-TO-SERVE	CAL (g)	FAT (g)	SAT FAT (g)	CHOL (mg)	SODIUM (mg)	CARB (g)	FIBER (g)
Chicken noodle, classic, Campbell's Chunky, 1 cup	130	3	1	20	1050	16	2
Chicken noodle, hearty, Campbell's Healthy Request, 1 cup	160	3	1	20	480	8	2
Chicken noodle, hearty, Old El Paso, 1 cup	110	3	1	25	720	10	0
Chicken noodle, microwave cup, Campbell's, 1 container	130	4	1	25	1320	18	2
Chicken noodle, microwave cup, Hormel, 1 cup	110	3	1	20	690	13	1
Chicken noodle, with mushroom, Campbell's Chunky, 1 cup	120	4	2	25	930	10	1
Chicken rice, Campbell's Chunky, 1 cup	140	3	1	25	840	18	2
Chicken rice, Campbell's Home Cookin', 1 cup	110	2	1	15	910	17	2
Chicken rice, hearty, Campbell's Healthy Request, 1 cup	120	3	1	15	480	17	0
Chicken rice, microwave cup, Campbell's, 1 container	120	3	1	10	1130	20	2
Chicken rice, with vegetables, Progresso Healthy Classics, 1 cup	90	1.5	0	10	450	12	1
Chicken rice vegetable, Progresso, 1 cup	110	3	1	15	750	12	<1
Chicken vegetable, Campbell's Chunky, 1 cup	90	1	0	10	870	13	3
Chicken vegetable, Campbell's Home Cookin', 1 cup	130	4	1	10	820	20	3
Chicken vegetable, Old El Paso, 1 cup	110	2.5	0.5	15	620	13	0
Chicken vegetable, hearty, Campbell's Healthy Request, 1 cup	120	3	1	15	480	17	2
Chicken vegetable, homestyle, Progresso, 1 cup	100	2.5	0.5	15	680	10	1

READY-TO-SERVE	CAL (g)	FAT (g)	SAT FAT (g)	CHOL (mg)	SODIUM (mg)	CARB (g)	FIBER (g)
Chicken vegetable and penne, Progresso Pasta Soups, 1 cup	100	2.5	0.5	10	780	11	3
Chicken with dumplings, frozen, Tabatchnick, 7.5 oz	70	2	0	20	830	13	1
Chicken with noodles, low sodium, Campbell's, 1 cup	140	5	1	40	95	14	2
Chicken with pasta, Healthy Choice, 1 cup	120	2.5	1	5	470	17	<1
Chicken with rice, Healthy Choice, 1 cup	110	3	1	5	430	15	<1
Chicken with rice, Old El Paso, 1 cup	90	2.5	0.5	15	680	10	0
Chicken with rice, Pepperidge Farm, 2/3 cup	80	4	2	15	960	8	1
Chili beef, Healthy Choice, 1 cup	170	1.5	0.5	10	380	30	5
Chili beef with beans, Campbell's Chunky, 1 cup	230	6	2	15	850	30	7
Clam chowder, Manhattan, Campbell's Chunky, 1 cup	130	4	1	5	900	20	3
Clam chowder, Manhattan, Pepperidge Farm, 2/3 cup	80	2	1	<5	860	12	2
Clam chowder, Manhattan, Progresso, 1 cup	110	2	0	10	710	11	3
Clam chowder, New England, Campbell's Chunky, 1 cup	220	14	5	15	1080	21	2
Clam chowder, New England, Campbell's Healthy Request, 1 cup	110	3	1	10	480	15	1
Clam chowder, New England, Campbell's Home Cookin', 1 cup	210	16	5	5	1120	12	2
Clam chowder, New England, Gorton's, 1 cup	140	6	1.5	15	730	15	0
Clam chowder, New England, Healthy Choice, 1 cup	130	2.5	2	<5	480	19	7
Clam chowder, New England, Pepperidge Farm, 2/3 cup	160	8	3	20	1160	13	1
Clam chowder, New England, Progresso, 1 cup	180	10	3	15	850	17	2

READY-TO-SERVE	CAL (g)	FAT (g)	SAT FAT (g)	CHOL (mg)	SODIUM (mg)	CARB (g)	FIBER (g)
Clam chowder, New England, Progresso Healthy Classics, 1 cup	120	2	0.5	5	530	20	1
Clam chowder, New England, microwave cup, Campbell's, 1 container	290	17	8	20	1150	26	3
Clam chowder, New England, microwave cup, Hormel, 1 cup	130	5	2.5	25	820	16	1
Clam and rotini chowder, Progresso Pasta Soups, 1 cup	200	9	2	10	800	21	0
Consomme Madrilene, Pepperidge Farm, ⅔ cup	50	1	0	0	910	6	0
Corn chowder, Pepperidge Farm, ⅔ cup	140	8	3	10	1050	14	2
Corn chowder, Progresso, 1 cup	180	10	4	10	780	20	2
Corn chowder, frozen, Tabatchnick, 7.5 oz	150	6	2	5	650	22	1
Country corn and vegetable, fat free, Health Valley, 1 cup	70	0	0	0	135	17	7
Crab, Pepperidge Farm, ⅔ cup	80	2	1	10	1150	9	2
Cream of broccoli, Pepperidge Farm, ⅔ cup	90	5	3	5	940	11	2
Cream of broccoli, Progresso Healthy Classics, 1 cup	90	3	0.5	<5	580	13	2
Cream of broccoli, frozen, Tabatchnick, 7.5 oz	90	4	2	5	740	12	3
Cream of chicken, Campbell's Home Cookin', 1 cup	210	18	6	15	1170	8	2
Cream of chicken, Progresso, 1 cup	170	10	3.5	35	880	11	0
Cream of mushroom, Campbell's Home Cookin', 1 cup	170	13	4	15	970	9	3
Cream of mushroom, Progresso, 1 cup	140	8	3.5	20	920	12	1
Cream of mushroom, low sodium, Campbell's, 1 cup	160	11	3	15	55	14	3
Cream of spinach, frozen, Tabatchnick, 7.5 oz	90	4	2	5	630	11	2

READY-TO-SERVE	CAL (g)	FAT (g)	SAT FAT (g)	CHOL (mg)	SODIUM (mg)	CARB (g)	FIBER (g)
Creamy chicken with mushroom, Campbell's Chunky, 1 cup	210	17	8	20	1020	12	1
Escarole in chicken broth, Progresso, 1 cup	25	1	0	<5	980	2	0
French onion, Pepperidge Farm, ⅔ cup	50	1	1	<5	1080	7	1
Garlic and pasta, Progresso Healthy Classics, 1 cup	100	1.5	0	<5	450	18	3
Gazpacho, Pepperidge Farm, ⅔ cup	70	2	0	0	1050	12	2
Green pea, low sodium, Campbell's, 1 cup	160	4	2	5	35	23	5
Green pea, with ham & sherry wine, Pepperidge Farm, ⅔ cup	210	6	4	10	1100	28	4
Hunters soup, with turkey, beef & burgundy, Pepperidge Farm, ⅔ cup	130	6	1	15	1150	9	2
Italian plus carotene, fat free, Health Valley, 1 cup	80	0	0	0	240	19	6
Lentil, Healthy Choice, 1 cup	150	1	0.5	0	420	29	5
Lentil, Progresso, 1 cup	140	2	0	0	750	22	7
Lentil, Progresso Healthy Classics, 1 cup	130	1.5	0	0	440	20	6
Lentil, Ultra Slim Fast, 1 can	230	3	1	5	990	40	3
Lentil, hearty, Campbell's Home Cookin', 1 cup	130	1	1	0	860	24	5
Lentil, savory, Campbell's Home Cookin', 1 cup	150	2	0.5	0	860	26	5
Lentil and carrots, fat free, Health Valley, 1 cup	90	0	0	0	220	25	14
Lentil and shells, Progresso Pasta Soups, 1 cup	130	1.5	0	0	840	22	4
Lentil with sausage, Progresso, 1 cup	170	7	2	15	780	19	5
Lobster bisque, with white wine, Pepperidge Farm, ⅔ cup	160	11	5	40	1090	12	1
Macaroni and bean, Progresso, 1 cup	160	4	1	<5	800	23	6

READY-TO-SERVE	CAL	FAT (g)	SAT FAT (g)	CHOL (mg)	SODIUM (mg)	CARB (g)	FIBER (g)
Meatballs and pasta pearls, Progresso Pasta Soups, 1 cup	140	7	3	15	700	13	0
Minestrone, Campbell's Chunky, 1 cup	140	5	2	5	800	22	2
Minestrone, Campbell's Home Cookin', 1 cup	120	2	1	5	990	19	3
Minestrone, Healthy Choice, 1 cup	110	1	0	0	390	23	3
Minestrone, Pepperidge Farm, 2/3 cup	100	4	1	<5	870	12	3
Minestrone, Progresso, 1 cup	130	2.5	0.5	0	960	22	5
Minestrone, Progresso Healthy Classics, 1 cup	120	2.5	0	0	510	20	1
Minestrone, Ultra Slim Fast, 1 can	240	3	1	<5	890	45	8
Minestrone, Weight Watchers, 10.5 oz	130	2	0.5	5	760	23	6
Minestrone, fat free, Health Valley, 1 cup	80	0	0	0	210	21	11
Minestrone, frozen, Tabatchnick, 7.5 oz	150	1	0	0	550	27	10
Minestrone, hearty, Campbell's Healthy Request, 1 cup	120	2	1	<5	480	24	3
Minestrone, Tuscany style, Campbell's Home Cookin', 1 cup	160	7	2	5	880	21	5
Minestrone, zesty, Progresso, 1 cup	150	6	2.5	10	790	17	4
Minestrone and shells, hearty, Progresso Pasta Soups, 1 cup	120	1.5	0	0	700	20	4
Mushroom, country, and rice, Campbell's Home Cookin', 1 cup	100	1	0	5	790	21	2
Mushroom, Shiitake, Pepperidge Farm, 2/3 cup	80	3	2	<5	1100	10	2
Oyster stew, Pepperidge Farm, 2/3 cup	160	10	7	30	1040	12	1
Pasta Bolognese, fat free, Health Valley, 1 cup	70	0	0	0	135	17	7

READY-TO-SERVE	CAL (g)	FAT (g)	SAT FAT (g)	CHOL (mg)	SODIUM (mg)	CARB (g)	FIBER (g)
Pasta cacciatore, fat free, Health Valley, 1 cup	90	0	0	0	210	19	4
Pasta fagioli, fat free, Health Valley, 1 cup	80	0	0	0	250	17	4
Pasta primavera, fat free, Health Valley, 1 cup	80	0	0	0	210	21	11
Pasta Romano, fat free, Health Valley, 1 cup	140	0	0	0	250	32	13
Pea, frozen, Tabatchnick, 7.5 oz	180	1.5	0	0	520	31	11
Pea, no salt added, frozen, Tabatchnick, 7.5 oz	180	1.5	0	0	80	31	11
Penne in chicken broth, hearty, Progresso Pasta Soups, 1 cup	70	1	0	<5	930	12	0
Penne pasta and vegetable, Campbell's Healthy Request, 1 cup	90	1	0	5	470	17	2
Pepper steak, Campbell's Chunky, 1 cup	140	3	1	20	830	18	3
Potato, New England, frozen, Tabatchnick, 7.5 oz	150	6	2.5	9	540	21	2
Potato, old fashioned, frozen, Tabatchnick, 7.5 oz	70	0	0	0	540	16	2
Potato cheese, with ham, microwave cup, Hormel, 1 cup	190	13	5	60	730	16	1
Potato ham chowder, Campbell's Chunky, 1 cup	220	14	8	20	840	16	3
Red beans & rice, Creole style, Campbell's Chunky, 1 cup	210	8	3	15	720	9	6
Rotini and vegetable, fat free, Health Valley, 1 cup	20	0	0	0	160	0	0
Salsa bean, Campbell's Home Cookin', 1 cup	190	1	1	0	850	38	6
Sirloin burger, Campbell's Chunky, 1 cup	190	9	4	20	930	20	4
Sirloin burger, chunky, microwave cup, Campbell's, 1 container	210	8	3	15	1090	24	5
Spicy chicken and penne, Progresso Pasta Soups, 1 cup	120	4	1	20	680	13	0

READY-TO-SERVE	CAL (g)	FAT (g)	SAT FAT (g)	CHOL (mg)	SODIUM (mg)	CARB (g)	FIBER (g)
Split pea, Progresso, 1 cup	170	3	1	5	870	25	5
Split pea, Progresso Healthy Classics, 1 cup	180	2.5	1	<5	420	30	5
Split pea, Ultra Slim Fast, 1 can	230	2.5	1	<5	1270	42	8
Split pea 'n' ham, Campbell's Chunky, 1 cup	190	3	1	20	1120	27	3
Split pea and carrots, fat free, Health Valley, 1 cup	110	0	0	0	230	17	4
Split pea with bacon, Grandma Brown's, 1 cup	210	4	1.5	0	520	31	6
Split pea with ham, Campbell's Healthy Request, 1 cup	170	3	1	10	480	27	6
Split pea with ham, Campbell's Home Cookin', 1 cup	170	2	1	5	880	30	6
Split pea with ham, Healthy Choice, 1 cup	160	2	1	10	400	25	2
Split pea with ham, Progresso, 1 cup	160	4	1.5	15	830	20	5
Steak 'n potato, Campbell's Chunky, 1 cup	160	4	1	20	890	20	3
Tomato, Progresso, 1 cup	90	2	0	0	990	15	4
Tomato, low sodium, Campbell's, 1 cup	170	6	3	10	60	28	2
Tomato and rotini, hearty, Progresso Pasta Soups, 1 cup	90	1	0	5	820	16	3
Tomato beef and rotini, Progresso, 1 cup	140	4.5	1.5	25	750	15	2
Tomato garden, Campbell's Home Cookin', 1 can	150	4	2	5	900	27	4
Tomato garden, Healthy Choice, 1 cup	110	1.5	0.5	0	420	21	3
Tomato garden vegetable, Progresso Healthy Classics, 1 cup	100	1	0	0	480	19	4
Tomato tortellini, Progresso Pasta Soups, 1 cup	120	5	1.5	10	910	13	2
Tomato vegetable, fat free, Health Valley, 1 cup	80	0	0	0	240	17	5

READY-TO-SERVE	CAL (g)	FAT (g)	SAT FAT (g)	CHOL (mg)	SODIUM (mg)	CARB (g)	FIBER (g)
Tomato vegetable with pasta, Campbell's Healthy Request, 1 cup	120	2	1	5	480	22	3
Tortellini, creamy, Progresso, 1 cup	210	15	8	30	830	15	0
Tortellini in chicken broth, Progresso, 1 cup	80	2	0.5	5	750	10	2
Turkey noodle, low sodium, Campbell's, 1 cup	60	3	1	10	30	8	1
Turkey vegetable, with wild rice, Campbell's Healthy Request, 1 cup	120	3	1	15	480	17	2
Turkey with white and wild rice, Healthy Choice, 1 cup	90	2.5	1	0	360	13	1
Vegetable, Campbell's Chunky, 1 cup	130	3	1	0	870	22	4
Vegetable, Progresso, 1 cup	90	2	0.5	<5	850	15	3
Vegetable, Progresso Healthy Classics, 1 cup	80	1.5	0	5	470	13	1
Vegetable, Weight Watchers, 10.5 oz	130	1	0	0	680	28	6
Vegetable, 5 bean, fat free, Health Valley, 1 cup	140	0	0	0	250	32	13
Vegetable, 14 garden, fat free, Health Valley, 1 cup	80	0	0	0	250	17	4
Vegetable, country, Campbell's Healthy Request, 1 cup	120	1	0	5	460	22	4
Vegetable, country, Campbell's Home Cookin', 1 cup	110	1	0	5	760	19	2
Vegetable, country, Healthy Choice, 1 cup	100	0.5	0	0	430	23	2
Vegetable, fiesta, Campbell's Home Cookin', 1 cup	130	2.5	0.5	0	750	24	4
Vegetable, frozen, Tabatchnick, 7.5 oz	110	1	0	0	580	20	4
Vegetable, garden, Healthy Choice, 1 cup	120	1	0	0	400	26	3
Vegetable, garden, Old El Paso, 1 cup	110	2.5	0.5	<5	710	17	0

READY-TO-SERVE	CAL (g)	FAT (g)	SAT FAT (g)	CHOL (mg)	SODIUM (mg)	CARB (g)	FIBER (g)
Vegetable, hearty, Campbell's Healthy Request, 1 cup	100	1	0	0	470	20	2
Vegetable, hearty, with pasta, Campbell's Chunky, 1 cup	130	3	0.5	0	1080	21	3
Vegetable, Italian, Campbell's Home Cookin', 1 cup	100	4	2	5	860	14	2
Vegetable, low sodium, Campbell's, 1 cup	90	2	1	0	50	14	2
Vegetable, Mediterranean, Campbell's Chunky, 1 cup	140	5	2	5	850	21	1
Vegetable, no salt added, frozen, Tabatchnick, 7.5 oz	110	1	0	0	75	20	4
Vegetable, plus carotene, fat free, Health Valley, 1 cup	70	0	0	0	240	17	6
Vegetable, Southwestern, Campbell's Home Cookin', 1 cup	130	3	1	0	750	24	4
Vegetable and rotini, hearty, Progresso Pasta Soups, 1 cup	110	1	0	0	720	20	3
Vegetable barley, fat free, Health Valley, 1 cup	90	0	0	0	210	19	4
Vegetable bean, Ultra Slim Fast, 1 can	240	3	1	<5	990	42	8
Vegetable beef, Campbell's Healthy Request, 1 cup	140	2	1	20	480	20	3
Vegetable beef, Campbell's Home Cookin', 1 cup	120	2	1	5	1010	18	3
Vegetable beef, Healthy Choice, 1 cup	130	1	0	<5	420	22	2
Vegetable beef, chunky, Campbell's, 1 cup	130	4	2	50	75	15	3
Vegetable beef, microwave cup, Campbell's, 1 container	140	1	0	10	1240	26	5
Vegetable beef, old fashioned, Campbell's Chunky, 1 cup	150	5	2	15	870	17	3
Vegetable broth, Swanson Natural Goodness, 1 cup	20	1	0	0	1000	3	0
Vichyssoise (cream of potato & onion), Pepperidge Farm, 2/3 cup	120	8	5	15	950	11	2

READY-TO-SERVE	CAL (g)	FAT (g)	SAT FAT (g)	CHOL (mg)	SODIUM (mg)	CARB (g)	FIBER (g)
Watercress, Pepperidge Farm, 1/3 cup	80	4	3	<5	930	11	2
Wisconsin cheddar vegetable, frozen, Tabatchnick, 7.5 oz	140	9	3	15	930	12	1

AT A GLANCE: READY-TO-SERVE SOUPS

Lowest in Sodium: Campbell's Turkey Noodle, Low Sodium
Highest in Fiber: Health Valley Lentil and Carrots, Fat Free

SOUP MIX *Serving size is for dry product.*

	CAL (g)	FAT (g)	SAT FAT (g)	CHOL (mg)	SODIUM (mg)	CARB (g)	FIBER (g)
Bean medley, Lipton Kettle Creations, 1/4 cup mix	130	1.5	0	0	690	23	4
Bean with bacon, mix to make 1 cup	110	2.5	1	<5	930	16	9
Beef, ground, vegetable, Borden Soup Starter, 1/8 pkg	80	0.5	0	0	990	17	2
Beef barley vegetable, Borden Soup Starter, 1/8 pkg	100	0.5	0	0	960	20	3
Beef bouillon, Herb-Ox, 1 packet	10	0	0	0	750	1	0
Beef bouillon, Knorr, 1/2 cube	20	1.5	0.5	ns	1290	<1	ns
Beef bouillon, Wyler's, 1 tsp	5	0	0	0	930	1	0
Beef bouillon, cube, Herb-Ox, cube	10	0	0	0	700	1	0
Beef bouillon, cube, Wyler's, cube	5	0	0	0	930	1	0
Beef bouillon, low sodium, Wyler's, 1 tsp	10	0	0	0	5	2	0
Beef broth, Romanoff-MBT/Wyler's, 1 packet	15	0	0	0	810	2	0
Beef broth, Weight Watchers, 16 oz	10	0	0	0	800	2	0
Beef broth, low sodium, Romanoff-MBT/Wyler's, packet	15	0	0	0	5	3	0
Beef broth & seasoning, Herb-Ox, 1 packet	10	0	0	0	900	1	0
Beef broth & seasoning, low sodium, Herb-Ox, 1 packet	15	0	0	0	5	2	0

SOUP MIX	CAL (g)	FAT (g)	SAT FAT (g)	CHOL (mg)	SODIUM (mg)	CARB (g)	FIBER (g)
Beef flavor noodle, Campbell's, 1 pkg	120	2	1	20	1260	22	1
Beef vegetable, Betty Crocker Hamburger Helper, ¼ cup	80	0.5	0	10	650	17	1
Beef vegetable, Borden Soup Starter, ⅛ pkg	90	0.5	0	0	990	19	2
Black bean, Knorr, 1 pkg	190	1	0	0	590	36	9
Black bean, Nile Spice, 1 pkg	190	1.5	0	0	570	34	2
Black bean, Jumpin', Fantastic Foods, 1 pkg	170	1	0	0	470	39	13
Black bean, Santa Fe, Campbell's Soupsations, 1 pkg	250	2	1	<5	1080	48	6
Black bean salsa, Nile Spice, 1 pkg	190	1	0	0	630	34	6
Black bean with couscous, spicy, fat free, Health Valley, ½ pkg	130	0	0	0	280	29	5
Black bean with rice, fat free, Health Valley, ½ pkg	100	0	0	0	280	22	4
Broccoli and cheddar, Fantastic Foods, 1 pkg	150	2	1	5	600	27	2
Broccoli and cheese, creamy, Lipton Cup-A-Soup, 1 envelope	70	3	1.5	<5	550	8	
Carrot dill, Nile Spice, 1 pkg	100	2	1	0	550	18	2
Cauliflower, mix to make 1 cup	70	2	0	0	840	11	1
Chicken & rice, Borden Soup Starter, ⅛ pkg	70	0.5	0	0	780	14	
Chicken bouillon, Herb-Ox, 1 packet	10	0	0	0	1040	1	
Chicken bouillon, Knorr, ½ cube	20	1.5	0.5	ns	1200	1	n
Chicken bouillon, Wyler's, 1 tsp	5	0	0	0	900	1	
Chicken bouillon, cube, Herb-Ox, 1 cube	10	0	0	0	1040	1	

SOUP MIX	CAL (g)	FAT (g)	SAT FAT (g)	CHOL (mg)	SODIUM (mg)	CARB (g)	FIBER (g)
Chicken bouillon, cube, Wyler's, 1 cube	5	0	0	0	900	1	0
Chicken bouillon, very low sodium, Wyler's/Steero, 1 tsp	10	0	0	0	0	2	0
Chicken broth, Lipton Cup-A-Soup, 1 envelope	20	1	0	0	580	3	0
Chicken broth, Romanoff-MBT/Wyler's, 1 packet	15	0	0	0	930	2	0
Chicken broth, Weight Watchers, 0.16 oz	10	0	0	0	830	2	0
Chicken broth, low sodium, Romanoff-MBT/Wyler's, 1 packet	15	0	0	0	0	3	0
Chicken broth & seasoning, Herb-Ox, 1 packet	10	0	0	0	760	1	0
Chicken broth & seasoning, low sodium, Herb-Ox, 1 packet	15	0	0	0	20	1	0
Chicken flavor, Campbell's, 1 pkg	130	2	1	25	1290	22	1
Chicken flavor, with rice, Mrs. Grass, ¼ of carton	80	1	0	0	1000	15	0
Chicken flavored vegetable, Nile Spice, 1 pkg	120	2	1	5	600	20	1
Chicken noodle, Borden Soup Starter, ⅛ pkg	80	0.5	0	5	960	17	1
Chicken noodle, Knorr, ⅓ pkg	90	1	0.5	15	800	17	0
Chicken noodle, Lipton Cup-A-Soup, 1 envelope	50	1	0.5	10	550	8	0
Chicken noodle, Lipton Soup Secrets, 3 Tbsp	80	2.5	1	15	650	12	0
Chicken noodle, hearty, Lipton Cup-A-Soup, 1 envelope	60	1	0.5	10	540	10	0
Chicken noodle, hearty, Lipton Soup Secrets, 2 Tbsp	80	2	0.5	20	670	14	0
Chicken noodle with vegetables, fat free, Health Valley, ½ pkg	80	0	0	0	360	18	2
Chicken rice, mix to make 1 cup	60	1.5	0	<5	980	9	0

SOUP MIX	CAL (g)	FAT (g)	SAT FAT (g)	CHOL (mg)	SODIUM (mg)	CARB (g)	FIBER (g)
Chicken supreme, hearty, Lipton Cup-A-Soup, 1 envelope	90	4	2	0	650	13	<1
Chicken vegetable, Knorr, 1 pkg	100	0	0	0	840	21	0
Chicken vegetable, Lipton Cup-A-Soup, 1 envelope	50	1	0.5	10	520	10	0
Chicken vegetable, hearty, Borden Soup Starter, ½ pkg	70	0	0	0	850	16	2
Chicken with onion and rice, Lipton Kettle Creations, ¼ cup	120	1	0	<5	690	24	1
Chicken with pasta & beans, Lipton Kettle Creations, ¼ cup	110	1.5	0	<5	690	20	3
Chicken with pasta & onion, Lipton Kettle Creations, ¼ cup	90	2	0	<5	700	19	1
Chili & corn, Nile Spice, 1 pkg	160	3	0.5	0	730	25	5
Clam chowder, Manhattan, mix to make 1 cup	70	1.5	0	0	1340	11	na
Clam chowder, New England, mix to make 1 cup	90	4	0.5	0	750	13	1
Corn chowder with tomatoes, fat free, Health Valley, ½ pkg	90	0	0	0	360	20	3
Corn and potato chowder, Fantastic Foods, 1 pkg	160	1	0	0	580	34	2
Couscous almondine, Nile Spice, 1 pkg	200	2.5	0	0	490	37	2
Couscous garbanzo, Nile Spice, 1 pkg	220	2.5	0	0	500	39	2
Couscous lentil curry, Nile Spice, 1 pkg	200	1.5	0	0	730	36	4
Couscous minestrone, Nile Spice, 1 pkg	180	1.5	0	0	590	34	2
Couscous parmesan, Nile Spice, 1 pkg	200	3	1.5	10	570	34	2
Couscous with lentils, Fantastic Foods, 1 pkg	220	1	0	0	480	44	7
Cream of asparagus, mix to make 1 cup	50	1.5	0	0	710	8	0

SOUP MIX	CAL (g)	FAT (g)	SAT FAT (g)	CHOL (mg)	SODIUM (mg)	CARB (g)	FIBER (g)
Cream of broccoli, Knorr Chef's Collection, ½ pkg	60	3	1	5	590	8	2
Cream of chicken, Lipton Cup-A-Soup, 1 envelope	70	2.5	0.5	0	650	11	0
Cream of chicken flavored vegetable, Lipton Cup-A-Soup, 1 envelope	90	4	1.5	0	590	10	<1
Cream of mushroom, Lipton Cup-A-Soup, 1 envelope	60	2	0	0	590	10	0
Cream of snow pea, Knorr Chef's Collection, ½ pkg	70	2	0.5	0	700	10	0
Cream of spinach, Knorr, ⅓ pkg	70	2.5	1	0	600	9	0
Cream of vegetable, mix to make 1 cup	110	6	1.5	0	1170	12	<1
Cream of wild mushroom, Knorr Chef's Collection, ½ pkg	90	3	0.5	0	670	12	0
Creamy potato with broccoli, fat free, Health Valley, ½ pkg	70	0	0	0	360	15	2
Curry lentil & rice, Nile Spice, 1 pkg	180	1	0	0	270	33	3
Egg noodles & vegetables in chicken broth, Campbell's Soupsations, 1 pkg	150	2	1	20	980	27	2
Fine herb, Knorr, ⅓ pkg	100	5	1.5	<5	1010	13	0
Fish bouillon, Knorr, ½ cube	10	1	ns	ns	960	0	ns
Five bean, Fantastic Foods, 1 pkg	200	1	0	0	480	44	11
French onion, Knorr, ⅓ pkg	45	1	0.5	<5	980	8	0
Giggle noodle with chicken broth, Lipton Soup Secrets, 2 Tbsp	80	2	1	15	730	11	0
Green pea, Lipton Cup-A-Soup, 1 envelope	110	3.5	1	0	620	17	3
Gumbo, New Orleans style, Campbell's Soupsations, 1 pkg	170	2	1	5	950	34	2

SOUP MIX	CAL (g)	FAT (g)	SAT FAT (g)	CHOL (mg)	SODIUM (mg)	CARB (g)	FIBER (g)
Herb, golden, with lemon, Lipton Recipe Secrets, 2 Tbsp	35	0.5	0	<5	510	7	0
Herb, Italian, with tomato, Lipton Recipe Secrets, 2 Tbsp	40	0.5	0	0	520	9	0
Herb, savory, with garlic, Lipton Recipe Secrets, 1 Tbsp	35	0.5	0	0	460	6	0
Hot and sour, Knorr, ⅓ pkg	50	1.5	0.5	0	810	8	0
Leek, Knorr, ⅓ pkg	70	3	1	<5	780	9	0
Lentil, Nile Spice, 1 pkg	180	1.5	0	0	500	34	3
Lentil, country, Fantastic Foods, 1 pkg	200	1	0	0	480	41	12
Lentil, hearty, Campbell's Soupsations, 1 pkg	240	1	1	<5	990	42	7
Lentil, hearty, Knorr, 1 pkg	220	0	0	0	900	40	6
Lentil with bow tie pasta, homestyle, Lipton Kettle Creations, ¼ cup	130	1	0	0	760	23	5
Lentil with couscous, fat free, Health Valley, ½ pkg	130	0	0	0	360	28	5
Mediterranean pasta, Nile Spice, 1 pkg	180	2.5	1	<5	350	33	2
Mexican bean & rice, Campbell's Soupsations, 1 pkg	210	2	1	<5	930	41	6
Minestrone, Fantastic Foods, 1 pkg	130	1	0	0	480	29	4
Minestrone, Lipton Kettle Creations, ¼ cup	110	1.5	0	0	750	22	4
Minestrone, Nile Spice, 1 pkg	160	1.5	0	0	550	29	4
Mushroom, Fantastic Foods, 1 pkg	130	0	0	0	600	27	2
Mushroom, beefy, Lipton Recipe Secrets, 2 Tbsp	35	0	0	0	650	7	0
Mushroom, country, Nile Spice, 1 pkg	140	2.5	1	10	580	26	<1
Navy bean, Knorr, 1 pkg	140	0	0	0	870	27	5
Noodle, chicken flavor, Borden Homestyle, ¼ of carton	70	1.5	0	15	730	11	0

SOUP MIX	CAL (g)	FAT (g)	SAT FAT (g)	CHOL (mg)	SODIUM (mg)	CARB (g)	FIBER (g)
Noodle, chicken free, Fantastic Foods, 1 pkg	140	0.5	0	0	540	26	4
Noodle, extra, Lipton Soup Secrets, 3 Tbsp	90	1.5	0.5	25	680	15	<1
Noodle, hearty, with vegetables, Lipton Soup Secrets, 3 Tbsp	70	2	1	10	710	11	<1
Noodle, Oriental, spring vegetable, House of Tsang, 1 container	120	1	0	0	1660	25	1
Noodle, vegetable beef flavor, Mrs. Grass, ¼ of carton	70	1	0	0	1030	11	0
Noodle, vegetable curry, Fantastic Foods, 1 pkg	140	1	0	0	490	28	3
Noodle, vegetable miso, Fantastic Foods, 1 pkg	130	1	0	0	540	25	3
Noodle, vegetable tomato, Fantastic Foods, 1 pkg	150	1	0	0	490	31	3
Noodle with chicken broth, Campbell's, 1 pkg	150	2	1	20	1050	28	1
Noodle with chicken broth, Lipton Soup Secrets, 2 Tbsp	60	2	1	15	710	9	0
Noodle with chicken broth, Mrs. Grass, ¼ of carton	60	1.5	0.5	20	880	10	0
Noodle with vegetables, hearty, Campbell's, 1 pkg	150	2	1	20	1050	28	1
Onion, Lipton Recipe Secrets, 1 Tbsp	20	0	0	0	610	4	<1
Onion, beefy, Lipton Recipe Secrets, 1 Tbsp	25	0.5	0	0	610	5	0
Onion, golden, Lipton Recipe Secrets, 2 Tbsp	60	1.5	0	0	650	10	0
Onion broth, Romanoff-MBT, 1 packet	15	0	0	0	800	3	ns
Onion mushroom, Lipton Recipe Secrets, 2 Tbsp	35	1	0	0	620	6	0
Onion-mushroom, Mrs. Grass, ⅓ pkg	60	1	0	0	1080	10	0

SOUP MIX	CAL (g)	FAT (g)	SAT FAT (g)	CHOL (mg)	SODIUM (mg)	CARB (g)	FIBER (g)
Oxtail, Knorr, ⅓ pkg	60	2.5	1	<5	910	9	0
Parmesan pasta, Nile Spice, 1 pkg	190	3	1.5	10	470	32	2
Pasta fasul, Casbah, 1 pkg	160	0	0	0	470	12	2
Pasta Italiano, fat free, Health Valley, ½ pkg	140	0	0	0	360	31	3
Potato leek, Knorr, 1 pkg	120	0	0	0	970	24	1
Potato leek, home style, Nile Spice, 1 pkg	130	3	2	10	500	21	3
Potato leek, with organic vegetables, Nile Spice, 1 pkg	160	6	4	20	490	21	2
Primavera pasta, Nile Spice, 1 pkg	190	2.5	2	5	350	35	3
Ramen noodle, beef flavor, Campbell's Caldo Picoso, ½ block	190	7	4	0	790	28	1
Ramen noodle, beef flavor, Sanwa, ½ block	180	7	4	0	870	26	1
Ramen noodle, beef flavor, low fat, Campbell's, 1 pkg	220	2	0	0	1370	45	2
Ramen noodle, chicken, low fat, Campbell's, 1 pkg	220	2	1	0	1340	44	1
Ramen noodle, chicken flavor, Campbell's Caldo Picoso, ½ block	190	7	4	0	850	28	1
Ramen noodle, chicken flavor, spicy, low fat, Campbell's, 1 pkg	140	1	0	0	910	29	1
Ramen noodle, chicken mushroom flavor, Thrifty Maid, ½ block	190	7	4	0	760	27	1
Ramen noodle, curry chicken flavor, Sanwa, ½ block	190	7	4	0	740	28	1
Ramen noodle, French onion flavor, Sanwa, ½ block	180	7	4	0	700	26	1
Ramen noodle, hot & spicy flavor, Thrifty Maid, ½ block	190	7	4	0	800	27	1
Ramen noodle, Oriental flavor, Sanwa, ½ block	180	7	4	0	850	26	1

SOUP MIX	CAL (g)	FAT (g)	SAT FAT (g)	CHOL (mg)	SODIUM (mg)	CARB (g)	FIBER (g)
Ramen noodle, Oriental flavor, low fat, Campbell's, 1 pkg	220	2	1	0	1360	45	2
Ramen noodle, pork flavor, Sanwa, ½ block	180	7	4	0	760	26	1
Ramen noodle, shrimp flavor, Campbell's, 1 pkg	310	14	4	0	1020	40	2
Ramen noodle, shrimp flavor, Campbell's Caldo Picoso, ½ block	190	7	4	0	1050	28	1
Ramen noodle, shrimp flavor, low fat, Campbell's, 1 pkg	220	2	0	5	1110	45	2
Ramen noodle, shrimp flavor, Thai style, Sanwa, ½ block	190	7	4	0	730	28	1
Ramen noodle, teriyaki flavor, Thrifty Maid, ½ block	190	7	4	0	670	27	1
Red beans & rice, Nile Spice, 1 pkg	190	1.5	0	0	560	36	3
Ring-o-noodle with chicken broth, Lipton Soup Secrets, 2 Tbsp	70	2	1	10	710	10	0
Ruffle pasta, Lipton Soup Secrets, 2 Tbsp	60	1	0	0	670	10	0
Split pea, Fantastic Foods, 1 pkg	160	0.5	0	0	470	37	2
Split pea, Nile Spice, 1 pkg	200	1.5	0	0	710	35	6
Split pea, low sodium, Campbell's, 1 cup	190	4	2	5	40	30	5
Split pea, with carrots, fat free, Health Valley, 1 pkg	130	0	0	0	360	25	2
Sweet corn chowder, Nile Spice, 1 pkg	120	3	1	0	420	20	0
Tomato, Lipton Cup-A-Soup, 1 envelope	90	2	1	<5	490	19	1
Tomato & rice, Nile Spice, 1 pkg	130	3	1.5	10	550	23	1
Tomato herb, Nile Spice, 1 pkg	120	3	1	0	420	19	3
Tomato rice parmesano, Fantastic Foods, 1 pkg	190	2	0.5	0	550	41	2

SOUP MIX	CAL (g)	FAT (g)	SAT FAT (g)	CHOL (mg)	SODIUM (mg)	CARB (g)	FIBER (g)
Tomato vegetable, mix to make 1 cup	60	1	0	0	1240	11	<1
Tomato vegetable, Campbell's Soupsations, 1 pkg	130	2	1	15	900	25	2
Vegetable, Knorr, ¼ pkg	30	0	0	0	730	6	1
Vegetable, Lipton Recipe Secrets, 2 Tbsp	30	0	0	0	580	7	1
Vegetable, Mrs. Grass Homestyle, ¼ pkt	35	0	0	0	900	7	1
Vegetable, harvest, Nile Spice, 1 pkg	110	1.5	0	<5	600	21	1
Vegetable, spring, Knorr, ⅓ pkg	25	0	0	0	570	5	0
Vegetable, spring, Lipton Cup-A-Soup, 1 envelope	50	1	0	10	500	9	1
Vegetable barley, Fantastic Foods, 1 pkg	140	0.5	0	0	470	29	6
Vegetable bouillon, Wyler's, 1 tsp	5	0	0	0	870	1	0
Vegetable bouillon, cube, Herb-Ox, 1 cube	10	0	0	0	1000	1	0
Vegetable broth, Romanoff-MBT, 1 packet	10	0	0	0	860	2	ns
Vegetable harvest, hearty, Lipton Cup-A-Soup, 1 envelope	90	1.5	0.5	0	450	17	2
Vegetarian vegetable bouillion, Knorr, ½ cube	15	1	ns	ns	910	1	ns
Virginia pea, Lipton Cup-A-Soup, 1 envelope	130	5	2	0	630	19	3

AT A GLANCE: SOUP MIX
Highest in Fiber: Fantastic Foods Jumpin' Black Bean

FAST FOODS

	CAL (g)	FAT (g)	SAT FAT (g)	CHOL (mg)	SODIUM (mg)	CARB (g)	FIBER (g)
ARBY'S, SANDWICHES							
Beef n' cheddar, 1 sandwich	510	27	8	50	1170	43	na
Chicken breast fillet, 1 sandwich	450	23	3	45	960	52	na
French dip sub, 1 sandwich	470	21	8	60	1310	42	na
Grilled chicken deluxe, 1 sandwich	430	20	3.5	45	900	42	na
Italian sub, 1 sandwich	660	36	13	80	1960	47	na
Light roast beef deluxe, 1 sandwich	290	10	3.5	40	830	33	na
Light roast chicken deluxe, 1 sandwich	280	7	2	35	780	33	na
Light roast turkey deluxe, 1 sandwich	260	6	1.5	35	1260	33	na
Roast beef, regular, 1 sandwich	380	18	7	45	940	35	na
Roast beef, junior, 1 sandwich	230	11	4	25	520	23	na
Roast beef, giant, 1 sandwich	540	26	11	70	1430	46	na
Roast beef, super, 1 sandwich	550	28	8	45	1170	54	na
Roast beef sub, 1 sandwich	670	39	14	80	2000	46	na
Turkey sub, 1 sandwich	530	26	7	55	1940	45	na

AT A GLANCE: ARBY'S, SANDWICHES
Lowest in Fat: Light Roast Turkey Deluxe

ARBY'S, SALADS & DRESSINGS

	CAL (g)	FAT (g)	SAT FAT (g)	CHOL (mg)	SODIUM (mg)	CARB (g)	FIBER (g)
Garden salad, 1 salad	120	5	3	15	135	11	na
Roast chicken salad, 1 salad	200	7	3.5	45	510	12	na
Side salad, 1 salad	25	0	0	0	30	4	na
Buttermilk dressing, 1 packet	350	39	6	5	470	2	na
Honey French dressing, 1 packet	320	27	4	0	490	22	na
Croutons, 1 order	60	2.5	0	0	160	9	na

	CAL	FAT (g)	SAT FAT (g)	CHOL (mg)	SODIUM (mg)	CARB (g)	FIBER (g)

ARBY'S, SIDE ORDERS

	CAL	FAT (g)	SAT FAT (g)	CHOL (mg)	SODIUM (mg)	CARB (g)	FIBER (g)
Curly fries, 1 order	340	18	7	0	170	43	na
Curly fries, cheddar, 1 order	400	22	9	10	440	46	na
French fries, 1 order	250	13	3	0	115	30	na
Potato cakes, 1 order	200	12	2.5	0	400	20	na

ARBY'S, SHAKES & DESSERTS

	CAL	FAT (g)	SAT FAT (g)	CHOL (mg)	SODIUM (mg)	CARB (g)	FIBER (g)
Apple turnover, 1 turnover	300	18	7	0	180	28	na
Cherry turnover, 1 turnover	280	18	5	0	200	25	na
Jamocha shake, 1 shake	370	11	2.5	35	260	59	na

BASKIN ROBBINS, ICE CREAM

	CAL	FAT (g)	SAT FAT (g)	CHOL (mg)	SODIUM (mg)	CARB (g)	FIBER (g)
Almond buttercrunch, light, ½ cup	120	4	2	10	55	18	1
Banana nut, ½ cup	140	9	4	25	40	15	0
Banana strawberry, ½ cup	130	6	4	25	40	18	0
Baseball Nut, ½ cup	150	8	4	25	55	18	0
Berries 'n banana, no sugar added, ½ cup	80	1	1	5	55	15	0
Black walnut, ½ cup	150	10	5	30	50	14	0
Blueberry cheesecake, ½ cup	150	7	4	25	80	20	0
Butter pecan, old fashion, ½ cup	160	10	5	30	50	14	1
Butter pecan, old fashion, regular scoop	280	18	na	40	120	25	na
Butterfinger, ½ cup	160	8	4	20	65	21	0
Butterfinger, regular scoop	300	15	na	31	65	39	na
Call Me Nuts, no sugar added, ½ cup	100	2	1	5	55	19	1
Caramel Ban Surprise, fat free, ½ cup	110	0	0	2	70	24	0
Caramel chocolate crunch, ½ cup	160	9	5	25	90	20	0
Cherries jubilee, ½ cup	130	6	4	25	40	17	0
Cherries jubilee, regular scoop	240	11	na	35	90	31	na
Cherry cheesecake, ½ cup	150	7	4	25	75	20	0

BASKIN ROBBINS, ICE CREAM	CAL (g)	FAT (g)	SAT FAT (g)	CHOL (mg)	SODIUM (mg)	CARB (g)	FIBER (g)
Cherry cordial, no sugar added, ½ cup	100	2	1.5	5	55	19	0
Chewy Baby Ruth, ½ cup	160	9	5	25	65	19	0
Chocolate, ½ cup	150	8	5	25	65	19	0
Chocolate, regular scoop	270	14	na	37	160	32	na
Chocolate almond, ½ cup	170	10	5	25	60	18	1
Chocolate almond, regular scoop	300	18	8	45	105	31	1
Chocolate caramel nut, light, ½ cup	130	4	1.5	10	70	20	1
Chocolate chip, ½ cup	150	9	5	30	50	16	0
Chocolate chip, regular scoop	260	15	10	55	85	28	0
Chocolate chip, no sugar added, ½ cup	100	2.5	1.5	6	70	17	0
Chocolate chip cookie dough, ½ cup	170	10	5	25	60	19	1
Chocolate chocolate chip, no sugar added, ½ cup	100	2.5	1.5	5	70	17	0
Chocolate fudge, ½ cup	160	9	5	30	75	20	0
Chocolate fudge, regular scoop	290	15	na	40	180	34	na
Chocolate marshmallow, fat free, ½ cup	110	0	0	<5	75	26	1
Chocolate mousse royale, ½ cup	170	9	6	25	65	21	0
Chocolate mousse royale, regular scoop	320	16	na	30	150	38	na
Chocolate ribbon, ½ cup	140	7	4	25	45	18	0
Chocolate vanilla twist, fat free, ½ cup	100	0	0	<5	75	22	1
Chocolate Wonder, fat free, ½ cup	90	0	0	<5	70	20	1
Chunks n Chips, ½ cup	160	9	6	30	80	17	0
Chunky banana, no sugar added, ½ cup	90	1.5	1	5	55	16	0
Chunky Heath bar, ½ cup	170	9	6	25	70	19	0
Cinnamon Tax Crunch, ½ cup	160	8	4	25	70	20	0
Coconut fudge, no sugar added, ½ cup	110	1.5	1	5	60	20	1

BASKIN ROBBINS, ICE CREAM	CAL (g)	FAT (g)	SAT FAT (g)	CHOL (mg)	SODIUM (mg)	CARB (g)	FIBER (g)
Cookies 'n cream, ½ cup	160	9	6	25	80	17	0
Cookies 'n cream, regular scoop	280	17	na	40	115	29	na
Double raspberry, light, ½ cup	90	2	1	10	40	16	0
Espresso 'n cream, light, ½ cup	110	4	2.5	10	55	18	0
French vanilla, ½ cup	160	11	6	70	45	15	0
French vanilla, regular scoop	280	18	na	90	90	25	na
Fudge brownie, ½ cup	170	10	6	25	75	20	1
Fudge brownie, regular scoop	320	18	na	35	na	35	na
German chocolate cake, ½ cup	170	11	5	25	80	21	1
German chocolate cake, regular scoop	310	15	na	30	na	39	na
Gold Medal Ribbon, ½ cup	140	7	4	25	85	19	0
Here Comes the Fudge, ½ cup	150	7	5	20	55	20	0
Jamoca, ½ cup	130	7	5	30	50	15	0
Jamoca, regular scoop	240	13	na	40	95	26	na
Jamoca almond fudge, ½ cup	150	8	4	25	40	18	1
Jamoca almond fudge, regular scoop	270	14	na	30	115	30	na
Jamoca swirl, fat free, ½ cup	110	0	0	<5	70	24	0
Jamoca Swiss almond, no sugar added, ½ cup	100	2.5	1.5	<5	65	16	0
Just Peachy, fat free, ½ cup	100	0	0	<5	65	23	0
Kookaberry Kiwi, fat free, ½ cup	100	0	0	<5	65	21	0
Lemon custard, ½ cup	140	7	4	40	55	17	3
Mint chocolate chip, ½ cup	150	9	5	30	50	16	0
Mint chocolate chip, regular scoop	260	15	na	40	85	27	na
Naughty New Year's Resolution, ½ cup	170	11	5	25	70	22	0
New York cheesecake, ½ cup	150	9	6	25	75	17	0
Nutty coconut, ½ cup	170	11	5	25	50	16	1

BASKIN ROBBINS, ICE CREAM	CAL (g)	FAT (g)	SAT FAT (g)	CHOL (mg)	SODIUM (mg)	CARB (g)	FIBER (g)
Oregon blackberry, ½ cup	130	7	4.5	30	40	16	0
Oregon blackberry, regular scoop	230	12	8	50	70	28	0
Peach, ½ cup	130	6	4	25	40	17	0
Peach, regular scoop	230	11	7	45	50	30	0
Peanut butter 'n chocolate, ½ cup	180	11	5	25	95	17	1
Peanut butter 'n chocolate, regular scoop	330	20	na	35	140	29	na
Peanut butter cream, fat free, ½ cup	90	0	0	<5	70	20	0
Peter, Peter, Pumpkin Cheezer, ½ cup	150	8	5	35	70	17	0
Pineapple coconut, no sugar added, ½ cup	90	1.5	1	5	60	16	0
Pink bubble gum, ½ cup	150	7	4	25	45	20	0
Pistachio-almond, ½ cup	160	11	5	25	45	14	1
Pistachio-almond, regular scoop	290	18	na	40	80	25	na
Pistachio creme chip, light, ½ cup	120	4	2.5	10	55	17	0
Praline dream, light, ½ cup	120	4	1.5	10	65	18	0
Pralines 'n cream, ½ cup	160	8	4	25	75	20	0
Pralines 'n cream, regular scoop	280	14	7	45	135	35	0
Pumpkin pie, ½ cup	130	6	4	25	50	17	0
Quarterback Crunch, ½ cup	160	9	6	25	75	19	0
Raspberry Revelation, no sugar added, ½ cup	100	1	0.5	5	55	20	1
Reese's peanut butter, ½ cup	170	10	5	25	75	18	0
Reese's peanut butter, regular scoop	300	18	12	45	110	32	0
Rocky Path, light, ½ cup	130	4	1.5	10	55	19	1
Rocky road, ½ cup	160	8	4	25	60	21	0
Rocky road, regular scoop	300	14	na	30	135	39	na
Rum raisin, ½ cup	140	6	4	25	40	19	0
S'crunchous Crunch, ½ cup	170	8	5	20	65	23	0

BASKIN ROBBINS, ICE CREAM	CAL (g)	FAT (g)	SAT FAT (g)	CHOL (mg)	SODIUM (mg)	CARB (g)	FIBER (g)
S'mores, ½ cup	170	8	5	15	55	23	0
S'mores, regular scoop	300	13	8	30	100	41	0
Snickidy Doo Dah, ½ cup	170	8	5	25	90	21	0
Strawberry cheesecake, ½ cup	150	7	4	25	75	20	0
Strawberry cheesecake, regular scoop	260	13	8	30	115	33	na
Strawberry shortcake, ½ cup	150	8	5	25	70	19	0
Thin mint, no sugar added, ½ cup	100	2.5	1.5	5	70	17	0
Transylvania Twist, ½ cup	160	8	4	20	55	22	0
Triple chocolate passion, ½ cup	180	10	6	35	70	22	0
Truly Free apple pie, fat free, reduced sugar, ½ cup	80	0	0	<5	75	16	1
Truly Free cafe mocha, fat free, reduced sugar, ½ cup	80	0	0	<5	75	15	1
Truly Free chocolate, fat free, reduced sugar, ½ cup	80	0	0	0	80	15	1
Truly Free triple berry delight, fat free, reduced sugar, ½ cup	90	0	0	<5	75	16	1
Truly Free vanilla, fat free, reduced sugar, ½ cup	80	0	0	<5	75	15	1
Truly Free Whata Banana, fat free, reduced sugar, ½ cup	80	0	0	<5	75	15	1
Vanilla, ½ cup	140	8	5	35	40	14	0
Vanilla, regular scoop	240	14	na	50	115	24	na
Vanilla Swiss almond, no sugar added, ½ cup	110	2	1.5	5	60	20	1
Very berry strawberry, ½ cup	120	6	4	20	45	16	0
Very berry strawberry, regular scoop	220	10	na	30	95	30	na
Winter white chocolate, ½ cup	150	8	5	20	50	18	0
World class chocolate, ½ cup	150	8	4	25	60	19	0
World class chocolate, regular scoop	280	14	na	35	140	35	na

	CAL (g)	FAT (g)	SAT FAT (g)	CHOL (mg)	SODIUM (mg)	CARB (g)	FIBER (g)
BASKIN ROBBINS, FROZEN YOGURT							
Blackberry, nonfat, ½ cup	110	0	0	0	50	24	1
Blueberry, lowfat, ½ cup	120	1.5	1	5	70	24	0
Cheesecake, lowfat, ½ cup	120	1.5	1	10	75	21	0
Chocolate, lowfat, ½ cup	120	1.5	1	5	75	23	0
Chocolate mint, nonfat, ½ cup	100	0	0	0	60	23	1
Dutch chocolate, nonfat, ½ cup	100	0	0	0	60	23	0
Kahlua, nonfat, ½ cup	100	0	0	0	55	21	0
Key lime, nonfat, ½ cup	100	0	0	0	55	22	0
Maple walnut, nonfat, ½ cup	100	0	0	0	55	22	0
Peach, nonfat, ½ cup	100	0	0	0	50	22	0
Peppermint twist, nonfat, ½ cup	100	0	0	0	55	22	0
Pina colada, nonfat, ½ cup	110	0	0	0	50	22	0
Raspberry, nonfat, ½ cup	100	0	0	0	55	22	0
Strawberry, nonfat, ½ cup	100	0	0	0	55	23	0
Vanilla, lowfat, ½ cup	120	2	1	10	75	22	0
Vanilla, nonfat, ½ cup	110	0	0	<5	65	23	0

AT A GLANCE: BASKIN ROBBINS, FROZEN YOGURT
Lowest in Fat: Most frozen yogurt selections are fat free.

	CAL (g)	FAT (g)	SAT FAT (g)	CHOL (mg)	SODIUM (mg)	CARB (g)	FIBER (g)
BASKIN ROBBINS, YOGURT GONE CRAZY							
Boom Choco Laka, ½ cup	160	5	4	10	75	24	1
For Heaven's Cake, ½ cup	120	2	1.5	10	75	24	0
Maui Brownie Madness, ½ cup	140	3	1	5	80	26	1
Perils of Praline, ½ cup	130	3	1.5	5	95	24	0
Raspberry Cheese Louise, ½ cup	130	3	2	10	95	24	0

	CAL (g)	FAT (g)	SAT FAT (g)	CHOL (mg)	SODIUM (mg)	CARB (g)	FIBER (g)
BASKIN ROBBINS, ICES & SHERBETS							
Daiquiri ice, ½ cup	110	0	0	0	10	27	0
Daiquiri ice, regular scoop	130	0	0	0	10	33	0
Grape ice, ½ cup	110	0	0	0	10	27	0

BASKIN ROBBINS, ICES & SHERBETS	CAL (g)	FAT (g)	SAT FAT (g)	CHOL (mg)	SODIUM (mg)	CARB (g)	FIBER (g)
Margarita ice, ½ cup	110	0	0	0	10	28	0
Orange sherbet, ½ cup	120	1.5	1	5	25	25	0
Orange sherbet, regular scoop	160	2	na	5	45	34	0
Rainbow sherbet, ½ cup	120	1.5	1	5	25	25	0
Rainbow sherbet, regular scoop	160	2	1.5	10	30	34	0
Red raspberry sorbet, ½ cup	120	0	0	0	10	30	0
Red raspberry sorbet, regular scoop	140	0	0	0	25	34	0

BASKIN ROBBINS, NOVELTY ITEMS

	CAL (g)	FAT (g)	SAT FAT (g)	CHOL (mg)	SODIUM (mg)	CARB (g)	FIBER (g)
Cappuccino Blast bar, 1 bar	120	5	3	20	35	18	0
Cappuccino Blast bar, mocha, 1 bar	120	4	2.5	15	35	21	0
Chillyburgers, chocolate chip, 1 sandwich	220	11	7	25	100	27	1
Chillyburgers, mint chocolate chip, 1 sandwich	220	11	7	25	100	27	1
Sundae bars, jamoca almond fudge, 1 bar	280	17	9	20	60	28	0
Sundae bars, peanut butter chocolate, 1 bar	340	27	11	20	115	22	2
Sundae bars, pralines 'n cream, 1 bar	280	17	10	10	105	28	2
Tiny Toon bars, chocolate chip, 1 bar	240	17	11	25	40	20	2
Tiny Toon bars, mint chocolate chip, 1 bar	240	17	11	25	40	20	2
Tiny Toon bars, vanilla, 1 bar	210	16	9	25	40	18	0

BASKIN ROBBINS, FOUNTAIN DRINKS

	CAL (g)	FAT (g)	SAT FAT (g)	CHOL (mg)	SODIUM (mg)	CARB (g)	FIBER (g)
Cappuccino Blast, 1 order	290	10	7	50	105	42	0
Cappuccino Blast, mocha, 1 order	330	11	7	50	130	55	1
Malt, with vanilla ice cream, 1 order	660	31	19	140	250	84	1

	CAL (g)	FAT (g)	SAT FAT (g)	CHOL (mg)	SODIUM (mg)	CARB (g)	FIBER (g)
BASKIN ROBBINS, CONES							
Sugar cone, 1 cone	60	0	0	0	50	7	0
Waffle cone, fresh baked, cone	150	2	0.5	15	5	30	<1
Waffle cone, large, 1 cone	120	1.5	0	0	55	14	0
BASKIN ROBBINS, TOPPINGS							
Baby gummy bears, 75 pieces	130	0	0	0	15	30	0
Butterscotch, 2 oz	200	2	na	5	160	47	na
Hot fudge, 1 oz	100	3	na	0	45	17	na
Hot fudge, fat free, no sugar added, 1 oz	90	0	0	<5	100	20	1
Praline caramel, 1 oz	90	0	0	0	105	19	na
Strawberry, 1 oz	60	0	0	0	5	14	na
Whipped cream, 2 tsp	30	2.5	1.5	5	0	1	0
BOSTON MARKET, ENTREES							
Chicken, dark meat, no skin, ¼ chicken	210	10	2.5	150	320	1	0
Chicken, dark meat, with skin, ¼ chicken	330	22	6	180	460	2	0
Chicken, white meat, no skin, ¼ chicken	160	4	1	95	350	0	0
Chicken, white meat, with skin, ¼ chicken	330	17	4.5	175	530	2	0
Chicken, with skin, ½ chicken	630	37	19	370	960	2	0
Chicken breast sandwich, 1 sandwich	420	5	1	100	900	50	4
Chicken pot pie, original, 1 order	750	34	9	115	2380	78	6
Chunky chicken salad sandwich, 1 sandwich	640	31	5	145	1330	53	5
Vegetable pot pie, 1 order	350	12	7	35	1450	52	7

AT A GLANCE: BOSTON MARKET, ENTREES
Lowest in Fat: Chicken, White Meat, No Skin

	CAL (g)	FAT (g)	SAT FAT (g)	CHOL (mg)	SODIUM (mg)	CARB (g)	FIBER (g)
BOSTON MARKET, SALADS & SIDE ORDERS							
BBQ baked beans, ¾ cup	330	9	3	10	630	53	9
Caesar salad, 10 oz	520	43	12	40	1420	16	3
Caesar salad, side, 4 oz	210	17	4.5	20	560	6	1
Caesar salad, with chicken, 13 oz	670	47	13	120	1860	16	3
Caesar salad, without dressing, 8 oz	240	13	7	25	780	14	3
Chicken soup, ¾ cup	80	3	1	25	470	4	1
Chunky chicken salad, ¾ cup	390	30	5	145	790	3	1
Cinnamon apples, hot, ¾ cup	250	4.5	0.5	0	45	56	3
Cole slaw, ¾ cup	280	16	2.5	25	520	32	3
Corn, whole kernel, ¾ cup	190	4	1	0	130	39	4
Cornbread, 1 loaf	200	6	1.5	25	390	33	1
Cranberrry relish, ¾ cup	370	5	0.5	0	5	84	5
Fruit salad, ¾ cup	70	0.5	0	0	10	17	2
Gravy, chicken, 1 oz	15	1	0	0	170	2	0
Homestyle mashed potatoes & gravy, ¾ cup	200	9	5	25	560	27	2
Macaroni & cheese, ¾ cup	280	10	6	20	760	36	1
Mashed potatoes, ⅔ cup	180	8	5	25	390	25	2
Mediterranean pasta salad, ¾ cup	170	10	2.5	10	490	16	2
New potatoes, ¾ cup	140	3	0.5	0	100	25	2
Rice pilaf, ⅔ cup	180	5	1	0	600	32	2
Spinach, creamed, ¾ cup	300	24	15	75	790	13	2
Squash, butternut, ¾ cup	160	6	4	15	580	25	3
Stuffing, ¾ cup	310	12	2	0	1140	44	3
Tortellini salad, ¾ cup	380	24	4.5	90	530	29	2
Vegetables, steamed, ⅔ cup	35	0.5	0	0	35	7	3
Zucchini marinara, ¾ cup	80	4	0.5	0	470	10	2

	CAL	FAT (g)	SAT FAT (g)	CHOL (mg)	SODIUM (mg)	CARB (g)	FIBER (g)

BOSTON MARKET, DESSERTS

	CAL	FAT (g)	SAT FAT (g)	CHOL (mg)	SODIUM (mg)	CARB (g)	FIBER (g)
Brownie, 1 piece	450	27	7	80	190	47	3
Chocolate chip cookie, 1 cookie	340	17	6	25	240	48	1
Oatmeal raisin cookie, 1 cookie	320	13	2.5	25	260	48	1

BROWN'S CHICKEN & PASTA, ENTREES

	CAL	FAT (g)	SAT FAT (g)	CHOL (mg)	SODIUM (mg)	CARB (g)	FIBER (g)
Chicken breast, 3.5 oz	280	15	na	70	530	12	na
Chicken gizzard, 3.5 oz	390	20	na	90	800	26	na
Chicken leg, 3.5 oz	290	16	na	50	540	9	na
Chicken liver, 3.5 oz	340	19	na	150	700	20	na
Chicken thigh, 3.5 oz	360	24	na	65	570	13	na
Chicken wing, 3.5 oz	390	25	na	80	650	17	na
Fettucini Alfredo, 12 oz	1510	64	na	50	3020	173	na
Italian sausage links, 1 link	320	26	9	70	1050	3	<1
Meatballs, Mamma Ranne Italian style, 3 oz	240	16	6	75	650	6	2
Mostaccioli, with meat, 12 oz	840	14	na	20	900	144	na
Mostaccioli, without meat, 12 oz	790	10	na	0	840	146	na
Pasta, all varieties, dry, 2 oz	210	1	na	0	0	41	0
Pasta sauce, 2 oz	50	2.5	na	na	280	8	1
Ravioli, with meat, 12 oz	870	20	na	20	930	138	na
Ravioli, without meat, 12 oz	820	16	na	0	880	140	na
Roast beef, Italian style, sliced, 3 oz	170	6	2.5	50	240	1	0
Shrimp, 3.5 oz	280	10	na	30	780	34	na

AT A GLANCE: BROWN'S CHICKEN & PASTA, ENTREES
Lowest in Fat: Italian Style Roast Beef

BROWN'S CHICKEN & PASTA, SIDE ORDERS

	CAL	FAT (g)	SAT FAT (g)	CHOL (mg)	SODIUM (mg)	CARB (g)	FIBER (g)
Cole slaw, 3.5 oz	130	10	na	5	210	9	na
Corn fritters, 3.5 oz	420	25	na	<5	550	42	na
Corn on the cob, 3.5 oz	130	3	na	0	25	22	na
French fries, 3.5 oz	500	22	na	0	240	44	na

BROWN'S CHICKEN & PASTA, SIDE ORDERS	CAL	FAT (g)	SAT FAT (g)	CHOL (mg)	SODIUM (mg)	CARB (g)	FIBER (g)
Mushrooms, 3.5 oz	290	16	na	0	670	30	na
Potato salad, 3.5 oz	90	4	na	10	640	13	na

BURGER KING, BREAKFAST

	CAL	FAT (g)	SAT FAT (g)	CHOL (mg)	SODIUM (mg)	CARB (g)	FIBER (g)
Croissan'wich, with bacon, egg & cheese, 1 order	350	24	8	225	790	18	<1
Croissan'wich, with ham, egg & cheese, 1 order	350	22	7	230	1390	19	<1
Croissan'wich, with sausage, egg & cheese, 1 order	530	41	14	255	1000	21	<1
French toast sticks, 1 order	500	27	7	0	490	60	1
Hash browns, 1 order	220	12	3	0	320	25	2
A.M. Express dip, 1 packet	80	0	0	0	20	21	0
A.M. Express grape jam, 1 packet	30	0	0	0	0	7	0
A.M. Express strawberry jam, 1 packet	30	0	0	0	5	8	0

BURGER KING, SANDWICHES

	CAL	FAT (g)	SAT FAT (g)	CHOL (mg)	SODIUM (mg)	CARB (g)	FIBER (g)
BK Big Fish sandwich, 1 order	720	43	8	60	1090	59	2
BK Broiler chicken sandwich, 1 order	540	29	6	80	480	41	2
Cheeseburger, 1 order	380	19	9	65	780	28	1
Chicken sandwich, 1 order	700	43	9	60	1400	54	2
Double cheeseburger, 1 order	600	36	17	135	1040	29	1
Double cheeseburger, with bacon, 1 order	640	39	18	145	1220	29	1
Hamburger, 1 order	330	15	6	55	570	28	1
Whopper, 1 order	640	39	11	90	870	45	3
Whopper, with cheese, 1 order	730	46	16	115	1300	46	3
Double Whopper, 1 order	870	56	19	170	940	45	3
Double Whopper, with cheese, 1 order	960	63	24	195	1360	46	3
Whopper Junior, 1 order	420	24	8	60	570	29	2
Whopper Junior, with cheese, 1 order	460	28	10	75	780	29	2

AT A GLANCE: BURGER KING SANDWICHES
Lowest in Fat: Hamburger

	CAL	FAT (g)	SAT FAT (g)	CHOL (mg)	SODIUM (mg)	CARB (g)	FIBER (g)
BURGER KING, SALADS & DRESSINGS							
Broiled chicken salad, 1 order	200	10	5	60	110	7	3
Chef salad, 1 order	210	11	4	180	730	na	na
Garden salad, 1 order	90	5	3	15	110	7	3
Side salad, 1 order	50	3	2	5	55	4	2
Bleu cheese dressing, 1 packet	160	16	4	30	260	1	<1
French dressing, 1 packet	140	10	2	0	190	11	0
Italian dressing, light, reduced calorie, 1 packet	15	0.5	0	0	50	3	0
Ranch dressing, 1 packet	180	19	4	10	170	2	<1
Thousand island dressing, 1 packet	140	12	3	15	190	7	<1
Bacon bits, 1 packet	15	1	0.5	5	0	0	0
Croutons, 1 packet	30	1	0	0	75	4	0
BURGER KING, CHICKEN TENDERS & SAUCE							
Chicken tenders (6 pc), 1 order	250	12	3	35	530	14	2
Barbecue dipping sauce, 1 packet	35	0	0	0	400	9	0
Honey dipping sauce, 1 packet	90	0	0	0	10	23	0
Ranch dipping sauce, 1 packet	170	17	3	0	200	2	0
Sweet & sour dipping sauce, 1 packet	45	0	0	0	50	11	0
BURGER KING, SIDE ORDERS							
French fries, medium, salted, 1 order	400	20	5	0	240	43	3
Onion rings, 1 order	310	14	2	0	810	41	5
BURGER KING, SHAKES & DESSERTS							
Chocolate shake, medium, 1 order	310	7	4	20	230	54	3
Chocolate shake, medium, syrup added, 1 order	460	7	4	20	300	87	1

BURGER KING, SHAKES & DESSERTS	CAL	FAT (g)	SAT FAT (g)	CHOL (mg)	SODIUM (mg)	CARB (g)	FIBER (g)
Strawberry shake, medium, syrup added, 1 order	430	7	4	20	260	83	1
Vanilla shake, medium, 1 order	310	7	4	20	230	53	1
Dutch apple pie, 1 pie	310	15	3	0	230	39	2

CARL'S JR., BREAKFAST

	CAL	FAT (g)	SAT FAT (g)	CHOL (mg)	SODIUM (mg)	CARB (g)	FIBER (g)
Bacon, 2 strips	40	3.5	1.5	10	125	0	0
Blueberry muffin, 1 muffin	340	14	2	40	340	49	1
Bran muffin, 1 muffin	370	13	2	45	410	61	6
Breakfast burrito, 1 order	430	26	12	460	810	29	<1
Breakfast quesadilla, 1 order	300	14	6	225	750	27	1
Cinnamon roll, 1 roll	420	13	4	15	570	68	4
Danish, cheese, 1 order	400	22	5	15	390	49	1
English muffin, with margarine, 1 muffin	230	10	1.5	0	330	30	2
French Toast Dips, without syrup, 1 order	410	25	6	0	380	40	3
Hash brown nuggets, 1 order	270	17	4	0	410	27	2
Sausage, 1 patty	200	18	7	35	530	0	0
Scrambled eggs, 1 order	160	11	4	425	125	1	0
Sunrise Sandwich (bacon/sausage not included), 1 order	370	21	6	225	710	31	2
Jam, strawberry, 1 packet	35	0	0	0	0	9	0
Jelly, grape, 1 packet	35	0	0	0	0	9	0
Salsa, 1 packet	10	0	0	0	160	2	0
Syrup, 1 packet	90	0	0	0	5	22	0

AT A GLANCE: CARL'S JR., BREAKFAST
Lowest in Fat: English Muffin

CARL'S JR., CHICKEN & DIPPING SAUCES

	CAL	FAT (g)	SAT FAT (g)	CHOL (mg)	SODIUM (mg)	CARB (g)	FIBER (g)
Chicken Stars, 6 pieces	230	14	3	85	450	11	0
BBQ sauce, 1 packet	50	0	0	0	270	11	0
Honey sauce, 1 packet	90	0	0	0	5	23	0
Mustard sauce, 1 packet	45	0.5	0	0	150	10	0
Sweet N' sour sauce, 1 packet	50	0	0	0	60	11	0

	CAL	FAT (g)	SAT FAT (g)	CHOL (mg)	SODIUM (mg)	CARB (g)	FIBER (g)
CARL'S JR., SANDWICHES							
BBQ chicken sandwich, 1 order	310	6	1.5	55	830	34	3
Big Burger, 1 order	470	20	8	55	810	46	2
Carl's Catch Fish Sandwich, 1 order	560	30	7	60	1220	54	5
Chicken club sandwich, 1 order	550	29	8	85	1160	37	3
Double Western bacon cheeseburger, 1 order	970	57	27	145	1810	58	2
Famous Big Star hamburger, 1 order	610	38	11	70	890	42	2
Hamburger, 1 order	200	8	4	25	500	23	1
Sante Fe chicken sandwich, 1 order	530	30	7	85	1230	36	3
Spicy Hot & Crispy Chicken Sandwich, 1 order	400	22	5	45	980	35	2
Super Star hamburger, 1 order	820	53	20	120	1030	41	2
Western Bacon Cheeseburger, 1 order	870	35	16	90	1490	59	2
CARL'S JR., SALADS & SALAD DRESSINGS							
Charbroiled Chicken Salad-To-Go, 1 order	260	9	5	70	530	11	4
Garden Salad-To-Go, 1 order	50	3	1.5	5	75	4	2
1000 island dressing, 2 oz	250	24	4	20	540	7	0
Bleu cheese dressing, 2 oz	310	34	6	25	360	1	0
French dressing, fat free, 2 oz	70	0	0	0	760	18	0
House dressing, 2 oz	220	22	4	20	440	3	0
Italian dressing, fat free, 2 oz	15	0	0	0	800	4	1
Croutons, 1 packet	35	1	0	0	65	5	0
CARL'S JR., SIDE ORDERS							
Breadsticks, 1 packet	35	0.5	0	0	60	7	1
CrissCut fries, large, 1 order	550	34	9	0	1280	55	3

CARL'S JR., SIDE ORDERS	CAL (g)	FAT (g)	SAT FAT (g)	CHOL (mg)	SODIUM (mg)	CARB (g)	FIBER (g)
French fries, regular, 1 order	370	20	7	0	240	44	3
Great Stuff Potatoes, bacon & cheese, 1 order	630	29	7	40	1720	76	6
Great Stuff Potatoes, broccoli & cheese, 1 order	530	22	5	15	930	76	8
Great Stuff Potatoes, plain, 1 order	290	0	0	0	40	68	6
Great Stuff Potatoes, sour cream & chive, 1 order	430	14	3	10	160	70	6
Onion rings, 1 order	520	26	6	0	840	63	3
Zucchini, 1 order	380	23	6	0	1040	38	3

CARL'S JR., SHAKES & DESSERTS

	CAL (g)	FAT (g)	SAT FAT (g)	CHOL (mg)	SODIUM (mg)	CARB (g)	FIBER (g)
Chocolate cake, 1 order	300	10	2.5	23	260	49	4
Chocolate chip cookie, 1 order	370	19	8	25	350	49	1
Chocolate shake, 1 order	390	7	5	30	280	74	0
Strawberry shake, 1 order	400	7	5	30	240	77	0
Vanilla shake, 1 order	330	8	5	35	250	54	0

CHURCHS FRIED CHICKEN

	CAL (g)	FAT (g)	SAT FAT (g)	CHOL (mg)	SODIUM (mg)	CARB (g)	FIBER (g)
Breast, 2.8 oz	200	12	na	65	510	4	0
Leg, 2 oz	140	9	na	45	160	2	0
Tender, 1.1 oz	80	4	na	15	140	5	<1
Thigh, 2.8 oz	230	16	na	80	520	5	0
Wing, 3.1 oz	250	16	na	60	540	8	0

CHURCHS FRIED CHICKEN, SIDE ORDERS

	CAL (g)	FAT (g)	SAT FAT (g)	CHOL (mg)	SODIUM (mg)	CARB (g)	FIBER (g)
Biscuits, 2.1 oz	250	16	na	<5	640	26	1
Cajun rice, 3.1 oz	130	7	na	<5	260	16	<1
Cole slaw, 3 oz	90	6	na	0	230	8	2
Corn on the cob, 5.7 oz	140	3.5	na	0	15	24	9
French fries, 2.7 oz	210	11	na	0	60	29	2
Okra, 2.8 oz	210	16	na	0	520	19	4
Potatoes & gravy, 3.7 oz	90	3.5	na	0	520	14	1

	CAL (g)	FAT (g)	SAT FAT (g)	CHOL (mg)	SODIUM (mg)	CARB (g)	FIBER (g)
CHURCHS FRIED CHICKEN, DESSERTS							
Apple pie, 3.1 oz	280	12	na	<5	340	41	1
DAIRY QUEEN							
Banana split, 1 order	510	11	8	30	250	93	na
Blizzard, Heath bar, regular, 1 order	820	36	17	60	410	114	na
Blizzard, Heath bar, small, 1 order	560	23	11	40	280	79	na
Blizzard, strawberry, regular, 1 order	570	16	11	50	230	92	na
Blizzard, strawberry, small, 1 order	400	12	8	35	160	64	na
Breeze, Heath, regular, 1 order	680	21	6	15	360	113	na
Breeze, Heath, small, 1 order	450	12	3	10	230	78	na
Breeze, strawberry, regular, 1 order	420	1	na	5	170	90	na
Buster Bar, 1 bar	450	29	9	15	220	40	na
Cone, chocolate, dipped, small, 1 cone	330	16	8	20	100	40	na
Cone, chocolate, regular, 1 cone	350	11	8	30	170	54	na
Cone, chocolate, small, 1 cone	230	7	5	20	115	36	na
Cone, vanilla, child's, 1 cone	140	4	3	15	60	22	na
Cone, vanilla, regular, 1 cone	340	10	7	30	140	53	na
Cone, vanilla, small, 1 cone	230	7	5	20	95	36	na
Dilly Bar, 1 bar	210	13	6	10	50	21	na
DQ frozen cake slice, undecorated, 1 slice	380	18	8	20	210	50	na
DQ sandwich, 1 order	140	4	2	5	135	24	na
Hot Fudge Brownie Delight, 1 order	710	29	14	35	340	102	na
Malt, vanilla, small, 1 order	610	14	8	45	230	106	na
Mr. Misty, small, 1 order	250	0	0	0	0	63	na

DAIRY QUEEN	CAL (g)	FAT (g)	SAT FAT (g)	CHOL (mg)	SODIUM (mg)	CARB (g)	FIBER (g)
Nutty Double Fudge, 1 order	580	22	10	35	170	85	na
Peanut Buster Parfait, 1 order	710	32	10	30	410	94	na
QC Chocolate Big Scoop, 1 order	310	14	10	35	100	40	na
QC Vanilla Big Scoop, 1 order	300	14	9	35	100	39	na
Shake, chocolate, small, 1 order	540	14	8	45	290	94	na
Shake, vanilla, regular, 1 order	600	16	10	50	260	101	na
Shake, vanilla, small, 1 order	520	14	8	45	230	88	na
Sundae, chocolate, small, 1 order	300	7	5	20	140	54	na
Sundae, waffle cone, strawberry, 1 order	350	12	5	20	220	56	na
Sundae, yogurt, strawberry, small, 1 order	200	na	na	na	80	43	na

AT A GLANCE: DAIRY QUEEN
Lowest in Fat: Mr. Misty

DAIRY QUEEN/BRAZIER, CHICKEN STRIPS

	CAL (g)	FAT (g)	SAT FAT (g)	CHOL (mg)	SODIUM (mg)	CARB (g)	FIBER (g)
Chicken strip basket, with BBQ sauce, 1 order	810	37	9	55	1590	88	5
Chicken strip basket, with gravy, 1 order	860	42	11	55	1820	88	5

DAIRY QUEEN/BRAZIER, SANDWICHES

	CAL (g)	FAT (g)	SAT FAT (g)	CHOL (mg)	SODIUM (mg)	CARB (g)	FIBER (g)
Cheese dog, 1 order	290	18	8	40	950	20	1
Chicken breast fillet sandwich, 1 order	430	20	4	55	760	37	2
Chicken breast fillet sandwich, with cheese, 1 order	480	25	7	70	980	38	2
Chili 'n' cheese dog, 1 order	330	21	9	45	1090	22	2
Chili dog, 1 order	280	16	6	35	870	21	2
DQ Homestyle bacon double cheeseburger, 1 order	610	36	18	130	1380	31	2
DQ Homestyle cheeseburger, 1 order	340	17	8	55	850	29	2

DAIRY QUEEN/BRAZIER, SANDWICHES	CAL	FAT (g)	SAT FAT (g)	CHOL (mg)	SODIUM (mg)	CARB (g)	FIBER (g)
DQ Homestyle deluxe double cheeseburger, 1 order	540	31	16	115	1130	31	2
DQ Homestyle deluxe double hamburger, 1 order	440	22	10	90	680	29	2
DQ Homestyle double cheeseburger, 1 order	540	31	16	115	1130	30	2
DQ Homestyle hamburger, 1 order	290	12	5	45	630	29	2
DQ Homestyle ultimate burger, 1 order	670	43	19	135	1210	29	2
Fish fillet sandwich, 1 order	370	16	3.5	45	630	39	2
Fish fillet sandwich, with cheese, 1 order	420	21	6	60	850	40	2
Grilled chicken breast fillet sandwich, 1 order	310	10	2.5	50	1040	30	3
Hot dog, 1 order	240	14	5	25	730	19	1

AT A GLANCE: DAIRY QUEEN/BRAZIER, SANDWICHES
Lowest in Fat: Grilled Chicken Breast Fillet Sandwich

DAIRY QUEEN/BRAZIER, SIDE ORDERS

French fries, small, 1 order	210	10	2	0	115	29	3
French fries, regular, 1 order	300	14	3	0	160	40	4
French fries, large, 1 order	390	18	4	0	200	52	6
Onion rings, 1 order	240	12	2.5	0	135	29	2

DOMINO'S PIZZA

12" deep dish, cheese, ¼ pizza	560	24	9	35	1180	63	3
12" deep dish, ham, ¼ pizza	580	25	9	40	1350	64	3
12" deep dish, Italian sausage & mushroom, ¼ pizza	620	28	11	45	1360	66	4
12" deep dish, pepperoni, ¼ pizza	620	29	11	45	1380	63	3
12" deep dish, veggie, ¼ pizza	580	25	9	35	1230	65	4
12" deep dish, x-tra cheese & pepperoni, ¼ pizza	670	33	13	55	1510	64	3

DOMINO'S PIZZA	CAL	FAT (g)	SAT FAT (g)	CHOL (mg)	SODIUM (mg)	CARB (g)	FIBER (g)
12" hand-tossed, cheese, ¼ pizza	340	10	4.5	20	980	50	2
12" hand-tossed, ham, ¼ pizza	360	10	4.5	25	1140	50	2
12" hand-tossed, Italian sausage & mushroom, ¼ pizza	400	14	6	30	1150	52	3
12" hand-tossed, pepperoni, ¼ pizza	410	15	7	35	1180	50	3
12" hand-tossed, veggie, ¼ pizza	360	10	4.5	20	1030	52	3
12" hand-tossed, x-tra cheese & pepperoni, ¼ pizza	460	19	9	40	1300	51	3
12" thin crust, cheese, ⅓ pizza	360	16	6	25	1010	40	2
12" thin crust, ham, ⅓ pizza	390	17	7	35	1230	41	2
12" thin crust, Italian sausage & mushroom, ⅓ pizza	440	21	9	40	1240	43	3
12" thin crust, pepperoni, ⅓ pizza	450	23	9	45	1280	40	2
12" thin crust, veggie, ⅓ pizza	390	17	7	25	1080	43	3
12" thin crust, x-tra cheese & pepperoni, ⅓ pizza	510	28	12	55	1440	41	2

AT A GLANCE: DOMINO'S PIZZA
Lowest in Calories & Fat, 12" Pizza: Hand-tossed Cheese

EL POLLO LOCO, ENTREES

	CAL	FAT (g)	SAT FAT (g)	CHOL (mg)	SODIUM (mg)	CARB (g)	FIBER (g)
Chicken breast, 3 oz	160	6	2	110	390	0	0
Chicken burrito, 7 oz	310	11	2	65	510	30	4
Chicken fajita meal, 17.5 oz	780	18	3	60	1060	120	17
Chicken leg, 1.75 oz	90	5	1.5	75	150	0	0
Chicken taco, 5 oz	180	7	1	35	300	18	2
Chicken thigh, 2 oz	180	12	4	130	230	0	0
Chicken wing, 1.5 oz	110	6	2	80	220	0	0
Steak burrito, 6 oz	450	22	9	70	740	31	4
Steak fajita meal, 17.5 oz	1040	38	14	100	1550	120	17
Steak taco, 4.5 oz	250	12	4	40	410	18	2

EL POLLO LOCO, ENTREES	CAL	FAT (g)	SAT FAT (g)	CHOL (mg)	SODIUM (mg)	CARB (g)	FIBER (g)
Vegetarian burrito, 6 oz	340	7	2	20	360	54	7

AT A GLANCE: EL POLLO LOCO, ENTREES
Lowest in Fat: Chicken Portions (Leg, Breast, or Wing); Chicken Taco, Vegetarian Burrito

EL POLLO LOCO, SIDE ORDERS

Beans, 4 oz	100	2.5	0.5	0	460	16	8
Coleslaw, 3 oz	100	8	1	10	160	7	1
Corn, 3 oz	110	2	1	0	110	20	1
Corn tortilla, 1 oz	60	0.5	0	0	25	13	<1
Flour tortilla, 1 oz	90	2.5	1.5	0	150	15	<1
Potato salad, 4 oz	180	10	1.5	10	340	21	1
Rice, 2 oz	110	1.5	0	0	220	19	0

EL POLLO LOCO, SALADS & DRESSINGS

Grilled chicken salad, 12 oz	160	4	1	45	440	11	4
Side salad, 9 oz	50	1	0	0	30	10	4
Blue cheese dressing, 1 oz	80	6	1	5	150	4	0
French dressing, deluxe, 1 oz	60	4	0	0	160	7	0
Italian dressing, reduced calorie, 1 oz	25	2	0	0	170	2	0
Ranch dressing, 1 oz	80	6	0	0	190	4	0
Thousand island dressing, 1 oz	110	10	0	5	240	4	0

EL POLLO LOCO, CONDIMENTS & TOPPINGS

Cheddar cheese, 1 oz	90	5	3	30	180	3	0
Guacamole, 1 oz	60	6	0	0	130	2	0
Honey dijon mustard, 1 oz	50	0.5	0	0	440	7	0
Salsa, 2 oz	10	0	0	0	180	3	1
Sour cream, 1 oz	60	6	4	15	15	1	0

EL POLLO LOCO, DESSERTS

Cheesecake, 3.5 oz	310	18	9	60	230	30	0
Churro, 1.25 oz	130	8	2	5	160	13	<1

	CAL	FAT (g)	SAT FAT (g)	CHOL (mg)	SODIUM (mg)	CARB (g)	FIBER (g)

GODFATHER'S PIZZA

	CAL	FAT (g)	SAT FAT (g)	CHOL (mg)	SODIUM (mg)	CARB (g)	FIBER (g)
Cheese, golden crust, medium, 1/8 pizza	230	9	na	20	270	28	na
Cheese, original crust, medium, 1/8 pizza	240	7	na	25	290	35	na
Cheese, original crust, mini, 1/4 pizza	140	4	na	15	160	20	na
Combo, golden crust, medium, 1/8 pizza	280	13	na	30	530	30	na
Combo, original crust, medium, 1/8 pizza	320	12	na	40	570	37	na
Combo, original crust, mini, 1/4 pizza	160	5	na	20	290	21	na

AT A GLANCE: GODFATHER'S PIZZA
Lowest in Fat, Medium Pizza: Original Crust, Cheese
Lowest in Fat, Mini Pizza: Cheese

HARDEE'S, BREAKFAST

	CAL	FAT (g)	SAT FAT (g)	CHOL (mg)	SODIUM (mg)	CARB (g)	FIBER (g)
Bacon & egg biscuit, 1 order	490	27	9	155	1250	44	na
Bacon, egg & cheese biscuit, 1 order	530	31	11	155	1470	45	na
Big Country Breakfast, with bacon, 1 order	740	43	13	305	1800	61	na
Big Country Breakfast, with sausage, 1 order	930	61	19	340	2240	61	na
Biscuit 'N' Gravy, 1 order	510	28	9	15	1500	55	na
Blueberry muffin, 1 muffin	400	17	4	65	310	56	na
Canadian Rise 'N' Shine biscuit, 1 order	570	32	11	175	1860	46	na
Chicken fillet biscuit, 1 order	510	25	7	45	1580	52	na
Cinnamon 'N' Raisin biscuit, 1 biscuit	370	18	5	0	450	48	na
Country ham biscuit, 1 order	430	22	6	25	1930	45	na
Frisco breakfast sandwich, ham, 1 order	460	22	8	175	1320	46	na
Ham biscuit, 1 order	400	20	6	15	1340	47	na

HARDEE'S BREAKFAST	CAL (g)	FAT (g)	SAT FAT (g)	CHOL (mg)	SODIUM (mg)	CARB (g)	FIBER (g)
Ham, egg & cheese biscuit, 1 order	500	27	10	170	1620	48	na
Hash Rounds, regular, 1 order	230	14	3	0	560	24	na
Pancakes (3 pc), 1 order	280	2	1	15	890	56	na
Pancakes (3 pc), with sausage patty, 1 order	430	16	6	40	1290	56	na
Pancakes (3 pc), with 2 bacon strips, 1 order	350	9	3	25	1130	56	na
Rise 'N Shine biscuit, 1 order	390	21	6	0	1000	44	na
Sausage & egg biscuit, 1 order	560	35	11	170	1400	44	na
Sausage biscuit, 1 order	510	31	10	25	1360	44	na
Steak biscuit, 1 order	580	32	10	30	1580	56	na

AT A GLANCE: HARDEE'S, BREAKFAST
Lowest in Fat: Pancakes

HARDEE'S, SANDWICHES

	CAL (g)	FAT (g)	SAT FAT (g)	CHOL (mg)	SODIUM (mg)	CARB (g)	FIBER (g)
Bacon cheeseburger, 1 order	600	36	15	50	950	35	na
Big Deluxe burger, 1 order	530	30	13	40	790	36	na
Big Roast Beef, 1 order	370	16	7	40	1050	34	na
Cheeseburger, 1 order	300	13	7	25	690	34	na
Chicken fillet, 1 order	400	14	3	55	1100	48	na
Fisherman's Fillet, 1 order	500	22	6	60	1170	51	na
Frisco burger, 1 order	760	50	18	70	1280	43	na
Frisco grilled chicken, 1 order	620	34	10	95	1730	44	na
Hamburger, 1 order	260	9	4	20	460	33	na
Hot dog, 1 order	450	20	6	35	1090	52	na
Hot Ham 'N' Cheese, 1 order	530	30	9	65	1710	49	na
Mushroom 'N' Swiss burger, 1 order	520	27	13	45	990	37	na
Quarter-pound cheeseburger, 1 order	490	25	12	35	860	37	na
Roast beef, regular, 1 order	270	11	5	25	780	28	na

AT A GLANCE: HARDEE'S, SANDWICHES
Lowest in Fat: Hamburger

	CAL (g)	FAT (g)	SAT FAT (g)	CHOL (mg)	SODIUM (mg)	CARB (g)	FIBER (g)

HARDEE'S, FRIED CHICKEN

	CAL (g)	FAT (g)	SAT FAT (g)	CHOL (mg)	SODIUM (mg)	CARB (g)	FIBER (g)
Breast, 1 order	370	15	4	75	1190	29	na
Leg, 1 order	170	7	2	45	570	15	na
Thigh, 1 order	330	15	4	60	1000	30	na
Wing, 1 order	200	8	2	30	740	23	na

HARDEE'S, SALADS & DRESSINGS

	CAL (g)	FAT (g)	SAT FAT (g)	CHOL (mg)	SODIUM (mg)	CARB (g)	FIBER (g)
Garden salad, 1 order	210	13	9	40	350	10	na
Grilled chicken salad, 1 order	150	3	1	60	610	11	na
Peppercorn steak salad, 1 order	180	5	2	30	300	13	na
Side salad, 1 order	25	ns	ns	0	45	4	na
Super chef salad, 1 order	230	12	7	45	800	11	na
French dressing, fat free, 1 order	70	0	0	0	580	17	na
Honey dijon dressing, fat free, 1 order	80	0	0	0	290	20	na
Italian dressing, 1 order	230	24	4	15	430	4	na
Parmesan peppercorn dressing, 1 order	330	34	5	25	560	3	na
Ranch dressing, 1 order	290	29	4	25	510	6	na
Thousand island dressing, 1 order	250	23	3	35	540	9	na

HARDEE'S, SIDE ORDERS

	CAL (g)	FAT (g)	SAT FAT (g)	CHOL (mg)	SODIUM (mg)	CARB (g)	FIBER (g)
Cole slaw, 1 order	240	20	3	10	340	13	na
Crispy Curls, 1 order	300	16	3	0	840	36	na
French fries, small, 1 order	240	10	3	0	100	33	na
French fries, medium, 1 order	350	15	4	0	150	49	na
French fries, large, 1 order	430	18	5	0	190	59	na
Gravy, 1 portion	20	na	na	0	260	3	na
Mashed potatoes, 1 portion	70	na	na	0	330	14	na

	CAL (g)	FAT (g)	SAT FAT (g)	CHOL (mg)	SODIUM (mg)	CARB (g)	FIBER (g)
HARDEE'S, SHAKES & DESSERTS							
Big Cookie, 1 order	280	12	4	15	150	41	na
Chocolate shake, 1 order	390	10	6	30	220	61	na
Peach shake, 1 order	530	11	7	45	220	95	na
Strawberry shake, 1 order	390	8	5	30	200	65	na
Vanilla shake, 1 order	370	9	6	25	210	59	na
Cool Twist cone, chocolate, 1 order	180	4	3	15	85	29	na
Cool Twist cone, vanilla, 1 order	180	4	3	15	80	29	na
Cool Twist cone, vanilla/chocolate, 1 order	170	4	3	15	85	29	na
Cool Twist sundae, hot fudge, 1 order	320	10	5	25	260	50	na
Cool Twist sundae, strawberry, 1 order	260	6	3	15	100	48	na
JACK IN THE BOX, BREAKFAST							
Breakfast Jack, 1 order	300	12	5	185	890	30	0
Hash browns, 1 order	160	11	2.5	0	310	14	1
Pancake platter, 1 order	400	12	3	30	980	59	3
Pancake syrup, 1 packet	120	0	0	0	5	30	0
Sausage croissant, 1 croissant	670	48	19	250	940	39	2
Scrambled egg pocket, 1 pocket	430	21	8	355	1060	31	0
Sourdough breakfast sandwich, 1 sandwich	380	20	7	235	1120	31	0
Supreme croissant, 1 croissant	570	36	15	245	1240	39	2
Ultimate breakfast sandwich, 1 sandwich	620	35	11	455	1800	39	<1

AT A GLANCE: JACK IN THE BOX, BREAKFAST
Lowest in Fat & Sat Fat: Pancake Platter

	CAL (g)	FAT (g)	SAT FAT (g)	CHOL (mg)	SODIUM (mg)	CARB (g)	FIBER (g)

JACK IN THE BOX, SANDWICHES

	CAL (g)	FAT (g)	SAT FAT (g)	CHOL (mg)	SODIUM (mg)	CARB (g)	FIBER (g)
¼ lb burger, 1 order	510	27	10	65	1080	39	0
Bacon bacon cheeseburger, 1 order	710	45	15	115	1280	41	0
Cheeseburger, 1 order	320	15	6	35	670	32	0
Chicken Caesar sandwich, 1 sandwich	520	26	6	55	1050	44	4
Chicken fajita pita, 1 sandwich	290	8	3	35	700	29	3
Chicken sandwich, 1 sandwich	400	18	4	45	1290	38	0
Chicken supreme sandwich, 1 sandwich	620	36	11	75	1520	48	0
Double cheeseburger, 1 order	450	24	12	75	970	35	0
The Colossus burger, 1 order	1100	84	28	220	1510	30	0
Fish supreme sandwich, 1 sandwich	590	34	6	70	1180	49	0
Grilled chicken fillet sandwich, 1 sandwich	430	19	5	65	1070	36	0
Grilled sourdough burger, 1 order	670	43	16	110	1180	39	0
Hamburger, 1 order	280	11	4	25	470	31	0
Jumbo Jack, 1 order	560	32	10	65	740	41	0
Jumbo Jack, with cheese, 1 order	650	40	14	90	1150	42	0
Monterey roast beef sandwich, 1 sandwich	540	30	9	75	1270	40	3
The Really Big Chicken Sandwich, 1 order	900	56	14	120	2150	58	1
Spicy crispy chicken sandwich, 1 sandwich	560	27	5	50	1020	55	0
Super taco, 1 taco	280	17	6	30	720	22	3
Taco, 1 taco	190	11	4	20	410	15	2
The Outlaw Burger, 1 order	720	40	17	95	1510	56	0
Ultimate cheeseburger, 1 order	1030	79	26	205	1200	30	0

AT A GLANCE: JACK IN THE BOX, SANDWICHES
Lowest in Fat: Chicken Fajita Pita

	CAL	FAT (g)	SAT FAT (g)	CHOL (mg)	SODIUM (mg)	CARB (g)	FIBER (g)
JACK IN THE BOX, CHICKEN							
Chicken strips, breaded (4 pc), 1 order	290	13	3	50	700	18	0
Chicken strips, breaded (6 pc), 1 order	450	20	5	80	1100	28	0
Chicken teriyaki bowl, 1 order	580	1.5	0.5	30	1220	115	6
JACK IN THE BOX, SIDES							
Curly fries, seasoned, 1 order	360	20	5	0	1070	39	4
Egg rolls (3 pc), 1 order	440	24	7	30	960	54	4
Egg rolls (5 pc), 1 order	750	41	12	50	1640	92	7
French fries, small, 1 order	220	11	2.5	0	120	28	3
French fries, regular, 1 order	350	17	4	0	190	45	4
French fries, jumbo, 1 order	400	19	5	0	220	51	4
French fries, super scoop, 1 order	590	29	7	0	330	76	6
Guacamole, 25 g	50	4	0.5	0	95	3	0
Jalapenos, stuffed (7 pc), 1 order	420	27	12	55	1620	29	3
Jalapenos, stuffed (10 pc), 1 order	600	39	16	75	2320	41	4
Onion rings, 1 order	380	23	6	0	450	38	0
Potato wedges, bacon & cheddar, 1 order	800	58	16	55	1470	49	4
JACK IN THE BOX, SALADS & DRESSINGS							
Garden chicken salad, 1 salad	200	9	4	65	420	8	3
Side salad, 1 salad	70	4	2.5	10	80	3	2
Blue cheese dressing, 1 packet	210	18	3.5	15	750	11	0
House dressing, buttermilk, 1 packet	290	30	11	20	560	6	0
Italian dressing, low calorie, 1 packet	25	1.5	0	0	670	2	0

JACK IN THE BOX, SALADS & DRESSINGS	CAL	FAT (g)	SAT FAT (g)	CHOL (mg)	SODIUM (mg)	CARB (g)	FIBER (g)
Thousand island dressing, 1 packet	250	24	4	20	570	10	0
Croutons, 1 order	50	2	0.5	0	105	8	0

JACK IN THE BOX, CONDIMENTS & SAUCES

	CAL	FAT (g)	SAT FAT (g)	CHOL (mg)	SODIUM (mg)	CARB (g)	FIBER (g)
Barbecue dipping sauce, 1 packet	45	0	0	0	300	11	0
Hot sauce, 1 packet	5	0	0	0	110	1	0
House dipping sauce, buttermilk, 1 packet	130	13	5	10	240	3	<1
Mustard, Chinese hot, 1 packet	10	0	0	0	50	1	0
Salsa, 1 packet	10	0	0	0	200	2	0
Sour cream, 30 g	60	6	4	20	30	1	0
Soy sauce, 9 g	5	0	0	0	480	<1	0
Sweet & sour dipping sauce, 1 packet	40	0	0	0	160	11	0
Tartar dipping sauce, 1 packet	150	15	1	10	200	2	0

JACK IN THE BOX, SHAKES & DESSERTS

	CAL	FAT (g)	SAT FAT (g)	CHOL (mg)	SODIUM (mg)	CARB (g)	FIBER (g)
Chocolate shake, regular, 1 shake	390	6	3.5	25	210	74	<1
Strawberry shake, regular, 1 shake	330	7	4	30	180	60	0
Vanilla shake, regular, 1 shake	350	7	4	30	180	62	0
Apple turnover, 1 turnover	350	19	4	0	460	48	0
Cheesecake, chocolate chip cookie dough, 1 order	360	18	8	45	200	44	1
Cheesecake, plain, 1 order	310	18	9	65	210	29	2

KENTUCKY FRIED CHICKEN, ENTREES

	CAL	FAT (g)	SAT FAT (g)	CHOL (mg)	SODIUM (mg)	CARB (g)	FIBER (g)
Colonel's Rotisserie Gold, ¼ chicken, breast & wing, skin removed, 1 order	200	6	2	100	670	0	0
Colonel's Rotisserie Gold, ¼ chicken, breast & wing, with skin, 1 order	340	19	5	160	1100	1	na

KENTUCKY FRIED CHICKEN, ENTREES	CAL	FAT (g)	SAT FAT (g)	CHOL (mg)	SODIUM (mg)	CARB (g)	FIBER (g)
Colonel's Rotisserie Gold, ¼ chicken, thigh & leg, skin removed, 1 order	220	12	3.5	130	770	0	0
Colonel's Rotisserie Gold, ¼ chicken, thigh & leg, with skin, 1 order	330	24	7	165	980	1	na
Extra Tasty Crispy, breast, 1 piece	470	28	7	80	930	25	1
Extra Tasty Crispy, drumstick, 1 piece	190	11	3	60	260	8	<1
Extra Tasty Crispy, thigh, 1 piece	370	25	6	70	540	18	2
Extra Tasty Crispy, whole wing, 1 piece	200	13	4	45	290	10	<1
Hot & spicy, breast, 1 piece	530	35	8	110	1110	23	2
Hot & spicy, drumstick, 1 piece	190	11	3	50	300	10	<1
Hot & spicy, thigh, 1 piece	370	27	7	90	570	13	1
Hot & spicy, whole wing, 1 piece	210	15	4	50	340	9	<1
Hot Wings (6 pc), 1 order	470	33	8	150	1230	18	na
Kentucky Nuggets (6 pc), 1 order	280	18	4	65	870	15	na
Original Recipe, breast, 1 piece	360	20	5	115	870	12	1
Original Recipe, drumstick, 1 piece	130	7	2	70	210	4	0
Original Recipe, thigh, 1 piece	260	17	5	110	570	9	1
Original Recipe, whole wing, 1 piece	150	8	3	40	380	7	0
Chicken sandwich, BBQ, 1 order	260	8	1	60	780	28	2
Colonel's chicken sandwich, 1 order	480	27	6	50	1060	39	na

AT A GLANCE: KENTUCKY FRIED CHICKEN, ENTREES
Lowest in Fat: Colonel's Rotisserie Gold, ¼ Chicken, Breast & Wing, Skin Removed

KENTUCKY FRIED CHICKEN, SIDE ORDERS

BBQ baked beans, 1 order	130	2	1	<5	540	24	4
Biscuit, 1 biscuit	200	12	3	<5	560	20	1

KENTUCKY FRIED CHICKEN, SIDE ORDERS	CAL	FAT (g)	SAT FAT (g)	CHOL (mg)	SODIUM (mg)	CARB (g)	FIBER (g)
Cole slaw, 1 order	110	6	1	<5	180	13	na
Corn on the cob, 1 piece	220	12	2	0	75	27	8
Cornbread, 1 piece	180	6	1.5	0	290	27	<1
Garden salad, 1 order	80	1	0	0	580	15	1
Green beans, 1 order	35	1	0	<5	560	5	2
Macaroni & cheese, 1 order	160	8	3	15	530	15	0
Mashed potatoes with gravy, 1 order	110	5	0.5	0	390	16	2
Mean Greens, 1 order	50	2	1	5	480	8	3
Potato salad, 1 order	180	11	2	10	420	18	2
Potato wedges, 1 order	190	9	3	<5	430	25	3
Red beans & rice, 1 order	110	3	1	<5	320	18	3

LITTLE CAESARS, PIZZA

	CAL	FAT (g)	SAT FAT (g)	CHOL (mg)	SODIUM (mg)	CARB (g)	FIBER (g)
Baby Pan! Pan!, 1 pizza	620	24	12	45	1470	67	4
Cheese, medium, Pan! Pan!, 1/9 pizza	180	6	3	15	380	22	1
Cheese, medium, round, 1/8 pizza	200	7	3.5	15	280	24	1
Cheese, pepperoni, medium, Pan! Pan!, 1/9 pizza	200	8	3.5	15	450	22	1
Cheese, pepperoni, medium, round, 1/8 pizza	220	9	4	15	360	24	1

LITTLE CAESARS, PASTA

	CAL	FAT (g)	SAT FAT (g)	CHOL (mg)	SODIUM (mg)	CARB (g)	FIBER (g)
Lasagna, 1 order	720	37	19	100	1610	58	4
Spaghetti, 1 order	260	6	1.5	10	400	44	3
Spaghetti, Little Bucket, 1 bucket	530	12	3.5	15	810	88	5

LITTLE CAESARS, SALADS

	CAL	FAT (g)	SAT FAT (g)	CHOL (mg)	SODIUM (mg)	CARB (g)	FIBER (g)
Antipasto salad, 1 order	180	12	2	20	540	7	2
Caesar salad, 1 order	140	5	3	10	370	14	2
Greek salad, 1 order	170	10	0	35	650	12	3
Tossed salad, 1 order	120	3	0.5	0	170	19	3

	CAL	FAT (g)	SAT FAT (g)	CHOL (mg)	SODIUM (mg)	CARB (g)	FIBER (g)
LITTLE CAESARS, SANDWICHES							
Big Veal Deal, 1 sandwich	530	26	5	55	910	51	3
Chicken sandwich, 1 sandwich	530	25	4	70	1040	44	2
Ham & cheese, 1 sandwich	670	37	3.5	40	1460	59	3
Italian sandwich, 1 sandwich	720	43	7	55	1610	59	3
Tuna sandwich, 1 sandwich	730	38	5	60	1300	61	3
Turkey sandwich, 1 sandwich	560	23	3.5	45	1920	59	3
Vegetarian sandwich, 1 sandwich	870	54	10	85	1980	62	3
LITTLE CAESARS, SIDE ORDERS							
Crazy Bread, 1 piece	110	3.5	0.5	0	115	16	<1
Crazy Sauce, 1 order	70	0	0	0	380	14	5
LITTLE CAESARS, VEAL PARMESAN							
Veal Parmesan, 1 order	510	23	6	60	1040	51	3
LONG JOHN SILVER'S, ENTREES							
Baked chicken, light herb, 3.5 oz	120	4	1.5	60	570	<1	na
Baked chicken, with rice, beans, slaw & roll, 15.9 oz	590	15	3.5	75	1620	82	na
Baked fish, lemon crumb, 3 pc, 5 oz	150	1	0.5	110	370	4	na
Baked fish (3 pc), lemon crumb, with rice, beans, slaw & roll, 17.4 oz	610	13	2.5	125	1420	86	na
Chicken Planks (2 pc), 4 oz	240	12	3.5	30	790	22	na
Chicken Planks (2 pc) & fries, 6.9 oz	490	26	6	30	1290	50	na
Chicken Planks (3 pc), with fries, slaw & Hushpuppies, 14.1 oz	890	44	10	55	2000	101	na
Clams (6 oz), with fries, slaw & Hushpuppies, 12.7 oz	990	52	11	75	1830	114	na
Crispy fish (3 pc), with fries, slaw & Hushpuppies, 13.5 oz	980	50	11	70	1530	92	na

LONG JOHN SILVER'S ENTREES	CAL (g)	FAT (g)	SAT FAT (g)	CHOL (mg)	SODIUM (mg)	CARB (g)	FIBER (g)
Fish & fries (2 pc), 9.2 oz	610	37	8	60	1480	52	na
Fish (1 pc) & chicken (1 pc) & fries, 8.1 oz	550	32	7	45	1380	51	na
Fish (1 pc) & chicken (2 pc), with fries, slaw & Hushpuppies, 15.2 oz	950	49	11	75	2090	102	na
Fish & More (2 pc) with fries, slaw & Hushpuppies, 14.4 oz	890	48	10	75	1790	92	na
Fish (2 pc) & shrimp (8 pc), with fries, slaw & Hushpuppies, 17.2 oz	1140	65	14	145	2440	108	na
Fish (2 pc), shrimp (5 pc) & chicken (1), with fries, slaw & Hushpuppies, 18.1 oz	1160	65	14	135	2590	113	na
Fish (2 pc), shrimp (4 pc) & clams (3 oz), with fries, slaw & Hushpuppies, 18.1 oz	1240	70	15	140	2630	123	na
Light Portion Fish (2 pc), lemon crumb, with rice & salad, 11.8 oz	330	5	1	75	640	46	na
Shrimp (10 pc), with fries, slaw & Hushpuppies, 11.7 oz	840	47	10	100	1630	88	na

AT A GLANCE: LONG JOHN SILVER'S, ENTREES
Lowest in Fat: Baked Lemon Crumb Fish

LONG JOHN SILVER'S, KIDS MEALS

Chicken Planks (2 pc) & fries, 7.8 oz	560	29	6	30	1310	60	na
Fish (1 pc) & chicken (1 pc) & fries, 8.9 oz	620	34	7	45	1400	61	na
Fish (1 pc) & fries, 7 oz	500	28	6	30	1010	50	na

LONG JOHN SILVER'S, SANDWICHES

Batter-dipped chicken sandwich, without sauce, 4.5 oz	280	8	2	15	790	39	na
Batter-dipped fish sandwich, without sauce, 5.6 oz	340	13	3.5	30	890	40	na

	CAL (g)	FAT (g)	SAT FAT (g)	CHOL (mg)	SODIUM (mg)	CARB (g)	FIBER (g)
LONG JOHN SILVER'S, SIDE ORDERS							
Batter-dipped fish (1 pc), 3.1 oz	180	11	3	30	490	12	na
Batter-dipped shrimp (1 pc), 0.4 oz	30	2	0.5	10	80	2	na
Chicken Plank (1 pc), 2 oz	120	6	1.5	15	400	11	na
Crispy fish, 1.8 oz	150	8	0	20	240	8	na
Flavorbaked chicken (1 pc), 3.5 oz	110	3	na	60	600	1	na
Flavorbaked fish (1 pc), 3.1 oz	90	2.5	na	35	320	1	na
Seafood chowder, with cod, 7 oz	140	6	2	20	590	10	na
Seafood gumbo, with cod, 7 oz	120	8	2	25	740	4	na
Baked potato, 8 oz	160	1	na	0	0	37	na
Cole slaw, drained on fork, 3.4 oz	140	6	1	15	260	20	na
Corn Cobbette (1 pc), 3.3 oz	140	8	na	0	0	18	na
French fries, 3 oz	250	15	2.5	0	500	28	na
Green beans, 3.5 oz	35	0.5	0	<5	350	6	na
Hushpuppies (1 pc), 0.8 oz	70	2	0	<5	25	10	na
Rice, 3 oz	140	3	na	0	210	25	na
Roll, 1.5 oz	110	0.5	0	0	170	23	na
LONG JOHN SILVER'S, SALADS & DRESSINGS							
Ocean chef salad, 8.3 oz	110	1	0	40	730	13	na
Seafood salad, 9.8 oz	380	31	na	55	980	12	na
Side salad, 4.4 oz	25	1	na	0	20	6	na
Creamy Italian dressing, 1 oz	30	3	na	na	280	<1	na
Ranch dressing, 1 oz	180	19	3.5	<5	230	<1	na
Sea salad dressing, 1 oz	140	15	6	<5	160	2	na
LONG JOHN SILVER'S, CONDIMENTS							
Honey mustard sauce, 0.42 oz	20	0.5	0	0	60	5	na
Malt vinegar, 0.28 oz	0	ns	na	na	15	0	na

LONG JOHN SILVER'S, CONDIMENTS	CAL	FAT (g)	SAT FAT (g)	CHOL (mg)	SODIUM (mg)	CARB (g)	FIBER (g)
Seafood sauce, 0.42 oz	15	0.5	0	0	180	3	na
Sweet n' sour sauce, 0.42 oz	20	0.5	0	0	45	5	na
Tartar sauce, 0.42 oz	50	5	1	0	35	2	na

LONG JOHN SILVER'S, DESSERTS

	CAL	FAT (g)	SAT FAT (g)	CHOL (mg)	SODIUM (mg)	CARB (g)	FIBER (g)
Apple pie, 4.5 oz	320	13	4.5	<5	420	45	na
Cherry pie, 4.5 oz	360	13	4.5	<5	200	55	na
Chocolate chip cookie, 1.8 oz	230	9	6	10	170	35	na
Lemon pie, 4 oz	340	9	3	45	130	60	na
Oatmeal raisin cookie, 1.8 oz	160	10	2	15	150	15	na
Pineapple cream cheese cake, 3.2 oz	310	18	9	10	105	34	na
Walnut brownie, 3.4 oz	440	22	5	20	150	54	na

McDONALD'S, BREAKFAST

	CAL	FAT (g)	SAT FAT (g)	CHOL (mg)	SODIUM (mg)	CARB (g)	FIBER (g)
Bacon, egg & cheese biscuit, 1 order	450	27	9	240	1310	na	na
Biscuit, 1 biscuit	260	13	3	0	840	na	na
Egg McMuffin, 1 order	290	13	4.5	235	730	na	na
English muffin, 1 order	140	2	0	0	220	na	na
Hash browns, 1 order	130	8	1.5	0	330	na	na
Hotcakes (plain), 1 order	290	4	0.5	10	600	na	na
Hotcakes, with syrup & 2 pats margarine, 1 order	560	14	2.5	10	750	na	na
Sausage biscuit, 1 order	430	29	9	35	1130	na	na
Sausage biscuit, with egg, 1 order	520	35	10	245	1200	na	na
Sausage McMuffin, 1 order	360	23	8	45	750	na	na
Sausage McMuffin, with egg, 1 order	440	29	10	255	820	na	na
Sausage patty, 1 order	170	16	5	35	290	na	na
Scrambled eggs, 2, 1 order	170	12	3.5	425	140	na	na
Apple bran muffin, fat-free, 1 order	180	0.5	0	0	210	na	na
Danish, apple, 1 order	360	16	5	40	290	na	na

McDONALD'S BREAKFAST	CAL	FAT (g)	SAT FAT (g)	CHOL (mg)	SODIUM (mg)	CARB (g)	FIBER (g)
Danish, cheese ,1 order	410	22	8	70	340	na	na
Danish, cinnamon raisin, 1 order	430	22	7	50	280	na	na
Danish, raspberry, 1 order	400	16	5	45	300	na	na

AT A GLANCE: MCDONALD'S, BREAKFAST
Lowest in Fat: Apple Bran Muffin, Fat Free

McDONALD'S, SANDWICHES

	CAL	FAT (g)	SAT FAT (g)	CHOL (mg)	SODIUM (mg)	CARB (g)	FIBER (g)
Big Mac, 1 order	510	26	9	75	930	na	na
Cheeseburger, 1 order	320	13	6	40	770	na	na
Filet-O-Fish, 1 order	360	16	3.5	35	710	na	na
Hamburger, 1 order	270	9	3	30	530	na	na
McChicken sandwich, 1 order	490	29	5	50	800	na	na
McGrilled Chicken sandwich, 1 order	250	3	0.5	45	510	na	na
McLean Deluxe, 1 order	340	12	4.5	60	810	na	na
McLean Deluxe, with cheese, 1 order	400	16	7	70	1040	na	na
Quarter Pounder, 1 order	420	20	8	70	690	na	na
Quarter Pounder, with cheese, 1 order	520	29	13	95	1160	na	na

AT A GLANCE: MCDONALD'S, SANDWICHES
Lowest in Fat: McGrilled Chicken Sandwich

McDONALD'S CHICKEN McNUGGETS & SAUCE

	CAL	FAT (g)	SAT FAT (g)	CHOL (mg)	SODIUM (mg)	CARB (g)	FIBER (g)
Chicken McNuggets, 4 piece	200	12	2.5	40	350	na	na
Chicken McNuggets, 6 piece	300	18	3.5	65	530	na	na
Chicken McNuggets, 9 piece	450	27	6	95	800	na	na
Barbecue sauce, 1 packet	50	0	0	0	280	na	na
Honey, 1 packet	45	0	0	0	0	na	na
Honey mustard, 1 packet	50	4.5	0.5	10	85	na	na
Hot mustard sauce, 1 packet	60	3.5	0	5	250	na	na
Sweet 'n sour sauce, 1 packet	50	0	0	0	160	na	na

McDONALD'S, SALADS & DRESSINGS

	CAL	FAT (g)	SAT FAT (g)	CHOL (mg)	SODIUM (mg)	CARB (g)	FIBER (g)
Chef salad, 1 order	210	11	4	180	610	na	na
Chunky chicken salad, 1 order	160	5	1.5	75	320	na	na

McDONALD'S SALADS & DRESSINGS	CAL (g)	FAT (g)	SAT FAT (g)	CHOL (mg)	SODIUM (mg)	CARB (g)	FIBER (g)
Garden salad, 1 order	80	4	1	140	60	na	na
Side salad, 1 order	45	2	0.5	70	35	na	na
1000 island dressing, 1 packet	190	13	2	25	510	na	na
Blue cheese dressing, 1 packet	190	17	3	30	650	na	na
Lite vinaigrette dressing, 1 packet	50	2	0	0	240	na	na
Ranch dressing, 1 packet	230	21	3	20	550	na	na
Red French dressing, reduced calorie, 1 packet	160	8	1	0	490	na	na
Bacon bits, 1 packet	15	1	0	5	90	na	na
Croutons, 1 packet	50	1.5	0	0	125	na	na

McDONALD'S, FRENCH FRIES

	CAL (g)	FAT (g)	SAT FAT (g)	CHOL (mg)	SODIUM (mg)	CARB (g)	FIBER (g)
French fries, small, 1 order	210	10	1.5	0	135	na	na
French fries, large, 1 order	450	22	4	0	290	na	na
French fries, super size, 1 order	540	26	4.5	0	350	na	na

McDONALD'S, DESSERTS/SHAKES

	CAL (g)	FAT (g)	SAT FAT (g)	CHOL (mg)	SODIUM (mg)	CARB (g)	FIBER (g)
Chocolate shake, small, 1 order	350	6	3.5	25	240	na	na
Strawberry shake, small, 1 order	340	5	3.5	25	170	na	na
Vanilla shake, small, 1 order	310	5	3.5	25	170	na	na
Apple pie, baked, 1 order	290	15	3.5	0	220	na	na
Chocolaty chip cookies, 1 order	280	14	4	5	230	na	na
Cone, vanilla, lowfat frozen yogurt, 1 order	120	0.5	0	5	85	na	na
McDonaldland Cookies, 1 order	260	9	2	0	260	na	na
Nuts for sundaes, 1 portion	40	3.5	0	0	0	na	na
Sundae, vanilla, lowfat frozen yogurt, 1 order	170	1	1	<5	105	na	1
Sundae topping, caramel, 1 order	140	2	1	0	95	na	1

MCDONALD'S, DESSERTS/SHAKES	CAL (g)	FAT (g)	SAT FAT (g)	CHOL (mg)	SODIUM (mg)	CARB (g)	FIBER (g)
Sundae topping, hot fudge, 1 order	130	4	4	0	85	na	1
Sundae topping, strawberry, 1 order	80	0	0	0	15	na	1

AT A GLANCE: MCDONALD'S, DESSERTS & SHAKES
Lowest in Fat: Vanilla Low Fat Frozen Yogurt Cone

PIZZA HUT, PIZZA *Values are based on medium pizza.*

	CAL	FAT	SAT FAT	CHOL	SODIUM	CARB	FIBER
Bigfoot, cheese, 1 slice	190	6	3	15	530	25	2
Bigfoot, pepperoni, 1 slice	210	7	3	20	590	25	2
Bigfoot, pepperoni, mushrooms and Italian sausage, 1 slice	210	8	4	20	670	25	2
Hand tossed, beef, 1 slice	260	9	4	25	800	29	2
Hand tossed, cheese, 1 slice	240	7	4	25	620	29	2
Hand tossed, ham, 1 slice	210	5	3	20	660	29	2
Hand tossed, Italian sausage, 1 slice	270	11	5	30	740	29	2
Hand tossed, Meat Lover's, 1 slice	310	11	6	40	960	29	2
Hand tossed, pepperoni, 1 slice	240	8	4	25	690	29	2
Hand tossed, Pepperoni Lover's, 1 slice	310	14	6	40	900	30	2
Hand tossed, pork topping, 1 slice	270	10	5	25	800	29	2
Hand tossed, super supreme, 1 slice	300	13	5	35	950	30	3
Hand tossed, supreme, 1 slice	280	12	5	30	880	30	3
Hand tossed, Veggie Lover's, 1 slice	220	6	3	20	630	30	3
Pan, beef, 1 slice	290	13	5	25	680	28	2
Pan, cheese, 1 slice	260	11	5	25	500	28	2
Pan, ham, 1 slice	240	9	3	20	540	28	2
Pan, Italian sausage, 1 slice	290	15	5	30	620	27	2
Pan, Meat Lover's, 1 slice	340	18	7	40	840	28	2
Pan, pepperoni, 1 slice	270	12	4	25	570	28	2

PIZZA HUT, PIZZA	CAL (g)	FAT (g)	SAT FAT (g)	CHOL (mg)	SODIUM (mg)	CARB (g)	FIBER (g)
Pan, Pepperoni Lover's, 1 slice	330	17	7	40	780	28	2
Pan, pork topping, 1 slice	290	14	5	25	680	28	2
Pan, super supreme, 1 slice	320	17	6	35	830	28	3
Pan, supreme, 1 slice	310	15	6	30	760	28	3
Pan, Veggie Lover's, 1 slice	240	10	3	20	510	29	3
Personal Pan, pepperoni, 1 whole	640	28	10	55	1340	69	5
Personal Pan, supreme, 1 whole	720	34	12	65	1760	70	6
Thin 'N Crispy, beef, 1 slice	230	11	5	25	710	21	2
Thin 'N Crispy, cheese, 1 slice	210	8	4	25	530	21	2
Thin 'N Crispy, ham, 1 slice	180	7	3	25	590	21	1
Thin 'N Crispy, Italian sausage, 1 slice	240	12	5	30	650	21	2
Thin 'N Crispy, Meat Lover's, 1 slice	290	13	6	40	890	21	2
Thin 'N Crispy, pepperoni, 1 slice	220	10	4	25	630	21	1
Thin 'N Crispy, Pepperoni Lover's, 1 slice	290	16	7	40	860	22	2
Thin 'N Crispy, pork topping, 1 slice	240	12	5	25	710	21	2
Thin 'N Crispy, super supreme, 1 slice	270	14	6	35	880	22	2
Thin 'N Crispy, supreme, 1 slice	260	13	5	30	800	21	2
Thin 'N Crispy, Veggie Lover's, 1 slice	190	7	3	20	550	22	2

AT A GLANCE: PIZZA HUT PIZZA
Lowest in Fat: Hand Tossed, Ham

POPEYES CHICKEN & BISCUITS, CHICKEN

	CAL	FAT	SAT FAT	CHOL	SODIUM	CARB	FIBER
Breast, mild, 3.7 oz	270	16	na	60	660	9	2
Breast, spicy, 3.7 oz	270	16	na	60	590	9	2
Leg, mild, 1.7 oz	120	7	na	40	240	4	0
Leg, spicy, 1.7 oz	120	7	na	40	240	4	0
Thigh, mild, 3.1 oz	300	23	na	70	620	9	<1

POPEYES CHICKEN & BISCUITS, CHICKEN	CAL (g)	FAT (g)	SAT FAT (g)	CHOL (mg)	SODIUM (mg)	CARB (g)	FIBER (g)
Thigh, spicy, 3.1 oz	300	23	na	70	450	9	<1
Wing, mild, 1.6 oz	160	11	na	40	290	7	0
Wing, spicy, 1.6 oz	160	11	na	40	290	7	0
Nuggets, 4.2 oz	410	32	na	55	660	18	3
Tender, mild, 1.2 oz	110	7	na	15	160	6	<1
Tender, spicy, 1.2 oz	110	7	na	15	220	6	<1

AT A GLANCE: POPEYE'S CHICKEN & BISCUITS, CHICKEN
Lowest in Calories & Fat: Chicken Tender

POPEYES CHICKEN & BISCUITS, SIDE ORDERS

	CAL (g)	FAT (g)	SAT FAT (g)	CHOL (mg)	SODIUM (mg)	CARB (g)	FIBER (g)
Biscuits, 2.3 oz	250	15	na	<5	430	26	1
Cajun rice, 3.9 oz	150	5	na	25	1260	17	3
Cole slaw, 4 oz	150	11	na	<5	270	14	3
Corn on the cob, 5.2 oz	130	3	na	0	20	21	9
French fries, 3 oz	240	12	na	10	610	31	3
Onion rings, 3.1 oz	310	19	na	25	210	31	2
Potatoes & gravy, 3.8 oz	100	6	na	<5	460	11	3
Red beans & rice, 5.9 oz	270	17	na	10	680	30	7

POPEYES CHICKEN & BISCUITS, DESSERT

	CAL (g)	FAT (g)	SAT FAT (g)	CHOL (mg)	SODIUM (mg)	CARB (g)	FIBER (g)
Apple pie, 3.1 oz	290	16	na	10	820	37	2

SUBWAY, 12" SUBS

	CAL (g)	FAT (g)	SAT FAT (g)	CHOL (mg)	SODIUM (mg)	CARB (g)	FIBER (g)
BMT sub, honey wheat roll, 1 sub	1010	57	20	135	3200	88	na
BMT sub, Italian roll, 1 sub	980	55	20	135	3200	83	na
Cold cut combo sub, honey wheat roll, 1 sub	880	41	12	170	2280	88	na
Cold cut combo sub, Italian roll, 1 sub	850	40	12	170	2220	83	na
Ham & cheese sub, honey wheat roll, 1 sub	670	22	7	75	2510	86	na
Ham & cheese sub, Italian roll, 1 sub	640	18	7	75	1710	81	na
Meatball sub, honey wheat roll, 1 sub	950	45	17	90	2060	101	na

SUBWAY, 12" SUBS	CAL (g)	FAT (g)	SAT FAT (g)	CHOL (mg)	SODIUM (mg)	CARB (g)	FIBER (g)
Meatball sub, Italian roll, 1 sub	920	44	17	90	2020	96	na
Roast beef sub, honey wheat roll, 1 sub	720	24	8	75	2350	89	na
Roast beef sub, Italian roll, 1 sub	690	23	8	75	2290	84	na
Seafood & crab sub, honey wheat roll, 1 sub	1020	58	11	55	2030	100	na
Seafood & crab sub, Italian roll, 1 sub	990	57	11	55	1970	94	na
Seafood & lobster sub, honey wheat roll, 1 sub	970	54	11	55	2140	100	na
Seafood & lobster sub, Italian roll, 1 sub	940	53	10	55	2070	94	na
Spicy Italian sub, honey wheat roll, 1 sub	1070	64	24	140	3080	88	na
Spicy Italian sub, Italian roll, 1 sub	1040	63	23	140	3020	83	na
Steak & cheese sub, honey wheat roll, 1 sub	710	33	12	80	1620	89	na
Steak & cheese sub, Italian roll, 1 sub	770	32	12	80	1570	83	na
Subway Club sub, honey wheat roll, 1 sub	720	23	7	85	2780	89	na
Subway Club sub, Italian roll, 1 sub	690	22	7	85	2720	83	na
Tuna sub, honey wheat roll, 1 sub	1130	73	10	85	1560	87	na
Tuna sub, Italian roll, 1 sub	1100	72	13	85	1500	81	na
Turkey breast sub, honey wheat roll, 1 sub	670	20	6	70	2520	88	na
Turkey breast sub, Italian roll, 1 sub	640	19	6	70	2460	83	na
Veggies & cheese sub, honey wheat roll, 1 sub	560	18	6	20	1140	86	na
Veggies & cheese sub, Italian roll, 1 sub	540	17	5	20	1080	81	na

AT A GLANCE: SUBWAY, 12" SUBS
Lowest in Fat: Veggie & Cheese Sub, Italian Roll

	CAL (g)	FAT (g)	SAT FAT (g)	CHOL (mg)	SODIUM (mg)	CARB (g)	FIBER (g)
SUBWAY, SALADS							
BMT salad, 1 salad	630	52	19	135	2400	14	na
Cold cut combo salad, 1 salad	510	37	11	170	1820	14	na
Ham & cheese salad, 1 salad	300	18	6	75	1710	12	na
Roast beef salad, 1 salad	340	20	7	75	1550	15	na
Seafood & crab salad, 1 salad	640	53	10	55	1230	26	na
Seafood & lobster salad, 1 salad	600	49	9	55	1340	26	na
Spicy Italian salad, 1 salad	900	60	22	140	2280	14	na
Subway Club salad, 1 salad	350	19	6	85	1980	14	na
Tuna salad, 1 salad	760	68	12	85	760	13	na
Turkey breast salad, 1 salad	300	16	4.5	70	1730	14	na
Veggies & cheese salad, 1 salad	190	14	4.5	20	340	12	na

AT A GLANCE: SUBWAY, SALADS
Lowest in Fat: Veggie & Cheese Salad

TACO BELL							
Bean burrito, 1 order	390	12	4	5	1140	58	8
Light bean burrito, 1 order	330	6	2	5	1340	55	8
Burrito Supreme, 1 order	440	19	9	45	1180	50	5
Light Burrito Supreme, 1 order	350	8	3	25	1300	50	4
Light 7-layer burrito, 1 order	440	9	3.5	5	1430	67	10
Light Chicken Burrito Supreme, 1 order	410	10	2	65	1190	62	2
Light Chicken Soft Taco, 1 order	180	5	1	30	570	26	1
Soft taco, 1 order	220	11	5	30	540	19	2
Light soft taco, 1 order	180	5	2.5	25	550	19	2
Soft Taco Supreme, 1 order	270	15	8	45	550	21	2
Light Soft Taco Supreme, 1 order	200	5	2.5	25	610	23	2
Taco, 1 order	180	11	4.5	30	280	11	1
Light taco, 1 order	140	5	1.5	20	280	11	2

TACO BELL	CAL (g)	FAT (g)	SAT FAT (g)	CHOL (mg)	SODIUM (mg)	CARB (g)	FIBER (g)
Taco Supreme, 1 order	230	15	8	45	290	12	1
Light Taco Supreme, 1 order	160	5	1.5	20	340	14	2
Taco salad, 1 order	860	55	16	80	1620	64	10
Light taco salad, with chips, 1 order	680	25	8	50	1620	81	10
Light taco salad, without chips, 1 order	330	9	4.5	50	1610	35	6

AT A GLANCE: TACO BELL
Lowest in Fat: Light Chicken Soft Taco

TACO JOHN'S, ENTREES

	CAL (g)	FAT (g)	SAT FAT (g)	CHOL (mg)	SODIUM (mg)	CARB (g)	FIBER (g)
Bean burrito, 1 order	340	11	3	15	650	45	na
Beef burrito, 1 order	420	19	6	45	700	39	na
Burrito platter, 1 order	970	38	15	60	2180	123	na
Chicken fajita burrito, 1 order	360	12	5	50	1200	41	na
Chicken fajita salad (no dressing), 1 order	560	35	10	55	1510	40	na
Chicken fajita softshell, 1 order	220	8	3	35	1080	20	na
Chimichanga platter, 1 order	920	35	14	50	2350	119	na
Combo burrito, 1 order	380	13	6	30	660	46	na
Crispy tacos, 1 order	180	10	4	25	260	13	na
Double enchilada platter, 1 order	900	37	13	75	2100	103	na
Heart Smart bean burrito, 1 order	290	4	1.5	10	640	na	na
Heart Smart beef burrito, 1 order	310	9	3.5	25	590	na	na
Heart Smart chicken fajita burrito, 1 order	290	6	2	35	880	na	na
Heart Smart chicken fajita salad, 1 order	250	4	1	40	1070	na	na
Heart Smart chicken fajita softshell, 1 order	150	2	1	25	640	na	na
Heart Smart softshell taco, 1 order	170	4.5	2	15	410	na	na
Heart Smart taco salad, 1 order	280	7	2.5	25	780	na	na

TACO JOHN'S, ENTREES	CAL	FAT (g)	SAT FAT (g)	CHOL (mg)	SODIUM (mg)	CARB (g)	FIBER (g)
Mexi Rolls, with guacamole, 1 order	840	46	12	45	1050	78	na
Mexi Rolls, with nacho cheese, 1 order	810	43	11	45	1200	77	na
Mexi Rolls, with salsa, 1 order	750	37	11	45	1390	77	na
Mexi Rolls, with sour cream, 1 order	850	47	11	45	850	74	na
Mexican pizza, 1 order	640	36	14	55	1330	53	na
Sampler platter, 1 order	1280	51	19	100	2740	149	na
Sierra Chicken Fillet Sandwich, 1 order	500	21	6	40	1490	46	na
Softshell taco, 1 order	280	11	4	25	560	32	na
Super burrito, 1 order	420	19	7	35	740	45	na
Taco Bravo, 1 order	330	14	4	20	650	38	na
Taco burger, 1 order	280	11	4.5	25	570	29	na
Taco salad (no dressing), 1 order	470	31	8	25	650	40	na

AT A GLANCE: TACO JOHN'S
Lowest in Fat: Heart Smart Chicken Fajita Softshell

TACO JOHN'S, KID'S MEALS

	CAL	FAT (g)	SAT FAT (g)	CHOL (mg)	SODIUM (mg)	CARB (g)	FIBER (g)
Kid's meal, with crispy taco, 1 order	580	33	10	30	770	55	na
Kid's meal, with softshell taco, 1 order	620	33	10	35	1020	66	na
Kid's meal, with taco burger, 1 order	670	34	10	35	1080	70	na

TACO JOHN'S, SIDE ORDERS

	CAL	FAT (g)	SAT FAT (g)	CHOL (mg)	SODIUM (mg)	CARB (g)	FIBER (g)
Beans (refried), 1 order	300	8	1.5	10	960	39	na
Chili, 1 order	300	14	7	50	1430	27	na
House salad dressing, 1 order	110	11	2	0	620	3	na
Mexican rice, 1 order	570	18	5	0	1290	94	na
Nacho cheese, 1 order	80	6	2	na	380	5	na
Nachos, 1 order	850	50	15	50	1230	77	na
Nachos, super, 1 order	290	17	4	5	450	31	na
Potato Oles, 1 order	440	28	7	0	390	45	na

TACO JOHN'S, SIDE ORDERS	CAL (g)	FAT (g)	SAT FAT (g)	CHOL (mg)	SODIUM (mg)	CARB (g)	FIBER (g)
Potato Oles, with nacho cheese, 1 order	520	34	9	5	830	50	na
Sour cream, 1 order	60	5	na	na	15	1	na

TACO JOHN'S, DESSERTS

	CAL (g)	FAT (g)	SAT FAT (g)	CHOL (mg)	SODIUM (mg)	CARB (g)	FIBER (g)
Apple flauta, 1 order	80	1	0	0	70	19	na
Cherry flauta, 1 order	140	3.5	1	0	110	27	na
Choco taco, 1 order	320	17	11	20	100	38	na
Churro, 1 order	150	8	2	<5	160	17	na
Cream cheese flauta, 1 order	180	8	3	10	135	27	na

WENDY'S, SANDWICHES

	CAL (g)	FAT (g)	SAT FAT (g)	CHOL (mg)	SODIUM (mg)	CARB (g)	FIBER (g)
Big Bacon Classic, 1 order	640	36	13	110	1500	44	3
Breaded chicken sandwich, 1 order	450	20	4	60	740	43	2
Cheeseburger, Kids' Meal, 1 order	310	13	5	45	770	33	2
Chicken club sandwich, 1 order	520	25	6	75	990	44	2
Grilled chicken sandwich, 1 order	290	7	1.5	55	720	35	2
Hamburger, Kids' Meal, 1 order	270	9	3	35	600	33	2
Junior bacon cheeseburger, 1 order	440	25	8	65	870	33	2
Junior cheeseburger, 1 order	320	13	5	45	770	34	2
Junior cheeseburger deluxe, 1 order	390	20	7	50	820	36	3
Junior hamburger, 1 order	270	9	3	35	600	34	2
Single, plain, 1 order	350	15	6	70	510	31	2
Single, with everything, 1 order	440	23	7	75	860	36	3

WENDY'S, CHICKEN NUGGETS & SAUCE

	CAL (g)	FAT (g)	SAT FAT (g)	CHOL (mg)	SODIUM (mg)	CARB (g)	FIBER (g)
Chicken nuggets, 6 nuggets	280	20	5	50	600	12	0
Barbecue sauce, 1 packet	50	0	na	0	100	11	na

WENDY'S, CHICKEN NUGGETS & SAUCE	CAL	FAT (g)	SAT FAT (g)	CHOL (mg)	SODIUM (mg)	CARB (g)	FIBER (g)
Honey, 1 packet	45	0	0	0	0	12	0
Sweet & sour sauce, 1 packet	45	0	0	0	55	11	0
Sweet mustard sauce, 1 packet	50	1	0	0	140	9	0

WENDY'S, SALADS & DRESSINGS

	CAL	FAT (g)	SAT FAT (g)	CHOL (mg)	SODIUM (mg)	CARB (g)	FIBER (g)
Caesar side salad, 1 order	110	5	2	15	580	7	2
Deluxe garden salad, 1 order	110	6	1	0	320	10	4
Grilled chicken salad, 1 order	200	8	1.5	50	690	10	4
Side salad, 1 order	60	3	0.5	0	160	5	2
Taco salad, 1 order	580	30	30	75	1060	51	11
Blue cheese dressing, 2 Tbsp	180	19	3	15	180	1	0
French dressing, fat free, 2 Tbsp	35	0	0	0	180	8	0
Hidden Valley Ranch dressing, reduced fat, reduced calorie, 2 Tbsp	60	5	1	10	280	2	0
Italian dressing, reduced fat, reduced calorie, 2 Tbsp	40	3	0.5	0	330	3	0
Italian Caesar dressing, 2 Tbsp	150	16	2.5	15	230	0	0
Thousand island dressing, 2 Tbsp	130	13	2	10	160	4	0
Croutons, 2 Tbsp	30	1	0	0	75	4	0

WENDY'S, SIDE ORDERS

	CAL	FAT (g)	SAT FAT (g)	CHOL (mg)	SODIUM (mg)	CARB (g)	FIBER (g)
Baked potato, bacon & cheese, 1 order	530	18	4	20	1280	77	7
Baked potato, broccoli & cheese, 1 order	460	14	2.5	0	440	79	9
Baked potato, cheese, 1 order	560	23	8	30	610	77	7
Baked potato, chili & cheese, 1 order	610	24	9	45	700	82	9
Baked potato, plain, 1 order	310	0	0	0	25	71	7
Baked potato, sour cream & chives, 1 order	380	6	4	15	40	74	8
Breadstick, soft, 1 piece	130	3	0.5	5	250	24	na

WENDY'S, SIDE ORDERS	CAL	FAT (g)	SAT FAT (g)	CHOL (mg)	SODIUM (mg)	CARB (g)	FIBER (g)
Chili, small, 8 oz	190	6	2.5	40	670	20	5
Chili, large, 12 oz	290	9	4	60	1000	31	7
French fries, small, 3.2 oz	240	12	2.5	0	150	33	3
French fries, medium, 4.6 oz	340	17	4	0	210	48	4
French fries, Biggie, 5.6 oz	420	20	4	0	260	58	5
Sour cream, 1 packet	60	6	4	10	15	1	0

WENDY'S, DESSERTS

	CAL	FAT (g)	SAT FAT (g)	CHOL (mg)	SODIUM (mg)	CARB (g)	FIBER (g)
Chocolate chip cookie, 1 order	270	11	8	0	150	38	3
Frosty, small, 12 oz	340	10	5	0	200	57	3
Frosty, medium, 16 oz	460	13	7	0	260	76	4
Frosty, large, 20 oz	570	17	9	0	330	95	5

AT A GLANCE: WENDY'S
Lowest in Fat: Grilled Chicken Sandwich

BY THE EDITORS OF CONSUMER GUIDE®
With the Nutrient Analysis Center,
Chicago Center for Clinical Research

THE COMPLETE

FOOD

COUNT

GUIDE

Publications International, Ltd.

The Nutrient Analysis Center is a division of the Chicago Center for Clinical Research, a unique, nationally recognized organization conducting clinical trials in food, nutrition, and pharmaceuticals.

Cover illustration: Tim Kilian

Editorial assistants: Amanda Johnson, Donna Shryer